£2 off

OXFORD
UNIVERSITY PRESS

Oxford Primary Grammar, Punctuation and Spelling Dictionary

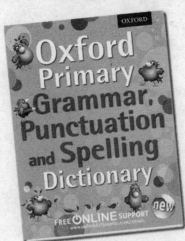

KT-452-396

Give your child a helping hand with improving grammar, punctuation and spelling skills

Ideal support for children preparing for Key Stage 2 tests

Take this voucher to the till when you purchase your book to receive **£2 off** the printed RRP.*

This offer is redeemable exclusively in **WHSmith** High Street stores from **2nd September and 29th September 2013.**

erms and conditions: This voucher entitles you to £2.00 off the full RRP rinted on the book of Oxford Primary Grammar, Punctuation and pelling Dictionary (9780192734211). Subject to availability. Voucher is alid from 2nd September – 29th September 2013 at WHSmith High treet stores only. Excludes outlet stores, online, 'Books by WHSmith' at elfridges, Harrods, Arnotts and Fenwick`s and all travel stores including ose at airports, railway stations, motorway service stations, hospitals nd workplaces. Vouchers must be surrendered upon use. Photocopies ill not be accepted. No cash alternative. WHSmith reserves the right to ject any voucher it deems, in its sole discretion, to have been forged, efaced or otherwise tampered with. Cannot be used in conjunction with ny other voucher offer.

*£9.99 RRP

3678 3366

WHSmith

Subject to availability. Most stores.

Oxford Popular School Dictionary

OXFORD
UNIVERSITY PRESS

OXFORD
UNIVERSITY PRESS

Great Clarendon Street, Oxford OX2 6DP

Oxford University Press is a department of the University of Oxford.
It furthers the University's objective of excellence in research,
scholarship, and education by publishing worldwide in

Oxford New York

Auckland Cape Town Dar es Salaam Hong Kong Karachi
Kuala Lumpur Madrid Melbourne Mexico City Nairobi
New Delhi Shanghai Taipei Toronto

with offices in

Argentina Austria Brazil Chile Czech Republic France Greece
Guatemala Hungary Italy Japan Poland Portugal Singapore
South Korea Switzerland Thailand Turkey Ukraine Vietnam

Oxford is a registered trade mark of Oxford University Press
in the UK and in certain other countries

© Oxford University Press 2008

This edition, based on the Oxford Mini School Dictionary & Thesaurus,
published 2008

Database right Oxford University Press (maker)

All rights reserved. No part of this publication may be reproduced,
stored in a retrieval system, or transmitted, in any form or by any means,
without the prior permission in writing of Oxford University Press, or as
expressly permitted by law, or under terms agreed with the appropriate
reprographic rights organization. Enquiries concerning reproduction
outside the scope of the above should be sent to the Rights Department,
Oxford University Press, at the address above

You must not circulate this book in any other binding or cover
and you must impose this same condition on any other acquirer

British Library cataloguing in Publication Data

Data available

ISBN 978-0-19-911874-8

20 19 18 17 16 15 14 13

Typeset in OUP Argo and OUP Swift

Printed in Great Britain by CPI Group (UK) Ltd, Croydon, CR0 4YY

Do you have a query about words, their origin, meaning, use, spelling,
pronunciation, or any other aspect of the English language? Visit our
website at www.askoxford.com where you will be able to find answers to
your language queries.

Paper used in the production of this book is a natural, recyclable product made from
wood grown in sustainable forests. The manufacturing process conforms to the
environmental regulations of the country of origin.

www.schooldictionaries.co.uk

Aa

a *DETERMINER* (**an** before most vowel sounds)
1 one but not any special one *Find me a pen.*
2 each, every *once a day*

aardvark *NOUN*
a nocturnal African animal with a long snout

aback *ADVERB*
taken aback surprised

abacus *NOUN* **abacuses**
a frame used for counting with beads sliding
on wires

abandon *VERB*
1 to give up an idea
2 to leave someone or something without
help
abandoned *ADJECTIVE* **abandonment** *NOUN*

abandon *NOUN*
a careless and uncontrolled manner

abbey *NOUN* **abbeys**
1 a monastery or convent
2 a church that was once part of a monastery

abbot *NOUN*
the head of an abbey

abbreviate *VERB*
to shorten something

abbreviation *NOUN*
a shortened form of a word or words,
e.g. GCSE, St., USA

abdicate *VERB*
1 to resign from a throne
2 to give up an important responsibility
abdication *NOUN*

abdomen *NOUN*
1 the lower front part of a person's or animal's
body, containing the stomach and intestines
2 the rear section of an insect's body
abdominal *ADJECTIVE*

abduct *VERB*
to take a person away illegally
abduction *NOUN* **abductor** *NOUN*

abet *VERB* **abetting**, **abetted**
to help or encourage someone to commit
a crime

abide *VERB*
to bear or tolerate something *I can't abide
wasps.*
abide by to keep to a law or a promise

abiding *ADJECTIVE*
lasting or permanent

ability *NOUN* **abilities**
1 being able to do something
2 a talent

abject *ADJECTIVE*
1 wretched or miserable *abject poverty*
2 humble *an abject apology*

ablaze *ADJECTIVE*
blazing; on fire

able *ADJECTIVE*
1 having the skill or opportunity to do
something
2 skilful or clever
ably *ADVERB*

abnormal *ADJECTIVE*
not normal; unusual
abnormally *ADVERB*

abnormality *NOUN* **abnormalities**
something that is not normal or usual

aboard *ADVERB, PREPOSITION*
on or into a ship or aircraft or train

abode *NOUN*
(*formal*) the place where someone lives

abolish *VERB*
to put an end to a law or custom
abolition *NOUN*

abominable *ADJECTIVE*
very bad or unpleasant
abominably *ADVERB*

abominate *VERB*
to hate something very much
abomination *NOUN*

aborigine *NOUN*
one of the original inhabitants of a country
aboriginal *ADJECTIVE, NOUN*
Aborigine one of the original inhabitants of
Australia who lived there before the
Europeans arrived

abort *VERB*
to stop something before it has been
completed

abortion *NOUN*
an operation to remove an unborn child from
the womb

abound *VERB*
1 to be plentiful or abundant
2 to have something in great quantities

about *ADVERB, PREPOSITION*
1 near in amount or time *about £5*
2 on the subject of *a book about animals*
3 in all directions *running about*
about to going to do something

above *ADVERB, PREPOSITION*
1 higher than something
2 more than something

abrasive *ADJECTIVE*
1 rough and used for rubbing or scraping
2 rude and unpleasant

abreast ADVERB
1 side by side
2 keeping up with something

abridge VERB
to shorten a book by using fewer words
abridgement NOUN

abroad ADVERB
in or to another country

abrupt ADJECTIVE
1 sudden or hasty *an abrupt departure*
2 rather rude and unfriendly; curt *an abrupt manner*
abruptly ADVERB **abruptness** NOUN

abscess NOUN
a painful swelling on the body where pus has formed

abscond VERB
to go away secretly

abseil VERB
to lower yourself down a steep cliff or rock by sliding down a rope

absent ADJECTIVE
not here; not present
absence NOUN

absent VERB
absent yourself to stay away

absent-minded ADJECTIVE
having your mind on other things; forgetful

absolute ADJECTIVE
complete; not restricted *absolute power*

absolutely ADVERB
completely; certainly

absolve VERB
1 to clear a person of blame or guilt
2 to release a person from a promise or obligation

absorb VERB
1 to soak up a liquid or gas
2 to deal with something and reduce its effect *The buffers absorbed the impact.*
3 to take up a person's attention or time
absorption NOUN

absorbent ADJECTIVE
able to soak up liquids easily

abstain VERB
1 to keep yourself from doing something
2 to choose not to vote
abstention NOUN

abstinence NOUN
not doing something, especially drinking alcohol

abstract ADJECTIVE
1 concerned with ideas and not solid objects
2 showing an artist's ideas or feelings and not a recognizable person or thing

abstract VERB
to take out or remove
abstraction NOUN

abstruse ADJECTIVE
hard to understand

absurd ADJECTIVE
ridiculous or foolish
absurdity NOUN **absurdly** ADVERB

abundance NOUN
a large amount of something

abundant ADJECTIVE
plentiful
abundantly ADVERB

abuse VERB
1 to use something badly or wrongly
2 to treat someone cruelly
3 to say unpleasant things about a person or thing

abuse NOUN
1 a wrong or bad use of something
2 physical harm or cruelty done to someone
3 offensive words or insults

abusive ADJECTIVE
rude and insulting *abusive remarks*

abysmal ADJECTIVE
extremely bad

abyss NOUN
an extremely deep pit

academic ADJECTIVE
1 to do with education or studying
2 theoretical; having no practical use *an academic point*

academic NOUN
a university or college teacher

academy NOUN **academies**
1 a school or college for specialized training
2 a society of scholars or artists

accelerate VERB
to become or cause to become faster

acceleration NOUN
the rate at which the speed of something increases

accelerator NOUN
the pedal that a driver presses to make a motor vehicle go faster

accent NOUN
1 the way a person pronounces the words of a language
2 emphasis or stress in a word
3 a mark placed over a letter to show how it is pronounced

accentuate VERB
to emphasize something
accentuation NOUN

accept VERB
1 to take a thing that is offered or presented
2 to say yes to an invitation or offer
acceptance NOUN

acceptable ADJECTIVE
pleasing or satisfactory
acceptably ADVERB

access VERB
to find information stored in a computer
access NOUN
1 a way to enter or reach something
2 the right to use or look at something

accessible ADJECTIVE
able to be reached or understood easily
accessibility NOUN **accessibly** ADVERB

accession NOUN
1 the act of becoming king or queen
2 something added

accessory NOUN **accessories**
1 an extra thing that goes with something
2 a person who helps another with a crime

accident NOUN
something unexpected that causes injury
or damage
by accident by chance

accidental ADJECTIVE
happening or done by chance
accidentally ADVERB

accolade NOUN
praise or a prize given for an achievement

accommodate VERB
1 to provide somebody with a place to live or
work, or to sleep for the night
2 to help someone by providing something

accommodating ADJECTIVE
willing to help or cooperate

accommodation NOUN
somewhere to live, work, or sleep overnight

accompanist NOUN
a musician who accompanies a singer or
another musician

accompany VERB **accompanies**,
accompanied
1 to go somewhere with somebody
2 to be present with something *Thunder
accompanied the storm.*
3 to play music that supports a singer or
another player
accompaniment NOUN

accomplice NOUN
a person who helps another to do wrong or
commit a crime

accomplish VERB
to do something successfully

accomplished ADJECTIVE
skilled in something

accomplishment NOUN
something you do well

accord NOUN
agreement or consent
of your own accord without being asked
or compelled
accord VERB
1 to be consistent with something
2 (*formal*) to award something *They were
accorded special privileges.*

accordance NOUN
in accordance with in agreement with
in accordance with the rules

according ADVERB
according to 1 as stated by 2 in relation to

accordingly ADVERB
1 in the way that is required
2 therefore

accordion NOUN
a portable musical instrument like a large
concertina with a keyboard, played by
squeezing it and pressing the keys

account NOUN
1 a statement of money owed, spent,
or received
2 an arrangement to keep money in a bank
3 a description or report
on account of because of
account VERB
account for to clarify why something
happens

accountable ADJECTIVE
having to explain why you have done
something
accountability NOUN

accountant NOUN
a person who keeps or inspects financial
accounts
accountancy NOUN

accumulate VERB
1 to collect or pile up
2 to increase in quantity
accumulation NOUN

accurate ADJECTIVE
correct or exact
accurately ADVERB **accuracy** NOUN

accusation NOUN
a statement accusing a person of a crime
or wrong

accuse VERB
to say that someone has committed a crime
or wrong
accuser NOUN

a

accustomed ADJECTIVE
1 usual; normal
2 used to something or familiar with it

ace NOUN
1 a playing card with one spot
2 a skilful person or action

acetylene NOUN
a gas that burns with a bright flame

ache NOUN
a dull continuous pain

ache VERB
to have an ache

achieve VERB
to succeed in doing or producing something
achievable ADJECTIVE

achievement NOUN
something you achieve

acid NOUN
a chemical substance that contains hydrogen
and neutralizes alkalis. The hydrogen can be
replaced by a metal to form a salt.
acidic ADJECTIVE **acidity** NOUN

acid ADJECTIVE
1 sharp-tasting; sour
2 sarcastic an acid reply

acknowledge VERB
1 to admit that something is true
2 to state that you have received something
They acknowledged my application.
3 to express thanks for something
acknowledgement NOUN

acne NOUN
inflamed red pimples on the face and neck

acorn NOUN
the seed of an oak tree

acoustic ADJECTIVE
1 to do with sound or hearing
2 (of a musical instrument) not electronically
amplified

acoustics PLURAL NOUN
1 the qualities of a room or building that
affect the way it carries sound
2 the properties of sound

acquaint VERB
to tell somebody about something Acquaint
me with the facts.

acquaintance NOUN
a person you know slightly

acquire VERB
to obtain something

acquisition NOUN
1 something acquired recently
2 the process of getting something

acquisitive ADJECTIVE
eager to get new things

acquit VERB **acquitting, acquitted**
to decide that someone is not guilty
acquit yourself well to do something well
acquittal NOUN

acre NOUN
an area of land measuring 4,840 square yards
or 0.405 hectares
acreage NOUN

acrid ADJECTIVE
sharp and bitter an acrid smell

acrobat NOUN
a person who performs spectacular
gymnastic stunts for entertainment
acrobatic ADJECTIVE **acrobatics** PLURAL NOUN

acronym NOUN
a word formed from the initial letters of other
words, e.g. Aids (acquired immune deficiency
syndrome)

across PREPOSITION, ADVERB
1 from one side to the other
2 on the opposite side the house across
the street

acrostic NOUN
a word puzzle or poem in which the first or
last letters of each line form a word or phrase

acrylic NOUN
a kind of fibre, plastic, or resin made from an
organic acid

act NOUN
1 something someone does
2 a pretence put on an act
3 one of the main divisions of a play or opera
4 each performance in a programme of
entertainment a juggling act
5 a law passed by a parliament

act VERB
1 to do something
2 to perform a part in a play or film
3 to function or have an effect

action NOUN
1 the process of doing something
2 something done
3 fighting in a war killed in action
4 a lawsuit a libel action
out of action not working or
functioning **take action** to do something

activate VERB
to start something working
activation NOUN

active ADJECTIVE
1 taking part in many activities; energetic
2 functioning or working
3 (of a verb) in the form used when the
subject of the verb is performing the action,
e.g. sells in The shop sells milk.
actively ADVERB **activeness** NOUN

activist NOUN
a person who is active in politics and social affairs

activity NOUN **activities**
1 an action or occupation
2 an active or lively state

actor NOUN
a person who acts in a play or film

actress NOUN
a woman who acts in a play or film

actual ADJECTIVE
really there or happening
actually ADVERB

acumen NOUN
a good ability to decide things

acupuncture NOUN
treatment of the body by pricking parts with needles to relieve pain or cure disease
acupuncturist NOUN

acute ADJECTIVE
1 sharp or strong *acute pain*
2 having a sharp mind
acutely ADVERB **acuteness** NOUN

acute accent NOUN
a mark over a vowel, e.g. *é* in *résumé*

acute angle NOUN
an angle of less than 90°

AD ABBREVIATION
Anno Domini (Latin = in the year of Our Lord), used in dates counted from the birth of Christ

adamant ADJECTIVE
firm and not giving way to persuasion

Adam's apple NOUN
the lump at the front of a man's neck

adapt VERB
1 to change something for a new purpose
2 to become used to a new situation
adaptable ADJECTIVE **adaptation** NOUN

adaptor NOUN
a device to connect pieces of equipment

add VERB
1 to put one thing with another
2 to make another remark
add up 1 to make or find a total **2** (*informal*) to make sense

adder NOUN
a small poisonous snake

addict NOUN
a person with a habit they cannot give up
addicted ADJECTIVE **addiction** NOUN

addictive ADJECTIVE
causing a habit that people cannot give up *an addictive drug*

addition NOUN
1 the process of adding
2 something added
in addition also; as an extra thing
additional ADJECTIVE **additionally** ADVERB

additive NOUN
a substance added to another in small amounts, e.g. as a flavouring in food

address NOUN
1 the details of the place where someone lives or can be contacted
2 a speech to an audience

address VERB
1 to write an address on a letter or parcel
2 to make a speech or remark to someone

adenoids PLURAL NOUN
thick spongy flesh at the back of the nose and throat

adept ADJECTIVE
very skilful

adequate ADJECTIVE
enough or good enough
adequately ADVERB **adequacy** NOUN

adhere VERB
to stick to something
adhesion NOUN

adhesive ADJECTIVE
sticky; making things stick

ad hoc ADJECTIVE, ADVERB
done or arranged for a particular purpose
ad hoc decisions

adjacent ADJECTIVE
near or next *an adjacent room*

adjective NOUN
a word that describes a noun or adds to its meaning, e.g. *big, square*
adjectival ADJECTIVE

adjoin VERB
to be next or joined to

adjourn VERB
1 to break off a meeting until a later time
2 to break off and go somewhere else *They adjourned to the library.*

adjournment NOUN
a temporary pause in a meeting or activity

adjust VERB
1 to put a thing into its proper position or order
2 to alter something so that it is suitable
adjustable ADJECTIVE

adjustment NOUN
a slight alteration to something

administer VERB
1 to give or provide something
2 to manage business affairs

a
b
c
d
e
f
g
h
i
j
k
l
m
n
o
p
q
r
s
t
u
v
w
x
y
z

administrate VERB
to manage public or business affairs
administrator NOUN **administrative** ADJECTIVE

administration NOUN
1 the management of public or business affairs
2 the people who manage an organization etc.
3 the government

admirable ADJECTIVE
worth admiring; excellent
admirably ADVERB

admiral NOUN
a naval officer of high rank

admire VERB
1 to look at something and enjoy it
2 to think that someone or something is very good
admiration NOUN **admirer** NOUN

admission NOUN
1 permission to go in
2 a charge for being allowed to go in
3 a statement admitting something

admit VERB **admitting, admitted**
1 to allow someone or something to come in
2 to state reluctantly that something is true

admittance NOUN
permission to go into a private place

admittedly ADVERB
as an agreed fact

ado NOUN
without more or **further ado** without wasting any more time

adolescent NOUN
a young person between being a child and being an adult
adolescence NOUN

adopt VERB
1 to take a child into your family as your own
2 to accept something and use it
adoption NOUN

adore VERB
to love a person or thing very much
adorable ADJECTIVE **adoration** NOUN

adorn VERB
to decorate
adornment NOUN

adrenalin NOUN
a hormone produced by the body when you are afraid or excited. It makes your heart beat faster and increases your energy.

adrift ADJECTIVE, ADVERB
drifting or floating freely

adult NOUN
a fully grown or mature person

adulterate VERB
to make a thing impure or less good by adding something to it
adulteration NOUN

adultery NOUN
the act of having sexual intercourse with someone other than your wife or husband
adulterer NOUN **adulterous** ADJECTIVE

advance NOUN
1 a forward movement
2 an increase
3 a loan or early payment
in advance beforehand

advance VERB
1 to move forward or make progress
2 to lend or pay money ahead of the proper time
advancement NOUN

advantage NOUN
1 something useful or helpful
2 (in tennis) the next point won after deuce
take advantage of to use a person or thing profitably or unfairly

advantageous ADJECTIVE
giving an advantage; beneficial

Advent NOUN
the four weeks before Christmas

adventure NOUN
an exciting or challenging experience
adventurer NOUN

adventurous ADJECTIVE
willing to take risks and do new things

adverb NOUN
a word that adds to the meaning of a verb, adjective, or another adverb, e.g. *slowly*, *often*, and *downstairs*
adverbial ADJECTIVE

adversary NOUN **adversaries**
an opponent or enemy

adverse ADJECTIVE
unfavourable or harmful *adverse effects*
adversely ADVERB
Do not confuse this word with *averse*.

adversity NOUN **adversities**
trouble or misfortune

advert NOUN
(*informal*) an advertisement

advertise VERB
1 to present and praise goods to the public to encourage them to buy or use them
2 to make something publicly known
3 to give information about a job vacancy
advertiser NOUN

advertisement NOUN
a public notice or announcement, especially one advertising goods or services in newspapers, on posters, or in broadcasts

advice NOUN
1 words that tell a person what they should do
2 a piece of information

advisable ADJECTIVE
that is the wise thing to do

advise VERB
1 to give somebody advice
2 to inform someone
adviser NOUN **advisory** ADJECTIVE

advocate VERB
to speak in favour of something
We advocate reform.

advocate NOUN
1 a person who advocates a policy
an advocate of reform
2 a lawyer representing a person in a lawcourt

aerate VERB
1 to add air to something
2 to add carbon dioxide to a liquid

aerial ADJECTIVE
1 in or from the air
2 to do with aircraft

aerial NOUN
a wire or rod for receiving or transmitting radio or television signals

aerobatics PLURAL NOUN
spectacular performances by flying aircraft
aerobatic ADJECTIVE

aerobics PLURAL NOUN
exercises to strengthen the heart and lungs
aerobic ADJECTIVE

aerodrome NOUN
a landing place for aircraft

aerodynamic ADJECTIVE
designed to move through the air quickly and easily

aeronautics NOUN
the study of aircraft and flying
aeronautic ADJECTIVE **aeronautical** ADJECTIVE

aeroplane NOUN
a flying vehicle with engines and wings

aerosol NOUN
a container that holds a liquid under pressure and can let it out in a fine spray

aerospace NOUN
the earth's atmosphere and space beyond it

aesthetic ADJECTIVE
to do with enjoying beautiful things

afar ADVERB
far away

affable ADJECTIVE
polite and friendly
affability NOUN **affably** ADVERB

affair NOUN
1 an event or matter *a grand affair*
2 a temporary sexual relationship outside marriage

affairs PLURAL NOUN
the business and activities that are part of private or public life

affect VERB
1 to have an effect on
2 to pretend *We affected ignorance.*

affectation NOUN
an unnatural manner that is intended to impress other people

affected ADJECTIVE
pretended and unnatural

affection NOUN
a strong liking for a person

affectionate ADJECTIVE
showing affection; loving
affectionately ADVERB

affidavit NOUN
a legal statement written down and sworn to be true

affiliated ADJECTIVE
officially connected with a larger organization

affinity NOUN **affinities**
attraction or similarity between people or things

affirm VERB
to state something definitely
affirmation NOUN

affix VERB
to attach or add

affix NOUN
a prefix or suffix

afflict VERB
to cause someone to suffer

affliction NOUN
something that causes pain or suffering

affluent ADJECTIVE
having a lot of money
affluence NOUN

afford VERB
1 to have enough money to pay for something
2 to have enough time or resources to do something
3 to be able to do something without a risk
You can't afford to wait.

affront VERB
to insult or offend someone

affront NOUN
an insult

afield ADVERB
at or to a distance *far afield*

afloat ADJECTIVE, ADVERB
floating; on the sea

afraid ADJECTIVE
frightened or alarmed
I'm afraid I regret *I'm afraid I can't come.*

afresh ADVERB
again; in a new way *start afresh*

African ADJECTIVE
to do with Africa or its people

African NOUN
an African person

aft ADVERB
at or towards the back of a ship or aircraft

after PREPOSITION
1 later than *after tea*
2 behind in place or order *the letter after A*
3 trying to catch; pursuing *Run after him.*
4 in imitation or honour of *She is named after her aunt.*
5 about or concerning *He asked after you.*

after ADVERB
1 behind
2 at a later time

aftermath NOUN
something that results from something bad or unpleasant *the aftermath of the earthquake*

afternoon NOUN
the time from noon or lunchtime to evening

afterthought NOUN
something you think of or add later

afterwards ADVERB
at a later time

again ADVERB
1 another time; once more
2 besides; moreover

against PREPOSITION
1 touching or hitting *leaning against a wall*
2 in opposition to *They voted against the proposal.*
3 in preparation for *protection against the cold*

age NOUN
1 the length of time a person or thing has existed
2 a special period of history or geology *the ice age*
for ages (*informal*) for a very long time

age VERB **ageing**
to make or become old

aged ADJECTIVE
1 having the age of *a girl aged 12*
2 very old *an aged man*

agency NOUN **agencies**
1 an office or business *a travel agency*
2 the means by which something is done

agenda NOUN
a list of things to be done or discussed

agent NOUN
1 a person who organizes things for other people *a travel agent*
2 a spy *a secret agent*

aggravate VERB
1 to make something worse or more serious
2 (*informal*) to annoy
aggravation NOUN

aggregate ADJECTIVE
combined or total *the aggregate amount*

aggregate NOUN
a total amount or score

aggression NOUN
hostile or attacking action or behaviour

aggressive ADJECTIVE
1 hostile or violent
2 very determined and forceful
aggressively ADVERB

aggressor NOUN
a person or nation that starts an attack

aggrieved ADJECTIVE
resentful because of being treated unfairly

aghast ADJECTIVE
horrified

agile ADJECTIVE
moving quickly and easily
agilely ADVERB **agility** NOUN

agitate VERB
1 to make someone feel upset or anxious
2 to stir up public interest
3 to shake something about
agitation NOUN **agitator** NOUN

ago ADVERB
in the past *long ago*

agog ADJECTIVE
eager and excited

agony NOUN **agonies**
great pain or suffering
agonizing ADJECTIVE

agree VERB
1 to think or say the same as another person
2 to say you will do something *I agreed to go.*
3 to suit a person's health or digestion

agreeable ADJECTIVE
1 willing
2 pleasant
agreeably ADVERB

agreement NOUN
1 the act of agreeing
2 an arrangement that people have agreed on

agriculture NOUN
the cultivating of land on a large scale and rearing livestock; farming
agricultural ADJECTIVE

aground ADVERB, ADJECTIVE
stranded on the bottom in shallow water

ah EXCLAMATION
an exclamation of surprise, pity, or admiration

ahead ADVERB
further forward; in front

ahoy EXCLAMATION
a cry used at sea to call attention

aid NOUN
1 help
2 something that helps
3 money and supplies sent to help another country
in aid of for the purpose of

aid VERB
to help

aide NOUN
an assistant

Aids NOUN
a disease caused by the HIV virus, which weakens a person's ability to resist infections, from the initial letters of 'acquired immune deficiency syndrome'

ailing ADJECTIVE
1 ill; in poor health
2 in difficulties; not successful

ailment NOUN
a slight illness

aim VERB
1 to point a weapon
2 to throw or kick in a particular direction
3 to try or intend to do something

aim NOUN
1 the pointing of a weapon
2 a purpose or intention

aimless ADJECTIVE
having no purpose
aimlessly ADVERB

air NOUN
1 the mixture of gases that surrounds the earth
2 the open space above the earth
3 a tune or melody
4 an appearance or impression of something
an air of secrecy
5 an impressive or haughty manner
put on airs

air VERB
1 to put washing in a warm place to finish drying
2 to ventilate a room
3 to express an opinion

airborne ADJECTIVE
1 (of an aircraft) flying
2 carried by the air or by aircraft

air conditioning NOUN
a system for controlling the temperature and quality of the air in a room or building
air-conditioned ADJECTIVE

aircraft NOUN **aircraft**
an aeroplane, glider, or helicopter

aircraft carrier NOUN
a large ship with a long deck where aircraft can take off and land

airfield NOUN
an area with runways where aircraft can take off and land

air force NOUN
the part of a country's armed forces that uses aircraft

airline NOUN
a company that provides a regular service of transport by aircraft

airmail NOUN
mail carried by air

airport NOUN
a place where aircraft land and take off, with passenger terminals and other buildings

air raid NOUN
an attack by aircraft dropping bombs

airship NOUN
a large balloon with engines and a passenger compartment underneath

airtight ADJECTIVE
sealed to prevent air escaping

airy ADJECTIVE
1 with plenty of fresh air
2 light as air
3 vague and insincere
airily ADVERB

aisle NOUN
a passage between rows of seats or between shelves in a large shop

ajar ADVERB, ADJECTIVE
slightly open

akin ADJECTIVE
related or similar

alabaster NOUN
a kind of hard white stone

alacrity NOUN
speed and willingness

alarm NOUN
1 a warning sound or signal
2 a feeling of fear or worry

alarm VERB
to make someone frightened or anxious
alarming ADJECTIVE

alarm clock NOUN
a clock that can be set to sound at a fixed time to waken someone who is asleep

alas EXCLAMATION
an exclamation of sorrow or regret

albatross NOUN
a large seabird with long wings

a

albino *NOUN* **albinos**
a person or animal with white skin and hair and pink eyes

album *NOUN*
1 a CD, record, or tape with a number of songs on it
2 a book with blank pages for keeping photographs or stamps

albumen *NOUN*
the white of an egg

alchemy *NOUN*
an early form of chemistry, concerned with turning ordinary metals into gold
alchemist *NOUN*

alcohol *NOUN*
1 a colourless liquid made by fermenting sugar or starch
2 drinks containing this, e.g. wine, beer, and spirits

alcoholic *ADJECTIVE*
containing alcohol

alcoholic *NOUN*
a person who is addicted to alcohol
alcoholism *NOUN*

alcove *NOUN*
a section of a room that is set back from the main part

ale *NOUN*
a kind of beer

alert *ADJECTIVE*
watching and ready to act
alertness *NOUN*

alert *NOUN*
a warning or alarm
on the alert keeping watch

alert *VERB*
to warn someone of danger or make them aware of something

A level *NOUN*
advanced level in GCSE

algae *PLURAL NOUN*
plants that grow in water, with no true stems or leaves

algebra *NOUN*
mathematics in which letters and symbols are used to represent quantities
algebraic *ADJECTIVE*

alias *NOUN*
a false or different name

alias *ADVERB*
also called

alibi *NOUN* **alibis**
evidence that a person accused of a crime was somewhere else when it took place

alien *NOUN*
1 a person from another country; a foreigner
2 (in science fiction) a being from another world

alien *ADJECTIVE*
1 foreign
2 not part of a person's experience or character

alienate *VERB*
to make a person unfriendly or unhelpful
alienation *NOUN*

alight [1] *ADJECTIVE*
1 on fire
2 lit up

alight [2] *VERB*
1 to step out of a vehicle
2 (of a bird or insect) to fly down and settle

align *VERB*
1 to arrange things in a line
2 to join as an ally

alignment *NOUN*
arrangement in a line or in a special way

alike *ADJECTIVE, ADVERB*
1 like one another
2 in the same way

alimony *NOUN*
(*American*) money that someone is ordered to pay their wife or husband after they are separated or divorced

alive *ADJECTIVE*
1 living
2 alert or aware

alkali *NOUN* **alkalis**
a chemical substance that neutralizes an acid to form a salt
alkaline *ADJECTIVE*

all *ADJECTIVE*
the whole number or amount of

all *NOUN*
1 everything or everyone
2 everybody

all *ADVERB*
1 completely *dressed all in white*
2 to each team or competitor *three goals all*

Allah *NOUN*
the Muslim name of God

allay *VERB*
to calm or relieve a fear or doubt

all-clear *NOUN*
a signal that a danger has passed

allegation *NOUN*
an accusation made without proof

allege *VERB*
to say something without being able to prove it
allegedly *ADVERB*

allegiance *NOUN*
loyalty to a person or country

allegory NOUN **allegories**
a story in which the characters and events represent a deeper meaning, e.g. to teach a moral lesson
allegorical ADJECTIVE

alleluia EXCLAMATION
praise to God

allergy NOUN **allergies**
intense sensitivity to something that can make you ill
allergic ADJECTIVE

alleviate VERB
to make something, e.g. pain or suffering, less severe
alleviation NOUN

alley NOUN **alleys**
1 a narrow street or passage
2 a place for playing bowls or skittles

alliance NOUN
an association formed by countries or groups who want to support each other

allied ADJECTIVE
1 joined as allies; on the same side
2 of the same kind

alligator NOUN
a large reptile of the crocodile family

allocate VERB
to set something aside for a particular purpose
allocation NOUN

allot VERB **allotting**, **allotted**
to give a share of something to different people

allotment NOUN
1 a small piece of rented land used for growing vegetables
2 an amount allotted

allow VERB
1 to permit
2 to provide someone with something
They are allowed £100 for books.
allow for to take into account
allowable ADJECTIVE

allowance NOUN
an amount of money given regularly for a particular purpose
make allowances to be especially considerate

alloy NOUN
a mixture of two or more metals

all right ADJECTIVE, ADVERB
1 satisfactory or adequate
2 in good condition

all-round ADJECTIVE
general; not specialist *an all-round athlete*
all-rounder NOUN

allude VERB
to mention something briefly or indirectly

allure VERB
to attract or fascinate someone
allure NOUN **alluring** ADJECTIVE

allusion NOUN
a reference to something without actually naming it

alluvium NOUN
sand and soil deposited by a river or flood
alluvial ADJECTIVE

ally NOUN **allies**
1 a country in alliance with another
2 a person who cooperates with another

ally VERB **allies**, **allied**
to form an alliance

almanac NOUN
an annual publication containing a calendar and other information

almighty ADJECTIVE
1 having complete power
2 (*informal*) very great *an almighty din*
the Almighty a name for God

almond NOUN
an oval edible nut

almost ADVERB
nearly but not quite

alms PLURAL NOUN
(*old use*) money and gifts given to the poor

alone ADJECTIVE, ADVERB
without any other people or things

along PREPOSITION
following the length of *along the path*

along ADVERB
1 on or onwards *Push it along.*
2 accompanying somebody
Bring them along.

alongside PREPOSITION, ADVERB
next to something; beside

aloof ADJECTIVE
unfriendly in manner

aloud ADVERB
in a voice that can be heard

alpha NOUN
the first letter of the Greek alphabet, equivalent to Roman *A, a*

alphabet NOUN
the letters used in a language, arranged in a set order
alphabetical ADJECTIVE **alphabetically** ADVERB

alpine ADJECTIVE
to do with high mountains *alpine plants*

already ADVERB
by now; before now

Alsatian NOUN
a German shepherd dog

also ADVERB
in addition; besides

altar NOUN
a table or similar structure used in religious ceremonies

alter VERB
to make or become different; to change
alteration NOUN

altercation NOUN
a noisy argument or quarrel

alternate ADJECTIVE
1 happening or coming one after the other
alternate layers of sponge and cream
2 one in every two *on alternate Fridays*
alternately ADVERB

alternate VERB
to use or come alternately
alternation NOUN

alternating current NOUN
electric current that reverses its direction at regular intervals

alternative ADJECTIVE
available instead of something else
alternatively ADVERB

alternative NOUN
one of two or more possibilities

alternative medicine NOUN
types of medical treatment that are not based on ordinary medicine, such as acupuncture and homeopathy

although CONJUNCTION
despite the fact that

altimeter NOUN
an instrument used in aircraft for showing the height above sea level

altitude NOUN
the height of something above sea level

altogether ADVERB
1 with all included; in total
2 completely
3 on the whole

aluminium NOUN
a lightweight silver-coloured metal

always ADVERB
1 at all times
2 often *You are always complaining.*
3 whatever happens *You can always sleep on the floor.*

a.m. ABBREVIATION
before noon

amalgam NOUN
1 an alloy of mercury
2 a mixture or combination

amalgamate VERB
to mix or combine
amalgamation NOUN

amass VERB
to heap up or collect

amateur NOUN
a person who does something out of interest and not as a professional

amateurish ADJECTIVE
not done or made very well

amaze VERB
to surprise somebody greatly
amazement NOUN

amazing ADJECTIVE
very surprising or remarkable

ambassador NOUN
a person sent to a foreign country to represent their own government

amber NOUN
a hard clear yellowish substance used for making jewellery

ambiguity NOUN **ambiguities**
uncertainty about the meaning of something

ambiguous ADJECTIVE
having more than one possible meaning
ambiguously ADVERB

ambition NOUN
a strong desire to be successful and achieve things

ambitious ADJECTIVE
having a strong desire to be successful

ambivalent ADJECTIVE
having conflicting feelings about a person or situation
ambivalence NOUN

amble VERB
to walk at a slow easy pace

ambulance NOUN
a vehicle equipped to carry sick or injured people

ambush NOUN
a surprise attack from a hidden position

ambush VERB
to attack someone from a hidden position

amen EXCLAMATION
a word used at the end of a prayer or hymn, meaning 'so be it'

amend VERB
to alter something to improve it

amendment NOUN
a change to improve something

amends PLURAL NOUN
make amends to make up for having done something wrong

amenity NOUN **amenities**
a pleasant or useful feature that a place has

American ADJECTIVE
to do with the continent of America, or the USA
American NOUN

amethyst NOUN
a purple precious stone

amiable ADJECTIVE
friendly and good-tempered
amiably ADVERB

amicable ADJECTIVE
friendly and likeable
amicably ADVERB

amid or **amidst** PREPOSITION
in the middle of; among

amino acid NOUN
an acid found in proteins

amiss ADJECTIVE, ADVERB
wrong or faulty
take something amiss to be offended by what someone says

ammonia NOUN
a colourless gas or liquid with a strong smell

ammunition NOUN
a supply of bullets, shells, and grenades

amnesia NOUN
a loss of memory

amnesty NOUN **amnesties**
a general pardon for people who have committed a crime

amoeba NOUN **amoebas**
a microscopic creature consisting of a single cell which constantly changes shape and can split itself in two

amok ADVERB
run amok to rush about wildly or violently

among or **amongst** PREPOSITION
1 surrounded by *weeds among the flowers*
2 between *sweets divided among the children*

amoral ADJECTIVE
having no moral standards

amorous ADJECTIVE
showing or feeling sexual love

amorphous ADJECTIVE
not having a definite shape

amount NOUN
a quantity or total

amount VERB
amount to to add up to or be equivalent to

amp NOUN
1 an ampere
2 (*informal*) an amplifier

ampere NOUN
a unit for measuring electric current

amphetamine NOUN
a drug used as a stimulant

amphibian NOUN
1 an animal able to live both on land and in water
2 a vehicle that can be used on land and in water

amphibious ADJECTIVE
able to live or move on land and in water

amphitheatre NOUN
a round open theatre with seats round a central arena

ample ADJECTIVE
1 quite enough
2 large
amply ADVERB

amplifier NOUN
a piece of equipment for making a sound or electrical signal louder or stronger

amplify VERB **amplifies**, **amplified**
1 to make a sound or electrical signal louder or stronger
2 to explain in more detail
amplification NOUN

amputate VERB
to cut off an arm or leg by a surgical operation
amputation NOUN

amuse VERB
1 to make a person laugh or smile
2 to make time pass pleasantly for someone
amusing ADJECTIVE

amusement NOUN
a way of passing time pleasantly

an DETERMINER
SEE **a**

anaemia NOUN
a poor condition of the blood that makes a person pale
anaemic ADJECTIVE

anaesthetic NOUN
a substance or gas that makes you unable to feel pain
anaesthesia NOUN

anaesthetist NOUN
a medical person qualified to give anaesthetics

anaesthetize VERB
to give an anaesthetic to

anagram NOUN
a word or phrase made by rearranging the letters of another word or phrase

anal ADJECTIVE
to do with the anus

analgesic NOUN
a substance that reduces pain

a

analogy NOUN **analogies**
a comparison between two things that are alike in some ways
analogous ADJECTIVE

analyse VERB
1 to examine and interpret something
2 to separate something into its parts

analysis NOUN **analyses**
1 a detailed examination of something
2 a separation of something into its parts
analytical ADJECTIVE

anarchy NOUN
1 lack of government or control
2 lawlessness or complete disorder

anathema NOUN
something you detest

anatomy NOUN
the structure of a person's or animal's body, or the study of this
anatomical ADJECTIVE **anatomist** NOUN

ancestor NOUN
someone from whom a person is descended
ancestral ADJECTIVE **ancestry** NOUN

anchor NOUN
a heavy object attached to a ship by a chain or rope and dropped to the bottom of the sea to hold the ship still

anchor VERB
1 to fix or be fixed by an anchor
2 to fix firmly

anchovy NOUN **anchovies**
a small fish with a strong flavour

ancient ADJECTIVE
1 very old
2 belonging to the distant past

ancillary ADJECTIVE
helping or supporting *ancillary staff*

and CONJUNCTION
a word used to link words and phrases
pens and pencils   better and better

anecdote NOUN
an entertaining story about a real person or thing

anemone NOUN
a plant with cup-shaped red, purple, or white flowers

anew ADVERB
again; in a new or different way

angel NOUN
1 an attendant or messenger of God
2 a kind or beautiful person
angelic ADJECTIVE

anger NOUN
a strong feeling that you want to quarrel or fight with someone

anger VERB
to make a person angry

angle NOUN
1 the space between two lines or surfaces that meet
2 the amount by which a line or surface must be turned to make it lie along another
3 a point of view

angle VERB
1 to put something in a slanting position
2 to present information from one point of view

angler NOUN
a person who fishes with a fishing rod and line
angling NOUN

angry ADJECTIVE **angrier, angriest**
feeling or showing anger
angrily ADVERB

anguish NOUN
severe suffering or misery
anguished ADJECTIVE

angular ADJECTIVE
having angles or sharp corners

animal NOUN
a living thing that can feel and move, usually other than a human

animate VERB
1 to make a thing lively
2 to produce something as an animated film

animated ADJECTIVE
1 lively and excited
2 (of a film) made by a process of animation

animation NOUN
1 a lively or excited state
2 the technique of making a film by photographing a series of still pictures and showing them rapidly one after another

animosity NOUN **animosities**
a feeling of hostility

aniseed NOUN
a sweet-smelling seed used for flavouring

ankle NOUN
the part of the leg where it joins the foot

annex VERB
1 to take something and add it to what you have already
2 to add or join a thing to something else

annexe NOUN
a building added to a larger or more important building

annihilate VERB
to destroy something completely
annihilation NOUN

anniversary NOUN **anniversaries**
a day when you remember something special that happened on the same day in a previous year

announce VERB
to make something known by saying it publicly or to an audience
announcement NOUN

announcer NOUN
a person who announces items on radio or television

annoy VERB
1 to make a person slightly angry
2 to be troublesome to someone
annoyance NOUN

annual ADJECTIVE
1 happening or done once a year
2 calculated over one year
3 living for one year or one season
annually ADVERB

annual NOUN
1 a book that comes out once a year
2 an annual plant

annuity NOUN **annuities**
a fixed annual allowance of money, especially from a kind of investment

annul VERB **annulling, annulled**
to end a contract or arrangement legally
annulment NOUN

anode NOUN
the electrode by which electric current enters a device COMPARE **cathode**

anoint VERB
to put oil or ointment on something in a religious ceremony

anomaly NOUN **anomalies**
something that does not follow the general rule or that is unlike the usual or normal kind

anonymous ADJECTIVE
without the name of the person responsible being known or made public *an anonymous donation*
anonymously ADVERB **anonymity** NOUN

anorak NOUN
a waterproof jacket with a hood

anorexia NOUN
an illness that makes a person so anxious to lose weight that they refuse to eat
anorexic ADJECTIVE

another ADJECTIVE, PRONOUN
a different or extra person or thing

answer NOUN
1 something said in return or reply
2 the solution to a problem

answer VERB
1 to give an answer to
2 to respond to a signal
answer back to reply cheekily or rudely **answer for** to be responsible for

ant NOUN
a small insect that lives as one of an organized group

antagonism NOUN
a feeling of being unfriendly or hostile

antagonist NOUN
an enemy or opponent

antagonistic ADJECTIVE
unfriendly or hostile

antagonize VERB
to make a person feel hostile or angry

anteater NOUN
an animal that feeds on ants and termites

antecedent NOUN
a person or thing that lived or occurred at an earlier time

antelope NOUN
a fast-running animal like a deer

antenna NOUN
1 (**antennae**) a feeler on the head of an insect or crustacean
2 (**antennas**) an aerial

anthem NOUN
a religious or patriotic song, usually sung by a choir or group of people

anthology NOUN **anthologies**
a collection of poems, stories, or songs

anthrax NOUN
a disease of sheep and cattle that can also infect people

anthropoid ADJECTIVE
like a human being

anthropology NOUN
the study of human beings and their customs
anthropological ADJECTIVE
anthropologist NOUN

antibiotic NOUN
a substance (e.g. penicillin) that destroys bacteria or prevents them from growing

antibody NOUN **antibodies**
a protein that forms in the blood as a defence against bacteria and other substances

anticipate VERB
1 to take action in advance about something you are aware of
2 to act before someone else does
3 to expect something
anticipation NOUN **anticipatory** ADJECTIVE

anticlimax NOUN
a feeble or disappointing ending to something exciting

anticlockwise ADVERB, ADJECTIVE
moving in a direction opposite to the hands of a clock

a
b
c
d
e
f
g
h
i
j
k
l
m
n
o
p
q
r
s
t
u
v
w
x
y
z

antics PLURAL NOUN
funny or foolish actions

anticyclone NOUN
an area where air pressure is high, usually producing fine settled weather

antidote NOUN
something that acts against the effects of a poison or disease

antifreeze NOUN
a liquid added to water to make its freezing point lower

antipathy NOUN
a strong dislike

antipodes PLURAL NOUN
places on opposite sides of the earth
the Antipodes Australia, New Zealand, and the areas near them, which are almost exactly opposite Europe
antipodean ADJECTIVE

antiquated ADJECTIVE
old-fashioned

antique ADJECTIVE
1 belonging to the distant past
2 very old

antique NOUN
a valuable object from an older time

antiquities PLURAL NOUN
objects that were made in ancient times

antiquity NOUN
ancient times, especially of the Greeks and Romans

antiseptic ADJECTIVE
1 able to destroy bacteria
2 thoroughly clean and free from germs

antiseptic NOUN
a substance that can destroy bacteria

antisocial ADJECTIVE
unfriendly or inconsiderate towards other people

antithesis NOUN **antitheses**
1 the exact opposite of something
2 a contrast of ideas

antler NOUN
the branching horn of a deer

antonym NOUN
a word that is opposite in meaning to another, e.g. *good* and *bad*

anus NOUN
the opening at the lower end of the alimentary canal, through which solid waste matter is passed out of the body

anvil NOUN
a large block of iron on which a blacksmith hammers metal

anxious ADJECTIVE
1 worried
2 keen or eager *anxious to please us*
anxiously ADVERB **anxiety** NOUN

any ADJECTIVE, PRONOUN
1 one or some
2 no matter which *Come any time.*

any ADVERB
at all *Is this any good?*

anybody PRONOUN
any person

anyhow ADVERB
1 in any case; whatever happens
2 in a careless way

anyone PRONOUN
anybody

anything PRONOUN
any thing

anyway ADVERB
in any case; whatever happens

anywhere ADVERB
in or to any place

aorta NOUN
the main artery that carries blood away from the left side of the heart

apart ADVERB
1 away from each other
2 into pieces *It has come apart.*
apart from excluding; other than

apartheid NOUN
the political policy of keeping people of different races apart

apartment NOUN
1 a set of rooms
2 a flat

apathy NOUN
lack of care or interest
apathetic ADJECTIVE

ape NOUN
an animal like a monkey but with no tail, e.g. a chimpanzee or gorilla

ape VERB
to imitate or mimic

aperture NOUN
an opening

apex NOUN
the tip or highest point

aphid NOUN
a tiny insect that sucks the juices from plants, e.g. a greenfly

aphorism NOUN
a short witty saying

apiary NOUN **apiaries**
a place where bees are kept

apiece ADVERB
to, for, or by each *We got five pounds apiece.*

aplomb NOUN
dignity and confidence

apologetic ADJECTIVE
expressing regret
apologetically ADVERB

apologize VERB
to make an apology

apology NOUN **apologies**
a statement that you are sorry for something you have done

apostle NOUN
a supporter of a person or belief, especially one of the twelve men sent out by Christ

apostrophe NOUN
a punctuation mark (') used to show that letters have been missed out (as in *I can't* = I cannot) or to show possession (as in *the boy's book*)

appal VERB **appalling, appalled**
to make a person shocked or horrified

appalling ADJECTIVE
shocking; very unpleasant

apparatus NOUN
the equipment for a particular experiment or task

apparent ADJECTIVE
1 clear or obvious
2 appearing to be true but not really so
their apparent indifference
apparently ADVERB

apparition NOUN
1 something strange or surprising that appears
2 a ghost

appeal VERB
1 to ask for something that you badly need
We'll appeal for more money.
2 to ask for a decision to be changed
3 to seem attractive or interesting

appeal NOUN
1 an act of asking for something you need
2 an act of asking for a decision to be changed
3 attraction or interest

appear VERB
1 to come into sight
2 to arrive
3 to seem

appearance NOUN
what somebody or something looks like or seems to be

appease VERB
to calm or pacify someone by agreeing to what they ask
appeasement NOUN

append VERB
to add at the end

appendage NOUN
something added or attached at the end

appendicitis NOUN
inflammation of the appendix

appendix NOUN
1 (**appendixes**) a small tube leading off from the intestine
2 (**appendices**) an extra section at the end of a book

appetite NOUN
1 a desire for food
2 an enthusiasm for something

appetizer NOUN
a small amount of food eaten before the main meal

appetizing ADJECTIVE
looking and smelling good to eat

applaud VERB
1 to show that you like something by clapping your hands
2 to express approval of

applause NOUN
a show of approval by clapping

apple NOUN
a round fruit with a red, yellow, or green skin

appliance NOUN
a device or piece of equipment

applicable ADJECTIVE
suitable or relevant

applicant NOUN
a person who applies for a job or position

application NOUN
1 the action of applying for something
2 a formal request
3 the ability to concentrate on working
4 (ICT) a program designed for a particular purpose

apply VERB **applies, applied**
1 to start using something
2 to make a formal request *I've applied for a job.*
3 to concern someone *This rule does not apply to you.*
4 to put one thing on another
apply yourself to concentrate on working

appoint VERB
1 to choose a person for a job
2 to arrange or decide something officially
They will appoint a time for the meeting.

appointment NOUN
1 an arrangement to meet or visit somebody at a particular time
2 a job or position

apposite ADJECTIVE
(of a remark) suitable or relevant

apposition NOUN
(*Grammar*) a construction in which two nouns referring to the same person or thing are placed together, e.g. *her dog Rufus*

appraise VERB
to estimate the value or quality of a person or thing
appraisal NOUN

appreciate VERB
1 to enjoy or value something
2 to understand something
3 to increase in value
appreciation NOUN **appreciative** ADJECTIVE

apprehend VERB
1 to seize or arrest someone
2 to understand something

apprehension NOUN
1 fear or worry
2 understanding
3 an arrest

apprehensive ADJECTIVE
anxious or worried

apprentice NOUN
a person who is learning a trade or craft from an employer
apprenticed ADJECTIVE **apprenticeship** NOUN

approach VERB
1 to come near
2 to go to someone with a request or offer
3 to set about doing something

approach NOUN
1 a way or road to a place
2 a method of doing something

approachable ADJECTIVE
friendly and easy to talk to

appropriate ADJECTIVE
suitable or relevant
appropriately ADVERB

appropriate VERB
to take something for yourself
appropriation NOUN

approval NOUN
1 a good opinion of somebody or something
2 formal agreement
on approval taken by a customer for a trial period before being bought

approve VERB
1 to have a good opinion of a person or thing
2 to agree formally to something

approximate ADJECTIVE
almost exact or correct but not completely so
approximately ADVERB

approximate VERB
to make or be almost the same as something
approximation NOUN

apricot NOUN
a juicy orange-coloured fruit with a stone in it

April NOUN
the fourth month of the year

apron NOUN
1 a piece of clothing worn over the front of the body to protect other clothes
2 an area on an airfield where aircraft are loaded and unloaded

apse NOUN
a domed semicircular part at the east end of a church

apt ADJECTIVE
1 likely; prone
2 suitable or relevant *an apt quotation*
aptly ADVERB

aptitude NOUN
a talent or ability

aquarium NOUN **aquariums**
a tank or building for keeping live fish and other water animals

aquatic ADJECTIVE
to do with water *aquatic sports*

aqueduct NOUN
a bridge carrying a water channel across a valley

aquiline ADJECTIVE
hooked like an eagle's beak

Arab NOUN
a member of a Semitic people living in parts of the Middle East and North Africa
Arabian ADJECTIVE

arabesque NOUN
1 (in dancing) a position with one leg stretched backwards in the air
2 an ornamental design of leaves and branches

Arabic ADJECTIVE
to do with the Arabs or their language
Arabic NOUN
the language of the Arabs

arabic numerals PLURAL NOUN
the figures 1, 2, 3, 4, etc.

arable ADJECTIVE
suitable for ploughing or growing crops on

arbiter NOUN
1 a person appointed to settle a disagreement
2 a person who is influential or sets standards

arbitrary ADJECTIVE
chosen or done on an impulse, not according to a rule or law
arbitrarily ADVERB

arbitrate VERB
to settle a disagreement by arbitration

arbitration NOUN
settlement of a disagreement by an impartial person who is not involved
arbitrator NOUN

arboretum NOUN **arboretums**
a place where trees are grown for study and display

arbour NOUN
a shady place among trees

arc NOUN
1 part of the circumference of a circle
2 a luminous electric current passing between two electrodes

arcade NOUN
a covered passage or area, usually with shops

arcane ADJECTIVE
secret or mysterious

arch¹ NOUN
1 a curved structure that supports a bridge or roof
2 something shaped like this
arch VERB
to form something into an arch

arch² ADJECTIVE
pretending to be playful
archly ADVERB

archaeology NOUN
the study of ancient civilizations from the remains of their buildings and artefacts
archaeological ADJECTIVE **archaeologist** NOUN

archaic ADJECTIVE
belonging to former or ancient times

archangel NOUN
an angel of the highest rank

archbishop NOUN
the chief bishop of a region

archer NOUN
a person who shoots with a bow and arrows

archery NOUN
the sport of shooting at a target with a bow and arrows

archipelago NOUN **archipelagos**
a large group of islands

architect NOUN
a person who designs buildings

architecture NOUN
1 the process of designing buildings
2 a particular style of building
architectural ADJECTIVE

archive NOUN
(ICT) a collection of computer files not in regular use

archives PLURAL NOUN
the historical records of an organization or community

archivist NOUN
a person trained to organize a set of archives

archway NOUN
an arched passage or entrance

arctic ADJECTIVE
very cold

ardent ADJECTIVE
enthusiastic or passionate
ardently ADVERB

ardour NOUN
enthusiasm or passion

arduous ADJECTIVE
needing much effort; laborious
arduously ADVERB

area NOUN
1 the extent or measurement of a surface
2 a particular region or piece of land
3 a subject or special activity

arena NOUN
the level area in the centre of an amphitheatre or sports stadium

aren't
are not

arguable ADJECTIVE
1 able to be stated as a possibility
2 open to doubt; not certain
arguably ADVERB

argue VERB
1 to disagree or exchange angry comments
2 to give reasons for a statement or opinion

argument NOUN
1 a disagreement or quarrel
2 a series of reasons for a statement or opinion

argumentative ADJECTIVE
fond of arguing

aria NOUN
a solo piece in an opera or oratorio

arid ADJECTIVE
dry and barren

arise VERB **arose**, **arisen**
1 to come into existence or to people's notice
A problem has arisen.
2 to rise from a sitting or kneeling position

aristocracy NOUN
people of the highest social rank; members of the nobility

aristocrat NOUN
a member of the aristocracy
aristocratic ADJECTIVE

arithmetic NOUN
the science or study of numbers; calculation with numbers
arithmetical ADJECTIVE

ark NOUN
1 (in the Bible) the ship in which Noah and his family escaped the Flood
2 a wooden box in which the writings of the Jewish Law were kept

arm[1] NOUN
1 each of the two limbs extending from the shoulder
2 something jutting out from a main part
3 the raised side part of a chair

arm[2] VERB
1 to supply with weapons
2 to prepare for war
armed ADJECTIVE

armada NOUN
a fleet of warships

armadillo NOUN **armadillos**
a small burrowing animal covered with a shell of bony plates

armaments PLURAL NOUN
the weapons of an army or country

armature NOUN
the current-carrying part of a dynamo or electric motor

armchair NOUN
a comfortable chair with arms

armed forces or **armed services**
PLURAL NOUN
a country's army, navy, and air force

armful NOUN **armfuls**
as much as you can carry in your arms

armistice NOUN
an agreement to stop fighting in a war or battle

armour NOUN
1 a protective covering for the body, formerly worn in fighting
2 a metal protective covering on a warship or heavy military vehicle
armoured ADJECTIVE

armoury NOUN **armouries**
a place where weapons and ammunition are stored

armpit NOUN
the hollow part below the top of the arm at the shoulder

arms PLURAL NOUN
1 weapons
2 a heraldic design on a shield

army NOUN **armies**
1 a large number of soldiers trained to fight on land
2 a large group of people

aroma NOUN
a pleasant smell
aromatic ADJECTIVE

around ADVERB, PREPOSITION
all round; about

arouse VERB
1 to stir up a feeling in someone
2 to wake someone up

arrange VERB
1 to put things into a certain order
2 to form plans for something
3 to prepare music for particular instruments or voices

arrangement NOUN
1 a particular pattern or ordering of things
2 an agreement to do something

array NOUN
1 a display
2 an orderly arrangement

array VERB
1 to arrange in order
2 to dress or decorate

arrears PLURAL NOUN
1 money owed that should have been paid earlier
2 a backlog of work
in arrears behind with payments

arrest VERB
1 to seize a person by the authority of the law
2 to stop or check a process or movement

arrest NOUN
1 the act of arresting somebody
2 the process of stopping something

arrive VERB
1 to reach the place you are going to
2 to reach a decision or agreement
3 to happen *The great day arrived.*
arrival NOUN

arrogant ADJECTIVE
unpleasantly proud and haughty
arrogantly ADVERB **arrogance** NOUN

arrow NOUN
1 a weapon with a pointed tip shot from a bow
2 a sign with a shape of an arrow, used for showing direction

arsenal NOUN
a place where weapons and ammunition are stored or produced

arsenic NOUN
a highly poisonous metallic substance

arson NOUN
the crime of deliberately setting fire to a building
arsonist NOUN

art NOUN
1 painting, drawing, or sculpture, or the things produced in this way
2 a skill *the art of debating*

artefact NOUN
an object made by humans, especially in the past and of historical interest

artery NOUN **arteries**
1 a tube that carries blood away from the heart
2 an important road or route
arterial ADJECTIVE

artful ADJECTIVE
clever and crafty
artfully ADVERB

arthritis NOUN
a disease that makes joints in the body stiff
and painful
arthritic ADJECTIVE

arthropod NOUN
an animal of the group that includes insects,
spiders, crabs, and centipedes

artichoke NOUN
a kind of plant with a flower head used as
a vegetable

article NOUN
1 a piece of writing published in a newspaper
or magazine
2 an object
3 (*Grammar*) any of the words *a* or *an* (the
indefinite article), or *the* (the definite article)

articulate ADJECTIVE
able to speak and express ideas clearly

articulate VERB
1 to say or speak clearly
2 to connect by a joint
articulation NOUN

articulated ADJECTIVE
(of a vehicle) having two sections connected
by a flexible joint

artificial ADJECTIVE
not natural; made by human beings in
imitation of a natural thing
artificially ADVERB **artificiality** NOUN

artillery NOUN
1 large guns
2 the part of an army that uses these

artisan NOUN
a skilled worker who makes things with their
hands

artist NOUN
1 a person who paints pictures
2 an entertainer
artistry NOUN

artistic ADJECTIVE
1 to do with art or artists
2 having a talent for art
artistically ADVERB

arts PLURAL NOUN
languages, literature, history, and other
non-scientific subjects in which opinion and
interpretation are very important
the arts creative work such as painting,
music, and writing

as ADVERB, CONJUNCTION
1 equally or similarly *This is just as easy.*
2 when or while *He fell as he got off the bus.*
3 because *As we were late, we missed the train.*
4 in a way that *Leave it as it is.*

as PREPOSITION
in the function of *It acts as a handle.*

asbestos NOUN
a fireproof material made up of fine soft fibres

ascend VERB
1 to go up
2 to rise or slope upwards
ascend the throne to become king or queen

ascent NOUN
1 an upward climb or movement
2 a way up

ascertain VERB
to find something out by asking

ascribe VERB
to regard something as having a particular
cause or reason *She ascribes her success to
hard work.*

aseptic ADJECTIVE
clean and free from bacteria that cause things
to become septic

ash [1] NOUN
the powder that is left after something has
been burned
ashes remains after something has been
burned, especially of a human body after
cremation

ash [2] NOUN
a tree with silver-grey bark

ashamed ADJECTIVE
feeling shame

ashen ADJECTIVE
grey or pale

ashore ADVERB
to or on the shore

Asian ADJECTIVE
to do with Asia or its people

Asian NOUN
an Asian person

aside ADVERB
1 to or at one side
2 in reserve

aside NOUN
words spoken so that only certain people
will hear

asinine ADJECTIVE
extremely stupid

ask VERB
1 to speak so as to find out or get something
2 to invite someone *Ask them to the party.*

askance ADVERB
look askance at to regard a person or situation with distrust or disapproval

askew ADVERB, ADJECTIVE
crooked; not straight or level

asleep ADVERB, ADJECTIVE
sleeping

asparagus NOUN
a plant whose young shoots are eaten as a vegetable

aspect NOUN
1 one part of a problem or situation
2 a person's or thing's appearance
3 the direction a room or building faces

asphalt NOUN
a sticky black substance like tar, mixed with gravel to make road surfaces

asphyxia NOUN
suffocation

asphyxiate VERB
to suffocate
asphyxiation NOUN

aspire VERB
to have an ambition to achieve something
He aspires to be prime minister.

aspirin NOUN
a drug used to relieve pain or reduce fever

ass NOUN
1 a donkey
2 (*informal*) a stupid person

assail VERB
to attack

assailant NOUN
an attacker

assassin NOUN
a person who kills an important person

assassinate VERB
to kill an important person, especially for political reasons
assassination NOUN

assault NOUN
a violent attack

assault VERB
to attack someone violently

assemble VERB
1 to bring or come together
2 to put the parts of something together

assembly NOUN **assemblies**
1 the process of coming together
2 a regular meeting, especially of all the members of a school
3 a parliament or other government body

assent VERB
1 to consent
2 to say you agree

assent NOUN
consent or approval

assert VERB
to state something firmly

assertion NOUN
something said with force or confidence

assertive ADJECTIVE
acting forcefully and with confidence

assess VERB
to decide or estimate the value or quality of a person or thing
assessment NOUN **assessor** NOUN

asset NOUN
something useful or valuable to someone

assets PLURAL NOUN
a person's or company's property that could be sold to pay debts or raise money

assign VERB
1 to give a task or duty to someone
2 to appoint a person to perform a task

assignation NOUN
an arrangement to meet someone, especially a lover

assignment NOUN
a task or duty given to someone

assimilate VERB
to take in and absorb something
assimilation NOUN

assist VERB
to help someone
assistance NOUN

assistant NOUN
1 a person who assists another
2 a person who serves customers in a shop

associate VERB
1 to connect things in your mind
2 to have dealings with a group of people

associate NOUN
a colleague or companion
associate ADJECTIVE

association NOUN
1 an organization of people; a society
2 a connection or link in your mind

assorted ADJECTIVE
of various sorts put together

assortment NOUN
a mixed collection of things

assume VERB
1 to accept something without proof
2 to undertake
3 to put on an expression
assumed name a false name
assumption NOUN

assurance NOUN
1 a promise or guarantee
2 a kind of life insurance
3 confidence in yourself

assure VERB
1 to tell somebody confidently
2 to make certain

asterisk NOUN
a star-shaped sign (*) used to draw attention to something

astern ADVERB
at or to the back of a ship or aircraft

asteroid NOUN
one of the small planets that orbit the sun between Mars and Jupiter

asthma NOUN
a disease that makes breathing difficult
asthmatic ADJECTIVE, NOUN

astigmatism NOUN
a defect that prevents an eye or lens from focusing properly
astigmatic ADJECTIVE

astonish VERB
to surprise somebody very much
astonishment NOUN

astound VERB
to astonish or shock somebody very much

astray ADVERB, ADJECTIVE
away from the right path or place or course of action
go astray to be lost or mislaid

astride ADVERB, PREPOSITION
with one leg on each side of something

astrology NOUN
the study of the stars and planets and how they are supposed to influence people's lives
astrologer NOUN **astrological** ADJECTIVE

astronaut NOUN
a person who travels in space

astronomical ADJECTIVE
1 to do with astronomy
2 (of a number or cost) extremely large

astronomy NOUN
the study of the stars and planets and their movements
astronomer NOUN

astute ADJECTIVE
clever at understanding situations quickly
astutely ADVERB

asylum NOUN
1 refuge and safety given to political refugees
2 (old use) a hospital for mentally ill people

at PREPOSITION
used to show: 1 position or direction *at the top Aim at the target.*
2 time *at midnight*
3 level or price *They are sold at £10 each.*
4 cause *We were surprised at his mistake.*
at all in any way **at once** 1 immediately *Come at once.* 2 at the same time *It all happened at once.*

atheist NOUN
a person who believes that there is no God
atheism NOUN

athlete NOUN
a person who is good at sport, especially athletics

athletic ADJECTIVE
1 physically strong and active
2 to do with athletes
athletically ADVERB

athletics PLURAL NOUN
physical exercises and sports, e.g. running, jumping, and throwing

atlas NOUN
a book of maps

atmosphere NOUN
1 the air around the earth
2 a feeling or mood *a friendly atmosphere*
atmospheric ADJECTIVE

atoll NOUN
a ring-shaped coral reef

atom NOUN
the smallest particle of a chemical element

atom bomb or **atomic bomb** NOUN
a bomb exploded by atomic energy

atomic ADJECTIVE
to do with an atom or atomic energy

atomic energy NOUN
energy created by splitting the nuclei of certain atoms

atomic number NOUN
(*Science*) the number of protons in the nucleus of an atom

atomizer NOUN
a device for making a liquid into a fine spray

atone VERB
to make amends for having done wrong
atonement NOUN

atrocious ADJECTIVE
extremely bad
atrociously ADVERB

atrocity NOUN **atrocities**
something extremely bad or wicked; wickedness

attach VERB
1 to fix or join something to something else
2 to think of something as relevant to a situation or topic *We attach great importance to fitness.*
attached to fond of

attachment NOUN
1 the process of attaching
2 something attached
3 (*ICT*) a file sent with an email

attack *NOUN*
1 a violent attempt to hurt or overcome somebody
2 a piece of strong criticism
3 sudden illness or pain
4 the players in a team whose job is to score goals; an attempt to score a goal

attack *VERB*
to make an attack on
attacker *NOUN*

attain *VERB*
to succeed in doing or getting something
attainable *ADJECTIVE* **attainment** *NOUN*

attainment *NOUN*
an achievement

attempt *VERB*
to make an effort to do something; to try

attempt *NOUN*
an effort to do something; a try

attend *VERB*
1 to be present somewhere or go somewhere regularly
2 to look after someone
3 to spend time dealing with something

attendance *NOUN*
1 the act of attending or being present
2 the number of people present at an event

attendant *NOUN*
a person who helps or accompanies someone

attention *NOUN*
1 concentration and careful thought
2 a position in which a soldier stands with feet together and arms straight downwards

attentive *ADJECTIVE*
giving attention to something
attentively *ADVERB*

attest *VERB*
to declare or prove that something is true or genuine
attestation *NOUN*

attic *NOUN*
a room in the roof of a house

attire *NOUN*
(*formal*) clothes

attired *ADJECTIVE*
(*formal*) dressed

attitude *NOUN*
1 a way of thinking or behaving
2 the position of the body; posture

attorney *NOUN* **attorneys**
1 a person appointed to act on behalf of another
2 (*American*) a lawyer

attract *VERB*
1 to seem pleasant or interesting to someone
2 to pull by a physical force *Magnets attract metal.*

attraction *NOUN*
1 the process of attracting, or the ability to attract
2 something that attracts visitors

attractive *ADJECTIVE*
1 pleasant or good-looking
2 interesting or appealing *an attractive idea*
attractively *ADVERB*

attribute *VERB*
to regard something as the cause or source *We attribute their success to hard work.*
attribution *NOUN*

attribute *NOUN*
a quality or characteristic

attuned *ADJECTIVE*
adjusted to something

aubergine *NOUN*
a deep purple fruit eaten as a vegetable

auction *NOUN*
a public sale at which things are sold to the person who bids highest

auction *VERB*
to sell something by auction
auctioneer *NOUN*

audacious *ADJECTIVE*
bold or daring
audaciously *ADVERB*

audacity *NOUN*
boldness or daring

audible *ADJECTIVE*
loud enough to be heard
audibility *NOUN* **audibly** *ADVERB*

audience *NOUN*
1 people who have gathered to hear or watch something
2 a formal interview with an important person

audio *NOUN*
the reproduction of recorded music or sounds

audio-visual *ADJECTIVE*
using both sound and pictures to give information

audit *NOUN*
an official examination of financial accounts to see that they are correct

audit *VERB*
to make an audit of accounts

audition *NOUN*
a test to see if an actor or musician is suitable for a job

audition *VERB*
to give someone an audition

auditor *NOUN*
a person qualified to audit accounts

auditorium *NOUN* **auditoriums**
the part of a theatre or hall where the audience sits

augment *VERB*
to increase or add to something
augmentation *NOUN*

augur *VERB*
to be a sign of what is to come *These successes augur well.*

August *NOUN*
the eighth month of the year

august *ADJECTIVE*
majestic or imposing

aunt *NOUN*
1 the sister of your father or mother
2 your uncle's wife

au pair *NOUN*
a young person from abroad who works for a time in someone's home

aura *NOUN*
a general feeling surrounding a person or thing *an aura of excitement*

aural *ADJECTIVE*
to do with the ear or hearing
aurally *ADVERB*

auspicious *ADJECTIVE*
fortunate or favourable

austere *ADJECTIVE*
very simple and plain
austerely *ADVERB* **austerity** *NOUN*

authentic *ADJECTIVE*
real; genuine
authentically *ADVERB* **authenticity** *NOUN*

authenticate *VERB*
to confirm something as being authentic
authentication *NOUN*

author *NOUN*
the writer of a book, play, poem, or article
authorship *NOUN*

authoritarian *ADJECTIVE*
strict in enforcing obedience

authoritative *ADJECTIVE*
having proper authority or expert knowledge

authority *NOUN* **authorities**
1 the right or power to give orders
2 a person or organization having this power
3 an expert or a book written by an expert

authorize *VERB*
to give official permission for something
authorization *NOUN*

autism *NOUN*
a disability that makes someone unable to communicate with other people or respond to surroundings
autistic *ADJECTIVE*

autobiography *NOUN* **autobiographies**
the story of a person's life written by himself or herself
autobiographical *ADJECTIVE*

autocracy *NOUN* **autocracies**
rule by one person with unlimited power

autocrat *NOUN*
a person who enforces rules harshly
autocratic *ADJECTIVE*

autocue *NOUN*
(*trademark*) a device that displays the script for a speaker or television presenter

autograph *NOUN*
the signature of a famous person

autograph *VERB*
to write a signature on

automated *ADJECTIVE*
working by automation

automatic *ADJECTIVE*
1 working on its own without needing control by people
2 done without thinking
automatically *ADVERB*

automation *NOUN*
the use of machines and automatic processes

automaton *NOUN*
1 a robot
2 a person who acts mechanically without thinking

automobile *NOUN*
(*American*) a car

autonomy *NOUN*
1 the right of a people to have their own government
2 the right to act independently
autonomous *ADJECTIVE*

autopsy *NOUN* **autopsies**
an examination of a body after death

autumn *NOUN*
the season between summer and winter
autumnal *ADJECTIVE*

auxiliary *ADJECTIVE*
giving help and support *auxiliary services*

auxiliary *NOUN* **auxiliaries**
a helper

auxiliary verb *NOUN*
a verb such as *do*, *have*, and *will*, used to form parts of other verbs, as in *I have finished.*

avail *NOUN*
to or **of no avail** of no use *Their pleas for mercy were all to no avail.*

avail *VERB*
avail yourself of to make use of

available *ADJECTIVE*
ready or able to be used
availability *NOUN*

avalanche *NOUN*
a mass of snow or rock falling down the side of a mountain

avarice NOUN
greed for money or possessions
avaricious ADJECTIVE

avenge VERB
to have revenge for something done to
harm you
avenger NOUN

avenue NOUN
1 a long wide street, often with trees down
the sides
2 a means of doing something

average NOUN
1 the value obtained by adding several
amounts together and dividing by the
number of amounts
2 the usual or ordinary standard

average ADJECTIVE
1 worked out as an average *Their average
age is 10.*
2 of the usual or ordinary standard

average VERB
to work out or amount to as an average

averse ADJECTIVE
opposed to something *I'm not averse to a bit
of hard work.*

aversion NOUN
a strong dislike

avert VERB
1 to turn something away *He averted his eyes.*
2 to prevent something

aviary NOUN
a large cage or building for keeping birds

aviation NOUN
the flying of aircraft
aviator NOUN

avid ADJECTIVE
keen or eager *an avid reader*
avidly ADVERB

avocado NOUN **avocados**
a pear-shaped fruit with a rough green skin
and creamy flesh

avoid VERB
1 to keep yourself away from someone or
something
2 to keep yourself from doing or saying
something
avoidable ADJECTIVE **avoidance** NOUN

avuncular ADJECTIVE
kind and friendly towards someone younger

await VERB
to wait for

awake VERB **awoke, awoken**
to wake up, or wake someone up
awake ADJECTIVE
not asleep

awaken VERB
1 to wake up, or wake someone up
2 to stimulate a feeling or interest
awakening NOUN

award VERB
to give something officially as a prize,
payment, or penalty

award NOUN
something awarded, such as a prize or a sum
of money

aware ADJECTIVE
knowing or realizing something *Are you
aware of the danger?*
awareness NOUN

away ADVERB
1 to or at a distance
2 not at the usual place
3 out of existence *The water had boiled away.*
4 continuously or persistently *We worked
away at it.*

away ADJECTIVE
(of a game) played on an opponent's ground

awe NOUN
fearful or deeply respectful wonder

awesome ADJECTIVE
causing awe

awful ADJECTIVE
1 very bad *an awful accident*
2 (*informal*) very great *an awful lot of money*
awfully ADVERB

awkward ADJECTIVE
1 difficult to use or deal with
2 not skilful; clumsy
awkwardly ADVERB

awl NOUN
a small pointed tool for making holes in
leather or wood

awning NOUN
a roof-like shelter made of canvas or plastic

awry ADVERB, ADJECTIVE
1 twisted to one side; crooked
2 not according to plan *go awry*

axe NOUN
1 a tool for chopping things
2 (*informal*) dismissal or redundancy
have an axe to grind have a personal
interest in something

axe VERB
1 to cancel or abolish something
2 to reduce something by a large amount

axiom NOUN
an established general truth or principle
axiomatic ADJECTIVE

axis NOUN axes

1 a line through the centre of a spinning object
2 a line dividing a thing in half
3 the horizontal or vertical line on a graph

axle NOUN

the rod through the centre of a wheel, on which the wheel turns

aye ADVERB

yes

Bb

babble VERB

1 to talk very quickly without making sense
2 to make a murmuring sound
babble NOUN

babe NOUN

a baby

baboon NOUN

a large monkey with a long muzzle and short tail

baby NOUN babies

a very young child or animal

babyish ADJECTIVE

childish or immature

babysit VERB babysitting, babysat

to look after a child while its parents are out
babysitter NOUN

bachelor NOUN

1 a man who has not married
2 someone who has a university degree
Bachelor of Arts

back NOUN

1 the part furthest from the front
2 the back part of the body from the shoulders to the base of the spine
3 the part of a chair etc. that your back rests against
4 a defending player near the goal in football etc.

back ADJECTIVE

placed at or near the back

back ADVERB

1 to or towards the back
2 to the place you have come from *Go back home.*
3 to an earlier time or position *Give it back.*

back VERB

1 to move backwards
2 to give someone support or help
3 to bet on something
4 to cover the back of something
back out to refuse to do what you agreed to do **back up 1** to give support or help to a

person or thing **2** (*ICT*) to make a spare copy of a file or disk
backer NOUN

backbone NOUN

1 the spine
2 the main support of an organization or undertaking

backfire VERB

1 (of a vehicle) to make a loud noise caused by an explosion in the exhaust pipe
2 (of a plan) to go wrong

background NOUN

1 the back part of a picture or scene
2 the conditions influencing something
3 a person's family and upbringing
in the background not noticeable or obvious

backhand NOUN

a stroke made in tennis with the back of the hand turned outwards

backing NOUN

1 help or support
2 a musical accompaniment

backlash NOUN

a violent reaction to an event

backlog NOUN

an amount of work that still has to be done

backpack NOUN

a pack carried on the back
backpacker NOUN

backside NOUN

(*informal*) the buttocks

backstroke NOUN

a swimming stroke done lying on your back

back-up NOUN

(*ICT*) a copy of a file or data kept for security

backward ADJECTIVE

1 going backwards
2 slow at learning or developing

backward ADVERB

backwards

The adverb *backward* is mainly used in American English.

backwards ADVERB

1 to or towards the back
2 with the back end going first
3 in reverse order *count backwards*

backwater NOUN

a quiet place not affected by progress or new ideas

bacon NOUN

smoked or salted meat from the back or sides of a pig

bacterium NOUN bacteria

a microscopic organism that can cause disease
bacterial ADJECTIVE

bad ADJECTIVE **worse**, **worst**
1 not good
2 wicked or evil
3 serious or severe　*a bad accident*
4 ill or unhealthy
5 harmful　*bad for your teeth*
6 (of food) decayed or rotten

bade *old past tense of* **bid** VERB

badge NOUN
a button or sign that you wear to show people who you are or what school or club etc. you belong to

badger NOUN
a grey burrowing animal with a black and white head

badger VERB
to pester or annoy someone

badly ADVERB **worse**, **worst**
1 in a bad way; not well
2 severely; causing much injury　*badly wounded*
3 very much　*We badly wanted to win.*

badminton NOUN
a game in which players use rackets to hit a light object called a shuttlecock across a high net

baffle VERB
to puzzle or confuse somebody
baffling ADJECTIVE

bag NOUN
a container made of a soft material
bags (informal) plenty　*bags of room*

bag VERB **bagging**, **bagged**
1 (informal) to catch or claim something
2 to put something into bags

bagatelle NOUN
a game played on a board in which small balls are struck into holes

baggage NOUN
luggage

baggy ADJECTIVE
(of clothes) large and loose

bagpipes PLURAL NOUN
a musical instrument in which air is squeezed out of a bag into pipes

bail[1] NOUN
money paid as a guarantee that a person accused of a crime will return for trial if they are released in the meantime

bail VERB
to provide bail for a person

bail[2] NOUN
each of two small pieces of wood placed on top of the stumps in cricket

bail[3] VERB
to scoop out water from a boat

bait NOUN
1 food that is put on a hook or in a trap to catch fish or animals
2 something that is meant to tempt someone

bait VERB
1 to put bait on a hook or in a trap
2 to try to make someone angry by teasing them

bake VERB
1 to cook in an oven
2 to make a thing hard by heating it
3 to make or become very hot

baker NOUN
a person who bakes or sells bread or cakes
bakery NOUN

balance NOUN
1 a steady position, with the weight or amount evenly distributed
2 the difference between money paid into an account and money paid out
3 an amount of money someone owes
4 a device for weighing

balance VERB
to make or be steady or equal

balcony NOUN **balconies**
1 a platform jutting out from the outside of a building
2 the upstairs part of a theatre or cinema

bald ADJECTIVE
1 having no hair on the top of the head
2 without details; blunt　*a bald statement*
baldly ADVERB

bale[1] NOUN
a large bundle of hay, straw, or cotton tied up tightly

bale[2] VERB
bale out to jump out of an aircraft with a parachute

ball[1] NOUN
1 a round object used in games
2 something with a round shape　*a ball of string*
3 the rounded part of the foot at the base of the big toe

ball[2] NOUN
a formal party where people dance

ballad NOUN
a simple song or poem that tells a story

ballast NOUN
heavy material carried in a ship to keep it steady

ball bearings PLURAL NOUN
small steel balls rolling in a groove on which machine parts can move easily

ballerina NOUN
a female ballet dancer

ballet (bal-ay) *NOUN*
a stage entertainment that tells a story with dancing, mime, and music

ballistic *ADJECTIVE*
to do with bullets and missiles

balloon *NOUN*
1 a thin rubber bag that can be inflated and used as a toy or decoration
2 a large round bag inflated with hot air or gas to make it rise in the air, often carrying a basket for passengers

ballot *NOUN*
1 a secret method of voting by making a mark on a piece of paper
2 a piece of paper on which a vote is made

ballroom *NOUN*
a large room for formal dances

balm *NOUN*
1 a sweet-smelling ointment
2 something that soothes you

balmy *ADJECTIVE* **balmier**, **balmiest**
soft and warm *a balmy breeze*

bamboo *NOUN*
1 a tall plant with hard hollow stems
2 a stem of the bamboo plant

ban *VERB* **banning**, **banned**
to forbid something officially

ban *NOUN*
an order that bans something

banal (ba-nahl) *ADJECTIVE*
ordinary and uninteresting
banality *NOUN*

banana *NOUN*
a long curved fruit with a yellow or green skin

band[1] *NOUN*
1 a strip or loop
2 a range of values or wavelengths

band[2] *NOUN*
1 an organized group of people
2 a group of people playing music together

band *VERB*
to form an organized group

bandage *NOUN*
a strip of material for binding up a wound
bandage *VERB*

bandit *NOUN*
a member of a gang of robbers who attack travellers

bandwagon *NOUN*
jump on the bandwagon to join other people in something that is successful

bandy[1] *ADJECTIVE*
having legs that curve outwards at the knees

bandy[2] *VERB* **bandies**, **bandied**
to mention a story or rumour to a lot of people

bane *NOUN*
a cause of trouble or worry *the bane of your life*

bang *NOUN*
1 a sudden loud noise like that of an explosion
2 a sharp blow or knock

bang *VERB*
1 to hit or shut something noisily
2 to make a sudden loud noise

bangle *NOUN*
a stiff bracelet

banish *VERB*
1 to punish a person by ordering them to leave a place
2 to drive away doubts or fears
banishment *NOUN*

banisters *PLURAL NOUN*
a rail with upright supports beside a staircase

banjo *NOUN* **banjos**
an instrument like a guitar with a round body

bank[1] *NOUN*
1 a slope
2 a long piled-up mass of sand, snow, or cloud
3 a row of lights or switches

bank *VERB*
1 to build or form a bank
2 (of an aircraft) to tilt sideways while changing direction

bank[2] *NOUN*
1 a business that looks after people's money
2 a reserve supply *a blood bank*

bank *VERB*
to put money in a bank
bank on to rely on

banker *NOUN*
a person who runs a bank

bankrupt *ADJECTIVE*
unable to pay your debts
bankruptcy *NOUN*

banner *NOUN*
1 a flag
2 a strip of cloth with a design or slogan on it, carried on two poles in processions

banns *PLURAL NOUN*
an announcement in a church that a marriage is going to take place

banquet *NOUN*
a large formal public meal
banqueting *NOUN*

banter *NOUN*
playful teasing or joking

bap *NOUN*
a soft flat bread roll

baptism *NOUN*
the ceremony of baptizing someone

baptize *VERB*
to receive a person into the Christian Church in a ceremony in which they are given a name and sprinkled with water

bar NOUN
1 a long piece of something hard
2 a counter or room where alcoholic drinks are served
3 a barrier or obstruction
4 each of the small equal sections into which music is divided *three beats to the bar*
5 the place in a lawcourt where the accused person stands
the Bar barristers

bar VERB **barring**, **barred**
1 to fasten something with a bar or bars
2 to block or obstruct something
3 to forbid or ban something

barb NOUN
a backward-pointing spike on a spear, arrow, or fish hook, which makes the point stay in

barbarian NOUN
an uncivilized or brutal person

barbaric or **barbarous** ADJECTIVE
savage and cruel
barbarity NOUN **barbarism** NOUN

barbecue NOUN
1 a frame for grilling food over an open fire outdoors
2 a party with food cooked in this way

barbed wire NOUN
wire with small spikes in it, used to make fences

barber NOUN
a men's hairdresser

bar code NOUN
a set of black lines printed on goods and read by a computer to give information about them

bard NOUN
(*literary*) a poet or minstrel

bare ADJECTIVE
1 without clothing or covering
2 empty *The cupboard was bare.*
3 plain; without details *the bare facts*
4 only just enough *the bare necessities*

bare VERB
to uncover or reveal

barefaced ADJECTIVE
bold or shameless *a barefaced lie*

barely ADVERB
only just; with difficulty

bargain NOUN
1 an agreement about buying or selling something
2 something that you buy cheaply

bargain VERB
to argue about a price
bargain for to be prepared for or expect
more than you bargained for

barge NOUN
a long flat-bottomed boat used on canals

barge VERB
to push or knock against someone roughly
barge in to rush into a room rudely

baritone NOUN
a male singer with a voice between a tenor and a bass

bark [1] NOUN
the short harsh sound made by a dog or fox

bark VERB
1 (of a dog or fox) to make its cry
2 (of a person) to speak angrily

bark [2] NOUN
the outer covering of a tree

barley NOUN
a cereal plant from which malt is made

barley sugar NOUN
a sweet made from boiled sugar

bar mitzvah NOUN
a religious ceremony for Jewish boys aged 13

barmy ADJECTIVE
(*informal*) crazy

barn NOUN
a farm building for storing hay or grain etc.

barnacle NOUN
a shellfish that attaches itself to rocks and the bottoms of ships

barometer NOUN
an instrument that measures air pressure

baron NOUN
1 a member of the lowest rank of noblemen
2 a powerful owner of an industry or business
a newspaper baron
baronial ADJECTIVE

baroness NOUN
a female baron or a baron's wife

baronet NOUN
a nobleman ranking below a baron but above a knight

baroque NOUN
a highly decorated style of architecture used in the 17th and 18th centuries

barracks NOUN
a large building or group of buildings for soldiers to live in

barrage NOUN
1 heavy gunfire
2 a large amount of something *a barrage of questions*
3 a dam built across a river

barrel NOUN
1 a large rounded container with flat ends
2 the metal tube of a gun

barren ADJECTIVE
1 (of a woman) not able to have children
2 (of land) not fertile

barricade NOUN
an improvised barrier across a street or door

barrier NOUN
1 a fence or wall that prevents people from getting past
2 something that stops you doing something

barrister NOUN
a lawyer who represents people in a lawcourt

barrow NOUN
1 a wheelbarrow
2 a small cart that is pushed or pulled by hand

barter VERB
to trade by exchanging goods for other goods

barter NOUN
the system of bartering

base [1] NOUN
1 the part on which something stands or rests
2 a starting point or foundation; a basis
3 a headquarters for an expedition or military operation
4 (*Chemistry*) a substance that can combine with an acid to form a salt
5 each of the four corners that must be reached by a runner in baseball

base VERB
to use something as a beginning or foundation *The story is based on facts.*

base [2] ADJECTIVE
1 dishonourable *base motives*
2 not of great value *base metals*

baseball NOUN
an American game in which runs are scored by hitting a ball and running round a series of four bases

basement NOUN
a room or storey below ground level

bash VERB
to hit hard

bash NOUN
1 a hard hit
2 (*informal*) a try *have a bash at it*

bashful ADJECTIVE
shy and self-conscious
bashfully ADVERB

basic ADJECTIVE
forming the first or most important part *Bread is a basic food.*

basically ADVERB
at the simplest or most fundamental level

basin NOUN
1 a deep bowl
2 a bowl with taps, for washing the hands and face
3 a sheltered area of water for mooring boats
4 the area from which water drains into a river

basis NOUN **bases**
something to start from or add to; the main principle or ingredient

bask VERB
to sit or lie comfortably in the sun

basket NOUN
a container made of strips of flexible material or wire woven together

basketball NOUN
a game in which goals are scored by putting a ball through a high net

bass [1] (bays) NOUN
1 the lowest part in music
2 a male singer with a deep voice

bass [2] (bas) NOUN **bass**
a fish of the perch family

bassoon NOUN
a bass woodwind instrument

baste VERB
to moisten meat with fat while it is cooking

bastion NOUN
1 a projecting part of a fortified building
2 something that protects a belief or way of life

bat [1] NOUN
a shaped piece of wood used to hit the ball in cricket or other games
off your own bat without help from other people

bat VERB **batting**, **batted**
to use a bat in cricket or other games

bat [2] NOUN
a flying animal that looks like a mouse with wings

batch NOUN
a set of things or people dealt with together

bated ADJECTIVE
with bated breath anxiously; hardly daring to speak

bath NOUN
1 a large container for water in which to wash the whole body
2 a washing of the body while sitting in water
3 a liquid in which something is placed *an acid bath*

bath VERB
to wash in a bath

bathe VERB
1 to go swimming
2 to wash something gently
bather NOUN

bathos NOUN
a sudden change from a serious subject or tone to a ridiculous or trivial one

bathroom NOUN
a room containing a bath

baths PLURAL NOUN
a public swimming pool

baton *NOUN*
1 a thin stick used to conduct an orchestra
2 a short thick stick used in a relay race

battalion *NOUN*
an army unit containing two or more companies

batten *NOUN*
a strip of wood or metal that holds something in place

batter *VERB*
to hit something hard and often

batter *NOUN*
a beaten mixture of flour, eggs, and milk, used in cooking

battery *NOUN* **batteries**
1 a device for storing and supplying electricity
2 a set of similar pieces of guns or other equipment
3 a series of cages in which poultry or animals are kept close together

battle *NOUN*
1 a fight between two armies
2 a struggle

battle *VERB*
to fight or struggle

battlefield or **battleground** *NOUN*
a place where a battle is fought

battlements *PLURAL NOUN*
the top of a castle wall, with gaps for firing at the enemy

battleship *NOUN*
a heavily armed warship

bauble *NOUN*
a showy ornament of little value

baulk *VERB*
1 to stop and refuse to go on
2 to prevent someone from doing or getting something

bawl *VERB*
to cry or shout noisily

bay [1] *NOUN*
1 a place where the shore curves inwards
2 an alcove in a room
3 a space or compartment for a special purpose *a parking bay*

bay [2] *VERB*
(of a hunting dog) to make a long deep cry
at bay cornered but defiant

bay [3] *NOUN*
a kind of laurel tree with leaves used in cooking

bayonet *NOUN*
a blade fixed to the end of a rifle for stabbing

bay window *NOUN*
a window that juts out from the main wall of a house

bazaar *NOUN*
1 a market place in an eastern country
2 a sale to raise money

bazooka *NOUN*
a portable weapon for firing anti-tank rockets

BC *ABBREVIATION*
before Christ (used with dates)
Some people prefer to use BCE ('before the common era').

be *VERB* **am**, **are**, **is**; **was** or **were**; **being**, **been**
1 to exist or occupy a position *The shop is on the corner.*
2 to happen or take place *The wedding is tomorrow.*
3 used to form parts of other verbs *They are coming. He was attacked.*

beach *NOUN*
the seashore by the water

beacon *NOUN*
a light or fire used as a signal or warning

bead *NOUN*
1 a small piece of a hard substance with a hole for threading on a string or wire to make jewellery
2 a drop of liquid *beads of sweat*

beady *ADJECTIVE*
(of the eyes) small and bright

beagle *NOUN*
a small hound used for hunting hares

beak *NOUN*
the hard horny part of a bird's mouth

beaker *NOUN*
1 a tall drinking mug
2 a glass container used in a laboratory

beam *NOUN*
1 a long thick bar of wood or metal
2 a ray or stream of light or other radiation
3 a happy smile

beam *VERB*
1 to smile happily
2 to send out a beam of light or other radiation

bean *NOUN*
1 a kind of plant with seeds growing in pods
2 its seed or pod eaten as food
3 the seed of coffee

bear [1] *NOUN*
a large heavy animal with thick fur and large teeth and claws

bear [2] *VERB* **bore**, **borne**
1 to carry or support something
2 to have or show a mark or sign *He still bears the scar.*
3 to endure or stand something unpleasant *I can't bear the noise.*

4 to produce or give birth to *She bore him two sons.*
to bear in mind to remember something and consider it **to bear out** to support or confirm an idea or argument
bearer NOUN

bearable ADJECTIVE
able to be endured; tolerable

beard NOUN
hair on a man's chin
bearded ADJECTIVE

beard VERB
to challenge someone face to face

bearing NOUN
1 the way a person stands, walks, or behaves
2 relevance or connection *This has no bearing on the matter.*
3 the direction or position of one thing in relation to another
4 a part in a machine that connects moving parts so they run smoothly

beast NOUN
1 a wild four-footed animal
2 a cruel or vicious person

beastly ADJECTIVE **beastlier, beastliest**
(*informal*) horrid or unpleasant

beat VERB **beat, beaten**
1 to hit a person or animal many times with a stick or weapon
2 to defeat someone or do better than them
3 to shape or flatten something by beating it
4 to stir a mixture vigorously in cooking
5 (of the heart) to make regular movements
to beat up to attack someone brutally

beat NOUN
1 a regular rhythm or stroke *the beat of your heart*
2 a strong rhythm in music
3 the regular route of a police officer

beautiful ADJECTIVE
very attractive to see or hear or think about
beautifully ADVERB

beauty NOUN **beauties**
1 the quality of being very attractive to see or hear or think about
2 a beautiful person or thing
3 a fine example of something

beaver NOUN
1 an animal with webbed feet and a large flat tail, that can gnaw through wood and dam streams
2 someone who works hard

beaver VERB
to work hard *They are beavering away.*

because CONJUNCTION
for the reason that

because of for the reason of *He limped because of his bad leg.*

beck NOUN
at someone's beck and call always ready to do what they ask

beckon VERB
to make a sign to a person to come

become VERB **became, become**
1 to begin to be *It became dark.*
2 to suit or make attractive
become of to happen to *What became of it?*

bed NOUN
1 a piece of furniture for lying on to sleep or rest
2 a piece of a garden where plants are grown
3 the bottom of the sea or of a river
4 a flat base or foundation
5 a layer of rock or soil

bedding NOUN
mattresses and bedclothes

bedraggled ADJECTIVE
very wet and untidy

bedridden ADJECTIVE
too weak or ill to get out of bed

bedrock NOUN
1 solid rock beneath soil
2 the fundamental facts or principles on which an idea or belief is based

bedroom NOUN
a room for sleeping in

bee NOUN
a winged insect that lives in a hive and makes honey

beech NOUN
a tree with smooth bark and glossy leaves

beef NOUN
meat from a cow or bull

beefy ADJECTIVE
having a solid muscular body
beefiness NOUN

beehive NOUN
a box or other container for bees to live in

beeline NOUN
make a beeline for to go straight towards something

beer NOUN
an alcoholic drink made with hops

beeswax NOUN
a yellow substance produced by bees, used for polishing wood

beet NOUN
a plant with a thick root used as a vegetable or for making sugar

beetle NOUN
an insect with hard shiny wing covers

beetroot NOUN beetroot
the dark red root of beet used as a vegetable

befall VERB befell, befallen
(formal) to happen to someone

before ADVERB
at an earlier time *Have you been here before?*

before PREPOSITION, CONJUNCTION
1 earlier than *I was here before you.*
2 in front of *He stood before the door.*

beforehand ADVERB
earlier; in readiness

beg VERB begging, begged
1 to ask to be given money or food
2 to ask for something seriously or desperately

beggar NOUN
1 a person who lives by begging
2 (informal) a person described in some way
You lucky beggar!
beggary NOUN

begin VERB began, begun
1 to do the earliest or first part of something
2 to come into existence *The problem began last year.*
3 to have something as the first part *The word begins with B.*

beginner NOUN
a person who is just beginning to learn a subject

beginning NOUN
the start of something

behalf NOUN
on behalf of for the benefit of someone else
or as their representative *collecting money on behalf of cancer research*

behave VERB
1 to act in a particular way *They behaved badly.*
2 to show good manners

behaviour NOUN
the way someone behaves
behavioural ADJECTIVE

behead VERB
to cut the head off a person or thing

behind ADVERB
1 at or to the back
2 at a place people have left *I'll leave it behind.*
3 late or not making good progress *behind with the rent*

behind PREPOSITION
1 at or to the back of
2 on the further side of
3 having made less progress than *behind the others at maths*
4 causing *What is behind all this trouble?*

behind NOUN
(informal) a person's bottom

behold VERB beheld
(old use) to see or look at
beholder NOUN

beige NOUN, ADJECTIVE
a pale brown colour

being NOUN
1 existence
2 a living person or animal

belated ADJECTIVE
coming late; late
belatedly ADVERB

belch VERB
1 to bring up wind from your stomach through your mouth
2 to send out a lot of fire or smoke
belch NOUN

beleaguered ADJECTIVE
experiencing a lot of difficulties or criticism

belfry NOUN belfries
a tower or part of a tower in which bells hang

belief NOUN
1 the act of believing
2 something a person believes

believe VERB
to think that something is true without having proof
believe in to think that something exists or is good or can be relied on **make believe** to pretend in your imagination
believable ADJECTIVE **believer** NOUN

bell NOUN
1 a cup-shaped metal instrument that makes a ringing sound when struck by a hanging piece inside it
2 a device that makes a ringing or buzzing sound

bellow NOUN
1 the loud deep sound made by a bull or other large animal
2 a deep shout

bellow VERB
to give a deep shout

bellows PLURAL NOUN
a device for blowing out air, especially to stimulate a fire

belly NOUN bellies
the abdomen or stomach

belong VERB
to have a proper place *These things belong on the shelf.*
belong to to be owned by

belongings PLURAL NOUN
a person's possessions

beloved ADJECTIVE
dearly loved

below ADVERB
at or to a lower position; underneath

below *PREPOSITION*
1 lower than
2 less than

belt *NOUN*
1 a strip of cloth, leather, or plastic worn round the waist
2 a band of flexible material used in machinery
3 a long narrow area *a belt of rain*

belt *VERB*
1 to put a belt round something
2 (*informal*) to hit

bench *NOUN*
1 a long seat
2 a long table for working at
the bench the judges in a lawcourt

bend *VERB* **bent**
1 to change from being straight
2 to stoop or turn downwards

bend *NOUN*
a place where something bends; a curve or turn *a bend in the road*

beneath *PREPOSITION*
1 under; lower than
2 considered unworthy of *Cheating is beneath you.*

beneath *ADVERB*
underneath

benefactor *NOUN*
a person who gives money or other help

beneficial *ADJECTIVE*
having a good or helpful effect

benefit *NOUN*
1 something that is helpful or profitable
2 a government payment to someone in need
3 a payment from an insurance policy

benefit *VERB*
1 to do good to a person or thing
2 to gain a benefit

benevolent *ADJECTIVE*
1 kind and helpful
2 formed for charitable purposes
a benevolent fund
benevolence *NOUN*

benign *ADJECTIVE*
1 kindly
2 favourable
3 (of a tumour) not malignant

bent *ADJECTIVE*
curved or crooked
bent on intending to do something

bent *NOUN*
a talent for something

bequeath *VERB*
to leave money or property to someone in a will

bequest *NOUN*
something left to a person, especially in a will

bereaved *ADJECTIVE*
suffering from the recent death of a close relative
bereavement *NOUN*

bereft *ADJECTIVE*
deprived of something *bereft of hope*

beret (**bair**-ay) *NOUN*
a round flat cap

berry *NOUN* **berries**
any small round juicy fruit without a stone

berserk *ADJECTIVE*
go berserk to become uncontrollably violent

berth *NOUN*
1 a sleeping place on a ship or train
2 a place where a ship can moor

berth *VERB*
to moor in a berth

beseech *VERB* **beseeched** or **besought**
to ask earnestly; to implore

beset *VERB* **besetting**, **beset**
to trouble or harass from all sides *They are beset with problems.*

beside *PREPOSITION*
1 by the side of; near
2 compared with
be beside yourself to be very excited or upset

besides *PREPOSITION, ADVERB*
in addition to; also

besiege *VERB*
1 to surround a place to capture it
2 to crowd round someone famous

besought *past tense* of **beseech**

best *ADJECTIVE*
of the most excellent kind; most able to do something

best *ADVERB*
1 in the best way; most
2 most usefully or sensibly *We had best go.*

best man *NOUN*
the bridegroom's chief attendant at a wedding

bestow *VERB*
to present something to someone
bestowal *NOUN*

bet *NOUN*
1 an agreement that you will receive money if you are correct in choosing the winner of a race or game or in predicting an event, and will lose your money if you are not correct
2 the money you risk losing in a bet

bet *VERB* **betting**, **bet** or **betted**
1 to make a bet
2 (*informal*) to think most likely *I bet he forgot.*

betide VERB
woe betide you you will be in trouble

betray VERB
1 to be disloyal to a person or country etc.
2 to reveal something by mistake
betrayal NOUN

betrothed ADJECTIVE
(*formal*) engaged to be married
betrothal NOUN

better ADJECTIVE
1 more excellent; more satisfactory
2 recovered from illness
get the better of to defeat or outwit

better ADVERB
1 in a better way; more
2 more usefully or sensibly *We had better go.*
be better off to have more money or be more fortunate

better VERB
1 to improve something
2 to do better than
betterment NOUN

between PREPOSITION, ADVERB
1 within two or more limits *between the walls*
2 from one place to another *the train line between London and Glasgow*
3 shared by *Divide the money between you.*
4 separating or comparing *I can't tell the difference between them.*

bevel VERB **bevelling, bevelled**
to give a sloping edge to

bevy NOUN **bevies**
a group of people

beware VERB
to be careful *Beware of forgeries.*

bewilder VERB
to puzzle someone completely
bewilderment NOUN

bewitch VERB
1 to put a magic spell on someone
2 to delight someone

beyond PREPOSITION, ADVERB
1 further than; further in *beyond the fence*
2 too difficult for *The problem is beyond us.*

biannual ADJECTIVE
happening twice a year
biannually ADVERB
Do not confuse this word with *biennial*.

bias NOUN
1 a tendency to favour one person or thing unfairly over another
2 a tendency to swerve
3 a slanting direction

biased ADJECTIVE
unfairly favouring one over another; prejudiced

bib NOUN
1 a cloth or covering put under a baby's chin when eating
2 the part of an apron above the waist

Bible NOUN
the sacred book of the Jews (the Old Testament) and of the Christians (the Old and New Testament)

biblical ADJECTIVE
to do with or in the Bible

bibliography NOUN **bibliographies**
1 a list of books about a subject
2 the study of books
bibliographical ADJECTIVE

bicentenary NOUN **bicentenaries**
a 200th anniversary

biceps NOUN
the large muscle at the front of the arm above the elbow

bicker VERB
to quarrel over unimportant things

bicycle NOUN
a two-wheeled vehicle driven by pedals

bid NOUN
1 the offer of an amount you are willing to pay for something
2 an attempt

bid VERB **bidding, bid** or **bade**
1 to make a bid
2 to say as a greeting or farewell *I bid you all good night.*
3 to command
bidder NOUN

bidding NOUN
do someone's bidding to do what they ask

bide VERB
bide your time to wait for the right time to act

biennial ADJECTIVE
1 lasting for two years
2 happening once every two years
biennially ADVERB
Do not confuse this word with *biannual*.

bier NOUN
a stand for a coffin

big ADJECTIVE **bigger, biggest**
1 large
2 important *the big match*
3 more grown-up; elder *my big sister*

bigamy NOUN
the crime of marrying a person when you are already married to someone else
bigamous ADJECTIVE **bigamist** NOUN

bigot NOUN
a narrow-minded and intolerant person
bigoted ADJECTIVE **bigotry** NOUN

bike NOUN
(informal) a bicycle or motorcycle

bikini NOUN **bikinis**
a woman's two-piece swimsuit

bilateral ADJECTIVE
1 of or on two sides
2 between two people or groups *a bilateral agreement*

bile NOUN
a bitter liquid produced by the liver, helping to digest fats

bilge NOUN
1 the bottom of a ship or the water that collects there
2 (informal) nonsense

bilingual ADJECTIVE
1 able to speak two languages well
2 written in two languages

bilious ADJECTIVE
feeling sick; sickly

bill NOUN
1 a statement of charges for goods or services supplied
2 a poster
3 a programme of entertainment
4 the draft of a proposed law to be discussed by parliament
5 (American) a banknote
6 a bird's beak

billet NOUN
a lodging for troops in a private house

billiards NOUN
a game in which three balls are struck with cues on a cloth-covered table

billion NOUN **billions** or **billion**
a thousand million (1,000,000,000)
billionth ADJECTIVE, NOUN

billow NOUN
a huge wave

billow VERB
to rise or roll like waves

billy goat NOUN
a male goat

bin NOUN
a large container for rubbish or litter

binary ADJECTIVE
1 involving sets of two
2 consisting of two parts

binary system NOUN
a system of expressing numbers by using the digits 0 and 1 only, used in computing

bind VERB
1 to fasten material round something
2 to fasten the pages of a book into a cover
3 to tie up or tie together
4 to make somebody agree to do something

bind NOUN
(informal) a nuisance; a bore

binder NOUN
a cover for loose sheets of paper

binding NOUN
the covers and stitching of a book

binding ADJECTIVE
(of an agreement or promise) that must be carried out or obeyed

bingo NOUN
a game with cards on which numbers are crossed out as they are randomly called out

binoculars PLURAL NOUN
an instrument with lenses for both eyes, for magnifying distant objects

biochemistry NOUN
the study of the chemical composition and processes of living things
biochemist NOUN

biodegradable ADJECTIVE
able to be broken down by bacteria in the environment

biography NOUN **biographies**
an account of a person's life
biographer NOUN **biographical** ADJECTIVE

biology NOUN
the scientific study of the life and structure of living things
biological ADJECTIVE **biologist** NOUN

bionic ADJECTIVE
(of a person or parts of the body) operated by electronic devices

biopsy NOUN **biopsies**
examination of tissue from a living body

birch NOUN
1 a tree with slender branches and a silver bark
2 a bundle of birch branches for flogging people

bird NOUN
an animal with feathers, two wings, and two legs

Biro NOUN **Biros**
(trademark) a kind of ballpoint pen

birth NOUN
1 the process of being born
2 a person's ancestry *of noble birth*

birth control NOUN
ways of avoiding becoming pregnant

birthday NOUN
the anniversary of the day a person was born

birthmark NOUN
a coloured mark that is on a person's skin from birth

birth rate NOUN
the number of children born in one year for every 1,000 people

biscuit NOUN
a small flat kind of cake that has been baked until it is crisp

bisect VERB
to divide something into two equal parts

bishop NOUN
1 an important member of the clergy in some churches
2 a chess piece shaped like a bishop's mitre

bison NOUN **bison**
a large wild ox with shaggy hair on its head

bistro NOUN **bistros**
a small restaurant

bit [1] NOUN
1 a small piece or amount
2 the part of a bridle that is put into a horse's mouth
3 the part of a tool that cuts or grips
a bit 1 a short distance or time **2** slightly *a bit nervous* **bit by bit** gradually

bit [2] *past tense* of **bite**

bit [3] NOUN
(*ICT*) the smallest unit of information in a computer, expressed as a choice between two possibilities

bitch NOUN
1 a female dog, fox, or wolf
2 (*informal*) a spiteful woman

bite VERB **bit**, **bitten**
1 to cut or take something with your teeth
2 to penetrate or sting

bite NOUN
1 an act of biting *take a bite*
2 a wound or mark made by biting *an insect bite*
3 a snack

bitter ADJECTIVE
1 tasting sharp, not sweet
2 feeling or causing mental pain or resentment
3 very cold
bitterly ADVERB

bizarre ADJECTIVE
strange in appearance or effect

blab VERB **blabbing**, **blabbed**
to let out a secret

black ADJECTIVE
1 of the darkest colour, like coal or soot
2 desperate or hopeless *The outlook is black.*
3 (of a person) having dark skin
4 (of coffee or tea) without milk

black NOUN
the darkest colour

black VERB
to make a thing black
black out 1 to lose consciousness **2** to cover windows so that no light can penetrate

blackberry NOUN **blackberries**
a sweet black berry

blackbird NOUN
a songbird, the male of which is black

blackboard NOUN
a dark board for writing on with chalk

blacken VERB
to make or become black

blackguard (blag-ard) NOUN
(*old use*) a wicked person

black hole NOUN
a region in space with such strong gravity that no matter or radiation can escape from it

black ice NOUN
thin transparent ice on roads

blacklist NOUN
a list of people who are disapproved of or not trusted

black magic NOUN
evil magic

blackmail NOUN
the crime of demanding money from someone by threatening to reveal a secret about them

blackmail VERB
to use blackmail on someone
blackmailer NOUN

black market NOUN
illegal buying and selling

blackout NOUN
1 darkness produced by covering windows
2 loss of consciousness

black sheep NOUN
a member of a family or other group who is considered a failure or disgrace

blacksmith NOUN
a person who makes and repairs iron things, especially horseshoes

bladder NOUN
1 the organ of the body in which urine collects
2 an inflatable bag inside a ball

blade NOUN
1 the flat cutting edge of a knife or tool
2 the flat wide part of an oar, spade, or propeller
3 a narrow leaf of grass or wheat

blame VERB
to say that somebody or something has caused something wrong or bad

blame NOUN
responsibility for what is wrong

blameless ADJECTIVE
not responsible for a wrong; innocent

blanch VERB
to make or become white or pale

blancmange (bla-**monj**) NOUN
a jelly-like pudding made with milk

bland ADJECTIVE
1 having a mild flavour
2 gentle and casual a bland manner

blank ADJECTIVE
1 not written or printed on; unmarked
2 without expression a blank look
3 empty of thoughts My mind's gone blank.

blank NOUN
1 an empty space
2 a cartridge that does not fire a bullet

blanket NOUN
1 a warm cloth covering used on a bed etc.
2 a thick soft covering a blanket of snow

blanket ADJECTIVE
covering all cases a blanket ban

blank verse NOUN
verse written without rhyme

blare VERB
to make a loud harsh sound
blare NOUN

blaspheme VERB
to talk or write in a disrespectful way about sacred things

blasphemy NOUN **blasphemies**
disrespectful talk about sacred things
blasphemous ADJECTIVE

blast NOUN
1 a strong rush of wind or air
2 a loud noise, e.g. on a trumpet

blast VERB
to blow up with explosives
blast off to launch by the firing of rockets

blast-off NOUN
the launching of a rocket

blatant ADJECTIVE
very obvious a blatant lie
blatantly ADVERB

blaze[1] NOUN
a very bright fire or light

blaze VERB
to burn or shine brightly

blaze[2] VERB
blaze a trail to show the way for others to follow

blazer NOUN
a jacket, often worn as part of a uniform

bleach VERB
to make or become white

bleach NOUN
a substance used to make things white or for cleaning

bleak ADJECTIVE
1 bare and cold a bleak hillside
2 dreary or miserable a bleak future

bleary ADJECTIVE
(of the eyes) watery and not seeing clearly
blearily ADVERB

bleat NOUN
the cry of a lamb, goat, or calf

bleat VERB
to make a bleat

bleed VERB **bled**
1 to lose blood
2 to draw blood or fluid from

bleep VERB
to give out a short high sound as a signal
bleep NOUN

blemish NOUN
a flaw; a mark that spoils a thing's appearance

blemish VERB
to spoil something

blench VERB
to flinch

blend VERB
to mix smoothly or easily

blend NOUN
a smooth mixture

blender NOUN
a machine for mixing food or turning it into liquid

bless VERB
1 to make sacred or holy
2 to bring God's favour on a person or thing

blessed (**bless**-id) ADJECTIVE
sacred or holy

blessing NOUN
1 a prayer that blesses a person or thing
2 something to be glad of

blight NOUN
1 a disease that withers plants
2 something that spoils or damages something

blight VERB
1 to affect with blight
2 to spoil or damage something Injuries blighted his career.

blind ADJECTIVE
1 without the ability to see
2 without any thought blind obedience
blindness NOUN

blind *VERB*
1 to make a person blind
2 to dazzle briefly

blind *NOUN*
1 a screen for a window
2 a deception *His journey was a blind.*

blindfold *NOUN*
a strip of cloth tied round someone's eyes to prevent them from seeing

blindfold *VERB*
to cover with a blindfold

blink *VERB*
to shut and open your eyes rapidly
blink *NOUN*

blinkers *PLURAL NOUN*
pieces fixed on a bridle to prevent a horse from seeing sideways
blinkered *ADJECTIVE*

bliss *NOUN*
perfect happiness

blissful *ADJECTIVE*
bringing great happiness
blissfully *ADVERB*

blister *NOUN*
a swelling like a bubble on skin

blister *VERB*
(of the skin) to produce blisters

blitz *NOUN*
1 a sudden violent attack
2 an attack by air with bombs

blizzard *NOUN*
a severe snowstorm

bloated *ADJECTIVE*
swollen by fat, gas, or liquid

blob *NOUN*
a small round mass of something
blobs of paint

bloc *NOUN*
a group of countries who have formed an alliance

block *NOUN*
1 a solid piece of something
2 an obstruction
3 a large building divided into flats or offices
4 a group of buildings

block *VERB*
to obstruct a place or prevent something from moving or being used
blockage *NOUN*

blockade *NOUN*
the blocking of a place to prevent people and goods from going in or out

blockade *VERB*
to set up a blockade of a place

block letters *PLURAL NOUN*
plain capital letters

bloke *NOUN*
(*informal*) a man

blond or **blonde** *ADJECTIVE*
having fair hair or skin

blonde *NOUN*
a girl or woman with fair hair

blood *NOUN*
1 the red liquid that flows through veins and arteries
2 ancestry *of royal blood*
in cold blood deliberately and cruelly

blood group *NOUN*
each of the classes or types of human blood

bloodhound *NOUN*
a large dog able to track people by their scent

bloodshed *NOUN*
the killing or wounding of people

bloodshot *ADJECTIVE*
(of the eyes) sore and streaked with red

blood sport *NOUN*
a sport that involves wounding or killing animals

bloodstream *NOUN*
the blood circulating in the body

bloodthirsty *ADJECTIVE*
eager for bloodshed

blood vessel *NOUN*
a tube carrying blood in the body, e.g. an artery or vein

bloody *ADJECTIVE* **bloodier**, **bloodiest**
1 stained with blood
2 involving much bloodshed *a bloody battle*

bloom *NOUN*
1 a flower
2 the fine powder on fruit

bloom *VERB*
(of a plant) to produce flowers

blossom *NOUN*
a mass of flowers on a fruit tree

blossom *VERB*
1 to produce flowers
2 to develop into something fine

blot *NOUN*
1 a spot of ink
2 an ugly flaw or fault

blot *VERB* **blotting**, **blotted**
to make a blot on something
blot out 1 to cross out thickly 2 to obscure

blotch *NOUN*
an untidy patch of colour
blotchy *ADJECTIVE*

blouse *NOUN*
a loose piece of clothing for the upper body, worn by women

blow [1] *VERB* **blew, blown**
1 to send out a current of air
2 to move in or with a current of air *Her hat blew off.*
3 to make or sound something by blowing *blow bubbles blow the whistle*
4 (of a fuse) to break
blow up 1 to inflate **2** to explode
blow *NOUN*
the action of blowing

blow [2] *NOUN*
1 a hard knock or hit
2 a shock or disaster

blowpipe *NOUN*
a tube for firing a dart or pellet by blowing

blubber *NOUN*
the fat of whales or seals

blue *ADJECTIVE*
1 of the colour of a cloudless sky
2 unhappy or depressed
blue *NOUN*
the colour of a cloudless sky
out of the blue unexpectedly

bluebell *NOUN*
a plant with blue bell-shaped flowers

blue blood *NOUN*
aristocratic or royal descent

bluebottle *NOUN*
a large fly with a dark blue body

blueprint *NOUN*
a detailed plan

blues *NOUN*
slow sad jazz music
the blues a sad feeling

bluff [1] *VERB*
to deceive someone by pretending to be confident about something
bluff *NOUN*
an act of bluffing; an unreal threat

bluff [2] *ADJECTIVE*
frank and cheerful in manner
bluff *NOUN*
a broad steep cliff

bluish *ADJECTIVE*
rather blue

blunder *NOUN*
a careless mistake
blunder *VERB*
1 to make a careless mistake
2 to move clumsily and uncertainly

blunderbuss *NOUN*
an old type of gun with a wide mouth

blunt *ADJECTIVE*
1 having an edge that is not sharp
2 speaking in plain terms *a blunt refusal*
bluntly *ADVERB*
blunt *VERB*
to make something blunt

blur *VERB* **blurring, blurred**
to make or become unclear or smeared
blur *NOUN*
an unclear appearance

blurt *VERB*
to say something suddenly or tactlessly

blush *VERB*
to become red in the face from shame or embarrassment
blush *NOUN*
a slight reddening

bluster *VERB*
1 to blow in windy gusts
2 to talk loudly and aggressively
blustery *ADJECTIVE*

boa constrictor *NOUN*
a large snake that curls round its prey and crushes it

boar *NOUN*
1 a wild pig
2 a male pig

board *NOUN*
1 a flat piece of wood
2 a flat piece of stiff material, e.g. for playing a game
3 daily meals supplied in return for payment or work
4 a group of people running an organization
on board on or in a ship, aircraft, or vehicle
board *VERB*
1 to go on board a ship, aircraft, or vehicle
2 to give or get meals and accommodation
board up to block with fixed boards

boarder *NOUN*
someone who receives board and lodging

boast *VERB*
1 to try to impress people about yourself or your achievements
2 to have something to be proud of *The town boasts a fine park.*
boast *NOUN*
a boasting statement

boastful *ADJECTIVE*
tending to boast
boastfully *ADVERB*

boat *NOUN*
a vehicle built to travel on water

boatswain (boh-sun) *NOUN*
a ship's officer in charge of rigging, boats, and other equipment

bob *VERB* **bobbing, bobbed**
to move quickly up and down

bobbin *NOUN*
a small spool holding thread or wire in a machine

a
b
c
d
e
f
g
h
i
j
k
l
m
n
o
p
q
r
s
t
u
v
w
x
y
z

bobble NOUN
a small round ornament, often made of wool

bobsleigh NOUN
a sledge with two sets of runners

bode VERB
to be a sign or omen of what is to come
It bodes well.

bodice NOUN
the upper part of a woman's dress

bodily ADJECTIVE
to do with your body

bodily ADVERB
by taking hold of the body *He was picked up bodily.*

bodkin NOUN
a thick blunt needle

body NOUN **bodies**
1 the structure of a person or animal, or the main part of this apart from the head and limbs
2 a corpse
3 the main part of something
4 a group of people acting together
5 a distinct object or piece of matter
heavenly bodies

bodyguard NOUN
a guard to protect a person from harm or attack

bog NOUN
an area of wet spongy ground

boggle VERB
to be amazed or puzzled *The mind boggles at the thought.*

bogus ADJECTIVE
not real; sham

bogy NOUN **bogies**
1 an evil spirit
2 something that frightens people

boil [1] VERB
1 to make or become hot enough to bubble and give off steam
2 to cook or wash something in boiling water
3 to be very hot

boil NOUN
boiling point *Bring the milk to the boil.*

boil [2] NOUN
an inflamed swelling under the skin

boiler NOUN
a container in which water is heated

boiling point NOUN
the temperature at which something boils

boisterous ADJECTIVE
noisy and lively

bold ADJECTIVE
1 confident and courageous

2 cheeky or disrespectful
3 (of colours or designs) strong and vivid
4 (of type) extra dark and thick
boldly ADVERB

bollard NOUN
a short post on the street for controlling the movement of traffic

bolster NOUN
a long pillow for placing across a bed

bolster VERB
to add extra support

bolt NOUN
1 a sliding bar for fastening a door
2 a thick metal pin used with a nut for joining things
3 a shaft of lightning
4 an arrow shot from a crossbow
a bolt from the blue an unwelcome surprise **bolt upright** with the back completely straight

bolt VERB
1 to fasten with a bolt
2 to run away or escape
3 to swallow food quickly

bomb NOUN
a device that explodes causing great damage
the bomb nuclear weapons

bomb VERB
to attack a place with bombs

bombard VERB
1 to attack with gunfire or many missiles
2 to direct a large number of questions at somebody
bombardment NOUN

bomber NOUN
1 someone who plants or sets off a bomb
2 an aeroplane from which bombs are dropped

bombshell NOUN
a great shock

bond NOUN
1 a close friendship or connection between two or more people
2 **bonds** ropes or chains used to tie someone up
3 a spoken or written agreement

bond VERB
to become closely linked or connected

bondage NOUN
slavery or captivity

bone NOUN
1 one of the hard whitish parts that make up the skeleton of a person's or animal's body
2 the substance from which these parts are made

bone VERB
to remove the bones from meat or fish

bone dry *ADJECTIVE*
extremely dry

bonfire *NOUN*
a large outdoor fire

bonnet *NOUN*
1 a hat with strings that tie under the chin
2 a Scottish beret
3 the cover over a car engine

bonny *ADJECTIVE* **bonnier**, **bonniest**
1 healthy-looking
2 (*Scottish*) good-looking

bonus *NOUN*
1 an extra payment in addition to a person's
normal wages
2 an extra benefit

bony *ADJECTIVE*
1 full of bones
2 thin without much flesh

boo *VERB* **boos**, **booing**, **booed**
to shout in disapproval
boo *NOUN*

booby *NOUN* **boobies**
a babyish or stupid person

booby prize *NOUN*
a prize given to someone who comes last in a
contest

booby trap *NOUN*
something designed to hit or injure someone
unexpectedly

book *NOUN*
a set of printed sheets of paper fastened
together inside a cover

book *VERB*
1 to reserve a seat or room in a theatre, train,
hotel, etc.
2 to make a note of a person's name when
they have committed an offence

booklet *NOUN*
a small thin book

bookcase *NOUN*
a piece of furniture with shelves for books

bookmark *NOUN*
1 something to mark a place in a book
2 (*ICT*) a record of the address of a file or
web page

boom *VERB*
1 to make a deep hollow sound
2 to be growing and prospering

boom *NOUN*
1 a deep hollow sound
2 prosperity or growth

boomerang *NOUN*
a curved piece of wood that returns when it is
thrown, originally used by Australian
Aborigines

boon *NOUN*
something helpful or pleasant

boor *NOUN*
a person with bad manners
boorish *ADJECTIVE*

boost *VERB*
to increase the strength or value of a person
or thing
booster *NOUN*

boost *NOUN*
1 an increase
2 a piece of encouragement

boot *NOUN*
1 a shoe that covers the foot and ankle or leg
2 the compartment for luggage in a car

boot *VERB*
1 to kick hard
2 (*ICT*) to switch on a computer

booth *NOUN*
an enclosed compartment for selling tickets,
telephoning, etc.

booty *NOUN*
valuable goods taken away by soldiers after a
battle

booze *NOUN*
(*informal*) alcoholic drink

border *NOUN*
1 the boundary of a country or the part near it
2 an edge
3 something placed round an edge
4 a strip of ground round a garden

border *VERB*
to put or be a border to something

borderline *NOUN*
a boundary

borderline *ADJECTIVE*
only just belonging to a particular group or
category *a borderline pass*

bore [1] *VERB*
to drill a hole

bore *NOUN*
1 the width of the inside of a gun barrel
2 a hole made by boring

bore [2] *VERB*
to seem dull and uninteresting to

bore *NOUN*
a boring person or thing
boredom *NOUN*

bore [3] *past tense* of **bear** [2]

bored *ADJECTIVE*
unhappy because something is uninteresting
or you have nothing to do

boring *ADJECTIVE*
dull and uninteresting

born *ADJECTIVE*
1 having come into existence by birth
2 having a certain natural quality or ability
a born leader

borne *past participle of* **bear** [2]

borough NOUN
an important town or district

borrow VERB
1 to get something to use for a time
2 to obtain money as a loan
borrower NOUN

bosom NOUN
1 a woman's breasts
2 the central part of something *the bosom of the family*

boss [1] NOUN
(*informal*) a manager or chief person

boss VERB
(*informal*) to order someone about

boss [2] NOUN
a round raised knob or stud

bossy ADJECTIVE
tending to order people about
bossiness NOUN

botany NOUN
the study of plants
botanical ADJECTIVE **botanist** NOUN

botch VERB
to spoil something by poor or clumsy work

both ADJECTIVE, PRONOUN
the two; all of two *both places I like both.*

both ADVERB
both ... and not only ... but also *both large and ugly*

bother VERB
1 to cause somebody trouble or worry
2 to take trouble *Don't bother to reply.*

bother NOUN
trouble or worry

bottle NOUN
1 a narrow-necked container for liquids
2 (*informal*) courage *They showed a lot of bottle.*

bottle VERB
to put or store something in bottles
bottle up to keep feelings to yourself

bottle bank NOUN
a large container for putting glass bottles in for recycling

bottleneck NOUN
1 a narrow place where traffic cannot flow freely
2 a stage in an activity in which progress is slow

bottom NOUN
1 the lowest part; the base
2 the part furthest away *the bottom of the garden*
3 a person's buttocks

bottom ADJECTIVE
lowest *the bottom shelf*

bough NOUN
a large branch coming from the trunk of a tree

bought *past tense of* **buy** VERB

boulder NOUN
a large smooth stone

bounce VERB
1 to spring back when thrown against something
2 to make something bounce
3 (of a cheque) to be sent back by the bank because there is not enough money in the account
4 to jump or move suddenly

bounce NOUN
1 the action or power of bouncing
2 a lively confident manner *full of bounce*
bouncy ADJECTIVE

bouncer NOUN
a person who stops unwanted people coming in a place

bound [1] VERB
1 to jump or spring
2 to run with jumping movements

bound NOUN
a bounding movement

bound [2] *past tense of* **bind**

bound ADJECTIVE
obstructed or hindered by something
The airport is fog-bound.
bound to certain to *He is bound to fail.*

bound [3] ADJECTIVE
going towards something *bound for India*

bound [4] VERB
to limit or be the boundary of *Their land is bounded by the river.*

boundary NOUN **boundaries**
an edge or limit

bounds PLURAL NOUN
limits *beyond the bounds of common sense*
out of bounds where you are not allowed to go

bounty NOUN **bounties**
1 a generous gift
2 generosity in giving things
3 a reward for doing something

bouquet (boh-**kay**) NOUN
a bunch of flowers

bout NOUN
1 a boxing or wrestling contest
2 a period of activity or illness

bovine ADJECTIVE
to do with or like cattle

bow[1] (rhymes with *go*) NOUN
1 a curved strip of wood with a tight string joining its ends, used for shooting arrows
2 a wooden rod with horsehair stretched between its ends, used for playing a stringed instrument
3 a knot made with loops

bow[2] (rhymes with *cow*) VERB
1 to bend the head or body forwards to show respect or as a greeting
2 to bend downwards *bowed by the weight*

bow NOUN
the act of bowing the head or body

bow[3] (rhymes with *cow*) NOUN
the front part of a ship

bowels PLURAL NOUN
the intestines

bowl[1] NOUN
1 a deep rounded container for food or liquid
2 the rounded part of something, e.g. a spoon

bowl[2] NOUN
a heavy ball used in the game of **bowls** or in bowling, in which it is rolled towards a target

bowl VERB
1 to send a ball to be played by a batsman
2 to get a batsman out by bowling
3 to send a ball rolling

bow-legged ADJECTIVE
having legs that curve outwards at the knees; bandy

bowler[1] NOUN
a person who bowls

bowler[2] NOUN
a man's stiff felt hat with a rounded top

bowling NOUN
1 the game of bowls
2 the game of knocking down skittles with a heavy ball

bow tie NOUN
a man's necktie tied into a bow

box[1] NOUN
1 a container with flat sides and usually a top or lid
2 a rectangular space to be filled in on a form, computer screen, etc.
3 a compartment in a public place such as a theatre
4 a hut or shelter
5 a small evergreen shrub

box VERB
to put something in a box

box[2] VERB
to fight with the fists as a sport
boxing NOUN

boxer NOUN
1 a person who boxes
2 a smooth-haired dog that looks like a bulldog

Boxing Day NOUN
the day after Christmas Day

boy NOUN
a male child
boyhood NOUN

boycott VERB
to refuse to have dealings with
boycott NOUN

boyfriend NOUN
a person's regular male friend or lover

boyish ADJECTIVE
like a boy; youthful and lively

bra NOUN
a piece of underwear worn by women to support their breasts

brace NOUN
1 a device for holding things in place
2 a pair *a brace of pheasants*

brace VERB
to support something or make it firm against something

bracelet NOUN
a piece of jewellery worn round the wrist

braces PLURAL NOUN
straps over the shoulders, to hold up a pair of trousers

bracing ADJECTIVE
making you feel refreshed and healthy

bracken NOUN
a type of large fern that grows in open country

bracket NOUN
1 a mark used in pairs to enclose words or figures. There are round brackets ( ) and square brackets [ ].
2 a support attached to a wall
3 a range between certain limits *a high income bracket*

brag VERB **bragging**, **bragged**
to boast

braid NOUN
1 a plait of hair
2 a strip of cloth with a woven decorative pattern

braid VERB
1 to plait
2 to trim with braid

Braille (rhymes with *mail*) NOUN
a system of representing letters by raised dots which blind people can read by touch

brain NOUN
1 the organ inside the top of the head that controls the body
2 the mind; intelligence

brainwash VERB
to force a person to accept new ideas or beliefs

brainwave NOUN
a sudden bright idea

brainy ADJECTIVE **brainier, brainiest**
clever or intelligent

braise VERB
to cook slowly in a small amount of liquid

brake NOUN
a device for slowing or stopping a vehicle

brake VERB
to use a brake

bramble NOUN
a blackberry bush or a prickly bush like it

bran NOUN
ground-up husks of corn

branch NOUN
1 a woody arm-like part of a tree or shrub
2 a part of a railway, road, or river that leads off from the main part
3 a shop or office that belongs to a large organization

branch VERB
to form a branch; to spread out
branch out to start something new

brand NOUN
1 a particular make of goods
2 a mark made by branding
3 a piece of burning wood

brand VERB
1 to mark cattle or sheep with a hot iron to identify them
2 to sell goods under a particular trademark

brandish VERB
to wave something about

brand new ADJECTIVE
completely new

brandy NOUN **brandies**
a strong alcoholic drink, usually made from wine

brash ADJECTIVE
loud and aggressive

brass NOUN
1 a metal alloy of copper and zinc
2 musical instruments made of brass, e.g. trumpets and trombones

brat NOUN
an unpleasant or unruly child

bravado NOUN
a display of boldness

brave ADJECTIVE
having or showing courage
bravely ADVERB

brave NOUN
a Native American warrior

brave VERB
to face and endure something bravely

bravery NOUN
the quality of being brave; courage

bravo EXCLAMATION
well done!

brawl NOUN
a noisy quarrel or fight

brawl VERB
to take part in a brawl

brawn NOUN
muscular strength

brawny ADJECTIVE
strong and muscular

bray VERB
to make the loud harsh cry of a donkey
bray NOUN

brazen ADJECTIVE
openly disrespectful or shameless

brazier NOUN
a metal framework for holding burning coals

breach NOUN
1 the breaking of an agreement or rule
2 a break or gap
Do not confuse this word with *breech*.

breach VERB
to break through or make a gap

bread NOUN
a food made by baking flour, water, and yeast

breadth NOUN
extent from side to side; width

break VERB **broke, broken**
1 to divide or fall into pieces by hitting or pressing
2 to damage or stop working properly
3 to fail to keep a promise or rule
4 to stop for a time *She broke her silence.*
5 to go suddenly or with force *They broke through.*
6 to appear suddenly *Day had broken.*
7 (of the weather) to change suddenly
8 (of a boy's voice) to deepen at puberty
9 (of waves) to fall in foam
break a record to do better than anyone else has done **break down 1** to stop working properly **2** to collapse **break in to**

train a wild animal **break into** to enter a place with force **break out 1** to begin suddenly **2** to escape **break the news** to make something known **break up 1** to break into small parts **2** to separate at the end of a school term **3** to end a relationship

break NOUN
1 a broken place; a gap
2 an escape or sudden dash
3 a short rest from work
4 (*informal*) a piece of luck; a fair chance
break of day dawn

breakage NOUN
1 the act of breaking something
2 something broken

breakdown NOUN
1 a sudden failure to work
2 a period of mental illness
3 an analysis

breakfast NOUN
the first meal of the day

break-in NOUN
an illegal entry into a place to steal from it

breakneck ADJECTIVE
dangerously fast *at breakneck speed*

breakthrough NOUN
an important advance or achievement

bream NOUN **bream**
a silvery fish with an arched back

breast NOUN
1 one of the two milk-producing fleshy parts on the upper front of a woman's body
2 a person's or animal's chest

breastbone NOUN
the flat bone down the centre of the chest or breast

breastplate NOUN
a piece of armour covering the chest

breaststroke NOUN
a swimming stroke done on the front with the arms and legs pushed forwards and sideways

breath NOUN
1 air drawn into the lungs and sent out again
2 a gentle blowing *a breath of wind*
out of breath panting **take your breath away** to surprise or delight you **under your breath** in a whisper

breathe VERB
to take air into the lungs and send it out again

breather NOUN
a pause for rest

breathless ADJECTIVE
out of breath

breathtaking ADJECTIVE
very surprising or beautiful

breech NOUN
the back part of a gun barrel where the bullets are put in

> Do not confuse this word with *breach*.

breeches PLURAL NOUN
trousers reaching to just below the knees

breed VERB
1 to produce children or young
2 to keep animals to produce young from them
3 to bring up or train
4 to create or produce *Poverty breeds disease.*
breeder NOUN

breed NOUN
a variety of animals with qualities inherited from their parents

breeze NOUN
a light wind
breezy ADJECTIVE

breve NOUN
a note in music, lasting eight times as long as a crotchet

brevity NOUN
shortness; briefness

brew VERB
1 to make beer or tea
2 to develop *Trouble is brewing.*

brew NOUN
a brewed drink

brewer NOUN
a person who brews beer

brewery NOUN **breweries**
a place where beer is brewed

briar NOUN
a thorny bush, especially the wild rose

bribe NOUN
money or a gift offered to influence a person

bribe VERB
to give a bribe to
bribery NOUN

brick NOUN
1 a small hard block of baked clay used in building
2 a rectangular block of something

brick VERB
to close something with bricks *We bricked up the gap in the wall.*

bricklayer NOUN
a builder who works with bricks

bride *NOUN*
a woman on her wedding day
bridal *ADJECTIVE*

bridegroom *NOUN*
a man on his wedding day

bridesmaid *NOUN*
a girl or woman who attends the bride at her wedding

bridge¹ *NOUN*
1 a structure built to take a path or road across a road, river, or railway
2 a high platform on a ship, for the officer in charge
3 the bony upper part of the nose
4 a piece of wood supporting the strings of a violin etc.
5 something that connects things

bridge *VERB*
to make or form a bridge over something

bridge² *NOUN*
a card game like whist, with bidding

bridle *NOUN*
the part of a horse's harness that fits over its head

bridleway *NOUN*
a road suitable only for horses

brief *ADJECTIVE*
short or concise
in brief in a few words
briefly *ADVERB*

brief *NOUN*
a set of instructions given to someone, especially to a barrister

brief *VERB*
1 to give a brief to a barrister
2 to instruct or inform someone concisely in advance

briefcase *NOUN*
a flat case for carrying papers

briefs *PLURAL NOUN*
short knickers or underpants

brier *NOUN*
another spelling of **briar**

brigade *NOUN*
1 a large unit of an army
2 a group of people organized for a special purpose *the fire brigade*

brigadier *NOUN*
an army officer who commands a brigade

brigand *NOUN*
a member of a band of robbers

bright *ADJECTIVE*
1 giving a strong light; shining
2 intelligent
3 cheerful
brightly *ADVERB*

brighten *VERB*
to make or become brighter

brilliant *ADJECTIVE*
1 very bright; sparkling
2 very clever
brilliance *NOUN* **brilliantly** *ADVERB*

brim *NOUN*
1 the edge of a cup, bowl, etc.
2 the bottom part of a hat that sticks out

brimful *ADJECTIVE*
full to the brim

brine *NOUN*
salt water
briny *ADJECTIVE*

bring *VERB* **brought**
to cause a person or thing to come; to lead or carry
bring about to cause to happen **bring off** to do successfully **bring up 1** to look after and train growing children **2** to mention a subject

brink *NOUN*
1 the edge of a steep place or of a stretch of water
2 the point beyond which something will happen *on the brink of war*

brisk *ADJECTIVE*
quick and lively
briskly *ADVERB*

bristle *NOUN*
a short stiff hair on an animal, brush, etc.
bristly *ADJECTIVE*

bristle *VERB*
1 (of an animal) to raise its bristles in anger or fear
2 to be indignant
bristle with to be full of *bristling with problems*

brittle *ADJECTIVE*
hard and easily broken

broach *VERB*
to begin talking about something *to broach the subject*

broad *ADJECTIVE*
1 large across; wide
2 full and complete *broad daylight*
3 in general terms; not detailed *in broad agreement*
4 strong and unmistakable *a broad hint* *a broad accent*
broadly *ADVERB*

broadband *NOUN*
(*ICT*) a continuous Internet connection using signals over a broad range of frequencies

broad bean *NOUN*
a bean with large flat seeds

broadcast NOUN
a programme transmitted on radio or television

broadcast VERB
to transmit on radio or on television
broadcaster NOUN

broaden VERB
to make or become broader

broadside NOUN
1 the firing of all guns on one side of a ship
2 a piece of fierce criticism

brocade NOUN
material woven with raised patterns

broccoli NOUN
a kind of cauliflower with small green flower heads

brochure NOUN
a booklet or pamphlet containing information

broil VERB
1 to cook on a fire or gridiron
2 to make or be very hot

broke ADJECTIVE
(*informal*) having no money left

broken VERB SEE **break**

broker NOUN
a person who buys and sells shares for other people

bronchitis NOUN
a disease with inflammation of the tubes leading from the windpipe to the lungs

bronze NOUN
1 a metal alloy of copper and tin
2 something made of bronze
3 yellowish-brown
bronze ADJECTIVE

Bronze Age NOUN
the time when tools and weapons were made of bronze

bronze medal NOUN
a medal awarded for third place in a competition

brooch (brohch) NOUN
a piece of jewellery with a hinged pin for fastening it on to clothes

brood NOUN
a group of young birds hatched together

brood VERB
1 to sit on eggs to hatch them
2 to keep thinking and worrying about something

broody ADJECTIVE
1 (of a hen) wanting to sit on eggs
2 (of a woman) longing to have children
3 thoughtful or brooding

brook[1] NOUN
a small stream

brook[2] VERB
to tolerate *She will brook no argument.*

broom NOUN
1 a sweeping brush with a long handle
2 a shrub with yellow, white, or pink flowers

broomstick NOUN
a long thick stick with twigs at one end, on which witches are said to fly

broth NOUN
a kind of thin soup

brother NOUN
1 a son of the same parents as another person
2 a fellow member or worker
brotherly ADJECTIVE

brotherhood NOUN
1 companionship between men
2 a society or association of men

brother-in-law NOUN **brothers-in-law**
1 the brother of a married person's husband or wife
2 the husband of a person's sister

brow NOUN
1 an eyebrow
2 the forehead
3 the top of a hill or cliff

brown ADJECTIVE
of a colour between orange and black, like the colour of dark wood

brown NOUN
the colour of dark wood

browse VERB
1 to read or look at something casually
2 (of an animal) to feed on grass or leaves

bruise NOUN
a dark mark made on the skin by hitting it

bruise VERB
to give or get a bruise

brunette NOUN
a woman with dark-brown hair

brunt NOUN
bear the brunt to take the chief impact or strain

brush NOUN
1 an implement used for cleaning or painting or for smoothing the hair, with pieces of hair, wire, etc. set in a handle
2 the bushy tail of a fox
3 the act of brushing *Give it a good brush.*
4 a brief fight *a brush with the enemy*

brush VERB
1 to use a brush on something
2 to touch gently in passing
brush up to revise a subject

brutal *ADJECTIVE*
very cruel
brutality *NOUN* **brutally** *ADVERB*

brute *NOUN*
1 a brutal person
2 an animal
brutish *ADJECTIVE*

bubble *NOUN*
1 a thin transparent ball of liquid filled with air or gas
2 a small ball of air in something
bubbly *ADJECTIVE*

bubble *VERB*
1 to send up or rise in bubbles
2 to be very lively

buccaneer *NOUN*
a pirate

buck [1] *NOUN*
a male deer, rabbit, or hare

buck *VERB*
(of a horse) to jump with its back arched
buck up (*informal*) 1 to hurry 2 to cheer up

buck [2] *NOUN*
pass the buck (*informal*) to pass the responsibility for something to another person

bucket *NOUN*
a deep container with a handle, for carrying liquids etc.
bucketful *NOUN*

buckle [1] *NOUN*
a device for passing a belt or strap through to fasten it

buckle *VERB*
to fasten with a buckle

buckle [2] *VERB*
to bend or crumple
buckle down to start working hard

bud *NOUN*
a flower or leaf before it opens

Buddhism (buud-izm) *NOUN*
a religion that follows the teachings of Gautama Buddha, who lived in the 5th century BC
Buddhist *NOUN*

budding *ADJECTIVE*
beginning to develop *a budding poet*

buddy *NOUN* **buddies**
(*informal*) a friend

budge *VERB*
to move slightly

budgerigar *NOUN*
an Australian bird kept as a pet in a cage

budget *NOUN*
1 a plan for spending money
2 an amount of money set aside for a purpose
budgetary *ADJECTIVE*

budget *VERB*
to plan how much you are going to spend

budgie *NOUN*
(*informal*) a budgerigar

buff *ADJECTIVE*
of a dull yellow colour

buff *VERB*
to polish with soft material

buffalo *NOUN* **buffalo** or **buffaloes**
a large ox of Asia, Africa, and North America

buffer *NOUN*
1 something that softens the force of a blow or impact
2 (*ICT*) a temporary memory for text or data

buffet [1] (buu-fay) *NOUN*
1 a cafe at a station
2 a meal at which guests serve themselves

buffet [2] (buf-it) *VERB*
to hit or knock strongly *Winds buffeted the coast.*

buffoon *NOUN*
a person who plays the fool
buffoonery *NOUN*

bug *NOUN*
1 an insect
2 an error in a computer program
3 a germ or virus
4 a hidden microphone for spying on people

bug *VERB* **bugging, bugged**
1 to fit with a hidden microphone
2 (*informal*) to annoy

bugbear *NOUN*
something you fear or dislike

buggy *NOUN* **buggies**
1 a pushchair for young children
2 a light horse-drawn carriage

bugle *NOUN*
a brass instrument like a small trumpet
bugler *NOUN*

build *VERB* **built**
to make something by putting the parts together
build in to include
build up 1 to establish gradually 2 to accumulate 3 to cover an area with buildings

build *NOUN*
the shape of someone's body *of slender build*

builder *NOUN*
someone who puts up buildings

building NOUN
1 the process of constructing houses and other structures
2 a permanent built structure that people can go into

bulb NOUN
1 a thick rounded part of a plant from which a stem grows up and roots grow down
2 a glass globe that produces electric light
3 a rounded part of something
bulbous ADJECTIVE

bulge NOUN
a rounded swelling; an outward curve

bulge VERB
to swell out

bulk NOUN
1 the size of something, especially when it is large
2 the greater portion; the majority *The bulk of the population voted for it.*
in bulk in large amounts

bulk VERB
to increase the size or thickness of something

bulky ADJECTIVE **bulkier**, **bulkiest**
taking up a lot of space

bull NOUN
1 the fully-grown male of cattle
2 a male seal, whale, or elephant

bulldog NOUN
a dog of a powerful breed with a short thick neck

bulldoze VERB
to clear with a bulldozer

bulldozer NOUN
a vehicle with a wide metal blade or scoop in front, used for shifting soil or clearing ground

bullet NOUN
a small piece of shaped metal shot from a rifle or revolver

bulletin NOUN
1 a short news announcement on radio or television
2 a regular newsletter or report

bulletproof ADJECTIVE
able to keep out bullets

bullfight NOUN
a public entertainment in which bulls are baited and killed in an arena
bullfighter NOUN

bullion NOUN
bars of gold or silver

bullock NOUN
a young castrated bull

bull's-eye NOUN
1 the centre of a target
2 a hard shiny peppermint sweet

bully VERB **bullies**, **bullied**
to use strength to hurt or frighten a weaker person

bully NOUN **bullies**
someone who bullies people

bulwark NOUN
1 a wall of earth built as a defence
2 a defence or protection

bulwarks PLURAL NOUN
a ship's side above the level of the deck

bum NOUN
(*informal*) a person's bottom

bumble VERB
to move or behave or speak clumsily

bumblebee NOUN
a large bee with a loud hum

bump VERB
1 to knock against something
2 to move along with jolts
bump into (*informal*) to meet by chance **bump off** (*informal*) to kill

bump NOUN
1 the action or sound of bumping
2 a swelling or lump
bumpy ADJECTIVE

bumper[1] NOUN
a protective bar along the front or back of a motor vehicle

bumper[2] ADJECTIVE
unusually large or plentiful *a bumper crop*

bumpkin NOUN
a country person with awkward manners

bumptious ADJECTIVE
conceited and self-important

bun NOUN
1 a small round sweet cake
2 hair twisted into a round bunch at the back of the head

bunch NOUN
a number of things joined or fastened together

bundle NOUN
a number of things tied or wrapped together

bundle VERB
1 to make a number of things into a bundle
2 to push hurriedly or carelessly *They bundled him into a taxi.*

bung NOUN
a stopper for closing a hole in a barrel or jar

bung VERB
(*informal*) throw *Bung it here.*
bunged up completely blocked

bungalow NOUN
a house on one floor

bungle VERB
to do something very badly
bungler NOUN

bunion NOUN
a swelling on the joint of the big toe

bunk[1] NOUN
a bed built like a shelf

bunk[2] NOUN
do a bunk (*informal*) to run away

bunker NOUN
1 a store for fuel
2 a sandy hollow built as an obstacle on a golf course
3 an underground shelter

bunny NOUN **bunnies**
(*informal*) a rabbit

Bunsen burner NOUN
a small gas burner used in scientific work

bunting NOUN
strips of small flags hung up to decorate streets and buildings

buoy (boi) NOUN
a floating object anchored as a guide or warning

buoyant (boi-ant) ADJECTIVE
1 able to float
2 light-hearted or cheerful
buoyancy NOUN

buoyed ADJECTIVE
buoyed up cheerfully eager and excited

bur NOUN
another spelling of **burr** (seed case)

burble VERB
to make a gentle murmuring sound
burble NOUN

burden NOUN
1 a heavy load
2 a worry or difficulty
burdensome ADJECTIVE

burden VERB
to put a burden on

bureau (bewr-oh) NOUN **bureaux**
1 a writing desk
2 a business office *an information bureau*

bureaucracy (bewr-ok-ra-see) NOUN
the use of too many rules and procedures, especially in government departments
bureaucratic ADJECTIVE

bureaucrat (bewr-ok-rat) NOUN
an official in a government department

burger NOUN
a flat round cake of fried meat, eaten in a bread roll

burglar NOUN
a person who breaks into a building in order to steal from it
burglary NOUN

burgle VERB
to steal from a place

burial NOUN
the placing of a dead body in the ground

burly ADJECTIVE **burlier**, **burliest**
strong and heavy

burn VERB **burned** or **burnt**
1 to glow with fire; to produce heat or light
2 to damage or destroy by fire, heat, or chemicals
3 to be damaged or destroyed by fire
4 to feel very hot

burn NOUN
a mark or injury made by burning

burner NOUN
the part of a lamp or cooker that gives out the flame

burning ADJECTIVE
extreme; intense *a burning ambition*

burr NOUN
1 a prickly seed case of a plant or flower
2 a soft country accent

burrow NOUN
a hole or tunnel dug by a small animal as a dwelling

burrow VERB
1 to dig a burrow
2 to search deeply

burst VERB **burst**
1 to break or force apart
2 to start suddenly *burst into flames burst out laughing*
3 to be very full *bursting with energy*

burst NOUN
1 a split caused by something bursting
2 something short and forceful *a burst of gunfire*

bury VERB **buries**, **buried**
1 to place a dead body in the ground
2 to put underground or cover up
bury the hatchet to agree to stop quarrelling or fighting

bus NOUN
a large public vehicle for carrying passengers

busby NOUN **busbies**
a tall ceremonial fur hat worn by some regiments

bush NOUN
1 a shrub
2 wild uncultivated land in Africa or Australia
bushy ADJECTIVE

bushel NOUN
a measure for grain and fruit (8 gallons or 36.4 litres)

business *NOUN*
1 a person's concern or responsibilities *That is my business.*
2 an affair or subject *tired of the whole business*
3 a shop or firm
4 the buying and selling of things

businesslike *ADJECTIVE*
practical and well-organized

businessman or **businesswoman**
NOUN **businessmen** or **businesswomen**
a man or woman who works in business

busker *NOUN*
a person who plays music in the street for money
busking *NOUN*

bust [1] *NOUN*
1 a sculpture of a person's head and shoulders
2 the upper front part of a woman's body

bust [2] *VERB* **bust**
(*informal*) to break something

bustle *VERB*
to hurry in a busy or excited way

bustle *NOUN*
hurried or excited activity

busy *ADJECTIVE* **busier**, **busiest**
1 having a lot to do
2 full of activity
3 (of a telephone line) engaged
busily *ADVERB*

busy *VERB* **busies**, **busied**
busy yourself to occupy yourself; to keep busy

busybody *NOUN* **busybodies**
a person who meddles or interferes

but *CONJUNCTION*
however; nevertheless *I wanted to go, but I couldn't.*

but *PREPOSITION*
except *no one but me*

but *ADVERB*
only; no more than *We can but try.*

butcher *NOUN*
1 a person who cuts up meat and sells it
2 a person who kills cruelly or needlessly
butchery *NOUN*

butcher *VERB*
to kill cruelly or needlessly

butler *NOUN*
the chief male servant in a large house

butt [1] *NOUN*
1 the thicker end of a weapon or tool
2 the stump of a used cigarette or cigar
3 a large cask or barrel
4 a target for ridicule or teasing

butt [2] *VERB*
to push or hit with the head
butt in to interrupt or meddle

butter *NOUN*
a soft fatty food made by churning cream
buttery *ADJECTIVE*

buttercup *NOUN*
a wild plant with bright yellow cup-shaped flowers

butterfly *NOUN* **butterflies**
1 an insect with large white or coloured wings
2 a swimming stroke in which both arms are lifted at the same time

butterscotch *NOUN*
a kind of hard toffee

buttocks *PLURAL NOUN*
the two fleshy rounded parts of your bottom

button *NOUN*
1 a knob or disc sewn on clothes as a fastening or ornament
2 a small knob pressed to work an electric device

button *VERB*
to fasten something with a button or buttons

buttonhole *NOUN*
1 a slit through which a button passes to fasten clothes
2 a flower worn on a lapel

buttress *NOUN*
a support built against a wall

buy *VERB* **bought**
to become the owner of something by paying for it
buyer *NOUN*

buy *NOUN*
something that is bought

buzz *NOUN*
a vibrating humming sound
get a buzz (*informal*) to find something exciting

buzz *VERB*
1 to make a buzz
2 to be full of excitement

buzzard *NOUN*
a large hawk

buzzer *NOUN*
a device that makes a buzzing sound as a signal

by *PREPOSITION*
1 near; close to *Sit by me.*
2 using or through the agency of *We came by a short cut. cooking by gas a poem by Byron*
3 during *They travel by night.*
4 to the extent of *I missed it by inches.*
by the way incidentally **by yourself** alone; without help

by ADVERB
1 near *He just stood by.*
2 past *People walked by.*
3 for future use *Put something by.*
by and by soon; later on **by and large** on the whole

bye NOUN
a run scored in cricket when the ball goes past the batsman without being touched

bye-bye EXCLAMATION
goodbye

by-election NOUN
an election to replace an MP who has died or resigned

bygone ADJECTIVE
belonging to the past
let bygones be bygones forgive and forget

bypass NOUN
a road taking traffic round a city or congested area

bypass VERB
to avoid something by going round it

bystander NOUN
a person who sees an event in the street without being involved in it

byte NOUN
(ICT) a unit for measuring computer data

byword NOUN
a person or thing used as a famous example
a byword for quality

Cc

cab NOUN
1 a taxi
2 a compartment for the driver of a lorry, train, bus, or crane

cabaret (kab-er-ay) NOUN
an entertainment for customers in a restaurant or nightclub

cabbage NOUN
a vegetable with green or purple leaves

cabin NOUN
1 a wooden hut or shelter
2 a room for sleeping on a ship
3 the part of an aircraft in which passengers sit

cabinet NOUN
1 a cupboard or container with drawers or shelves
2 the group of senior government ministers who meet regularly to decide policy

cable NOUN
1 a thick rope of fibre or wire
2 a covered group of wires laid underground for transmitting electrical signals
3 a telegram sent overseas

cable television NOUN
a broadcasting service with signals transmitted by cable to subscribers

cacao (ka-kay-oh) NOUN
a tree with a seed from which cocoa and chocolate are made

cache (kash) NOUN
a hidden store of valuable things

cackle VERB
1 to make a loud silly laugh
2 to chatter noisily
3 to cluck loudly as a hen does
cackle NOUN

cacophony NOUN **cacophonies**
a loud unpleasant sound
cacophonous ADJECTIVE

cactus NOUN **cacti**
a type of prickly fleshy plant

cad NOUN
(old use) a man who treats others badly

caddie NOUN
a person who carries a golfer's clubs during a game

caddy NOUN **caddies**
a small box for holding tea

cadet NOUN
a young trainee in the armed forces or the police

cadge VERB
to get something by asking for it without wanting to pay for it or work for it

cadmium NOUN
a metal that looks like tin

Caesarean (siz-air-ee-an) NOUN
a surgical operation for delivering a baby by cutting through the wall of the mother's womb

cafe (kaf-ay) NOUN
a small restaurant serving drinks and light meals

cafeteria NOUN
a self-service cafe

caffeine (kaf-een) NOUN
a stimulant substance found in tea and coffee

caftan NOUN
a long loose coat or dress

cage NOUN
an enclosure with bars, in which birds or animals are kept

cage VERB
to enclose in a cage

cagoule (kag-**ool**) NOUN
a light waterproof jacket

cairn NOUN
a pile of loose stones set up as a landmark or monument

cake NOUN
1 a baked food made from a mixture of flour, fat, eggs, and sugar
2 a shaped lump or mass *a cake of soap*

caked ADJECTIVE
heavily covered with something thick such as mud

calamity NOUN **calamities**
a disaster

calcium NOUN
a chemical substance found in teeth, bones, and lime

calculate VERB
1 to work something out with mathematics
2 to plan or intend something
calculation NOUN

calculating ADJECTIVE
planning things carefully and selfishly

calculator NOUN
a small electronic device for making calculations

calculus NOUN
mathematics for working out problems about rates of change

calendar NOUN
a chart or set of pages showing the dates of the month or year

calf[1] NOUN **calves**
a young cow, bull, elephant, whale, or seal

calf[2] NOUN **calves**
the fleshy back part of the leg below the knee

calibrate VERB
to mark a gauge or instrument with a scale of measurements
calibration NOUN

calibre (kal-ib-er) NOUN
1 the diameter of a tube or gun barrel
2 ability or importance *someone of your calibre*

call NOUN
1 a shout or cry
2 a visit
3 a telephone conversation
4 a summons

call VERB
1 to shout or speak loudly, especially to attract attention
2 to telephone someone
3 to name a person or thing

4 to tell somebody to come to you
5 to make a short visit
call for 1 to come and collect 2 to need *The work calls for great care.* **call off** to cancel or postpone **call up** to summon to join the armed forces
caller NOUN

call centre NOUN
an office that deals with telephone enquiries from the public

calligraphy NOUN
the art of fine handwriting

calling NOUN
a profession or career

callipers PLURAL NOUN
compasses for measuring the width of tubes or of round objects

callous ADJECTIVE
hard-hearted or unsympathetic
callously ADVERB

calm ADJECTIVE
1 quiet and still; not windy
2 not excited or agitated
calmly ADVERB

calm VERB
to make or become calm

calorie NOUN
a unit for measuring an amount of heat or the energy produced by food
calorific ADJECTIVE

calve VERB
to give birth to a calf

calypso NOUN **calypsos**
a West Indian song improvised by the singer on a topical theme

camber NOUN
a slight upward curve on a road to allow drainage

camcorder NOUN
a combined video camera and sound recorder

camel NOUN
a large desert animal with a long neck and humped back, used for transport

cameo (kam-ee-oh) NOUN **cameos**
1 a small hard piece of stone carved with a raised design
2 a short special part for a well-known actor in a play or film

camera NOUN
a device for taking photographs, films, or television pictures

camouflage (kam-off-lah*zh*) NOUN
a natural or artificial way of making things look like part of their surroundings, as a protection

camouflage VERB
to disguise with camouflage

camp NOUN
a place where people live in tents or huts for a short time

camp VERB
1 to put up a tent or tents
2 to have a holiday in a tent
camper NOUN

campaign NOUN
1 a series of battles in one area or with one purpose
2 a planned series of actions to arouse interest in something *an advertising campaign*

campaign VERB
to take part in a campaign
campaigner NOUN

campus NOUN
the grounds of a university or college

can[1] AUXILIARY VERB **could**
1 to be able to *He can speak three languages.*
2 to be allowed to *You can go if you like.*

can[2] NOUN
1 a sealed tin in which food or drink is preserved
2 a metal or plastic container for liquids

can VERB **canning**, **canned**
to preserve food in a sealed can

canal NOUN
1 an artificial waterway for boats or drainage
2 a tube in a plant or animal body

canary NOUN **canaries**
a small yellow songbird

cancan NOUN
a lively dance in which the legs are kicked very high

cancel VERB **cancelling**, **cancelled**
1 to stop something planned from happening
2 to stop an order or instruction
3 to mark a stamp or ticket as used
cancel out to balance each other's effect
The good and harm cancel each other out.
cancellation NOUN

cancer NOUN
1 a disease in which harmful growths form in the body
2 a harmful growth or tumour
cancerous ADJECTIVE

candid ADJECTIVE
frank and honest
candidly ADVERB

candidate NOUN
1 a person who wants to be elected or chosen for a particular job or position etc.
2 a person taking an examination
candidacy NOUN **candidature** NOUN

candle NOUN
a stick of wax with a wick through it, giving light when burning

candlestick NOUN
a holder for a candle or candles

candour (kan-der) NOUN
frankness; honesty

candy NOUN **candies**
(*American*) sweets or a sweet

candyfloss NOUN
a fluffy mass of thin strands of spun sugar

cane NOUN
1 the stem of a reed or tall grass
2 a thin stick

cane VERB
to beat with a cane

canine ADJECTIVE
to do with dogs

canister NOUN
a metal container

canker NOUN
a disease that rots the wood of trees and plants or causes ulcers and sores on animals

cannabis NOUN
hemp smoked as a narcotic drug

cannibal NOUN
1 a person who eats human flesh
2 an animal that eats animals of its own kind
cannibalism NOUN

cannibalize VERB
to take a machine or vehicle apart to provide spare parts for others
cannibalization NOUN

cannon NOUN
a large heavy gun mounted on a carriage

cannonball NOUN
a large solid ball fired from a cannon

cannot VERB
can not

canny ADJECTIVE **cannier**, **canniest**
shrewd and cautious
cannily ADVERB

canoe NOUN
a narrow lightweight boat, moved forwards with paddles
canoeing NOUN **canoeist** NOUN

canon NOUN
1 a general principle or rule
2 a clergyman at a cathedral

canonize VERB
to declare officially that a dead person is a saint
canonization NOUN

canopy NOUN **canopies**
a hanging cover above a throne or bed

cant NOUN
1 insincere or hypocritical talk
2 the slang or jargon of a particular group

can't
cannot

cantankerous ADJECTIVE
bad-tempered and quarrelsome

canteen NOUN
1 a restaurant for workers in a factory or office
2 a case or box containing a set of cutlery
3 a water flask

canter NOUN
a gentle gallop

canter VERB
to go or ride at a canter

canticle NOUN
a song or chant with words taken from
the Bible

cantilever NOUN
a beam or girder fixed at one end and
supporting a bridge

canton NOUN
each of the districts into which Switzerland
is divided

canvas NOUN
1 a kind of strong coarse cloth
2 a piece of canvas for painting on

canvass VERB
to ask people for their support, e.g. in
an election
canvasser NOUN

canyon NOUN
a deep river valley

cap NOUN
1 a soft hat with a peak
2 a cover or top
3 a small explosive strip used in a toy pistol
4 a cap awarded to players selected for a
sports team

cap VERB **capping, capped**
1 to put a cap or cover on something
2 to award a sports cap to someone chosen
for a team
3 to do better than something
4 to put a limit on something

capability NOUN **capabilities**
the ability or skill to do something

capable ADJECTIVE
able to do something
capably ADVERB

capacity NOUN **capacities**
1 the amount that something can hold
2 ability or capability
3 the position that someone occupies *in his
capacity as commander-in-chief*

cape[1] NOUN
a short cloak

cape[2] NOUN
a piece of high land jutting into the sea

caper[1] VERB
to jump about playfully

caper NOUN
a playful prank or adventure

caper[2] NOUN
a bud of a prickly shrub, pickled for use in
cooking

capillary ADJECTIVE
very narrow or fine

capital NOUN
1 the most important city in a country
2 a large letter used at the start of a name or
sentence
3 the top part of a pillar
4 money or property that can be used to
produce more wealth

capitalism NOUN
an economic system in which trade and
industry are controlled by private owners for
profit, and not by the state

capitalist NOUN
a person who supports capitalism

capitalize VERB
1 to write or print as a capital letter
2 to use something to your advantage
You should capitalize on your language skills.
capitalization NOUN

capital punishment NOUN
punishment by being put to death

capitulate VERB
to admit that you are defeated and surrender
capitulation NOUN

cappuccino NOUN **cappuccinos**
milky coffee made frothy with
pressurized steam

capricious ADJECTIVE
deciding or changing your mind impulsively
capriciously ADVERB

capsize VERB
(of a boat) to overturn

capstan NOUN
a thick post used for winding a thick rope
or cable

capsule NOUN
1 a gelatine case containing a dose of
medicine, swallowed whole
2 a seed case on a plant, which splits open
when ripe
3 a detachable compartment of a spacecraft

captain NOUN
1 a person in command of a ship or aircraft
2 the leader in a sports team

a
b
c
d
e
f
g
h
i
j
k
l
m
n
o
p
q
r
s
t
u
v
w
x
y
z

3 an army officer ranking next below a major
4 a naval officer ranking next below a commodore
captaincy NOUN

caption NOUN
1 the words printed with a picture to describe it
2 a short title or heading in a newspaper or magazine

captivate VERB
to charm or delight
captivation NOUN

captive NOUN
a person taken prisoner
captive ADJECTIVE
1 taken prisoner
2 unable to escape

captivity NOUN
1 the state of being captured
2 the confined state of an animal in a zoo

captor NOUN
someone who has captured a person or animal

capture VERB
1 to take someone prisoner
2 to take or obtain by force, trickery, or charm
3 (*ICT*) to put data in a form that can be stored in a computer

capture NOUN
the act of capturing someone or something

car NOUN
1 a motor car
2 a carriage of a train *dining car*

carafe (ka-**raf**) NOUN
a glass bottle for serving wine or water

caramel NOUN
1 a kind of toffee tasting like burnt sugar
2 burnt sugar used for colouring and flavouring food

carat NOUN
1 a measure of weight for precious stones
2 a measure of the purity of gold

caravan NOUN
1 a vehicle towed by a car and used for living in
2 a group of people travelling together across desert country
caravanning NOUN

carbohydrate NOUN
a compound of carbon, oxygen, and hydrogen (e.g. sugar or starch)

carbolic NOUN
a kind of disinfectant

carbon NOUN
an element present in all living things and occurring in its pure form as diamond and graphite

carbonate NOUN
a compound that gives off carbon dioxide when mixed with acid

carbonated ADJECTIVE
(of a drink) having added carbon dioxide to make it fizzy

carbon dioxide NOUN
a gas formed when things burn, or breathed out by humans and animals

carbuncle NOUN
1 an abscess in the skin
2 a bright-red gem

carburettor NOUN
a device for mixing fuel and air in an engine

carcass NOUN
the dead body of an animal

card NOUN
1 thick stiff paper or thin cardboard
2 a small piece of stiff paper for writing or printing on to send messages or greetings or to record information
3 a small oblong piece of plastic with machine-readable information, issued to customers by banks and shops
4 a playing card
cards PLURAL NOUN a game using playing cards **on the cards** likely; possible

cardboard NOUN
a kind of thin board made of layers of paper or wood fibre

cardiac ADJECTIVE
to do with the heart

cardigan NOUN
a knitted jacket

cardinal NOUN
a senior priest in the Roman Catholic Church
cardinal ADJECTIVE
1 chief or most important
2 deep scarlet, like a cardinal's cassock

cardinal number NOUN
a number used for counting things, e.g. one, two, three, etc.

care NOUN
1 attention and thought *Proceed with care.*
2 protection or supervision *a child in her care*
3 worry or anxiety *free from care*
take care to be especially careful **take care of** to look after
care VERB
1 to feel interested or concerned
2 to feel affection
care for 1 to have in your care **2** to be fond of

career NOUN
the series of jobs that someone has as they make progress in their occupation

career *VERB*
to rush along wildly

carefree *ADJECTIVE*
without worries or responsibilities

careful *ADJECTIVE*
1 giving serious thought and attention to
something
2 avoiding damage or danger; cautious
carefully *ADVERB*

careless *ADJECTIVE*
not taking proper care
carelessly *ADVERB*

carer *NOUN*
someone who looks after a person in need
of care

caress *NOUN*
a fond and gentle touch

caress *VERB*
to touch fondly

caretaker *NOUN*
a person employed to look after a school or
other large building

cargo *NOUN* **cargoes**
goods carried in a ship or aircraft

caricature *NOUN*
an amusing or exaggerated picture of someone

caries *NOUN* **caries**
decay in the teeth or bones

carnage *NOUN*
the killing of many people

carnal *ADJECTIVE*
to do with the body as opposed to the spirit

carnation *NOUN*
a garden flower with a sweet smell

carnival *NOUN*
a festival with a procession of people in
fancy dress

carnivorous *ADJECTIVE*
eating meat
carnivore *NOUN*

carol *NOUN*
a religious hymn sung at Christmas

carousel (ka-roo-**sel**) *NOUN*
1 a rotating conveyor belt for baggage at
an airport
2 (*American*) a roundabout at a fair

carp¹ *NOUN* **carp**
an edible freshwater fish

carp² *VERB*
to complain constantly about trivial things

carpenter *NOUN*
a person who makes things out of wood
carpentry *NOUN*

carpet *NOUN*
a thick soft covering for a floor
carpeted *ADJECTIVE* **carpeting** *NOUN*

carriage *NOUN*
1 each of the separate parts of a passenger
train
2 a passenger vehicle pulled by horses
3 the process or cost of transporting goods
4 a moving part carrying or holding
something in a machine

carriageway *NOUN*
the part of a road on which vehicles travel

carrier *NOUN*
1 a person or thing that carries something
2 someone who transmits an illness without
catching it

carrion *NOUN*
dead and decaying flesh

carrot *NOUN*
a plant with a thick orange-coloured root
used as a vegetable

carry *VERB* **carries**, **carried**
1 to take something from one place to another
2 to support the weight of something
3 to take an amount into the next column
when adding figures
4 (of sound) to reach a long way away
5 to approve a proposal at a meeting
be carried away to be very excited **carry
on** to continue **carry out** to put into
practice

cart *NOUN*
an open vehicle for carrying loads

cart *VERB*
1 to carry in a cart
2 (*informal*) to carry something heavy or
tiring

cartilage *NOUN*
tough white flexible tissue attached to a bone

cartography *NOUN*
the process of drawing maps
cartographer *NOUN* **cartographic** *ADJECTIVE*

carton *NOUN*
a cardboard or plastic container

cartoon *NOUN*
1 a funny or comic drawing
2 a series of drawings that tell a story
3 an animated film
cartoonist *NOUN*

cartridge *NOUN*
1 a case containing the explosive for a bullet
or shell
2 a container holding film, ink, etc.

a
b
c
d
e
f
g
h
i
j
k
l
m
n
o
p
q
r
s
t
u
v
w
x
y
z

cartwheel NOUN
a handstand balancing on each hand in turn with arms and legs spread like spokes of a wheel

carve VERB
1 to make something by cutting wood or stone
2 to cut cooked meat into slices

cascade NOUN
1 a small waterfall
2 a lot of things falling or hanging down

cascade VERB
to fall like a cascade

case NOUN
1 a container or covering
2 a suitcase
3 an example of something existing or occurring *in all cases*
4 a police investigation *a murder case*
5 a set of facts or arguments *They put forward a good case.*
6 the form of a word that shows how it is used in a sentence, e.g. *him* is the objective case of *he*
in any case whatever happens **in case** because something may happen

casement NOUN
a window that opens on hinges at its side

cash NOUN
1 money in coin or notes
2 immediate payment for goods

cash VERB
to change a cheque etc. for cash

cashew NOUN
a kind of small nut

cashier NOUN
a person who deals with money in a bank or shop

cashmere NOUN
very fine soft wool

cashpoint NOUN
a cash dispenser

casing NOUN
a protective covering

casino NOUN **casinos**
a public building or room for gambling

cask NOUN
a barrel for wine or other alcoholic drink

casket NOUN
a small box for jewellery

casserole NOUN
1 a covered dish in which food is cooked and served
2 food cooked in a casserole

cassette NOUN
a small sealed case containing recording tape, film, etc.

cast VERB **cast**
1 to throw with force
2 to shed or throw off
3 to record a vote
4 to make something of metal or plaster in a mould
5 to choose performers for a play or film

cast NOUN
1 a shape made by pouring liquid metal or plaster into a mould
2 the performers in a play or film

castanets PLURAL NOUN
a pair of curved pieces of wood held in one hand by Spanish dancers and snapped together to make a clicking sound

castaway NOUN
a shipwrecked person

cast iron NOUN
a hard alloy of iron made by casting it in a mould

castle NOUN
1 a large old fortified building
2 a piece in chess, also called a *rook*

castor NOUN
a small wheel on the leg of a piece of furniture

castor oil NOUN
oil from the seeds of a tropical plant, used as a laxative

castor sugar NOUN
finely-ground white sugar

castrate VERB
to remove the testicles of a male animal
castration NOUN

casual ADJECTIVE
1 happening by chance; not planned
2 not careful or methodical
3 informal; suitable for informal occasions *casual clothes*
4 not permanent *casual work*
casually ADVERB

casualty NOUN **casualties**
someone who is killed or injured in war or in an accident

cat NOUN
1 a small furry domestic animal
2 a wild animal of the same family as a domestic cat, e.g. a lion, tiger, or leopard
let the cat out of the bag to reveal a secret

catacombs (kat-a-koomz) PLURAL NOUN
underground passages with compartments for tombs

catalogue *NOUN*
1 a list of items arranged in order
2 a book containing a list of things for sale
catalogue *VERB*
to enter something in a catalogue

catamaran *NOUN*
a boat with two parallel hulls

catapult *NOUN*
1 a device with elastic for shooting small stones
2 an ancient military weapon for hurling stones etc.
catapult *VERB*
to hurl or rush violently

cataract *NOUN*
1 a large waterfall or rush of water
2 a cloudy area that forms in the eye and prevents clear sight

catarrh (ka-**tar**) *NOUN*
inflammation in the nose that makes it drip a watery fluid

catastrophe *NOUN*
a sudden great disaster
catastrophic *ADJECTIVE*

catch *VERB* **caught**
1 to take and hold something
2 to arrest or capture
3 to overtake
4 to be in time to get on a bus or train etc.
5 to be infected with an illness
6 to hear *I didn't catch what you said.*
7 to discover someone doing something wrong
8 to make or become held or entangled on something sharp
9 to hit or strike *The blow caught him on the nose.*
catch fire to start burning **catch on 1** to become popular **2** to understand
catch *NOUN*
1 the act of catching something
2 something caught or worth catching
3 a hidden difficulty
4 a device for fastening something

catching *ADJECTIVE*
(of an illness) infectious

catchment area *NOUN*
1 the area from which a hospital takes patients or a school takes pupils
2 the whole area from which water drains into a river or reservoir

catchphrase *NOUN*
a familiar or popular phrase

catchy *ADJECTIVE*
(of a tune) pleasant and easy to remember

categorical *ADJECTIVE*
definite and absolute *a categorical refusal*
categorically *ADVERB*

category *NOUN* **categories**
a set of people or things classified as being similar to each other

cater *VERB*
1 to provide food
2 to provide what is needed
caterer *NOUN*

caterpillar *NOUN*
the wormlike larva of a butterfly or moth

cathedral *NOUN*
the most important church of a district, usually the seat of a bishop

Catherine wheel *NOUN*
a firework that spins round

cathode *NOUN*
the electrode by which electric current leaves a device COMPARE **anode**

cathode ray tube *NOUN*
a tube used in televisions and monitors, in which a beam of electrons from a cathode produces an image on a fluorescent screen

Catholic *ADJECTIVE*
belonging to the Roman Catholic Church
Catholicism *NOUN*
Catholic *NOUN*
a Roman Catholic
catholic *ADJECTIVE*
including most things *catholic tastes*

catkin *NOUN*
a spike of small soft flowers on trees such as hazel and willow

Catseye *NOUN*
(*trademark*) one of a line of reflecting studs marking the centre or edge of a road

cattle *PLURAL NOUN*
animals with horns and hoofs, kept by farmers for milk and beef

catty *ADJECTIVE* **cattier**, **cattiest**
speaking or spoken spitefully

cauldron *NOUN*
a large deep pot for boiling

cauliflower *NOUN*
a cabbage with a large head of white flowers

cause *NOUN*
1 a person or thing that produces a result or effect
2 a reason *no cause for worry*
3 an aim or purpose for which people work
cause *VERB*
to be the cause of

causeway *NOUN*
a raised road across low or marshy ground

caustic *ADJECTIVE*
1 able to burn or wear things away by chemical action
2 sarcastic

caution *NOUN*
1 care taken in order to avoid danger etc.
2 a warning

caution *VERB*
to warn

cautionary *ADJECTIVE*
giving a warning

cautious *ADJECTIVE*
showing caution
cautiously *ADVERB*

cavalcade *NOUN*
a large procession

Cavalier *NOUN*
a supporter of King Charles I in the English Civil War (1642–9)

cavalry *NOUN*
soldiers who fight on horseback or in armoured vehicles

cave *NOUN*
a large hollow place in a hill or cliff or underground

cave *VERB*
cave in 1 to fall inwards 2 to give way in an argument

caveman *NOUN* **cavemen**
a person living in a cave in prehistoric times

cavern *NOUN*
a large cave

cavernous *ADJECTIVE*
(of a space) large and hollow

caviar or **caviare** (kav-ee-ar) *NOUN*
the pickled roe of sturgeon or other large fish

cavil *VERB* **cavilling, cavilled**
to raise petty objections

cavity *NOUN* **cavities**
a hollow or hole

cavort *VERB*
jump or run about excitedly

cc *ABBREVIATION*
cubic centimetre(s)

CD *ABBREVIATION*
compact disc

CD-ROM *ABBREVIATION*
compact disc read-only memory; a compact disc on which large amounts of data can be stored and then displayed on a computer screen

CDT *ABBREVIATION*
craft, design, and technology

cease *VERB*
to stop or end

ceasefire *NOUN*
a signal for armies to stop fighting or firing weapons

ceaseless *ADJECTIVE*
not stopping

cedar *NOUN*
an evergreen tree with hard fragrant wood

cede *VERB*
to give up your rights to something

ceilidh (kay-lee) *NOUN*
an informal gathering for music and dancing, especially in Scotland

ceiling *NOUN*
1 the flat surface under the top of a room
2 the highest limit of something

celebrate *VERB*
1 to do something enjoyable on a special day
2 to perform a religious ceremony
celebration *NOUN*

celebrated *ADJECTIVE*
famous

celebrity *NOUN* **celebrities**
1 a famous person
2 fame

celery *NOUN*
a vegetable with crisp white or green stems

celibate *ADJECTIVE*
remaining unmarried or not having sex
celibacy *NOUN*

cell *NOUN*
1 a small room in a prison, monastery, etc.
2 a microscopic unit of living matter
3 a device for producing electric current chemically
4 a small group or unit in an organization

cellar *NOUN*
an underground room

cello (chel-oh) *NOUN* **cellos**
a musical instrument like a large violin, placed between the knees of a player
cellist *NOUN*

Cellophane *NOUN*
(*trademark*) a thin transparent wrapping material

cellular *ADJECTIVE*
to do with or containing cells

celluloid *NOUN*
a kind of plastic

cellulose *NOUN*
tissue that forms the main part of all plants and trees

Celsius (sel-see-us) *ADJECTIVE*
measuring temperature on a scale using 100 degrees, in which water freezes at 0° and boils at 100°

Celtic (**kel**-tik) *ADJECTIVE*
1 to do with the peoples of ancient Britain and France before the Romans, or of their descendants in Ireland, Scotland, and Wales
2 of the languages of these peoples

cement *NOUN*
1 a mixture of lime and clay used in building
2 a strong glue

cement *VERB*
1 to put cement on
2 to join firmly

cemetery *NOUN* **cemeteries**
a place where people are buried

cenotaph *NOUN*
a monument to people who are buried elsewhere

censor *NOUN*
an official who examines films, books, etc. and removes or bans anything that seems harmful
censorship *NOUN*

censor *VERB*
to ban or remove material from films, books, etc.
Do not confuse this word with *censure*.

censure *NOUN*
strong criticism or disapproval of something

censure *VERB*
to criticize or disapprove of someone or something
Do not confuse this word with *censor*.

census *NOUN*
an official count of the population

cent *NOUN*
a coin worth one-hundredth of a dollar

centaur *NOUN*
(in Greek myths) a creature with the upper body, head, and arms of a man and the lower body of a horse

centenary *NOUN* **centenaries**
a 100th anniversary

centigrade *ADJECTIVE*
a temperature scale based on 100 degrees, especially Celsius

centilitre *NOUN*
one hundredth of a litre

centimetre *NOUN*
one hundredth of a metre

centipede *NOUN*
a small crawling creature with many legs

central *ADJECTIVE*
1 to do with or at the centre
2 most important
centrally *ADVERB*

central heating *NOUN*
a system of heating a building by circulating hot water or hot air or steam from a central source

centralize *VERB*
to bring under the control of a central authority
centralization *NOUN*

centre *NOUN*
1 the middle point or part
2 an important place
3 a building or place for a special purpose
a shopping centre

centre *VERB*
to place something at the centre
centre on 1 to be concentrated in 2 to have as the main subject or concern

centre of gravity *NOUN*
the point in an object around which its mass is perfectly balanced

centrifugal *ADJECTIVE*
moving away from the centre

century *NOUN* **centuries**
1 a period of 100 years
2 100 runs scored in cricket

ceramic *ADJECTIVE*
to do with or made of pottery

ceramics *PLURAL NOUN*
the art of making pottery

cereal *NOUN*
1 a grass producing seeds which are used as food, e.g. wheat, barley, rice
2 a breakfast food made from these seeds
Do not confuse this word with *serial*.

cerebral *ADJECTIVE*
to do with the brain

cerebral palsy *NOUN*
a condition caused by brain damage before birth, causing spasms of the muscles

ceremonial *ADJECTIVE*
to do with a ceremony; formal
ceremonially *ADVERB*

ceremonious *ADJECTIVE*
full of ceremony; elaborately performed

ceremony *NOUN* **ceremonies**
the formal actions carried out on an important occasion

certain *ADJECTIVE*
1 sure; without doubt
2 known but not named *a certain person*

certainly *ADVERB*
1 for certain
2 yes; of course

certainty NOUN **certainties**
1 something that is sure to happen
2 the state of being sure

certificate NOUN
an official written or printed statement giving information about a person etc. *a birth certificate*

certify VERB **certifies**, **certified**
to declare formally that something is true
certification NOUN

cessation NOUN
(*formal*) the ending of something

CFC ABBREVIATION
chlorofluorocarbon; a gas that is thought to be harmful to the environment

chafe VERB
1 to make or become sore by rubbing
2 to become impatient

chaff [1] NOUN
husks of corn, separated from the seed

chaff [2] VERB
to tease pleasantly

chaffinch NOUN
a kind of finch

chain NOUN
1 a row of linked metal rings
2 a connected series of things *a mountain chain*
3 a number of shops or other businesses owned by the same company

chain VERB
to fasten with a chain

chain reaction NOUN
a series of happenings in which each causes the next

chair NOUN
1 a seat with a back, for one person
2 the person in charge of a meeting

chair VERB
to be in charge of a meeting

chairman or **chairperson** NOUN
chairmen or **chairpersons**
the person in charge of a meeting

chalet (**shal**-ay) NOUN
1 a Swiss hut or cottage
2 a small house in a holiday camp

chalice NOUN
a large goblet for holding wine, especially in Christian services

chalk NOUN
1 soft white limestone
2 a soft white or coloured stick used on blackboards
chalky ADJECTIVE

challenge NOUN
1 an exciting but difficult task or activity
2 a call to someone to take part in a contest

challenge VERB
1 to make a challenge to
2 to be a challenge to
3 to question whether something is true or correct
challenger NOUN

challenging ADJECTIVE
exciting but difficult

chamber NOUN
1 a room
2 a hall used for meetings of a parliament or a judicial body
3 a compartment in a weapon or piece of machinery

chambermaid NOUN
a woman employed to clean bedrooms at a hotel

chameleon (ka-**mee**-lee-on) NOUN
a small lizard that can change its colour to match its surroundings

chamois NOUN
1 (**sham**-wa) a small wild antelope living in the mountains
2 (**sham**-ee) a piece of soft yellow leather used for washing and polishing

champ VERB
to munch or bite noisily

champagne (sham-**payn**) NOUN
a sparkling white French wine

champion NOUN
1 a person, animal, or thing that has defeated all the others in a sport or competition
2 someone who actively supports a cause
championship NOUN

champion VERB
to support a cause by fighting or speaking for it

chance NOUN
1 an opportunity or possibility
2 the way things happen without being planned
take a chance to take a risk

chance VERB
1 to happen by chance *I chanced to meet her.*
2 to risk something

chancellor NOUN
1 an important government or legal official
2 the chief minister of the government in some European countries

Chancellor of the Exchequer NOUN
the government minister in charge of a country's finances and taxes

chancy *ADJECTIVE* **chancier**, **chanciest**
risky

chandelier *NOUN*
a support for several lights or candles that hangs from the ceiling

change *VERB*
1 to make or become different
2 to exchange
3 to put on different clothes
4 to go from one train or bus etc. to another
5 to give smaller units of money, or money in another currency, for an amount of money

change *NOUN*
1 the process of changing
2 a difference in doing something
3 coins or notes of small values
4 money given back when the price is less than the amount handed over
5 a fresh set of clothes
6 a variation in routine

changeable *ADJECTIVE*
likely to change; often changing

channel *NOUN*
1 a way for water to flow
2 a stretch of water connecting two seas
3 a broadcasting wavelength
4 the part of a river or sea deep enough for ships

channel *VERB* **channelling**, **channelled**
1 to make a channel in something
2 to direct through a channel or in a particular direction

chant *NOUN*
1 a simple repeated tune in church music
2 a rhythmic call or shout

chant *VERB*
1 to sing a chant
2 to call out words in a rhythm

chaos (**kay**-oss) *NOUN*
great confusion or disorder

chaotic *ADJECTIVE*
in a state of great confusion
chaotically *ADVERB*

chap *NOUN*
(*informal*) a man

chapel *NOUN*
1 a small building or room used for Christian worship
2 a section of a large church with its own altar

chaplain *NOUN*
a member of the clergy attached to a college, hospital, army regiment, etc.

chapped *ADJECTIVE*
with skin split or cracked from cold

chapter *NOUN*
1 a division of a book
2 the clergy of a cathedral or members of a monastery

char[1] *VERB* **charring**, **charred**
to make or become black by burning

char[2] *NOUN*
(*informal*) a woman employed as a cleaner

character *NOUN*
1 a person in a story, film, or play
2 all the qualities a person or thing has
3 a letter of the alphabet or other written symbol

characteristic *NOUN*
a quality that forms part of a person's or thing's character

characteristic *ADJECTIVE*
typical of a person or thing
characteristically *ADVERB*

characterize *VERB*
1 to be a characteristic of
2 to describe the character of
characterization *NOUN*

charade (sha-**rahd**) *NOUN*
1 a scene in the game (*charades*) in which people try to guess a word from other people's acting
2 a pretence

charcoal *NOUN*
a black substance made from burnt wood, used for drawing

charge *NOUN*
1 the price asked for something
2 a rushing attack
3 the amount of explosive needed to fire a gun
4 an amount of stored electricity
5 an accusation that someone has committed a crime
6 a person or thing in someone's care
in charge in control or authority

charge *VERB*
1 to ask a particular price
2 to rush forward in an attack
3 to give an electric charge to
4 to accuse of committing a crime
5 to entrust with a responsibility or task

chariot *NOUN*
a horse-drawn vehicle with two wheels, used in ancient times for fighting and racing
charioteer *NOUN*

charity *NOUN* **charities**
1 an organization helping people who are poor, ill, or disabled
2 the act of giving money or help to those in need
3 kindness and sympathy towards others
charitable *ADJECTIVE*

charlatan (shar-la-tan) *NOUN*
a person who falsely claims knowledge or ability

charm *NOUN*
1 the power to please or delight people
2 a magic spell
3 a small object believed to bring good luck
4 an ornament worn on a bracelet etc.

charm *VERB*
1 to give pleasure or delight to people
2 to put a spell on someone
charmer *NOUN* **charming** *ADJECTIVE*

chart *NOUN*
1 a map used in sailing ships or flying aircraft
2 an outline map showing special information
a weather chart
3 a diagram, list, or table of information
the charts a list of the records that are
most popular

chart *VERB*
to make a chart of

charter *NOUN*
1 an official document granting rights
2 the act of chartering an aircraft, ship, or
vehicle

chary (chair-ee) *ADJECTIVE*
cautious about doing or giving something

chase *VERB*
to go quickly after a person or thing to
capture or catch them up
chase *NOUN*

chasm (kazm) *NOUN*
a deep opening in the ground

chassis (shass-ee) *NOUN*
the framework on which a vehicle is built

chaste *ADJECTIVE*
not having sex outside marriage or at all

chasten (chay-sen) *VERB*
to make someone realize that they have
done wrong

chastise *VERB*
to punish or scold severely
chastisement *NOUN*

chastity (chas-ti-ti) *NOUN*
the state of being chaste or sexually pure

chat *NOUN*
a friendly conversation

chat *VERB* **chatting**, **chatted**
to have a friendly conversation

chatter *VERB*
1 to talk about unimportant things
2 (of the teeth) to make a rattling sound from
cold or fright

chatter *NOUN*
chattering talk or sound

chatterbox *NOUN*
a talkative person

chauffeur (shoh-fer) *NOUN*
a person employed to drive a car

chauvinism *NOUN*
1 unthinking support for your own country
2 the belief that men are superior to women
chauvinist *NOUN* **chauvinistic** *ADJECTIVE*

cheap *ADJECTIVE*
1 low in price; not expensive
2 of poor quality
cheaply *ADVERB*

cheapen *VERB*
to make cheap

cheat *VERB*
1 to act dishonestly to gain an advantage
2 to trick or deceive somebody out of
something

cheat *NOUN*
a person who cheats

check [1] *VERB*
1 to make sure that something is correct or in
good condition
2 to make something stop or go slower

check *NOUN*
1 the act of checking something
2 a pause or act of stopping
3 (*American*) a bill in a restaurant
4 the situation in chess when the king is
directly threatened

check [2] *NOUN*
a pattern of squares
checked *ADJECTIVE*

checkmate *NOUN*
the winning situation in chess

checkout *NOUN*
a place where goods are paid for in a
supermarket

checkpoint *NOUN*
a place on a road where traffic is stopped and
checked

cheek *NOUN*
1 the side of the face below the eye
2 rude or disrespectful behaviour

cheeky *ADJECTIVE*
rude or disrespectful
cheekily *ADVERB*

cheer *NOUN*
a shout of praise or encouragement

cheer *VERB*
1 to give a cheer
2 to gladden or encourage
cheer up to make or become cheerful

cheerful *ADJECTIVE*
1 looking or sounding happy
2 pleasantly bright or colourful
cheerfully *ADVERB*

cheerio *EXCLAMATION*
(*informal*) goodbye

cheerless *ADJECTIVE*
gloomy or dreary

cheers *EXCLAMATION* (*informal*)
1 good health
2 goodbye
3 thank you

cheery *ADJECTIVE* **cheerier**, **cheeriest**
bright and cheerful

cheese *NOUN*
a solid food made from milk

cheesecake *NOUN*
a dessert made of a mixture of sweetened curds on a layer of biscuit

cheetah *NOUN*
a large fast-running spotted animal of the cat family

chef *NOUN*
the cook in a hotel or restaurant

chemical *ADJECTIVE*
to do with or produced by chemistry

chemical *NOUN*
a substance obtained by or used in chemistry

chemist *NOUN*
1 a person who makes or sells medicines
2 a shop selling medicines and toiletries
3 an expert in chemistry

chemistry *NOUN*
the study of how substances combine and react with one another

cheque *NOUN*
a printed form for writing instructions to a bank to pay money from an account

chequered *ADJECTIVE*
marked with a pattern of squares

cherish *VERB*
1 to look after a person or thing lovingly
2 to be fond of

cherry *NOUN* **cherries**
a small soft round fruit with a stone

cherub *NOUN*
an angel shown as a chubby child with wings

chess *NOUN*
a game for two players with sixteen pieces each (called *chessmen*) on a board of 64 squares (a *chessboard*)

chest *NOUN*
1 the front part of the body between the neck and the waist
2 a large strong box for storing things

chestnut *NOUN*
1 a tree that produces hard brown nuts
2 the nut of this tree
3 an old joke

chevron (shev-ron) *NOUN*
a V-shaped stripe on a sign or road marking

chew *VERB*
to grind food between the teeth
chewy *ADJECTIVE*

chic (sheek) *ADJECTIVE*
stylish and elegant

chick *NOUN*
a young bird

chicken *NOUN*
1 a young hen
2 a hen's flesh used as food

chicken *ADJECTIVE*
(*informal*) lacking courage; cowardly

chicken *VERB*
chicken out (*informal*) to fail to do something from fear

chickenpox *NOUN*
a disease that produces red spots on the skin

chickpea *NOUN*
the yellow seed of a plant of the pea family, eaten as a vegetable

chicory *NOUN*
a plant with leaves that are used in salads

chide *VERB*
to scold

chief *NOUN*
1 a leader or ruler of a people
2 a person with the highest rank or authority

chief *ADJECTIVE*
most important; main
chiefly *ADVERB*

chieftain *NOUN*
the leader of a tribe or clan

chiffon (shif-on) *NOUN*
a thin almost transparent fabric

chilblain *NOUN*
a sore swollen place on a hand or foot, caused by cold

child *NOUN* **children**
1 a young person; a boy or girl
2 a person's son or daughter

childhood *NOUN*
the time when a person is a child

childish *ADJECTIVE*
1 like a child; unsuitable for a grown person
2 silly and immature
childishly *ADVERB*

childless *ADJECTIVE*
having no children

childlike *ADJECTIVE*
like a child in appearance or behaviour

childminder *NOUN*
a person who is paid to look after children while their parents are out

a
b
c
d
e
f
g
h
i
j
k
l
m
n
o
p
q
r
s
t
u
v
w
x
y
z

chill *NOUN*
1 unpleasant coldness
2 an illness that makes you shiver

chill *VERB*
1 to make a person or thing cold
2 (*informal*) to relax

chilli *NOUN* **chillies**
the hot-tasting pod of a red pepper

chilly *ADJECTIVE* **chillier**, **chilliest**
1 rather cold
2 unfriendly
chilliness *NOUN*

chime *NOUN*
a series of notes sounded by a set of bells

chime *VERB*
to make a chime

chimney pot *NOUN*
a pipe fitted to the top of a chimney

chimney *NOUN* **chimneys**
a tall pipe or structure that carries smoke
away from a fire

chimpanzee *NOUN*
a small African ape

chin *NOUN*
the lower part of the face below the mouth

china *NOUN*
thin delicate pottery

chink *NOUN*
1 a narrow opening
2 a chinking sound

chink *VERB*
to make a sound like glasses or coins being
struck together

chintz *NOUN*
a shiny cotton cloth used for making curtains

chip *NOUN*
1 a thin piece cut or broken off
something hard
2 a fried oblong strip of potato
3 a place where a small piece has been
knocked off
4 a small counter used in games
5 a microchip
a chip on your shoulder resentment about
something

chip *VERB* **chipping**, **chipped**
to knock small pieces off something

chipboard *NOUN*
board made from chips of wood pressed and
stuck together

chirp *VERB*
to make short sharp sounds like a bird
chirp *NOUN*

chirpy *ADJECTIVE* **chirpier**, **chirpiest**
lively and cheerful

chisel *NOUN*
a tool with a sharp end for shaping wood or
stone

chisel *VERB* **chiselling**, **chiselled**
to shape or cut with a chisel

chivalry *NOUN*
kindness and consideration towards people
less strong than yourself
chivalrous *ADJECTIVE*

chive *NOUN*
a small herb with leaves that taste like onions

chivvy *VERB* **chivvies**, **chivvied**
to hurry someone along

chlorine *NOUN*
a greenish-yellow gas used to disinfect
water etc.

chloroform *NOUN*
a liquid with a vapour that makes people
unconscious

chlorophyll *NOUN*
a substance in plants that traps sunlight and
makes them green

chock-a-block *ADJECTIVE*
crammed or crowded together

chock-full *ADJECTIVE*
crammed full

chocolate *NOUN*
1 a solid brown food or powder made from
roasted cacao seeds
2 a drink made with this powder
3 a sweet made of or covered with chocolate

choice *NOUN*
1 the act of choosing between things
2 the range of things from which someone
can choose *a wide choice of holidays*
3 a person or thing chosen

choice *ADJECTIVE*
of the best quality

choir *NOUN*
a group of people trained to sing together,
especially in a church

choke *VERB*
1 to be unable to breathe; to stop someone
breathing
2 to clog or block up

choke *NOUN*
a device controlling the flow of air into an
engine

cholera (kol-er-a) *NOUN*
a serious infectious disease causing vomiting
and diarrhoea

cholesterol (kol-est-er-ol) *NOUN*
a fatty substance that can clog the arteries

choose *VERB* **chose**, **chosen**
1 to decide from several possibilities
2 to decide to do something

choosy ADJECTIVE **choosier**, **choosiest**
fussy and difficult to please

chop VERB **chopping**, **chopped**
to cut or hit with a heavy blow

chop NOUN
1 a chopping blow
2 a small thick slice of meat

chopper NOUN
1 a small axe
2 (*informal*) a helicopter

choppy ADJECTIVE **choppier**, **choppiest**
(of the sea) not smooth; full of small waves

chopsticks PLURAL NOUN
a pair of thin sticks used for eating Chinese
and Japanese food

choral ADJECTIVE
to do with or sung by a choir or chorus

chord (kord) NOUN
1 a number of musical notes sounded
together
2 a straight line joining two points on a curve

chore NOUN
a regular or dull task

chortle VERB
to give a loud chuckle
chortle NOUN

chorus NOUN
1 the words repeated after each verse of a
song or poem
2 music sung by a group of people
3 a group singing together

chorus VERB
to sing or speak the same words at the
same time

christen (kris-en) VERB
1 to baptize
2 to give a name to
christening NOUN

Christian NOUN
a person who believes in Jesus Christ and his
teachings

Christian ADJECTIVE
to do with Christians or their beliefs
Christianity NOUN

Christmas NOUN
the day (25 December) when Christians
commemorate the birth of Jesus Christ

chromatic ADJECTIVE
1 to do with colours
2 (of a musical scale) going up or down in
semitones

chrome NOUN
chromium

chromium (kroh-mee-um) NOUN
a shiny silvery metal

chromosome (kroh-mos-ohm) NOUN
a tiny thread-like part of an animal cell or
plant cell, carrying genes

chronic ADJECTIVE
(of an illness) lasting for a long time
chronically ADVERB

chronicle NOUN
a record of events in the order in which they
happened

chronological ADJECTIVE
arranged in the order in which things
happened
chronologically ADVERB

chronology NOUN **chronologies**
the arrangement of events according to their
dates or the order in which they happened

chronometer (kron-om-it-er) NOUN
a device for measuring time accurately

chrysalis NOUN
the hard cover a caterpillar makes round itself
before it changes into a butterfly or moth

chrysanthemum NOUN
a garden flower that blooms in autumn

chubby ADJECTIVE **chubbier**, **chubbiest**
plump

chuck [1] VERB
(*informal*) to throw clumsily

chuck [2] NOUN
1 the gripping part of a lathe
2 the part of a drill that holds the bit

chuckle NOUN
a quiet laugh

chuckle VERB
to laugh quietly

chug VERB **chugging**, **chugged**
to make the sound of an engine running slowly

chum NOUN
(*informal*) a friend

chunk NOUN
a thick piece of something
chunky ADJECTIVE

church NOUN
1 a public building for Christian worship
2 a particular Christian religion

churlish ADJECTIVE
bad-mannered and unfriendly

churn NOUN
1 a large can for transporting milk
2 a machine for beating milk to make butter

churn VERB
1 to make butter in a churn
2 to stir or swirl vigorously
churn out to produce something in large
quantities

chute NOUN
a steep channel for people or things to slide down

chutney NOUN **chutneys**
a strong-tasting sauce made with fruit, peppers, etc.

cider NOUN
an alcoholic drink made from apples

cigar NOUN
a roll of compressed tobacco leaves for smoking

cigarette NOUN
a roll of shredded tobacco in thin paper for smoking

cinder NOUN
a piece of partly burnt coal or wood

cine camera (sin-ee) NOUN
a camera used for taking moving pictures

cinema NOUN
1 a place where films are shown
2 the business or art of making films

cinnamon NOUN
a reddish-brown spice

cipher NOUN
1 a kind of code
2 the symbol 0, for nought or zero

circle NOUN
1 a perfectly round flat shape or thing
2 the balcony of a cinema or theatre
3 a number of people with similar interests

circle VERB
1 to move in a circle
2 to go round something

circuit (ser-kit) NOUN
1 a circular line or journey
2 a track for motor racing
3 the path of an electric current

circular ADJECTIVE
1 shaped like a circle; round
2 moving round a circle

circular NOUN
a letter or advertisement sent to a number of people

circulate VERB
1 to go round continuously *Blood circulates in the body.*
2 to pass from place to place
3 to send something to several people

circulation NOUN
1 the movement of blood around the body
2 the number of copies of a newspaper or magazine that are sold or distributed

circumcise VERB
to cut off the fold of skin at the tip of the penis
circumcision NOUN

circumference NOUN
the line or distance round a circle

circumspect ADJECTIVE
cautious and vigilant
circumspection NOUN

circumstance NOUN
a fact or condition connected with an event or person or action

circumstantial ADJECTIVE
consisting of facts that suggest something but do not prove it *circumstantial evidence*

circus NOUN
a travelling show performed in a tent, with clowns, acrobats, and sometimes performing animals

cistern NOUN
a tank for storing water

citadel NOUN
a fortress protecting a city

cite VERB
to quote as an example
citation NOUN

citizen NOUN
a person belonging to a particular city or country

citizenry NOUN
all the citizens of a place

citizenship NOUN
the rights or duties of a citizen

citrus fruit NOUN
a sharp-tasting fruit such as a lemon or orange

city NOUN **cities**
a large important town, often having a cathedral

civic ADJECTIVE
1 to do with a city or town
2 to do with citizens

civics NOUN
the study of the rights and duties of citizens

civil ADJECTIVE
1 polite and courteous
2 to do with citizens
3 to do with civilians; not military
civilly ADVERB

civil engineering NOUN
the work of designing roads, bridges, dams, etc.
civil engineer NOUN

civilian NOUN
a person who is not serving in the armed forces

civility NOUN
politeness

civilization *NOUN*
1 a society or culture at a particular time in history *ancient civilizations*
2 a developed or organized way of life

civilize *VERB*
1 to bring culture and education to a primitive community
2 to improve a person's behaviour and manners

civil service *NOUN*
people employed by the government in various departments other than the armed forces

civil war *NOUN*
war between groups of people of the same country

clad *ADJECTIVE*
clothed or covered

claim *VERB*
1 to ask for something you believe you have a right to
2 to state something without being able to prove it
claimant *NOUN*

claim *NOUN*
1 an act of claiming
2 something claimed

clairvoyant *NOUN*
a person who can supposedly predict future events
clairvoyance *NOUN*

clam *NOUN*
a large shellfish

clamber *VERB*
to climb with difficulty

clammy *ADJECTIVE* **clammier, clammiest**
damp and slimy

clamour *NOUN*
1 a loud confused noise
2 a loud protest or demand

clamour *VERB*
to make a loud protest or demand

clamp *NOUN*
a device for holding things tightly

clamp *VERB*
1 to fix with a clamp
2 to fix firmly
clamp down on to become stricter about something

clan *NOUN*
a group of families having the same ancestor

clandestine *ADJECTIVE*
done secretly; kept secret

clang *VERB*
to make a loud ringing sound
clang *NOUN*

clank *VERB*
to make a sound like heavy pieces of metal banging together
clank *NOUN*

clap *VERB* **clapping, clapped**
1 to strike the palms of the hands together loudly, especially as applause
2 to slap in a friendly way *I clapped him on the shoulder.*
3 to put quickly *They clapped him into jail.*

clap *NOUN*
1 a sudden sharp noise, especially of thunder
2 a round of clapping
3 a friendly slap

clapper *NOUN*
the hanging piece inside a bell that strikes it to make it sound

claptrap *NOUN*
insincere or foolish talk

claret *NOUN*
a kind of French red wine

clarify *VERB* **clarifies, clarified**
to make something clear or easier to understand
clarification *NOUN*

clarinet *NOUN*
a woodwind instrument
clarinettist *NOUN*

clarity *NOUN*
the state of being clear or understandable

clash *VERB*
1 to make a loud sound like cymbals banging together
2 to happen inconveniently at the same time
3 to have a fight or argument
4 (of colours) to look unpleasant together
clash *NOUN*

clasp *NOUN*
1 a device for fastening things
2 a tight grasp

clasp *VERB*
1 to grasp or hold tightly
2 to fasten with a clasp

class *NOUN*
1 a group of children or students who are taught together
2 a group of similar people, animals, or things
3 people of the same social or economic level
4 level of quality *first class*

class *VERB*
to arrange things in classes or groups

classic *ADJECTIVE*
generally regarded as excellent or important

classic *NOUN*
a classic book, film, writer, etc.

classical ADJECTIVE
1 to do with ancient Greek or Roman literature, art, etc.
2 (of music) serious or conventional in style

classics NOUN
the study of ancient Greek and Latin languages and literature

classified ADJECTIVE
1 put into classes or groups
2 (of information) officially secret and available only to certain people

classify VERB **classifies**, **classified**
to arrange things in classes or groups
classification NOUN

classroom NOUN
a room in a school where lessons are held

clatter VERB
to make a sound like hard objects rattling together

clatter NOUN
a clattering noise

clause NOUN
1 a single part of a treaty, law, or contract
2 (Grammar) a part of a sentence, with its own verb

claustrophobia NOUN
fear of being inside an enclosed space

claw NOUN
1 a sharp nail on a bird's or animal's foot
2 a claw-like part or device

claw VERB
to grasp, pull, or scratch with a claw or hand

clay NOUN
a stiff sticky earth that becomes hard when baked

clean ADJECTIVE
1 free of dirt or stains
2 fresh; not yet used
3 honourable; not unfair a clean fight
4 neat and effective a clean catch

clean VERB
to make clean

clean ADVERB
completely I clean forgot.

cleaner NOUN
1 a person who cleans rooms
2 something used for cleaning

cleanliness (klen-li-nis) NOUN
the quality of being clean

cleanly (kleen-lee) ADVERB
in a clean way

cleanse (klenz) VERB
1 to clean
2 to make pure
cleanser NOUN

clear ADJECTIVE
1 transparent; not muddy or cloudy
2 easy to see or hear or understand; distinct
3 free from obstacles or unwanted things
4 free from guilt a clear conscience
clearly ADVERB **clearness** NOUN

clear ADVERB
1 distinctly; clearly We heard you loud and clear.
2 completely He got clear away.
3 apart; not in contact Stand clear of the doors.

clear VERB
1 to make or become clear
2 to remove everything from clear the table
3 to show that someone is innocent or reliable
4 to jump over without touching
5 to get approval for
clear off or **out** (informal) to leave **clear up 1** to make things tidy **2** to become better or brighter

clearance NOUN
1 the process of getting rid of unwanted things
2 the space between two things

clearing NOUN
an open space in a forest

cleavage NOUN
the hollow between a woman's breasts

cleave VERB **clove** or **cleft** or **cleaved**, **cloven** or **cleft** or **cleaved**
to divide by chopping

cleaver NOUN
a butcher's chopping tool

clef NOUN
a symbol on a stave in music, showing the pitch of the notes as treble or bass

cleft NOUN
a split in something

clemency NOUN
gentle or merciful treatment

clench VERB
to close the teeth or fingers tightly

clergy NOUN
the priests and ministers of the Christian Church

clergyman or **clergywoman** NOUN **clergymen** or **clergywomen**
a Christian minister

cleric NOUN
a member of the clergy

clerical ADJECTIVE
1 to do with routine office work
2 to do with the clergy

clerk NOUN
an office worker who writes letters and keeps records

clever ADJECTIVE
1 quick at learning and understanding
2 skilful
cleverly ADVERB

cliché (klee-shay) NOUN
a phrase or idea that is used so often that it has little meaning

click VERB
to make a short sharp sound
click NOUN

client NOUN
a person who gets help or advice from a professional person such as a lawyer or accountant

clientele (klee-on-tel) NOUN
customers or clients

cliff NOUN
a steep rock face on a coast

climate NOUN
the regular weather conditions of an area
climatic ADJECTIVE

climax NOUN
the most interesting or important point of a story or series of events

climb VERB
1 to go up or over or down something
2 to grow upwards
3 to go higher
climb down to admit that you have been wrong
climb NOUN **climber** NOUN

clinch VERB
1 to settle something definitely
2 to clasp tightly
clinch NOUN

cling VERB **clung**
to hold on tightly

cling film NOUN
a thin clinging transparent film, used to wrap food

clinic NOUN
a place where patients see doctors for treatment or advice

clinical ADJECTIVE
1 to do with the medical treatment of patients
2 cool and unemotional
clinically ADVERB

clink VERB
to make a thin sharp sound like glasses being struck together
clink NOUN

clip¹ NOUN
a fastener for keeping things together

clip VERB **clipping**, **clipped**
to fasten with a clip

clip² VERB **clipping**, **clipped**
1 to cut with shears or scissors
2 (informal) to hit someone

clip NOUN
a short piece of film shown on its own

clipper NOUN
an old type of fast sailing ship

clippers PLURAL NOUN
an instrument for cutting hair

clique (kleek) NOUN
a small group of people who stick together and keep others out

cloak NOUN
a piece of outdoor clothing that hangs loosely from the shoulders

cloak VERB
to cover or conceal

cloakroom NOUN
1 a place where coats and bags can be left by visitors
2 a toilet in a large building

clock NOUN
1 a device that shows the time
2 a measuring device with a dial or digital display

clock VERB
clock in or **out** to register the time you arrive at or leave work

clockwise ADVERB, ADJECTIVE
moving in the same direction as the hands of a clock

clockwork NOUN
a mechanism with a spring that has to be wound up
like clockwork very regularly

clod NOUN
a lump of earth or clay

clog NOUN
a shoe with a wooden sole

clog VERB **clogging**, **clogged**
to block up

clone NOUN
an animal or plant made from the cells of another and exactly like it

clone VERB
to produce a clone of an animal or plant

close¹ ADJECTIVE
1 near
2 detailed or concentrated *close attention*
3 with little empty space *a close fit*
4 in which competitors are nearly equal
a close contest
5 (of the weather) humid and stuffy
closely ADVERB

a b c d e f g h i j k l m n o p q r s t u v w x y z

close ADVERB
closely　*close behind*　*He held her close.*

close NOUN
1 a street that is closed at one end
2 an enclosed area in a town

close [2] VERB
1 to shut
2 to end
close in to get nearer

close NOUN
the end of a performance or event

closet NOUN
(*American*) a cupboard or storeroom

closet VERB
to shut yourself away in private

close-up NOUN
a photograph or piece of film taken at
close range

closure NOUN
the process of closing

clot NOUN
1 a small mass of blood, cream, etc. that has
become solid
2 (*informal*) a silly person

clot VERB **clotting, clotted**
to form clots

cloth NOUN
1 woven material or felt
2 a piece of this material
3 a tablecloth

clothe VERB
to put clothes on someone

clothes PLURAL NOUN
things worn to cover the body

clothing NOUN
clothes

cloud NOUN
1 a mass of condensed water vapour floating
in the sky
2 a mass of smoke or dust in the air

cloud VERB
to become cloudy

cloudburst NOUN
a sudden heavy rainstorm

cloudy ADJECTIVE **cloudier, cloudiest**
1 full of clouds
2 not clear or transparent

clout VERB
(*informal*) to hit

clout NOUN (*informal*)
1 a hit
2 power or influence

clove [1] NOUN
1 the dried bud of a tropical tree, used as a
spice
2 a section of a garlic bulb

clove [2] *past tense* of **cleave** [1]

cloven *past participle* of **cleave** [1]

clover NOUN
a small plant usually with three leaves on each
stalk
in clover in ease and luxury

clown NOUN
1 a performer of amusing tricks and actions in
a circus
2 a silly person

clown VERB
to do silly things

cloying ADJECTIVE
sickeningly sweet

club NOUN
1 a heavy stick used as a weapon
2 a stick with a shaped head used to hit the
ball in golf
3 an organized group of people with a
common interest
4 a playing card with black clover leaves on it

club VERB **clubbing, clubbed**
to hit with a heavy stick
club together to join with other people to
pay for something

cluck VERB
to make the cry of a hen
cluck NOUN

clue NOUN
something that helps to solve a puzzle or a
mystery
not have a clue (*informal*) to be ignorant
or baffled

clump NOUN
1 a cluster or mass of things
2 a clumping sound

clump VERB
1 to form a cluster or mass
2 to walk with a heavy tread

clumsy ADJECTIVE **clumsier, clumsiest**
1 heavy and awkward
2 not skilful or tactful　*a clumsy apology*
clumsily ADVERB

cluster NOUN
a small close group

cluster VERB
to form a cluster

clutch [1] VERB
to grasp tightly

clutch NOUN
1 a tight grasp
2 a device for connecting and disconnecting
the engine of a motor vehicle to and from its
gears

clutch [2] NOUN
a set of eggs for hatching

clutter *NOUN*
things lying about untidily

clutter *VERB*
to fill with clutter

coach *NOUN*
1 a bus used for long journeys
2 a carriage of a railway train
3 a horse-drawn carriage with four wheels
4 an instructor in sports
5 a teacher giving private specialized tuition

coach *VERB*
to instruct or train in sports

coal *NOUN*
a hard black mineral substance used for burning to supply heat

coalition *NOUN*
a temporary alliance of political parties to form a government

coarse *ADJECTIVE*
1 not smooth or delicate; rough or harsh
2 composed of large particles; not fine
3 rude or vulgar

coarsen *VERB*
to make or become coarse

coast *NOUN*
the seashore or the land close to it
coastal *ADJECTIVE*

coast *VERB*
to ride downhill without using power

coat *NOUN*
1 a piece of outer clothing with sleeves
2 the hair or fur on an animal's body
3 a covering layer

coat *VERB*
to cover something with a coating

coating *NOUN*
a covering layer

coat of arms *NOUN*
a crest on a shield

coax *VERB*
to persuade gently or patiently

cob *NOUN*
1 the central part of an ear of maize, on which the corn grows
2 a sturdy horse for riding

cobalt *NOUN*
a hard silvery-white metal

cobble[1] *NOUN*
(also **cobblestone**) a rounded stone used for paving roads
cobbled *ADJECTIVE*

cobble[2] *VERB*
to make or mend roughly

cobbler *NOUN*
someone who mends shoes

cobra *NOUN*
a poisonous snake that can rear up

cobweb *NOUN*
a thin sticky net made by a spider to trap insects

cocaine *NOUN*
an addictive drug made from the leaves of a tropical plant

cock *NOUN*
1 a male chicken or other bird
2 a lever in a gun

cock *VERB*
1 to make a gun ready to fire by raising the cock
2 (of a dog) to turn the ears upwards when on the alert

cockatoo *NOUN* **cockatoos**
a crested parrot

cockerel *NOUN*
a young male chicken

cock-eyed *ADJECTIVE*
(*informal*) crooked; not straight

cockle *NOUN*
an edible shellfish

cockney *NOUN*
1 a person born in the East End of London
2 the speech of cockneys

cockpit *NOUN*
the compartment for the pilot and crew of an aircraft

cockroach *NOUN*
a dark brown beetle-like insect, often found in dirty houses

cocksure *ADJECTIVE*
very sure; too confident

cocktail *NOUN*
a mixed alcoholic drink

cocky *ADJECTIVE* **cockier, cockiest**
(*informal*) too self-confident

cocoa *NOUN*
a hot drink made from a powder of crushed cacao seeds

coconut *NOUN*
a large round nut from a palm tree, with a white flesh and milky juice

cocoon *NOUN*
1 the covering round a chrysalis
2 a protective wrapping

cocoon *VERB*
to protect something by wrapping it up

cod *NOUN* **cod**
a large edible sea fish

coddle *VERB*
to cherish and protect carefully

code NOUN
1 a word or phrase used to represent a message to keep its meaning secret
2 a set of signs used in sending messages
3 a set of numbers or letters used to identify something
4 a set of laws or rules

code VERB
to put a message into code

codify VERB **codifies**, **codified**
to arrange laws or rules into a code or system
codification NOUN

coeducation NOUN
the education of boys and girls together
coeducational ADJECTIVE

coefficient NOUN
a number by which another number is multiplied

coerce (koh-**erss**) VERB
to compel someone with threats or force
coercion NOUN

coffee NOUN
1 a hot drink made from the roasted ground seeds of a tropical plant
2 these seeds

coffer NOUN
a large strong box for holding money and valuables

coffin NOUN
a long box in which a dead body is buried or cremated

cog NOUN
a tooth-like part on the edge of a gear wheel

cogent (koh-jent) ADJECTIVE
convincing *a cogent argument*

cognac (kon-yak) NOUN
a kind of French brandy

cohere VERB
to stick together
cohesion NOUN **cohesive** ADJECTIVE

coherent ADJECTIVE
clear, reasonable, and making sense
coherently ADVERB

coil NOUN
something wound into a spiral

coil VERB
to wind something into a coil

coin NOUN
a round piece of metal used as money

coin VERB
1 to manufacture coins
2 to invent a word or phrase

coinage NOUN
1 a system of money
2 a new word or phrase

coincide VERB
1 to happen at the same time as something else
2 to be in the same place
3 to be the same *My opinion coincides with yours.*

coincidence NOUN
the happening of similar events at the same time by chance

coke NOUN
solid fuel left when gas and tar have been extracted from coal

colander NOUN
a bowl with holes in it, used for straining water from vegetables after cooking

cold ADJECTIVE
1 having a low temperature; not warm
2 unfriendly or unenthusiastic
get cold feet to have doubts about doing something bold or ambitious
coldly ADVERB **coldness** NOUN

cold NOUN
1 a low temperature
2 an infectious illness that makes your nose run and your throat sore

cold-blooded ADJECTIVE
1 having a body temperature that changes according to the surroundings
2 callous; deliberately cruel

cold war NOUN
a situation of hostility between nations without open fighting

colic NOUN
pain in a baby's stomach

collaborate VERB
1 to work together on a task
2 to cooperate with an enemy of your country
collaboration NOUN **collaborator** NOUN

collage (kol-ahzh) NOUN
a picture made by fixing small objects to a surface

collapse VERB
1 to break or fall to pieces
2 to become very weak or ill
3 to fold up

collapse NOUN
1 the act of collapsing
2 a breakdown

collapsible ADJECTIVE
able to be folded up

collar NOUN
1 the part of a piece of clothing that goes round your neck
2 a band round the neck of an animal

collar VERB
(*informal*) to seize or catch someone

colleague NOUN
a person you work with

collect VERB
1 to bring people or things together
2 to find examples of things as a hobby
3 to come together
4 to ask for money or contributions from people
5 to go and fetch
collector NOUN

collection NOUN
1 the process of collecting
2 things collected
3 money collected for a charity

collective ADJECTIVE
to do with a group as a whole *our collective opinion*

collective noun NOUN
a singular noun that refers to many individuals taken as a unit, e.g. *army* or *herd*

college NOUN
a place where people can take courses after they have left school

collide VERB
to crash into something
collision NOUN

collie NOUN
a dog with a long pointed face

colliery NOUN **collieries**
a coal mine and its buildings

colloquial (col-**oh**-kwee-al) ADJECTIVE
used in conversation but not in formal speech or writing
colloquially ADVERB

collusion NOUN
a secret agreement between two or more people who are trying to deceive or cheat someone

colon[1] NOUN
a punctuation mark (:), often used to introduce a list

colon[2] NOUN
the largest part of the intestine

colonel (**ker**-nel) NOUN
an army officer in charge of a regiment

colonial ADJECTIVE
to do with a colony or colonies abroad

colonize VERB
to establish a colony in a country
colonist NOUN **colonization** NOUN

colonnade NOUN
a row of columns

colony NOUN **colonies**
1 an area of land that people of another country settle in and control
2 the people of a colony
3 a group of people or animals of the same kind living together

colossal ADJECTIVE
very large; enormous

colour NOUN
1 the effect produced by waves of light of a particular wavelength
2 the use of various colours
3 the complexion of a person's skin
4 a substance used to colour things

colour VERB
1 to put colour on; to paint or stain
2 to blush
3 to influence what someone says or believes

colour-blind ADJECTIVE
unable to see the difference between certain colours

coloured ADJECTIVE
having a particular colour

colourful ADJECTIVE
1 full of colour
2 lively; having vivid details

colouring NOUN
the colour of something

colourless ADJECTIVE
without colour

colt NOUN
a young male horse

column NOUN
1 a pillar
2 something long or tall and narrow *a column of smoke*
3 a vertical section of a page
4 a regular article in a newspaper

columnist NOUN
a journalist who writes regularly for a newspaper

coma (**koh**-ma) NOUN
a state of deep unconsciousness caused by illness or injury

comb NOUN
1 a toothed strip of wood or plastic used to tidy the hair
2 the red crest on the head of a hen or turkey

comb VERB
1 to tidy the hair with a comb
2 to search thoroughly

combat NOUN
a fight

combat VERB
to fight or resist

combatant NOUN
someone who takes part in a fight

combination NOUN
1 the process of joining together
2 a number of people or things combined
3 a series of numbers or letters needed to open a lock

combine VERB
to join or mix together

combustible ADJECTIVE
able to be set on fire

combustion NOUN
the process of burning

come VERB came, come
1 to move towards this place
2 to reach a condition or result *to come to a decision*
3 to happen *How did you come to lose it?*
4 to occur or be present *It comes on the next page.*
5 to result *This comes of being careless.*
come across to find or meet by chance **come by** to obtain **come in for** to receive a share of **come to** 1 to amount to 2 to become conscious again

comedian NOUN
a performer who entertains by making the audience laugh

comedy NOUN comedies
1 a play or film that makes people laugh
2 humour

comet NOUN
an object moving across the sky with a bright tail of light

comfort NOUN
1 a comfortable feeling or condition
2 a person or thing that gives comfort

comfort VERB
to make a person less unhappy; to soothe

comfortable ADJECTIVE
1 free from worry or pain
2 pleasant to use or wear *comfortable shoes*
comfortably ADVERB

comic ADJECTIVE
making people laugh
comical ADJECTIVE **comically** ADVERB

comic NOUN
1 a children's magazine containing comic strips
2 a comedian

comic strip NOUN
a series of drawings telling a story, especially a funny one

comma NOUN
a punctuation mark (,) used to mark a pause in a sentence or to separate items in a list

command NOUN
1 a statement telling somebody to do something
2 authority or control
3 the ability to use or do something *a good command of Japanese*

command VERB
1 to give a command to
2 to have authority over
3 to deserve and get *They command our respect.*

commandant NOUN
a military officer in charge of a place or group of people

commandeer VERB
to take or seize something for use in a war

commander NOUN
1 a person who has command
2 a naval officer

commandment NOUN
a sacred command, especially one of the Ten Commandments in the Old Testament of the Bible

commando NOUN commandos
a soldier trained to carry out dangerous raids

commemorate VERB
to be a celebration or reminder of some past event or person
commemoration NOUN
commemorative ADJECTIVE

commence VERB
(*formal*) to begin
commencement NOUN

commend VERB
1 to praise *He was commended for bravery.*
2 to entrust *We commend him to your care.*
commendation NOUN

commendable ADJECTIVE
deserving praise

comment NOUN
a brief opinion or explanation

comment VERB
to make a comment

commentary VERB
1 a description of an event by someone who is watching it
2 a set of explanatory notes
commentator NOUN

commerce NOUN
trade and the services that assist it, e.g. banking and insurance

commercial ADJECTIVE
1 to do with commerce
2 paid for by advertising *commercial television*
3 profitable
commercially ADVERB

commercial NOUN
an advertisement on radio or television

commercialized ADJECTIVE
changed in order to make more money

commiserate VERB
to sympathize
commiseration NOUN

commission NOUN
1 a task formally given to someone
2 an appointment to be an officer in the armed forces
3 a group of people given authority to do or investigate something
4 a payment to someone for providing a service on your behalf
commission VERB
to give a commission to

commissionaire NOUN
an attendant in uniform at the entrance to a large building

commissioner NOUN
1 an official appointed by commission
2 a member of a commission

commit VERB **committing**, **committed**
1 to do or perform to commit a crime
2 to place in someone's care or custody
3 to promise to use time or money available for a particular purpose

commitment NOUN
1 the work, belief, and loyalty that a person gives to a system or organization
2 something that you have to do regularly work commitments

committal NOUN
1 the act of committing a person to prison
2 the act of giving a body for burial or cremation

committee NOUN
a group of people appointed to deal with a particular matter

commodity NOUN **commodities**
a product for buying and selling

commodore NOUN
1 a naval officer ranking next below a rear admiral
2 the commander of part of a fleet

common ADJECTIVE
1 ordinary or usual
2 occurring often a common mistake
3 for all or most people the common good
4 shared a common interest
5 vulgar
in common shared by two or more people or things
commonly ADVERB
common NOUN
a piece of land for public use

commoner NOUN
a member of the ordinary people

commonplace ADJECTIVE
ordinary or usual

common room NOUN
an informal room for students or teachers at a school or college

common sense NOUN
normal good sense in thinking or behaviour

commonwealth NOUN
1 a group of independent countries
2 a country made up of several states
the Commonwealth an association of Britain and countries that used to be part of the British Empire

commotion NOUN
a noisy uproar

communal ADJECTIVE
shared by several people
communally ADVERB

commune[1] NOUN
a group of people living together and sharing everything

commune[2] VERB
to talk together

communicate VERB
1 to pass news or information to other people
2 (of rooms) to have a connecting door

communication NOUN
1 the process of communicating
2 something communicated; a message
communications PLURAL NOUN links between places (e.g. roads, railways, telephones, radio)

communicative ADJECTIVE
willing to talk or give information

communion NOUN
religious fellowship
Communion the Christian ceremony in which consecrated bread and wine are given to worshippers

Communism NOUN
a political system in which the state controls property and the means of production
Communist NOUN

communism NOUN
a system in which property is shared by the community

community NOUN **communities**
1 the people living in an area
2 a group with similar interests or origins

commute VERB
to travel daily to and from work
commuter NOUN

compact ADJECTIVE
closely or neatly packed together
compact NOUN
a small flat container for face powder

compact VERB
to join or press firmly together or into a small space

compact disc NOUN
a small plastic disc on which music or data is stored as digital signals and is read by a laser beam

companion NOUN
1 a person you spend time with or travel with
2 one of a matching pair of things
companionship NOUN

company NOUN **companies**
1 a number of people together
2 a business firm
3 having people with you
4 visitors
5 a section of a battalion

comparable ADJECTIVE
able to be compared, similar
comparably ADVERB

comparative ADJECTIVE
compared with others *They live in comparative comfort.*
comparatively ADVERB

compare VERB
to put things together to see how they are similar or different
compare with to be similar to or as good as

comparison NOUN
the act of comparing

compartment NOUN
one of the spaces into which something is divided

compass NOUN
a device that shows direction, with a magnetized needle pointing to the north
compasses or **pair of compasses** a device for drawing circles

compassion NOUN
pity or mercy
compassionate ADJECTIVE

compatible ADJECTIVE
1 able to live or exist together
2 able to be used together
compatibility NOUN

compatriot NOUN
a person from the same country as another

compel VERB **compelling**, **compelled**
to force somebody to do something

compelling ADJECTIVE
1 convincing *a compelling argument*
2 interesting or attractive

compensate VERB
1 to give a person money etc. to make up for a loss or injury
2 to have a balancing effect
compensation NOUN

compère (kom-pair) NOUN
a person who introduces the performers in a show or broadcast

compete VERB
to take part in a competition

competent ADJECTIVE
able to do a particular thing
competence NOUN **competently** ADVERB

competition NOUN
1 a game or race or other contest in which people try to win
2 the people competing with you
competitive ADJECTIVE

competitor NOUN
someone who competes; a rival

compile VERB
to put things together into a list or collection
compiler NOUN **compilation** NOUN

complacent ADJECTIVE
smugly satisfied
complacency NOUN **complacently** ADVERB

complain VERB
to say that you are annoyed or unhappy about something

complaint NOUN
1 a statement complaining about something
2 an illness

complement NOUN
1 the quantity needed to fill or complete something
2 (*Grammar*) the word or words used after verbs such as *be* and *become* to complete the sense

complement VERB
to go well together with something else or make it complete

complementary ADJECTIVE
completing or adding to something else

complementary angle NOUN
either of two angles that add up to 90°

complete ADJECTIVE
1 having all its parts
2 finished
3 thorough; in every way *a complete surprise*
completely ADVERB

complete VERB
1 to make a thing complete
2 to add what is needed
completion NOUN

complex ADJECTIVE
1 difficult to understand or do
2 made up of parts
complexity NOUN

complex NOUN
1 a set of related buildings or facilities on the same site
2 a group of feelings or ideas that influence a person's behaviour

complexion NOUN
the natural colour and appearance of the skin of the face

complicate VERB
to make a thing more complicated or difficult

complicated ADJECTIVE
1 difficult to understand or do
2 made up of many parts

complication NOUN
something that complicates things or adds difficulties

complicity NOUN
the state of being involved in a crime or bad action

compliment NOUN
something good you say about a person or thing
compliments PLURAL NOUN good wishes given in a message

compliment VERB
to pay someone a compliment; to congratulate

complimentary ADJECTIVE
1 expressing a compliment
2 given free of charge *complimentary tickets*

comply VERB **complies**, **complied**
to obey laws or rules

component NOUN
one of the parts from which a thing is made

compose VERB
1 to form or make up *The class is composed of 20 students.*
2 to write music or poetry
3 to arrange in good order

composed ADJECTIVE
calm or quiet

composer NOUN
a person who writes music

composite ADJECTIVE
made up of different parts or styles

composition NOUN
1 the process of composing
2 a piece of music or writing
3 the parts that make something

compost NOUN
decayed leaves and grass used as a fertilizer

composure NOUN
a calm manner

compound[1] ADJECTIVE
made of two or more parts or ingredients

compound NOUN
a compound substance

compound VERB
to put together; to combine

compound[2] NOUN
a fenced area containing buildings

comprehend VERB
1 to understand
2 to include

comprehensible ADJECTIVE
understandable

comprehensive ADJECTIVE
including all or many kinds of people or things

compress (kom-**press**) VERB
to press together or into a smaller space
compression NOUN **compressor** NOUN

compress (**kom**-press) NOUN
a soft pad or cloth pressed on the body to stop bleeding or reduce inflammation

comprise VERB
to include or consist of *The pentathlon comprises five events.*

compromise NOUN
the settling of a dispute by each side accepting less than it wanted

compromise VERB
1 to settle by a compromise
2 to expose someone to danger or suspicion

compulsion NOUN
a strong and uncontrollable desire to do something

compulsive ADJECTIVE
having a strong and uncontrollable desire

compulsory ADJECTIVE
required to be done; not optional

compunction NOUN
a guilty feeling about doing something
had no compunction about leaving them

compute VERB
to calculate
computation NOUN

computer NOUN
an electronic machine that stores and analyses information

comrade NOUN
a companion who shares in your activities
comradeship NOUN

con VERB **conning**, **conned**
(*informal*) to swindle

concave ADJECTIVE
curved like the inside of a ball or circle

conceal VERB
to hide something or keep something secret
concealment NOUN

a
b
c
d
e
f
g
h
i
j
k
l
m
n
o
p
q
r
s
t
u
v
w
x
y
z

concede VERB
1 to admit that something is true
2 to grant or allow a right

conceit NOUN
too much pride in yourself

conceited ADJECTIVE
having too high an opinion of yourself

conceivable ADJECTIVE
able to be imagined or believed
conceivably ADVERB

conceive VERB
1 to become pregnant
2 to form an idea or plan; to imagine

concentrate VERB
1 to give your full attention or effort to something
2 to bring or come together in one place

concentration NOUN
1 the process of concentrating
2 the amount dissolved in each part of a liquid

concentric ADJECTIVE
having the same centre

concept NOUN
an idea
conceptual ADJECTIVE

conception NOUN
1 the process of conceiving
2 an idea

concern VERB
1 to affect or be important to somebody
2 to worry somebody
3 to have as its subject

concern NOUN
1 something that concerns you
2 a worry
3 a business

concerned ADJECTIVE
1 worried
2 involved in or affected by something

concerning PREPOSITION
on the subject of; about

concert NOUN
a musical entertainment

concerted ADJECTIVE
done in cooperation with others
a concerted effort

concertina NOUN
a musical instrument with bellows, played by squeezing

concerto (kon-chert-oh) NOUN **concertos**
or **concerti**
a piece of music for a solo instrument and an orchestra

concession NOUN
1 the process of conceding
2 something conceded
3 a reduction in price for certain types of people
concessionary ADJECTIVE

conciliate VERB
1 to win over by friendliness
2 to help people to agree
conciliation NOUN

concise ADJECTIVE
giving much information in a few words
concisely ADVERB

conclude VERB
1 to bring or come to an end
2 to form an opinion by reasoning

conclusion NOUN
1 an ending
2 an opinion formed by reasoning

conclusive ADJECTIVE
putting an end to all doubt
conclusively ADVERB

concoct VERB
1 to make something by putting ingredients together
2 to invent *to concoct an excuse*
concoction NOUN

concord NOUN
friendly agreement or harmony

concordance NOUN
an index of the words used in a book or an author's works

concourse NOUN
an open area through which people pass, e.g. at an airport

concrete NOUN
cement mixed with sand and gravel, used in building

concrete ADJECTIVE
1 able to be touched and felt; not abstract
2 definite *concrete evidence*

concur VERB **concurring, concurred**
to agree
concurrence NOUN

concussion NOUN
a temporary injury to the brain caused by a blow to the head
concussed ADJECTIVE

condemn VERB
1 to say that you strongly disapprove of something
2 to sentence to a particular punishment
3 to declare a building unfit for use
condemnation NOUN

condensation NOUN
1 the process of condensing
2 drops of liquid formed by vapour condensing

condense VERB
1 to make a liquid denser or more compact
2 to put something into fewer words
3 to change from gas or vapour to liquid

condescend VERB
to act in a superior way towards someone
condescension NOUN

condition NOUN
1 the state or fitness of a person or thing
in good condition
2 the situation or surroundings that affect
something *working conditions*
3 something required as part of an
agreement
on condition that only if

condition VERB
1 to put something into a healthy or proper
condition
2 to train someone to behave or react in a
particular way

conditional ADJECTIVE
depending on certain actions or events
conditionally ADVERB

conditioner NOUN
a substance put on the hair to keep it in good
condition

condolence NOUN
an expression of sympathy for someone

condone VERB
to forgive or ignore a wrong or bad action

conducive ADJECTIVE
helping to cause or produce something *Noisy
surroundings are not conducive to work.*

conduct VERB
1 to lead or guide
2 to be the conductor of an orchestra or choir
3 to manage or direct something
4 to allow heat, light, sound, or electricity to
pass along or through
5 to behave *They conducted themselves
with dignity.*

conduct NOUN
behaviour

conduction NOUN
the process of conducting heat or electricity

conductor NOUN
1 a person who directs the performance of an
orchestra or choir
2 a person who collects the fares on a bus
3 something that conducts heat or electricity

cone NOUN
1 a circular object that narrows to a point at
one end
2 an ice cream cornet
3 the dry fruit of a pine or other tree
4 a plastic cone-shaped marker on a road

confectionery NOUN
sweets and chocolates

confer VERB **conferring, conferred**
1 to grant a right or title on someone
2 to hold a discussion

conference NOUN
a meeting for discussion

confess VERB
to state that you have done something wrong

confession NOUN
an admission of having done wrong

confetti NOUN
small pieces of coloured paper thrown by
guests at a wedding

confide VERB
to tell someone a secret *I will confide in you.*

confidence NOUN
1 a feeling of belief in yourself and your ability
to do things well
2 firm trust
3 something told confidentially
in confidence as a secret

confidence trick NOUN
a trick to swindle someone after persuading
them to trust you

confident ADJECTIVE
showing or feeling confidence
confidently ADVERB

confidential ADJECTIVE
meant to be kept secret
confidentially ADVERB

confine VERB
1 to keep something within limits *Confine
your remarks to the subject.*
2 to keep someone in a place

confined ADJECTIVE
narrow or restricted

confinement NOUN
1 imprisonment
2 the time when a woman gives birth to a
baby

confines PLURAL NOUN
the limits or boundaries of an area

confirm VERB
1 to show that something is true or correct
2 to make a thing definite *to confirm
a booking*
3 to make a person a full member of a
Christian Church
confirmation NOUN

confiscate VERB
to take something away as a punishment
confiscation NOUN

conflict NOUN
a fight or disagreement

conflict *VERB*
to differ or disagree

conform *VERB*
to keep to accepted rules or customs
conformist *NOUN* **conformity** *NOUN*

confound *VERB*
to puzzle or confuse

confront *VERB*
1 to come or bring face to face in a hostile way
2 to face up to and deal with
confrontation *NOUN*

confuse *VERB*
1 to make a person puzzled or muddled
2 to mistake one thing for another
confusion *NOUN*

congeal *VERB*
to become jelly-like in cooling

congenial *ADJECTIVE*
pleasant or agreeable *a congenial companion*
congenially *ADVERB*

congenital *ADJECTIVE*
existing from birth
congenitally *ADVERB*

congested *ADJECTIVE*
crowded or blocked up
congestion *NOUN*

congratulate *VERB*
to tell a person that you are pleased about their success or good fortune
congratulation *NOUN*

congregate *VERB*
to assemble or come together

congregation *NOUN*
a group of people who have come together for religious worship

Congress *NOUN*
the parliament of the USA

congress *NOUN*
a meeting for discussion

conical *ADJECTIVE*
shaped like a cone
conically *ADVERB*

conifer *NOUN*
an evergreen tree with cones
coniferous *ADJECTIVE*

conjecture *NOUN*
a guess
conjectural *ADJECTIVE*

conjugal *ADJECTIVE*
to do with marriage

conjunction *NOUN*
a word that joins words or groups of words, e.g. *and* or *but*

conjure *VERB*
to perform tricks that look like magic
conjuror *NOUN*

conker *NOUN*
the hard shiny brown nut of the horse chestnut tree

connect *VERB*
to join together or link

connection *NOUN*
1 a point where two things are connected; a link
2 a train, bus, etc. that leaves a station soon after another arrives

connive (kon-**yv**) *VERB*
connive at to take no notice of a wrong or bad action
connivance *NOUN*

connoisseur (kon-a-**ser**) *NOUN*
a person with great experience and knowledge of something

conquer *VERB*
to defeat or overcome
conqueror *NOUN*

conquest *NOUN*
1 a victory
2 conquered territory

conscience *NOUN*
a feeling of what is right and wrong in what you do

conscientious *ADJECTIVE*
careful and honest about doing your work properly
conscientiously *ADVERB*

conscious *ADJECTIVE*
1 awake and knowing what is happening
2 aware of something *I was not conscious of the time.*
3 done deliberately *a conscious decision*
consciously *ADVERB* **consciousness** *NOUN*

consecutive *ADJECTIVE*
following one after another
consecutively *ADVERB*

consensus *NOUN*
the opinion of most people

consent *VERB*
to say that you are willing to do or allow what someone wants

consent *NOUN*
agreement to what someone wants

consequence *NOUN*
1 something that happens as the result of an event or action
2 importance *of no consequence*

consequent *ADJECTIVE*
happening as a result
consequently *ADVERB*

conservation NOUN
preservation of the natural environment or old buildings
conservationist NOUN

Conservative NOUN
a person who supports the Conservative Party, a British political party that favours private business and industry
Conservative ADJECTIVE

conservative ADJECTIVE
1 liking traditional ways and disliking changes
2 moderate or cautious; not extreme
a conservative estimate
conservatism NOUN

conservatory NOUN **conservatories**
a room with a glass roof and large windows, built against an outside wall of a house

conserve VERB
to prevent something valuable from being changed or wasted

consider VERB
1 to think carefully about something, especially to make a decision
2 to think *Consider yourself lucky.*

considerable ADJECTIVE
fairly large *a considerable amount*
considerably ADVERB

considerate ADJECTIVE
taking care not to inconvenience or hurt others
considerately ADVERB

consideration NOUN
1 careful thought
2 a fact that must be kept in mind

considering PREPOSITION
taking something into consideration *The car runs well, considering its age.*

consign VERB
to hand something over formally

consignment NOUN
a batch of goods sent to someone

consist VERB
to be made up or composed of *The flat consists of three rooms.*

consistency NOUN **consistencies**
1 thickness or stiffness, especially of a liquid
2 the quality of being regular

consistent ADJECTIVE
1 keeping to a regular pattern or style
2 not contradictory
consistently ADVERB

consolation NOUN
something that makes you feel less unhappy or disappointed

console [1] (kon-**sohl**) VERB
to comfort someone who is unhappy or disappointed

console [2] (kon-sohl) NOUN
a panel of controls or switches

consolidate VERB
to make or become secure and strong
consolidation NOUN

consonant NOUN
a letter that is not a vowel, e.g. b, c, d, and f

consort (**kon**-sort) NOUN
the husband or wife of a monarch

consort (kon-**sort**) VERB
to be in someone's company

consortium NOUN **consortiums**
a group of business companies acting together

conspicuous ADJECTIVE
easily seen; noticeable
conspicuously ADVERB

conspiracy NOUN **conspiracies**
a plot to do something illegal

conspire VERB
to take part in a conspiracy
conspirator NOUN

constable NOUN
a police officer of the lowest rank

constant ADJECTIVE
1 not changing; happening all the time
2 faithful or loyal
constancy NOUN **constantly** ADVERB

constant NOUN
something that does not change, especially a number

constellation NOUN
a group of stars

constipated ADJECTIVE
unable to empty the bowels easily or regularly
constipation NOUN

constituency NOUN **constituencies**
a district represented by a Member of Parliament elected by the people who live there

constituent NOUN
1 one of the parts that form a whole thing
2 someone who lives in a constituency
constituent ADJECTIVE

constitute VERB
to make up or form something *Twelve months constitute a year.*

constitution NOUN
1 a set of laws or principles about how a country is organized and governed
2 the condition of the body in regard to health *a strong constitution*
3 the composition of something
constitutional ADJECTIVE

constraint NOUN
1 force or compulsion
2 a restriction

constrict VERB
to squeeze or tighten something by making it narrower
constriction NOUN

construct VERB
to make something by putting the parts together
constructor NOUN

construction NOUN
1 the process of constructing
2 a building or other thing put together
3 words put together to form a phrase or sentence
4 an interpretation of what someone says

constructive ADJECTIVE
helpful and positive

construe VERB
to interpret or explain

consul NOUN
a government official who represents their country in another country
consular ADJECTIVE

consulate NOUN
the office of a consul

consult VERB
to go to a person or book for information or advice
consultation NOUN

consultant NOUN
1 a person who gives expert advice
2 a senior hospital doctor

consume VERB
1 to eat or drink something
2 to use up
3 to destroy

consumer NOUN
a person who buys goods or services

consumption NOUN
1 the act of consuming
2 an amount consumed

contact NOUN
1 the act of touching
2 communication between people
3 a person you can communicate with

contact VERB
to get in touch with a person

contagious ADJECTIVE
spreading by contact with an infected person

contain VERB
1 to have inside
2 to consist of
3 to hold back *Try to contain your laughter.*

container NOUN
1 a box or bottle etc. designed to contain something
2 a large box-like object for transporting goods

contaminate VERB
to make dirty or impure or diseased
contamination NOUN

contemplate VERB
1 to look at something thoughtfully
2 to consider or think about doing something
contemplation NOUN
contemplative ADJECTIVE

contemporary ADJECTIVE
1 belonging to the same period
2 modern or up-to-date *contemporary furniture*

contemporary NOUN **contemporaries**
a person of roughly the same age as someone else

contempt NOUN
a feeling of despising a person or thing

contemptible ADJECTIVE
deserving contempt

contemptuous ADJECTIVE
feeling or showing contempt
contemptuously ADVERB

contend VERB
1 to struggle in a fight or against difficulties
2 to compete
3 to state or declare *We contend that he is innocent.*
contender NOUN

content[1] (kon-**tent**) ADJECTIVE
pleased or satisfied

content NOUN
happiness or satisfaction

content VERB
to make a person pleased or satisfied

content[2] (**kon**-tent) NOUN or **contents**
PLURAL NOUN
what something contains

contented ADJECTIVE
pleased with what you have; satisfied
contentedly ADVERB

contest (**kon**-test) NOUN
a competition or struggle

contest (kon-**test**) VERB
1 to dispute or argue about something
2 to compete in

contestant NOUN
a person taking part in a contest

context NOUN
1 the words that come before and after a particular word or phrase and help to fix its meaning
2 the background to an event that helps to explain it

continent NOUN
one of the main masses of land in the world (Europe, Asia, Africa, North America, South America, Australia, and Antarctica)
the Continent the mainland of Europe
continental ADJECTIVE

contingency NOUN **contingencies**
something that may happen but cannot be known for certain

contingent NOUN
a section of a larger group

continual ADJECTIVE
happening all the time at intervals *continual interruptions*
continually ADVERB

continue VERB
1 to do something without stopping
2 to begin again after stopping
continuation NOUN

continuous ADJECTIVE
going on without a break *continuous rain*
continuously ADVERB **continuity** NOUN

contort VERB
to twist or force out of the usual shape
contortion NOUN

contortionist NOUN
a person who can twist their body into unusual positions

contour NOUN
1 a line on a map joining the points that are the same height above sea level
2 an outline

contraband NOUN
smuggled goods

contraception NOUN
prevention of pregnancy

contraceptive NOUN
a substance or device that prevents pregnancy

contract (kon-trakt) NOUN
a legal agreement to do something
contract (kon-**trakt**) VERB
1 to make or become smaller
2 to make a contract
3 to catch an illness

contraction NOUN
1 the process of contracting
2 a shortened form of a word or words, e.g. *can't* for *cannot*

contractor NOUN
a person who makes a contract to do work or supply goods

contradict VERB
1 to say that something said is not true or that someone is wrong
2 to say the opposite of
contradiction NOUN

contradictory ADJECTIVE
saying or meaning the opposite of something else

contraption NOUN
a strange-looking device or machine

contrary ADJECTIVE
1 (**kon**-tra-ree) of the opposite kind or direction
2 (kon-**trair**-ee) awkward and obstinate
contrary (**kon**-tra-ree) NOUN
the opposite
on the contrary the opposite is true

contrast (kon-trahst) NOUN
1 a clear difference between things
2 something showing a clear difference
contrast (kon-**trahst**) VERB
1 to compare or oppose two things to show they are different
2 to be clearly different

contribute VERB
1 to give money or help jointly with others
2 to write something for a newspaper or magazine
3 to help to cause something
contributor NOUN **contributory** ADJECTIVE

contribution NOUN
something given or offered jointly with others

contrite ADJECTIVE
sorry for having done wrong

contrivance NOUN
an ingenious device

contrive VERB
1 to plan cleverly
2 to find a way of doing or making something

control NOUN
power or authority to make someone or something do what you want
control VERB **controlling**, **controlled**
1 to have control over
2 to hold a feeling in check
controller NOUN

controls PLURAL NOUN
the switches and instruments used to control a machine

controversial ADJECTIVE
causing argument or disagreement

controversy NOUN **controversies**
a long argument or disagreement

conundrum NOUN **conundrums**
a riddle or difficult question

convalesce VERB
to be recovering from an illness
convalescence NOUN

convalescent NOUN
someone who is recovering from an illness

convection NOUN
the passing through of heat within liquid, air, or gas

convector NOUN
a heater that circulates warm air by convection

convene VERB
to summon or assemble for a meeting
convener NOUN

convenience NOUN
1 the quality of being convenient
2 something that is convenient
3 a public lavatory

convenient ADJECTIVE
easy to use or deal with or reach
conveniently ADVERB

convent NOUN
a place where nuns live and work

convention NOUN
1 an accepted way of doing things
2 a formal assembly

conventional ADJECTIVE
1 done or doing things in the accepted way
2 (of weapons) not nuclear
conventionally ADVERB

converge VERB
to come towards the same point
convergence NOUN **convergent** ADJECTIVE

conversant ADJECTIVE
(formal) familiar with something *conversant with the rules*

conversation NOUN
talk between people
conversational ADJECTIVE

converse [1] (kon-**verss**) VERB
to have a conversation

converse [2] (kon-verss) ADJECTIVE
opposite; contrary
conversely ADVERB

converse NOUN
the opposite of something *the converse is true*

conversion NOUN
the process of converting

convert (kon-**vert**) VERB
1 to change something
2 to cause a person to change their beliefs
3 to kick a goal after scoring a try in rugby football
converter NOUN

convert (kon-vert) NOUN
a person who has changed their beliefs

convertible ADJECTIVE
able to be converted

convertible NOUN
a car with a folding roof

convex ADJECTIVE
curved like the outside of a ball or circle

convey VERB
1 to transport
2 to communicate a message or idea
conveyor NOUN

conveyance NOUN
1 the process of conveying
2 a vehicle for transporting people

conveyancing NOUN
the process of transferring ownership of land or buildings from one person to another

conveyor belt NOUN
a continuous moving belt for moving objects from one place to another

convict (kon-**vikt**) VERB
to declare that a person is guilty of a crime

convict (kon-vikt) NOUN
a convicted person in prison

conviction NOUN
1 the process of being convicted of a crime
2 a firm opinion or belief

convince VERB
to make a person feel certain that something is true

convoy NOUN
a group of ships or lorries travelling together

convulse VERB
to make violent movements of the body
convulsive ADJECTIVE

convulsion NOUN
1 a violent movement of the body
2 a violent upheaval

coo VERB **coos**, **cooing**, **cooed**
to make a soft murmuring sound
coo NOUN

cook VERB
to prepare food by heating it

cook NOUN
a person who cooks

cooker NOUN
a piece of kitchen equipment for cooking

cookery NOUN
the cooking of food

cool ADJECTIVE
1 fairly cold
2 calm; not enthusiastic
3 (informal) good or fashionable
coolly ADVERB

cool VERB
to make or become cool
cooler NOUN

coop NOUN
a cage for poultry

cooped up ADJECTIVE
having to stay in a small uncomfortable place

cooperate VERB
to work helpfully with other people
cooperation NOUN **cooperative** ADJECTIVE

coordinate VERB
to organize people or things to work together
coordination NOUN **coordinator** NOUN

coordinate NOUN
one of a set of numbers or letters used to fix
the position of a point on a graph or map

coot NOUN
a waterbird with a white patch on its forehead

cop VERB **copping, copped**
cop it (informal) to get into trouble

cop NOUN
(informal) a police officer

cope VERB
to manage or deal with something
successfully

copier NOUN
a device for copying documents

copious ADJECTIVE
plentiful; in large amounts
copiously ADVERB

copper NOUN
1 a reddish-brown metal
2 a reddish-brown colour
3 a coin made of copper

copse NOUN
a small group of trees

copy NOUN **copies**
1 a thing made to look like another
2 something written or printed out again
from its original form
3 one of a number of specimens of the same
book etc.

copy VERB **copies, copied**
1 to make a copy of something
2 to do the same as someone else

copyright NOUN
the legal right to print a book, reproduce a
picture, record a piece of music, etc.

coral NOUN
1 a hard substance formed by the skeletons of
tiny sea creatures massed together
2 a pink colour

cord NOUN
1 a long thin flexible strip of twisted threads
or strands
2 a piece of flex
3 a cord-like structure in the body
the spinal cord
4 corduroy

cordial NOUN
a fruit-flavoured drink

cordial ADJECTIVE
warm and friendly
cordially ADVERB

cordon NOUN
a line of people, ships, fortifications, etc.
placed round an area to guard or enclose it

corduroy NOUN
cotton cloth with velvety ridges

core NOUN
the part in the middle of something,
especially of fruit

corgi NOUN **corgis**
a small dog with short legs and upright ears

cork NOUN
1 the lightweight bark of a kind of oak tree
2 a stopper for a bottle

cork VERB
to close with a cork

corkscrew NOUN
1 a device for removing corks from bottles
2 a spiral

corn NOUN
1 the seed of wheat and similar plants
2 a plant, such as wheat, grown for
its grain
3 a small hard lump on the foot

cornea NOUN
the transparent covering over the pupil of
the eye

corner NOUN
1 the angle or area where two lines or walls or
roads meet
2 a free hit or kick from the corner of a hockey
or football field

corner VERB
1 to drive someone into a position from
which it is difficult to escape
2 to travel round a corner
3 to get hold of all or most of something

cornerstone NOUN
1 a stone built into the corner at the base of a
building
2 something that is a vital foundation

cornet NOUN
1 a cone-shaped wafer holding ice cream
2 a musical instrument like a trumpet

cornflakes PLURAL NOUN
toasted maize flakes eaten as a breakfast
cereal

cornflour NOUN
flour made from maize or rice

cornflower NOUN
a wild plant with blue flowers

cornice NOUN
an ornamental moulding on walls below the ceiling

corny ADJECTIVE **cornier**, **corniest**
(*informal*) (of a joke) repeated so often that it is no longer funny

coronation NOUN
a ceremony to crown a king or queen

coroner NOUN
an official who holds an inquiry into the cause of a death

coronet NOUN
a small crown

corporal[1] NOUN
a soldier ranking next below a sergeant

corporal[2] ADJECTIVE
to do with the body

corporal punishment NOUN
physical punishment such as spanking or caning

corporation NOUN
1 a group of people elected to govern a town
2 a group of people legally authorized to act as an individual in business

corps (kor) NOUN
1 a unit in an army
2 a group of people in a job

corpse NOUN
a dead body

corpuscle NOUN
a red or white cell in the blood

correct ADJECTIVE
1 true or accurate
2 done or said in the right way
correctly ADVERB

correct VERB
1 to make a thing correct
2 to mark the mistakes in something
correction NOUN **corrective** ADJECTIVE

correspond VERB
1 to write letters
2 to agree or match
3 to be similar or equivalent

correspondence NOUN
1 letters or the writing of letters
2 similarity or agreement

correspondent NOUN
1 a person who writes letters
2 a person who writes news reports for a newspaper or broadcasting station

corridor NOUN
a passage in a building

corroborate VERB
to help to confirm a statement
corroboration NOUN

corrode VERB
to destroy metal gradually by chemical action
corrosion NOUN

corrosive ADJECTIVE
able to corrode something

corrugated ADJECTIVE
shaped into alternate ridges and grooves

corrupt ADJECTIVE
1 dishonest; accepting bribes
2 bad; wicked
3 decaying

corrupt VERB
1 to make dishonest or wicked
2 to spoil or cause to decay
corruptible ADJECTIVE

corruption NOUN
dishonesty; the practice of bribery

corset NOUN
a close-fitting piece of underwear worn to support the body

cosh NOUN
a heavy weapon

cosmetic NOUN
a substance (e.g. powder or lipstick) put on the skin to make it look more attractive

cosmetic ADJECTIVE
done only for appearance

cosmic ADJECTIVE
to do with the universe or outer space

cosmopolitan ADJECTIVE
including people from many countries

cosset VERB
to treat someone very kindly and lovingly

cost NOUN
1 the amount of money needed to buy or do
2 the effort or loss needed to achieve something

cost VERB **cost**
1 to have a certain amount as its price or charge
2 to cause the loss of *The war has cost many lives.*
3 (*past tense* is **cost** or **costed**) to estimate the cost of something

costly ADJECTIVE **costlier**, **costliest**
having a high price

costume NOUN
clothes for a particular purpose or of a particular date

cosy ADJECTIVE **cosier**, **cosiest**
warm and comfortable
cosily ADVERB

cosy NOUN **cosies**
a cover placed over a teapot or boiled egg to keep it hot

cot NOUN
a baby's bed with high sides

cottage NOUN
a small simple house

cottage cheese NOUN
soft white cheese made from skimmed milk

cotton NOUN
1 a soft white substance covering the seeds of a tropical plant
2 a thread made from this substance
3 cloth made from cotton thread

cotton wool NOUN
soft fluffy wadding originally made from cotton

couch NOUN
a long soft seat with one end raised

cough VERB
to send out air from the lungs with a sudden sharp sound
cough NOUN

could *past tense of* **can**[1] AUXILIARY VERB

couldn't
could not

council NOUN
a group of people elected to organize or discuss something, especially to organize the affairs of a town or county

councillor NOUN
a member of a town or county council

counsel NOUN
1 expert advice
2 a barrister representing someone in a lawsuit

counsel VERB **counselling**, **counselled**
to give expert advice to

counsellor NOUN
an adviser

count[1] VERB
1 to say numbers in their correct order
2 to find the total of
3 to include in a total *six of us, counting the dog*
4 to be important
5 to regard or consider *to count it an honour*
count on to rely on

count NOUN
1 an instance of counting
2 a number reached by counting
3 a charge or accusation

count[2] NOUN
a foreign nobleman

countdown NOUN
a count backwards to zero before an event

countenance NOUN
a person's face or expression

countenance VERB
to tolerate or approve of

counter[1] NOUN
1 a flat surface over which customers are served in a shop
2 a small round playing piece used in board games
3 a device for counting things

counter[2] VERB
1 to counteract
2 to return an opponent's blow

counteract VERB
to act against something and reduce or prevent its effects
counteraction NOUN

counter-attack VERB
to attack to oppose an enemy's attack
counter-attack NOUN

counterfeit (**kownt**-er-feet) ADJECTIVE
fake; not genuine

counterfeit NOUN
a forgery or imitation

counterfeit VERB
to forge or make an imitation of

counterpart NOUN
a person or thing that corresponds to another

counterpoint NOUN
a method of combining melodies in harmony

countess NOUN
1 a woman with the rank of count
2 the wife or widow of a count or earl

countless ADJECTIVE
too many to count

country NOUN **countries**
1 the land a nation occupies
2 all the people of a country
3 areas away from towns and cities

countryside NOUN
areas away from towns and cities, with fields, trees, and villages

county NOUN **counties**
a major division of a country

coup (koo) NOUN
a sudden action taken to win power

couple NOUN
two people or things considered together; a pair

couple VERB
to fasten or link two things

couplet NOUN
a pair of lines in rhyming verse

coupon NOUN
a piece of paper that gives you the right to receive or do something

courage NOUN
the ability to face danger or difficulty or pain when you are afraid
courageous ADJECTIVE

courgette NOUN
a kind of small vegetable marrow

courier NOUN
1 a messenger
2 a person employed to guide tourists

course NOUN
1 the direction which something takes
2 a series of events or actions
3 a series of lessons or exercises
4 a part of a meal
5 a racecourse or golf course
of course without a doubt; as we expected

course VERB
to move or flow freely

court NOUN
1 the royal household
2 a lawcourt or the judges and lawyers in it
3 an enclosed area for games such as tennis or netball
4 a courtyard

court VERB
to try to win somebody's love or support

courteous (ker-tee-us) ADJECTIVE
polite and helpful
courteously ADVERB **courtesy** NOUN

courtier NOUN
(old use) a companion of a king or queen at court

courtly ADJECTIVE
dignified and polite

court martial NOUN **courts martial**
1 a court for trying people who have broken military law
2 a trial in this court

court-martial VERB **court-martialling**, **court-martialled**
to try a person by a court martial

courtship NOUN
1 the process of courting someone
2 the mating ritual of some birds and animals

courtyard NOUN
a space surrounded by walls or buildings

cousin NOUN
a child of your uncle or aunt

cove NOUN
a small bay

coven (kuv-en) NOUN
a group of witches

cover VERB
1 to place one thing over or round another
2 to travel a certain distance
3 to aim a gun at or near somebody
4 to protect by insurance or a guarantee
5 to be enough money to pay for something
6 to deal with or include
cover up to hide an awkward fact or piece of information

cover NOUN
1 a thing used for covering something else
2 the binding of a book
3 something that hides or shelters

coverage NOUN
the amount of time or space given to reporting an event in a newspaper or broadcast

covert ADJECTIVE
done secretly

covet (kuv-it) VERB
to want very much to have something belonging to someone else
covetous ADJECTIVE

cow [1] NOUN
1 the female of cattle
2 the female of an elephant, whale, or seal

cow [2] VERB
to subdue by bullying

coward NOUN
a person who has no courage and shows fear in a shameful way
cowardly ADJECTIVE

cowardice NOUN
lack of courage

cowboy NOUN
a man in charge of grazing cattle on a ranch in the USA

cower VERB
to crouch or shrink back in fear

cowl NOUN
1 a monk's hood
2 a hood-shaped covering on a chimney

cowslip NOUN
a wild plant with small yellow flowers

cox NOUN
a person who steers a rowing boat

coy ADJECTIVE
pretending to be shy or modest
coyly ADVERB

coyote (koi-oh-ti) NOUN
a North American wolf

crab NOUN
a shellfish with ten legs, the first pair being a set of pincers

crab apple NOUN
a small sour apple

crack NOUN
1 a line on the surface of something that has broken but not come apart
2 a narrow gap
3 a sudden sharp noise
4 a knock
5 (informal) a joke
6 a drug made from cocaine
crack ADJECTIVE
(informal) first-class a crack shot
crack VERB
1 to make or get a crack
2 to make a sudden sharp noise
3 to break down
4 to tell a joke
crack down on (informal) to stop something illegal or against the rules **get cracking** (informal) to get busy

cracker NOUN
1 a paper tube that bangs when pulled apart
2 a thin biscuit

crackle VERB
to make small cracking sounds
crackle NOUN

crackling NOUN
crisp skin on roast pork

cradle NOUN
1 a small cot for a baby
2 a supporting framework
cradle VERB
to hold gently

craft NOUN
1 a job needing skilful use of the hands
2 skill
3 cunning or trickery
4 a boat or small ship

craftsman NOUN **craftsmen**
a person who is good at a craft
craftsmanship NOUN

crafty ADJECTIVE **craftier**, **craftiest**
cunning
craftily ADVERB

crag NOUN
a steep piece of rough rock
craggy ADJECTIVE

cram VERB **cramming**, **crammed**
1 to push many things into a space so that it is too full
2 to learn facts quickly for an exam

cramp NOUN
pain caused by a muscle tightening suddenly
cramp VERB
to hinder someone's freedom or growth

cramped ADJECTIVE
in a space that is too small or tight

cranberry NOUN **cranberries**
a small sour red berry

crane NOUN
1 a machine for lifting and moving heavy objects
2 a large wading bird with long legs and neck
crane VERB
to stretch your neck to try to see something

crane fly NOUN **crane flies**
a flying insect with long thin legs

cranium NOUN
the skull

crank NOUN
1 an L-shaped part used for changing the direction of movement in machinery
2 an eccentric person
cranky ADJECTIVE
crank VERB
to move by means of a crank

cranny NOUN **crannies**
a small crack or opening

crash NOUN
1 the loud noise of something breaking or colliding
2 a violent collision or fall
3 a sudden drop or failure
crash VERB
1 to make or have a crash
2 to cause to crash
3 to move with a crash
4 (of a computer) to stop working suddenly
crash ADJECTIVE
short and intensive a crash course

crass ADJECTIVE
1 very obvious or shocking crass ignorance
2 very stupid

crate NOUN
1 a packing case made of wooden strips
2 an open container for carrying bottles

crater NOUN
1 the mouth of a volcano
2 a hollow caused by an explosion or impact

cravat NOUN
a short wide scarf worn by men round the neck instead of a tie

crave VERB
to want very much

craving NOUN
a strong desire or longing

crawl VERB
1 to move with the body close to the ground
2 to move slowly
3 to be covered with crawling things
crawler NOUN
crawl NOUN
1 a crawling movement
2 a very slow pace
3 an overarm swimming stroke

crayon NOUN
a coloured stick or pencil for drawing

craze NOUN
a temporary enthusiasm

crazed ADJECTIVE
driven insane

crazy ADJECTIVE **crazier, craziest**
insane or foolish
crazily ADVERB

creak NOUN
a harsh squeak like a stiff door hinge
creaky ADJECTIVE

creak VERB
to make a creak

cream NOUN
1 the fatty part of milk
2 a yellowish-white colour
3 a food containing or looking like cream
4 a soft substance
5 the best part of something
creamy ADJECTIVE

cream VERB
to take the cream off
cream off to remove the best part of
something

crease NOUN
1 a line made in something by folding
2 a line on a cricket pitch marking a batsman's
or bowler's position

crease VERB
to make creases in

create VERB
1 to bring into existence; to make or produce
2 (*informal*) to make a fuss

creation NOUN
1 the act of creating something
2 something created

creative ADJECTIVE
showing imagination and thought as well
as skill
creativity NOUN

creator NOUN
a person who creates something

creature NOUN
a living being

crèche (kresh) NOUN
a place where babies and young children are
looked after while their parents are at work

credentials PLURAL NOUN
documents showing a person's identity,
qualifications, etc.

credible ADJECTIVE
able to be believed; convincing
credibility NOUN **credibly** ADVERB

credit NOUN
1 a source of pride or honour
2 praise or acknowledgement for an
achievement or good quality
3 an arrangement by which a person pays for
something at a later time
4 an amount of money in an account at a bank
5 belief or trust *I put no credit in this rumour.*
credits a list of people involved in a film or
television programme

credit VERB
1 to believe
2 to say that a person has done or achieved
something *Columbus is credited with the
discovery of America.*
3 to enter something as a credit in a
financial account

credit card NOUN
a card authorizing a person to buy on credit

creditor NOUN
a person to whom money is owed

credulous ADJECTIVE
too ready to believe things; gullible

creed NOUN
a set or formal statement of beliefs

creek NOUN
1 a narrow inlet
2 a small stream

creep VERB **crept**
1 to move along close to the ground
2 to move quietly
3 to come gradually
4 (of the flesh) to prickle with fear

creep NOUN
1 a creeping movement
2 (*informal*) an unpleasant person
the creeps (*informal*) a nervous feeling
caused by fear or dislike

creeper NOUN
a plant that grows along the ground or up a
wall etc.

creepy ADJECTIVE **creepier, creepiest**
frightening and sinister

cremate VERB
to burn a dead body to ashes
cremation NOUN

crematorium NOUN **crematoriums**
a place where corpses are cremated

creosote NOUN
an oily brown liquid painted on wood to
preserve it

crêpe paper NOUN
paper with a wrinkled surface

crescendo (krish-**en**-doh) NOUN
crescendos
a gradual increase in loudness

crescent NOUN
1 a narrow curved shape coming to a point at each end
2 a curved street

cress NOUN
a plant with hot-tasting leaves, used in salads

crest NOUN
1 a tuft of hair, skin, or feathers on a bird's head
2 the top of a hill or wave
3 a badge or design
crested ADJECTIVE

crestfallen ADJECTIVE
disappointed or dejected

crevasse (kri-**vass**) NOUN
a deep open crack in a glacier

crevice NOUN
a narrow opening in a rock or wall

crew [1] NOUN
1 the people working in a ship or aircraft
2 a group working together a camera crew

crew [2] past tense of **crow** [2]

crib NOUN
1 a baby's cot
2 a manger
3 a translation used by students
crib VERB cribbing, cribbed
to copy someone else's work

cribbage NOUN
a card game

crick NOUN
painful stiffness in the neck or back

cricket [1] NOUN
a game played outdoors between teams of 11 with a ball, bats, and two wickets
cricketer NOUN

cricket [2] NOUN
a brown insect like a grasshopper

crime NOUN
1 an action that breaks the law
2 unlawful activity

criminal NOUN
a person who has committed a crime
criminal ADJECTIVE

crimson ADJECTIVE
of a deep red colour
crimson NOUN

cringe VERB
to shrink back in fear

crinkle VERB
to make or become wrinkled
crinkly ADJECTIVE

cripple VERB
1 to make a person lame
2 to weaken or damage seriously

crisis NOUN crises
a time of great danger or difficulty

crisp ADJECTIVE
1 very dry and breaking with a snap
2 fresh and stiff
3 cold and dry a crisp morning
4 brisk and sharp a crisp manner
crisply ADVERB

crisp NOUN
a thin fried slice of potato, sold in packets

criss-cross ADJECTIVE, ADVERB
with crossing lines

criss-cross VERB
to move backwards and forwards across

criterion NOUN criteria
a standard for judging or deciding something

critic NOUN
1 a person who gives opinions on books, plays, films, music, etc.
2 a person who finds fault

critical ADJECTIVE
1 criticizing
2 to do with critics or criticism
3 at a crisis; very serious
critically ADVERB

criticism NOUN
1 the process of criticizing
2 the work of a critic

criticize VERB
to say that a person or thing has faults

croak VERB
to make a deep hoarse sound like a frog
croak NOUN

crochet (**kroh**-shay) NOUN
a kind of needlework done with a hooked needle
crochet VERB
to make with crochet

crock NOUN
1 a piece of crockery
2 (informal) a decrepit person or thing

crockery NOUN
household china

crocodile NOUN
1 a large tropical reptile with a thick skin, long tail, and huge jaws
2 a line of schoolchildren walking in pairs

crocus NOUN
a small plant with yellow, purple, or white flowers

croft NOUN
a small rented farm in Scotland
crofter NOUN

croissant (**krwah**-son) NOUN
a flaky crescent-shaped bread roll

crone NOUN
an old woman

crony NOUN **cronies**
a close friend or companion

crook NOUN
1 a shepherd's stick with a curved end
2 something bent or curved
3 (*informal*) a person who makes a living dishonestly

crook VERB
to bend or make into a hook

crooked ADJECTIVE
1 bent or twisted; not straight
2 dishonest

croon VERB
to sing softly and gently

crop NOUN
1 something grown for food
2 a whip with a loop instead of a lash
3 part of a bird's throat
4 a short haircut

crop VERB **cropping, cropped**
1 to cut or bite off
2 to produce a crop
crop up to happen unexpectedly

cropper NOUN
come a cropper (*informal*) 1 to have a bad fall 2 to fail badly

croquet (kroh-kay) NOUN
a game in which players use mallets to drive wooden balls through hoops in the ground

cross NOUN
1 a mark or shape made like + or X
2 an upright post with another piece of wood across it, used in ancient times for crucifixion; this as a symbol of Christianity
3 a mixture of two different things

cross VERB
1 to go across something
2 to draw a line or lines across something
3 to make the sign or shape of a cross
4 to produce something from two different kinds
cross out to draw a line across unwanted writing

cross ADJECTIVE
1 annoyed or bad-tempered
2 going from one side to another *cross winds*
crossly ADVERB

crossbar NOUN
a horizontal bar, especially between two uprights

crossbow NOUN
a powerful bow with a mechanism for pulling and releasing the string

cross-examine VERB
to question someone carefully to test answers given to previous questions, especially in a lawcourt
cross-examination NOUN

cross-eyed ADJECTIVE
with eyes that look or seem to look towards the nose

crossfire NOUN
lines of gunfire that cross each other

crossing NOUN
a place where people can cross a road or railway

cross-legged ADJECTIVE, ADVERB
with ankles crossed and knees spread apart

crossroads NOUN
a place where two or more roads cross one another

cross-section NOUN
1 a drawing of something as if it has been cut through
2 a typical sample

crosswise ADVERB, ADJECTIVE
with one thing crossing another

crossword NOUN
a puzzle in which words have to be found from clues and written into blank squares in a grid

crotch NOUN
the part between the legs where they join the body

crotchet NOUN
a note in music, usually representing one beat (♩)

crotchety ADJECTIVE
bad-tempered

crouch VERB
to lower your body, with your arms and legs bent

croup (kroop) NOUN
a disease causing a hard cough and difficulty in breathing

crow[1] NOUN
a large black bird
as the crow flies in a straight line

crow[2] VERB **crowed** or **crew**
1 to make a shrill cry as a cock does
2 to boast
crow NOUN

crowbar NOUN
an iron bar used as a lever

crowd NOUN
a large number of people in one place

crowd VERB
1 to come together in a crowd
2 to cram

crown NOUN
1 an ornamental headdress worn by a king or queen
2 (often **Crown**) the sovereign
3 the highest part of a road or hill
4 a former coin worth 5 shillings (25p)
Crown Prince or **Crown Princess** the heir to the throne

crown VERB
1 to place a crown on someone as a symbol of royal power or victory
2 to form or cover or decorate the top of
3 to be a successful end to something
4 (informal) to hit on the head

crow's nest NOUN
a lookout platform high up on a ship's mast

crucial (kroo-shal) ADJECTIVE
most important
crucially ADVERB

crucible NOUN
a melting pot for metals

crucifix NOUN
a model of Christ on the cross

crucify VERB **crucifies**, **crucified**
to put a person to death by nailing or binding the hands and feet to a cross
crucifixion NOUN

crude ADJECTIVE
1 in a natural state; not yet refined
2 not well finished; rough
3 vulgar
crudely ADVERB **crudity** NOUN

cruel ADJECTIVE **crueller**, **cruellest**
causing pain or suffering
cruelly ADVERB **cruelty** NOUN

cruet NOUN
a set of small containers for salt, pepper, oil, etc. for use at the table

cruise NOUN
a pleasure trip in a ship

cruise VERB
1 to sail or travel at a moderate speed
2 to go on a cruise

cruiser NOUN
1 a fast warship
2 a large motor boat

crumb NOUN
a tiny piece of bread, cake, or biscuit

crumble VERB
to break or fall into small pieces

crumble NOUN
a pudding made with fruit cooked with a crumbly topping

crumbly ADJECTIVE
easily breaking into small pieces

crumpet NOUN
a soft flat cake made with yeast, eaten toasted with butter

crumple VERB
1 to crush or become crushed into creases
2 to collapse loosely

crunch VERB
to crush noisily, e.g. between your teeth

crunch NOUN
a crunching sound
the crunch (informal) a crucial event or turning point
crunchy ADJECTIVE

Crusade NOUN
a military expedition made by Christians in the Middle Ages to recover Palestine from the Muslims who had conquered it
Crusader NOUN

crusade NOUN
a campaign in a good cause

crush VERB
1 to press something so that it breaks or is damaged
2 to squeeze tightly
3 to defeat completely

crush NOUN
1 a crowd of people pressed together
2 a drink made with crushed fruit

crust NOUN
1 the hard outer layer of something, e.g. bread
2 the rocky outer layer of the earth

crustacean NOUN
an animal with a shell, e.g. a crab, lobster, or shrimp

crusty ADJECTIVE **crustier**, **crustiest**
1 having a crisp crust
2 irritable or bad-tempered
crustily ADVERB

crutch NOUN
a support like a long walking stick for helping a lame person

cry NOUN **cries**
1 a loud wordless sound expressing pain, grief, joy, etc.
2 a shout
3 a spell of crying

cry VERB **cries**, **cried**
1 to shed tears
2 to call out loudly

crypt NOUN
a room under a church

cryptic *ADJECTIVE*
having a secret meaning that is hard to find
cryptically *ADVERB*

crystal *NOUN*
1 a clear transparent mineral like glass
2 very clear high-quality glass
3 a small solid piece of a substance with a symmetrical shape *ice crystals*

crystalline *ADJECTIVE*
made of crystals

crystallize *VERB*
1 to form into crystals
2 to become definite in form
crystallization *NOUN*

cub *NOUN*
a young lion, tiger, fox, or bear

Cub or **Cub Scout** *NOUN*
a member of the junior branch of the Scout Association

cubby hole *NOUN*
a small compartment

cube *NOUN*
1 an object that has six equal square sides, like a box or dice
2 the number produced by multiplying something by itself twice *The cube of 3 is 3 x 3 x 3 = 27.*

cube *VERB*
1 to multiply a number by itself twice *4 cubed is 4 x 4 x 4 = 64.*
2 to cut into cubes

cube root *NOUN*
the number that gives a particular number if it is multiplied by itself twice *The cube root of 27 is 3.*

cubic *ADJECTIVE*
1 three-dimensional
2 denoting volume *cubic metre*

cubicle *NOUN*
a compartment within a room

cuboid (kew-boid) *NOUN*
an object with six rectangular sides

cuckoo *NOUN* **cuckoos**
a bird with a two-note cry that lays its eggs in the nests of other birds

cucumber *NOUN*
a long vegetable with a green skin

cud *NOUN*
half-digested food that a sheep or cow brings back from its first stomach to chew again

cuddle *VERB*
to put your arms closely round; to hug
cuddly *ADJECTIVE*

cudgel *NOUN*
a short thick stick used as a weapon

cudgel *VERB* **cudgelling**, **cudgelled**
to beat with a cudgel

cue [1] *NOUN*
a signal for an actor to speak or come on stage

cue [2] *NOUN*
a long stick for striking the ball in billiards or snooker

cuff *NOUN*
1 the end of a sleeve round the wrist
2 a sharp slap with the hand
off the cuff without rehearsal or preparation

cuff *VERB*
to hit with the hand

cufflink *NOUN*
each of a pair of fasteners for shirt cuffs

cuisine (kwiz-een) *NOUN*
a style of cooking

cul-de-sac *NOUN*
a street that is closed at one end

culinary *ADJECTIVE*
to do with cooking

cull *VERB*
1 to pick out and kill a number of animals from a larger number
2 to select and use
cull *NOUN*

culminate *VERB*
to reach the highest or last point
culmination *NOUN*

culpable *ADJECTIVE*
deserving blame

culprit *NOUN*
the person who is to blame for something

cult *NOUN*
1 a religious sect
2 a film, rock group, etc. that is popular with a particular group of people

cultivate *VERB*
1 to use land to grow crops
2 to grow or develop things by looking after them
cultivation *NOUN* **cultivator** *NOUN*

cultivated *ADJECTIVE*
having good manners and education

culture *NOUN*
1 appreciation and understanding of literature and the arts
2 the customs and traditions of a people
3 (*Science*) a quantity of bacteria or cells grown for study
4 the cultivation of plants
cultural *ADJECTIVE*

cultured *ADJECTIVE*
educated to appreciate literature, art, music, etc.

cumbersome ADJECTIVE
clumsy to carry or manage

cumulative ADJECTIVE
increasing by continuous additions

cunning ADJECTIVE
1 clever at deceiving people
2 cleverly designed or planned

cunning NOUN
1 skill in deceiving people
2 skill or ingenuity

cup NOUN
1 a small container for drinking from
2 anything shaped like a cup
3 a goblet-shaped ornament given as a prize

cup VERB **cupping**, **cupped**
to form your hands into the shape of a cup

cupboard NOUN
a piece of furniture with a door, for storage

cupful NOUN **cupfuls**
the amount a cup will hold

curable ADJECTIVE
able to be cured

curate NOUN
a member of the clergy who helps a vicar

curator (kewr-ay-ter) NOUN
a person in charge of a museum or gallery or a part of one

curb VERB
to restrain *curb your impatience*

curb NOUN
a restraint *a curb on spending*
  Do not confuse this word with *kerb*.

curd NOUN or **curds** PLURAL NOUN
a thick substance formed when milk turns sour

curdle VERB
to form into curds

cure VERB
1 to free someone from an illness
2 to stop something bad
3 to preserve food by drying or smoking it

cure NOUN
1 the process of freeing from an illness
2 something that cures a person or thing

curfew NOUN
1 an order for people to remain indoors after a certain time until the next day
2 the time fixed for this

curiosity NOUN **curiosities**
1 the state of being curious
2 something unusual and interesting

curious ADJECTIVE
1 wanting to find out about things; inquisitive
2 strange or unusual
curiously ADVERB

curl NOUN
a curve or coil, e.g. of hair

curl VERB
to form into curls
curl up to sit or lie with your knees drawn up

curling NOUN
a game played on ice with large flat stones

curly ADJECTIVE **curlier**, **curliest**
having many curls

currant NOUN
1 a small black dried grape used in cookery
2 a small round red, black, or white berry

currency NOUN **currencies**
1 the money in use in a country
2 the general use of something

current ADJECTIVE
happening now; used now
currently ADVERB

current NOUN
1 water or air etc. moving in one direction
2 the flow of electricity along a wire etc. or through something

current affairs PLURAL NOUN
political events in the news

curriculum NOUN **curricula**
a course of study in a school or university

curry [1] NOUN **curries**
food cooked with spices that taste hot
curried ADJECTIVE

curry [2] VERB **curries**, **curried**
curry favour to seek favour by flattery

curse NOUN
1 a call for a person or thing to be harmed
2 something very unpleasant
3 an angry word or words

curse VERB
1 to make a curse
2 to use a curse against

cursor NOUN
a flashing symbol on a computer screen, that moves to show where new data will be put

cursory ADJECTIVE
hasty and not thorough
cursorily ADVERB

curt ADJECTIVE
brief and hasty or rude *a curt reply*
curtly ADVERB

curtail VERB
1 to cut short
2 to reduce or limit
curtailment NOUN

curtain NOUN
a piece of material hung at a window or door or at the front of a stage

curtsy *NOUN* **curtsies**
a bow made by putting one foot behind the other and bending the knees

curtsy *VERB* **curtsies**, **curtsied**
to make a curtsy

curve *VERB*
to bend smoothly

curve *NOUN*
a curved line or shape
curvy *ADJECTIVE*

cushion *NOUN*
1 a cloth cover filled with soft material for resting on
2 anything soft or springy that acts as a support

cushion *VERB*
to protect from the effects of a knock or shock

cushy *ADJECTIVE*
(*informal*) pleasant and easy

cusp *NOUN*
a pointed end where two curves meet

custard *NOUN*
a sweet yellow sauce made with milk and eggs

custody *NOUN*
1 care and supervision
2 imprisonment

custom *NOUN*
1 the usual way of behaving or acting
2 regular business from customers

customary *ADJECTIVE*
according to custom; usual
customarily *ADVERB*

customer *NOUN*
a person who uses a shop, bank, or other business

customs *PLURAL NOUN*
1 taxes charged on goods brought into a country
2 the officials who collect these

cut *VERB* **cutting**, **cut**
1 to divide or separate by using a sharp implement
2 to wound
3 to reduce in amount or size
4 to divide a pack of playing cards
5 to hit a ball with a chopping movement
6 to go through or across something
7 to switch off electrical power or an engine etc.
8 (in a film) to move to another shot or scene
9 to make a sound recording
cut a corner to pass round it very closely **cut and dried** already decided **cut in** to interrupt **cut off 1** to remove by cutting **2** to stop a supply of

cut *NOUN*
1 an act of cutting; the result of cutting
2 a small wound
3 (*informal*) a share

cute *ADJECTIVE* (*informal*)
1 attractive in a pretty way
2 smart; clever

cuticle *NOUN*
the skin round a nail

cutlass *NOUN*
a short sword with a broad curved blade

cutlery *NOUN*
knives, forks, and spoons

cutlet *NOUN*
a thick slice of meat for cooking

cut-out *NOUN*
a shape cut out of paper, cardboard, etc.

cut-price *ADJECTIVE*
sold at a reduced price

cutting *NOUN*
1 a steep-sided passage cut through high ground for a road or railway
2 a piece cut out of a newspaper or magazine
3 a piece cut from a plant to form a new plant

cuttlefish *NOUN*
a sea creature with ten arms

cyanide *NOUN*
a highly poisonous chemical

cycle *NOUN*
1 a bicycle or motorcycle
2 a series of events regularly repeated
cyclic *ADJECTIVE* **cyclical** *ADJECTIVE*

cycle *VERB*
to ride a bicycle
cyclist *NOUN*

cyclone *NOUN*
a wind that rotates round a calm central area
cyclonic *ADJECTIVE*

cygnet (**sig**-nit) *NOUN*
a young swan

cylinder *NOUN*
an object with straight sides and circular ends
cylindrical *ADJECTIVE*

cymbal *NOUN*
a percussion instrument consisting of a metal plate that is struck to make a ringing sound
Do not confuse this word with *symbol*.

cynic (**sin**-ik) *NOUN*
a person who believes that people act for selfish or bad reasons
cynical *ADJECTIVE* **cynicism** *NOUN*

cypress *NOUN*
an evergreen tree with dark leaves

cyst (sist) *NOUN*
a swelling containing fluid or soft matter

czar (zar) *NOUN*
another spelling of **tsar**

Dd

dab *NOUN*
1 a quick gentle touch with something damp
2 a small lump *a dab of butter*

dab *VERB* **dabbing**, **dabbed**
to touch quickly and gently

dabble *VERB*
1 to splash something about in water
2 to do something as a hobby

dachshund (daks-huund) *NOUN*
a small dog with a long body and short legs

dad or **daddy** *NOUN*
(*informal*) father

daddy-long-legs *NOUN*
a crane fly

daffodil *NOUN*
a yellow flower that grows from a bulb

daft *ADJECTIVE*
(*informal*) silly or stupid

dagger *NOUN*
a stabbing weapon like a short sword

dahlia (day-lee-a) *NOUN*
a garden plant with brightly-coloured flowers

daily *ADVERB, ADJECTIVE*
every day

dainty *ADJECTIVE* **daintier**, **daintiest**
small and pretty
daintily *ADVERB*

dairy *NOUN* **dairies**
a place where milk, butter, and cheese are
produced or sold

daisy *NOUN* **daisies**
a small flower with white petals and a yellow
centre

dale *NOUN*
a valley

dally *VERB* **dallies**, **dallied**
to dawdle or waste time

dam *NOUN*
a wall built to hold back water

dam *VERB* **damming**, **dammed**
to hold back water with a dam

damage *NOUN*
harm or injury done to something

damage *VERB*
to harm or spoil something

damages *PLURAL NOUN*
money paid as compensation for an injury or
loss

Dame *NOUN*
the title of a lady who has been given the
equivalent of a knighthood

dame *NOUN*
a comic middle-aged woman in a
pantomime, played by a man

damn *VERB*
to curse or condemn
damnation *NOUN*

damp *ADJECTIVE*
slightly wet; not quite dry

damp *NOUN*
moisture in the air or on a surface

damp *VERB*
1 to make slightly wet
2 to reduce the strength of

dampen *VERB*
1 to make damp
2 to reduce the strength of

damper *NOUN*
a metal plate that can be moved to increase
or decrease the amount of air flowing into a
fire or furnace etc.
put a damper on to make less enjoyable

damsel *NOUN*
(*old use*) a young woman

damson *NOUN*
a small dark-purple plum

dance *VERB*
to move in time to music

dance *NOUN*
1 a set of movements used in dancing
2 a piece of music for dancing
3 a party with dancing
dancer *NOUN*

dandelion *NOUN*
a yellow wild flower with jagged leaves

dandruff *NOUN*
tiny white flakes of dead skin in a person's hair

D and T *ABBREVIATION*
design and technology

dandy *NOUN* **dandies**
a man who likes to look well-dressed

danger *NOUN*
1 something unsafe or harmful
2 the possibility of suffering harm or death

dangerous *ADJECTIVE*
likely to cause harm or difficulty
dangerously *ADVERB*

dangle *VERB*
to hang or swing loosely

dank *ADJECTIVE*
damp and chilly

dappled ADJECTIVE
marked with patches of a different colour

dare VERB
1 to be brave or bold enough to do something
2 to challenge someone to do something risky

dare NOUN
a challenge to someone to do something risky

daredevil NOUN
a person who is very bold and reckless

dark ADJECTIVE
1 with little or no light
2 not light in colour *a dark suit*
3 having dark hair
4 sinister or evil
darkness NOUN

dark NOUN
1 the absence of light *to see in the dark*
2 the time when the sun has set *after dark*

darken VERB
to make or become dark

darling NOUN
someone who is loved very much

darn VERB
to mend a hole in material by weaving threads across it

darn NOUN
a place that has been darned

dart NOUN
1 an object with a sharp point, thrown at a target
2 a quick movement

dart VERB
to run suddenly and quickly

darts NOUN
a game in which darts are thrown at a circular target (a *dartboard*)

dash VERB
1 to run quickly
2 to throw a thing violently against something

dash NOUN
1 a short quick run; a rush
2 energy or liveliness
3 a small amount *a dash of lemon juice*
4 a short line (-) used in writing or printing

dashboard NOUN
a panel with dials and controls in front of the driver of a vehicle

dashing ADJECTIVE
lively and showy

data (**day**-ta) NOUN
pieces of information

database NOUN
(*ICT*) a store of information held in a computer

date[1] NOUN
1 the time when something happens or happened or was done
2 an appointment to meet someone at an agreed time

date VERB
1 to give a date to
2 to have existed from a particular time *The building dates from 1684.*
3 to seem old-fashioned

date[2] NOUN
a small sweet brown fruit from a palm tree

daub VERB
to paint or smear clumsily
daub NOUN

daughter NOUN
a female child

daughter-in-law NOUN
daughters-in-law
a son's wife

daunting ADJECTIVE
difficult or alarming

dawdle VERB
to go slowly and lazily
dawdler NOUN

dawn NOUN
the time when the sun rises

dawn VERB
1 to grow light in the morning
2 to begin to be realized *The truth dawned on them.*

day NOUN
1 the 24 hours between midnight and the next midnight
2 the light part of this time
3 a particular day *sports day*
4 a period of time *in my day*

daybreak NOUN
dawn

daydream NOUN
pleasant thoughts of something you would like to happen

daydream VERB
to have daydreams

daylight NOUN
1 the light of day
2 dawn

day-to-day ADJECTIVE
ordinary; happening every day

dazed ADJECTIVE
unable to think or see clearly
daze NOUN

dazzle VERB
1 to make you unable to see clearly because of too much bright light
2 to amaze or impress

DC ABBREVIATION
direct current

dead ADJECTIVE
1 no longer alive
2 not lively
3 not functioning; no longer in use
4 exact or complete *a dead loss*

deaden VERB
to make pain or noise weaker

dead end NOUN
1 a road or passage with one end closed
2 a situation where no progress can be made

dead heat NOUN
a race in which two or more winners finish exactly together

deadline NOUN
a time limit

deadlock NOUN
a situation in which no progress can be made

deadly ADJECTIVE **deadlier, deadliest**
likely to kill

deaf ADJECTIVE
1 unable to hear
2 unwilling to listen
deafness NOUN

deafen VERB
to be so loud that it is difficult to hear anything else
deafening ADJECTIVE

deal VERB **dealt**
1 to hand out
2 to give out cards for a card game
3 to do business *to deal in antiques*
deal with 1 to be concerned with *The book deals with whales and dolphins.* **2** to take action about *I'll deal with the washing-up.*
dealer NOUN

deal NOUN
1 an agreement or bargain
2 someone's turn to deal at cards
a good deal or **a great deal** a large amount

dean NOUN
1 a member of the clergy
2 the head of a university or department

dear ADJECTIVE
1 loved very much
2 a polite greeting in letters
3 expensive
dearly ADVERB

dearth (derth) NOUN
a shortage or lack of something

death NOUN
the end of life

deathly ADJECTIVE
like death

debar VERB **debarring, debarred**
to forbid or ban

debatable ADJECTIVE
questionable; that can be argued against

debate NOUN
a formal discussion
debate VERB
to hold a debate

debilitating ADJECTIVE
causing weakness

debit NOUN
an entry in an account showing how much money is owed
debit VERB
to remove money from an account

debonair (deb-on-**air**) ADJECTIVE
carefree and confident

debris (**deb**-ree) NOUN
scattered fragments or wreckage

debt (det) NOUN
something that you owe someone
in debt owing money

debtor (**det**-or) NOUN
a person who owes money

debut (**day**-bew) NOUN
the first public appearance, e.g. of an actor

decade NOUN
a period of ten years

decadent ADJECTIVE
abandoning normal moral standards
decadence NOUN

decaffeinated ADJECTIVE
(of coffee or tea) with the caffeine removed

decanter NOUN
a decorative glass bottle for serving wine

decathlon NOUN
an athletic contest in which each competitor takes part in ten events

decay VERB
1 to rot or go bad
2 to become less good or less strong
decay NOUN

deceased ADJECTIVE
dead

deceit (dis-**eet**) NOUN
the act of making a person believe something that is not true

deceitful ADJECTIVE
using deceit
deceitfully ADVERB

deceive VERB
to make a person believe something that is not true
deceiver NOUN

December NOUN
the twelfth month of the year

decent ADJECTIVE
1 respectable and honest
2 reasonable or adequate *a decent income*
3 (*informal*) kind or helpful
decency NOUN **decently** ADVERB

deception NOUN
the act of deceiving someone

deceptive ADJECTIVE
misleading
deceptively ADVERB

decibel (**dess**-ib-el) NOUN
a unit for measuring the loudness of sound

decide VERB
1 to make a choice about what to do or have
2 to settle a contest or argument
decider NOUN

decided ADJECTIVE
1 having clear and definite opinions
2 noticeable *a decided difference*
decidedly ADVERB

deciduous ADJECTIVE
(of a tree) losing its leaves in autumn

decimal ADJECTIVE
using tens or tenths

decimal NOUN
a fraction with tenths shown as numbers after a point (e.g. 0.3, 1.5)

decimal point NOUN
the dot in a decimal fraction

decimate VERB
to kill or destroy a large part of

decipher VERB
1 to work out the meaning of a coded message
2 to work out the meaning of untidy writing
decipherment NOUN

decision NOUN
1 the act of deciding
2 what you have decided
3 determination

decisive ADJECTIVE
1 settling or ending something
a decisive victory
2 able to make decisions quickly and firmly
decisively ADVERB

deck NOUN
1 a floor on a ship or bus
2 a pack of playing cards
3 a turntable on a record player

deck VERB
to decorate

deckchair NOUN
a folding chair with a canvas or plastic seat

declare VERB
1 to say something clearly or firmly
2 to admit to income or goods on which a tax has to be paid
3 to end a cricket innings before all the batsmen are out
declare war to announce that you are starting a war
declaration NOUN

decline VERB
1 to refuse
2 to become weaker or smaller
3 to slope downwards
4 to give the various forms of a noun, pronoun, or adjective

decline NOUN
a gradual decrease or loss of strength

decode VERB
to work out the meaning of something written in code
decoder NOUN

decompose VERB
to decay or rot
decomposition NOUN

decompression NOUN
reducing air pressure

decor (**day**-kor) NOUN
the style of furnishings and decorations

decorate VERB
1 to make something look more beautiful or colourful
2 to put fresh paint or paper on walls
3 to give someone a medal
decoration NOUN **decorator** NOUN

decorative ADJECTIVE
pretty or ornamental

decorum (dik-**or**-um) NOUN
polite and dignified behaviour

decoy (**dee**-koi) NOUN
something used to tempt a person or animal into a trap or into danger

decoy (dik-**oi**) VERB
to tempt a person or animal into a trap etc.

decrease VERB
to make or become smaller or fewer

decrease NOUN
the amount by which something decreases

decree NOUN
an official order or decision

decree VERB
to make a decree

decrepit ADJECTIVE
old and weak

dedicate VERB
1 to devote all your time or energy to something
2 to name a person at the beginning of a book, as a tribute
dedication NOUN

deduce VERB
to work something out from known facts
deducible ADJECTIVE

deduct VERB
to subtract part of something

deduction NOUN
1 the process of deducting; something deducted
2 the process of deducing; a conclusion reached

deed NOUN
1 something that someone has done
2 a legal document

deem VERB
(formal) to consider *I deem it an honour.*

deep ADJECTIVE
1 going a long way down or back or in *a deep well* *deep cupboards*
2 measured from top to bottom or front to back *six feet deep*
3 intense or strong *deep colours* *deep feelings*
4 low-pitched, not shrill
deeply ADVERB

deepen VERB
to make or become deeper

deep-freeze NOUN
a freezer

deer NOUN deer
a fast-running animal, the male of which has antlers

deface VERB
to spoil the surface of something
defacement NOUN

defamatory ADJECTIVE
attacking a person's good reputation
defamation NOUN

default VERB
to fail to do what you have agreed to do
defaulter NOUN

default NOUN
1 failure to do something
2 (ICT) the action a computer performs unless given another command

defeat VERB
1 to win a victory over someone
2 to baffle or be too difficult for

defeat NOUN
1 the process of defeating someone
2 a lost game or battle

defect (dif-ekt or dee-fekt) NOUN
a flaw or imperfection

defect (dif-ekt) VERB
to desert your own country and join the enemy
defection NOUN **defector** NOUN

defective ADJECTIVE
having defects; not working properly
defectiveness NOUN

defence NOUN
1 the act of defending something
2 the soldiers, weapons, etc. that a country uses to protect itself
3 something that defends or protects
4 the case put forward on behalf of a defendant in a lawsuit
5 the players in a defending position in a game

defenceless ADJECTIVE
having no defences

defend VERB
1 to protect against an attack or accusation
2 to try to prove that an accused person is not guilty
defender NOUN

defendant NOUN
a person accused in a lawcourt

defensive ADJECTIVE
1 used or done for defence
2 anxious about being criticized
defensively ADVERB

defer[1] VERB **deferring**, **deferred**
to postpone
deferment NOUN **deferral** NOUN

defer[2] VERB **deferring**, **deferred**
to give way to a person's wishes or authority

defiance NOUN
open opposition or disobedience

defiant ADJECTIVE
defying; openly disobedient
defiantly ADVERB

deficiency NOUN **deficiencies**
1 a lack or shortage
2 a defect
deficient ADJECTIVE

deficit (def-iss-it) NOUN
1 the amount by which a total is too small
2 the amount by which spending is greater than income

define VERB
1 to explain what a word or phrase means
2 to show clearly what something is
3 to show a thing's outline
definable ADJECTIVE

definite ADJECTIVE
1 clearly stated; exact *a definite promise*
2 certain or settled

definite article NOUN
the word 'the'

definitely ADVERB
certainly; without any doubt

definition NOUN
1 an explanation of what a word or phrase means
2 clearness of outline in a photograph or picture

definitive ADJECTIVE
1 finally settling something *a definitive victory*
2 not able to be bettered *the definitive history of the war*

deflate VERB
1 to let out air from a tyre or balloon
2 to make someone feel less proud or less confident

deflation NOUN
1 the process of deflating
2 a feeling of disappointment

deflect VERB
to make something turn aside
deflection NOUN **deflector** NOUN

deforestation NOUN
the process of clearing away trees from an area

deformed ADJECTIVE
badly or abnormally shaped
deformity NOUN

defraud VERB
to take something from a person by fraud; to cheat or swindle

defrost VERB
1 to thaw out something frozen
2 to remove the ice and frost from a refrigerator or windscreen

deft ADJECTIVE
skilful and quick
deftly ADVERB **deftness** NOUN

defunct ADJECTIVE
no longer in use or existing

defuse VERB
1 to remove the fuse from a bomb
2 to make a situation less dangerous or tense

defy VERB **defies**, **defied**
1 to resist openly; to refuse to obey
2 to challenge a person to do something you think impossible *I defy you to prove this.*

degenerate VERB
to become worse or lower in standard
degeneration NOUN

degenerate ADJECTIVE
having become immoral or bad
degeneracy NOUN

degrading ADJECTIVE
humiliating

degree NOUN
1 a unit for measuring temperature
2 a unit for measuring angles
3 amount or extent *to some degree*
4 an award to someone at a university or college who has successfully finished a course

dehydrated ADJECTIVE
dried up; with all moisture removed
dehydration NOUN

deign (dayn) VERB
to be gracious enough to do something

deity (dee-it-ee) NOUN **deities**
a god or goddess

dejected ADJECTIVE
sad or depressed
dejection NOUN

delay VERB
1 to make someone or something late
2 to postpone

delay NOUN
the process of delaying, or the time this lasts *an hour's delay*

delegate NOUN
a person who represents others and acts on their instructions

delegate VERB
to give someone a task or duty to do

delegation NOUN
1 the act of delegating
2 a group of delegates

delete VERB
to cross out or remove something written or printed or stored on a computer
deletion NOUN

deliberate ADJECTIVE
1 done on purpose; intentional
2 slow and careful
deliberately ADVERB

deliberate VERB
to discuss or think carefully
deliberation NOUN

delicacy NOUN **delicacies**
1 a delicate state
2 a piece of delicious food

delicate ADJECTIVE
1 fine and graceful
2 fragile and easily damaged
3 pleasant and not strong or intense
4 becoming ill easily
5 needing great care or tact *a delicate situation*
delicately ADVERB

delicatessen *NOUN*
a shop that sells cooked meats, cheeses, salads, etc.

delicious *ADJECTIVE*
tasting or smelling very pleasant
deliciously *ADVERB*

delight *VERB*
1 to please someone very much
2 to take great pleasure in something

delight *NOUN*
great pleasure

delightful *ADJECTIVE*
very pleasing
delightfully *ADVERB*

delinquent *NOUN*
a young person who breaks the law
delinquent *ADJECTIVE* **delinquency** *NOUN*

delirious *ADJECTIVE*
1 in a state of mental confusion
2 extremely excited or enthusiastic
deliriously *ADVERB*

delirium *NOUN*
1 a state of mental confusion caused by fever
2 wild excitement

deliver *VERB*
1 to take letters or goods to a place
2 to give a speech or lecture
3 to help with the birth of a baby
4 to aim or strike a blow or attack
5 to rescue or set free

delivery *NOUN* **deliveries**
1 the process of delivering
2 something delivered

dell *NOUN*
a small valley with trees

delta *NOUN*
a triangular area at the mouth of a river

delude *VERB*
to deceive or mislead

deluge *NOUN*
1 a large flood
2 a heavy fall of rain
3 something coming in great numbers

deluge *VERB*
to overwhelm

delusion *NOUN*
a false belief

de luxe *ADJECTIVE*
of very high quality

delve *VERB*
to search deeply

demand *VERB*
1 to ask for something firmly or forcefully
2 to need *The work demands great skill.*

demand *NOUN*
1 a firm or forceful request
2 a desire to have something *a great demand for computers*
in demand wanted or needed

demanding *ADJECTIVE*
1 needing skill or effort
2 needing a lot of attention

demeaning *ADJECTIVE*
lowering a person's dignity; humiliating

demeanour (dim-**een**-er) *NOUN*
a person's behaviour or manner

demented *ADJECTIVE*
driven mad; crazy

demise (dim-**yz**) *NOUN*
(*formal*) death

demo *NOUN* **demos**
(*informal*) a demonstration

democracy *NOUN* **democracies**
1 government of a country by representatives elected by the people
2 a country governed in this way

Democrat *NOUN*
a member of the Democratic Party in the USA

democrat *NOUN*
a supporter of democracy
democratic *ADJECTIVE* **democratically** *ADVERB*

demography (dim-**og**-ra-fee) *NOUN*
the study of statistics to do with populations
demographic *ADJECTIVE*

demolish *VERB*
1 to knock a building down and break it up
2 to destroy completely
demolition *NOUN*

demon *NOUN*
1 a devil; an evil spirit
2 a fierce or forceful person
demonic *ADJECTIVE*

demonstrate *VERB*
1 to show or prove something
2 to take part in a demonstration
demonstrator *NOUN*

demonstration *NOUN*
1 the process of demonstrating
2 a march or meeting to promote an opinion or cause

demonstrative *ADJECTIVE*
1 showing or proving something
2 showing feelings or affection openly

demoralize *VERB*
to dishearten someone or weaken their confidence
demoralization *NOUN*

demote VERB
to reduce to a lower position or rank
demotion NOUN

den NOUN
1 an animal's lair
2 a private room

denial NOUN
the act of denying or refusing

denigrate VERB
to blacken the reputation of
denigration NOUN

denim NOUN
a kind of strong blue cotton cloth used to
make jeans or other clothes

denomination NOUN
1 a name or title
2 a religious group with a special name
3 a unit of weight or of money

denominator NOUN
the number below the line in a fraction,
showing how many parts the whole is divided
into, e.g. 4 in ¼

denote VERB
to mean or indicate *P denotes parking.*
denotation NOUN

denounce VERB
to speak strongly against; to accuse
denunciation NOUN

dense ADJECTIVE
1 thick or packed closely *dense fog*
dense crowds
2 (*informal*) stupid
densely ADVERB

density NOUN
1 thickness
2 (*Science*) the proportion of mass to volume

dent NOUN
a hollow left in a surface where something has
pressed or hit it

dent VERB
to make a dent in

dental ADJECTIVE
to do with the teeth

dentist NOUN
a person who is trained to take care of teeth
dentistry NOUN

dentures NOUN
a set of false teeth

denude VERB
to make bare or naked
denudation NOUN

denunciation NOUN
the act of denouncing

deny VERB **denies**, **denied**
1 to say that something is not true

2 to refuse to give or allow something
deny yourself to go without something
you want

deodorant NOUN
a substance that removes unpleasant smells

depart VERB
to go away; to leave

department NOUN
one section of a large organization or shop

departure NOUN
the act of departing

depend VERB
depend on to rely on or be controlled by

dependable ADJECTIVE
reliable

dependant NOUN
a person who depends on another, especially
financially

> Do not confuse this word with *dependent*,
> which is an adjective.

dependency NOUN **dependencies**
1 dependence
2 a country that is controlled by another

dependent ADJECTIVE
relying or depending *two dependent children*
They are dependent on us.
dependence NOUN

> Do not confuse this word with *dependant*,
> which is a noun.

depict VERB
1 to show something in a painting or drawing
2 to describe
depiction NOUN

deplete (dip-**leet**) VERB
to reduce the amount of
depletion NOUN

deplore VERB
to think something very bad or unwelcome
deplorable ADJECTIVE

deploy VERB
1 to place troops or weapons in positions
for use
2 to use something effectively
deployment NOUN

deport VERB
to send an unwanted foreign person out of
a country
deportation NOUN

depose VERB
to remove a person from power

deposit NOUN
1 an amount of money paid into a bank
2 money paid as a first instalment
3 a layer of solid matter in or on the earth

deposit VERB
1 to put something down
2 to pay money as a deposit
depositor NOUN

depot (**dep**-oh) NOUN
1 a place where things are stored
2 a place where buses or trains are kept and repaired
3 a headquarters

depraved ADJECTIVE
behaving wickedly
depravity NOUN

deprecate (**dep**-rik-ayt) VERB
to say that you disapprove of something
Do not confuse this word with *depreciate*.

depreciate (dip-ree-shee-ayt) VERB
to make or become lower in value
depreciation NOUN
Do not confuse this word with *deprecate*.

depress VERB
to make you sad or unhappy

depression NOUN
1 a feeling of great sadness or hopelessness
2 a long period when trade is slack

deprive VERB
to take or keep something away from somebody
deprivation NOUN

depth NOUN
1 deepness; how deep something is
2 the deepest or lowest part

deputation NOUN
a group of people sent as representatives

deputize VERB
to act as someone's deputy

deputy NOUN **deputies**
a person appointed to act as a substitute for another

derail VERB
to cause a train to leave the rails
derailment NOUN

deranged ADJECTIVE
insane
derangement NOUN

derby (**dar**-bi) NOUN **derbies**
a sports match between two teams from the same area

derelict ADJECTIVE
abandoned and left to fall into ruin
dereliction NOUN

deride VERB
to laugh at with contempt or scorn

derision NOUN
scorn or ridicule

derisive ADJECTIVE
mocking; scornful
derisively ADVERB

derisory ADJECTIVE
absurdly inadequate *a derisory offer*

derivation NOUN
the origin of a word

derivative ADJECTIVE
derived from something; not original
derivative NOUN

derive VERB
1 to obtain something from a source
2 to form or originate from something
words that are derived from Latin

dermatology NOUN
the study of the skin and its diseases
dermatologist NOUN

derogatory ADJECTIVE
scornful or severely critical

descant NOUN
a tune sung or played above the main tune

descend VERB
to go down
be descended from to have as an ancestor

descendant NOUN
a person who is descended from someone

descent NOUN
the act of descending

describe VERB
1 to say what someone or something is like
2 to draw in outline

description NOUN
1 a statement that describes someone or something
2 sort or kind *houses of every description*
descriptive ADJECTIVE

desert (**dez**-ert) NOUN
a large area of dry often sandy land
Do not confuse this word with *dessert*.

desert (diz-ert) VERB
1 to leave a person or place without intending to return
2 to run away from the army
deserter NOUN **desertion** NOUN

desert island NOUN
an uninhabited tropical island

deserts (diz-erts) PLURAL NOUN
what a person deserves

deserve VERB
to have a right to; to be worthy of
deservedly ADVERB

desiccated ADJECTIVE
dried *desiccated coconut*

a b c d e f g h i j k l m n o p q r s t u v w x y z

design NOUN
1 a drawing or pattern
2 the way something is made or arranged

design VERB
1 to draw a design for
2 to plan or intend for a special purpose
designer NOUN

designate VERB
to mark or describe as something particular
designation NOUN

desirable ADJECTIVE
1 pleasing; worth having
2 worth doing; advisable

desire NOUN
a feeling of wanting something
desirous ADJECTIVE

desire VERB
to wish for

desist (diz-ist) VERB
to stop doing something

desk NOUN
a piece of furniture with a flat top, used for writing or working

desktop ADJECTIVE
small enough to use on a desk

desolate ADJECTIVE
1 lonely and sad
2 uninhabited
desolation NOUN

despair NOUN
a feeling of hopelessness

despair VERB
to feel despair

despatch VERB
another spelling of **dispatch**
despatch NOUN

desperate ADJECTIVE
1 extremely serious or hopeless
2 having a great need for something
3 reckless and ready to do anything
desperation NOUN

despicable ADJECTIVE
hateful; contemptible

despise VERB
to feel contempt for a person or thing

despite PREPOSITION
in spite of

despondent ADJECTIVE
sad or gloomy
despondency NOUN

despot NOUN
a tyrant

dessert (diz-ert) NOUN
a sweet course served as the last part of a meal
Do not confuse this word with *desert*.

destination NOUN
the place to which a person or thing is travelling

destined ADJECTIVE
having a certain destiny; intended

destiny NOUN **destinies**
what will happen or has happened to somebody or something

destitute ADJECTIVE
having no home or food or money
destitution NOUN

destroy VERB
to ruin or put an end to
destruction NOUN **destructive** ADJECTIVE

destroyer NOUN
a fast warship

detach VERB
to unfasten or separate

detachment NOUN
1 the state of being impartial
2 a small group of soldiers sent on a special duty

detail NOUN
1 a small part of a design or plan or decoration
2 a small piece of information
detailed ADJECTIVE

detain VERB
1 to keep someone waiting
2 to keep someone confined to a place
detention NOUN

detect VERB
to notice or discover
detection NOUN

detective NOUN
a person who investigates crimes

detention NOUN
1 the act of detaining someone
2 a punishment in which a pupil is made to stay late at school

deter VERB **deterring, deterred**
to discourage or prevent from doing something

detergent NOUN
a substance used for cleaning or washing things

deteriorate VERB
to become worse
deterioration NOUN

determination NOUN
1 a firm intention to achieve something
2 the act of deciding something

determine *VERB*
1 to decide *The time of the meeting is yet to be determined.*
2 to cause or influence
3 to find out or calculate

determined *ADJECTIVE*
fully decided; having a firm intention

determiner *NOUN*
(*Grammar*) a word (such as *a*, *the*, *some*) that modifies a noun

deterrent *NOUN*
something that may deter people from a particular action
deterrence *NOUN*

detest *VERB*
to dislike something very much

detonate *VERB*
to explode or cause to explode
detonation *NOUN* **detonator** *NOUN*

detour *NOUN*
a roundabout route instead of the normal one

detract *VERB*
to lessen the amount or value
detraction *NOUN*

detriment *NOUN*
harm or disadvantage

detrimental *ADJECTIVE*
harmful or disadvantageous
detrimentally *ADVERB*

deuce *NOUN*
a score of 40 points on each side in tennis

devalue *VERB*
1 to reduce the value of
2 to reduce the value of a country's currency
devaluation *NOUN*

devastate *VERB*
1 to destroy completely
2 to make someone extremely upset
devastation *NOUN*

develop *VERB*
1 to make or become bigger or better
2 to come gradually into existence
Storms developed.
3 to begin to have or use *to develop bad habits*
4 to use an area of land for building
5 to produce pictures on photographic film

development *NOUN*
1 the process of growing or becoming better
2 use of land for building
3 a new or unexpected occurrence

deviate *VERB*
to turn aside from a course or from what is usual
deviation *NOUN*

device *NOUN*
1 something made for a particular purpose
2 a design used as a decoration or emblem

devil *NOUN*
1 an evil spirit
2 a wicked or cruel person
devilish *ADJECTIVE* **devilry** *NOUN*

devious *ADJECTIVE*
1 roundabout; not direct *a devious route*
2 not straightforward; underhand

devise *VERB*
to invent or plan

devoid *ADJECTIVE*
lacking or without something
work devoid of merit

devolution *NOUN*
the process of giving power to local or regional government

devote *VERB*
to give completely *He devoted his time to sport.*

devoted *ADJECTIVE*
loving or loyal

devotee *NOUN*
an enthusiast

devotion *NOUN*
great love or loyalty

devour *VERB*
1 to eat hungrily or greedily
2 to destroy

devout *ADJECTIVE*
earnestly religious or sincere
devoutly *ADVERB*

dew *NOUN*
tiny drops of water that form at night on surfaces in the open air

dexterity (deks-**te**rri-tee) *NOUN*
skill in handling things

diabetes *NOUN*
a disease in which there is too much sugar in the blood
diabetic *ADJECTIVE, NOUN*

diabolical *ADJECTIVE*
very bad or wicked

diagnose *VERB*
to find out what disease a person has
diagnosis *NOUN*

diagonal *NOUN*
a straight line joining opposite corners
diagonal *ADJECTIVE* **diagonally** *ADVERB*

diagram *NOUN*
a drawing or picture that shows the parts or working of something

a b c **d** e f g h i j k l m n o p q r s t u v w x y z

dial

dial NOUN
a circular object with numbers or letters round it

dial VERB **dialling**, **dialled**
to call a telephone number by using a dial or buttons

dialect NOUN
the words and pronunciations used by people in one district but not in the rest of a country

dialogue NOUN
1 the words spoken by characters in a play, film, or story
2 a conversation

diameter NOUN
1 a line drawn straight across a circle or sphere and passing through its centre
2 the length of this line

diamond NOUN
1 a hard precious stone
2 a shape with four equal sides and four angles that are not right angles
3 a playing card with red diamond shapes on it

diaper NOUN
(*American*) a baby's nappy

diaphragm (**dy**-a-fram) NOUN
a layer of muscle separating the chest from the abdomen and used in breathing

diarrhoea (dy-a-**ree**-a) NOUN
frequent watery emptying of the bowels

diary NOUN **diaries**
a book in which the events of each day are written

dice NOUN **dice**
a small cube marked with dots on its sides, used in games

dice VERB
to cut food into small cubes

dictate VERB
1 to speak or read something aloud for someone else to write down
2 to give firm orders
dictation NOUN

dictator NOUN
a ruler with unlimited power

dictatorial ADJECTIVE
like a dictator; domineering

diction NOUN
1 a way of speaking words
2 a writer's choice of words

dictionary NOUN **dictionaries**
a book that contains words in alphabetical order with their meanings

didn't
did not

dig

die[1] VERB **dying**
1 to stop living or existing
2 to stop burning or functioning *The fire died down.*
be dying for or **to** (*informal*) to want to have or do something very much

die[2] NOUN
a device that stamps a design on coins or medals

diesel NOUN
1 an engine that works by burning oil in compressed air
2 fuel for this kind of engine

diet NOUN
1 a course of special meals followed for health or to lose weight
2 the sort of foods someone eats

diet VERB
to follow a diet

differ VERB
1 to be different
2 to disagree

difference NOUN
1 the state of being different; the way in which things differ
2 the remainder left after one number is subtracted from another
3 a disagreement

different ADJECTIVE
1 unlike; not the same
2 separate or distinct *three different occasions*
differently ADVERB

differentiate VERB
to make or recognize differences

difficult ADJECTIVE
needing a lot of effort or skill; not easy

difficulty NOUN **difficulties**
1 the state of being difficult
2 something that causes a problem

diffident ADJECTIVE
shy and not self-confident
diffidence NOUN

diffuse (dif-**yooz**) VERB
to spread widely or thinly *diffused lighting*
diffusion NOUN

diffuse (dif-**yooss**) ADJECTIVE
1 spread widely
2 using many words

dig VERB **digging**, **dug**
1 to take up soil with a spade or fork
2 to poke something in
3 to seek or discover by investigating

dig NOUN
1 an archaeological excavation
2 a poke
3 an unpleasant remark

digest (dy-**jest**) VERB
1 to soften and change food in the stomach for the body to absorb
2 to take information into your mind
digestion NOUN

digest (dy-jest) NOUN
a summary of news or information

digestive ADJECTIVE
to do with digestion

digger NOUN
a machine for digging

digit (dij-it) NOUN
1 any of the numbers from 0 to 9
2 a finger or toe

digital ADJECTIVE
1 to do with or using digits
2 (of a watch or clock) showing the time with a row of figures
3 (of a computer, recording, etc.) storing data or sound as a series of binary digits

dignified ADJECTIVE
having dignity

dignitary NOUN **dignitaries**
an important official

dignity NOUN
a calm and serious manner

digress VERB
to stray from the main subject
digression NOUN

dike NOUN
another spelling of **dyke**

dilapidated ADJECTIVE
falling to pieces

dilate VERB
to make or become wider or larger
dilation NOUN

dilemma NOUN
a situation in which it is difficult to choose between two possibilities, both unwelcome

diligent ADJECTIVE
hard-working
diligence NOUN

dilute VERB
to make a liquid weaker by adding water or other liquid
dilution NOUN

dim ADJECTIVE **dimmer**, **dimmest**
1 not bright or clear; only faintly lit
2 (informal) stupid
dimly ADVERB

dim VERB **dimming**, **dimmed**
to make or become dim

dime NOUN
(American) a ten-cent coin

dimension NOUN
1 a measurement such as length, width, area, or volume
2 size or extent
dimensional ADJECTIVE

diminish VERB
to make or become smaller
diminution NOUN

diminutive ADJECTIVE
very small

dimple NOUN
a small hollow or dent in the skin
dimpled ADJECTIVE

din NOUN
a loud annoying noise

dine VERB
to have dinner

diner NOUN
1 someone eating dinner
2 (American) a small inexpensive restaurant

dinghy (ding-ee) NOUN **dinghies**
a kind of small boat

dingo NOUN **dingoes**
an Australian wild dog

dingy (din-jee) ADJECTIVE **dingier**, **dingiest**
dirty-looking

dinner NOUN
the main meal of the day, at midday or in the evening

dinosaur (dy-noss-or) NOUN
a prehistoric reptile, often of enormous size

dip VERB **dipping**, **dipped**
to put down or go down, especially into a liquid

dip NOUN
1 the act of dipping
2 a downward slope
3 a quick swim
4 a substance into which things are dipped

diphtheria (dif-**theer**-ee-a) NOUN
a serious disease that causes inflammation in the throat

diphthong (dif-thong) NOUN
a vowel sound made up of two sounds, e.g. oi in point or ou in loud

diploma NOUN
a certificate awarded by a college for completing a course

diplomacy NOUN
1 the work of making agreements with other countries
2 skill in dealing with people

a b c **d** e f g h i j k l m n o p q r s t u v w x y z

diplomat *NOUN*
1 a person employed in diplomacy
2 a tactful person

diplomatic *ADJECTIVE*
1 to do with diplomats or diplomacy
2 tactful
diplomatically *ADVERB*

dire *ADJECTIVE*
dreadful or serious *in dire need*

direct *ADJECTIVE*
1 as straight as possible
2 going straight to the point; frank
3 exact *the direct opposite*

direct *VERB*
1 to tell someone the way
2 to guide or aim in a certain direction
3 to control or manage
4 to order

direct current *NOUN*
electric current flowing only in one direction

direction *NOUN*
1 the line along which something moves or faces
2 the process of directing
directional *ADJECTIVE*

directions *PLURAL NOUN*
information on how to use or do something or how to get somewhere

directive *NOUN*
a command

directly *ADVERB*
1 by a direct route *Go directly home.*
2 immediately *Please come directly.*

director *NOUN*
1 a person in charge of a business
2 a person who directs the making of a film, programme, or play

directory *NOUN* **directories**
1 a book containing a list of people with their addresses and telephone numbers
2 (*ICT*) a group of files

direct speech *NOUN*
a person's words expressed in the form in which they were said

dirge *NOUN*
a slow sad song

dirt *NOUN*
earth or soil; anything that is not clean

dirty *ADJECTIVE* **dirtier**, **dirtiest**
1 not clean; soiled
2 unfair; dishonourable *a dirty trick*
3 indecent; obscene
dirtily *ADVERB*

disable *VERB*
to make something unable to work or act

disabled *ADJECTIVE*
unable to use part of the body properly because of illness or injury
disability *NOUN*

disadvantage *NOUN*
something that hinders or is unhelpful
disadvantageous *ADJECTIVE*

disadvantaged *ADJECTIVE*
suffering from a disadvantage, especially having less money or fewer opportunities than most people

disagree *VERB*
1 to have or express a different opinion
2 to have a bad effect
Rich food disagrees with me.
disagreement *NOUN*

disagreeable *ADJECTIVE*
unpleasant

disappear *VERB*
to stop being visible; to vanish
disappearance *NOUN*

disappoint *VERB*
to fail to do what someone hopes for
disappointment *NOUN*

disappointed *ADJECTIVE*
unhappy because a hope has not been achieved

disapprove *VERB*
to have an unfavourable opinion of
disapproval *NOUN*

disarm *VERB*
1 to give up using weapons
2 to take away someone's weapons

disarmament *NOUN*
reduction of a country's armed forces or weapons

disarray *NOUN*
a state of disorder

disaster *NOUN*
1 a bad accident or misfortune
2 a complete failure
disastrous *ADJECTIVE*

disband *VERB*
to stop working as a group

disbelieve *VERB*
to be unwilling to believe something
disbelief *NOUN*

disc *NOUN*
1 a round flat object
2 a layer of cartilage between vertebrae in the spine
3 a CD or record

discard *VERB*
to throw away or put aside

discern VERB
to see or recognize clearly
discernible ADJECTIVE

discerning ADJECTIVE
showing good judgement

discharge VERB
1 to release a person
2 to dismiss from a job
3 to send out a liquid or substance
4 to pay a debt

discharge NOUN
1 the process of discharging
2 something that is discharged

disciple NOUN
1 a person who follows the teachings of a leader
2 any of the original followers of Christ

disciplinarian NOUN
a person who believes in strict discipline

discipline NOUN
1 orderly and obedient behaviour
2 a subject for study
disciplinary ADJECTIVE

discipline VERB
1 to train to be orderly and obedient
2 to punish

disc jockey NOUN
a person who introduces and plays records

disclose VERB
to reveal or make known
disclosure NOUN

disco NOUN
a place where CDs or records are played for dancing

discolour VERB
to spoil the colour of; to stain
discoloration NOUN

discomfort NOUN
a lack of comfort

disconcert VERB
to make a person feel uneasy

disconnect VERB
to break the connection between; to detach
disconnection NOUN

disconnected ADJECTIVE
not having a connection between its parts

discontent NOUN
lack of contentment; dissatisfaction
discontented ADJECTIVE **discontentment** NOUN

discontinue VERB
to stop doing something; to end

discord NOUN
1 disagreement; quarrelling
2 musical notes producing a harsh or unpleasant sound
discordant ADJECTIVE

discount NOUN
a sum taken off a price

discount VERB
to ignore or disregard something

discourage VERB
1 to take away someone's enthusiasm or confidence
2 to try to persuade someone not to do something
discouragement NOUN

discourteous ADJECTIVE
not courteous; rude
discourtesy NOUN

discover VERB
1 to find or find out
2 to be the first person to find something

discovery NOUN **discoveries**
1 the process of discovering
2 something discovered

discredit VERB
1 to cause to be doubted
2 to damage the reputation of

discreet ADJECTIVE
1 cautious about what you say
2 not showy
discreetly ADVERB
Do not confuse this word with *discrete*.

discrepancy NOUN **discrepancies**
a difference between things which should be the same

discrete ADJECTIVE
separate or distinct
Do not confuse this word with *discreet*.

discretion (dis-**kresh**-on) NOUN
1 caution in what you say or do
2 freedom to decide for yourself about something

discriminate VERB
1 to notice the differences between things
2 to treat people unfairly because of their race, sex, or religion

discrimination NOUN
1 unfair treatment because of race, sex, or religion
2 sensitive taste or judgement

discus NOUN
a thick heavy disc thrown in athletic contests

discuss VERB
to talk with other people about a subject
discussion NOUN

disease NOUN
an unhealthy condition; an illness
diseased ADJECTIVE

disentangle *VERB*
to free from tangles or confusion

disfigure *VERB*
to spoil the appearance of
disfigurement *NOUN*

disgorge *VERB*
to pour or send out

disgrace *NOUN*
1 shame; loss of approval or respect
2 something that causes shame

disgrace *VERB*
to bring disgrace on

disgraceful *ADJECTIVE*
shameful; very bad
disgracefully *ADVERB*

disgruntled *ADJECTIVE*
discontented or resentful

disguise *NOUN*
something used to disguise

disguise *VERB*
1 to make a person or thing look different
2 to conceal your feelings

disgust *NOUN*
a feeling that something is very unpleasant or disgraceful

disgust *VERB*
to cause disgust in

dish *NOUN*
1 a plate or bowl for food
2 something having this shape
3 food prepared for eating

dish *VERB*
dish out (*informal*) to give out; to distribute

dishcloth *NOUN*
a cloth for washing dishes

dishearten *VERB*
to cause to lose hope or confidence

dishevelled *ADJECTIVE*
ruffled and untidy

dishonest *ADJECTIVE*
not honest
dishonesty *NOUN*

dishonour *NOUN, VERB*
to bring disgrace to
dishonourable *ADJECTIVE*

disillusion *VERB*
to correct a wrong belief that someone has

disinclined *ADJECTIVE*
unwilling to do something

disinfect *VERB*.
to destroy the germs in
disinfection *NOUN*

disinfectant *NOUN*
a substance used for disinfecting

disintegrate *VERB*
to break up into small parts or pieces
disintegration *NOUN*

disinterested *ADJECTIVE*
not influenced by personal interest; impartial
disinterested advice

> This word does not mean the same as *uninterested*.

disjointed *ADJECTIVE*
(of talk or writing) not fitting together well and so difficult to understand

disk *NOUN*
(*ICT*) a circular storage device for data

dislike *NOUN*
a feeling of not liking someone or something

dislike *VERB*
to feel that you do not like someone or something

dislocate *VERB*
to move or force a bone from its proper position
dislocation *NOUN*

dislodge *VERB*
to move or force something from its place

disloyal *ADJECTIVE*
not loyal
disloyally *ADVERB* **disloyalty** *NOUN*

dismal *ADJECTIVE*
1 gloomy
2 of poor quality
dismally *ADVERB*

dismantle *VERB*
to take to pieces

dismay *NOUN*
a feeling of surprise and disappointment
dismayed *ADJECTIVE*

dismiss *VERB*
1 to send away
2 to remove from a job
3 to stop thinking about
dismissal *NOUN* **dismissive** *ADJECTIVE*

dismount *VERB*
to get off a horse or bicycle

disobedient *ADJECTIVE*
not obedient
disobediently *ADVERB* **disobedience** *NOUN*

disobey *VERB*
to refuse to do what you are told

disorder *NOUN*
1 untidiness
2 public fighting or rioting
3 an illness

disorderly *ADJECTIVE*
disorganized; untidy

disorganized ADJECTIVE
muddled and badly organized
disorganization NOUN

disown VERB
to refuse to acknowledge as yours

disparage VERB
to speak of in a belittling way

dispatch VERB
1 to send off to a destination
2 to kill

dispatch NOUN
1 the act of dispatching
2 a report or message sent

dispel VERB **dispelling**, **dispelled**
to scatter or drive away

dispense VERB
1 to distribute or deal out
2 to prepare medicine according to
prescriptions
dispense with to do without something

dispenser NOUN
a device or machine that supplies a quantity
of something *a cash dispenser*

disperse VERB
to scatter
dispersal NOUN

displace VERB
1 to shift from its place
2 to take a person's or thing's place
displacement NOUN

display VERB
to show clearly

display NOUN
1 an exhibition
2 something displayed

displease VERB
to annoy or not please someone
displeasure NOUN

disposable ADJECTIVE
made to be thrown away after use

disposal NOUN
the process of getting rid of something
at your disposal ready for you to use

dispose VERB
to place in position; to arrange
dispose of to get rid of

disposed ADJECTIVE
ready and willing
be well disposed to be friendly

disposition NOUN
1 a person's nature or qualities
2 an arrangement

disproportionate ADJECTIVE
out of proportion; too large or too small

disprove VERB
to show that something is not true

dispute VERB
1 to argue or debate
2 to quarrel
3 to raise an objection to

dispute NOUN
1 an argument or debate
2 a quarrel
in dispute being argued about

disqualify VERB **disqualifies**, **disqualified**
to bar someone from a competition for
breaking the rules
disqualification NOUN

disquiet NOUN
anxiety or worry
disquieting ADJECTIVE

disregard VERB
to ignore

disregard NOUN
the act of ignoring something

disrepair NOUN
bad condition from being neglected

disreputable ADJECTIVE
not respectable

disrepute NOUN
bad reputation

disrespect NOUN
lack of respect; rudeness
disrespectful ADJECTIVE

disrupt VERB
to put into disorder
disruption NOUN **disruptive** ADJECTIVE

dissatisfied ADJECTIVE
not satisfied
dissatisfaction NOUN

dissect VERB
to cut something up in order to examine it
dissection NOUN

dissent NOUN
strong disagreement

dissent VERB
to disagree strongly

dissident NOUN
a person who disagrees with those in
authority

dissipate VERB
1 to disappear or scatter
2 to waste or squander
dissipation NOUN

dissolute ADJECTIVE
having an immoral way of life

dissolution NOUN
the formal ending of an arrangement,
especially a marriage

dissolve VERB
1 to make or become liquid; to melt
2 to end a marriage or partnership
3 to end a parliament or assembly

dissuade VERB
to persuade somebody not to do something
dissuasion NOUN

distance NOUN
the amount of space between two places
in the distance far away but visible

distant ADJECTIVE
1 far away
2 not friendly or sociable
3 not closely related
distantly ADVERB

distaste NOUN
dislike

distasteful ADJECTIVE
unpleasant

distil VERB **distilling**, **distilled**
to purify a liquid by boiling it and condensing
the vapour
distillation NOUN

distiller NOUN
a person or firm that makes alcoholic drinks
by distilling
distillery NOUN

distinct ADJECTIVE
1 easily heard or seen; noticeable
2 clearly separate or different
distinctly ADVERB
Do not confuse this word with *distinctive*.

distinction NOUN
1 a difference
2 excellence or honour
3 an award or high mark

distinctive ADJECTIVE
easy to recognize or identify
a distinctive uniform
distinctively ADVERB
Do not confuse this word with *distinct*.

distinguish VERB
1 to make or notice differences between things
2 to see or hear something clearly
3 to bring honour to
distinguishable ADJECTIVE

distinguished ADJECTIVE
1 excellent and famous
2 dignified in appearance

distort VERB
1 to pull or twist out of its normal shape
2 to give a false account of
distortion NOUN

distract VERB
to take a person's attention away from
something

distraction NOUN
1 something that distracts your attention
2 an amusement
3 great worry or distress

distraught (dis-**trawt**) ADJECTIVE
very worried or upset

distress NOUN
great sorrow or trouble

distress VERB
to cause distress to

distribute VERB
1 to deal or share out
2 to spread or scatter
distribution NOUN **distributor** NOUN

district NOUN
part of a town or country

distrust NOUN
lack of trust; suspicion
distrustful ADJECTIVE

distrust VERB
not to trust

disturb VERB
1 to spoil the peace or rest of
2 to cause to worry
3 to move something from its position

disturbance NOUN
1 an argument or an outbreak of violence
2 the act of disturbing or interrupting

disuse NOUN
the state of not being used any more

disused ADJECTIVE
no longer used

ditch NOUN
a trench dug to hold water or carry it away

ditch VERB
1 (*informal*) to bring an aircraft down in a
forced landing on the sea
2 (*informal*) to abandon or discard
something

dither VERB
to hesitate nervously

ditto NOUN
(used in lists) the same again

ditty NOUN **ditties**
a short song

divan NOUN
a bed or couch without a raised back or sides

dive VERB
1 to go underwater, especially head first
2 to move down quickly
dive NOUN

diver NOUN
a person who works underwater in a special suit with an air supply

diverge VERB
to separate and go in different directions
divergent ADJECTIVE **divergence** NOUN

diverse ADJECTIVE
of several different kinds
diversity NOUN

diversify VERB **diversifies**, **diversified**
1 to make or become varied
2 to involve yourself in different things
diversification NOUN

diversion NOUN
1 an alternative route for traffic
2 a recreation or entertainment

divert VERB
1 to turn something aside from its course
2 to entertain or amuse
diverting ADJECTIVE

divide VERB
1 to separate into smaller parts
2 to share among several people
3 to find how many times one number is contained in another
divider NOUN

dividend NOUN
1 a share of business profits
2 a number that is to be divided by another

dividers PLURAL NOUN
a pair of compasses for measuring distances

divine ADJECTIVE
1 belonging to or coming from God
2 like a god
3 (*informal*) excellent; extremely beautiful
divinely ADVERB

divinity NOUN **divinities**
1 a divine state
2 a god or goddess
3 the study of religion

division NOUN
1 the process of dividing
2 a dividing line or thing
3 a section

divisive ADJECTIVE
causing disagreement within a group

divisor NOUN
a number by which another is to be divided

divorce NOUN
the legal ending of a marriage

divorce VERB
1 to separate from a husband or wife by divorce
2 to separate

divulge VERB
to reveal secret or sensitive information

Diwali (di-**wah**-lee) NOUN
a Hindu religious festival of lamps, held in October or November

DIY ABBREVIATION
do-it-yourself

dizzy ADJECTIVE **dizzier**, **dizziest**
confused or giddy, or causing this state
dizzily ADVERB **dizziness** NOUN

DJ ABBREVIATION
disc jockey

DNA ABBREVIATION
deoxyribonucleic acid, a substance in chromosomes that stores genetic information

do VERB **does**, **did**, **done**
1 to perform or carry out *Do your work.*
2 to deal with *I'll do the dinner.*
3 to act or behave *They do as they please.*
4 to succeed or manage *You are doing very well.*
5 used to form negative statements and questions *I do not like this. Do you want it?*
6 used for emphasis *I do hope you can come.*
7 used to avoid repeating a verb that has just been used *We work as hard as they do.*
do away with to get rid of **do up 1** to fasten **2** to repair or redecorate

do NOUN
(*informal*) a party or other social event

docile ADJECTIVE
willing to obey

dock[1] NOUN
1 a part of a harbour where ships are loaded and repaired
2 an enclosure for the accused or witnesses in a lawcourt

dock VERB
1 to bring or come into a dock
2 (of a spacecraft) to join with another in space

dock[2] NOUN
a weed with broad leaves

dock[3] VERB
1 to cut short an animal's tail
2 to reduce someone's wages or supplies

docker NOUN
a labourer who loads and unloads ships

docket NOUN
a document or label listing the contents of a package

dockyard NOUN
an open area with docks and equipment for ships

doctor NOUN
1 a person who is trained to treat sick or injured people
2 a person who holds an advanced degree at a university *Doctor of Music*

doctrine NOUN
a belief held by a religious or political group

document NOUN
a written or printed paper giving information or evidence about something
documentation NOUN

documentary ADJECTIVE
1 consisting of documents
documentary evidence
2 showing real events or situations

documentary NOUN **documentaries**
a film giving information about real events

doddery ADJECTIVE
unsteady from old age

dodge VERB
to move quickly to avoid someone or something

dodge NOUN
1 a dodging movement
2 (*informal*) a clever way of doing something

dodgem NOUN
a small electric car at a funfair, driven to bump or avoid others

dodgy ADJECTIVE **dodgier, dodgiest**
(*informal*)
1 awkward or tricky
2 not working properly
3 dishonest

dodo NOUN **dodos**
a large extinct bird that was unable to fly

doe NOUN
a female deer, rabbit, or hare

doesn't
does not

dog NOUN
a four-legged animal that barks, often kept as a pet

dog VERB **dogging, dogged**
to follow closely

dog-eared ADJECTIVE
(of a book) with the corners worn from use

dogged (dog-id) ADJECTIVE
persistent or obstinate
doggedly ADVERB

dogma NOUN
a belief or principle that must be accepted by members of a religion

dogmatic ADJECTIVE
expressing ideas in a firm way and not willing to accept other ideas
dogmatically ADVERB

doh NOUN
a name for the keynote of a scale in music, or the note C

do-it-yourself ADJECTIVE
suitable for an amateur to do or make at home

doldrums PLURAL NOUN
an uninteresting or depressing time

dole VERB
dole out to distribute

dole NOUN
(*informal*) money paid by the state to unemployed people

doleful ADJECTIVE
sad or sorrowful
dolefully ADVERB

doll NOUN
a toy model of a person

dollar NOUN
a unit of money in the USA and some other countries

dollop NOUN
(*informal*) a lump of something soft

dolphin NOUN
a sea animal like a small whale with a beak-like snout

domain (dom-**ayn**) NOUN
1 a kingdom
2 an area of knowledge or interest

dome NOUN
a roof shaped like the top half of a ball
domed ADJECTIVE

domestic ADJECTIVE
1 to do with the home or household
2 (of animals) kept by people; not wild
domestically ADVERB

domesticated ADJECTIVE
(of animals) trained to live with humans

dominate VERB
1 to control by being stronger or more powerful
2 to be conspicuous or prominent
dominant ADJECTIVE **domination** NOUN

domineering ADJECTIVE
behaving in a dominating way

dominion NOUN
1 authority or control over others
2 an area over which someone rules

domino NOUN **dominoes**
a small flat oblong piece of wood or plastic marked with dots or a blank space at each end, used in the game called *dominoes*

don VERB **donning, donned**
to put on a coat etc.

donate VERB
to present money or a gift to a fund or institution
donation NOUN

donkey NOUN **donkeys**
an animal that looks like a small horse with long ears

donor NOUN
someone who gives something *a blood donor*

don't
do not

doodle VERB
to scribble or draw absent-mindedly
doodle NOUN

doom NOUN
a grim fate that you cannot avoid

doomed ADJECTIVE
1 destined to a grim fate
2 bound to fail or be destroyed

doomsday NOUN
the end of the world

door NOUN
a hinged or movable barrier used to open or close an entrance

doorstep NOUN
the step or piece of ground just outside a door

doorway NOUN
the opening into which a door fits

dope NOUN (*informal*)
1 an illegal drug
2 a stupid person
dopey ADJECTIVE

dope VERB
(*informal*) to give a drug to

dormant ADJECTIVE
1 sleeping
2 living or existing but not active

dormitory NOUN **dormitories**
a room for several people to sleep in

dormouse NOUN **dormice**
an animal like a large mouse that hibernates in winter

dosage NOUN
the size of a dose of medicine

dose NOUN
an amount of medicine taken at one time

dose VERB
to give a dose of medicine to

dossier (doss-ee-ay) NOUN
a set of documents containing information about a person or event

dot NOUN
a tiny spot

dot VERB **dotting, dotted**
to mark with dots

dotage (doh-tij) NOUN
a condition of weakness of mind caused by old age

dote VERB
dote on to be very fond of

double ADJECTIVE
1 twice as much or as many
2 having two things or parts that form a pair
a double-barrelled gun
3 suitable for two people *a double bed*
doubly ADVERB

double NOUN
1 a double quantity or thing
2 a person or thing that looks exactly like another

double VERB
1 to make or become twice as much or as many
2 to bend or fold in two
3 to turn back sharply

double bass NOUN
a musical instrument with strings, like a large cello

double-cross VERB
to deceive or cheat

double-decker NOUN
a bus with two floors, one above the other

double glazing NOUN
a window of two sheets of glass with a space between, to retain heat or keep out noise

doubt NOUN
a feeling of not being sure about something

doubt VERB
to feel doubt

doubtful ADJECTIVE
1 feeling doubt
2 making you feel doubt
doubtfully ADVERB

doubtless ADVERB
probably

dough NOUN
1 a thick mixture of flour and water used for making bread or pastry
2 (*informal*) money
doughy ADJECTIVE

doughnut NOUN
a round bun that has been fried and covered in sugar

dour (doo-er) ADJECTIVE
stern and gloomy-looking

douse VERB
1 to put into water or pour water over
2 to put out a light

dove NOUN
a kind of pigeon

dowager NOUN
a woman who holds a title or property after her husband has died

dowdy ADJECTIVE **dowdier, dowdiest**
shabby or unfashionable
dowdily ADVERB

down [1] *ADVERB*
1 to or in a lower place or position or level *to fall down*
2 to a source or place etc. *to track down*
3 in writing *Take down these instructions.*
4 as an immediate payment *£50 down*

down *PREPOSITION*
downwards through or along or into *down the stairs*

down *ADJECTIVE*
unhappy or depressed *feeling down*

down [2] *NOUN*
fine soft feathers or hair
downy *ADJECTIVE*

downcast *ADJECTIVE*
1 (of the eyes) looking down
2 dejected

downfall *NOUN*
1 a fall from power or prosperity
2 a heavy fall of rain or snow

downgrade *VERB*
to make less important or valuable

downhill *ADVERB, ADJECTIVE*
down a slope

download *VERB*
to transfer data from a large computer system to a smaller one

downpour *NOUN*
a heavy fall of rain

downright *ADVERB, ADJECTIVE*
complete or completely *a downright lie*

downs *PLURAL NOUN*
grass-covered hills

downstairs *ADVERB, ADJECTIVE*
to or on a lower floor

downstream *ADJECTIVE, ADVERB*
in the direction in which a stream flows

down-to-earth *ADJECTIVE*
sensible and practical

downward *ADJECTIVE, ADVERB*
going towards what is lower
downwards *ADVERB*

dowry *NOUN* **dowries**
property or money brought by a bride to her husband when she marries him

doze *VERB*
to sleep lightly
doze *NOUN* **dozy** *ADJECTIVE*

dozen *NOUN*
a set of twelve

drab *ADJECTIVE* **drabber, drabbest**
1 not colourful
2 dull or uninteresting

draft *NOUN*
1 a rough sketch or plan
2 a written order for a bank to pay out money

draft *VERB*
1 to prepare a draft
2 to select for a special duty

drag *VERB* **dragging, dragged**
1 to pull something heavy along
2 to search a river or lake

drag *NOUN*
1 something tedious or unpleasant
2 (*informal*) women's clothes worn by men

dragon *NOUN*
1 (in stories) a fire-breathing monster with wings
2 a fierce person

dragonfly *NOUN* **dragonflies**
an insect with a long thin body and two pairs of transparent wings

drain *NOUN*
1 a pipe or ditch for taking away water or other liquid
2 something that uses up strength or resources

drain *VERB*
1 to take away water through a drain
2 to flow or trickle away
3 to empty liquid out of a container
4 to use up strength or resources
drainage *NOUN*

drake *NOUN*
a male duck

drama *NOUN*
1 a play
2 the writing or performing of plays
3 a series of exciting events

dramatic *ADJECTIVE*
1 to do with drama
2 exciting and impressive *a dramatic change*
dramatically *ADVERB*

dramatist *NOUN*
a person who writes plays

dramatize *VERB*
1 to make a story into a play
2 to make something seem exciting
dramatization *NOUN*

drape *VERB*
to hang loosely over something

drapery *NOUN*
cloth arranged in loose folds

drastic *ADJECTIVE*
having a strong or violent effect
drastically *ADVERB*

draught (drahft) *NOUN*
1 a current of cold air indoors
2 the depth of water needed to float a ship
3 a swallow of liquid
draughty *ADJECTIVE*

draughts NOUN
a game played with 24 round pieces on a chessboard

draughtsman NOUN **draughtsmen**
1 a person who makes drawings
2 a piece used in the game of draughts

draw VERB **drew**, **drawn**
1 to make a picture or outline by making marks on a surface
2 to pull
3 to take out *draw water*
4 to attract *The fair drew large crowds.*
5 to have the same score on both sides
6 to move or come *to draw near*
7 to write out a cheque to be cashed
8 to form a conclusion

draw NOUN
1 the drawing of lots
2 the drawing out of a gun *He was quick on the draw.*
3 an attraction
4 a drawn game

drawback NOUN
a disadvantage

drawbridge NOUN
a bridge over a moat, hinged to be raised or lowered

drawer NOUN
1 a sliding compartment in a piece of furniture
2 a person who draws

drawing NOUN
a picture or outline

drawl VERB
to speak slowly or lazily
drawl NOUN

dread NOUN
great fear

dread VERB
to fear very much
dreaded ADJECTIVE

dreadful ADJECTIVE
1 terrible
2 (*informal*) very bad *had a dreadful time*
dreadfully ADVERB

dreadlocks PLURAL NOUN
hair worn in ringlets or plaits

dream NOUN
1 a series of pictures or events in the mind during sleep
2 an ambition or ideal

dream VERB **dreamt** or **dreamed**
1 to have a dream or dreams
2 to have an ambition
3 to think something might happen *I never dreamt she would leave.*
dream up to invent or imagine
dreamer NOUN

dreamy ADJECTIVE **dreamier**, **dreamiest**
1 half-asleep
2 vague or unclear
dreamily ADVERB

dreary ADJECTIVE **drearier**, **dreariest**
1 dull or tedious
2 gloomy
drearily ADVERB

dredge VERB
to drag up by scooping at the bottom of a river or the sea
dredger NOUN

dregs PLURAL NOUN
the last drops and sediment at the bottom of a glass or bottle

drench VERB
to make wet all through; soak

dress NOUN
1 a woman's or girl's piece of clothing with a bodice and skirt
2 clothes or costume *fancy dress*

dress VERB
1 to put clothes on
2 to prepare food for cooking or eating
3 to put a dressing on a wound

dresser NOUN
a sideboard with shelves for dishes

dressing NOUN
1 a bandage or plaster for a wound
2 a mixture of oil, vinegar, etc. for a salad

dressing gown NOUN
a loose garment for wearing over pyjamas or a nightdress

dribble VERB
1 to let saliva trickle out of your mouth
2 (of a liquid) to flow in drops
3 to move the ball forward with short movements in football or hockey
dribble NOUN

drier NOUN
a device for drying things

drift VERB
1 to be carried gently along by water or air
2 to move along slowly and casually
3 to live aimlessly
drifter NOUN

drift NOUN
1 a drifting movement
2 a mass of snow or sand piled up by the wind
3 the general meaning of what someone says

drill NOUN
1 a tool or machine for making holes
2 repeated exercises in training

drill VERB
1 to make a hole with a drill
2 to teach with repeated exercises

drily ADVERB
in a dry way

drink VERB **drank**, **drunk**
1 to swallow liquid
2 to drink alcoholic drinks, especially in large amounts
drinker NOUN

drink NOUN
1 an amount of liquid for drinking
2 an alcoholic drink

drip VERB **dripping**, **dripped**
to fall or let something fall in drops

drip NOUN
1 a drop of falling liquid
2 apparatus for dripping liquid into the veins

dripping NOUN
fat from roasted meat

drive VERB **drove**, **driven**
1 to make something or someone move
2 to operate a motor vehicle or a train etc.
3 to force someone to do something
Hunger drove them to steal.
4 to force someone into a state
You are driving me crazy.
5 to move with force *Rain drove against the window.*
driver NOUN

drive NOUN
1 a journey in a vehicle
2 a track for vehicles through the grounds of a house
3 the transmitting of power to machinery
4 energy or enthusiasm
5 a hard stroke in cricket or golf etc.
6 an organized effort *a sales drive*

drivel NOUN
silly talk; nonsense

drizzle NOUN
fine light rain

droll ADJECTIVE
amusing in an odd way

drone VERB
1 to make a deep humming sound
2 to talk in a deep dull voice

drone NOUN
1 a droning sound
2 a male bee

drool VERB
to dribble
drool over to be very emotional about liking something

droop VERB
to hang down weakly

drop NOUN
1 a tiny amount of liquid
2 a fall or decrease
3 a descent
4 a small round sweet

drop VERB **dropping**, **dropped**
1 to fall
2 to let something fall
3 to become lower or less
4 to abandon or stop dealing with
5 to set down a passenger from a vehicle
drop in to visit someone casually
drop out to stop taking part in something

droppings PLURAL NOUN
the dung of animals or birds

drought (drout) NOUN
a long period of dry weather

drove NOUN
a moving herd or flock
droves a large number of people

drown VERB
1 to die or kill by suffocation underwater
2 to flood or drench
3 to suppress a sound with a louder one

drowsy ADJECTIVE **drowsier**, **drowsiest**
slightly sleepy
drowsily ADVERB

drubbing NOUN
a severe defeat

drudge NOUN
a person who does hard or tedious work
drudgery NOUN

drug NOUN
1 a substance used in medicine
2 a substance taken because it affects the senses or the mind, e.g. a narcotic or stimulant, especially one causing addiction such as heroin or cocaine

drug VERB **drugging**, **drugged**
to give a drug to

Druid (droo-id) NOUN
a priest of an ancient Celtic religion in Britain and France

drum NOUN
1 a musical instrument made of a skin or parchment stretched over a round frame, beaten with sticks
2 a cylindrical object or container

drum VERB **drumming**, **drummed**
1 to beat a drum
2 to tap repeatedly with the fingers
drummer NOUN

drunk ADJECTIVE
not able to control your behaviour through
drinking too much alcohol

drunk NOUN
a person who is drunk

drunkard NOUN
a person who is often drunk

drunken ADJECTIVE
1 drunk
2 caused by drinking alcohol *a drunken brawl*

dry ADJECTIVE **drier**, **driest**
1 without water or moisture
2 thirsty
3 tedious or dull
4 (of remarks or humour) said in a
matter-of-fact or ironical way
drily ADVERB **dryness** NOUN

dry VERB **dries**, **dried**
to make or become dry

dual ADJECTIVE
composed of two parts; double
Do not confuse this word with *duel*.

dub[1] VERB **dubbing**, **dubbed**
1 to make someone a knight by touching him
on the shoulder with a sword
2 to give a nickname to

dub[2] VERB **dubbing**, **dubbed**
to change or add new sound to the
soundtrack of a film or to a recording

dubious (dew-bee-us) ADJECTIVE
doubtful or uncertain
dubiously ADVERB

duchess NOUN
1 a woman with the same rank as a duke
2 the wife or widow of a duke

duchy NOUN **duchies**
the territory of a duke

duck NOUN
1 a swimming bird with a flat beak
2 a batsman's score of no runs at cricket
3 a ducking movement

duck VERB
1 to bend down quickly to avoid something
2 to go or push quickly underwater
3 to dodge or avoid doing something

duckling NOUN
a young duck

duct NOUN
a tube or channel through which liquid, gas,
air, or cables can pass

ductile ADJECTIVE
(of metal) able to be drawn out into fine
strands

dud NOUN
(informal) something useless or broken

due ADJECTIVE
1 expected or scheduled *due in ten minutes*
2 owing; needing to be paid
3 that ought to be given; rightful *due respect*
due to as a result of

due ADVERB
exactly *due east*

due NOUN
1 something you deserve or have a right to
2 a fee *harbour dues*

duel NOUN
a fight between two people, especially with
pistols or swords
duelling NOUN **duellist** NOUN
Do not confuse this word with *dual*.

duet NOUN
a piece of music for two players or singers

duffel coat NOUN
a thick overcoat with a hood, fastened with
toggles

dugout NOUN
1 an underground shelter
2 a bench for coaches and substitutes beside
a sports pitch
3 a canoe made by hollowing out a tree trunk

duke NOUN
a member of the highest rank of nobility
dukedom NOUN

dull ADJECTIVE
1 not bright or clear *dull weather*
2 stupid
3 uninteresting *a dull concert*
4 not sharp *a dull pain a dull thud*
dully ADVERB

duly ADVERB
1 in the due or proper way
2 at the expected time

dumb ADJECTIVE
1 without the ability to speak
2 silent
3 (informal) stupid

dumbfounded ADJECTIVE
too astonished to speak

dummy NOUN **dummies**
1 something made to look like a person
or thing
2 an imitation teat given to a baby to suck

dump NOUN
1 a place where rubbish is left or stored
2 (informal) a dull or unattractive place
in the dumps depressed or unhappy

dump VERB
1 to get rid of something unwanted
2 to put down carelessly

dumpling NOUN
a piece of dough cooked in a stew

dumpy ADJECTIVE **dumpier**, **dumpiest**
short and fat

dunce NOUN
a person who is slow at learning

dune NOUN
a mound of loose sand shaped by the wind

dung NOUN
solid waste matter excreted by an animal

dungarees PLURAL NOUN
trousers with a piece in front covering the chest and held up by straps

dungeon (dun-jon) NOUN
an underground prison cell

dunk VERB
to dip something into liquid

duo (dew-oh) NOUN **duos**
a pair of people, especially musicians

dupe VERB
to deceive

duplicate NOUN
an exact copy or imitation

duplicate VERB
to make or be a duplicate
duplication NOUN

durable ADJECTIVE
strong and likely to last
durability NOUN

duration NOUN
the length of time something lasts

duress (dewr-ess) NOUN
the use of force or threats to get your way

during PREPOSITION
1 through the course of *It rained during the night.*
2 at a point in the course of *They arrived during our meal.*

dusk NOUN
twilight in the evening

dusky ADJECTIVE
dark or shadowy

dust NOUN
tiny particles of earth or other solid material

dust VERB
1 to wipe away dust
2 to sprinkle with dust or powder

dustbin NOUN
a bin for household rubbish

duster NOUN
a cloth for dusting things

dustman NOUN
a person employed to take away household rubbish

dusty ADJECTIVE **dustier**, **dustiest**
1 covered with dust
2 like dust

dutiful ADJECTIVE
doing your duty; obedient
dutifully ADVERB

duty NOUN
1 what you ought to do or must do
2 a task that must be done
3 a tax charged on some goods
on or **off duty** actually doing (or not doing) your regular work

duvet (doo-vay) NOUN
a thick quilt used on a bed instead of blankets

DVD ABBREVIATION
digital video (or versatile) disc, a disc used for storing audio or video information, especially films

dwarf NOUN **dwarfs** or **dwarves**
a very small person or thing

dwarf VERB
to make something seem small by contrast

dwell VERB **dwelt**
to live in a place
dwell on to think or talk about constantly
dweller NOUN

dwelling NOUN
a building for living in

dwindle VERB
to get smaller gradually

dye NOUN
a substance used to colour fabrics etc.

dye VERB **dyeing**
to colour something with dye

dyke NOUN
1 a long wall or embankment holding back water
2 a ditch for draining water from land

dynamic ADJECTIVE
1 energetic or forceful
2 (of a force) producing motion
dynamically ADVERB

dynamics NOUN
1 the study of force and motion
2 (*Music*) different levels of loudness and softness

dynamite NOUN
a powerful explosive

dynamo NOUN **dynamos**
a machine that generates electricity

dynasty NOUN **dynasties**
a line of rulers or leaders from the same family
dynastic ADJECTIVE

dysentery (dis-en-tree) NOUN
a disease causing fever and diarrhoea

dyslexia NOUN
special difficulty in being able to read and spell
dyslexic ADJECTIVE

Ee

each ADJECTIVE, PRONOUN
every; every one *each child each of you*

eager ADJECTIVE
strongly wanting to do something
eagerly ADVERB **eagerness** NOUN

eagle NOUN
a large bird of prey with keen sight

ear¹ NOUN
1 the organ of the body used for hearing
2 hearing ability *a good ear*

ear² NOUN
the spike of seeds at the top of a stalk of corn

eardrum NOUN
a membrane in the ear that vibrates when
sounds reach it

earl NOUN
a member of the British nobility below
a marquess
earldom NOUN

early ADJECTIVE, ADVERB **earlier**, **earliest**
1 before the usual or expected time
2 near the beginning *early in the book*

earn VERB
1 to receive money for doing work
2 to deserve

earnest ADJECTIVE
showing serious feelings or intentions
earnestly ADVERB

earnings PLURAL NOUN
money paid for work

earphones PLURAL NOUN
a listening device that fits over the ears

earring NOUN
a piece of jewellery worn on the ear

earshot NOUN
the distance within which a sound can
be heard

earth NOUN
1 the planet that we live on
2 the ground; soil
3 the hole where a fox or badger lives
4 connection to the ground to complete an
electrical circuit

earth VERB
to connect an electrical circuit to the ground

earthenware NOUN
pottery made of coarse baked clay

earthly ADJECTIVE
concerned with life on earth rather than with
life after death

earthquake NOUN
a violent movement of part of the
earth's surface

earthworm NOUN
a worm that lives in the soil

earthy ADJECTIVE **earthier**, **earthiest**
1 like earth or soil
2 coarse and vulgar

earwig NOUN
a crawling insect with pincers at the end of
its body

ease NOUN
freedom from trouble or effort or pain

ease VERB
1 to make less painful or less tight or
troublesome
2 to move gently into position
3 to become less severe *The pain has eased.*

easel NOUN
a stand for supporting a blackboard or painting

easily ADVERB
1 without difficulty; with ease
2 by far *easily the best*
3 very likely *They could easily be wrong.*

east NOUN
1 the direction where the sun rises
2 the eastern part of a country, city, etc.

east ADJECTIVE, ADVERB
towards or in the east; coming from the east

Easter NOUN
the Sunday (in March or April) when
Christians commemorate the resurrection
of Christ

easterly ADJECTIVE
1 coming from the east
2 facing the east

eastern ADJECTIVE
of or in the east

eastward ADJECTIVE, ADVERB
towards the east
eastwards ADVERB

easy ADJECTIVE **easier**, **easiest**
able to be done or used or understood
without trouble
take it easy to relax

eat VERB **ate**, **eaten**
1 to chew and swallow as food
2 to have a meal
3 to use up or destroy gradually

eaves PLURAL NOUN
the overhanging edges of a roof

eavesdrop VERB **eavesdropping, eavesdropped**
to listen secretly to a private conversation
eavesdropper NOUN

ebb NOUN
1 the movement of the tide when it is going out
2 a low point *Our courage was at a low ebb.*

ebb VERB
1 to flow away from the land
2 to weaken or become less

ebony NOUN
a hard black wood

eccentric (ik-**sen**-trik) ADJECTIVE
behaving strangely
eccentrically ADVERB **eccentricity** NOUN

echo NOUN **echoes**
a sound that is heard again as it is reflected off a surface

echo VERB **echoes, echoing, echoed**
1 to make an echo
2 to repeat a sound or saying

éclair (ay-**klair**) NOUN
a finger-shaped cake of pastry with a creamy filling

eclipse NOUN
the blocking of the sun's or moon's light when the moon or the earth is in the way

eclipse VERB
1 to block the light and cause an eclipse
2 to be much better or more important than

ecology (ee-**kol**-o-jee) NOUN
the study of living things in relation to their environment
ecological ADJECTIVE **ecologist** NOUN

economic (ee-kon-**om**-ik) ADJECTIVE
1 to do with economy or economics
2 profitable

economical ADJECTIVE
careful with resources
economically ADVERB

economics NOUN
the study of how money is earned and used
economist NOUN

economize VERB
to be economical; to use or spend less

economy NOUN **economies**
1 the management of a country's or household's income and spending
2 the careful use of resources
3 a saving

ecosystem NOUN
all the plants and animals in a particular area considered in terms of their relationship with their environment

ecstasy NOUN
1 a feeling of great delight
2 an illegal drug that causes hallucinations
ecstatic (ik-**stat**-ik) ADJECTIVE

eczema (**eks**-im-a) NOUN
a skin disease causing rough itching patches

eddy NOUN **eddies**
a swirling patch of water or air or smoke etc.

eddy VERB **eddies, eddied**
to swirl

edge NOUN
1 the part along the side or end of something
2 the sharp part of a knife or other cutting instrument
3 special interest or excitement

edge VERB
1 to be the edge or border of
2 to put a border on
3 to move gradually *He edged away.*

edgeways ADVERB
with the edge forwards or outwards

edgy ADJECTIVE **edgier, edgiest**
tense and irritable
edginess NOUN

edible ADJECTIVE
suitable for eating; not poisonous

edict NOUN
an official command

edit VERB
1 to be the editor of a newspaper or other publication
2 to make written material ready for publishing
3 to choose and put the parts of a film or tape recording etc. into order

edition NOUN
1 the form in which something is published
2 all the copies of a book

editor NOUN
a person who edits something

editorial ADJECTIVE
to do with editing or editors

editorial NOUN
a newspaper article giving the editor's opinions

educate VERB
to provide with education
educated ADJECTIVE

education NOUN
the training of people's minds and abilities to acquire knowledge and develop skills
educational ADJECTIVE

eel NOUN
a long snake-like fish

eerie *ADJECTIVE* **eerier**, **eeriest**
strange in a frightening or mysterious way
eerily *ADVERB*

efface *VERB*
to wipe or rub out
effacement *NOUN*

effect *NOUN*
1 a change or result
2 an impression that is produced by something *a cheerful effect*

effect *VERB*
to make something happen *to effect changes*
Do not confuse this word with *affect*.

effective *ADJECTIVE*
1 producing the effect that is wanted
2 impressive and striking

effeminate *ADJECTIVE*
(of a man) having feminine qualities
effeminacy *NOUN*

effervesce (ef-er-**vess**) *VERB*
to give off bubbles of gas
effervescence *NOUN* **effervescent** *ADJECTIVE*

efficient *ADJECTIVE*
doing work well; effective
efficiency *NOUN* **efficiently** *ADVERB*

effigy *NOUN* **effigies**
a model or sculptured figure

effort *NOUN*
1 the use of energy; the energy used
2 something difficult or tiring
3 an attempt *a good effort*

effusive *ADJECTIVE*
making a great show of affection or enthusiasm
effusively *ADVERB*

e.g. *ABBREVIATION*
for example

egg [1] *NOUN*
1 an oval object containing an embryo, produced by a bird, fish, reptile, or insect
2 a hen's or duck's egg used as food
3 an ovum

egg [2] *VERB*
to urge or encourage

eggplant *NOUN*
(*American*) an aubergine

ego (eeg-oh) *NOUN*
a person's self or self-respect

egotist (eg-oh-tist) *NOUN*
a conceited person who is always talking about himself or herself
egotism *NOUN* **egotistic** *ADJECTIVE*

Eid (eed) *NOUN*
a Muslim festival marking the end of Ramadan

eiderdown *NOUN*
a quilt stuffed with feathers or other soft material

eight *NOUN, ADJECTIVE*
the number 8
eighth *ADJECTIVE, NOUN*

eighteen *NOUN, ADJECTIVE*
the number 18
eighteenth *ADJECTIVE, NOUN*

eighty *NOUN, ADJECTIVE* **eighties**
the number 80
eightieth *ADJECTIVE, NOUN*

either *ADJECTIVE, PRONOUN*
1 one or the other of two *Either team can win. either of them*
2 both of two *on either side of the road*

either *ADVERB*
also; similarly *If you won't go, I won't either.*

either *CONJUNCTION* (used with **or**)
the first of two possibilities *He is either ill or drunk. Either come in or go away.*

ejaculate *VERB*
1 (of a man) to produce semen from the penis
2 (*formal*) to suddenly say something
ejaculation *NOUN*

eject *VERB*
1 to send out forcefully
2 to force someone to leave
ejection *NOUN*

eke (eek) *VERB*
eke out to make something last by using small amounts

elaborate (il-**ab**-er-at) *ADJECTIVE*
having many parts or details; complicated
elaborately *ADVERB*

elaborate (il-**ab**-er-ayt) *VERB*
to explain or work out in detail
elaboration *NOUN*

elapse *VERB*
(of time) to pass

elastic *NOUN*
cord or material woven with strands of rubber so that it can stretch

elastic *ADJECTIVE*
able to be stretched and return to its original length

elated *ADJECTIVE*
feeling very pleased
elation *NOUN*

elbow *NOUN*
the joint in the middle of the arm

elbow *VERB*
to push with the elbow

elder [1] *ADJECTIVE*
older *my elder brother*

elder NOUN
1 an older person
2 an official in certain Churches

elder [2] NOUN
a tree with white flowers and black berries

elderberry NOUN **elderberries**
a berry from an elder tree

elderly ADJECTIVE
rather old

eldest ADJECTIVE
oldest

elect VERB
1 to choose by voting
2 to choose to do something

elect ADJECTIVE
chosen by a vote but not yet in office
the president elect

election NOUN
the process of electing people, especially
Members of Parliament

electorate NOUN
all the people who can vote

electric ADJECTIVE
1 to do with or worked by electricity
2 causing sudden excitement *an electric effect*
electrical ADJECTIVE

electrician NOUN
a person skilled in working with electrical
equipment

electricity NOUN
a form of energy carried by certain particles of
matter (electrons and protons), used for
lighting, heating, and power

electrify VERB **electrifies**, **electrified**
1 to give an electric charge to
2 to supply with electric power
3 to thrill with excitement
electrification NOUN

electrocute VERB
to kill by electricity
electrocution NOUN

electrode NOUN
a solid conductor through which electricity
enters or leaves a vacuum tube

electromagnet NOUN
a magnet worked by electricity
electromagnetic ADJECTIVE

electron NOUN
a particle of matter with a negative
electric charge

electronic ADJECTIVE
produced or worked by a flow of electrons
electronically ADVERB

electronics NOUN
the use or study of electronic devices

elegant ADJECTIVE
graceful and dignified
elegance NOUN

elegy NOUN **elegies**
a sorrowful or serious poem

element NOUN
1 (*Science*) a substance that cannot be split
up into simpler substances, composed of
atoms that have the same number of protons
2 each of the parts that make up a thing
3 a basic or elementary principle
the elements of algebra
4 a wire or coil that gives out heat in an
electric fire or cooker
the elements weather conditions, such as
rain, wind, and cold

elementary ADJECTIVE
dealing with the simplest stages of
something; easy

elephant NOUN
a large animal with a trunk, large ears,
and tusks

elevate VERB
to lift or raise to a higher position
elevation NOUN

elevator NOUN
(*American*) a lift in a building

eleven ADJECTIVE, NOUN
the number 11
eleventh ADJECTIVE, NOUN

elf NOUN
(in fairy tales) a small being with magic powers

eligible ADJECTIVE
qualified or suitable for something
eligibility NOUN

eliminate VERB
to get rid of
elimination NOUN

élite (ay-leet) NOUN
a group of people given privileges which are
not given to others

elk NOUN
a large kind of deer

ellipse NOUN
an oval shape

elm NOUN
a tall tree with rough leaves

elocution NOUN
the art of speaking clearly and correctly

elongated ADJECTIVE
made longer; lengthened
elongation NOUN

elope VERB
to run away secretly to get married
elopement NOUN

eloquent ADJECTIVE
speaking fluently and expressing ideas vividly
eloquence NOUN

else ADVERB
1 besides; other *Someone else did it.*
2 otherwise; if not *Run or else you'll be late.*

elsewhere ADVERB
somewhere else

elude VERB
1 to avoid being caught by
2 to be too difficult to remember or understand *The name eludes me.*
elusive ADJECTIVE

email NOUN
1 a system of sending messages and data from one computer to another by means of a network
2 a message sent in this way
email VERB
to send by email

emancipation NOUN
the process of setting people free from slavery or other restraints

embalm VERB
to preserve a dead body from decay by using spices or chemicals

embankment NOUN
a bank of earth or stone holding back water or supporting a road or railway

embargo NOUN **embargoes**
an official ban on trade with a country

embark VERB
to put or go on board a ship or aircraft
embark on to begin something new or challenging
embarkation NOUN

embarrass VERB
to make someone feel awkward or ashamed
embarrassment NOUN

embassy NOUN **embassies**
the office and staff of an ambassador in a foreign country

embed VERB **embedding**, **embedded**
to fix firmly in something solid

embellish VERB
to decorate or add details to
embellishment NOUN

embers PLURAL NOUN
small pieces of glowing coal or wood in a dying fire

embezzle VERB
to take dishonestly money that was left in your care
embezzlement NOUN

emblem NOUN
a symbol that represents something
an emblem of friendship

embody VERB **embodies**, **embodied**
1 to include or contain
2 to express in a visible form *art that embodies a view of life*
embodiment NOUN

embossed ADJECTIVE
decorated with a raised design

embrace VERB
1 to hold closely in your arms
2 to include
3 to accept or adopt a cause or belief
embrace NOUN
a hug

embroider VERB
1 to decorate cloth with needlework
2 to add details to a story to make it more interesting
embroidery NOUN

embryo (em-bree-oh) NOUN **embryos**
a baby or young animal in its earliest stages

emend VERB
to remove errors from a piece of writing

emerald NOUN
a bright-green precious stone

emerge VERB
1 to come out or appear
2 to become known
emergence NOUN

emergency NOUN **emergencies**
a sudden serious event that needs immediate action

emigrant NOUN
a person who goes to live in another country

emigrate VERB
to leave your own country to live in another
emigration NOUN

eminent ADJECTIVE
famous and respected
eminently ADVERB

emission NOUN
fumes or radiation

emit VERB **emitting**, **emitted**
to send out light, heat, fumes, etc.

emotion NOUN
a strong feeling in the mind, such as love, anger, or hate

emotional ADJECTIVE
having or causing strong feelings

emotive ADJECTIVE
likely to cause strong feelings

empathize VERB
to share the feelings of another person

empathy NOUN
the ability to understand and share in someone else's feelings

emperor NOUN
a man who rules an empire

emphasis NOUN **emphases**
1 special importance given to something
2 stress put on a word or part of a word

emphasize VERB
to put emphasis on

emphatic ADJECTIVE
using emphasis; spoken strongly
emphatically ADVERB

empire NOUN
1 a group of countries ruled by one country
2 a large business organization controlled by one person or group

employ VERB
1 to pay a person to do work
2 to make use of to employ modern methods

employee NOUN
a person who works for a person or organization

employer NOUN
a person or organization that employs people

employment NOUN
paid work

empower VERB
to give someone the power to do something

empress NOUN
1 a woman who rules an empire
2 the wife of an emperor

empty ADJECTIVE **emptier**, **emptiest**
1 containing nothing or nobody
2 not likely to have any effect empty promises
emptiness NOUN

empty VERB **empties**, **emptied**
to make or become empty

emu NOUN **emus**
a large Australian bird like an ostrich

emulate VERB
to try to do as well as someone
emulation NOUN

emulsion NOUN
1 a creamy or slightly oily liquid
2 a kind of water-based paint

enable VERB
to give the means or ability to do something

enact VERB
1 to make a law
2 to perform
enactment NOUN

enamel NOUN
1 a shiny substance for coating metal
2 paint that dries hard and shiny
3 the hard shiny surface of teeth

enamel VERB **enamelling**, **enamelled**
to coat or decorate with enamel

enamoured ADJECTIVE
fond

encapsulate VERB
to express an idea clearly and concisely

enchant VERB
1 to put under a magic spell
2 to fill with delight and wonder

encircle VERB
to surround

enclave NOUN
a country's territory lying entirely within another country

enclose VERB
1 to put a wall or fence round
2 to include in a letter or package

enclosure NOUN
1 the act of enclosing
2 an enclosed area
3 something included with a letter or parcel

encompass VERB
1 to surround
2 to contain or include

encore (on-kor) NOUN
an extra item performed at a concert after applause for the main items

encounter VERB
1 to meet unexpectedly
2 to experience We encountered some difficulties.

encounter NOUN
1 an unexpected meeting
2 a battle

encourage VERB
1 to give confidence or hope to
2 to try to persuade
3 to help something happen or develop to encourage healthy eating
encouragement NOUN

encroach VERB
1 to intrude on someone's rights
2 to go further than the proper limits
encroachment NOUN

encrypt VERB
to put information into a special code for security
encryption NOUN

encumber VERB
to be a burden to
encumbrance NOUN

encyclopedia *NOUN*
a book or set of books containing information on many subjects

encyclopedic *ADJECTIVE*
giving information about many different things

end *NOUN*
1 the last part of something
2 each half of a sports pitch
3 destruction or death
4 a purpose *for your own ends*

end *VERB*
to bring or come to an end

endanger *VERB*
to cause danger to

endear *VERB*
to make someone fond of you
endearing *ADJECTIVE*

endearment *NOUN*
a word or phrase expressing love or affection

endeavour (en-**dev**-er) *VERB*
to try hard

endeavour *NOUN*
a strong attempt

endemic (en-**dem**-ik) *ADJECTIVE*
(of a disease) often found in a certain area or group of people

ending *NOUN*
the last part

endless *ADJECTIVE*
never stopping
endlessly *ADVERB*

endorse *VERB*
1 to confirm or give your approval to something
2 to sign your name on the back of a document
endorsement *NOUN*

endow *VERB*
1 to provide a source of income to establish something *to endow a scholarship*
2 to provide with an ability or quality *They were endowed with great talent.*
endowment *NOUN*

endurance *NOUN*
the ability to put up with difficulty or pain for a long period

endure *VERB*
1 to suffer or put up with difficulty or pain
2 to continue to exist
endurable *ADJECTIVE*

enemy *NOUN* **enemies**
1 someone who opposes or seeks to harm another
2 a nation or army at war with another

energetic *ADJECTIVE*
full of energy
energetically *ADVERB*

energy *NOUN* **energies**
1 strength to do things; liveliness
2 (*Science*) the ability of matter or radiation to do work
3 power obtained from fuel and other resources

enfold *VERB*
to surround or be wrapped round something

enforce *VERB*
to make people obey a law or rule
enforcement *NOUN*

engage *VERB*
1 to arrange to employ or use
2 to occupy the attention of *to engage someone in conversation*
3 to begin a battle with

engaged *ADJECTIVE*
1 having promised to marry somebody
2 in use; occupied

engagement *NOUN*
1 a promise to marry
2 an arrangement to meet
3 a battle

engaging *ADJECTIVE*
attractive or charming

engine *NOUN*
1 a machine that provides power
2 a vehicle that pulls a railway train

engineer *NOUN*
an expert in engineering

engineer *VERB*
1 to plan and build machines and large structures
2 to cause to happen by clever planning

engineering *NOUN*
the design and building of machines and large structures such as roads and bridges

engrave *VERB*
to carve something on a surface

engross *VERB*
to occupy the whole attention of

engulf *VERB*
to flow over and cover completely

enhance *VERB*
to make a thing more attractive or increase its value
enhancement *NOUN*

enigma *NOUN*
something difficult to understand; a mystery

enigmatic (en-ig-**mat**-ik) *ADJECTIVE*
mysterious and puzzling
enigmatically *ADVERB*

enjoy VERB
to get pleasure from something
enjoyment NOUN

enjoyable ADJECTIVE
pleasant and satisfying

enlarge VERB
to make bigger
enlargement NOUN

enlighten VERB
to give more knowledge or information to
enlightenment NOUN

enlist VERB
1 to join the armed forces
2 to obtain the support or help of

enliven VERB
to make more lively

enmity NOUN
a state of being an enemy; hostility

enormity NOUN
1 great wickedness *the enormity of the crime*
2 great size; hugeness *the enormity of the task*
Many people regard the use of sense 2 as
incorrect, and it is usually better to use
magnitude instead.

enormous ADJECTIVE
very large; huge
enormously ADVERB

enough ADJECTIVE, NOUN, ADVERB
as much or as many as necessary *enough food*
I have had enough. Are you warm enough?

enquire VERB
1 to ask for information *He enquired if I
was well.*
2 to investigate carefully
See the note at **inquire**.

enquiry NOUN
1 a question
2 an investigation

enrage VERB
to make very angry

enrich VERB
make richer or more satisfying
enrichment NOUN

enrol VERB **enrolling**, **enrolled**
1 to become a member of a society
2 to make someone a member
enrolment NOUN

ensemble (on-**som**bl) NOUN
1 a group of things that go together
2 a group of musicians
3 a matching set of clothes

ensign NOUN
a military or naval flag

enslave VERB
to make a slave of
enslavement NOUN

ensue VERB
to happen afterwards or as a result

ensure VERB
to make certain of *The right diet can ensure
good health.*
Do not confuse this word with *insure*.

entail VERB
to involve as a result *This plan entails danger.*

entangle VERB
1 to tangle
2 to make complicated
entanglement NOUN

enter VERB
1 to come in or go in
2 to put into a list or book
3 to key into a computer
4 to register as a competitor

enterprise NOUN
1 the ability to act independently and set up
new projects
2 business activity *private enterprise*

enterprising ADJECTIVE
willing to try new or adventurous projects

entertain VERB
1 to amuse
2 to have as guests
3 to consider
entertainer NOUN

entertainment NOUN
something performed before an audience

enthral VERB **enthralling**, **enthralled**
to give great pleasure or interest to

enthusiasm NOUN
a strong liking, interest, or excitement
enthusiast NOUN

enthusiastic ADJECTIVE
full of enthusiasm
enthusiastically ADVERB

entice VERB
to attract or persuade by offering
something pleasant
enticement NOUN

entire ADJECTIVE
whole or complete
entirely ADVERB

entirety (int-I-rit-ee) NOUN
the whole of something

entitle VERB
to give the right to have or do something
entitlement NOUN

entitled ADJECTIVE
having as a title

entity NOUN **entities**
something that exists separately from other things

entrails PLURAL NOUN
the intestines

entrance[1] (en-trans) NOUN
1 the way into a place
2 the act of entering

entrance[2] (in-trahns) VERB
to fill with intense delight

entrant NOUN
someone who enters for an examination or competition

entreat VERB
to ask earnestly

entreaty NOUN **entreaties**
an earnest request

entrenched ADJECTIVE
(of an idea) firmly established

entrust VERB
to place in someone's care

entry NOUN **entries**
1 an entrance
2 an item entered in a list, diary, or reference book
3 something entered in a competition

envelop (en-**vel**-op) VERB
to cover or wrap round completely

envelope (en-vel-ohp) NOUN
a wrapper or covering, especially for a letter

enviable ADJECTIVE
likely to be envied

envious ADJECTIVE
feeling envy

environment NOUN
1 surroundings, especially as they affect people's lives
2 the natural world of the land, sea, and air
environmental ADJECTIVE

environmentalist NOUN
a person who wishes to protect or improve the environment

envisage VERB
1 to picture in the mind
2 to imagine as being possible

envoy NOUN
an official representative sent by one government to another

envy NOUN **envies**
1 a feeling of discontent when someone else is more fortunate than you
2 something that causes this feeling

envy VERB **envies**, **envied**
to feel envy towards

enzyme NOUN
a kind of substance that assists chemical processes

ephemeral ADJECTIVE
lasting only a short time

epic NOUN
1 a long poem or story about heroic deeds
2 a spectacular film

epicentre NOUN
the point where an earthquake reaches the earth's surface

epidemic NOUN
an outbreak of a disease among the people of an area

epigram NOUN
a short witty saying

epilepsy NOUN
a disease of the nervous system, causing convulsions
epileptic ADJECTIVE, NOUN

epilogue NOUN
a short section at the end of a book or play

episode NOUN
1 one event in a series of happenings
2 one programme in a radio or television serial

epistle NOUN
a letter, especially one in the New Testament of the Bible

epitaph NOUN
words written on a gravestone or describing a person who has died

epithet NOUN
an adjective or special name

epitome (ip-**it**-um-ee) NOUN
a perfect example of something *the epitome of kindness*

epoch NOUN
a long period of time

equal ADJECTIVE
1 the same in amount, size, or value
2 having the necessary strength or ability *equal to the task*
equally ADVERB

equal NOUN
a person or thing that is equal to another

equal VERB **equalling**, **equalled**
1 to be the same as in amount, size, or value
2 to match or be as good as

equality NOUN
the state of being equal

equalize VERB
to make equal

equate VERB
to regard as equal or equivalent

equation NOUN
(*Maths*) a statement that two things are equal, e.g. 3 + 4 = 2 + 5

equator NOUN
an imaginary line round the earth at an equal distance from the North and South Poles
equatorial ADJECTIVE

equestrian ADJECTIVE
to do with horse riding

equilateral (ee-kwi-**lat**-er-al) ADJECTIVE
(of a triangle) having all sides equal

equilibrium NOUN
1 a balance between different forces, influences, etc.
2 a balanced state of mind

equine ADJECTIVE
of or like a horse

equinox NOUN
the time of year when day and night are equal in length (about 20 March in spring, about 22 September in autumn)

equip VERB **equipping**, **equipped**
to supply with what is needed

equipment NOUN
the things needed for a particular purpose

equitable ADJECTIVE
fair and sensible

equity (ek-wit-ee) NOUN
fairness

equivalent ADJECTIVE
equal in importance, meaning, value, etc.

equivalent NOUN
something that is equivalent

era (eer-u) NOUN
a major period of history

eradicate VERB
to get rid of
eradication NOUN

erase VERB
1 to rub out
2 to remove or wipe out
eraser NOUN

erect ADJECTIVE
standing straight up

erect VERB
to set up or build

erection NOUN
1 the process of erecting
2 something erected

ermine NOUN
1 a kind of weasel
2 its white fur

erode VERB
to wear away

erosion NOUN
the wearing away of the earth's surface by the action of water, wind, etc.

erotic ADJECTIVE
arousing sexual feelings
erotically ADVERB

err (er) VERB
1 to make a mistake
2 to do wrong

errand NOUN
a short journey to take a message, fetch goods, etc.

erratic (ir-**at**-ik) ADJECTIVE
1 not regular
2 not reliable
erratically ADVERB

erroneous ADJECTIVE
incorrect; mistaken
erroneously ADVERB

error NOUN
a mistake

erupt VERB
1 to burst out
2 (of a volcano) to shoot out lava
eruption NOUN

escalate VERB
to make or become greater or more extreme
escalation NOUN

escalator NOUN
a staircase with steps moving up or down

escapade NOUN
an adventure

escape VERB
1 to get free or away
2 to avoid something unpleasant *to escape punishment*
3 to be forgotten by *Her name escapes me for the moment.*

escape NOUN
1 an act of escaping
2 a way to escape

escarpment NOUN
a steep slope at the edge of high level ground

escort (ess-kort) NOUN
someone accompanying a person or thing for company or protection

escort (iss-**kort**) VERB
to act as an escort to

Eskimo NOUN
a name formerly used for *Inuit*
The name *Inuit* is preferred.

especially ADVERB
specially; more than anything else

espionage NOUN
spying

essay *NOUN*
a short piece of writing in prose

essence *NOUN*
1 the most important quality or element of something
2 a concentrated liquid

essential *ADJECTIVE*
completely necessary
essentially *ADVERB*

essential *NOUN*
an essential thing

establish *VERB*
1 to set up an organization or relationship
2 to show to be true *He established his innocence.*

establishment *NOUN*
a business firm or other institution

estate *NOUN*
1 an area of land with houses or factories on it
2 a large area of land owned by one person
3 the property of someone who has died

estate agent *NOUN*
a person whose business is selling or letting houses and land

estate car *NOUN*
a car with a door at the back giving access to an inside luggage compartment

esteem *VERB*
to think very highly of

esteem *NOUN*
respect and admiration

esteemed *ADJECTIVE*
highly respected and admired

ester *NOUN*
a kind of chemical compound

estimate (ess-tim-at) *NOUN*
a rough calculation or guess about an amount or value

estimate (ess-tim-ayt) *VERB*
to make an estimate
estimation *NOUN*

estranged *ADJECTIVE*
unfriendly after having been friendly or loving
estrangement *NOUN*

estuary *NOUN* **estuaries**
the mouth of a river where it reaches the sea

etc. *ABBREVIATION*
(short for **et cetera**) and other similar things; and so on

etch *VERB*
to engrave a picture with acid on a metal plate, especially for printing

etching *NOUN*
a picture printed from an etched metal plate

eternal *ADJECTIVE*
lasting for ever
eternally *ADVERB*

eternity *NOUN* **eternities**
1 a time that has no end
2 (*informal*) a very long time

ether (ee-ther) *NOUN*
1 a colourless liquid with fumes that are used as an anaesthetic
2 the upper air

ethereal *ADJECTIVE*
light and delicate
ethereally *ADVERB*

ethical *ADJECTIVE*
1 to do with ethics
2 morally right; honourable
ethically *ADVERB*

ethics (eth-iks) *PLURAL NOUN*
standards of right behaviour

ethnic *ADJECTIVE*
belonging to a particular race or group of people

etiquette (et-ik-et) *NOUN*
the rules of correct behaviour

etymology *NOUN* **etymologies**
1 the origin of a word and its meaning
2 the study of the origins of words

EU *ABBREVIATION*
European Union

eucalyptus (yoo-kal-ip-tus) *NOUN*
1 a kind of evergreen tree
2 a strong-smelling oil obtained from its leaves

Eucharist (yoo-ker-ist) *NOUN*
the Christian ceremony commemorating the Last Supper of Christ and his disciples

eulogy (yoo-loj-ee) *NOUN* **eulogies**
a speech or piece of writing praising a person or thing

eunuch (yoo-nuk) *NOUN*
a man who has been castrated

euphemism (yoo-fim-izm) *NOUN*
a mild word or phrase used instead of an offensive or frank one, e.g. *pass away* instead of *die*
euphemistic *ADJECTIVE*

euphoria (yoo-for-ee-a) *NOUN*
a feeling of general happiness

euro *NOUN* **euros**
the basic unit of currency used by some members of the EU since 1999

European *ADJECTIVE*
to do with Europe or its people
European *NOUN*

euthanasia (yooth-an-**ay**-zee-a) NOUN
the act of causing a person with a terminal illness to die gently and without pain

evacuate VERB
1 to move people away from a dangerous place
2 to make empty
evacuation NOUN

evacuee NOUN
a person who has been evacuated

evade VERB
to avoid by cleverness or trickery

evaluate VERB
estimate the value of something; assess
evaluation NOUN

evaporate VERB
1 to change from liquid into steam or vapour
2 to cease to exist *Their enthusiasm evaporated.*
evaporation NOUN

evasion NOUN
1 the act of evading
2 an evasive answer or excuse

evasive ADJECTIVE
trying to avoid giving an answer; not frank or straightforward

eve NOUN
the day or evening before an important day or event *New Year's Eve*

even[1] ADJECTIVE
1 level and smooth
2 not varying
3 calm; not easily upset *an even temper*
4 equal *The scores were even.*
5 (of a number) able to be divided exactly by two
get even to take revenge
evenly ADVERB **evenness** NOUN

even VERB
to make or become even

even ADVERB
used to emphasize a word or statement *They ran even faster.*

even-handed ADJECTIVE
fair and impartial

evening NOUN
the time at the end of the day before the night

event NOUN
1 something important that happens
2 an item forming part of a sports contest

eventful ADJECTIVE
full of happenings

eventual ADJECTIVE
happening at last *our eventual success*
eventually ADVERB

eventuality NOUN **eventualities**
something that may happen

ever ADVERB
1 at any time *the best thing I ever did*
2 always *ever hopeful*
3 (informal) used for emphasis *Why ever not?*

evergreen ADJECTIVE
having green leaves all the year
evergreen NOUN

everlasting ADJECTIVE
lasting for ever or for a long time

every ADJECTIVE
each without any exceptions *We enjoyed every minute.*
every one each one **every other** every second one

Every should be used with a singular verb and singular pronouns: *Every house has its own garden.*

everybody or **everyone** PRONOUN
every person

everyday ADJECTIVE
ordinary; usual *everyday clothes*

everything PRONOUN
all things; all

everywhere ADVERB
in every place

evict VERB
to force someone to leave the house they are living in
eviction NOUN

evidence NOUN
1 anything that gives people reason to believe something
2 information given in a lawcourt to prove something

evident ADJECTIVE
obvious; clearly seen
evidently ADVERB

evil ADJECTIVE
morally bad; wicked
evilly ADVERB

evil NOUN
1 wickedness
2 something unpleasant or harmful

evocative ADJECTIVE
inspiring memories or feelings

evoke VERB
to produce or inspire memories or feelings

evolution NOUN
1 gradual change into something different
2 the development of animals and plants from earlier or simpler forms of life
evolutionary ADJECTIVE

evolve VERB
to develop gradually

ewe (yoo) NOUN
a female sheep

ewer (yoo-er) NOUN
a large water jug

exacerbate (eks-**ass**-er-bayt) VERB
to make worse

exact ADJECTIVE
1 correct; precise
2 giving all details *exact instructions*

exact VERB
to insist on and obtain

exacting ADJECTIVE
making great demands *an exacting task*

exactly ADVERB
1 precisely; with all details
2 used in reply as a strong form of agreement

exaggerate VERB
to make something seem bigger, better, or
worse than it really is
exaggeration NOUN

exalt VERB
1 to raise in rank or status
2 to praise highly
exaltation NOUN

exam NOUN
an examination

examination NOUN
1 a test of a person's knowledge or skill
2 an act of examining or inspecting *a medical
examination*

examine VERB
1 to test a person's knowledge or skill
2 to look at closely or in detail
examiner NOUN

example NOUN
1 anything that represents things of the
same kind
2 a person or thing worth imitating

exasperate VERB
to annoy very much
exasperation NOUN

excavate VERB
to dig out or uncover by digging
excavation NOUN **excavator** NOUN

exceed VERB
1 to be greater than
2 to go beyond the limit of

exceedingly ADVERB
very; extremely

excel VERB **excelling**, **excelled**
1 to be better than
2 to do very well

Excellency NOUN
the title of high officials such as ambassadors
and governors

excellent ADJECTIVE
of high quality; extremely good
excellence NOUN

except PREPOSITION
not including *They all left except me.*

except VERB
to exclude or leave out
Do not confuse this word with *accept*.

excepting PREPOSITION
except

exception NOUN
a person or thing that is left out or does not
follow the general rule
take exception to to object to or resent

exceptional ADJECTIVE
1 very unusual
2 outstandingly good
exceptionally ADVERB

excerpt (ek-serpt) NOUN
a passage taken from a book or speech
or film etc.

excess NOUN
too much of something

excessive ADJECTIVE
too much or too great
excessively ADVERB

exchange VERB
to give something and get something else in
return

exchange NOUN
1 the act of exchanging
2 a place where stocks and shares are bought
and sold
3 a place where telephone connections
are made

exchequer NOUN
a national treasury into which taxes and other
public funds are paid

excise [1] (eks-I'z) NOUN
a tax charged on certain goods

excise [2] (iks-I'z) VERB
to remove by cutting

excitable ADJECTIVE
easily excited

excite VERB
1 to make eager and enthusiastic about
something
2 to cause a feeling or reaction
to excite great interest

excitement NOUN
a strong feeling of eagerness or pleasure

exclaim _VERB_
to shout or cry out in eagerness or surprise

exclamation _NOUN_
1 the act of exclaiming
2 a word or words cried out

exclamation mark _NOUN_
the punctuation mark (!) placed after an exclamation

exclude _VERB_
1 to shut somebody or something out
2 to leave out of consideration
exclusion _NOUN_

exclusive _ADJECTIVE_
1 including only certain people
an exclusive club
2 not existing elsewhere _an exclusive offer_
exclusive of not including
the cost exclusive of tax
exclusively _ADVERB_

excrement _NOUN_
waste matter excreted from the bowels

excrete _VERB_
to get rid of waste matter from the body
excretion _NOUN_

excruciating _ADJECTIVE_
1 extremely painful
2 hard to put up with

excursion _NOUN_
a short journey made for pleasure

excuse (iks-kewz) _VERB_
1 to forgive
2 to release from a duty or commitment
excuse (iks-kewss) _NOUN_
a reason given to explain a wrongdoing or mistake

execute _VERB_
1 to put to death as a punishment
2 to perform or produce
execution _NOUN_

executioner _NOUN_
an official who executes a condemned person

executive _NOUN_
1 a senior person in a business organization
2 the part of a government that puts decisions into effect
executive _ADJECTIVE_
having the authority to carry out plans or laws

executor (ig-zek-yoo-ter) _NOUN_
an official appointed to carry out the instructions in a will

exemplary (ig-zem-pler-ee) _ADJECTIVE_
good as an example to others _exemplary conduct_

exemplify _VERB_ **exemplifies**, **exemplified**
to be an example of

exempt _ADJECTIVE_
not having to do something that others have to do

exempt _VERB_
to make exempt
exemption _NOUN_

exercise _NOUN_
1 the practice of using your body to make it strong and healthy
2 a piece of work done for practice

exercise _VERB_
1 to do exercises
2 to give exercise to an animal
3 to use _Exercise more care._

exert _VERB_
to bring into use _to exert authority_
exertion _NOUN_

exhale _VERB_
to breathe out
exhalation _NOUN_

exhaust _VERB_
1 to make very tired
2 to use up completely
exhaustion _NOUN_

exhaust _NOUN_
1 the waste gases or steam from an engine
2 the system they pass through

exhaustive _ADJECTIVE_
thorough _an exhaustive search_
exhaustively _ADVERB_

exhibit _VERB_
to show or display in public
exhibitor _NOUN_

exhibit _NOUN_
an item on display in a gallery or museum

exhibition _NOUN_
a collection of things put on display for people to look at

exhibitionist _NOUN_
a person who behaves in a way that is meant to attract attention
exhibitionism _NOUN_

exhilarate _VERB_
to make someone happy and excited
exhilarating _ADJECTIVE_ **exhilaration** _NOUN_

exhort _VERB_
to try hard to persuade someone
exhortation _NOUN_

exhume _VERB_
to dig up a body that has been buried
exhumation _NOUN_

exile _VERB_
to banish

exile _NOUN_
1 a period of having to live away from your own country
2 a person sent away from their own country

exist VERB
1 to be present as part of what is real
2 to stay alive

existence NOUN
1 the state of being
2 life or a particular type of life
a miserable existence

exit NOUN
1 the way out of a building
2 the act of leaving

exit VERB
to leave; to go out

exodus NOUN
the departure of many people, especially
from their country

exonerate VERB
to free from blame or guilt

exorbitant ADJECTIVE
(of an amount charged) much too great

exorcize VERB
to drive out an evil spirit
exorcism NOUN **exorcist** NOUN

exotic ADJECTIVE
1 strange or unusual *exotic clothes*
2 from another part of the world *exotic plants*

expand VERB
to make or become larger or fuller
expansion NOUN **expansive** ADJECTIVE

expanse NOUN
a wide area

expansive ADJECTIVE
1 wide and large
2 talkative

expect VERB
1 to think or believe that something is likely
to happen
2 to want or demand *to expect courtesy*

expectant ADJECTIVE
1 expecting something to happen
2 (of a woman) pregnant

expectation NOUN
1 belief that something will happen
2 something you expect to happen

expedient ADJECTIVE
practical and convenient rather than fair

expedient NOUN
a means of doing something difficult

expedite VERB
to make something happen more quickly

expedition NOUN
1 a journey made for a special purpose
2 speed or promptness

expel VERB **expelling**, **expelled**
1 to send or force out *a fan to expel stale air*
2 to make a person leave a school or country

expend VERB
to spend or use up

expenditure NOUN
the spending or using up of money or effort

expense NOUN
1 a cost
2 something that causes a cost

expensive ADJECTIVE
costing a lot

experience NOUN
1 knowledge gained from doing or
seeing things
2 an event you have taken part in

experience VERB
to take part in an event

experienced ADJECTIVE
having skill or knowledge from experience

experiment NOUN
a test to get information or try to prove
something

experiment VERB
to carry out an experiment
experimentation NOUN

experimental ADJECTIVE
done as a trial or experiment
experimentally ADVERB

expert NOUN
a person with great knowledge or skill
in a subject

expert ADJECTIVE
having great knowledge or skill
expertly ADVERB

expertise (eks-per-**teez**) NOUN
expert ability

expire VERB
1 to come to an end
2 to die
3 to breathe out air

expiry NOUN
the time when something ends

explain VERB
1 to make clear to someone; to show the
meaning of
2 to account for

explanation NOUN
a statement explaining something

explanatory (iks-**plan**-at-er-ee) ADJECTIVE
giving an explanation

explicit ADJECTIVE
stated or stating something openly and exactly
explicitly ADVERB

explode VERB
1 to burst or suddenly release energy with a loud noise
2 to cause a bomb to go off
3 to increase suddenly or quickly

exploit (eks-ploit) NOUN
a brave or exciting deed

exploit (iks-ploit) VERB
1 to use or develop to good effect
2 to make use of a person selfishly
exploitation NOUN

exploratory ADJECTIVE
for the purpose of exploring

explore VERB
1 to travel to make discoveries
2 to examine a subject or idea carefully
exploration NOUN **explorer** NOUN

explosion NOUN
1 the exploding of a bomb etc.; the noise made by exploding
2 a sudden great increase

explosive ADJECTIVE
able to explode

explosive NOUN
a substance that can explode

export (ek-spawt) VERB
to send goods abroad to be sold
exportation NOUN **exporter** NOUN

export (ek-spawt) NOUN
1 the exporting of goods
2 something exported

expose VERB
1 to reveal or uncover
2 to allow light to reach a photographic film

exposure NOUN
1 the harmful effects of being exposed to cold weather without protection
2 the exposing of photographic film to the light
3 a piece of film exposed in this way

express ADJECTIVE
1 going or sent quickly
2 clearly stated express orders

express NOUN
a fast train or bus

express VERB
1 to put into words
2 to press or squeeze out

expression NOUN
1 the look on a person's face
2 a word or phrase
3 a way of speaking or of playing music to show your feelings
4 the act of expressing

expressive ADJECTIVE
expressing meaning clearly or vividly

expressly ADVERB
1 clearly and plainly expressly forbidden
2 specially designed expressly for you

expulsion NOUN
the act of expelling or being expelled, especially from a school

exquisite (eks-kwiz-it) ADJECTIVE
very beautiful and delicate
exquisitely ADVERB

extend VERB
1 to stretch out
2 to make or become longer or larger
3 to offer or give
extendible ADJECTIVE

extension NOUN
1 a part added on, especially to a building
2 an extra telephone linked to the main one

extensive ADJECTIVE
covering a large area or range
extensively ADVERB

extent NOUN
1 the area or length of something
2 level or scope the full extent of his power

extenuating ADJECTIVE
making something bad seem less so
extenuating circumstances
extenuation NOUN

exterior ADJECTIVE
outer; outside
exterior NOUN
the outside of a building

exterminate VERB
to destroy or kill all of
extermination NOUN

external ADJECTIVE
outside
externally ADVERB

extinct ADJECTIVE
not existing or active any more an extinct bird
an extinct vocano

extinction NOUN
the process of making or becoming extinct

extinguish VERB
1 to put out a fire or light
2 to put an end to

extol VERB **extolling, extolled**
to praise highly

extort VERB
to obtain by force or threats
extortion NOUN

extortionate ADJECTIVE
charging far too much

extra ADJECTIVE
more than is needed or usual

a b c d e f g h i j k l m n o p q r s t u v w x y z

extra ADVERB
more than usually *extra strong*

extra NOUN
1 an extra person or thing
2 a person acting as part of a crowd in a film or play

extract (iks-**trakt**) VERB
to take out or remove
extractor NOUN

extract (**eks**-trakt) NOUN
1 a passage taken from a book, speech, film, etc.
2 a substance separated or obtained from another

extraction NOUN
1 the process of extracting
2 a person's descent *of Russian extraction*

extradite VERB
to hand over a person accused of a crime to the country where the crime was committed
extradition NOUN

extraneous (iks-**tray**-nee-us) ADJECTIVE
added from outside *extraneous noises*

extraordinary ADJECTIVE
very unusual or strange
extraordinarily ADVERB

extraterrestrial ADJECTIVE
from beyond the earth's atmosphere

extraterrestrial NOUN
a being from outer space

extravagant ADJECTIVE
spending or using too much
extravagance NOUN

extravaganza NOUN
a spectacular show or display

extreme ADJECTIVE
1 very great or intense *extreme cold*
2 furthest away *the extreme north*
3 going to great lengths in actions or opinions
extremely ADVERB

extreme NOUN
1 something extreme
2 either end of something

extremity (iks-**trem**-it-ee) NOUN
extremities
1 an extreme point; the very end
2 extreme danger

extricate VERB
to free from a difficult position or situation
extrication NOUN

extrovert NOUN
a person who is sociable and communicative

exuberant (ig-**zew**-ber-ant) ADJECTIVE
lively and cheerful
exuberance NOUN

exude VERB
1 to give off moisture, a smell, etc.
2 to display openly *to exude confidence*

exult VERB
to rejoice greatly
exultant ADJECTIVE **exultation** NOUN

eye NOUN
1 the organ of the body used for seeing
2 the ability to see *keen eyes*
3 the small hole in a needle
4 the centre of a storm

eye VERB **eyeing**
to look at closely

eyeball NOUN
the ball-shaped part of the eye inside the eyelids

eyebrow NOUN
the fringe of hair growing above each eye

eyelash NOUN
each of the short hairs that grow on an eyelid

eyelid NOUN
each of the two folds of skin that close over the eyeball

eyesight NOUN
the ability to see

eyesore NOUN
something large and ugly

eyewitness NOUN
a person who saw an accident or crime take place

eyrie (**eer**-ee) NOUN
the nest of an eagle or other bird of prey

Ff

fable NOUN
a short story, often about animals, with a moral or lesson

fabric NOUN
1 cloth
2 the basic framework of a building

fabricate VERB
1 to construct or manufacture something
2 to invent a story or excuse
fabrication NOUN

fabulous ADJECTIVE
1 great or wonderful
2 told of in fables and myths
fabulously ADVERB

facade (fas-**ahd**) NOUN
1 the front of a building
2 a deceptive outward appearance

face NOUN
1 the front part of the head
2 the expression on a person's face
3 the front or upper side of something
4 a surface of a block or cube
facial ADJECTIVE

face VERB
1 to look or have the front towards something *The house faces the sea.*
2 to have to deal with *Explorers face many dangers.*
3 to cover with a layer of different material

facelift NOUN
1 surgery to remove wrinkles, done to make someone look younger
2 a renovation or improvement to the appearance of something

facet (fas-it) NOUN
1 each side of a cut stone or jewel
2 one aspect of a situation or problem

facetious (fas-ee-shus) ADJECTIVE
trying to be funny at an unsuitable time
facetious remarks
facetiously ADVERB

facile (fas-yl) ADJECTIVE
done or produced easily or with little thought

facilitate VERB
to make easier to do
facilitation NOUN

facility (fas-il-it-ee) NOUN **facilities**
1 buildings and equipment for doing things
sports facilities
2 ease or skill

facsimile (fak-**sim**-il-ee) NOUN
an exact copy

fact NOUN
something that is certainly true

faction NOUN
a small united group within a larger one

factor NOUN
1 something that affects a situation or result
Hard work is an important factor.
2 a number by which a larger number can be divided exactly

factory NOUN **factories**
a large building where machines are used to make goods

factual ADJECTIVE
based on facts; containing facts
factually ADVERB

faculty NOUN **faculties**
1 any of the powers of the body or mind (e.g. sight, speech, understanding)

2 a department teaching a particular subject in a university or college

fad NOUN
1 an unusual like or dislike
2 a temporary fashion or craze
faddy ADJECTIVE

fade VERB
1 to lose colour or strength
2 to disappear gradually
3 to make something become gradually weaker or stronger

faeces (fee-seez) PLURAL NOUN
solid waste matter passed out of the body

fag NOUN
1 something tiring or tedious
2 (*informal*) a cigarette
fagged out tired out; exhausted

Fahrenheit ADJECTIVE
measuring temperature on a scale on which water freezes at 32° and boils at 212°

fail VERB
1 to be unable to do something
2 to become weak or useless; to break down
3 not to do something you should have done
They failed to warn me.
4 to be unsuccessful in an exam or test
without fail for certain; whatever happens

failing NOUN
a weakness or fault

failure NOUN
1 the act of failing
2 a person or thing that has failed

faint ADJECTIVE
1 pale or dim; not distinct
2 weak or giddy; nearly unconscious
3 slight *a faint hope*
faintly ADVERB

faint VERB
to become unconscious for a short time
Do not confuse this word with *feint*.

fair[1] ADJECTIVE
1 right or just; according to the rules
a fair fight
2 (of hair or skin) light in colour
3 (of weather) fine or favourable
4 moderate; quite good *a fair number*
fairness NOUN

fair[2] NOUN
1 a group of outdoor entertainments including sideshows and stalls
2 an exhibition or market

fairground NOUN
an open space for holding a fair

fairly ADVERB
1 justly; according to the rules
2 moderately *fairly good*

fairy NOUN **fairies**
an imaginary small creature with magic powers

fairy story or **fairy tale** NOUN
a traditional story about fairies, giants, etc.

faith NOUN
1 strong belief or trust
2 a religion

faithful ADJECTIVE
1 loyal and trustworthy
2 true to the facts *a faithful account*
faithfully ADVERB

fake NOUN
something that looks genuine but is not;
a forgery

fake VERB
1 to make a copy or forgery of
2 to pretend *to fake illness*

falcon NOUN
a bird of prey used to hunt other birds or game

fall VERB **fell**, **fallen**
1 to come or go down under its own weight
2 to decrease or become lower
3 (of a place) to be captured in war
4 to die in battle
5 to happen *A silence fell.*
6 to become *She fell asleep.*

fall NOUN
1 the action of falling
2 (*American*) autumn, when leaves fall

fallacy (fal-a-see) NOUN **fallacies**
a false or mistaken idea or belief

fallible (fal-ib-ul) ADJECTIVE
liable to make mistakes
fallibility NOUN

fallout NOUN
radioactive material carried in the air after a
nuclear explosion

fallow ADJECTIVE
(of land) ploughed and left without crops for
a time

falls PLURAL NOUN
a waterfall

false ADJECTIVE
1 untrue or incorrect
2 not genuine; artificial
3 treacherous or deceitful

falsehood NOUN
a lie

falsetto NOUN **falsettos**
a man's voice forced into speaking or singing
higher than is natural

falsify VERB **falsifies**, **falsified**
to alter dishonestly; to make false
falsification NOUN

falter VERB
1 to hesitate when you move or speak
2 to become weaker *His courage faltered.*

fame NOUN
the state of being very well-known
famed ADJECTIVE

familiar ADJECTIVE
1 well-known; often seen or experienced
2 knowing something well
3 very friendly
familiarity NOUN

familiarize VERB
to make yourself familiar with something

family NOUN **families**
1 parents and their children
2 a group of related plants or things

famine NOUN
a serious shortage of food in an area

famished ADJECTIVE
very hungry

famous ADJECTIVE
known to many people

fan[1] NOUN
a device or machine for making air move
about

fan VERB **fanning**, **fanned**
to send a current of air on

fan[2] NOUN
an enthusiastic admirer or supporter

fanatic NOUN
a person who is extremely or wildly
enthusiastic about something

fanatical ADJECTIVE
extremely or wildly enthusiastic

fanciful ADJECTIVE
1 imagining things
2 imaginary

fancy NOUN **fancies**
1 a liking
2 imagination

fancy ADJECTIVE
decorated or elaborate; not plain

fancy VERB **fancies**, **fancied**
1 to have a liking or desire for
2 to imagine or believe

fancy dress NOUN
unusual costume worn for a party, e.g. to look
like a famous person

fanfare NOUN
a short piece of loud music played on trumpets

fang NOUN
a long sharp tooth

fantasize VERB
to imagine something pleasant or strange

145

fantastic ADJECTIVE
  1 (*informal*) excellent
  2 strange or unusual
  3 designed in a fanciful way

fantasy NOUN **fantasies**
  something imaginary or fantastic

far ADVERB
  1 at or to a great distance
  2 much; by a great amount *far worse*

far ADJECTIVE
  distant or remote *on the far side*

farce NOUN
  1 a comedy based on ridiculous situations
  2 an absurd or false situation or series of events
  farcical ADJECTIVE

fare NOUN
  1 the price charged to make a journey
  2 food and drink

fare VERB
  to make progress

farewell EXCLAMATION, NOUN
  goodbye

far-fetched ADJECTIVE
  unlikely, difficult to believe

farm NOUN
  1 an area of land for growing crops or keeping animals for food
  2 a farmer's house

farm VERB
  1 to grow crops or keep animals for food
  2 to use land for growing crops

farmer NOUN
  a person who owns or manages a farm

farrow NOUN
  a litter of young pigs

farther ADVERB, ADJECTIVE
  at or to a greater distance; more distant

farthest ADVERB, ADJECTIVE
  at or to the greatest distance; most distant

farthing NOUN
  a former British coin worth one-quarter of an old penny

fascinate VERB
  to be very attractive or interesting to
  fascination NOUN

fascism (fash-izm) NOUN
  an extreme dictatorial form of government
  fascist NOUN

fashion NOUN
  1 the popular style of clothes or other things
  2 a way of doing something

fashion VERB
  to make in a particular shape or style

fashionable ADJECTIVE
  following the fashion of the time; popular
  fashionably ADVERB

fast [1] ADJECTIVE
  1 moving or done quickly; rapid
  2 allowing fast movement *a fast road*
  3 showing a time later than the correct time *Your watch is fast.*
  4 firmly fixed or attached
  5 (of colour) not likely to fade

fast ADVERB
  1 quickly
  2 firmly *stuck fast*
  fast asleep in a deep sleep

fast [2] VERB
  to go without food
  fast NOUN

fasten VERB
  to fix one thing firmly to another
  fastener NOUN **fastening** NOUN

fast food NOUN
  hot food that is quickly prepared and served

fastidious ADJECTIVE
  1 fussy and hard to please
  2 very careful about small details

fat NOUN
  1 the white greasy part of meat
  2 oil or grease used in cooking

fat ADJECTIVE **fatter**, **fattest**
  1 having a thick round body
  2 thick *a fat book*
  3 full of fat

fatal ADJECTIVE
  causing death or disaster
  fatally ADVERB

fatality (fa-**tal**-it-ee) NOUN **fatalities**
  a death caused by an accident or war

fate NOUN
  1 a power that is thought to make things happen
  2 what will happen or has happened to a person

fated ADJECTIVE
  certain to do or suffer something bad or unpleasant

fateful ADJECTIVE
  bringing events that are important and usually unpleasant *that fateful day*
  fatefully ADVERB

father NOUN
  1 a male parent
  2 a priest
  fatherhood NOUN

father VERB
  to be the father of

father-in-law NOUN **fathers-in-law**
the father of a married person's husband or wife

fathom NOUN
a unit used to measure the depth of water, equal to 1.83 metres or 6 feet

fathom VERB
1 to measure the depth of
2 to work out a problem

fatigue NOUN
1 tiredness
2 weakness in metals

fatten VERB
to make or become fat

fatty ADJECTIVE **fattier, fattiest**
like fat; containing fat

fatuous ADJECTIVE
silly or foolish
fatuously ADVERB

fault NOUN
1 anything that makes a person or thing imperfect
2 the responsibility for something wrong
3 a break in a layer of rock
faultless ADJECTIVE

fault VERB
to find faults in; to criticize

faulty ADJECTIVE **faultier, faultiest**
having a fault or faults

faun NOUN
an ancient country god with a goat's legs, horns, and tail

fauna NOUN
the animals of a certain area or period of time

favour NOUN
1 a kind or helpful act
2 approval or goodwill
3 friendly support shown to one person or group

favour VERB
to like or support

favourable ADJECTIVE
1 helpful or advantageous
2 showing approval
favourably ADVERB

favourite ADJECTIVE
liked more than others

favourite NOUN
a person or thing that is favoured

favouritism NOUN
a tendency to be kinder to one person than to others

fawn[1] NOUN
1 a young deer
2 a light-brown colour

fawn[2] VERB
to get someone to like you by flattering them

fax NOUN
1 a machine that sends an exact copy of a document electronically
2 a copy produced by this

fax VERB
to send a copy of a document using a fax machine

faze VERB
(informal) to make someone feel confused or shocked

fear NOUN
a feeling that something unpleasant may happen
fearless ADJECTIVE

fear VERB
to feel fear; to be afraid

fearful ADJECTIVE
1 feeling fear; afraid
2 causing fear or horror
fearfully ADVERB

fearsome ADJECTIVE
frightening

feasible ADJECTIVE
able to be done
feasibility NOUN **feasibly** ADVERB

feast NOUN
1 a large splendid meal
2 a religious festival

feast VERB
to have a feast

feat NOUN
a brave or clever deed

feather NOUN
one of the light coverings that grow from a bird's skin
feathery ADJECTIVE

feather VERB
to cover or line with feathers

feature NOUN
1 any part of the face (e.g. the mouth, nose, or eyes)
2 an important or noticeable part
3 a special newspaper article or programme
4 the main film in a cinema programme

feature VERB
to make or be a noticeable part of something

February NOUN
the second month of the year

fed past tense of **feed**
fed up (informal) unhappy or bored

federal ADJECTIVE
of a system in which several states are ruled by a central government but are responsible for their own internal affairs

federation *NOUN*
a group of federal states

fee *NOUN*
a charge for work or a service

feeble *ADJECTIVE*
weak; without strength
feebly *ADVERB*

feed *VERB* **fed**
1 to give food to a person or animal
2 to eat
feeder *NOUN*

feed *NOUN*
food for animals or babies

feedback *NOUN*
comments from users of something

feel *VERB* **felt**
1 to touch something to find out what it is like
2 to be aware of
3 to experience an emotion
4 to give a certain sensation *feels warm*
feel like to want

feel *NOUN*
the sensation caused by feeling something

feeler *NOUN*
1 a long thin projection on an insect's or
crustacean's body; an antenna
2 a cautious question or suggestion

feeling *NOUN*
1 the ability to feel things; the sense of touch
2 an emotion
3 a thought or opinion

feign (fayn) *VERB*
to pretend

feint (faynt) *NOUN*
a pretended attack or punch

feint *VERB*
to make a feint
Do not confuse this word with *faint*.

feisty *ADJECTIVE* **feistier**, **feistiest**
lively and rather aggressive

feline *ADJECTIVE*
to do with cats

fell [1] *past tense of* **fall**

fell [2] *VERB*
to cut or knock down

fell [3] *NOUN*
a piece of wild hilly country

fellow *NOUN*
1 a friend or companion
2 a man or boy
3 a member of a learned society

fellow *ADJECTIVE*
of the same group or kind *fellow teachers*

fellowship *NOUN*
1 friendship
2 a group of friends

felony (fel-on-ee) *NOUN* **felonies**
a serious crime

felt [1] *past tense of* **feel**

felt [2] *NOUN*
a thick fabric made of fibres of wool or fur

female *ADJECTIVE*
of the sex that can bear offspring or produce
eggs or fruit

female *NOUN*
a female person, animal, or plant

feminine *ADJECTIVE*
1 to do with or like women
2 (in some languages) belonging to the
class of words which includes words referring
to women
femininity *NOUN*

feminist *NOUN*
a person who believes that women should
have the same rights and status as men
feminism *NOUN*

fen *NOUN*
an area of low-lying wet ground

fence *NOUN*
1 a flat upright barrier round an area
2 a structure for a horse to jump over

fence *VERB*
1 to put a fence round
2 to fight with swords as a sport
fencer *NOUN*

fend *VERB*
fend for yourself to take care of
yourself **fend off** to keep a person or thing
away

fender *NOUN*
a low barrier round a fireplace

fennel *NOUN*
a herb with yellow flowers

ferment (fer-ment) *VERB*
to bubble and change chemically, e.g. by the
action of yeast
fermentation *NOUN*
Do not confuse this word with *foment*.

ferment (fer-ment) *NOUN*
an excited or agitated condition

fern *NOUN*
a plant with feathery leaves and no flowers

ferocious *ADJECTIVE*
fierce or savage
ferociously *ADVERB* **ferocity** *NOUN*

ferret *NOUN*
a small weasel-like animal

ferret *VERB*
to search for something in small spaces

ferry *NOUN* **ferries**
a ship used for transporting people or things across water

ferry *VERB* **ferries, ferried**
to transport across water

fertile *ADJECTIVE*
1 (of soil) producing good crops
2 able to produce offspring
3 able to produce ideas *a fertile imagination*
fertility *NOUN*

fertilize *VERB*
1 to add substances to the soil to make it more fertile
2 to put pollen into a plant or sperm into an egg or female animal so that it develops seed or young
fertilization *NOUN*

fertilizer *NOUN*
chemicals or manure added to the soil to make it more fertile

fervent *ADJECTIVE*
showing warm or strong feeling

fester *VERB*
1 to become septic and filled with pus
2 to cause resentment

festival *NOUN*
1 a time of religious celebration
2 an organized series of concerts, films, performances, etc.

festive *ADJECTIVE*
1 to do with a festival
2 joyful

festivity *NOUN* **festivities**
a festive occasion or celebration

fetch *VERB*
1 to go for and bring back
2 to be sold for a particular price

fete (fayt) *NOUN*
an outdoor entertainment with stalls and sideshows

fete *VERB*
to honour with celebrations

fetus (**fee**-tuhs) *NOUN*
a developing embryo; an unborn baby
fetal *ADJECTIVE*

feud (fewd) *NOUN*
a long-lasting quarrel

feudal (**few**-duhl) *ADJECTIVE*
to do with the system used in the Middle Ages in which people could farm land in exchange for work done for the owner
feudalism *NOUN*

fever *NOUN*
1 a high body temperature, with an illness
2 excitement or agitation
feverish *ADJECTIVE*

few *ADJECTIVE*
not many

few *NOUN*
a small number of people or things

fiancé or **fiancée** (fee-**ahn**-say) *NOUN*
a man or woman who is engaged to be married

fiasco (fee-**as**-koh) *NOUN* **fiascos**
a complete failure

fib *NOUN*
a lie about something unimportant

fib *VERB* **fibbing, fibbed**
to lie about something trivial

fibre *NOUN*
1 a fine thread
2 a substance made of thin threads
3 material in food that stimulates the action of the intestines

fibreglass *NOUN*
1 fabric made from glass fibres
2 plastic containing glass fibres

fickle *ADJECTIVE*
constantly changing; not loyal

fiction *NOUN*
stories about made-up events
fictional *ADJECTIVE*

fictitious *ADJECTIVE*
imagined or untrue

fiddle *VERB*
1 to play the violin
2 to tinker with something
3 (*informal*) to alter accounts dishonestly
fiddler *NOUN*

fiddle *NOUN*
1 a violin
2 (*informal*) a swindle or deception

fiddly *ADJECTIVE* **fiddlier, fiddliest**
small and awkward to use or do

fidelity *NOUN*
1 faithfulness or loyalty
2 accuracy, especially of sound reproduction

fidget *VERB*
to make small restless movements
fidgety *ADJECTIVE*

fidget *NOUN*
a person who fidgets

field *NOUN*
1 a piece of land with grass or crops
2 an area of interest or study

field *VERB*
1 to stop or catch the ball in cricket or other ball games
2 to deal with a difficult question effectively

field marshal *NOUN*
an army officer of the highest rank

fieldwork NOUN
practical work or research

fiend (feend) NOUN
1 an evil spirit; a devil
2 a wicked or cruel person
3 an enthusiast *a fresh-air fiend*

fiendish ADJECTIVE
1 very wicked or cruel
2 extremely difficult

fierce ADJECTIVE **fiercer, fiercest**
1 angry and violent or cruel
2 intense *fierce heat*

fiery ADJECTIVE
1 full of flames or heat
2 full of emotion
3 easily made angry

fife NOUN
a small shrill flute

fifteen NOUN, ADJECTIVE
1 the number 15
2 a team in rugby union football
fifteenth ADJECTIVE, NOUN

fifth ADJECTIVE, NOUN
next after the fourth
fifthly ADVERB

fifty NOUN, ADJECTIVE **fifties**
the number 50
fiftieth ADJECTIVE, NOUN

fifty-fifty ADJECTIVE, ADVERB
1 shared equally between two
2 evenly balanced *a fifty-fifty chance*

fig NOUN
a soft fruit full of small seeds

fight NOUN
1 a struggle against somebody using hands
or weapons
2 an attempt to achieve or overcome
something *the fight against poverty*

fight VERB **fought**
1 to have a fight
2 to attempt to overcome a difficulty
fighter NOUN

figment NOUN
something imagined *a figment of the
imagination*

figurative ADJECTIVE
using a figure of speech; metaphorical, not
literal

figure NOUN
1 the symbol of a number
2 an amount or value
3 a diagram or illustration
4 a shape
5 the shape of a person's body
6 a person
7 a representation of a person or animal in
painting etc.

figure VERB
to appear or take part in something
figure out to work something out

figurehead NOUN
an important person with no real power

figure of speech NOUN **figures of speech**
a word or phrase used for special effect,
e.g. *a flood of letters*

filament NOUN
a thin wire in a light bulb, which gives out light

filch VERB
(*informal*) to steal in a sly way

file¹ NOUN
a metal tool with a rough surface, rubbed on
wood or metal to shape or smooth it

file VERB
to shape or smooth with a file

file² NOUN
1 a folder or box for keeping papers in order
2 a collection of data stored under one name
in a computer
3 a line of people one behind the other

file VERB
1 to put into a file
2 to walk in a file

fill VERB
1 to make or become full
2 to block up a hole or cavity
3 to do the work involved in a job

fillet NOUN
a piece of fish or meat without bones

fillet VERB
to remove the bones from fish or meat

filling NOUN
1 something used to fill a hole or gap
2 something put in a pie or sandwich

filling station NOUN
a place where petrol is sold from pumps

filly NOUN **fillies**
a young female horse

film NOUN
1 a motion picture shown in cinemas or on
television
2 a strip of thin plastic coated with material
that is sensitive to light, used for taking
photographs
3 a thin layer *a film of grease*

film VERB
to record on film

filter NOUN
a device for holding back dirt or other
unwanted material from a liquid or gas etc.
that passes through it

filter VERB
to pass through a filter

filth NOUN
disgusting dirt

filthy ADJECTIVE **filthier, filthiest**
1 disgustingly dirty
2 obscene or offensive

fin NOUN
1 a thin flat part on the body of a fish
2 a flat piece on an aircraft or rocket

final ADJECTIVE
1 last
2 not allowing disagreement
finally ADVERB

final NOUN
the last in a series of contests

finale (fin-**ah**-lee) NOUN
the last section of a piece of music

finalist NOUN
a competitor in a final

finalize VERB
to put into a final form

finance NOUN
1 the use of money
2 money paying for something
finances PLURAL NOUN
money resources; funds
finance VERB
to provide the money for
financier NOUN

financial ADJECTIVE
to do with finance
financially ADVERB

finch NOUN
a small bird with a short bill

find VERB **found**
1 to get or see by looking or by chance
2 to learn by experience *He found that it was hard work.*
3 to decide and give a verdict *The jury found him guilty.*
find out to get or discover information
find NOUN
something useful that has been found

findings PLURAL NOUN
conclusions from an investigation

fine [1] ADJECTIVE
1 of high quality; excellent
2 (of weather) dry and sunny
3 very thin; consisting of small particles
4 in good health
finely ADVERB

fine [2] NOUN
money which has to be paid as a punishment
fine VERB
to impose a fine on

fine arts PLURAL NOUN
painting, sculpture, and music

finery NOUN
fine clothes or decorations

finesse (fin-**ess**) NOUN
skill and elegance in doing something

finger NOUN
1 each of the separate parts of the hand
2 a narrow piece of something
finger VERB
to touch or feel with your fingers

fingerprint NOUN
a mark made by the tiny ridges on the fingertip, used as a means of identification

finicky ADJECTIVE
fussy about details

finish VERB
to bring or come to an end
finish NOUN
1 the last stage of something
2 the surface or coating on a surface

finite (**fy**-nyt) ADJECTIVE
limited in amount or size

fir NOUN
an evergreen tree that produces cones

fire NOUN
1 the process of burning that produces light and heat
2 material burning to give heat
3 a device using electricity or gas to heat a room
4 the shooting of guns *Hold your fire!*
fire VERB
1 to set fire to
2 to bake pottery or bricks in a kiln
3 to shoot a gun or missile
4 to dismiss from a job
5 to excite

firearm NOUN
a small gun or pistol

fire brigade NOUN
a team of firefighters

fire drill NOUN
a rehearsal of the procedure that needs to be followed in case of a fire

fire engine NOUN
a large vehicle that carries firefighters and equipment to put out large fires

firefighter NOUN
a person trained to put out fires

firefly NOUN **fireflies**
a kind of beetle that gives off a glowing light

fireman NOUN **firemen**
a male firefighter

fireplace NOUN
an open structure for holding a fire in a room

firework NOUN
a device containing chemicals that shoot out coloured patterns when lit

firing squad NOUN
a group of soldiers ordered to shoot a condemned person

firm NOUN
a business organization

firm ADJECTIVE
1 not giving way when pressed
2 steady; not shaking or moving
3 definite and not changing *a firm belief*
firmly ADVERB

first ADJECTIVE
coming before all others in time or order
firstly ADVERB

first ADVERB
before everything else *Finish this first.*

first NOUN
a person or thing that is first

first aid NOUN
treatment given to an injured person

first-class ADJECTIVE
1 using the best class of a service
2 excellent

first-hand ADJECTIVE, ADVERB
obtained directly *first-hand experience*

fish NOUN **fish** or **fishes**
an animal that lives in water and breathes through gills

fish VERB
to try to catch fish

fisherman NOUN **fishermen**
a person who tries to catch fish

fishmonger NOUN
a shopkeeper who sells fish

fishy ADJECTIVE **fishier, fishiest**
1 smelling or tasting of fish
2 (*informal*) doubtful or suspicious

fission NOUN
the splitting of the nucleus of an atom to release energy

fissure (fish-er) NOUN
a narrow opening or crack

fist NOUN
a tightly closed hand

fit [1] ADJECTIVE **fitter, fittest**
1 suitable or good enough *a meal fit for a king*
2 in good physical condition
3 ready or likely *fit to collapse*
fitness NOUN

fit VERB
1 to be the right size and shape
2 to put into place *to fit a lock*
3 to alter or make suitable

fit NOUN
the way something fits *a good fit*

fit [2] NOUN
an attack of an illness, laughter, etc.

fitful ADJECTIVE
happening in short periods, not steadily
fitfully ADVERB

fitting ADJECTIVE
proper or suitable

fitting NOUN
something fixed or fitted

five NOUN, ADJECTIVE
the number 5

fix VERB
1 to fasten or place firmly
2 to make permanent
3 to decide or arrange *fix a date for the party*
4 to repair

fix NOUN
(*informal*) an awkward situation

fixation NOUN
a strong interest or a concentration on one idea

fixture NOUN
1 something fixed in its place
2 a sports event arranged for a particular day

fizz VERB
to make a hissing sound

fizzle VERB
to make a slight fizzing sound

fizzy ADJECTIVE **fizzier, fizziest**
(of a drink) having a lot of small bubbles

flabbergasted ADJECTIVE
very surprised

flabby ADJECTIVE **flabbier, flabbiest**
fat and soft, not firm
flabbiness NOUN

flag NOUN
1 a piece of cloth with a distinctive pattern on it, used as the symbol of a country or organization
2 a slab of stone

flag VERB **flagging, flagged**
1 to become tired or weak
2 to signal with a flag or by waving

flagon NOUN
a large bottle or container for wine or cider

flagrant (flay-gruhnt) ADJECTIVE
very bad and noticeable *flagrant rudeness*

flagship NOUN
a ship that carries an admiral

flair NOUN
a natural ability or talent *a flair for languages*
Do not confuse this word with *flare*.

flak NOUN
1 shells fired by anti-aircraft guns
2 strong criticism

flake NOUN
1 a very light thin piece of something
2 a small flat piece of falling snow
flaky ADJECTIVE

flake VERB
come off in flakes

flamboyant ADJECTIVE
very showy in appearance or manner

flame NOUN
a tongue-shaped portion of fire or burning gas

flame VERB
to produce flames

flamenco NOUN
a lively Spanish style of guitar playing and dance

flamingo NOUN **flamingos**
a wading bird with long legs and pale pink feathers

flammable ADJECTIVE
able to be set on fire

flan NOUN
a tart open on top

flank NOUN
the side of an animal's body or an army

flannel NOUN
1 a soft cloth for washing
2 a soft woollen material

flap VERB **flapping, flapped**
1 to wave about
2 (informal) to fuss or panic

flap NOUN
1 a covering part that is fixed at one edge
2 the action or sound of flapping
3 (informal) a fuss or panic

flare VERB
1 to blaze with a sudden bright flame
2 to become angry suddenly
3 to become gradually wider

flare NOUN
1 a sudden bright flame or light, especially one used as a signal
2 a gradual widening
Do not confuse this word with *flair*.

flash NOUN
1 a sudden bright flame or light
2 a device for making a sudden bright light for taking photographs
3 a sudden display of anger, wit, etc.

flash VERB
1 to make a flash
2 to appear or move quickly

flashback NOUN
a scene in a film or story that goes back to earlier events

flashy ADJECTIVE **flashier, flashiest**
gaudy or showy

flask NOUN
1 a bottle with a narrow neck
2 a container for keeping drinks hot

flat ADJECTIVE **flatter, flattest**
1 having no curves or bumps; smooth and level
2 lying at full length *flat on the ground*
3 (of a tyre) having no air inside
4 (of the feet) without the normal arch underneath
5 complete *a flat refusal*
6 dull; not changing
7 (of a drink) no longer fizzy
8 (of a battery) unable to produce any more electric current
9 (*Music*) one semitone lower than the natural note
flat out as fast as possible

flat NOUN
1 a set of rooms on one floor for living in
2 a punctured tyre

flatten VERB
to make or become flat

flatter VERB
1 to praise someone insincerely
2 to make a person or thing seem more attractive than they really are
flattery NOUN

flaunt VERB
to display in a showy way
Do not confuse this word with *flout*.

flavour NOUN
1 the taste of something
2 a characteristic quality

flavour VERB
to give a flavour to
flavouring NOUN

flaw NOUN
a fault or imperfection
flawed ADJECTIVE

flawless ADJECTIVE
without a flaw; perfect

flax NOUN
a plant producing fibres from which linen is made

flay VERB
to strip the skin from a dead animal

flea NOUN
a small jumping insect that sucks blood

fleck NOUN
1 a small patch of colour
2 a particle or speck
flecked ADJECTIVE

fledgling *NOUN*
a young bird when its feathers have grown

flee *VERB* **fled**
to run or hurry away

fleece *NOUN*
1 the woolly hair of a sheep or similar animal
2 a soft warm article of clothing
fleecy *ADJECTIVE*

fleet *NOUN*
a number of ships, aircraft, or vehicles

fleeting *ADJECTIVE*
passing quickly

flesh *NOUN*
1 the soft substance of the bodies of people and animals
2 the body as opposed to the mind or soul
3 the soft part of fruit
fleshy *ADJECTIVE*

flex *VERB*
to bend or stretch

flex *NOUN*
flexible insulated wire for carrying electric current

flexible *ADJECTIVE*
1 easy to bend or stretch
2 able to be changed
flexibility *NOUN*

flick *NOUN*
a quick light hit or movement

flick *VERB*
to hit or move with a flick

flicker *VERB*
1 to burn or shine unsteadily
2 to move quickly to and fro

flicker *NOUN*
a flickering light or movement

flight *NOUN*
1 the act of flying
2 a journey in an aircraft
3 an escape
4 a series of stairs or steps
5 a group of flying birds or aircraft

flighty *ADJECTIVE* **flightier, flightiest**
silly and frivolous

flimsy *ADJECTIVE* **flimsier, flimsiest**
thin and weak

flinch *VERB*
to move or shrink back from fear or pain

fling *VERB* **flung**
to throw hard or carelessly

fling *NOUN*
1 a brief time of enjoyment
2 a brief romantic affair
3 a vigorous dance

flint *NOUN*
a hard kind of stone

flip *VERB* **flipping, flipped**
1 to flick
2 (*informal*) to lose your temper

flip *NOUN*
a flipping movement

flippant *ADJECTIVE*
not showing proper seriousness
flippancy *NOUN*

flipper *NOUN*
1 a limb that some water-living animals use for swimming
2 a flat rubber shoe worn for swimming

flirt *VERB*
to behave as though sexually attracted to someone to amuse yourself
flirtation *NOUN*

flirt *NOUN*
a person who flirts
flirtatious *ADJECTIVE*

flit *VERB* **flitting, flitted**
to fly or move lightly and quickly
flit *NOUN*

flitter *VERB*
to flit about

float *VERB*
1 to stay on the surface of a liquid or in air
2 to make something float

float *NOUN*
1 a device that floats
2 a display vehicle in a procession

flock[1] *NOUN*
a group of sheep, goats, or birds

flock *VERB*
to gather or move in a crowd

flock[2] *NOUN*
a tuft of wool or cotton

floe *NOUN*
a sheet of floating ice

flog *VERB* **flogging, flogged**
1 to beat or whip
2 (*informal*) to sell

flood *NOUN*
1 a large amount of water spreading over a place
2 a huge amount

flood *VERB*
1 to cover with a flood
2 to come in great amounts

floodlight *NOUN*
a lamp with a broad bright beam to light up a building or public place
floodlit *ADJECTIVE*

floor *NOUN*
1 the part of a room that people walk on
2 a storey of a building; all the rooms at the same level

floor

floor VERB
1 to put a floor into a building
2 (*informal*) to knock someone down
3 (*informal*) to baffle someone

floorboard NOUN
one of the boards forming the floor of a room

flop VERB **flopping**, **flopped**
1 to fall or sit down clumsily
2 to hang or sway heavily and loosely
3 (*informal*) to fail

flop NOUN
1 a flopping movement or sound
2 (*informal*) a failure

floppy ADJECTIVE **floppier**, **floppiest**
hanging loosely; not firm or rigid
floppiness NOUN

floppy disk NOUN
(*ICT*) a flexible disc holding data for use in a computer

flora NOUN
the plants of a particular area or period

floral ADJECTIVE
made with flowers

florid (**flo**-rid) ADJECTIVE
1 red and flushed
2 elaborate and ornate

florist NOUN
a seller of flowers

floss NOUN
1 silky thread or fibres
2 a soft medicated thread pulled between the teeth to clean them

flotilla NOUN
a fleet of boats or small ships

flotsam NOUN
objects found floating after a shipwreck

flounce[1] VERB
to move in an impatient or annoyed manner
flounce NOUN

flounce[2] NOUN
a wide frill

flounder VERB
1 to move clumsily
2 to make mistakes

flour NOUN
a fine powder of wheat or other grain, used in cooking
floury ADJECTIVE

flourish VERB
1 to grow or develop strongly
2 to be successful
3 to wave about dramatically

flourish NOUN
a showy or dramatic sweeping movement or stroke

fluorescent

flout VERB
to disobey a rule or instruction openly
Do not confuse this word with *flaunt*.

flow VERB
1 to move along smoothly or continuously
2 to gush out
3 to hang loosely *flowing hair*
4 (of the tide) to come in towards the land

flow NOUN
1 a flowing movement or mass
2 a steady continuous stream *a flow of ideas*
3 the movement of the tide when it is coming in

flower NOUN
1 the part of a plant from which seed and fruit develop
2 a blossom and its stem
flowery ADJECTIVE

flower VERB
to produce flowers

flu NOUN
influenza

fluctuate VERB
to rise and fall
fluctuation NOUN

flue NOUN
a pipe or tube through which smoke or hot gases are drawn off

fluent (**floo**-ent) ADJECTIVE
1 skilful at speaking clearly
2 able to speak a foreign language well
fluency NOUN

fluff NOUN
a fluffy substance

fluff VERB
(*informal*) to make a small mistake

fluffy ADJECTIVE **fluffier**, **fluffiest**
having a mass of soft fur or fibres

fluid NOUN
a substance able to flow freely as liquids and gases do

fluid ADJECTIVE
1 able to flow freely
2 not fixed or definite
fluidity NOUN

fluke NOUN
a success achieved by luck

flummox VERB
(*informal*) to baffle

fluorescent ADJECTIVE
creating light from radiation
fluorescence NOUN

fluoridation NOUN
the process of adding fluoride to drinking water

fluoride NOUN
a chemical substance that is thought to prevent tooth decay

flurry NOUN **flurries**
1 a sudden whirling gust of wind, rain, or snow
2 a short period of activity or excitement

flush[1] VERB
1 to blush
2 to clean or remove with a fast flow of water

flush NOUN
1 a blush
2 a fast flow of water
3 (in card games) a hand of cards of the same suit

flush[2] ADJECTIVE
1 level with the surrounding surface
2 having plenty of money

fluster VERB
to make nervous and confused
fluster NOUN

flute NOUN
a musical instrument consisting of a long pipe held across the mouth, with holes stopped by fingers or keys

flutter VERB
1 to flap the wings quickly
2 to move or flap quickly and irregularly

flutter NOUN
a fluttering state or movement

flux NOUN
constant change or flow

fly[1] NOUN **flies**
1 a small flying insect
2 an artificial fly used as bait in fishing
3 the front opening of a pair of trousers

fly[2] VERB **flies**, **flew**, **flown**
1 to move through the air with wings or in an aircraft
2 (of a flag) to wave in the air
3 to move or pass quickly
4 to flee from a place
flyer NOUN

flyover NOUN
a bridge carrying one road or railway over another

flywheel NOUN
a heavy wheel used to regulate machinery

foal NOUN
a young horse

foam NOUN
1 a white mass of tiny bubbles on liquid
2 a spongy kind of rubber or plastic
foamy ADJECTIVE

foam VERB
to form bubbles

fob[1] NOUN
1 a chain for a pocket watch
2 a tab on a key ring

fob[2] VERB **fobbing**, **fobbed**
fob off to get rid of someone with an excuse

focal ADJECTIVE
to do with or at a focus

focus NOUN
1 the distance from an eye or lens at which an object appears clearest
2 the point at which rays seem to meet
3 something that is a centre of interest or attention

focus VERB
1 to adjust the focus of
2 to concentrate

fodder NOUN
food for horses and farm animals

foe NOUN
(*literary*) an enemy

fog NOUN
thick mist
foggy ADJECTIVE

fogy NOUN **fogies**
a person with old-fashioned ideas

foible NOUN
a slight peculiarity in someone's character

foil[1] NOUN
1 a thin sheet of metal
2 a person or thing that makes another look better in contrast

foil[2] NOUN
a long narrow sword used in fencing

foil[3] VERB
to prevent from being successful

foist VERB
to make a person accept something inferior or unwelcome

fold[1] VERB
to bend or move so that one part lies on another part

fold NOUN
a line where something is folded

fold[2] NOUN
an enclosure for sheep

folder NOUN
a folding cover for loose papers

foliage NOUN
the leaves of a tree or plant

folk PLURAL NOUN
people

folklore NOUN
old beliefs and legends

follow VERB
1 to go or come after
2 to do a thing after something else
3 to take as a guide or example
4 to take an interest in the progress of
5 to understand
6 to result from

follower NOUN
a supporter or disciple

folly NOUN **follies**
1 foolishness
2 a foolish action

foment (fo-**ment**) VERB
to arouse or stimulate deliberately
  Do not confuse this word with *ferment*.

fond ADJECTIVE
1 loving or liking a person or thing
2 (of hopes) foolishly optimistic

fondle VERB
to touch or stroke lovingly

font NOUN
1 a basin in a church, for holding water
for baptism
2 a set of characters in printing

food NOUN
a substance that an animal or plant can take
into its body to help it to grow

fool NOUN
1 a silly person
2 a jester or clown
3 a creamy pudding with crushed fruit in it

fool VERB
1 to behave in a joking way
2 to trick or deceive

foolhardy ADJECTIVE
bold but foolish; reckless

foolish ADJECTIVE
not having good sense or judgement; unwise

foolproof ADJECTIVE
easy to use or do correctly

foot NOUN
1 the lower part of the leg below the ankle
2 the lowest part *the foot of the hill*
3 a measure of length, 12 inches or about 30
centimetres
4 a unit of rhythm in a line of poetry

footage NOUN
a length of film

football NOUN
1 a game played by two teams which try to
kick a ball into their opponents' goal
2 the ball used in this game
footballer NOUN

foothold NOUN
a place to put your foot when climbing

footing NOUN
1 balance with the foot *to lose your footing*
2 the nature of a relationship
on a friendly footing

footnote NOUN
a note printed at the bottom of the page

footpath NOUN
a path for pedestrians

footprint NOUN
a mark made by a foot or shoe

footstep NOUN
1 a step taken in walking or running
2 the sound of this

for PREPOSITION
1 sent to or intended for *a letter for you*
2 in the direction of *set out for home*
3 during or over *walk for three hours*
4 at the price of *We bought it for £50.*
5 because of *fined for speeding*
6 in support of *to play for your country*
7 in order to get *doing it for the money*
for ever for all time; always

for CONJUNCTION
because *They hesitated, for they were afraid.*

forage VERB
to go searching for food or fuel

foray NOUN
a sudden attack or raid

forbear VERB **forbears**, **forbearing**,
forbore, **forborne**
to refrain from something *We forbore to
mention it.*

forbearance NOUN
patience with someone or something difficult
or tiresome

forbid VERB **forbade**, **forbidden**
1 to order someone not to do something
2 to refuse to allow

forbidding ADJECTIVE
unfriendly in appearance

force NOUN
1 strength or power
2 (*Science*) an influence, which can be
measured, that causes something to move
3 an organized group of police, soldiers, etc.

force VERB
1 to use force to get or do something; to
make or compel
2 to break open by force

forceful ADJECTIVE
strong and vigorous

forceps NOUN
pincers or tongs used by surgeons and
dentists

forcible ADJECTIVE
done by force; forceful
forcibly ADVERB

ford NOUN
a shallow place for crossing a river on foot

fore ADJECTIVE, ADVERB
at or towards the front *fore and aft*

fore NOUN
the front part

forearm NOUN
the arm from the elbow to the wrist or
fingertips

forebears PLURAL NOUN
ancestors

foreboding NOUN
a feeling that trouble is coming

forecast NOUN
a statement about the future

forecast VERB **forecast**
to make a forecast

forecourt NOUN
an enclosed area in front of a building

forefathers PLURAL NOUN
ancestors

forefinger NOUN
the finger next to the thumb

forefront NOUN
the very front

foregoing ADJECTIVE
preceding; previously mentioned

foregone conclusion NOUN
a result that is inevitable

foreground NOUN
the part of a scene, picture, or view that is
nearest to you

forehand NOUN
a stroke made in tennis with the palm of the
hand turned forwards

forehead NOUN
the part of the face above the eyes

foreign ADJECTIVE
1 belonging to another country
2 not belonging naturally *a foreign body*

foreigner NOUN
a person from another country

foreleg NOUN
an animal's front leg

foreman NOUN **foremen**
1 a worker in charge of a group of workers
2 the leader of a jury

foremost ADJECTIVE, ADVERB
first in position or rank

forensic (fer-**en**-sik) ADJECTIVE
to do with or used in lawcourts

forerunner NOUN
a person or thing that comes before another

foresee VERB **foresaw**, **foreseen**
to realize what is going to happen

foreshadow VERB
to be a sign of something to come

foresight NOUN
the ability to foresee and prepare for
future needs

foreskin NOUN
the fold of skin covering the tip of the penis

forest NOUN
trees and undergrowth covering a large area
forested ADJECTIVE

forestall VERB
to prevent somebody or something by taking
action first

forestry NOUN
the planting and care of forests

foretell VERB **foretold**
to tell in advance; to prophesy

forethought NOUN
careful thought and planning for the future

forewarn VERB
to warn beforehand

foreword NOUN
a preface

forfeit (for-fit) VERB
to pay or give up something as a penalty
forfeiture NOUN

forfeit NOUN
something forfeited

forge¹ NOUN
a place where metal is heated and shaped;
a blacksmith's workshop

forge VERB
1 to shape metal by heating and hammering
2 to copy something in order to
deceive people
forgery NOUN

forge² VERB
forge ahead to move forward steadily

forget VERB **forgetting**, **forgot**, **forgotten**
1 to fail to remember
2 to stop thinking about

forgetful ADJECTIVE
tending to forget
forgetfully ADVERB

forget-me-not NOUN
a plant with small blue flowers

forgive VERB **forgave**, **forgiven**
to stop feeling angry with somebody about
something
forgiveness NOUN

forgo *VERB* **forgoes**, **forwent**, **forgone**
to give up or go without

fork *NOUN*
1 a small tool with prongs for lifting food to your mouth
2 a large tool with prongs used for digging or lifting
3 a place where something divides into two or more parts

fork *VERB*
1 to lift or dig with a fork
2 to divide into branches
3 to follow one of these branches *Fork left after a mile.*
fork out (*informal*) to pay out money

forlorn *ADJECTIVE*
alone and unhappy
forlorn hope the only faint hope left

form *NOUN*
1 the shape, appearance, or condition of something
2 the way something exists
Ice is a form of water.
3 a class in school
4 a bench
5 a piece of paper with spaces to be filled in

form *VERB*
1 to shape or construct something
2 to come into existence *Icicles formed.*

formal *ADJECTIVE*
1 strictly following the accepted rules or customs
2 serious and stiff in manner
formally *ADVERB*

formality *NOUN* **formalities**
1 formal behaviour
2 something done to obey a rule or custom

format *NOUN*
1 the shape and size of something
2 the way something is arranged or organized
3 (*ICT*) the way data is organized for processing or storage by a computer

format *VERB* **formatting**, **formatted**
(*ICT*) to organize data in the correct format

formation *NOUN*
a special arrangement or pattern

formative *ADJECTIVE*
forming or developing something

former *ADJECTIVE*
of an earlier time
the former the first of two people or things mentioned

formerly *ADVERB*
at an earlier time; previously

formidable (for-mid-a-bul) *ADJECTIVE*
1 difficult to deal with or do *a formidable task*
2 frightening

formula *NOUN* **formulae** or **formulas**
1 (*Science*) a set of chemical symbols
2 a list of substances
3 a fixed wording

formulate *VERB*
to express an idea or plan clearly and exactly
formulation *NOUN*

forsake *VERB* **forsook**, **forsaken**
to desert or abandon

fort *NOUN*
a fortified building

forth *ADVERB*
onwards or forwards
and so forth and so on

forthcoming *ADJECTIVE*
1 happening soon
2 willing to give information

forthright *ADJECTIVE*
frank and outspoken

forthwith *ADVERB*
immediately

fortification *NOUN*
a wall or building built to make a place strong against attack

fortify *VERB* **fortifies**, **fortified**
1 to make a place strong against attack
2 to strengthen

fortitude *NOUN*
courage in bearing pain or trouble

fortnight *NOUN*
a period of two weeks
fortnightly *ADVERB*, *ADJECTIVE*

fortress *NOUN*
a fortified building or town

fortuitous *ADJECTIVE*
happening by chance; accidental
fortuitously *ADVERB*
Note that this word does not mean the same as *fortunate*.

fortunate *ADJECTIVE*
lucky
fortunately *ADVERB*

fortune *NOUN*
1 good luck
2 a large amount of money

forty *NOUN*, *ADJECTIVE* **forties**
the number 40
forty winks a short light sleep
fortieth *ADJECTIVE*, *NOUN*

forum *NOUN*
a meeting for public discussion

forward *ADJECTIVE*
1 placed or going forwards
2 having made more than the normal progress
3 too bold

forward ADVERB
forwards

forward NOUN
a player in the front line of a team

forward VERB
1 to send on a letter to a new address
2 to help to make progress

forwards ADVERB
1 to or towards the front
2 in the direction you are facing

fossil NOUN
the remains or traces of a prehistoric animal
hardened in rock
fossilized ADJECTIVE

fossil fuel NOUN
a natural fuel such as coal or gas that is
formed from the remains of plants and
animals

fossilize VERB
to turn into a fossil
fossilization NOUN

foster VERB
1 to bring up someone else's child as your own
2 to help to grow or develop

foster child NOUN
a child who is fostered

foster parent NOUN
a parent who fosters a child

foul ADJECTIVE
1 tasting or smelling unpleasant
2 (of weather) rough or stormy
3 breaking the rules of a game
foully ADVERB

foul NOUN
an action that breaks the rules of a game

foul VERB
1 to make or become foul
2 to commit a foul against

foul play NOUN
a violent crime, especially murder

found[1] *past tense* of **find**

found[2] VERB
to establish or provide money for

foundation NOUN
1 the solid base on which a building stands
2 the founding of something
3 a charitable institution

founder[1] NOUN
a person who founds an institution

founder[2] VERB
1 (of a ship) to fill with water and sink
2 to stumble or fall
3 to fail completely

foundling NOUN
a child found abandoned

foundry NOUN **foundries**
a factory or workshop where metal or glass
is made

fount NOUN
a fountain

fountain NOUN
a structure in which a jet of water shoots up
into the air

four NOUN, ADJECTIVE
the number 4
fourth ADJECTIVE, NOUN

fourteen NOUN, ADJECTIVE
the number 14
fourteenth ADJECTIVE, NOUN

fowl NOUN
a bird, especially one kept for its eggs or meat

fox NOUN
a wild animal that looks like a dog with a long
furry tail

fox VERB
to deceive or puzzle

foxglove NOUN
a tall plant with flowers like the fingers
of gloves

foyer (foy-ay) NOUN
the entrance hall of a theatre or large building

fraction NOUN
1 a number that is not a whole number,
e.g. ½, 0.5
2 a tiny part

fractious (frak-shus) ADJECTIVE
irritable
fractiously ADVERB **fractiousness** NOUN

fracture NOUN
the breaking of a bone in the body

fracture VERB
to break

fragile ADJECTIVE
easy to break or damage
fragility NOUN

fragment NOUN
1 a small piece broken off
2 a small part
fragmentary ADJECTIVE

fragrant ADJECTIVE
having a pleasant smell
fragrance NOUN

frail ADJECTIVE
1 not strong or healthy
2 fragile
frailty NOUN

frame NOUN
1 a holder that fits round the outside of a picture
2 a rigid structure that supports something
3 a human or animal body *He has a small frame.*
4 a single exposure on a cinema film
frame of mind the way you think or feel for a while

frame VERB
1 to put a frame on or round
2 to incriminate

framework NOUN
1 a frame supporting something
2 a basic plan or system

franchise NOUN
1 the right to vote in elections
2 a licence to sell a firm's goods or services in a certain area

frank ADJECTIVE
making your thoughts and feelings clear
frankly ADVERB

frantic ADJECTIVE
wildly agitated or excited
frantically ADVERB

fraternal (fra-**tern**-al) ADJECTIVE
to do with brothers; brotherly
fraternally ADVERB

fraternity NOUN **fraternities**
1 a brotherly feeling
2 a group of people with the same interest

fraternize VERB
to associate with other people in a friendly way
fraternization NOUN

fraud NOUN
1 the crime of swindling people
2 a fake

fraudulent (**fraw**-dew-lent) ADJECTIVE
involving fraud; deceitful or dishonest

fraught ADJECTIVE
1 tense or upset
2 filled with *fraught with danger*

fray [1] NOUN
a fight or conflict *ready for the fray*

fray [2] VERB
1 to become ragged with loose threads
2 (of tempers or nerves) to become strained

freak NOUN
a strange or abnormal person or thing
freakish ADJECTIVE

freckle NOUN
a small brown spot on the skin
freckled ADJECTIVE

free ADJECTIVE **freer**, **freest**
1 able to do what you want
2 not costing any money
3 not fixed
4 not having or being affected by something
5 not being used or occupied
6 generous *very free with their money*
freely ADVERB

free VERB
to set free

freedom NOUN
the state of being free; independence

freehand ADJECTIVE, ADVERB
(of a drawing) done without the aid of instruments

freehold NOUN
the possession of land or a house as its absolute owner

free-range ADJECTIVE
(of poultry) not caged but allowed to move about freely

freeway NOUN
(*American*) a motorway

freewheel VERB
to ride a bicycle without pedalling

freeze VERB **froze**, **frozen**
1 to turn into ice
2 to make or be very cold
3 to keep at a fixed level
4 to become still

freeze NOUN
1 a period of freezing weather
2 the freezing of wages or prices

freezer NOUN
a refrigerator in which food can be frozen quickly and stored

freight (frayt) NOUN
goods transported as cargo

freighter NOUN
a ship or aircraft carrying cargo

frenzy NOUN **frenzies**
a state of wild excitement
frenzied ADJECTIVE

frequency NOUN **frequencies**
1 the rate at which something happens
2 the number of vibrations made each second by a wave of sound, radio, or light

frequent (**freek**-went) ADJECTIVE
happening often
frequently ADVERB

frequent (frik-**wuhnt**) VERB
to visit a place often

fresco NOUN **frescoes**
a picture painted on a wall or ceiling when the plaster is still wet

fresh ADJECTIVE
1 newly made or arrived; not stale
2 not tinned or preserved *fresh fruit*
3 cool and clean *fresh air*
4 (of water) not salty
5 cheeky

freshen VERB
to make or become fresh

freshwater ADJECTIVE
living in rivers or lakes, not the sea

fret¹ VERB
to worry or be upset
fretful ADJECTIVE

fret² NOUN
a bar or ridge on the neck of a guitar

friar NOUN
a male member of a Roman Catholic religious
order who has vowed to live a life of poverty
friary NOUN

friction NOUN
1 the rubbing of one thing against another
2 bad feeling between people
frictional ADJECTIVE

Friday NOUN
the day of the week following Thursday

fridge NOUN
a refrigerator

friend NOUN
a person you like who likes you

friendly ADJECTIVE **friendlier, friendliest**
behaving like a friend
friendliness NOUN

friendship NOUN
being friends

frieze (freez) NOUN
a strip of designs round a wall

fright NOUN
1 a sudden great fear
2 a person or thing that looks ugly or
ridiculous

frighten VERB
to make or become afraid
frightened ADJECTIVE

frightful ADJECTIVE
awful; very great or bad
frightfully ADVERB

frigid ADJECTIVE
1 extremely cold
2 unfriendly

frill NOUN
1 a gathered or pleated trimming on a dress
or curtain
2 an unnecessary extra benefit
frilly ADJECTIVE

fringe NOUN
1 a decorative edging with threads hanging
down loosely
2 a straight line of hair over the forehead
3 the edge of something

frisk VERB
1 to jump or run about playfully
2 to search somebody by running the hands
over their clothes

frisky ADJECTIVE **friskier, friskiest**
playful or lively
friskily ADVERB

fritter¹ NOUN
a slice of meat, potato, or fruit coated in
batter and fried

fritter² VERB
to waste time or money gradually

frivolous ADJECTIVE
seeking pleasure in a light-hearted way
frivolity NOUN

frizzy ADJECTIVE **frizzier, frizziest**
(of hair) in tight curls

fro ADVERB
to and fro backwards and forwards

frock NOUN
a girl's or woman's dress

frog NOUN
a small jumping animal that can live both in
water and on land

frogman NOUN **frogmen**
a swimmer equipped to swim underwater

frolic NOUN
a lively cheerful game or entertainment

frolic VERB **frolicking, frolicked**
to play about in a lively cheerful way

from PREPOSITION
1 used to show a starting point in space or
time or order *from London to Paris*
from 9 a.m. to 5 p.m.
2 used to show separation *Take the gun
from him.*
3 used to show origin or cause *I suffer from
headaches.*

front NOUN
1 the part or side that comes first or is the
most important or furthest forward
2 the place where fighting is happening in a
war
3 an approaching mass of air
frontal ADJECTIVE

front ADJECTIVE
of the front; in front

frontier NOUN
the boundary between two countries or
regions

frost NOUN
1 powdery ice that forms on surfaces in freezing weather
2 weather with a temperature below freezing point

frost VERB
to cover with frost

frostbite NOUN
harm done to the body by very cold weather
frostbitten ADJECTIVE

frosty ADJECTIVE **frostier, frostiest**
1 cold with frost
2 unfriendly and unwelcoming
frostily ADVERB

froth NOUN
a white mass of tiny bubbles on liquid
frothy ADJECTIVE

frown VERB
to wrinkle your forehead when angry or worried

frown NOUN
a frowning movement or look

frugal (froo-gal) ADJECTIVE
1 spending little money
2 costing very little *a frugal meal*
frugally ADVERB

fruit NOUN
1 the seed container that grows on a tree or plant
2 a good result of doing something
fruity ADJECTIVE

fruitful ADJECTIVE
having good results

fruitless ADJECTIVE
producing no results

frustrate VERB
to prevent from doing something or from happening
frustration NOUN

fry[1] VERB **fries, fried**
to cook in hot fat
fryer NOUN

fry[2] PLURAL NOUN
very young fish

fudge[1] NOUN
a soft sugary sweet

fudge[2] VERB
to avoid giving clear information

fuel NOUN
something that is burned to produce heat or power

fuel VERB **fuelling, fuelled**
to supply with fuel

fug NOUN
(*informal*) a stuffy atmosphere in a room

fugitive (few-jit-iv) NOUN
a person who is running away from the authorities

fulcrum NOUN
the point on which a lever is placed

fulfil VERB **fulfilling, fulfilled**
to perform or complete
fulfilment NOUN

full ADJECTIVE
1 containing as much or as many as possible
2 having many people or things *full of ideas*
3 complete *the full story*
4 the greatest possible *at full speed*
5 fitting loosely; with many folds *a full skirt*
in full with nothing left out

full ADVERB
completely and directly *It hit him full in the face.*

full moon NOUN
the moon when it is visible as a complete disc

full stop NOUN
the dot used as a punctuation mark at the end of a sentence

fully ADVERB
completely

fumble VERB
to hold or handle clumsily

fume VERB
1 to give off fumes
2 to be very angry

fumes PLURAL NOUN
strong-smelling smoke or gas

fun NOUN
amusement or enjoyment
make fun of to make people laugh at

function NOUN
1 a role or purpose
2 an important event
3 a basic computer operation
4 (*Maths*) a variable quantity whose value depends on the value of other variable quantities

function VERB
1 to perform a function
2 to work properly

functional ADJECTIVE
1 working properly
2 useful

fund NOUN
1 money collected
2 a stock or supply

fund VERB
to supply with money

fundamental ADJECTIVE
basic; essential
fundamentally ADVERB

funeral NOUN
the ceremony of burying or cremating a dead person

funereal (few-**neer**-ee-al) ADJECTIVE
gloomy or depressing

funfair NOUN
a fair consisting of amusements and sideshows

fungus NOUN **fungi**
a plant that grows on decayed material, such as a mushroom or a toadstool

funk NOUN
a style of popular music with a strong beat, based on jazz and blues

funky ADJECTIVE **funkier**, **funkiest**
1 (of music) having a strong beat
2 fashionable; trendy

funnel NOUN
1 a metal chimney on a ship or steam engine
2 a narrowing tube for pouring things into a narrow opening

funny ADJECTIVE **funnier**, **funniest**
1 that makes you laugh or smile
2 strange or odd *a funny smell*
funnily ADVERB

fur NOUN
1 the soft hair on some animals
2 animal skin with the fur on it, used for clothing

furious ADJECTIVE
1 very angry
2 violent or intense *furious heat*
furiously ADVERB

furlong NOUN
one-eighth of a mile, 220 yards

furniture NOUN
tables, chairs, and other movable things in a building

furrow NOUN
1 a long cut in the ground made by a plough
2 a deep groove
3 a wrinkle

furrow VERB
to make furrows in

furry ADJECTIVE **furrier**, **furriest**
like fur; covered with fur

further ADVERB, ADJECTIVE
1 at or to a greater distance
2 more; additional *further enquiries*
further VERB
to help or develop *to further your career*

furthermore ADVERB
also; moreover

furthest ADVERB, ADJECTIVE
at or to the greatest distance; most distant

furtive ADJECTIVE
stealthy; trying not to be seen

fury NOUN **furies**
wild anger or rage

furze NOUN
gorse

fuse NOUN
1 a safety device that breaks an electric circuit
2 a length of material used for setting off an explosive

fuse VERB
1 to stop working because a fuse has melted
2 to blend together

fuselage (**few**-zel-ahzh) NOUN
the main body of an aircraft

fusion NOUN
1 the action of blending or merging
2 the uniting of atomic nuclei, releasing energy

fuss NOUN
1 unnecessary excitement or bustle
2 an agitated protest

fuss VERB
to make a fuss

fussy ADJECTIVE **fussier**, **fussiest**
1 inclined to make a fuss
2 choosing very carefully
3 full of unnecessary details
fussily ADVERB **fussiness** NOUN

fusty ADJECTIVE **fustier**, **fustiest**
smelling stale or stuffy

futile ADJECTIVE
useless; having no result
futility NOUN

futon (**foo**-ton) NOUN
a padded mattress that rolls out to form a bed

future NOUN
1 the time that will come; what is going to happen
2 (*Grammar*) the tense of a verb that indicates something happening in the future, expressed by using 'shall', 'will', or 'be going to'

future ADJECTIVE
belonging or referring to the future

futuristic ADJECTIVE
very modern, as if belonging to the future

fuzz NOUN
something light or fluffy

fuzzy ADJECTIVE **fuzzier**, **fuzziest**
1 like fuzz; covered with fuzz
2 blurred; not clear

Gg

gabble *VERB*
to talk too quickly to be understood

gable *NOUN*
the pointed part at the top of an outside wall

gadget *NOUN*
a small useful tool

Gaelic (**gay**-lik) *NOUN*
the Celtic languages of Scotland and Ireland

gaffe *NOUN*
an embarrassing blunder

gag *NOUN*
1 something put into a person's mouth to prevent them speaking
2 a joke

gag *VERB* **gagging**, **gagged**
1 to put a gag on
2 to prevent from making comments
3 to retch

gaggle *NOUN*
a flock of geese

gaiety *NOUN*
cheerfulness

gaily *ADVERB*
in a cheerful way

gain *VERB*
1 to get something you did not have before
2 (of a clock or watch) to become ahead of the correct time
gain on to come closer to someone else moving

gain *NOUN*
something gained; a profit or improvement

gait *NOUN*
a way of walking or running *a shuffling gait*

gala (**gah**-la) *NOUN*
1 a festival or celebration
2 a set of sports contests

galaxy *NOUN* **galaxies**
a large group of stars
galactic *ADJECTIVE*

gale *NOUN*
a strong wind

gall *NOUN*
boldness or impudence

gallant *ADJECTIVE*
brave or heroic
gallantry *NOUN*

galleon *NOUN*
in former times, a large Spanish sailing ship

gallery *NOUN* **galleries**
1 a room or building for showing works of art
2 the highest balcony in a cinema or theatre
3 a long room or passage

galley *NOUN* **galleys**
1 an old type of ship driven by oars
2 the kitchen in a ship or aircraft

galling *ADJECTIVE*
annoying or humiliating

gallivant *VERB*
to wander about for fun

gallon *NOUN*
a unit used to measure liquids, 8 pints or 4.546 litres

gallop *NOUN*
a fast pace by a horse

gallop *VERB*
to go or ride at a gallop

gallows *NOUN*
a framework with a noose for hanging criminals

galore *ADVERB*
in large numbers *bargains galore*

galvanize *VERB*
1 to stimulate into activity
2 to coat iron with zinc to protect it from rust

gamble *VERB*
1 to bet on the result of a game, race, or other event
2 to take risks
gambler *NOUN*

gamble *NOUN*
1 a bet or chance
2 a risky attempt

gambol *VERB* **gambolling**, **gambolled**
to jump or skip about in play

game *NOUN*
1 a form of play or sport, especially one with rules
2 a scheme or trick
3 wild animals or birds hunted for sport or food

game *ADJECTIVE*
brave and enterprising

gamma *NOUN*
the third letter of the Greek alphabet, equivalent to Roman G, g

gamma rays *PLURAL NOUN*
very short X-rays emitted by radioactive substances

gammon *NOUN*
ham that has been cured like bacon

gander *NOUN*
a male goose

gang *NOUN*
1 a group of people who do things together
2 a group of criminals

gang *VERB*
gang up on to join together to fight or bully someone

gangling *ADJECTIVE*
tall, thin, and awkward-looking

gangrene (**gang**-green) *NOUN*
decay of body tissue in a living person

gangster *NOUN*
a member of a gang of violent criminals

gangway *NOUN*
1 a gap for passing between rows of seats
2 a bridge for walking on and off a ship

gannet *NOUN*
a large seabird which catches fish by diving

gaol (jayl) *NOUN*
a different spelling of **jail**
gaol *VERB* **gaoler** *NOUN*

gap *NOUN*
1 a break or opening
2 an interval

gape *VERB*
to stare with your mouth open

garage *NOUN*
1 a building for a vehicle
2 a place that services and repairs vehicles

garbage *NOUN*
household rubbish

garble *VERB*
to give a confused account of

garden *NOUN*
a piece of ground where flowers, fruit, or vegetables are grown

gardener *NOUN*
someone who looks after a garden
gardening *NOUN*

gargle *VERB*
to wash the throat by breathing air through a liquid at the back of the mouth

gargoyle *NOUN*
an ugly or comical face carved on a building

garish (**gair**-ish) *ADJECTIVE*
very bright or highly coloured

garland *NOUN*
a wreath of flowers worn or hung as a decoration

garlic *NOUN*
a plant with a bulb divided into cloves, used for flavouring food

garment *NOUN*
a piece of clothing

garnish *VERB*
to decorate food

garnish *NOUN*
a decoration on food

garrison *NOUN*
troops guarding a fortified building

garter *NOUN*
a band of elastic to hold up a sock or stocking

gas [1] *NOUN* **gases**
1 a substance, such as oxygen, that can move freely and is not liquid or solid at ordinary temperatures
2 a gas that can be burned, used as a fuel

gas *VERB* **gasses**, **gassing**, **gassed**
to kill or injure with gas

gas [2] *NOUN*
(*informal*) (*American*) short for **gasoline**

gaseous (**gas**-ee-us) *ADJECTIVE*
in the form of a gas

gash *NOUN*
a long deep cut or wound

gash *VERB*
to make a gash in

gasket *NOUN*
a layer of soft material sealing a joint between metal surfaces

gasoline *NOUN*
(*American*) petrol

gasp *VERB*
1 to breathe in suddenly from shock or surprise
2 to struggle to breathe
gasp *NOUN*

gassy *ADJECTIVE* **gassier**, **gassiest**
fizzy

gastric *ADJECTIVE*
to do with the stomach

gate *NOUN*
1 a movable barrier on hinges, used as a door in a wall or fence
2 a place for waiting to board an aircraft
3 the number of people attending a sports event

gateau (gat-oh) *NOUN* **gateaus** or **gateaux**
a large rich cream cake

gatecrash *VERB*
to go to a private party without being invited

gateway *NOUN*
an opening containing a gate

gather *VERB*
1 to come or bring together
2 to collect gradually
3 to collect as harvest
4 to understand or learn *I gather you've been ill.*
5 to pull cloth into folds

gathering *NOUN*
a meeting of people

gaudy ADJECTIVE **gaudier, gaudiest**
showy and bright
gaudily ADVERB

gauge (gayj) NOUN
1 a standard measurement
2 the distance the rails of a railway
3 a measuring instrument

gauge VERB
1 to measure
2 to estimate

gaunt ADJECTIVE
looking thin and unwell

gauntlet NOUN
a glove with a wide cuff over the wrist

gauze NOUN
1 thin transparent woven material
2 fine wire mesh

gave VERB past tense of **give**

gay ADJECTIVE
1 homosexual
2 cheerful
3 brightly coloured

gaze VERB
to look at something steadily

gaze NOUN
a long steady look

gazelle NOUN
a small antelope

gazette NOUN
1 a newspaper
2 an official journal

gazetteer NOUN
a list of place names

GCSE ABBREVIATION
General Certificate of Secondary Education

gear NOUN
1 a set of wheels with cogs that transmit power
2 (informal) equipment or clothing

gear VERB
gear to to make something match or be suitable

gearbox NOUN
a case enclosing gears

gel NOUN
a jelly-like substance

gelatin NOUN
a clear jelly-like substance used to make jellies

gem NOUN
1 a precious stone
2 an excellent person or thing

gender NOUN
1 (Grammar) the group in which a noun is classed in some languages, e.g. masculine, feminine, or neuter
2 a person's sex

gene (jeen) NOUN
the part of a living cell that controls which characteristics are inherited from parents

genealogy (jeen-ee-**al**-o-jee) NOUN **genealogies**
the study of family history and ancestors

genera (**jen**-e-ra) PLURAL NOUN
plural of **genus**

general ADJECTIVE
1 to do with most people or things
2 not detailed; broad the general idea

general NOUN
a senior army officer

general election NOUN
an election of Members of Parliament for the whole country

generalize VERB
to make a statement that is true in most cases
generalization NOUN

generally ADVERB
1 usually
2 in a general sense

general practitioner NOUN
a doctor who treats all kinds of diseases

generate VERB
to produce or create

generation NOUN
1 the process of producing
2 a single stage in a family
3 all the people born at about the same time

generator NOUN
a machine for producing electricity

generic (jin-e-rik) ADJECTIVE
belonging to a whole class or group

generous ADJECTIVE
1 willing to give or share
2 plentiful
generosity NOUN

genetic (jin-**et**-ik) ADJECTIVE
1 to do with genes
2 to do with inherited characteristics
genetically ADVERB

genetics NOUN
the study of genes and genetic behaviour

genial (**jee**-nee-al) ADJECTIVE
kindly and cheerful

genie (**jee**-nee) NOUN
(in stories) a spirit who can grant wishes

genitals PLURAL NOUN
the external sexual organs

genius NOUN
1 an unusually able person
2 a great ability a genius for music

genocide (jen-o-syd) *NOUN*
deliberate extermination of a race of people

genome (jen-ohm) *NOUN*
(*Science*) all the genes in one cell of a living thing

genteel (jen-**teel**) *ADJECTIVE*
trying to seem polite and refined

gentle *ADJECTIVE*
1 mild or kind; not rough
2 not harsh or severe *a gentle breeze*
gently *ADVERB*

gentleman *NOUN* **gentlemen**
1 a well-mannered man
2 a man of good social position

gentry *PLURAL NOUN*
upper-class people

genuine *ADJECTIVE*
real; not faked or pretending

genus (jee-nus) *NOUN* **genera**
a group of similar animals or plants

geography *NOUN*
the study of the earth's surface and of its climate and products
geographer *NOUN* **geographical** *ADJECTIVE*

geology *NOUN*
the study of the structure of the earth's crust and its layers
geological *ADJECTIVE* **geologist** *NOUN*

geometric *ADJECTIVE*
1 to do with geometry
2 made up of straight lines and angles
geometrical *ADJECTIVE*

geometry *NOUN*
the study of lines, angles, surfaces, and solids in mathematics

geranium *NOUN*
a garden plant with red, pink, or white flowers

gerbil (jer-bil) *NOUN*
a small brown rodent kept as a pet

geriatric (je-ree-**at**-rik) *ADJECTIVE*
to do with the care of old people

germ *NOUN*
1 a small organism causing disease
2 a tiny living structure from which a plant or animal may develop

German measles *NOUN*
rubella

German shepherd *NOUN*
a large strong dog, often used by the police

germicide *NOUN*
a substance that kills germs

germinate *VERB*
(of a seed) to produce roots and shoots
germination *NOUN*

gestation (jes-**tay**-shun) *NOUN*
the process of carrying a fetus in the womb

gesticulate *VERB*
to make expressive movements
gesticulation *NOUN*

gesture (jes-cher) *NOUN*
1 a movement that expresses what a person feels
2 an action that shows goodwill

gesture *VERB*
to say something by making a gesture

get *VERB* **getting**, **got**
1 to obtain or receive *to get first prize*
2 to become *Don't get angry!*
3 to reach a place *We'll get there soon.*
4 to put or move *I can't get my shoe on.*
5 to prepare *Will you get the tea?*
6 to persuade or order *Get him to come here.*
7 to catch an illness
8 (*informal*) to understand *I don't get that.*
get over to recover from an illness **get up**
1 to stand up 2 to get out of bed in the morning

getaway *NOUN*
an escape after committing a crime

geyser (gee-zer or gy-zer) *NOUN*
a natural hot spring

ghastly *ADJECTIVE*
1 very unpleasant or bad
2 looking pale and ill
ghastliness *NOUN*

gherkin (ger-kin) *NOUN*
a small pickled cucumber

ghetto (get-oh) *NOUN* **ghettos**
a deprived area of a city where immigrants or other minorities live

ghost *NOUN*
the spirit of a dead person that appears to the living
ghostly *ADJECTIVE*

ghoulish (gool-ish) *ADJECTIVE*
enjoying things that are grisly or unpleasant

giant *NOUN*
(in stories) a creature like a huge person

giant *ADJECTIVE*
very large

gibberish (jib-er-ish) *NOUN*
nonsense

gibbon *NOUN*
an ape with long arms

giddy *ADJECTIVE* **giddier**, **giddiest**
feeling unsteady and dizzy
giddiness *NOUN*

gift NOUN
1 something you give someone
2 a natural talent *a gift for music*

gifted ADJECTIVE
having a special talent

gigabyte (gi-ga-byt) NOUN
(*ICT*) a unit of information equal to one thousand million bytes, or (more precisely) 2^{30} bytes

gigantic (jy-gan-tik) ADJECTIVE
extremely large

giggle VERB
to laugh in a silly way
giggle NOUN

gild VERB
to cover with a thin layer of gold

gills PLURAL NOUN
the part of the body through which a fish breathes

gilt NOUN
a thin covering of gold or gold paint

gilt ADJECTIVE
gilded; gold-coloured

gimmick NOUN
something unusual done to attract attention

gin NOUN
an alcoholic drink flavoured with juniper berries

ginger NOUN
the hot-tasting root of a tropical plant, used for flavouring
ginger ADJECTIVE

ginger VERB
to make more lively

gingerbread NOUN
a ginger-flavoured cake or biscuit

gingerly ADVERB
cautiously

Gipsy NOUN **Gipsies**
another spelling of **Gypsy**

giraffe NOUN
an African animal with long legs and a long neck

girder NOUN
a metal beam supporting part of a building or bridge

girdle NOUN
1 a belt or cord worn round the waist
2 a tight corset

girl NOUN
a female child or young woman
girlhood NOUN

girlfriend NOUN
a person's regular female friend or lover

girlish ADJECTIVE
like a girl; young and attractive

giro (jy-roh) NOUN
a system of sending money directly from one bank account to another

girth NOUN
the distance round something

gist (jist) NOUN
the essential points or general sense of a story or argument

give VERB **gave**, **given**
1 to let someone have something
2 to make or do *give a laugh*
3 to bend or collapse when pressed
give in to admit defeat **give up** to stop
giver NOUN

glacial ADJECTIVE
made of or produced by ice

glacier NOUN
a mass of ice that moves slowly down a mountain valley

glad ADJECTIVE
1 pleased; expressing joy
2 giving pleasure *the glad news*

gladden VERB
to make glad

glade NOUN
an open space in a forest

gladiator (glad-ee-ay-ter) NOUN
a man trained to fight for public entertainment in ancient Rome

glamorize VERB
to make something seem glamorous or romantic

glamorous ADJECTIVE
excitingly attractive

glamour NOUN
attractiveness; romantic charm

glance VERB
1 to look briefly
2 to strike at an angle and slide off
The ball glanced off his bat.
glance NOUN

gland NOUN
an organ of the body that separates substances from the blood so that they can be used or passed out of the body
glandular ADJECTIVE

glare VERB
1 to shine with a bright or dazzling light
2 to stare angrily
glare NOUN

glaring ADJECTIVE
very obvious *a glaring error*

a b c d e f **g** h i j k l m n o p q r s t u v w x y z

glass NOUN
1 a hard brittle substance that allows light to pass through
2 a drinking container made of glass
3 a mirror or lens
glassy ADJECTIVE

glasses PLURAL NOUN
a pair of lenses in a frame, worn over the eyes to improve eyesight

glaze VERB
1 to fit a window or building with glass
2 to give a shiny surface to

glaze NOUN
a shiny surface or coating

glazier (glay-zee-er) NOUN
a person who fits glass

gleam VERB
to shine brightly

gleam NOUN
1 a beam of soft light
2 a small amount of hope

glean VERB
to gather information bit by bit

glee NOUN
mischievous delight
gleeful ADJECTIVE **gleefully** ADVERB

glen NOUN
a narrow valley in Scotland

glib ADJECTIVE
speaking or writing readily but not sincerely or thoughtfully

glide VERB
1 to move along smoothly
2 to fly without using an engine
glide NOUN

glider NOUN
an aircraft without an engine that flies by floating on warm air currents

glimmer NOUN
1 a faint light
2 a small sign or trace

glimmer VERB
to shine with a faint, flickering light

glimpse VERB
to see briefly
glimpse NOUN

glint NOUN
a brief flash of light

glint VERB
to shine with a flash of light

glisten (glis-en) VERB
to shine like something wet or oily

glitter VERB
to shine or sparkle

glitter NOUN
tiny sparkling pieces used for decoration

gloat VERB
to be pleased in an unkind way about someone's misfortune

global ADJECTIVE
1 to do with the whole world
2 to do with the whole of a system
globally ADVERB

globalization NOUN
the process by which a business or organization becomes international

global warming NOUN
the increase in the temperature of the earth's atmosphere

globe NOUN
1 a map of the whole world on a ball
2 something shaped like a ball

globule (glob-yool) NOUN
a small rounded drop

gloom NOUN
1 darkness
2 sadness or despair

gloomy ADJECTIVE **gloomier, gloomiest**
1 almost dark
2 depressed or depressing
gloomily ADVERB

glorify VERB **glorifies, glorified**
1 to give great praise or honour to
2 to make a thing seem more splendid or attractive than it really is *a film that glorifies war*
glorification NOUN

glorious ADJECTIVE
splendid or magnificent

glory NOUN **glories**
1 fame and honour
2 praise
3 beauty or magnificence

glory VERB **glories, gloried**
to rejoice or take great pleasure

gloss [1] NOUN
the shine on a smooth surface

gloss VERB
to make a thing glossy

gloss [2] VERB
gloss over to mention a fault or mistake only briefly

glossary NOUN **glossaries**
a list of difficult words with their meanings explained

glossy ADJECTIVE **glossier, glossiest**
smooth and shiny

glove NOUN
a covering for the hand with divisions for each finger and the thumb

glow NOUN
1 brightness and warmth without flames
2 a warm or cheerful feeling *a glow of pride*

glow VERB
to shine with a soft warm light

glower (rhymes with *flower*) VERB
to stare angrily

glucose NOUN
a form of sugar found in fruit juice and honey

glue NOUN
a sticky substance used for sticking things together
gluey ADJECTIVE

glue VERB
to stick with glue

glum ADJECTIVE
miserable or depressed

glut NOUN
an excessive supply

glutinous ADJECTIVE
glue-like or sticky

glutton NOUN
a person who eats too much
gluttonous ADJECTIVE **gluttony** NOUN

glycerine (glis-er-een) NOUN
a thick sweet colourless liquid

gnash (nash) VERB
to grind the teeth together

gnat (nat) NOUN
a tiny fly that bites

gnaw (naw) VERB
to keep on biting something hard

gnome (nohm) NOUN
(in stories) a dwarf that lives underground

gnu (noo) NOUN **gnu** or **gnus**
a large ox-like antelope

go VERB **goes**, **going**, **went**, **gone**
1 to move from one place to another
2 to leave
3 to lead from one place to another
The road goes to Bristol.
4 to become *He went pale.*
5 to make a sound *The gun went bang.*
6 to belong *Plates go on that shelf.*
go off 1 to explode 2 to become stale 3 to stop liking something **go on** to continue **go out** to stop burning or shining **go through** to experience something unpleasant or difficult

go NOUN **goes**
1 a turn or try
2 (*informal*) energy or liveliness *full of go*

goad VERB
to stir into action by annoying

goal NOUN
1 the place where a ball must go to score a point in football, hockey, etc.
2 a point scored in this way
3 something you are trying to achieve

goalkeeper NOUN
a player who defends the goal

goat NOUN
an animal related to the sheep, with horns and a beard and long hair

gobble VERB
to eat quickly and greedily

gobbledegook NOUN
(*informal*) technical language or jargon that is difficult to understand

goblet NOUN
a drinking glass with a long stem and a base

goblin NOUN
(in stories) a mischievous ugly elf

God NOUN
the creator of the universe in Christian, Jewish, and Muslim belief

god NOUN
a divine male being who is worshipped

godchild NOUN **godchildren**
a child who has a godparent
god-daughter NOUN **godson** NOUN

goddess NOUN
a divine female being who is worshipped

godparent NOUN
a person at a child's christening who agrees to take responsibility for the child's religious upbringing
godfather NOUN **godmother** NOUN

godsend NOUN
a piece of unexpected good luck

goggles PLURAL NOUN
large glasses for protecting the eyes from wind, water, dust, etc.

going NOUN
good going quick progress

gold NOUN
1 a precious yellow metal
2 a deep yellow colour
gold ADJECTIVE

golden ADJECTIVE
1 made of gold
2 coloured like gold
3 precious or excellent *a golden opportunity*

goldfinch NOUN
a bird with yellow feathers in its wings

goldfish NOUN
a small red or orange fish

a b c d e f **g** h i j k l m n o p q r s t u v w x y z

gold medal NOUN
a medal awarded for first place in a competition

goldsmith NOUN
a person who makes articles in gold

golf NOUN
an outdoor game played by hitting a small white ball with a club into a series of holes on a prepared ground
golfer NOUN

gondola (gond-uhl-uh) NOUN
a boat with high pointed ends used on the canals in Venice

gondolier NOUN
the person who moves a gondola along with a pole

gong NOUN
a large metal disc that makes an echoing sound when it is hit

good ADJECTIVE **better**, **best**
1 having the right qualities *a good book*
2 kind *good of you to help*
3 well-behaved *a good boy*
4 skilled or talented *a good pianist*
5 healthy; giving benefit *Exercise is good for you.*
6 thorough *a good clean*
7 large; considerable *a good distance away*

good NOUN
1 something good *to do good*
2 benefit *for your own good*
for good for ever **no good** useless

goodbye EXCLAMATION
a word used when you leave somebody

goodness NOUN
1 the quality of being good
2 the good part of something

goods PLURAL NOUN
1 things that are bought and sold
2 things that are transported by train or road

goodwill NOUN
a kindly feeling towards others

goody NOUN **goodies** (*informal*)
1 something good to eat
2 a hero or good person in a story

gooey ADJECTIVE
sticky or slimy

goose NOUN **geese**
a large water bird with webbed feet and a long neck

gooseberry NOUN **gooseberries**
a small green fruit that grows on a prickly bush

goose pimples or **goosebumps** PLURAL NOUN
small bumps on the skin caused by cold or fear

gore[1] VERB
to wound by piercing with a horn or tusk

gore[2] NOUN
thickened blood from a cut or wound

gorge NOUN
a narrow valley with steep sides

gorge VERB
to eat greedily

gorgeous ADJECTIVE
magnificent or beautiful

gorilla NOUN
a large powerful ape
Do not confuse this word with *guerrilla*.

gorse NOUN
a prickly bush with small yellow flowers

gory ADJECTIVE **gorier**, **goriest**
1 covered with blood
2 with much bloodshed *a gory battle*

gosh EXCLAMATION
an exclamation of surprise

gosling NOUN
a young goose

gospel NOUN
1 the teachings of Christ
2 something you can safely believe to be true

gossip VERB
to talk trivially about other people

gossip NOUN
1 trivial talk or rumours about other people
2 a person who enjoys gossip
gossipy ADJECTIVE

got *past tense* of **get**
have got to possess *Have you got a car?* **have got to** must *I have got to go now.*

gouge (gowj) VERB
to scoop or force out by pressing

goulash (goo-lash) NOUN
a meat stew seasoned with paprika

gourd (goord) NOUN
the rounded hard-skinned fruit of a climbing plant

gourmet (goor-may) NOUN
a person who appreciates good food and drink

gout NOUN
a disease that causes painful swelling of the toes, knees, and fingers

govern VERB
1 to be in charge of the affairs of a country or region
2 to control or determine

governess _NOUN_
a woman who teaches children at their home

government _NOUN_
1 the group of people who are in charge of the affairs of a country
2 the process of governing

governor _NOUN_
1 a person who governs a state or colony
2 a person who runs or helps to run an institution

gown _NOUN_
1 a woman's long dress
2 a loose robe worn by lawyers, members of a university, etc.

GP _ABBREVIATION_
general practitioner

grab _VERB_ **grabbing, grabbed**
to take hold of firmly or suddenly

grace _NOUN_
1 beauty of movement
2 goodwill or favour
3 dignity or good manners _He had the grace to apologize._
4 a short prayer of thanks at a meal
5 the title of a duke, duchess, or archbishop _Your Grace_

grace _VERB_
to bring honour or dignity to someone or something _The mayor graced us with his presence._

graceful _ADJECTIVE_
beautiful and elegant
gracefully _ADVERB_

gracious _ADJECTIVE_
kind and honourable

grade _NOUN_
1 a step in a scale of quality or rank
2 a mark showing the quality of work

grade _VERB_
to sort or divide into grades

gradient (gray-dee-uhnt) _NOUN_
a slope or the steepness of a slope

gradual _ADJECTIVE_
happening slowly but steadily
gradually _ADVERB_

graduate (grad-yoo-ayt) _VERB_
1 to be awarded a university or college degree
2 to divide into graded sections
graduation _NOUN_

graduate (grad-yoo-at) _NOUN_
a person who has a university or college degree

graffiti _NOUN_
words or drawings scribbled or sprayed on a wall

graft _NOUN_
1 a shoot from a plant or tree fitted into another to form a new growth
2 a piece of transplanted body tissue

graft _VERB_
to insert or transplant as a graft

grain _NOUN_
1 a small hard seed or similar particle
2 cereal plants
3 a small amount _a grain of truth_
4 the pattern of lines made by the fibres in a piece of wood or paper

gram _NOUN_
a unit of mass or weight in the metric system

grammar _NOUN_
1 the rules for using words correctly
2 a book about these rules

grammar school _NOUN_
a secondary school for children with academic ability

grammatical _ADJECTIVE_
following the rules of grammar
grammatically _ADVERB_

granary _NOUN_ **granaries**
a storehouse for grain

grand _ADJECTIVE_
1 splendid and impressive
2 most important or highest-ranking
3 including everything _a grand total_

grandad _NOUN_
(_informal_) grandfather

grandchild _NOUN_ **grandchildren**
the child of a person's son or daughter
granddaughter _NOUN_ **grandson** _NOUN_

grandeur (grand-yer) _NOUN_
impressive beauty

grandfather _NOUN_
the father of a person's father or mother

grandiose (grand-ee-ohss) _ADJECTIVE_
large and impressive

grandma _NOUN_
(_informal_) grandmother

grandmother _NOUN_
the mother of a person's father or mother

grandpa _NOUN_
(_informal_) grandfather

grandparent _NOUN_
a grandfather or grandmother

grandstand _NOUN_
a building open at the front with seats for spectators at a racecourse or sports ground

granite _NOUN_
a very hard kind of rock used for building

granny _NOUN_ **grannies**
(_informal_) grandmother

a
b
c
d
e
f
g
h
i
j
k
l
m
n
o
p
q
r
s
t
u
v
w
x
y
z

grant VERB
1 to give or allow *to grant a request*
2 to admit that something is true

grant NOUN
a sum of money awarded for a special purpose

Granth (grunt) NOUN
the sacred scriptures of the Sikhs

granular ADJECTIVE
like grains

granule NOUN
a small grain

grape NOUN
a small green or purple berry that grows in bunches on a vine, used to make wine

grapefruit NOUN
a large round yellow citrus fruit

grapevine NOUN
1 a vine with grapes growing
2 a means of spreading news

graph NOUN
a diagram showing how two quantities or variables are related

graphic ADJECTIVE
1 to do with drawing or painting *a graphic artist*
2 (of a description) lively and vivid
graphically ADVERB

graphics PLURAL NOUN
diagrams, lettering, and drawings, especially pictures that are produced by a computer

graphite NOUN
a soft black form of carbon used for the lead in pencils

grapple VERB
1 to struggle with
2 to seize
3 to try to deal with a problem

grasp VERB
1 to seize and hold firmly
2 to understand

grasp NOUN
1 a person's understanding of a subject
2 a firm hold

grasping ADJECTIVE
greedy

grass NOUN
1 a plant with green blades and stalks that are eaten by animals
2 ground covered with grass; lawn
grassy ADJECTIVE

grasshopper NOUN
a jumping insect that makes a shrill noise

grate¹ NOUN
1 a metal framework that keeps fuel in a fireplace
2 a fireplace

grate² VERB
1 to shred into small pieces by rubbing on a rough surface
2 to make a harsh unpleasant sound
3 to sound harshly

grateful ADJECTIVE
thankful for something that has been done for you
gratefully ADVERB

grater NOUN
a device for grating food

gratify VERB **gratifies**, **gratified**
to please or satisfy
gratification NOUN

grating NOUN
a framework of metal bars across an opening

gratitude NOUN
a feeling of being grateful

gratuitous (gra-tew-it-us) ADJECTIVE
done without good reason; uncalled for

grave¹ NOUN
the place where a dead body is buried

grave² ADJECTIVE
serious or solemn
gravely ADVERB

grave accent (rhymes with *starve*) NOUN
a backward-sloping mark over a vowel, as in *à*

gravel NOUN
small stones mixed with coarse sand
gravelled ADJECTIVE

gravestone NOUN
a stone monument over a grave

graveyard NOUN
a burial ground

gravitate VERB
to move or be attracted towards something

gravitation NOUN
1 the process of gravitating
2 the force of gravity

gravity NOUN
1 the force that pulls everything towards the earth
2 seriousness

gravy NOUN
a hot brown sauce made from meat juices

graze VERB
1 to feed on growing grass
2 to scrape the skin slightly
3 to touch lightly in passing

graze NOUN
a raw place where skin has been scraped

grease NOUN
1 any thick oily substance
2 melted fat

grease VERB
to put grease on

greasy ADJECTIVE **greasier**, **greasiest**
containing or covered in grease

great ADJECTIVE
1 very large; much more than normal
2 very important or talented *a great writer*
3 (*informal*) very good or enjoyable
great to see you
4 older or younger by one generation
great-grandmother
greatly ADVERB

greed NOUN
a constant desire for more than you need

greedy ADJECTIVE **greedier greediest**
wanting more food, money, or other things
than you need
greedily ADVERB

green ADJECTIVE
1 of the colour of grass, leaves, etc.
2 concerned with protecting the environment
3 inexperienced

green NOUN
1 the colour of grass, leaves, etc.
2 an area of land with grass

greenery NOUN
green leaves or plants

greenfly NOUN **greenfly**
a small green insect that sucks the juice
from plants

greengrocer NOUN
someone who sells fruit and vegetables

greenhouse NOUN
a glass building in which plants are protected
from the cold

greens PLURAL NOUN
green vegetables, such as cabbage and spinach

greet VERB
1 to meet and welcome
2 to receive *They greeted the song with
applause.*
3 to present itself to *A strange sight greeted
our eyes.*

greeting NOUN
words or actions used to greet someone

greetings PLURAL NOUN
good wishes

gregarious (grig-**air**-ee-us) ADJECTIVE
fond of company

grenade (grin-**ayd**) NOUN
a small bomb thrown by hand

grey ADJECTIVE
of a colour between black and white
grey NOUN

greyhound NOUN
a slender racing dog with smooth hair

grid NOUN
1 a pattern of bars or lines crossing each other
2 a network of cables carrying electricity over
a large area

grief NOUN
deep sorrow, especially at a person's death

grievance NOUN
a cause for complaining

grieve VERB
1 to feel deep sorrow at a person's death
2 to make a person feel very sad

grievous (gree-vus) ADJECTIVE
1 causing grief
2 serious

grill NOUN
1 a heated element on a cooker, sending heat
downwards
2 food cooked under this

grill VERB
1 to cook under a grill
2 to question closely

grille NOUN
a metal grating over a window or opening

grim ADJECTIVE **grimmer**, **grimmest**
1 stern or severe
2 unpleasant or unattractive
grimly ADVERB

grimace NOUN
a twisted expression on the face

grimace VERB
to make a grimace

grime NOUN
dirt in a layer on a surface

grimy ADJECTIVE **grimier**, **grimiest**
covered in a layer of dirt

grin NOUN
a broad smile

grin VERB **grinning**, **grinned**
to smile broadly

grind VERB
1 to crush into powder
2 to sharpen on a rough surface
3 to rub harshly together

grip VERB **gripping**, **gripped**
to hold firmly

grip NOUN
1 a firm hold
2 a handle
3 a travelling bag
get to grips with to begin to deal with

gripe VERB
(*informal*) to grumble or complain

gripe NOUN
a complaint

gripping ADJECTIVE
(of a story etc.) exciting

grisly ADJECTIVE **grislier**, **grisliest**
causing horror or disgust
Do not confuse this word with *grizzly*.

gristle NOUN
tough rubbery tissue in meat
gristly ADJECTIVE

grit NOUN
1 tiny pieces of stone or sand
2 courage and endurance

grit VERB **gritting**, **gritted**
1 to spread grit over
2 to clench your teeth

gritty ADJECTIVE **grittier**, **grittiest**
1 like grit or covered in grit
2 showing courage

grizzle VERB
to whimper or whine

grizzled ADJECTIVE
streaked with grey hairs

grizzly ADJECTIVE **grizzlier**, **grizzliest**
grey or grey-haired
Do not confuse this word with *grisly*.

grizzly bear NOUN
a large fierce bear of North America

groan VERB
to make a long deep sound in pain or
disapproval
groan NOUN

grocer NOUN
a person who sells food and household goods

groceries PLURAL NOUN
goods sold by a grocer

groggy ADJECTIVE **groggier**, **groggiest**
dizzy and unsteady after illness or injury

groin NOUN
the hollow between the thigh and the trunk
of the body

groom NOUN
1 a person who looks after horses
2 a bridegroom

groom VERB
1 to clean and brush a horse
2 to train for a job or position

groove NOUN
a long narrow channel cut in a surface
grooved ADJECTIVE

grope VERB
to feel about for something you cannot see

gross (grohss) ADJECTIVE
1 fat and ugly
2 obvious or shocking *gross stupidity*
3 bad-mannered
4 total *gross income*
grossly ADVERB

gross NOUN
twelve dozen (144)

grotesque (groh-**tesk**) ADJECTIVE
strange and ugly in appearance

grotto NOUN **grottoes**
an artificial cave

ground[1] *past tense* of **grind**

ground[2] NOUN
1 the solid surface of the earth
2 a sports field
3 land of a certain kind *marshy ground*

ground VERB
1 to keep an aircraft from flying
2 to stop a child from going out

grounding NOUN
basic training or instruction

groundless ADJECTIVE
without reason

grounds PLURAL NOUN
1 the gardens of a large house
2 solid particles that sink to the bottom
of liquid
3 reasons *grounds for suspicion*

groundwork NOUN
the first work done for a task

group NOUN
a number of people or things that come or
belong together

group VERB
to put together in a group or groups

grouse[1] NOUN **grouse**
a bird with feathered feet, hunted as game

grouse[2] VERB
(*informal*) to grumble or complain
grouse NOUN

grove NOUN
a small group of trees

grovel VERB **grovelling**, **grovelled**
1 to crawl on the ground
2 to act in an excessively humble way

grow VERB **grew**, **grown**
1 to become bigger or greater
2 to develop
3 to plant and look after
4 to become *grew tired*
grow up to become an adult

growl VERB
to make a deep angry sound in the throat
growl NOUN

grown-up NOUN
an adult person
grown-up ADJECTIVE

growth NOUN
1 the process of growing
2 something that has grown
3 a lump or tumour on or inside a person's body

grub NOUN
1 a tiny worm-like creature that will become an insect; a larva
2 (*informal*) food

grubby ADJECTIVE **grubbier**, **grubbiest**
rather dirty
grubbiness NOUN

grudge NOUN
a feeling of resentment or ill will
to bear a grudge

grudge VERB
to resent having to give or allow

gruelling ADJECTIVE
exhausting

gruesome ADJECTIVE
horrible or disgusting

gruff ADJECTIVE
having a rough voice or manner

grumble VERB
to complain in a bad-tempered way
grumble NOUN

grumpy ADJECTIVE **grumpier**, **grumpiest**
bad-tempered
grumpily ADVERB

grunt VERB
to make the gruff snort of a pig
grunt NOUN

guarantee NOUN
1 a formal promise
2 a statement by the maker of a product that it will be put right if faulty

guarantee VERB
1 to give a guarantee
2 to make something certain
guarantor NOUN

guard VERB
1 to protect or keep safe
2 to watch over and prevent from escaping

guard NOUN
1 the act of guarding *under close guard*
2 someone guarding a person or place
3 a group of soldiers or police acting as a guard
4 a railway official in charge of a train
5 a protecting device

guardian NOUN
1 someone who guards
2 a person who is legally in charge of a child in place of the child's parents
guardianship NOUN

guerrilla (ger-il-a) NOUN
a member of a small unofficial army that fights by making surprise attacks
Do not confuse this word with *gorilla*.

guess NOUN
an opinion or answer given without certain knowledge

guess VERB
to make a guess

guesswork NOUN
something you do by guessing

guest NOUN
a person who is staying at another person's house or hotel etc.

guffaw VERB
to laugh noisily
guffaw NOUN

guidance NOUN
1 the act of guiding
2 advice on problems

Guide NOUN
a member of the Girl Guides Association, an organization for girls

guide NOUN
1 a person who shows others the way or points out interesting sights
2 a book giving information about a place

guide VERB
to show someone the way or how to do something

guide dog NOUN
a dog trained to lead a blind person

guidelines PLURAL NOUN
rules or information about how something should be done

guild (gild) NOUN
a society of people with similar skills or interests

guile (rhymes with *mile*) NOUN
craftiness; cunning

guillotine (gil-ot-een) NOUN
1 a machine with a heavy blade for beheading criminals
2 a machine for cutting paper

guillotine VERB
to behead or cut with a guillotine

guilt NOUN
1 the fact of having committed an offence
2 a feeling that you are to blame

guilty ADJECTIVE **guiltier**, **guiltiest**
1 having done wrong
2 feeling or showing guilt *a guilty conscience*
guiltily ADVERB

guinea (gin-ee) NOUN
1 a former British gold coin worth 21 shillings (£1.05)
2 this amount of money

guinea pig NOUN
1 a small furry animal without a tail
2 someone used as the subject of an experiment

guise (guys) NOUN
an outward disguise or pretence

guitar NOUN
a musical instrument played by plucking the strings
guitarist NOUN

gulf NOUN
1 a large area of the sea partly surrounded by land
2 a large difference

gull NOUN
a seagull

gullet NOUN
the passage from the throat to the stomach

gullible ADJECTIVE
easily deceived

gully NOUN **gullies**
a narrow channel carrying water

gulp VERB
1 to swallow hastily or greedily
2 to make a loud swallowing noise from fear

gulp NOUN
1 the act of gulping
2 a large mouthful of liquid

gum NOUN
1 the firm flesh in which the teeth are rooted
2 a sticky substance produced by some trees and shrubs, used as glue
3 a sweet made with gum or gelatin
4 chewing gum
gummy ADJECTIVE

gum VERB **gumming**, **gummed**
to cover or stick with gum

gumption NOUN
(informal) common sense

gun NOUN
a weapon that fires shells or bullets

gun VERB **gunning**, **gunned**
gun down to shoot and kill with a gun

gunfire NOUN
the firing of guns

gunpowder NOUN
an explosive powder

gunshot NOUN
a shot fired from a gun

gurdwara NOUN
a Sikh temple

gurgle VERB
to make a low bubbling sound
gurgle NOUN

guru NOUN
1 a Hindu religious leader
2 an influential teacher

gush VERB
1 to flow suddenly or quickly
2 to talk too enthusiastically or emotionally
gush NOUN

gust NOUN
a sudden rush of wind, rain, or smoke
gusty ADJECTIVE

gust VERB
to blow in gusts

gusto NOUN
great enjoyment or enthusiasm

gut NOUN
the lower part of the digestive system; the intestine

gut VERB **gutting**, **gutted**
1 to remove the guts from
2 to remove or destroy the inside of
Fire gutted the building.

guts PLURAL NOUN
1 the digestive system; the insides of a person or thing
2 (informal) courage

gutted ADJECTIVE
(informal) extremely disappointed or upset

gutter NOUN
a long narrow water channel at the side of a street or along the edge of a roof

guttural ADJECTIVE
throaty and harsh-sounding

guy [1] NOUN
1 a figure representing Guy Fawkes, burned on 5 November in memory of a plot to blow up Parliament on that day in 1605
2 (informal) a man

guy [2] NOUN
a rope used to secure a tent

guzzle VERB
to eat or drink greedily
guzzler NOUN

gym (jim) NOUN
1 a gymnasium
2 gymnastics

gymkhana (jim-kah-na) NOUN
a series of horse-riding contests and other sports events

gymnasium NOUN
a place equipped for gymnastics

gymnast NOUN
an expert in gymnastics

gymnastics PLURAL NOUN
exercises to develop the muscles
gymnastic ADJECTIVE

Gypsy NOUN **Gypsies**
a member of a community of people, also called travellers, who travel from place to place

gyrate (jy-rayt) VERB
to move in circles or spirals
gyration NOUN

gyroscope (jy-ro-skohp) NOUN
a navigation device that keeps steady in a rolling ship

Hh

habit NOUN
1 something that you do often and are used to
2 something that is hard to give up
3 the dress worn by a monk or nun

habitat NOUN
the place in which an animal or plant lives naturally

habitation NOUN
a place to live in

habitual ADJECTIVE
done by habit; usual
habitually ADVERB

hack VERB
1 to chop or cut roughly
2 (*informal*) to break into a computer system

hacker NOUN
a person who breaks into a computer system, especially that of a company or government

hackles PLURAL NOUN
make someone's hackles rise to make them angry

hackneyed ADJECTIVE
(of a word or phrase) used often and no longer interesting

hacksaw NOUN
a saw for cutting metal

haddock NOUN **haddock**
a small sea fish used as food

hadn't
had not

haemoglobin (heem-a-gloh-bin) NOUN
the red substance that carries oxygen in the blood

haemophilia (heem-o-fil-ee-a) NOUN
a condition that causes dangerous bleeding from even a slight cut
haemophiliac NOUN, ADJECTIVE

haemorrhage (hem-er-ij) NOUN
bleeding, especially inside a person's body

hag NOUN
an ugly old woman

haggard ADJECTIVE
looking ill or very tired

haggis NOUN
a Scottish food made from sheep's offal

haggle VERB
to argue about a price or agreement

haiku (hy-koo) NOUN
a Japanese form of poem, written in three lines of five, seven, and five syllables

hail[1] NOUN
frozen drops of rain

hail VERB
to fall as hail

hail[2] VERB
to call out to
hail from to come from *He hails from Ireland.*

hailstone NOUN
a piece of hail

hair NOUN
1 a soft covering growing on the heads and bodies of people and animals
2 one of the threads forming part of this

hairbrush NOUN
a brush for grooming the hair

haircut NOUN
1 the act of cutting a person's hair
2 a hairstyle

hairdresser NOUN
a person who cuts and arranges people's hair

hair-raising ADJECTIVE
terrifying

hairstyle NOUN
a way of cutting and arranging the hair

hairy ADJECTIVE **hairier**, **hairiest**
covered with hair

hajj NOUN
the Muslim pilgrimage to Mecca

hake NOUN **hake**
a sea fish used as food

halal ADJECTIVE
keeping to Muslim law about the preparation of meat

hale ADJECTIVE
strong and healthy *hale and hearty*

half NOUN **halves**
each of two equal parts into which something can be divided

half ADVERB
partly; not completely *only half cooked*

half-brother or **half-sister** NOUN
a brother or sister by one parent only

half-hearted ADJECTIVE
not enthusiastic

half mast NOUN
the position of a flag halfway up the flagpole as a mark of respect for a person who has died

half-term NOUN
a short holiday in the middle of a term

half-time NOUN
the point or interval halfway through a game

halfway ADJECTIVE, ADVERB
at a point half the distance or amount between two places or times

halibut NOUN
a large flat fish used as food

hall NOUN
1 a space or passage inside the front entrance of a house
2 a large room or building used for public events

hallmark NOUN
1 an official mark on gold and silver showing its quality
2 a characteristic by which something is recognized

hallo EXCLAMATION
a word of greeting

hallowed ADJECTIVE
honoured as being holy

Hallowe'en NOUN
31 October, traditionally a time when ghosts and spirits are believed to be present

hallucinate VERB
to see something that is not really there
hallucination NOUN

halo NOUN **haloes**
a circle of light round the head of a holy person in paintings

halt VERB
to stop

halt NOUN
1 a stop or standstill *come to a halt*
2 a small stopping place on a railway

halter NOUN
a rope or strap put round a horse's head for guiding it

halve VERB
1 to divide into halves
2 to reduce to half

ham NOUN
meat from a pig's leg

hamburger NOUN
a fried cake of minced beef

hamlet NOUN
a small village

hammer NOUN
a tool with a heavy metal head for driving in nails

hammer VERB
1 to hit with a hammer
2 to knock loudly

hammock NOUN
a bed made of a length of cloth or netting hung up by the ends

hamper[1] NOUN
a large box-shaped basket with a lid

hamper[2] VERB
to hinder or prevent from working freely

hamster NOUN
a small furry animal with cheek pouches for carrying grain

hamstring NOUN
a tendon at the back of the knee

hand NOUN
1 the end part of the arm below the wrist
2 a pointer on a clock or dial
3 a worker; a member of a ship's crew
4 the cards held by a player in a card game
5 side or direction *the right-hand side*
6 help or aid *Give me a hand.*
7 applause *a big hand*
at hand near; available **by hand** using your hand or hands **hands down** winning easily **in hand** being dealt with **on hand** available **out of hand** out of control

hand VERB
to give or pass to someone

handbag NOUN
a small bag for holding a purse and personal articles

handcuffs PLURAL NOUN
a pair of metal rings linked by a chain, for fastening the wrists of a prisoner

handcuff VERB
to fasten with handcuffs

handful NOUN **handfuls**
1 as much as can be carried in one hand
2 a few people or things
3 a troublesome person or task

handicap NOUN
a disability or disadvantage
handicapped ADJECTIVE

handicraft NOUN
artistic work done with the hands

handiwork NOUN
1 something made by hand
2 something someone has done

handkerchief NOUN **handkerchieves**
a small square of cloth for wiping the nose or face

handle NOUN
the part of a thing by which it is held or controlled

handle VERB
1 to touch or feel with your hands
2 to deal with
handler NOUN

handlebars PLURAL NOUN
a bar with handles for steering at the front of a bicycle or motorcycle

handout NOUN
1 money given to a needy person
2 a sheet of information given out in a lesson or talk

handsome ADJECTIVE
1 good-looking
2 generous *a handsome gift*

hands-on ADJECTIVE
involving actual experience

handstand NOUN
an act of balancing on your hands with your feet in the air

handwriting NOUN
writing done by hand
handwritten ADJECTIVE

handy ADJECTIVE **handier**, **handiest**
1 convenient or useful
2 good at using the hands

handyman NOUN **handymen**
a person who does odd jobs

hang VERB **hung**
1 to fix or be fixed at the top or side so it is off the ground
2 to stick wallpaper to a wall
3 to decorate with ornaments
4 to remain in the air or as something unpleasant *Smoke hung over the city.*
5 (with *past tense* & *past participle* **hanged**) to execute a condemned person by hanging them from a rope round the neck

hangar NOUN
a large shed for aircraft

hanger NOUN
a device for hanging clothes

hang-glider NOUN
a framework in which a person can glide through the air
hang-gliding NOUN

hangover NOUN
an unpleasant feeling after drinking too much alcohol

hank NOUN
a coil or piece of wool, thread, etc.

hanker VERB
to feel a longing for something

hanky NOUN **hankies**
(*informal*) a handkerchief

Hanukkah (hah-noo-ka) NOUN
the eight-day Jewish festival of lights beginning in December

haphazard ADJECTIVE
done or chosen at random, without planning

hapless ADJECTIVE
having no luck

happen VERB
1 to take place; to occur
2 to do something by chance *I happened to see him.*

happening NOUN
something that happens; an event

happy ADJECTIVE **happier**, **happiest**
1 pleased or contented
2 fortunate *a happy coincidence*
3 willing *happy to help*
happily ADVERB **happiness** NOUN

harangue (ha-rang) VERB
to make a long aggressive speech to
harangue NOUN

harass (ha-ras) VERB
to trouble or annoy persistently
harassment NOUN

harbour NOUN
a place where ships can shelter or unload

harbour VERB
1 to keep in your mind *to harbour a grudge*
2 to give shelter to

hard ADJECTIVE
1 firm or solid; not soft
2 difficult to do or understand
3 severe or stern
4 causing suffering *hard luck*
5 using great effort *a hard worker*
6 (of drugs) strong and addictive
7 (of water) containing minerals that reduce lathering

hard ADVERB
with great effort *to work hard*

hardboard NOUN
stiff board made of compressed wood pulp

hard disk NOUN
(*ICT*) a computer disk able to store large amounts of data

harden VERB
to make or become hard

hard-hearted ADJECTIVE
unkind or unsympathetic

hardly ADVERB
only just; only with difficulty *can hardly speak*

hardship NOUN
difficult conditions or suffering

hardware NOUN
1 metal implements and tools
2 (*ICT*) the machinery of a computer as opposed to the software

hardy ADJECTIVE **hardier, hardiest**
able to endure cold or difficult conditions
hardiness NOUN

hare NOUN
an animal like a rabbit but larger

harem (har-eem) NOUN
the part of a Muslim palace or house where the women live

hark VERB
to listen

harlequin NOUN
a pantomime character who wears a costume of mixed colours

harm VERB
to damage or injure

harm NOUN
damage or injury

harmful ADJECTIVE
causing harm or injury

harmless ADJECTIVE
not causing any harm; safe

harmonic ADJECTIVE
to do with harmony in music

harmonica NOUN
a mouth organ

harmonious ADJECTIVE
1 combining together in a pleasant or effective way
2 sounding pleasant
3 peaceful and friendly

harmonize VERB
to combine together in a pleasant way
harmonization NOUN

harmony NOUN **harmonies**
1 a pleasant combination of musical notes
2 a state of being friendly

harness NOUN
the straps put round a horse's head and neck for controlling it

harness VERB
1 to put a harness on a horse
2 to control and use

harp NOUN
a musical instrument with strings stretched down a triangular frame and plucked with the fingers
harpist NOUN

harpoon NOUN
a spear attached to a rope, used for killing whales

harpsichord NOUN
an instrument like a piano but with strings that are plucked

harrow NOUN
a heavy device pulled over the ground to break up the soil

harrowing ADJECTIVE
upsetting or distressing

harry VERB **harries, harried**
to harass or worry

harsh ADJECTIVE
1 rough and unpleasant
2 severe or cruel
harshly ADVERB

hart NOUN
a male deer

harvest NOUN
1 the time when ripened corn, fruit, or vegetables are gathered in
2 the crop that is gathered in

harvest VERB
to gather in a crop

hash NOUN
1 a dish of small pieces of fried meat and vegetables
2 the symbol #

hashish NOUN
a drug made from hemp

hasn't
has not

hassle NOUN
(*informal*) something difficult or annoying

hassle VERB
(*informal*) to annoy or pester someone

haste NOUN
a hurry
make haste to act promptly

hasten VERB
to hurry

hasty ADJECTIVE **hastier, hastiest**
hurried; done too quickly
hastily ADVERB

hat NOUN
a covering for the head

hatch[1] NOUN
a covered opening in a floor, wall, etc.

hatch[2] VERB
1 to break out of an egg
2 to keep an egg warm until a young bird comes out
3 to form a plot

hatchback *NOUN*
a car with a sloping back hinged to open at the top

hatchet *NOUN*
a small axe

hate *VERB*
to dislike very strongly

hate *NOUN*
extreme dislike

hateful *ADJECTIVE*
arousing hatred

hatred *NOUN*
extreme dislike

hat-trick *NOUN*
three successes in a row

haughty *ADJECTIVE* **haughtier, haughtiest**
proud and arrogant
haughtily *ADVERB*

haul *VERB*
to pull or drag with great effort

haul *NOUN*
an amount of booty

haulage *NOUN*
1 the transporting of goods
2 a charge for this

haunch *NOUN*
the buttock and top part of the thigh

haunt *VERB*
1 (of ghosts) to appear often in a place
2 to visit a place often
3 (of a memory) to linger in the mind
haunted *ADJECTIVE*

haunt *NOUN*
a place that you often visit

have *VERB* **has, had**
1 to possess or own *We have two dogs.*
2 to contain *The tin has tea in it.*
3 to experience *He had a shock.*
4 to be obliged to do something *We have to go now.*
5 to allow *I won't have him disturbed.*
6 receive or accept *Will you have a sweet?*
7 to get something done *I'm having my watch mended.*
8 used to form the past tense of verbs *He has gone.*

haven *NOUN*
a safe place or refuge

haven't
have not

havoc *NOUN*
great destruction or disorder

hawk [1] *NOUN*
a bird of prey with very good eyesight

hawk [2] *VERB*
to carry goods about to sell
hawker *NOUN*

hawthorn *NOUN*
a thorny tree with small red berries

hay *NOUN*
dried grass for feeding to animals

hay fever *NOUN*
irritation of the nose, throat, and eyes, caused by pollen or dust

haystack or **hayrick** *NOUN*
a large neat pile of hay packed for storing

haywire *ADJECTIVE*
out of control

hazard *NOUN*
1 a danger or risk
2 an obstacle on a golf course

hazard *VERB*
to chance or risk

hazardous *ADJECTIVE*
risky or dangerous

haze *NOUN*
thin mist

hazel *NOUN*
1 a shrub or small tree with small nuts
2 a light brown colour

hazelnut *NOUN*
a nut of a hazel tree

hazy *ADJECTIVE* **hazier, haziest**
1 misty
2 vague or uncertain
hazily *ADVERB*

H-bomb *NOUN*
a hydrogen bomb

he *PRONOUN*
the male person or animal being talked about

head *NOUN*
1 the part of the body containing the brains, eyes, and mouth
2 the brains or mind
3 a talent or ability *a good head for figures*
4 the side of a coin on which someone's head is shown
5 a person *It costs £5 a head.*
6 the top or front of something
7 the person in charge
8 a headteacher

head *VERB*
1 to be at the top or front of something
2 to hit a ball with the head
3 to move in a particular direction
head off to force someone to turn aside by getting in front of them

headache *NOUN*
1 a pain in the head
2 (*informal*) a worrying problem

headdress NOUN
a covering or decoration for the head

header NOUN
the act of heading the ball in football

heading NOUN
a word or words put at the top of a piece of
printing or writing

headland NOUN
a large piece of high land jutting into the sea

headlight NOUN
a powerful light at the front of a vehicle

headline NOUN
a heading in large print in a newspaper

headlong ADVERB, ADJECTIVE
1 falling head first
2 hastily

headmaster NOUN
a male headteacher

headmistress NOUN
a female headteacher

head-on ADVERB, ADJECTIVE
(of a collision) with the front parts meeting

headphones PLURAL NOUN
a pair of earphones on a band that fits over
the head

headquarters NOUN
the place from which an organization is
controlled

headstone NOUN
a stone set up on a grave; a gravestone

headstrong ADJECTIVE
determined to do what you want

headteacher NOUN
the person in charge of a school

headway NOUN
progress

heal VERB
to make or become healthy

health NOUN
1 the condition of a person's body or mind
2 a good state of health in sickness and
in health

healthy ADJECTIVE healthier, healthiest
1 being well and free from illness
2 producing good health a healthy diet
healthily ADVERB

heap NOUN
an untidy pile
heaps PLURAL NOUN (informal) plenty heaps
of time

heap VERB
1 to put into a heap
2 to put on large amounts

hear VERB heard
1 to take in sounds through the ears
2 to receive news or information
3 to try a case in a lawcourt
hearer NOUN

hearing NOUN
1 the ability to hear
2 a legal trial or investigation

hearsay NOUN
rumour or gossip

hearse NOUN
a vehicle for taking a coffin to a funeral

heart NOUN
1 the organ of the body that pumps the blood
2 a person's feelings or emotions; sympathy
3 courage take heart
4 the middle or most important part
5 a curved shape representing a heart
6 a playing card with red heart shapes on it
break a person's heart to make them very
unhappy **by heart** memorized

heart attack NOUN
a sudden and painful failure of the heart to
work properly

heartbroken ADJECTIVE
very upset or unhappy

hearten VERB
to make a person feel encouraged

heartfelt ADJECTIVE
felt deeply

hearth NOUN
the floor of a fireplace

heartless ADJECTIVE
without pity or sympathy

hearty ADJECTIVE heartier, heartiest
1 strong and vigorous
2 enthusiastic and sincere hearty thanks
3 (of a meal) large
heartily ADVERB

heat NOUN
1 a hot condition, or the form of energy
causing this
2 hot weather
3 anger or other strong feeling
4 a first round in a contest

heat VERB
to make or become hot

heater NOUN
a device for heating

heath NOUN
open land with low shrubs

heathen NOUN
a person who does not believe in any of the
world's chief religions

heather NOUN
an evergreen plant with small purple, pink, or
white flowers

heatwave NOUN
a long period of hot weather

heave VERB **heaved** (*when used of ships* **hove**)
1 to lift or move something heavy
2 (*informal*) to throw
3 to rise and fall
heave NOUN

heaven NOUN
1 the place believed in some religions to be the dwelling of God
2 a very pleasant state
the heavens the sky

heavenly ADJECTIVE
1 to do with heaven
2 in the sky *heavenly bodies*
3 (*informal*) very pleasing

heavy ADJECTIVE **heavier**, **heaviest**
1 weighing a lot
2 great in amount or force *heavy rain*
3 large or massive *a heavy door*
4 needing much effort *heavy work*
heavily ADVERB

heavyweight NOUN
1 a heavy person
2 a boxer of the heaviest weight
heavyweight ADJECTIVE

Hebrew NOUN
the language of the Jews in ancient Palestine and modern Israel

heckle VERB
to interrupt a public speaker with awkward questions
heckler NOUN

hectare (hek-tar) NOUN
a unit of area equal to 10,000 square metres or nearly 2 acres

hectic ADJECTIVE
full of activity

hector VERB
to talk to someone in a bullying way

hedge NOUN
a row of bushes forming a barrier or boundary
hedge VERB
1 to surround with a hedge
2 to avoid giving an answer

hedgehog NOUN
a small animal covered with long prickles

hedgerow NOUN
a hedge of bushes bordering a field

heed VERB
to pay attention to
heed NOUN
take or **pay heed** to give attention to something

heedless ADJECTIVE
taking no notice

heel [1] NOUN
the back part of the foot
heel VERB
1 to repair the heel of a shoe
2 to kick with your heel

heel [2] VERB
(of a ship) to lean over to one side

hefty ADJECTIVE **heftier**, **heftiest**
large and strong

heifer (hef-er) NOUN
a young cow

height NOUN
1 extent from top to bottom or foot
2 a high place
3 the most intense part *the height of the season*

heighten VERB
to make or become higher or more intense

heinous (hay-nus or hee-nus) ADJECTIVE
very wicked *a heinous crime*

heir (say as air) NOUN
a person who inherits property

heiress (air-ess) NOUN
a female heir to a fortune

heirloom (air-loom) NOUN
a valued possession handed down in a family for several generations

helicopter NOUN
a kind of aircraft with a large horizontal propeller or rotor

helium (hee-lee-um) NOUN
a light colourless gas that does not burn

helix (hee-liks) NOUN **helices**
a spiral

hell NOUN
1 a place where, in some religions, wicked people are thought to be punished after they die
2 a very unpleasant place

hellish ADJECTIVE
(*informal*) very difficult or unpleasant

hello EXCLAMATION
a word of greeting

helm NOUN
the handle or wheel used to steer a ship

helmet NOUN
a strong covering worn to protect the head

help VERB
1 to do something useful for someone
2 to make better or easier *This will help you to sleep.*
3 to prevent yourself *can't help coughing*
4 to serve food to
helper NOUN

help NOUN
1 the act of helping
2 a person or thing that helps

helpful ADJECTIVE
giving help; useful
helpfully ADVERB

helping NOUN
a portion of food

helpless ADJECTIVE
unable to act without help

helpline NOUN
a telephone service giving advice to callers

helter-skelter ADVERB
in great haste
helter-skelter NOUN
a spiral slide at a fair

hem NOUN
the edge of a piece of cloth, folded over and
sewn down

hem VERB **hemming**, **hemmed**
put a hem on
hem in to surround and restrict

hemisphere NOUN
1 half a sphere
2 half the earth *the southern hemisphere*

hemp NOUN
1 a plant that produces fibres for making
cloth and ropes
2 the drug cannabis, made from this plant

hen NOUN
1 a female bird
2 a female fowl

hence ADVERB
1 from this time or place
2 therefore

henceforth ADVERB
from now on

henna NOUN
a reddish-brown dye used for colouring hair

hepatitis NOUN
inflammation of the liver

heptagon NOUN
a flat shape with seven sides
heptagonal ADJECTIVE

her PRONOUN
the form of **she** used as the object of a verb or
after a preposition

her ADJECTIVE
belonging to her *her house*

herald NOUN
1 in former times, an official who made
announcements and carried important
messages
2 a person or thing that is a sign of something
to come

herald VERB
to show that something is coming

heraldry NOUN
the study of coats of arms
heraldic (hir-**al**-dik) ADJECTIVE

herb NOUN
a plant used for flavouring or for making
medicine
herbal ADJECTIVE

herbivorous (her-**biv**-er-us) ADJECTIVE
eating plants
herbivore NOUN

herd NOUN
1 a group of animals that feed together
2 a mass of people

herd VERB
to gather or move together

here ADVERB
in or to this place

hereafter ADVERB
from now on

hereby ADVERB
by this act

hereditary ADJECTIVE
passed from one generation to the next

heredity NOUN
the inheriting of physical or mental
characteristics from parents or ancestors

heresy (herri-see) NOUN **heresies**
a religious opinion that disagrees with the
main beliefs

heretic (herri-tik) NOUN
a person who supports a heresy

heritage NOUN
the property that someone has inherited

hermit NOUN
a person who lives alone, usually for religious
reasons

hernia NOUN
a condition in which an internal part of the
body pushes through a weak point in
another part

hero NOUN **heroes**
1 a person who is admired for bravery
2 the chief male character in a story

heroic ADJECTIVE
brave like a hero
heroically ADVERB

heroin NOUN
a strong addictive drug made from morphine

heroine NOUN
1 a woman who is admired for bravery
2 the chief female character in a story

heroism NOUN
bravery

heron NOUN
a wading bird with long legs and a long neck

herring NOUN **herring** or **herrings**
a sea fish used as food

hers POSSESSIVE PRONOUN
belonging to her *The house is hers.*
It is incorrect to write *her's.*

herself PRONOUN
she or her and nobody else *She cut herself.*
She herself has said it.
by herself alone; on her own

hertz NOUN
a unit of frequency of electromagnetic waves

hesitant ADJECTIVE
hesitating; undecided about what to do
hesitancy NOUN

hesitate VERB
to be slow or uncertain in speaking,
moving, etc.
hesitation NOUN

heterosexual ADJECTIVE
attracted to people of the opposite sex; not
homosexual
heterosexual NOUN

hew VERB **hewn**
to chop or cut with an axe etc.

hexagon NOUN
a flat shape with six sides
hexagonal ADJECTIVE

hey EXCLAMATION
an exclamation used to attract attention or to
express surprise or interest

heyday NOUN
the time of a thing's greatest success or
prosperity

hi EXCLAMATION
an exclamation used as a friendly greeting

hiatus (hy-**ay**-tuhs) NOUN
a gap in something that is otherwise
continuous

hibernate VERB
(of an animal) to spend the winter in a state
like deep sleep
hibernation NOUN

hiccup NOUN
1 a high gulping sound made when the breath
is briefly interrupted
2 a hitch or setback

hiccup VERB **hiccuping**, **hiccuped**
to make the sound of a hiccup

hide[1] VERB
1 to go where you cannot be seen
2 to keep from being seen
3 to keep secret

hide[2] NOUN
an animal's skin

hide-and-seek NOUN
a game of looking for people who are hiding

hideous ADJECTIVE
very ugly or unpleasant

hideout NOUN
a place to hide from other people

hiding[1] NOUN
a state of being hidden *go into hiding*

hiding[2] NOUN
a beating

hierarchy (**hyr**-ark-ee) NOUN **hierarchies**
an organization that puts people one above
another in rank

hieroglyphics (hyr-o-**glif**-iks) PLURAL NOUN
pictures or symbols used in ancient Egypt to
represent words

hi-fi NOUN
equipment for reproducing recorded sound
with high quality

higgledy-piggledy ADVERB, ADJECTIVE
mixed up; in great disorder

high ADJECTIVE
1 reaching a long way upwards *high hills*
2 far above the ground or sea *high clouds*
3 measuring from top to bottom
two metres high
4 above average level in importance, quality,
amount, etc. *high rank high prices*
5 (of meat) beginning to go bad
6 (*informal*) affected by a drug

high ADVERB
at or to a high level or position etc.
high above them

highbrow ADJECTIVE
intellectual

higher education NOUN
education at a university or college

high jump NOUN
an athletic contest in which competitors
jump over a high bar

highlands PLURAL NOUN
mountainous country
highland ADJECTIVE **highlander** NOUN

highlight NOUN
1 the most interesting part of something
2 a light-coloured area or streak

highlight VERB
to draw special attention to

a b c d e f g **h** i j k l m n o p q r s t u v w x y z

highly *ADVERB*
1 extremely *highly amusing*
2 very favourably *thought highly of them*

highly strung *ADJECTIVE*
nervous and easily upset

Highness *NOUN*
the title of a prince or princess

high-rise *ADJECTIVE*
(of a building) having many storeys

high road *NOUN*
a main road

high school *NOUN*
a secondary school

high spirits *PLURAL NOUN*
cheerful and lively behaviour
high-spirited *ADJECTIVE*

high street *NOUN*
the main street of a town

highway *NOUN*
a main road or route

highwayman *NOUN* **highwaymen**
a man who robbed travellers on highways

hijack *VERB*
to seize control of an aircraft or vehicle during
a journey
hijack *NOUN* **hijacker** *NOUN*

hike *VERB*
to walk a long distance in the countryside
hike *NOUN* **hiker** *NOUN*

hilarious *ADJECTIVE*
very funny
hilariously *ADVERB* **hilarity** *NOUN*

hill *NOUN*
a piece of land that is higher than the ground
around it
hilly *ADJECTIVE*

hillock *NOUN*
a small hill

hilt *NOUN*
the handle of a sword or dagger

him *PRONOUN*
the form of **he** used as the object of a verb or
after a preposition

himself *PRONOUN*
he or him and nobody else *He cut himself. He
himself has said it.*
by himself alone; on his own

hind[1] *ADJECTIVE*
at the back *hind legs*

hind[2] *NOUN*
a female deer

hinder *VERB*
to get in the way of or make things difficult for
hindrance *NOUN*

Hindi *NOUN*
one of the languages of India

hindmost *ADJECTIVE*
furthest behind

hindquarters *PLURAL NOUN*
an animal's hind legs and rear parts

hindsight *NOUN*
knowledge or understanding about
something after it has happened

Hinduism *NOUN*
one of the religions of India

hinge *NOUN*
a joining device on which a lid or door turns
when it opens

hinge *VERB*
1 to fix with a hinge
2 to depend

hint *NOUN*
1 a useful idea or piece of advice
2 a slight indication or suggestion

hint *VERB*
to make a hint

hinterland *NOUN*
the district lying inland from the coast

hip[1] *NOUN*
the bony side of the body between the waist
and the thigh

hip[2] *NOUN*
the fruit of the wild rose

hippie *NOUN*
a young person who joins with others to live in
an unconventional way, often based on ideas
of peace and love

hippo *NOUN* **hippos**
(*informal*) a hippopotamus

hippopotamus *NOUN*
a large African animal that lives near water

hire *VERB*
1 to pay to have use of something
2 to lend for payment
hirer *NOUN*

hire *NOUN*
the act of hiring

his *ADJECTIVE, POSSESSIVE PRONOUN*
belonging to him *his house The house is his.*

hiss *VERB*
to make a sound like an *s*
hiss *NOUN*

historian *NOUN*
a person who writes or studies history

historic *ADJECTIVE*
famous or important in history

historical *ADJECTIVE*
1 to do with history
2 that actually existed or took place *historical
events*
historically *ADVERB*

history NOUN **histories**
the study or description of what happened in the past

hit VERB **hitting**, **hit**
1 to come forcefully against a person or thing
2 to have a bad effect on *Famine hit the country.*

hit NOUN
1 an act of hitting; a blow or stroke
2 a shot that hits the target
3 something very successful

hitch VERB
1 to raise or pull with a slight jerk
2 to fasten with a loop or hook
3 to hitch-hike

hitch NOUN
1 a slight difficulty causing delay
2 a hitching movement
3 a knot

hitch-hike VERB
to travel by getting lifts from passing vehicles
hitch-hiker NOUN

hither ADVERB
to or towards this place

hitherto ADVERB
until this time

HIV ABBREVIATION
human immunodeficiency virus; the virus that causes Aids

hive NOUN
1 a box or other container for bees to live in
2 the bees living in a beehive

hoard NOUN
a carefully saved store of money, treasure, food, etc.

hoard VERB
to store away
hoarder NOUN
Do not confuse this word with *horde*.

hoarding NOUN
a tall fence covered with advertisements

hoar frost NOUN
a white frost

hoarse ADJECTIVE
having a rough or croaking voice

hoary ADJECTIVE
white or grey from age

hoax VERB
to deceive somebody as a joke
hoax NOUN

hob NOUN
a flat surface on a cooker, for cooking food

hobble VERB
to limp or walk with difficulty

hobby NOUN **hobbies**
an activity done for pleasure

hobgoblin NOUN
a mischievous or evil spirit

hobnob VERB **hobnobbing**, **hobnobbed**
to spend time together

hockey NOUN
a game played by two teams with curved sticks and a hard ball

hoe NOUN
a tool for scraping up weeds

hoe VERB **hoes**, **hoeing**, **hoed**
to scrape or dig with a hoe

hog NOUN
1 a male pig
2 (*informal*) a greedy person

hog VERB **hogging**, **hogged**
(*informal*) to take more than your share of

Hogmanay NOUN
New Year's Eve in Scotland

hoist VERB
to lift up with ropes or pulleys

hold VERB **held**
1 to have and keep in your hands
2 to have room for *The jug holds two pints.*
3 to support *won't hold my weight*
4 to believe or consider *to hold us responsible*
5 to cause something to take place *to hold a meeting*
6 to keep in custody
hold up 1 to hinder 2 to stop and rob

hold NOUN
1 the act of holding; a grasp
2 something to hold on to
3 the part of a ship where cargo is stored

holdall NOUN
a large portable bag or case

holder NOUN
a person or thing that holds something

hold-up NOUN
1 a delay
2 a robbery with force

hole NOUN
1 a hollow place; a gap or opening
2 a burrow
3 (*informal*) an unpleasant place

hole VERB
to make a hole or holes in

holiday NOUN
1 a day or time when people d⟨o not⟩ work or school
2 a time to enjoy you⟨r⟩

holiness NOUN
the state of being holy or sacred
His Holiness the title of the Pope

hollow ADJECTIVE
with an empty space inside; not solid

hollow ADVERB
completely *beat them hollow*

hollow NOUN
a hollow or sunken place

hollow VERB
to make hollow

holly NOUN
an evergreen bush with shiny prickly leaves
and red berries

hollyhock NOUN
a plant with large flowers on a very tall stem

holocaust NOUN
a huge destruction by fire
the Holocaust the mass killing of Jews by the
Nazis from 1939 to 1945

hologram NOUN
a laser photograph with a three-dimensional
image

holster NOUN
a leather case in which a pistol or revolver is
carried

holy ADJECTIVE **holier, holiest**
1 belonging or devoted to God
2 consecrated *holy water*

homage NOUN
an act or expression of respect or honour

home NOUN
1 the place where a person lives or was born
2 a place where those who need help are
looked after
3 the place to be reached in a race or game

home ADJECTIVE
1 to do with your own home or country
home industries
2 played on a team's own ground *a home
match*

home ADVERB
1 to or at home *Is she home yet?*
2 to the point aimed at *Push the bolt home.*

home VERB
home in on to move towards a target

homeless ADJECTIVE
having no home

homely ADJECTIVE
simple and ordinary

home-made ADJECTIVE
made at home, not bought

homeopathy NOUN
the treatment of disease by tiny doses of
drugs that produce symptoms similar to the
disease
homeopathic ADJECTIVE

homesick ADJECTIVE
sad when away from home

homework NOUN
school work that is done at home

homicide NOUN
the killing of one person by another
homicidal ADJECTIVE

homing ADJECTIVE
(of a pigeon) trained to fly home

homogeneous (hom-o-**jeen**-ee-us)
ADJECTIVE
formed of people or things of the same kind

homograph NOUN
a word that is spelt like another but has a
different meaning or origin, e.g. *bat* (a flying
animal) and *bat* (for hitting a ball)

homophone NOUN
a word with the same sound as another but a
different spelling or meaning , e.g. *son* and *sun*

homosexual ADJECTIVE
attracted to people of the same sex
homosexual NOUN **homosexuality** NOUN

honest ADJECTIVE
being truthful and not cheating
honestly ADVERB **honesty** NOUN

honey NOUN
a sweet sticky food made by bees

honeycomb NOUN
a wax structure made by bees to hold their
honey and eggs

honeymoon NOUN
a holiday spent together by a newly-married
couple

honeysuckle NOUN
a climbing plant with fragrant yellow or pink
flowers

honk NOUN
a loud sound like that made by a goose or an
old car horn

honk VERB
to make a honk

honorary ADJECTIVE
1 given as an honour *an honorary degree*
2 unpaid *the honorary treasurer*

honour NOUN
1 great respect or reputation
2 a person or thing that brings honour
3 something a person is proud to do
an honour to meet you
4 honesty and loyalty *a person of honour*
5 an award given as a mark of respect

honour *VERB*
1 to feel or show honour for
2 to keep to the terms of an agreement or promise
3 to acknowledge and pay a cheque etc.

honourable *ADJECTIVE*
deserving honour; honest and loyal
honourably *ADVERB*

hood *NOUN*
1 a covering of soft material for the head and neck
2 a folding roof or cover
3 (*American*) the bonnet of a car
hooded *ADJECTIVE*

hoodwink *VERB*
to deceive

hoof *NOUN* **hoofs** or **hooves**
the horny part of the foot of a horse etc.

hook *NOUN*
a bent or curved piece of metal etc. for hanging things on or for catching hold of something

hook *VERB*
1 to fasten with or on a hook
2 to catch a fish with a hook
3 to hit a ball in a curving path
hooked *ADJECTIVE*

hooligan *NOUN*
a rough and violent young person
hooliganism *NOUN*

hoop *NOUN*
a large ring used as a toy

hooray *EXCLAMATION*
a shout of joy or approval

hoot *VERB*
1 to make a sound like that made by an owl
2 to laugh loudly
hoot *NOUN*

hooter *NOUN*
a horn or siren that makes a hooting sound

hop[1] *VERB* **hopping**, **hopped**
1 to jump on one foot
2 (of an animal) to spring from all feet at once
hop *NOUN*
a hopping movement

hop[2] *NOUN*
a climbing plant used to give beer its flavour

hope *NOUN*
1 the feeling of wanting and expecting something to happen
2 a person or thing that gives hope
hope *VERB*
to want and expect something

hopeful *ADJECTIVE*
1 feeling hope
2 likely to be good or successful
hopefully *ADVERB*

hopeless *ADJECTIVE*
1 without hope
2 very bad at something
hopelessly *ADVERB*

hopscotch *NOUN*
a game of hopping into squares drawn on the ground

horde *NOUN*
a large group or crowd
Do not confuse this word with *hoard*.

horizon *NOUN*
the line where the earth and the sky appear to meet

horizontal *ADJECTIVE*
level; parallel to the horizon
horizontally *ADVERB*

hormone *NOUN*
a substance produced in the body and carried by the blood to stimulate other organs in the body
hormonal *ADJECTIVE*

horn *NOUN*
1 a hard growth on the head of a bull, cow, ram, etc.
2 a brass instrument played by blowing
3 a device for making a warning sound
horned *ADJECTIVE* **horny** *ADJECTIVE*

hornet *NOUN*
a large kind of wasp

hornpipe *NOUN*
a sailors' dance

horoscope *NOUN*
a prediction of future events based on the positions of stars

horrendous *ADJECTIVE*
extremely unpleasant

horrible *ADJECTIVE*
1 horrifying
2 very unpleasant or nasty
horribly *ADVERB*

horrid *ADJECTIVE*
horrible

horrific *ADJECTIVE*
horrifying
horrifically *ADVERB*

horrify *VERB* **horrifies**, **horrified**
1 to make someone feel afraid or disgusted
2 to shock

horror *NOUN*
1 great fear or disgust
2 a person or thing causing horror

horse NOUN
1 a large four-legged animal used for riding on and for pulling carts etc.
2 a piece of gymnastic equipment for vaulting over

horsepower NOUN
a unit for measuring the power of an engine, equal to 746 watts

horseshoe NOUN
a curved piece of metal nailed to a horse's hoof

horticulture NOUN
the art of gardening
horticultural ADJECTIVE

hose NOUN
a flexible tube for directing a flow of water

hose VERB
to water or spray with a hose

hospice (hosp-iss) NOUN
a nursing home for people who are very ill or dying

hospitable ADJECTIVE
welcoming; liking to give hospitality
hospitably ADVERB

hospital NOUN
a place providing medical treatment for people who are ill or injured

hospitality NOUN
the welcoming of guests or strangers with food and entertainment

host[1] NOUN
1 a person who has guests and looks after them
2 the presenter of a television or radio programme

host VERB
to organize and take charge of a party or other event

host[2] NOUN
a large number of people or things

host[3] NOUN
(in Christianity) the bread consecrated at Holy Communion

hostage NOUN
a person who is held prisoner until demands are met

hostel NOUN
a building where travellers, students, or other groups can stay or live

hostess NOUN
a woman who has guests and looks after them

hostile ADJECTIVE
1 unfriendly a hostile glance
2 opposed to something
3 to do with an enemy hostile aircraft
hostility NOUN

hot ADJECTIVE hotter, hottest
1 having great heat or a high temperature
2 (of food) highly spiced
3 passionate or excitable a hot temper

hot VERB hotting, hotted
hot up (informal) to become more exciting

hot dog NOUN
a hot sausage in a bread roll

hotel NOUN
a building where people pay to stay for a night or several nights

hothead NOUN
an impetuous person
hotheaded ADJECTIVE

hothouse NOUN
a heated greenhouse

hotly ADVERB
intensely a hotly disputed point

hotplate NOUN
a heated surface for cooking food

hotpot NOUN
a kind of stew

hound NOUN
a dog used in hunting or racing

hound VERB
to pursue or harass

hour NOUN
one twenty-fourth part of a day and night; sixty minutes

hourly ADVERB, ADJECTIVE
every hour

house (howss) NOUN
1 a building for people to live in
2 a building for a special purpose opera house
3 a government assembly House of Commons
4 one of the divisions in some schools
5 a family or dynasty the House of Tudor

house (howz) VERB
to provide accommodation for

houseboat NOUN
a boat for living in

household NOUN
all the people living in the same house

housekeeper NOUN
a person employed to look after a household

housekeeping NOUN
the business of looking after a household

housewife NOUN housewives
a woman who does the housekeeping for her family

housework NOUN
cleaning and cooking and other work done in a house

housing NOUN
accommodation; houses

hovel NOUN
a small shabby house

hover VERB
1 to stay in one place in the air
2 to wait about nearby

hovercraft NOUN
a vehicle that travels on a cushion of air produced by its engines

how ADVERB
1 in what way; by what means *How do you do it?*
2 to what extent or amount *How high can you jump?*
3 in what condition *How are you?*

however ADVERB
1 regardless of how *You can never win, however hard you try.*
2 all the same *Later, however, he left.*

howl NOUN
a long loud cry or sound, like that made by a dog or wolf

howl VERB
1 to make a howl
2 to weep loudly

howler NOUN
(*informal*) a foolish mistake

HQ ABBREVIATION
headquarters

hub NOUN
1 the central part of a wheel
2 the central point of interest or activity

hubbub NOUN
a loud confused noise of voices

huddle VERB
1 to crowd closely together
2 to curl your body closely
huddle NOUN

hue NOUN
a colour or tint

huff NOUN
a period of sulking

huff VERB
to blow hard

hug VERB **hugging, hugged**
1 to clasp tightly in your arms
2 to keep close to

hug NOUN
a tight embrace

huge ADJECTIVE
extremely large; enormous
hugely ADVERB

hulk NOUN
1 the body or wreck of an old ship
2 a large clumsy person or thing
hulking ADJECTIVE

hull NOUN
the framework of a ship

hullabaloo NOUN
an uproar

hullo EXCLAMATION
a word of greeting

hum VERB **humming, hummed**
1 to sing a tune with your lips closed
2 to make a low continuous sound like that of a bee

hum NOUN
a humming sound

human ADJECTIVE
to do with human beings

human NOUN
a human being

human being NOUN
a man, woman, or child

humane ADJECTIVE
kind-hearted and merciful
humanely ADVERB

humanist NOUN
a person who is concerned with people's needs and with finding rational ways to solve human problems rather than relying on religious belief
humanism NOUN

humanitarian ADJECTIVE
concerned with people's welfare
humanitarian NOUN

humanity NOUN
1 people in general
2 the state of being human
3 being humane
humanities PLURAL NOUN arts subjects such as history, literature, and music, not sciences

humble ADJECTIVE
1 modest; not proud or showy
2 of low rank or importance
humbly ADVERB

humble VERB
to make a person feel humble

humbug NOUN
1 insincere or dishonest talk
2 a hard peppermint sweet

humdrum ADJECTIVE
dull and not exciting

humid (**hew**-mid) ADJECTIVE
(of air) warm and damp
humidity NOUN

humiliate VERB
to make a person feel disgraced or ashamed
humiliation NOUN

humility NOUN
a humble state

hummingbird NOUN
a small tropical bird that makes a humming sound by beating its wings rapidly

humorous ADJECTIVE
full of humour; amusing

humour NOUN
1 an amusing aspect of something; what makes people laugh
2 the ability to enjoy comical things *a sense of humour*
3 a person's mood *a good humour*

humour VERB
to keep a person happy by agreeing to what they want

hump NOUN
1 a rounded lump or mound
2 a growth at the top of a person's back

hump VERB
to carry with difficulty

humus (**hew**-mus) NOUN
rich earth made by decayed plants

hunch [1] NOUN
a feeling about what is true or is going to happen

hunch [2] VERB
to bend your shoulders with your back rounded

hunchback NOUN
someone with a hump on their back
hunchbacked ADJECTIVE

hundred NOUN, ADJECTIVE
the number 100
hundredth ADJECTIVE, NOUN

hundredweight NOUN
a unit of weight equal to 112 pounds (about 50.8 kilograms)

hunger NOUN
1 a feeling of needing food
2 a strong desire

hunger VERB
to have a strong desire

hungry ADJECTIVE **hungrier, hungriest**
feeling hunger
hungrily ADVERB

hunk NOUN
a large piece of something

hunt VERB
1 to chase and kill animals for food or as a sport
2 to search for
hunter NOUN

hunt NOUN
1 an act of hunting
2 a group of hunters

hurdle NOUN
1 an upright frame to be jumped over in a race
2 an obstacle or difficulty

hurl VERB
to throw with great force

hurly-burly NOUN
busy noisy activity

hurray or **hurrah** EXCLAMATION
another spelling of **hurray**

hurricane NOUN
a storm with a strong wind

hurried ADJECTIVE
done in a hurry
hurriedly ADVERB

hurry VERB **hurries, hurried**
1 to move or act quickly
2 to try to make someone be quick

hurry NOUN
1 the act of hurrying
2 a need to hurry

hurt VERB **hurt**
1 to cause pain or injury to
2 to suffer pain *My leg hurts.*
3 to upset or offend

hurt NOUN
physical or mental pain or injury

hurtful ADJECTIVE
causing pain or offence

hurtle VERB
to move very rapidly

husband NOUN
the man to whom a woman is married

husbandry NOUN
1 farming
2 management of resources

hush VERB
to make or become quiet

hush NOUN
silence

hush-hush ADJECTIVE
(*informal*) highly secret

husk NOUN
the dry outer covering of some seeds and fruits

husky [1] ADJECTIVE **huskier, huskiest**
1 hoarse
2 big and strong; burly

husky [2] NOUN **huskies**
a large dog used in the Arctic for pulling sledges

hustle *VERB*
1 to hurry
2 to push or shove rudely

hut *NOUN*
a small roughly-made house or shelter

hutch *NOUN*
a box-like cage for a pet animal

hyacinth *NOUN*
a sweet-smelling flower that grows from a bulb

hybrid *NOUN*
1 a plant or animal produced by combining two different species or varieties
2 something that combines parts of two different things

hydrangea (hy-**drayn**-ja) *NOUN*
a shrub with clusters of pink, blue, or white flowers

hydrant *NOUN*
a special tap in the street for attaching a large hose to draw off water

hydraulic *ADJECTIVE*
worked by the force of water or other fluid

hydroelectric *ADJECTIVE*
using water power to produce electricity
hydroelectricity *NOUN*

hydrofoil *NOUN*
a boat designed to skim over the surface of water

hydrogen *NOUN*
a lightweight gas that combines with oxygen to form water

hydrogen bomb *NOUN*
a powerful bomb using energy created by the fusion of hydrogen nuclei

hydrolysis *NOUN*
(*Science*) the chemical reaction of a substance with water

hyena *NOUN*
a wild animal that makes a shrieking howl

hygiene (**hy**-jeen) *NOUN*
the practice of keeping things clean to remain healthy and prevent disease
hygienic *ADJECTIVE*

hymn *NOUN*
a religious song of praise

hype *NOUN*
(*informal*) extravagant publicity or advertising

hyperactive *ADJECTIVE*
always active and unable to relax

hyperbole (hy-**per**-bol-ee) *NOUN*
dramatic exaggeration for special effect, e.g. 'I've had thousands of letters'

hyperlink *NOUN*
(*ICT*) a place in a computer document that provides a link to another document

hypertext *NOUN*
(*ICT*) a computer document that contains links to other documents

hyphen *NOUN*
a short dash used to join words or parts of words together (e.g. in *hit-and-miss*)

hyphenate *VERB*
to join or spell with a hyphen
hyphenation *NOUN*

hypnosis *NOUN*
a condition like a deep sleep in which a person's actions may be controlled by another person
hypnotic *ADJECTIVE*

hypnotism *NOUN*
the process of producing hypnosis in a person
hypnotist *NOUN*

hypnotize *VERB*
to produce hypnosis in

hypochondriac (hy-po-**kon**-dree-ak) *NOUN*
a person who constantly worries that they are ill
hypochondria *NOUN*

hypocrite (**hip**-o-krit) *NOUN*
a person who pretends to be more virtuous than they really are
hypocrisy (hip-**ok**-riss-ee) *NOUN*
hypocritical *ADJECTIVE*

hypodermic *ADJECTIVE*
injecting drugs under the skin

hypotenuse (hy-**pot**-i-newz) *NOUN*
the longest side in a right-angled triangle

hypothermia *NOUN*
the condition of having a body temperature well below normal

hypothesis (hy-**poth**-i-sis) *NOUN*
hypotheses
a suggestion or argument that has not yet been proved true or correct
hypothetical *ADJECTIVE*

hysterectomy (hist-er-**ek**-tom-ee) *NOUN*
hysterectomies
the surgical removal of the womb

hysteria *NOUN*
wild uncontrollable excitement or panic

hysterical *ADJECTIVE*
1 in a state of hysteria
2 (*informal*) extremely funny
hysterically *ADVERB*

hysterics (hiss-**te**-riks) *PLURAL NOUN*
a fit of hysteria

a b c d e f g **h** i j k l m n o p q r s t u v w x y z

I *PRONOUN*
a word used to refer to the person speaking
or writing

ice *NOUN*
1 frozen water
2 an ice cream
icy *ADJECTIVE*

ice *VERB*
1 to make or become icy
2 to put icing on a cake

iceberg *NOUN*
a large mass of ice floating in the sea

ice cream *NOUN*
a sweet creamy frozen food

ice hockey *NOUN*
a form of hockey played on ice

ice rink *NOUN*
a place made for skating

icicle *NOUN*
a pointed hanging piece of ice formed when
dripping water freezes

icing *NOUN*
a sugary substance for decorating cakes

icon *NOUN*
1 a sacred painting or mosaic of a holy person
2 (*ICT*) a small symbol or picture on a
computer screen

ICT *ABBREVIATION*
information and communication technology

idea *NOUN*
1 a plan or thought formed in the mind
2 an opinion or belief
3 a feeling that something is likely

ideal *ADJECTIVE*
perfect; completely suitable
ideally *ADVERB*

ideal *NOUN*
1 a standard that people try to achieve
2 a person or thing regarded as perfect

idealist *NOUN*
a person with high ideals
idealism *NOUN* **idealistic** *ADJECTIVE*

identical *ADJECTIVE*
exactly the same
identically *ADVERB*

identification *NOUN*
1 a document that proves who you are
2 the process of identifying someone or
something

identify *VERB* **identifies**, **identified**
1 to recognize as being a certain person or
thing
2 to treat as identical to something else
3 to share someone's feelings
identifiable *ADJECTIVE*

identity *NOUN* **identities**
1 who or what a person or thing is
2 the state of being the same
3 distinctive character

ideology *NOUN* **ideologies**
a set of political beliefs and aims
ideological *ADJECTIVE*

idiocy *NOUN*
foolishness

idiom *NOUN*
a phrase with a meaning that cannot be
guessed from the words in it, e.g. *in hot water*
(= in trouble)
idiomatic *ADJECTIVE*

idiosyncrasy *NOUN* **idiosyncrasies**
a person's own way of behaving or doing
something

idiot *NOUN*
a stupid or foolish person

idiotic *ADJECTIVE*
stupid or foolish
idiotically *ADVERB*

idle *ADJECTIVE*
1 doing no work; lazy
2 not in use or working
3 useless or pointless *idle gossip*
idly *ADVERB*

idle *VERB*
1 to be idle
2 (of an engine) to be working slowly
idler *NOUN*

idol *NOUN*
1 an image that is worshipped as a god
2 a famous person who is widely admired

idolize *VERB*
to admire someone very much
idolization *NOUN*

idyll *NOUN*
1 a beautiful scene or situation
2 a poem describing a peaceful or romantic
scene

idyllic *ADJECTIVE*
very happy or beautiful

i.e. *ABBREVIATION*
that is

if *CONJUNCTION*
1 on condition that; supposing that
2 whether

igloo *NOUN*
an Inuit round house built of snow

ignite *VERB*
1 to set fire to
2 to catch fire

ignition *NOUN*
1 the process of igniting
2 the part of a motor engine that starts the fuel burning

ignoble *ADJECTIVE*
not noble; shameful

ignominious *ADJECTIVE*
humiliating; bringing disgrace
ignominy *NOUN*

ignorant *ADJECTIVE*
not knowing much or anything
ignorance *NOUN*

ignore *VERB*
to take no notice of

iguana (ig-**wah**-na) *NOUN*
a large tree-climbing tropical lizard

ilk *NOUN*
of that ilk (*informal*) of that kind

ill *ADJECTIVE*
1 unwell; in bad health
2 bad or harmful *no ill effects*

ill *ADVERB*
badly
ill at ease uncomfortable

ill *NOUN*
harm

illegal *ADJECTIVE*
not legal; against the law
illegality *NOUN* **illegally** *ADVERB*

illegible *ADJECTIVE*
impossible to read
illegibility *NOUN* **illegibly** *ADVERB*

illegitimate *ADJECTIVE*
born of parents who are not married to each other

illicit *ADJECTIVE*
against the law; not allowed
illicitly *ADVERB*

illiterate *ADJECTIVE*
unable to read or write
illiteracy *NOUN*

illness *NOUN*
a form of bad health

illogical *ADJECTIVE*
not logical; not reasoning correctly
illogicality *NOUN* **illogically** *ADVERB*

illuminate *VERB*
1 to light up
2 to decorate with lights
3 to help to explain
illumination *NOUN*

illusion *NOUN*
1 something that appears to be real but is not
2 a false idea or belief
illusory *ADJECTIVE*

illusionist *NOUN*
a conjuror

illustrate *VERB*
1 to show something by pictures, examples, etc.
2 to put illustrations in a book
illustrator *NOUN*

illustration *NOUN*
a picture in a book or magazine

illustrious *ADJECTIVE*
famous and distinguished

image *NOUN*
1 a picture or statue of a person or thing
2 a mental picture of something
3 a strong likeness to someone else
4 the public reputation of a person or organization

imagery *NOUN*
a writer's or speaker's use of words to produce pictures in the mind

imaginable *ADJECTIVE*
able to be imagined

imaginary *ADJECTIVE*
existing in the imagination; not real

imagination *NOUN*
the ability to imagine things in a creative way

imaginative *ADJECTIVE*
having or showing imagination

imagine *VERB*
1 to form pictures or ideas in the mind
2 to suppose

imam *NOUN*
a Muslim religious leader

imbalance *NOUN*
a lack of balance

imbecile *NOUN*
an idiot
imbecile *ADJECTIVE* **imbecility** *NOUN*

imitate *VERB*
to copy or mimic
imitator *NOUN*

imitation *NOUN*
1 the process of imitating
2 a copy that imitates

immaculate *ADJECTIVE*
1 perfectly clean; spotless
2 without any fault or blemish

immaterial *ADJECTIVE*
unimportant; not mattering

a
b
c
d
e
f
g
h
i
j
k
l
m
n
o
p
q
r
s
t
u
v
w
x
y
z

immature ADJECTIVE
not mature
immaturity NOUN

immediate ADJECTIVE
1 happening or done without any delay
2 nearest *our immediate neighbours*
immediacy NOUN

immediately ADVERB
without delay; straight away

immense ADJECTIVE
exceedingly great; huge
immensity NOUN

immerse VERB
1 to put completely into a liquid
2 to absorb in thought
immersion NOUN

immigrant NOUN
a person who comes to live in a country

immigrate VERB
to come into a country to live there
immigration NOUN

imminent ADJECTIVE
likely to happen at any moment

immobile ADJECTIVE
not moving; not able to move
immobility NOUN

immobilize VERB
to stop from moving or working
immobilization NOUN

immoral ADJECTIVE
morally wrong; improper
immorality NOUN

Do not confuse this word with *amoral*, which means 'having no moral standards'.

immortal ADJECTIVE
1 living for ever; not mortal
2 famous for all time
immortal NOUN **immortality** NOUN

immune ADJECTIVE
1 safe from catching a disease
2 not affected by *immune to his charms*
immunity NOUN

immunize VERB
to make a person immune from a disease,
e.g. by vaccination
immunization NOUN

imp NOUN
1 a small devil
2 a mischievous child
impish ADJECTIVE

impact NOUN
1 a collision; the force of a collision
2 an influence or effect

impair VERB
to damage or weaken

impala NOUN
an African antelope

impale VERB
to pierce or fix on a pointed object

impart VERB
to tell information or news

impartial ADJECTIVE
not favouring one side more than the other;
not biased
impartiality NOUN **impartially** ADVERB

impassable ADJECTIVE
(of a road) not able to be travelled along

impasse (am-pass) NOUN
a situation in which no progress can be made

impassive ADJECTIVE
not showing any emotion
impassively ADVERB

impatient ADJECTIVE
1 not patient; in a hurry
2 eager to do something without waiting
impatience NOUN **impatiently** ADVERB

impeach VERB
to bring a person to trial for a serious crime
against their country
impeachment NOUN

impeccable ADJECTIVE
faultless; perfect
impeccably ADVERB

impede VERB
to hinder or get in the way of

impediment NOUN
1 a hindrance
2 a defect

impel VERB **impelling, impelled**
1 to urge or drive someone to do something
2 to drive forward

impending ADJECTIVE
soon to happen; imminent

impenetrable ADJECTIVE
1 impossible to get through
2 incomprehensible

imperative ADJECTIVE
1 essential
2 (*Grammar*) expressing a command

imperceptible ADJECTIVE
too small or gradual to be noticed

imperfect ADJECTIVE
not perfect
imperfectly ADVERB

imperfection NOUN
a fault or weakness

imperial ADJECTIVE
to do with an empire or its rulers

imperialism NOUN
the policy of extending a country's empire or its influence
imperialist NOUN

impersonal ADJECTIVE
not affected by personal feelings
impersonally ADVERB

impersonate VERB
to pretend to be another person
impersonation NOUN

impertinent ADJECTIVE
insolent; not showing proper respect
impertinence NOUN

impervious ADJECTIVE
not affected by something *impervious to criticism*

impetuous ADJECTIVE
acting hastily without thinking

impetus NOUN
1 the force that makes an object start moving
2 an influence causing something to happen or develop

impinge VERB
impinge on to have an effect on

implacable ADJECTIVE
determined to remain hostile or opposed
implacably ADVERB

implant (im-plahnt) VERB
to insert or fix in
implantation NOUN

implant (im-plahnt) NOUN
an organ or piece of tissue inserted in the body

implement NOUN
a tool

implement VERB
to put into action
implementation NOUN

implicate VERB
to involve in a crime or wrongdoing

implication NOUN
something implied without being said

implicit ADJECTIVE
1 implied without being said
2 unquestioning *implicit obedience*
implicitly ADVERB

implode VERB
to burst or explode inwards
implosion NOUN

implore VERB
to beg somebody to do something

imply VERB **implies**, **implied**
to suggest something without actually saying it
implication NOUN

import (im-pawt) VERB
to bring in goods from abroad to be sold

import (im-pawt) NOUN
1 the importing of goods
2 something imported

important ADJECTIVE
1 having or able to have a great effect
2 having great authority or influence
importance NOUN

impose VERB
to put or inflict *It imposes a strain upon us.*
impose on to put an unfair burden on someone

imposition NOUN
an unfair burden or inconvenience

impossible ADJECTIVE
1 not possible
2 (*informal*) annoying; unbearable
impossibility NOUN **impossibly** ADVERB

impostor NOUN
a person who dishonestly pretends to be someone else

impotent ADJECTIVE
powerless; unable to take action
impotence NOUN **impotently** ADVERB

impound VERB
to confiscate or take possession of

impoverished ADJECTIVE
made poor or weak

impractical ADJECTIVE
not practical

impregnable ADJECTIVE
strong enough to be safe against attack

impregnate VERB
to fertilize or make pregnant

impress VERB
1 to make a person admire something
2 to fix firmly in the mind

impression NOUN
1 an effect produced on the mind *can make a big impression*
2 a vague idea
3 an imitation of a person or a sound

impressive ADJECTIVE
making a strong impression; important or good

imprint NOUN
a mark pressed into or on something

imprison VERB
to put or keep in prison
imprisonment NOUN

improbable ADJECTIVE
unlikely
improbability NOUN **improbably** ADVERB

impromptu ADJECTIVE, ADVERB
without any rehearsal or preparation

improper ADJECTIVE
1 unsuitable or wrong
2 indecent

improve VERB
to make or become better
improvement NOUN

improvise VERB
to make or perform without preparation
improvisation NOUN

impudent ADJECTIVE
cheeky or disrespectful
impudence NOUN

impulse NOUN
a sudden strong desire to do something

impulsive ADJECTIVE
done or acting on impulse

impunity (im-**pewn**-it-ee) NOUN
freedom from punishment

impure ADJECTIVE
not pure or clean
impurity NOUN

in PREPOSITION
1 at or inside in a box
2 within the limits of in two hours
3 into fall in a puddle
4 consisting of a serial in four parts
5 occupied with; a member of He is in the army.
6 by means of to pay in cash
in all in total number; altogether

in ADVERB
1 so as to be inside Do come in.
2 at home
3 in action or power
be in for to be likely to get be in for a shock

inability NOUN
lack of ability or power

inaccurate ADJECTIVE
not accurate

inactive ADJECTIVE
not active
inaction NOUN **inactivity** NOUN

inadequate ADJECTIVE
1 not enough
2 not able to cope or deal with something
inadequacy NOUN

inane ADJECTIVE
silly; without sense
inanely ADVERB **inanity** NOUN

inappropriate ADJECTIVE
not appropriate

inaudible ADJECTIVE
not loud enough to be heard
inaudibly ADVERB

inaugurate VERB
1 to start or introduce something new and important
2 to formally establish in office
inauguration NOUN

inborn ADJECTIVE
existing from birth

inbred ADJECTIVE
1 inborn
2 produced by inbreeding

incapable ADJECTIVE
not able to do something

incapacitate VERB
to make a person or thing unable to do something

incense (**in**-sens) NOUN
a substance making a spicy smell when it is burnt

incense (in-**sens**) VERB
to make angry

incentive NOUN
something that encourages a person to do something

inception NOUN
the beginning of something

incessant ADJECTIVE
continuing without a pause; unceasing

inch NOUN
a measure of length, one twelfth of a foot (about 2.5 centimetres)

inch VERB
to move gradually

incidence NOUN
the extent or frequency of something

incident NOUN
an event

incidental ADJECTIVE
happening as a minor part of something else
incidentally ADVERB

incinerator NOUN
a device for burning rubbish

incise VERB
to cut or engrave into a surface

incision NOUN
a cut made in a surgical operation

incisive ADJECTIVE
clear and sharp

incite VERB
to urge a person to act
incitement NOUN

inclination NOUN
1 a tendency
2 a liking or preference

incline (in-**klyn**) VERB
1 to lean or slope
2 to bend forward in a nod or bow
3 to cause or influence
be inclined to to tend to

incline (**in**-klyn) NOUN
a slope

include

include *VERB*
to make or consider as part of a group of things
inclusion *NOUN*

inclusive *ADJECTIVE*
including everything

incoherent *ADJECTIVE*
not speaking or reasoning in an orderly way

income *NOUN*
money received regularly from work or investments

incomparable (in-komp-er-abul) *ADJECTIVE*
without an equal

incompatible *ADJECTIVE*
not able to exist or be used together

incompetent *ADJECTIVE*
unable to do something well

incomplete *ADJECTIVE*
not complete

incomprehensible *ADJECTIVE*
not able to be understood
incomprehension *NOUN*

inconceivable *ADJECTIVE*
not able to be imagined; most unlikely

inconclusive *ADJECTIVE*
not conclusive

incongruous *ADJECTIVE*
out of place or unsuitable

inconsiderate *ADJECTIVE*
not considerate towards other people

inconsistent *ADJECTIVE*
not consistent
inconsistency *NOUN*

inconspicuous *ADJECTIVE*
not attracting attention

incontinent *ADJECTIVE*
not able to control the bladder or bowels
incontinence *NOUN*

inconvenience *NOUN*
something inconvenient

inconvenience *VERB*
to cause inconvenience to

inconvenient *ADJECTIVE*
not convenient

incorporate *VERB*
to include as a part of something larger
incorporation *NOUN*

incorrect *ADJECTIVE*
not correct
incorrectly *ADVERB*

incorrigible *ADJECTIVE*
not able to be reformed

independent

increase (in-krees) *VERB*
to make or become larger or more

increase (in-krees) *NOUN*
1 the process of increasing
2 the amount by which a thing increases

incredible *ADJECTIVE*
impossible to believe
incredibly *ADVERB*

incredulous *ADJECTIVE*
unwilling to believe something
incredulity *NOUN*

incriminate *VERB*
to show a person to have been involved in a crime
incrimination *NOUN*

incubate *VERB*
to hatch eggs by keeping them warm
incubation *NOUN*

incubator *NOUN*
1 a device for keeping a premature baby warm and supplied with oxygen
2 a device for incubating eggs

incur *VERB* **incurring, incurred**
to bring something on yourself *to incur expenses*

incurable *ADJECTIVE*
not able to be cured
incurably *ADVERB*

indebted *ADJECTIVE*
owing money or gratitude

indecent *ADJECTIVE*
not decent; improper
indecency *NOUN*

indeed *ADVERB*
1 used to strengthen a meaning *very hot indeed*
2 really; truly *I am indeed surprised.*

indefinite *ADJECTIVE*
not definite; vague
indefinitely *ADVERB*

indefinite article *NOUN*
the word 'a' or 'an'

indelible *ADJECTIVE*
impossible to rub out or remove

indent *VERB*
to start a line of writing or printing further in from the margin than other lines
indentation *NOUN*

independent *ADJECTIVE*
1 not dependent on any other person or thing
2 (of a country) free of foreign rule
3 not connected with something
independence *NOUN*

indescribable ADJECTIVE
too extraordinary to be described

indeterminate ADJECTIVE
not fixed or decided exactly

index NOUN
1 (**indexes**) an alphabetical list of subjects in a book
2 (**indices**) (*Maths*) the raised number written to the right of another (e.g. 3 in 2^3) showing how many times the first one is to be multiplied by itself

index VERB
to put into an index

index finger NOUN
the forefinger

indicate VERB
1 to point out or make known
2 to be a sign of
indication NOUN **indicator** NOUN

indicative ADJECTIVE
giving an indication

indict (ind-yt) VERB
to charge a person with a crime
indictment NOUN

indifferent ADJECTIVE
1 not caring or interested
2 not good
indifference NOUN

indigenous ADJECTIVE
growing or originating in a particular country

indigestible ADJECTIVE
difficult to digest

indigestion NOUN
pain or discomfort while digesting food

indignant ADJECTIVE
angry at something unfair
indignation NOUN

indignity NOUN **indignities**
treatment that makes a person feel humiliated

indigo NOUN
a deep-blue colour

indirect ADJECTIVE
not direct
indirectly ADVERB

indiscreet ADJECTIVE
not discreet; revealing secrets
indiscretion NOUN

indiscriminate ADJECTIVE
not choosing carefully; haphazard
indiscriminately ADVERB

indispensable ADJECTIVE
essential

indisposed ADJECTIVE
slightly unwell

indistinct ADJECTIVE
not clear

indistinguishable ADJECTIVE
not able to be told apart

individual ADJECTIVE
1 of or for one person
2 single or separate *each individual word*
individually ADVERB

individual NOUN
one person, animal, or plant

indivisible ADJECTIVE
not able to be divided or separated

indoctrinate VERB
to fill someone's mind with ideas or beliefs which they accept unthinkingly
indoctrination NOUN

indolent ADJECTIVE
lazy
indolence NOUN

indoor ADJECTIVE
used or done inside a building *indoor games*

indoors ADVERB
inside a building

indubitable ADJECTIVE
not able to be doubted
indubitably ADVERB

induce VERB
1 to persuade
2 to produce or cause
induction NOUN

inducement NOUN
an incentive

indulge VERB
to allow someone what they want

indulgent ADJECTIVE
kind and lenient
indulgence NOUN

industrial ADJECTIVE
to do with industry

industrialized ADJECTIVE
(of a country or district) having many industries
industrialization NOUN

industrious ADJECTIVE
working hard

industry NOUN **industries**
1 the making of goods in factories
2 a branch of this
3 hard work

inedible ADJECTIVE
not edible

ineffective ADJECTIVE
not effective; inefficient
ineffectively ADVERB

inefficient ADJECTIVE
not efficient
inefficiency NOUN

ineligible ADJECTIVE
not eligible or qualified

inept ADJECTIVE
lacking skill
ineptitude NOUN

inequality NOUN **inequalities**
an unequal or unfair state

inert ADJECTIVE
1 not moving or reacting
2 (*Science*) (of a gas) not combining with
other substances

inertia (in-er-sha) NOUN
1 the state of being inert or slow to take
action
2 (*Science*) the tendency for a moving thing
to keep moving

inescapable ADJECTIVE
unavoidable

inevitable ADJECTIVE
unavoidable; sure to happen
inevitably ADVERB

inexorable ADJECTIVE
relentless
inexorably ADVERB

inexpensive ADJECTIVE
not expensive; cheap
inexpensively ADVERB

inexperience NOUN
lack of experience
inexperienced ADJECTIVE

inexplicable ADJECTIVE
impossible to explain
inexplicably ADVERB

infallible ADJECTIVE
never wrong or failing
infallibility NOUN **infallibly** ADVERB

infamous (in-fam-us) ADJECTIVE
having a bad reputation; wicked
infamy NOUN

infancy NOUN
early childhood

infant NOUN
a baby or young child

infantile ADJECTIVE
1 to do with infants
2 childish

infantry NOUN
soldiers fighting on foot

infatuated ADJECTIVE
filled with foolish love
infatuation NOUN

infect VERB
to pass on a disease to

infection NOUN
an infectious disease or condition

infectious ADJECTIVE
1 (of a disease) able to be spread by air or
water
2 quickly spreading *infectious laughter*

infer VERB **inferring**, **inferred**
to draw a conclusion from what someone
says or does
inference NOUN
Do not use this word to mean *imply* or
suggest.

inferior ADJECTIVE
less good or important
inferiority NOUN

inferior NOUN
a person who is lower in position or rank

infernal ADJECTIVE
to do with or like hell *infernal regions*
infernally ADVERB

inferno NOUN **infernos**
a huge fire that is out of control

infertile ADJECTIVE
not fertile
infertility NOUN

infest VERB
(of pests) to be present in large numbers in a
place
infestation NOUN

infidelity NOUN
unfaithfulness

infiltrate VERB
to get into an organization gradually in order
to control it
infiltration NOUN **infiltrator** NOUN

infinite ADJECTIVE
endless; without a limit
infinitely ADVERB

infinitesimal ADJECTIVE
extremely small

infinitive NOUN
(*Grammar*) the basic form of a verb
(e.g. *come* and *kill*, sometimes preceded
by *to* (e.g. *I want to come*)

infinity *NOUN*
an infinite number or distance or time

infirm *ADJECTIVE*
weak from old age or illness
infirmity *NOUN*

infirmary *NOUN* **infirmaries**
a hospital

inflamed *ADJECTIVE*
1 red and swollen
2 angry

inflammable *ADJECTIVE*
able to be set on fire

inflammation *NOUN*
painful redness or swelling in a part of
the body

inflammatory *ADJECTIVE*
likely to make people angry

inflate *VERB*
1 to fill with air or gas
2 to increase too much
inflatable *ADJECTIVE*

inflation *NOUN*
a general rise in prices

inflection *NOUN*
(*Grammar*) an ending or form of a word used
to change its role in a sentence, e.g. *take*,
takes, *taking*, *took*

inflexible *ADJECTIVE*
1 not able to be bent
2 unable to be persuaded

inflict *VERB*
to make a person suffer something

influence *NOUN*
1 the power to affect other people or things
2 a person or thing with this power

influence *VERB*
to have an influence on

influential *ADJECTIVE*
having great influence

influenza *NOUN*
an infectious disease causing fever

influx *NOUN*
the arrival of people or things

inform *VERB*
to give information to

informal *ADJECTIVE*
not formal
informality *NOUN* **informally** *ADVERB*

informant *NOUN*
someone who gives information

information *NOUN*
knowledge or facts

informative *ADJECTIVE*
giving a lot of information

informed *ADJECTIVE*
knowing about something

informer *NOUN*
a person who gives information to the police

infrared *ADJECTIVE*
below or beyond red in the spectrum

infrastructure *NOUN*
the basic services and systems of a country

infringe *VERB*
1 to break a rule or law
2 to encroach on a person's rights
infringement *NOUN*

infuriate *VERB*
to make angry

ingenious *ADJECTIVE*
1 clever at inventing things
2 cleverly made
ingenuity *NOUN*

ingot *NOUN*
a lump of gold or silver in the form of a brick

ingrained *ADJECTIVE*
(of feelings or habits) deeply fixed

ingratitude *NOUN*
lack of gratitude

ingredient *NOUN*
one of the parts of a mixture

inhabit *VERB*
to live in a place
inhabitant *NOUN*

inhale *VERB*
to breathe in
inhaler *NOUN*

inherent *ADJECTIVE*
existing naturally in someone or something

inherit *VERB*
1 to receive property when someone dies
2 to receive from parents
inheritance *NOUN*

inhibit *VERB*
to hinder or restrain
inhibited *ADJECTIVE*

inhibition *NOUN*
a feeling of embarrassment or worry that
prevents a person from acting in a natural way

inhuman *ADJECTIVE*
cruel; without pity or kindness
inhumanity *NOUN*

inhumane *ADJECTIVE*
not humane

initial *NOUN*
the first letter of a word or name

initial *VERB* **initialling**, **initialled**
to mark or sign with the initials of your name

initial ADJECTIVE
at the beginning   *the initial stages*
initially ADVERB

initiate VERB
1 to start
2 to admit to a group
initiation NOUN

initiative NOUN
the right or ability to take action

inject VERB
to put a medicine or drug into the body
injection NOUN

injunction NOUN
a legal order not to do something

injure VERB
to harm or hurt someone

injury NOUN **injuries**
an instance of harm or damage

injustice NOUN
an unjust action or treatment

ink NOUN
a black or coloured liquid used in writing and
printing

inkling NOUN
a slight idea or suspicion

inland ADJECTIVE, ADVERB
in or towards the interior of a country

inlet NOUN
a strip of water reaching into the land from a
sea or lake

inmost ADJECTIVE
most inward; furthest in

inn NOUN
a country hotel or pub

innards PLURAL NOUN
(*informal*) the internal organs of a person or
animal

innate ADJECTIVE
inborn or natural

inner ADJECTIVE
inside; nearer to the centre
innermost ADJECTIVE

innings NOUN
the turn of a cricket team or player to bat

innocent ADJECTIVE
1 not guilty or bad
2 harmless
innocence NOUN

innocuous ADJECTIVE
harmless

innovation NOUN
something completely new
innovative ADJECTIVE

innuendo NOUN **innuendoes**
an indirect reference to something insulting
or rude

innumerable ADJECTIVE
too many to be counted

inoculate VERB
to inject with a vaccine or serum as a
protection against a disease
inoculation NOUN

inoffensive ADJECTIVE
not giving offence

inordinate ADJECTIVE
excessive
inordinately ADVERB

inorganic ADJECTIVE
not of living organisms; of mineral origin

input NOUN
data put into a computer

inquest NOUN
an official inquiry into a sudden death

inquire VERB
1 to investigate carefully
2 to ask for information

inquiry NOUN **inquiries**
1 an official investigation
2 a question

inquisition NOUN
a detailed investigation

inquisitive ADJECTIVE
fond of asking questions

insane ADJECTIVE
mad
insanity NOUN

insatiable ADJECTIVE
impossible to satisfy

inscribe VERB
to write or carve

inscription NOUN
words written or carved

inscrutable ADJECTIVE
mysterious

insect NOUN
a small animal with six legs and no backbone

insecure ADJECTIVE
not secure or safe
insecurity NOUN

insensible ADJECTIVE
unconscious or unaware

insensitive ADJECTIVE
not sensitive

inseparable ADJECTIVE
not able or wanting to be separated
inseparably ADVERB

insert VERB
to put a thing into something else
insertion NOUN

inshore ADVERB, ADJECTIVE
near or nearer to the shore

inside NOUN
the inner side, surface, or part

inside ADJECTIVE, ADVERB
on or to the inside

inside PREPOSITION
on or to the inside of *inside the box*

insidious ADJECTIVE
causing harm gradually

insight NOUN
the ability to understand things

insignificant ADJECTIVE
not important or influential
insignificance NOUN

insincere ADJECTIVE
not sincere
insincerity NOUN

insinuate VERB
1 to hint something unpleasant
2 to become gradually involved
insinuation NOUN

insipid ADJECTIVE
lacking flavour or interest

insist VERB
to be firm in saying or asking
insistent ADJECTIVE

insolent ADJECTIVE
rude and insulting
insolence NOUN

insoluble ADJECTIVE
impossible to solve or dissolve

insomnia NOUN
an inability to sleep
insomniac NOUN

inspect VERB
to examine carefully
inspection NOUN **inspector** NOUN

inspiration NOUN
1 a sudden good idea
2 an inspiring influence

inspire VERB
to fill a person with ideas or enthusiasm

install VERB
to put in position
installation NOUN

instalment NOUN
1 each of several payments
2 each part of a story

instance NOUN
an example

instant ADJECTIVE
happening or ready immediately

instant NOUN
a moment

instantaneous ADJECTIVE
happening immediately

instead ADVERB
in place of something else

instep NOUN
the top of the foot between the toes and
the ankle

instigate VERB
to cause to happen
instigation NOUN

instil VERB **instilling**, **instilled**
to put ideas into a person's mind gradually

instinct NOUN
a natural tendency or ability
instinctive ADJECTIVE

institute NOUN
a society or organization

institute VERB
to establish or found

institution NOUN
1 a public organization
2 a habit or custom

instruct VERB
1 to teach a person a subject or skill
2 to tell a person what they must do
instruction NOUN **instructor** NOUN

instructive ADJECTIVE
giving knowledge or information

instrument NOUN
1 a device for producing musical sounds
2 a tool or device

instrumental ADJECTIVE
1 performed on musical instruments
2 helping to make something happen

insubordinate ADJECTIVE
disobedient or rebellious
insubordination NOUN

insufferable ADJECTIVE
unbearable

insufficient ADJECTIVE
not enough

insular ADJECTIVE
like an island

insulate VERB
to cover or protect to prevent heat, cold,
electricity, etc. from passing in or out
insulation NOUN

insulin NOUN
a substance that controls the amount of
sugar in the blood

insult (in-sult) VERB
to hurt a person's feelings or pride

insult (in-sult) NOUN
an insulting remark

insuperable ADJECTIVE
unable to be overcome *an insuperable difficulty*

insurance NOUN
an agreement to compensate someone for a loss, damage, injury, etc., in return for a payment made in advance

insure VERB
to protect with insurance
Do not confuse this word with *ensure*.

intact ADJECTIVE
not damaged; complete

intake NOUN
the number of people or things accepted

intangible ADJECTIVE
not able to be touched; not solid

integer NOUN
a whole number (e.g. 0, 3, 19), not a fraction

integral (in-tig-ral) ADJECTIVE
1 being an essential part of something
2 whole or complete

integrate VERB
1 to make into a whole
2 to bring people together
integration NOUN

integrity NOUN
honesty

intellect NOUN
the ability to reason

intellectual ADJECTIVE
1 to do with or using the intellect
2 having a good intellect

intellectual NOUN
a person with a good intellect

intelligence NOUN
1 the state of being intelligent
2 information of military value

intelligent ADJECTIVE
able to learn and understand well

intelligible ADJECTIVE
able to be understood
intelligibility NOUN

intend VERB
to have something in mind as what you want to do

intense ADJECTIVE
1 very strong or great
2 feeling things strongly
intensity NOUN

intensify VERB **intensifies, intensified**
to make or become more intense

intensive ADJECTIVE
concentrated; using a lot of effort over a short time

intent NOUN
intention

intent ADJECTIVE
intent on determined to do something

intention NOUN
a purpose or plan

intentional ADJECTIVE
deliberate
intentionally ADVERB

inter VERB **interring, interred**
to bury

interactive ADJECTIVE
(ICT) allowing information to be sent immediately between a computer system and its user

intercede VERB
to intervene on behalf of another person
intercession NOUN

intercept VERB
to stop or catch a person or thing that is going from one place to another
interception NOUN

interchange VERB
to exchange or alternate
interchangeable ADJECTIVE

interchange NOUN
a major road junction

intercom NOUN
a system of telephone communication between parts of a building

intercourse NOUN
communication between people

interest NOUN
1 a feeling of wanting to know about something
2 something that interests someone
3 an advantage
4 money paid in return for money lent

interest VERB
to attract the interest of

interface NOUN
(ICT) a connection between parts of a computer system

interfere VERB
1 to take part in something that is not your concern
2 to get in the way

interference NOUN
1 the act of interfering
2 distortion of a radio or television signal

interim ADJECTIVE
temporary *an interim arrangement*

interior ADJECTIVE
inner

interior NOUN
the inside of something

interject VERB
to interrupt someone
interjection NOUN

interlude NOUN
1 an interval
2 something happening between other events

intermediary NOUN **intermediaries**
someone who tries to settle a dispute

intermediate ADJECTIVE
coming between two things

interminable ADJECTIVE
long and tedious
interminably ADVERB

intermission NOUN
an interval or pause

intermittent ADJECTIVE
happening at intervals; not continuous
intermittently ADVERB

internal ADJECTIVE
happening or situated inside
internally ADVERB

international ADJECTIVE
1 to do with or belonging to more than one country
2 agreed between nations
internationally ADVERB

international NOUN
a sports contest between different countries

Internet NOUN
an international computer network that allows users to communicate and exchange information

interpret VERB
1 to explain or translate
2 to perform music
interpretation NOUN **interpreter** NOUN

interrogate VERB
to question someone closely or formally
interrogation NOUN **interrogator** NOUN

interrogative ADJECTIVE
expressing a question

interrupt VERB
1 to break in on what someone is saying
2 to prevent from continuing
interruption NOUN

intersect VERB
1 to divide a thing by passing or lying across it
2 (of lines or roads) to cross each other
intersection NOUN

interval NOUN
1 a time between two events or parts
2 a space between two things

intervene VERB
1 to come between two events
2 to try to stop something
intervention NOUN

interview NOUN
a formal meeting with someone to obtain information

interview VERB
to hold an interview with someone

intestine NOUN
the tube along which food passes after the stomach

intimate (in-tim-at) ADJECTIVE
1 friendly
2 private and personal
intimacy NOUN

intimate (in-tim-ayt) VERB
to hint at something
intimation NOUN

intimidate VERB
to frighten with threats
intimidation NOUN

into PREPOSITION
1 to the inside of *went into the house*
2 to a different condition *It broke into pieces.*

intolerable ADJECTIVE
unbearable
intolerably ADVERB

intonation NOUN
the tone or pitch of the voice in speaking

intone VERB
to recite in a chanting voice

intoxicate VERB
1 to make drunk
2 to excite
intoxication NOUN

intransitive ADJECTIVE
(of a verb) not having a direct object, e.g. *walk* in *We walked to the station.*

intrepid ADJECTIVE
fearless and brave

intricate ADJECTIVE
very complicated
intricacy NOUN **intricately** ADVERB

intrigue (in-treeg) VERB
1 to interest very much
2 to plot or scheme

intrigue NOUN
secret plotting

intrinsic ADJECTIVE
being part of the essential nature of
something *intrinsic value*
intrinsically ADVERB

introduce VERB
1 to bring into use
2 to make a person known to other people

introduction NOUN
1 the act of introducing
2 a piece at the beginning of a book
explaining its contents
introductory ADJECTIVE

introspective ADJECTIVE
examining your own thoughts and feelings
introspection NOUN

introvert NOUN
someone who does not like to talk about their
own thoughts and feelings with other people

intrude VERB
to join in without being wanted
intrusion NOUN **intrusive** ADJECTIVE

intruder NOUN
1 someone who intrudes
2 a burglar

intuition NOUN
the power to know or understand things
naturally
intuitive ADJECTIVE

Inuit (in-yoo-it) NOUN
1 a member of a people living in northern
Canada and Greenland; an Eskimo
2 the language of the Inuit
Inuit is preferred to *Eskimo*.

inundate VERB
to flood or overwhelm
inundation NOUN

inured (in-yoord) ADJECTIVE
used to something unpleasant

invade VERB
to attack and enter a country
invader NOUN

invalid (in-va-leed) NOUN
a person who is ill or weakened by illness

invalid (in-**val**-id) ADJECTIVE
not valid
invalidity NOUN

invalidate VERB
to make invalid
invalidation NOUN

invaluable ADJECTIVE
extremely valuable
This is not the opposite of *valuable*, which is
valueless.

invasion NOUN
the act of invading a country

invent VERB
to make or think of something new
invention NOUN **inventive** NOUN
inventor NOUN

inventory (in-ven-ter-ee) NOUN
inventories
a detailed list of things

inverse ADJECTIVE
opposite or reverse

invert VERB
to turn something upside down
inversion NOUN

invertebrate NOUN
an animal without a backbone
invertebrate ADJECTIVE

inverted commas PLURAL NOUN
a pair of punctuation marks (' ' or " ") put
round quotations and spoken words

invest VERB
1 to use money to make a profit
2 to give someone an honour
investor NOUN

investigate VERB
to find out as much as you can about
investigation NOUN **investigator** NOUN

investment NOUN
1 an amount of money invested
2 something in which money is invested

inveterate ADJECTIVE
firmly established *an inveterate liar*

invidious ADJECTIVE
causing resentment because of unfairness

invigorate VERB
to give a person strength or courage

invincible ADJECTIVE
not able to be defeated
invincibility NOUN

invisible ADJECTIVE
not able to be seen

invite VERB
1 to ask a person to come or do something
2 to be likely to cause *to invite disaster*
invitation NOUN

inviting ADJECTIVE
attractive or tempting

invoice NOUN
a written request for payment

invoke VERB
to appeal or pray to
invocation NOUN

involuntary ADJECTIVE
not deliberate
involuntarily ADVERB

i

a
b
c
d
e
f
g
h
i
j
k
l
m
n
o
p
q
r
s
t
u
v
w
x
y
z

involve *VERB*
1 to have as a part or make necessary
2 to make someone take part in something
involvement *NOUN*

involved *ADJECTIVE*
1 complicated
2 taking part

inward *ADJECTIVE*
1 on the inside
2 going or facing inwards

inward *ADVERB*
inwards

inwards *ADVERB*
towards the inside

iodine *NOUN*
a chemical substance used as an antiseptic

ion *NOUN*
an electrically charged particle

iota *NOUN*
a tiny amount of something *not an iota of truth in the story*

IQ *ABBREVIATION*
intelligence quotient; a number indicating a person's intelligence

irascible *ADJECTIVE*
easily becoming angry

irate *ADJECTIVE*
angry

iridescent *ADJECTIVE*
coloured like a rainbow
iridescence *NOUN*

iris *NOUN*
1 the coloured part of the eyeball
2 a plant with long pointed leaves and large flowers

irk *VERB*
to bother or annoy

irksome *ADJECTIVE*
annoying or tiresome

iron *NOUN*
1 a hard grey metal
2 a device for pressing clothes or cloth
3 a tool made of iron
iron *ADJECTIVE*

iron *VERB*
to smooth clothes or cloth with an iron

Iron Age *NOUN*
the time when tools and weapons were made of iron

ironic *ADJECTIVE*
using irony; full of irony
ironical *ADJECTIVE* **ironically** *ADVERB*

ironmonger *NOUN*
a shopkeeper who sells tools and household equipment
ironmongery *NOUN*

irons *PLURAL NOUN*
shackles or fetters

irony *NOUN* **ironies**
1 saying the opposite of what you mean in order to emphasize it
2 an oddly contradictory situation

irrational *ADJECTIVE*
not rational; illogical
irrationally *ADVERB*

irregular *ADJECTIVE*
1 not regular; uneven
2 against the rules or custom
irregularity *NOUN*

irrelevant *ADJECTIVE*
not relevant
irrelevance *NOUN*

irreparable *ADJECTIVE*
unable to be repaired
irreparably *ADVERB*

irreplaceable *ADJECTIVE*
unable to be replaced

irrepressible *ADJECTIVE*
always lively and cheerful

irresistible *ADJECTIVE*
too strong or attractive to be resisted
irresistibly *ADVERB*

irrespective *ADJECTIVE*
not taking something into account
irrespective of cost

irresponsible *ADJECTIVE*
not showing a proper sense of responsibility
irresponsibly *ADVERB*

irreverent *ADJECTIVE*
not reverent or respectful
irreverence *NOUN*

irrevocable (ir-ev-ok-a-bul) *ADJECTIVE*
unable to be altered
irrevocably *ADVERB*

irrigate *VERB*
to supply land with water for crops
irrigation *NOUN*

irritable *ADJECTIVE*
easily annoyed; bad-tempered

irritant *NOUN*
something that annoys or causes itching

irritate *VERB*
1 to annoy
2 to cause itching
irritation *NOUN*

Islam *NOUN*
the religion of Muslims
Islamic *ADJECTIVE*

island *NOUN*
a piece of land surrounded by water
islander *NOUN*

isle (*say as* I'll) *NOUN*
an island

isn't
is not

isobar (I-so-bar) *NOUN*
a line on a map connecting places that have the same atmospheric pressure

isolate *VERB*
to place apart or alone
isolation *NOUN*

isosceles (I-**soss**-il-eez) *ADJECTIVE*
(of a triangle) having two sides of equal length

isotope *NOUN*
(*Science*) a form of an element that differs from other forms in the structure of its nucleus but has the same chemical properties as the other forms

issue *VERB*
1 to supply or give out
2 to send out information or a warning
3 to publish
4 to come or go out

issue *NOUN*
1 a subject for discussion or concern
2 a particular edition of a newspaper or magazine
3 the process of issuing
4 (*formal*) children *He died without issue.*

isthmus *NOUN*
a narrow strip of land connecting two larger pieces of land

IT *ABBREVIATION*
information technology

it *PRONOUN*
the thing being talked about

italic *ADJECTIVE*
printed with sloping letters (called *italics*, *like this*)

itch *VERB*
1 to feel a tickling sensation in the skin
2 to long to do something

itch *NOUN*
an itching feeling
itchy *ADJECTIVE*

item *NOUN*
one thing in a list or group of things

itinerant *ADJECTIVE*
travelling from place to place

itinerary *NOUN* **itineraries**
a list of places to be visited on a journey

its *POSSESSIVE PRONOUN*
belonging to it *The cat hurt its paw.*
Do not use an apostrophe unless you mean 'it is' or 'it has' (see the next entry).

it's
it is or it has
Do not confuse *its* and *it's*.

itself *PRONOUN*
it and nothing else
by itself on its own; alone

ivory *NOUN* **ivories**
the hard white substance forming elephants' tusks

ivy *NOUN* **ivies**
a climbing plant with shiny leaves

Jj

jab *VERB* **jabbing**, **jabbed**
to push or poke roughly

jab *NOUN*
1 a jabbing movement
2 (*informal*) an injection

jabber *VERB*
to speak quickly and indistinctly
jabber *NOUN*

jack *NOUN*
1 a device for lifting a heavy weight
2 a playing card with a picture of a young man

jack *VERB*
to lift with a jack

jackal *NOUN*
a wild animal like a dog

jackass *NOUN*
1 a male donkey
2 a stupid person

jackdaw *NOUN*
a kind of small crow

jacket *NOUN*
1 a short coat reaching to the hips
2 a paper wrapper for a book

jack-in-the-box *NOUN*
a toy figure on a spring that leaps from a box when the lid is lifted

jackknife *VERB*
(of an articulated lorry) to skid and swing against itself

jackpot *NOUN*
an amount of prize money that increases until someone wins it

Jacobite *NOUN*
a supporter of the exiled Stuarts after the abdication of James II (1688)

Jacuzzi (ja-**koo**-zi) *NOUN*
(*trademark*) a large bath with underwater jets of water

jade NOUN
a green stone that is carved to make ornaments

jaded ADJECTIVE
tired and bored

jagged (jag-id) ADJECTIVE
having a rough uneven edge

jaguar NOUN
a South American animal like a leopard

jail NOUN
a prison

jail VERB
to put into prison
jailer NOUN

Jain (say as Jane) NOUN
a believer in an Indian religion similar to Buddhism

jam NOUN
1 a thick sweet food made of fruit boiled with sugar
2 a crush of people or vehicles
in a jam in a difficult situation

jam VERB **jamming, jammed**
1 to make or become unable to move
2 to crowd or squeeze into a space

jamb (jam) NOUN
a side post of a doorway or window frame

jamboree NOUN
a large party or celebration

jam-packed ADJECTIVE
tightly packed; congested

jangle VERB
to make a harsh ringing sound
jangle NOUN

janitor NOUN
a caretaker

January NOUN
the first month of the year

jar[1] NOUN
a container made of glass or pottery

jar[2] VERB **jarring, jarred**
1 to cause an unpleasant jolt
2 to sound unpleasantly harsh

jargon NOUN
special words used by a profession or group

jasmine NOUN
a shrub with yellow or white flowers

jaundice NOUN
a disease in which the skin becomes yellow
jaundiced ADJECTIVE

jaunt NOUN
a short trip for pleasure

jaunty ADJECTIVE **jauntier, jauntiest**
lively and cheerful
jauntily ADVERB

javelin NOUN
a light spear for throwing

jaw NOUN
the lower part of the face round the mouth

jay NOUN
a brightly coloured bird

jazz NOUN
a kind of music with strong rhythm, often improvised

jazzy ADJECTIVE **jazzier, jazziest**
bright and colourful

jealous ADJECTIVE
1 unhappy because someone is better or luckier than you
2 careful in keeping something
jealousy NOUN

jeans PLURAL NOUN
trousers made of strong cotton fabric

jeep NOUN
(trademark) a small sturdy army vehicle

jeer VERB
to scoff at
jeer NOUN

jelly NOUN **jellies**
1 a soft transparent food
2 a soft slippery substance
jellied ADJECTIVE

jellyfish NOUN
a sea animal with a body like jelly

jemmy NOUN **jemmies**
a burglar's crowbar

jeopardize (jep-er-dyz) VERB
to put in danger or at risk

jeopardy (jep-er-dee) NOUN
danger of harm or failure

jerk VERB
1 to make a sudden sharp movement
2 to pull suddenly

jerk NOUN
a sudden sharp movement

jerkin NOUN
a sleeveless jacket

jerky ADJECTIVE **jerkier, jerkiest**
moving in jerks
jerkily ADVERB

jersey NOUN **jerseys**
1 a pullover with sleeves
2 a plain machine-knitted material

jest NOUN
a joke

jest VERB
to make jokes

jester NOUN
a professional entertainer at a royal court in the Middle Ages

jet[1] *NOUN*
1 a stream of water, gas, flame, etc.
2 an aircraft driven by engines that send out a jet of hot gases

jet[2] *NOUN*
1 a hard black mineral substance
2 a deep glossy black colour

jetsam *NOUN*
goods thrown overboard and washed ashore

jettison *VERB*
1 to throw overboard
2 to get rid of

jetty *NOUN* **jetties**
a small landing stage

Jew *NOUN*
a member of a people descended from the ancient tribes of Israel
Jewish *ADJECTIVE*

jewel *NOUN*
a precious stone
jewelled *ADJECTIVE*

jeweller *NOUN*
a person who sells or makes jewellery

jewellery *NOUN*
jewels and similar ornaments for wearing

jib[1] *NOUN*
1 a triangular sail stretching forward from a ship's front mast
2 the arm of a crane

jib[2] *VERB* **jibbing**, **jibbed**
to be reluctant or unwilling to do something

jiffy *NOUN* **jiffies**
(*informal*) a moment

jig *NOUN*
a lively jumping dance

jig *VERB* **jigging**, **jigged**
to move up and down quickly

jigsaw *NOUN*
a puzzle in which pieces have to be put together to make a picture

jihad *NOUN*
a war or struggle undertaken by Muslims

jilt *VERB*
to abandon a boyfriend or girlfriend

jingle *VERB*
to make or cause to make a tinkling sound

jingle *NOUN*
1 a jingling sound
2 a simple verse or tune

jingoism *NOUN*
an unreasonable belief that your country is superior to others
jingoistic *ADJECTIVE*

jinx *NOUN*
a person or thing that brings bad luck

jitters *PLURAL NOUN*
(*informal*) a nervous feeling

jittery *ADJECTIVE*
nervous

job *NOUN*
1 work that someone does regularly to earn a living
2 a piece of work to be done

jockey *NOUN* **jockeys**
a person who rides horses in races

jocular *ADJECTIVE*
joking
jocularity *NOUN*

jodhpurs (jod-perz) *PLURAL NOUN*
trousers for horse riding, fitting closely from the knee to the ankle

jog *VERB* **jogging**, **jogged**
1 to run or trot slowly
2 to give a slight push
jogger *NOUN*

jog *NOUN*
1 a slow run or trot
2 a slight knock or push

join *VERB*
1 to put or come together
2 to take part with others in an activity
I joined the search party.
3 to become a member of

join *NOUN*
a place where things join

joiner *NOUN*
a person who makes wooden furniture
joinery *NOUN*

joint *NOUN*
1 a place where two things are joined
2 a large piece of meat cut ready for cooking

joint *ADJECTIVE*
shared or done by two or more people or groups
jointly *ADVERB*

joist *NOUN*
a beam supporting a floor or ceiling

joke *NOUN*
something said or done to make people laugh

joke *VERB*
1 to make jokes
2 to tease or not be serious

joker *NOUN*
1 someone who jokes
2 an extra playing card with a jester on it

jolly *ADJECTIVE* **jollier**, **jolliest**
cheerful and good-humoured

jolly *ADVERB*
(*informal*) very *jolly good*

a
b
c
d
e
f
g
h
i
j
k
l
m
n
o
p
q
r
s
t
u
v
w
x
y
z

jolly

jolly *VERB* **jollies**, **jollied**
(*informal*) **jolly along** to keep someone
cheerful

jolt *VERB*
1 to shake with a sudden movement
2 to move along jerkily
3 to give someone a shock

jolt *NOUN*
1 a jolting movement
2 a shock

jostle *VERB*
to push roughly in a crowd

jot *VERB* **jotting**, **jotted**
to write quickly

jotter *NOUN*
a notepad or notebook

joule (jool) *NOUN*
(*Science*) a unit of work or energy

journal *NOUN*
1 a newspaper or magazine
2 a diary

journalist *NOUN*
a person who writes for a newspaper or
magazine
journalism *NOUN*

journey *NOUN* **journeys**
the process of going from one place to
another

journey *VERB*
to make a journey

joust (jowst) *VERB*
(in medieval times) to fight on horseback
with lances
joust *NOUN*

jovial *ADJECTIVE*
cheerful and good-humoured
joviality *NOUN*

jowl *NOUN*
the jaw or cheek

joy *NOUN*
1 a feeling of pleasure or happiness
2 a thing that causes this

joyful *ADJECTIVE*
very happy
joyfully *ADVERB*

joyous *ADJECTIVE*
full of joy

joyride *NOUN*
a drive in a stolen car
joyrider *NOUN*

joystick *NOUN*
1 the control lever of an aircraft
2 a control device in computer games

jumble

jubilant *ADJECTIVE*
rejoicing or triumphant
jubilation *NOUN*

jubilee (joo-bil-ee) *NOUN*
a special anniversary

Judaism (joo-day-izm) *NOUN*
the religion of the Jewish people

judder *VERB*
to shake noisily or violently

judge *NOUN*
1 a person who hears cases in a lawcourt
2 a person who applies the rules in a
competition
3 someone who is good at forming opinions

judge *VERB*
1 to act as a judge
2 to form and give an opinion
3 to estimate

judgement *NOUN*
1 the process of judging
2 the decision made by a lawcourt
3 an opinion
4 the ability to judge wisely

judicial *ADJECTIVE*
to do with lawcourts or judges
judicially *ADVERB*

judiciary *NOUN*
the judges of a country

judicious *ADJECTIVE*
showing good sense or judgement
judiciously *ADVERB*

judo *NOUN*
a Japanese method of self-defence

jug *NOUN*
a container for liquids, with a handle and a lip

juggernaut *NOUN*
a large articulated lorry

juggle *VERB*
1 to toss and catch objects skilfully
2 to rearrange things
juggler *NOUN*

jugular *ADJECTIVE*
to do with the throat or neck

juice *NOUN*
1 the liquid from fruit or vegetables
2 a liquid produced by the stomach

juicy *ADJECTIVE* **juicier**, **juiciest**
containing a lot of juice

jukebox *NOUN*
a machine that automatically plays a record
you have selected when you put a coin in

July *NOUN*
the seventh month of the year

jumble *VERB*
to mix up into a confused mass

jumble *NOUN*
a confused mixture or muddle

jumble sale NOUN
a sale of second-hand goods

jumbo NOUN **jumbos**
1 something very large
2 an elephant

jump VERB
1 to move up suddenly from the ground into the air
2 to go over something by jumping
3 to pass over or miss out
4 to move suddenly in surprise

jump NOUN
1 a jumping movement
2 a sudden rise or change

jumper NOUN
a jersey

jumpy ADJECTIVE **jumpier**, **jumpiest**
nervous and edgy

junction NOUN
1 a join
2 a place where roads or railway lines meet

juncture NOUN
a point of time

June NOUN
the sixth month of the year

jungle NOUN
a thick tangled forest in a tropical country
jungly ADJECTIVE

junior ADJECTIVE
1 younger
2 for young children *a junior school*
3 lower in rank *junior officers*

junior NOUN
a junior person

juniper NOUN
an evergreen shrub

junk [1] NOUN
things of no value

junk [2] NOUN
a Chinese sailing boat

junk food NOUN
food that is not nourishing

junk mail NOUN
unwanted advertising sent by post

jurisdiction NOUN
authority or official power

juror NOUN
a member of a jury

jury NOUN **juries**
a group of people appointed to give a verdict in a lawcourt

just ADJECTIVE
1 giving proper consideration to everyone's claims
2 deserved *a just reward*
justly ADVERB

just ADVERB
1 exactly *just what I wanted*
2 only; simply *I just wanted to see him.*
3 by a small amount *just below the knee*
4 only a little while ago *She has just gone.*

justice NOUN
1 fair treatment
2 a judge or magistrate

justification NOUN
good reason

justify VERB **justifies**, **justified**
1 to show that something is fair or just
2 to arrange lines of text with an even margin
justifiable ADJECTIVE

jut VERB **jutting**, **jutted**
to stick out

jute NOUN
fibre from tropical plants

juvenile ADJECTIVE
1 of or for young people
2 childish

juvenile NOUN
a young person

juxtapose VERB
to put things side by side
juxtaposition NOUN

Kk

kaleidoscope (kal-y-dos-kohp) NOUN
a tube to look through to see changing patterns

kangaroo NOUN
an Australian animal that jumps on its hind legs

karaoke (ka-ri-**oh**-ki) NOUN
an entertainment of singing against a pre-recorded backing

karate (ka-**rah**-tee) NOUN
a Japanese method of self-defence using the hands and feet

kayak NOUN
a small canoe

KB or **Kb** ABBREVIATION
kilobytes

kebab NOUN
small pieces of meat or vegetables cooked on a skewer

keel NOUN
the long piece of wood or metal along the bottom of a boat

keel VERB
keel over to fall down or overturn

keen [1] *ADJECTIVE*
1 enthusiastic or interested
2 sharp *a keen edge keen eyesight*
3 (of the wind) very cold
keenness *NOUN*

keen [2] *VERB*
to wail in mourning

keep *VERB* **kept**
1 to have and look after
2 to stay or cause to stay in the same condition
3 to do something continually *He keeps laughing.*
4 (of food) to last without going bad
5 to respect and not break *keep your word*

keep *NOUN*
1 the food etc. that are needed to live
2 a strong tower in a castle

keeper *NOUN*
1 a person who looks after an animal, building, etc.
2 a goalkeeper or wicketkeeper

keeping *NOUN*
care and attention *in safe keeping*

keepsake *NOUN*
a gift in memory of the person who gave it

keg *NOUN*
a small barrel

kelvin *NOUN*
(*Science*) the SI unit of thermodynamic temperature

kennel *NOUN*
a shelter for a dog

kerb *NOUN*
the edge of a pavement

kernel *NOUN*
the part inside the shell of a nut or fruit

kerosene *NOUN*
paraffin

kestrel *NOUN*
a small falcon

ketchup *NOUN*
a thick sauce made from tomatoes

kettle *NOUN*
a container with a spout for boiling water

kettledrum *NOUN*
a drum made of a large metal bowl with a skin stretched over the top

key *NOUN*
1 a piece of metal shaped to open a lock
2 a device for winding up a clock or clockwork mechanism
3 a small lever to be pressed by a finger on a piano or computer
4 a system of notes in music
5 an explanation
6 a list of symbols used in a map or table

key *VERB*
to type information into a computer

keyboard *NOUN*
the set of keys on a piano, typewriter, or computer

keyhole *NOUN*
the hole through which a key is put into a lock

keypad *NOUN*
a small keyboard or set of buttons used to operate a telephone, television, etc.

kg *ABBREVIATION*
kilogram

khaki *NOUN*
a dull yellowish-brown colour used for military uniforms

kibbutz *NOUN*
a farming commune in Israel

kick *VERB*
to hit or move with your foot

kick *NOUN*
1 a kicking movement
2 (*informal*) a thrill

kick-off *NOUN*
the start of a football match

kid *NOUN*
1 (*informal*) a child
2 a young goat
3 the skin of a young goat

kid *VERB* **kidding, kidded**
(*informal*) to deceive playfully

kidnap *VERB* **kidnapping, kidnapped**
to take someone away by force
kidnapper *NOUN*

kidney *NOUN* **kidneys**
an organ in the body that removes waste products from the blood

kill *VERB*
1 to end the life of
2 to destroy or put an end to
killer *NOUN*

kill *NOUN*
the act of killing an animal

killing *NOUN*
an act causing death

kiln *NOUN*
an oven for hardening pottery or bricks

kilo *NOUN*
a kilogram

kilobyte *NOUN*
a unit of computer data equal to 1,024 bytes

kilogram *NOUN*
a unit of mass or weight equal to 1,000 grams

kilohertz *NOUN*
a unit of frequency of electromagnetic waves, equal to 1,000 cycles per second

kilometre *NOUN*
a unit of length equal to 1,000 metres

kilowatt *NOUN*
a unit of electrical power equal to 1,000 watts

kilt *NOUN*
a kind of pleated skirt worn by men

kimono *NOUN* **kimonos**
a long loose Japanese robe

kin *NOUN*
a person's relatives
next of kin a person's closest relative

kind [1] *NOUN*
a sort or type

kind [2] *ADJECTIVE*
friendly and helpful
kindly *ADVERB* **kindness** *NOUN*

kindergarten *NOUN*
a school or class for young children

kind-hearted *ADJECTIVE*
kind and considerate

kindle *VERB*
1 to start a flame
2 to begin burning

kindly *ADJECTIVE* **kindlier**, **kindliest**
kind

kinetic *ADJECTIVE*
to do with or produced by movement
kinetic energy

king *NOUN*
1 a country's male ruler who reigns because
of his birth
2 the most important piece in chess
3 a playing card with a picture of a king

kingdom *NOUN*
1 a country ruled by a king or queen
2 a major division of the natural world

kingfisher *NOUN*
a bird with blue feathers that dives to catch fish

king-size or **king-sized** *ADJECTIVE*
extra large

kink *NOUN*
a short twist in a rope, wire, etc.

kinsman or **kinswoman** *NOUN* **kinsmen**
or **kinswomen**
a male or female relation

kiosk *NOUN*
1 a telephone box
2 a stall for selling newspapers etc.

kip *NOUN*
(*informal*) a short sleep

kipper *NOUN*
a smoked herring

kiss *NOUN*
the act of touching lips as a sign of affection

kiss *VERB*
to give someone a kiss

kit *NOUN*
1 equipment or clothes
2 a set of parts for fitting together

kitchen *NOUN*
a room in which meals are prepared and
cooked

kite *NOUN*
1 a light covered framework flown in the wind
on a string
2 a large hawk

kith and kin
friends and relatives

kitten *NOUN*
a young cat

kitty *NOUN* **kitties**
a fund of money for a special purpose

kiwi (**kee-wee**) *NOUN* **kiwis**
a New Zealand bird that cannot fly

kiwi fruit *NOUN*
a fruit with thin hairy skin and green flesh

kleptomania *NOUN*
an uncontrollable urge to steal
kleptomaniac *NOUN*

km *ABBREVIATION*
kilometre

knack *NOUN*
a special skill

knapsack *NOUN*
a bag carried on the back by soldiers and
hikers

knave *NOUN*
1 a rogue
2 a jack in playing cards

knead *VERB*
to press and stretch dough with the hands

knee *NOUN*
the joint in the middle of the leg

kneecap *NOUN*
the bone covering the front of the knee joint

kneel *VERB* **knelt**
to be or get yourself in a position on your
knees

knell *NOUN*
the sound of a bell rung solemnly after a death

knickers *PLURAL NOUN*
underpants worn by women and girls

knick-knack *NOUN*
a small ornament

knife *NOUN* **knives**
a tool with a blade for cutting

knife VERB
to stab with a knife

knight NOUN
1 a man who has been given the rank can put *Sir* before his name
2 (in the Middle Ages) a warrior of high social rank
3 a piece in chess, with a horse's head
knighthood NOUN

knit VERB **knitting**, **knitted** or **knit**
to make clothing by looping wool with needles or a machine
knitting NOUN

knob NOUN
1 the round handle of a door, drawer, etc.
2 a round lump
3 a round button or switch
4 a small round piece *a knob of butter*
knobbly ADJECTIVE **knobby** ADJECTIVE

knock VERB
1 to hit hard to make a noise
2 to produce by hitting *to knock a hole in the wall*
3 (*informal*) to criticize unfavourably
knock out to make unconscious

knock NOUN
the act or sound of knocking

knocker NOUN
a hinged device on a door, for knocking

knockout NOUN
1 the act of knocking someone out
2 a contest in which the loser in each round has to drop out

knoll NOUN
a small round hill

knot NOUN
1 a place where a piece of string, rope, etc. is twisted round itself or another piece
2 a tangle or lump
3 a round spot on a piece of wood where a branch joined it
4 a cluster of people or things
5 a unit of speed for ships and aircraft, equal to 1.85 kilometres per hour

knot VERB
1 to tie or fasten with a knot
2 to entangle

knotty ADJECTIVE **knottier**, **knottiest**
1 full of knots
2 difficult or puzzling

know VERB **knew**, **known**
1 to have something in your mind that you have learned or discovered
2 to recognize or be familiar with

knowing ADJECTIVE
showing that you know something

knowledge NOUN
1 the fact of knowing
2 all that is known

knowledgeable ADJECTIVE
having a lot of knowledge
knowledgeably ADVERB

knuckle NOUN
a joint in the finger

knuckle VERB
knuckle down to begin to work hard

koala (koh-**ah**-la) NOUN
an Australian animal like a small bear

Koran NOUN
the sacred book of Islam

kosher ADJECTIVE
keeping to Jewish laws about the preparation of food

krypton NOUN
an inert gas present in the earth's atmosphere and used in fluorescent lights

kudos (**kew**-doss) NOUN
honour and glory

kung fu NOUN
a Chinese method of self-defence

Ll

lab NOUN
(*informal*) a laboratory

label NOUN
a small piece of paper, cloth, etc. attached to something to give information about it

label VERB **labelling**, **labelled**
1 to put a label on
2 to identify with a name

laboratory NOUN **laboratories**
a place equipped for scientific experiments

laborious ADJECTIVE
1 needing a lot of hard work
2 lengthy and tedious

labour NOUN
1 hard work
2 a task
3 workers
4 the contractions of the womb during childbirth

labour VERB
1 to work hard
2 to explain or discuss at tedious length

labourer NOUN
a person who does heavy manual work

Labrador NOUN
a large black or light-brown dog

laburnum NOUN
a tree with hanging yellow flowers

labyrinth NOUN
a complicated set of passages or paths

lace NOUN
1 net-like material with decorative patterns of holes in it
2 a piece of thin cord for fastening shoes etc.

lace VERB
1 to fasten with a lace
2 to thread a cord through

lack NOUN
the state of being without something

lack VERB
to be without

lackadaisical ADJECTIVE
lacking energy; feeble

lackey NOUN **lackeys**
1 a male servant
2 a person who behaves or is treated like a servant

lacking ADJECTIVE
not having something, or not having enough

laconic ADJECTIVE
using few words
laconically ADVERB

lacquer NOUN
a hard glossy varnish
lacquered ADJECTIVE

lacrosse NOUN
a game using a stick with a net on it to catch and throw a ball

lad NOUN
a boy or youth

ladder NOUN
1 a set of rungs between two upright pieces of wood or metal, used for climbing up or down
2 a row of undone stitches in a pair of tights or stockings

laden ADJECTIVE
carrying a load

ladle NOUN
a large deep spoon for lifting and pouring liquids

ladle VERB
to lift and pour a liquid with a ladle

lady NOUN **ladies**
1 a well-mannered woman
2 a woman of good social position
ladyship NOUN

ladybird NOUN
a small flying beetle, usually red with black spots

ladylike ADJECTIVE
(of a woman) well-mannered

lag[1] VERB **lagging**, **lagged**
to fail to keep up with others

lag NOUN
a delay

lag[2] VERB **lagging**, **lagged**
to wrap pipes or boilers etc. in insulating material

lager (lah-ger) NOUN
a light beer

lagoon NOUN
a salt-water lake separated from the sea by sandbanks or reefs

laid *past tens* of **lay** VERB

laid-back ADJECTIVE
(*informal*) relaxed and easy-going

lain *past participle* of **lie**[2] VERB

lair NOUN
a sheltered place where a wild animal lives

lake NOUN
a large area of water surrounded by land

lama NOUN
a Buddhist priest or monk in Tibet and Mongolia

lamb NOUN
1 a young sheep
2 meat from a lamb

lame ADJECTIVE
1 unable to walk normally
2 weak; not convincing *a lame excuse*
lamely ADVERB **lameness** NOUN

lament NOUN
a statement, song, or poem expressing grief or regret

lament VERB
to express grief or regret about
lamentation NOUN

lamentable (lam-in-ta-bul) ADJECTIVE
regrettable or deplorable

laminated ADJECTIVE
made of thin layers or sheets pressed together *laminated plastic*

lamp NOUN
a device for producing light from electricity, gas, or oil

lamppost NOUN
a tall post with a lamp at the top

lamprey NOUN **lampreys**
a small eel-like water animal

lance NOUN
a long spear

lance *VERB*
to cut open a boil etc. with a knife

lance corporal *NOUN*
a soldier ranking between a private and a corporal

lancet *NOUN*
a pointed two-edged knife used in surgery

land *NOUN*
1 the part of the earth's surface not covered by sea
2 the ground or soil
3 a country

land *VERB*
1 to arrive on land or the shore
2 to bring an aircraft to the ground
3 (*informal*) to obtain *to land a job*
4 (*informal*) to present with a problem

landed *ADJECTIVE*
1 owning land
2 consisting of land

landing *NOUN*
1 the level area at the top of a staircase
2 the act of bringing or coming to land
3 a place where people can get on and off a boat

landlady *NOUN* **landladies**
1 a woman who lets rooms to lodgers
2 a woman who runs a pub

landlocked *ADJECTIVE*
almost or entirely surrounded by land

landlord *NOUN*
1 a person who lets a house, room, or land to a tenant
2 a person who runs a pub

landlubber *NOUN*
(*informal*) a person who is not used to the sea

landmark *NOUN*
1 an object that is easily seen in the distance
2 an important event

landmine *NOUN*
an explosive mine laid near the surface of the ground

landowner *NOUN*
a person who owns a large amount of land

landscape *NOUN*
1 a view of a particular area of countryside or town
2 a picture of the countryside

landslide *NOUN*
1 a mass of soil and rocks sliding down a slope
2 an overwhelming victory in an election

lane *NOUN*
1 a narrow country road
2 a strip of road for a single line of traffic

language *NOUN*
1 words and their use
2 the words used by a particular people

languid *ADJECTIVE*
slow and lacking energy
languor *NOUN*

languish *VERB*
1 to live in miserable conditions
2 to become weak or listless

lank *ADJECTIVE*
(of hair) long and limp

lanky *ADJECTIVE* **lankier**, **lankiest**
awkwardly thin and tall

lantern *NOUN*
a transparent case for holding a light

lap [1] *NOUN*
1 the level place between the knees and the waist of someone sitting
2 one circuit round a racetrack

lap *VERB* **lapping**, **lapped**
to overtake another competitor in a race to become one or more laps ahead

lap [2] *VERB* **lapping**, **lapped**
1 to take up liquid by moving the tongue
2 to make a gentle splash against

lapel (la-**pel**) *NOUN*
a flap folded back at the front edge of a coat or jacket

lapse *NOUN*
1 a slight mistake or failure
2 an amount of time between two events
a lapse of two months

lapse *VERB*
1 to pass or slip gradually *to lapse into unconsciousness*
2 to be no longer valid

laptop *NOUN*
a portable computer for use while travelling

lapwing *NOUN*
a black and white bird with a crested head and a shrill cry

larceny *NOUN*
the crime of stealing possessions

larch *NOUN*
a tall deciduous tree that bears small cones

lard *NOUN*
melted pig fat used in cooking

larder *NOUN*
a cupboard or small room for storing food

large *ADJECTIVE*
of more than the ordinary size
at large free; not captured

largely *ADVERB*
to a great extent *is largely responsible*

a b c d e f g h i j k l m n o p q r s t u v w x y z

lark[1] NOUN
a light brown songbird

lark[2] NOUN
(*informal*) a bit of fun

lark VERB
lark about (*informal*) to have fun

larva NOUN **larvae**
an insect in the first stage of its life

laryngitis NOUN
inflammation of the larynx, causing hoarseness

larynx (la-rinks) NOUN **larynxes** or **larynges**
the part of the throat that contains the vocal cords

lasagne (laz-an-ya) NOUN
a dish made from sheets of pasta with minced meat and cheese

laser NOUN
a device that makes a strong narrow beam of light or other electromagnetic radiation

lash NOUN
1 a stroke with a whip or stick
2 the cord or cord-like part of a whip
3 an eyelash

lash VERB
1 to beat with a whip
2 to tie with cord
lash out to speak or hit out angrily

lashings PLURAL NOUN
plenty

lass NOUN
a girl or young woman

lasso NOUN **lassos**
a rope with a sliding noose at the end, used for catching cattle or wild horses

lasso VERB **lassoes**, **lassoing**, **lassoed**
to catch an animal with a lasso

last[1] ADJECTIVE, ADVERB
1 coming after all others; final
2 latest; most recent *last night*
3 least likely *the last person I'd have thought of*
the last straw a final thing that makes a problem unbearable

last NOUN
1 a person or thing that is last
2 the end *fighting to the last*

last[2] VERB
1 to continue or go on existing
2 to be enough for

last[3] NOUN
a block used for repairing shoes or making them by hand

lastly ADVERB
in the last place; finally

latch NOUN
a small bar fastening a door or gate

latch VERB
to fasten with a latch

late ADJECTIVE, ADVERB
1 after the usual or expected time
2 near the end *late in the afternoon*
3 recent *the latest news*
4 recently dead *the late king*

lately ADVERB
recently

latent (lay-tent) ADJECTIVE
existing but not active or visible

lateral ADJECTIVE
1 to do with the side or sides
2 sideways *lateral movement*
laterally ADVERB

latex NOUN
the milky juice of the rubber tree

lath NOUN
a narrow thin strip of wood

lathe (layth) NOUN
a machine for holding and turning pieces of wood while they are being shaped

lather NOUN
a mass of froth

lather VERB
to form a lather

Latin NOUN
the language of the ancient Romans

latitude NOUN
1 the distance of a place from the equator, measured in degrees
2 freedom of action

latrine (la-treen) NOUN
a toilet in a camp or barracks

latter ADJECTIVE
later *the latter part of the year*
the latter the second of two people or things mentioned

latterly ADVERB
recently

lattice NOUN
a framework of crossed strips or bars

laud VERB
(*formal*) to praise

laudable ADJECTIVE
deserving praise
laudably ADVERB

laudatory ADJECTIVE
expressing praise

laugh VERB
to make the sounds that show you are happy or think something is funny
laughable ADJECTIVE

laugh NOUN
the sound of laughing

laughter NOUN
the act, sound, or manner of laughing

launch [1] VERB
1 to send a ship from the land into the water
2 to send a rocket into space
3 to set a thing moving
4 to make available
5 to start *to launch an attack*

launch NOUN
the launching of a ship, spacecraft, or new product

launch [2] NOUN
a large motor boat

launder VERB
to wash and iron clothes etc.

launderette NOUN
a place fitted with washing machines that people pay to use

laundry NOUN **laundries**
1 a place where clothes etc. are washed
2 clothes etc. for washing

laurel NOUN
an evergreen shrub with smooth shiny leaves

lava NOUN
molten rock that flows from a volcano and becomes solid when it cools

lavatory NOUN **lavatories**
a toilet

lavender NOUN
1 a shrub with sweet-smelling purple flowers
2 a light-purple colour

lavish ADJECTIVE
1 generous
2 plentiful

lavish VERB
to give generously

law NOUN
1 a rule or set of rules
2 the profession of lawyers
3 (*informal*) the police
4 a scientific principle *the law of gravity*

lawcourt NOUN
a room or building in which a judge or magistrate hears evidence and decides whether someone has broken the law

lawful ADJECTIVE
allowed by the law
lawfully ADVERB

lawless ADJECTIVE
not having or obeying laws

lawn NOUN
an area of closely cut grass in a garden or park

lawyer NOUN
a person qualified to give advice about the law

lax ADJECTIVE
slack; not strict
laxity NOUN

laxative NOUN
a medicine that stimulates the bowels to empty

lay [1] VERB **laid**
1 to put something down in a particular place or way
2 to arrange things
3 to place *laid the blame on his sister*
4 to form or prepare *We laid our plans.*
5 to produce an egg
lay off to stop employing someone for a while **lay on** to supply or provide

lay [2] *past tense* of **lie** [2]

lay [3] ADJECTIVE
1 not belonging to the clergy
2 not professional

layabout NOUN
an idle person who avoids work

lay-by NOUN
a place where vehicles can stop beside a main road

layer NOUN
a single thickness or coating

layman NOUN **laymen**
a person who does not have special knowledge of a subject

layout NOUN
an arrangement of parts according to a plan

laze VERB
to spend time in a lazy way

lazy ADJECTIVE **lazier**, **laziest**
not wanting to work
lazily ADVERB **laziness** NOUN

lead [1] (leed) VERB **led**
1 to take or guide by going in front
2 to be winning in a race or contest
3 to be in charge of
4 to be a way or route *a path leading to the beach*
5 to live or experience *to lead a dull life*

lead (leed) NOUN
1 a leading place or part or position *She took the lead on the final bend.*
2 guidance or example *We should be taking a lead on this issue.*
3 a clue to be followed
4 a strap or cord for leading a dog or other animal
5 an electrical wire attached to something

lead [2] (led) NOUN
1 a soft heavy grey metal
2 the substance in a pencil, made of graphite, that marks the paper

leaden ADJECTIVE
1 made of lead
2 heavy and slow
3 dark grey *leaden skies*

leader NOUN
1 the person in charge of a group
2 the person who is winning
3 a leading article in a newspaper
leadership NOUN

leaf NOUN **leaves**
1 a flat green part growing from a branch or stem
2 the paper forming one page of a book
3 a thin sheet or flap
leafy ADJECTIVE

leaflet NOUN
a piece of paper printed with information

league NOUN
1 a group of competing teams
2 a group of people or nations working together

leak NOUN
1 an escape of liquid or gas
2 the revealing of secret information
leaky ADJECTIVE

leak VERB
1 to escape or let out through a leak
2 to reveal secret information
leakage NOUN

lean¹ ADJECTIVE
thin or lacking fat

lean² VERB **leaned** or **leant**
1 to bend your body
2 to put or be in a sloping position
3 to rest against something
4 to rely or depend on for help

leaning NOUN
a tendency or preference

leap VERB **leaped** or **leapt**
to jump vigorously
leap NOUN

leapfrog NOUN
a game in which players jump with legs apart over others bending down

leap year NOUN
a year with an extra day in it (29 February)

learn VERB **learned** or **learnt**
1 to get knowledge or skill
2 to find out about something

learned (ler-nid) ADJECTIVE
having or showing much knowledge

learner NOUN
a person who is learning something

learning NOUN
knowledge got by study

lease NOUN
an agreement to allow someone to use a building or land etc. for a fixed period in return for payment

lease VERB
to allow or obtain the use of by lease

leash NOUN
a dog's lead

least ADJECTIVE, ADVERB
very small in amount etc.

least NOUN
the smallest amount or degree

leather NOUN
material made from animal skins
leathery ADJECTIVE

leave VERB **left**
1 to go away from a person or place
2 to cause something to stay as it is
3 to go away without taking
4 to give responsibility for something *left the decision to you*
5 to put something to be collected or passed on
leave out to omit or exclude

leave NOUN
official permission to be away

lecherous ADJECTIVE
showing strong sexual desire

lectern NOUN
a stand for a large book

lecture NOUN
1 a formal talk
2 a serious warning

lecture VERB
to give a lecture to
lecturer NOUN

led *past tense* of **lead**¹

ledge NOUN
a narrow shelf

ledger NOUN
an account book

lee NOUN
the sheltered side away from the wind

leech NOUN
a blood-sucking worm

leek NOUN
a long green and white vegetable of the onion family

leer VERB
to look at someone in a lustful or unpleasant way
leer NOUN

leeway NOUN
extra space or time available

a b c d e f g h i j k l m n o p q r s t u v w x y z

left [1] ADJECTIVE, ADVERB
1 on or towards the west if you are facing north
2 (of politics) in favour of socialist or radical views
left-hand ADJECTIVE

left NOUN
the left-hand side or part etc.

left [2] *past tense* of **leave**

left-handed ADJECTIVE
using the left hand in preference

leg NOUN
1 one of the limbs on which a person or animal stands or moves
2 each of the supports of a chair or table
3 one stage of a journey
4 each of a pair of sports matches

legacy NOUN **legacies**
property left to a person in a will

legal ADJECTIVE
1 lawful
2 to do with the law
legally ADVERB

legality NOUN
the state of being legal

legalize VERB
to make legal

legate NOUN
an official representative

legend NOUN
a traditional story

legendary ADJECTIVE
1 existing in legend
2 famous for a long time

leggings PLURAL NOUN
tight-fitting trousers worn by women

legible ADJECTIVE
clear enough to read
legibility NOUN **legibly** ADVERB

legion NOUN
1 a division of an army
2 a large number of people

legionnaire NOUN
a member of an association of former soldiers

legionnaires' disease NOUN
a serious form of pneumonia caused by bacteria

legislate VERB
to make laws
legislation NOUN **legislative** ADJECTIVE

legislature NOUN
a country's parliament or law-making assembly

legitimate ADJECTIVE
1 born of married parents
2 acceptable or reasonable
legitimacy NOUN

leisure NOUN
time that is free from work
leisured ADJECTIVE

leisurely ADJECTIVE
done without hurrying *a leisurely stroll*

lemming NOUN
a small mouse-like animal of Arctic regions that is said to run headlong into the sea and drown during its mass migration

lemon NOUN
1 an yellow fruit with a sour taste
2 a pale yellow colour

lemonade NOUN
a lemon-flavoured drink

lemur (**lee**-mer) NOUN
a monkey-like animal

lend VERB **lent**
1 to give someone something they have to give back
2 to give or add a quality *lent dignity to the occasion*
lend a hand to help in a task

length NOUN
1 extent from one end to the other
2 a strip cut from a larger piece

lengthen VERB
to make or become longer

lengthways or **lengthwise** ADVERB
from end to end; along the longest part

lengthy ADJECTIVE
going on for a long time

lenient ADJECTIVE
not strict
leniency NOUN

lens NOUN
1 a curved piece of glass or plastic used to focus in glasses, cameras, etc.
2 the transparent part of the eye

Lent NOUN
a time of fasting observed by Christians before Easter

lent *past tense* of **lend**

lentil NOUN
a kind of small bean

leopard (**lep**-erd) NOUN
a large spotted animal of the cat family

leotard (**lee**-o-tard) NOUN
a close-fitting piece of clothing worn for dancing, gymnastics, etc.

leper NOUN
a person who has leprosy

leprechaun (**lep**-rek-awn) NOUN
an elf that looks like a little old man

leprosy NOUN
an infectious disease that makes parts of the body waste away
leprous ADJECTIVE

lesbian NOUN
a homosexual woman

less ADJECTIVE, ADVERB
smaller in amount; not so much

less NOUN
a smaller amount

less PREPOSITION
minus; deducting *£100 less tax*

lessen VERB
to make or become less

lesser ADJECTIVE
not so great as the other *the lesser evil*

lesson NOUN
1 a period of teaching
2 something to be learned
3 an example or experience

lest CONJUNCTION
(*old use*) to prevent *Remind us, lest we forget.*

let VERB **letting**, **let**
1 to allow
2 to leave *Let it alone.*
3 to give someone use of a house or building in return for payment
let down to disappoint or fail **let off 1** to excuse from a duty or punishment **2** to cause to explode **let up** (*informal*) **1** to relax **2** to become less intense

lethal (**lee**-thal) ADJECTIVE
causing death
lethally ADVERB

lethargy NOUN
lack of energy
lethargic ADJECTIVE

letter NOUN
1 a symbol representing a sound
2 a written message

lettering NOUN
letters drawn or painted

lettuce NOUN
a garden plant with broad crisp leaves used in salads

leukaemia (lew-**kee**-mee-a) NOUN
a disease of the white corpuscles in the blood

level ADJECTIVE
1 flat or horizontal
2 at the same height or position

level NOUN
1 height, depth, position, or value in relation to other things
2 a level surface
3 a tool that shows whether something is level

level VERB **levelling**, **levelled**
1 to make or become level
2 to aim or direct

level crossing NOUN
a place where a road crosses a railway at the same level

lever NOUN
1 a bar for lifting or forcing something
2 a handle for operating machinery

lever VERB
to lift or move with a lever

leverage NOUN
1 the force of a lever
2 power or influence

levitate VERB
to rise in the air
levitation NOUN

levity NOUN
unsuitable humour

levy VERB **levies**, **levied**
to impose a tax or other payment

levy NOUN **levies**
an amount of money paid in tax

lewd ADJECTIVE
indecent or crude

liability NOUN **liabilities**
1 legal responsibility
2 a debt or obligation
3 a disadvantage

liable ADJECTIVE
1 likely to do or suffer something
2 legally responsible

liaise (lee-**ayz**) VERB
(*informal*) to act in cooperation with someone

liaison (lee-**ay**-zon) NOUN
communication and cooperation

liar NOUN
a person who tells lies

libel NOUN
an untrue statement that damages a person's reputation
libellous ADJECTIVE

libel VERB **libelling**, **libelled**
to make a libel about someone

liberal ADJECTIVE
1 giving or given generously
2 not strict; tolerant
liberally ADVERB

liberate VERB
to set free
liberation NOUN **liberator** NOUN

liberty NOUN **liberties**
freedom to speak and act
take liberties to behave impolitely

librarian NOUN
a person in charge of or working in a library

library NOUN **libraries**
1 a place where books are kept for use or loan
2 a collection of books, records, films, etc.

libretto NOUN **libretti** or **librettos**
the words of an opera

lice *plural* of **louse**

licence NOUN
1 an official permit to do or use or own
something
2 special freedom to avoid the usual rules or
customs

license VERB
to authorize by law

lichen (ly-ken) NOUN
a dry-looking plant growing on rocks,
walls, etc.

lick VERB
1 to pass the tongue over
2 to touch lightly
3 (*informal*) to defeat

lick NOUN
1 an act of licking
2 a slight application of paint etc.

lid NOUN
a cover for a box or pot etc.

lie [1] NOUN
an deliberate untrue statement

lie VERB **lies**, **lied**
to tell a lie

lie [2] VERB **lies**, **lay**, **lain**
1 to be or get in a flat or resting position
2 to be or remain

lieutenant (lef-ten-ant) NOUN
1 an officer in the army or navy
2 a deputy

life NOUN **lives**
1 the period between birth and death
2 the state of being alive
3 living things
4 liveliness *full of life*

lifebelt NOUN
a ring of buoyant material to support a person
in water

lifeboat NOUN
a boat for rescuing people at sea

lifebuoy NOUN
a device to support a person needing rescue
in water

lifeguard NOUN
a person qualified to rescue swimmers in
difficulty

life jacket NOUN
a jacket of buoyant material to support a
person in water

lifeless ADJECTIVE
unconscious or without life

lifelike ADJECTIVE
looking like a real person or thing

lifelong ADJECTIVE
lasting for a whole life

lifetime NOUN
the time someone is alive

lift VERB
1 to raise or pick up
2 to rise up
3 to remove a restriction

lift NOUN
1 a device for taking people or goods from
one floor or level to another in a building
2 a ride in someone else's car

lift-off NOUN
the launch of a rocket or spacecraft

ligament NOUN
a tough flexible tissue that holds the bones of
the body together

light [1] NOUN
1 radiation that makes things visible
2 a lamp or other source of light
3 a flame

light ADJECTIVE
1 full of light; not dark
2 pale

light VERB **lit** or **lighted**
1 to start a thing burning
2 to provide light for

light [2] ADJECTIVE
1 having little weight; not heavy
2 small in amount or force *light rain*
3 needing little effort *light work*
4 cheerful, not sad *with a light heart*
5 not serious or profound *light music*
lightly ADVERB

lighten VERB
to make or become brighter or less heavy

light-hearted ADJECTIVE
cheerful

lighthouse NOUN
a tower with a bright light to guide or
warn ships

lighting NOUN
lamps, or the light they provide

lightning NOUN
a flash of bright light produced during a
thunderstorm

lightweight *NOUN*
unimportant

light year *NOUN*
the distance light travels in one year (about 6 million million miles)

like[1] *VERB*
1 to think a person or thing is pleasant or satisfactory
2 to wish *I'd like to come.*

like[2] *PREPOSITION*
1 in the manner of *swims like a fish*
2 in a suitable state for *It looks like rain. I feel like a cup of tea.*
3 such as *things like art and music*

like *ADJECTIVE*
similar

likeable *ADJECTIVE*
easy to like; pleasant

likelihood *NOUN*
being likely; probability

likely *ADJECTIVE* **likelier, likeliest**
1 expected to happen or be true
2 expected to do something

liken *VERB*
to compare

likeness *NOUN*
1 a similarity in appearance
2 a portrait

likewise *ADVERB*
similarly; in the same way

liking *NOUN*
a feeling that you like something

lilac *NOUN*
a bush with purple or white flowers

lilt *NOUN*
a light pleasant rhythm
lilting *ADJECTIVE*

lily *NOUN* **lilies**
a garden plant with trumpet-shaped flowers

limb *NOUN*
1 a leg, arm, or wing
2 a large branch of a tree

limber *VERB*
limber up to exercise in preparation for a sport

limbo[1] *NOUN*
in limbo in an uncertain situation

limbo[2] *NOUN*
a West Indian dance in which the dancer bends backwards to pass under a low bar

lime[1] *NOUN*
a white chalky substance used in making cement

lime[2] *NOUN*
a green fruit like a small round lemon

lime[3] *NOUN*
a tree with yellow flowers

limelight *NOUN*
in the limelight getting publicity

limerick *NOUN*
an amusing poem with five lines

limestone *NOUN*
a kind of rock from which lime is obtained

limit *NOUN*
1 a line or point where something ends
2 the greatest amount allowed

limit *VERB*
1 to keep within certain limits
2 to be a limit to

limitation *NOUN*
a limit or restriction

limited *ADJECTIVE*
kept within limits *a limited choice*

limousine (lim-oo-**zeen**) *NOUN*
a large luxurious car

limp[1] *VERB*
to walk lamely
limp *NOUN*
a limping walk

limp[2] *ADJECTIVE*
not stiff or firm

limpet *NOUN*
a small shellfish that clings to rocks

limpid *ADJECTIVE*
(of liquids) clear or transparent

linchpin *NOUN*
a pin through the end of an axle keeping a wheel in position

line[1] *NOUN*
1 a long thin mark
2 a row or series of people or things
3 a length of rope, string, wire, etc.
4 a railway
5 a company operating a transport service
6 a way of doing things or behaving
7 a telephone connection

line *VERB*
1 to mark with lines
2 to form into a line

line[2] *VERB*
to cover the inside of

lineage (lin-ee-ij) *NOUN*
a line of descendants from an ancestor

linear (lin-ee-er) *ADJECTIVE*
1 arranged in a line
2 to do with a line or length

linen *NOUN*
1 cloth made from flax
2 shirts, sheets, and other items originally made of linen

liner NOUN
a large passenger ship

linesman NOUN **linesmen**
an official in football or tennis etc. who
decides whether the ball has crossed a line

linger VERB
to be slow to leave

lingerie (lan-zher-ee) NOUN
women's underwear

linguist NOUN
an expert in languages

linguistics NOUN
the study of languages and of language
linguistic ADJECTIVE

liniment NOUN
a soothing body lotion

lining NOUN
a layer that covers the inside of something

link NOUN
1 a ring or loop in a chain
2 a connection or relationship

link VERB
to join together
linkage NOUN

links NOUN
a golf course near the sea

linnet NOUN
a kind of finch

lino NOUN
linoleum

linoleum NOUN
a stiff shiny floor covering

linseed oil NOUN
oil obtained from the seeds of flax plants

lint NOUN
a soft material for covering wounds

lintel NOUN
a horizontal piece of wood or stone etc. above
a door or other opening

lion NOUN
a large strong flesh-eating animal of the cat
family found in Africa and India

lioness NOUN
a female lion

lip NOUN
1 either of the two fleshy edges of the mouth
2 the edge of a cup or crater
3 the pointed part at the top of a jug for
pouring

lip-read VERB **lip-read**
to understand what a person says by
watching the lips

lipstick NOUN
a stick of a waxy substance for colouring
the lips

liquefy VERB **liquefies**, **liquefied**
to make or become liquid

liqueur (lik-yoor) NOUN
a strong sweet alcoholic drink

liquid NOUN
a substance that flows freely but has a
constant volume

liquid ADJECTIVE
1 in the form of a liquid
2 easily converted into cash
liquidity NOUN

liquidate VERB
1 to pay off or settle a debt
2 to close down a bankrupt business
liquidation NOUN **liquidator** NOUN

liquidize VERB
to make into a liquid or pulp
liquidizer NOUN

liquor NOUN
an alcoholic drink

liquorice NOUN
a black substance from a plant, used as a
sweet

lisp NOUN
a fault in speech in which s and z are
pronounced like th

lisp VERB
to speak with a lisp

list [1] NOUN
a number of items written one after another

list VERB
to make a list of

list [2] VERB
(of a ship) to lean over to one side
list NOUN

listen VERB
to try to hear
listener NOUN

listless ADJECTIVE
too tired to do much

lit past tense of **light** [1] VERB

litany NOUN **litanies**
a formal prayer with fixed responses

literacy NOUN
the ability to read and write

literal ADJECTIVE
1 meaning exactly what is said
2 word for word

literally ADVERB
really; exactly as stated

literary (lit-er-er-i) ADJECTIVE
to do with literature

literate ADJECTIVE
able to read and write

literature *NOUN*
1 novels, plays, and other written works
2 the books and writings on a subject

lithe *ADJECTIVE*
flexible and supple

litmus *NOUN*
a blue substance that is turned red by acids
and can be turned back to blue by alkalis

litre *NOUN*
a measure of liquid, about 1.75 pints

litter *NOUN*
1 rubbish or untidy things lying about
2 young animals born to a mother at one time
3 a tray of absorbent material used as a cat's
toilet

litter *VERB*
to leave litter about in a place

little *ADJECTIVE* **less**, **least**
small in amount or size

little *NOUN*
a small amount

liturgy *NOUN* **liturgies**
a form of public worship used in churches
liturgical *ADJECTIVE*

live[1] (rhymes with *give*) *VERB*
1 to have life; to be alive
2 to have a home *lives in Glasgow*
3 to pass your life in a certain way
lived as a hermit

live[2] (rhymes with *hive*) *ADJECTIVE*
1 alive
2 connected to an electric current
3 (of a broadcast) transmitted while it is
actually happening
4 burning *live coals*

livelihood *NOUN*
a way of earning money to support yourself

lively *ADJECTIVE* **livelier**, **liveliest**
full of life or action
liveliness *NOUN*

liven *VERB*
to make or become lively

liver *NOUN*
an organ of the body that purifies the blood

livery *NOUN* **liveries**
a uniform worn by male servants

livestock *NOUN*
farm animals

livid *ADJECTIVE*
1 bluish-grey
2 furious

living *NOUN*
1 the state of being alive
2 the way a person lives
3 a way of earning money

lizard *NOUN*
a reptile with a rough skin and a long tail

llama (lah-ma) *NOUN*
a South American animal like a camel but with
no hump

load *NOUN*
1 something carried; a burden
2 the total amount of an electric current
3 (*informal*) a large amount *a load of
nonsense*

load *VERB*
1 to put a bullet or shell into a gun or film
into a camera
2 to enter programs or data into a computer
3 to put a load in or on
4 to fill heavily
5 to add a weight to

loaf[1] *NOUN* **loaves**
a shaped mass of bread

loaf[2] *VERB*
to spend time idly
loafer *NOUN*

loam *NOUN*
rich soil
loamy *ADJECTIVE*

loan *NOUN*
something lent, especially money
on loan being lent

loan *VERB*
to lend

loath (rhymes with *both*) *ADJECTIVE*
unwilling

loathe (rhymes with *clothe*) *VERB*
to hate very much
loathing *NOUN*

loathsome *ADJECTIVE*
causing disgust; revolting

lob *VERB* **lobbing**, **lobbed**
to throw, hit, or kick a ball high into the air

lobby *NOUN* **lobbies**
1 an entrance hall
2 a group who try to influence MPs or officials

lobby *VERB* **lobbies**, **lobbied**
to try to persuade an MP or other person to
support your cause

lobe *NOUN*
1 a rounded part of an organ of the body
2 the soft part at the bottom of the ear

lobster *NOUN*
a large shellfish with eight legs and two
long claws

local *ADJECTIVE*
belonging to a particular place or a small area
locally *ADVERB*

local NOUN (*informal*)
1 someone who lives in a particular district
2 a pub near a person's home

locality NOUN **localities**
a district or location

locate VERB
to discover where something is *have located the fault*
be located to be situated in a particular place

location NOUN
the place where something is

loch NOUN
a lake in Scotland

lock [1] NOUN
1 a fastening that is opened with a key or other device
2 a section of a canal in which boats can be raised or lowered to a different level
3 the distance that a vehicle's front wheels can turn
lock, stock, and barrel completely

lock VERB
1 to fasten or secure with a lock
2 to store away securely
3 to become fixed in one place
lock up to shut in or imprison

lock [2] NOUN
a clump of hair

locker NOUN
a small cupboard with a lock, for leaving your belongings in

locket NOUN
a small ornamental case for a portrait or lock of hair, worn on a chain round the neck

locks PLURAL NOUN
the hair of the head

locksmith NOUN
a person who makes and mends locks

locomotive NOUN
a railway engine

locomotive ADJECTIVE
to do with movement *locomotive power*
locomotion NOUN

locum NOUN
a doctor who takes the place of another for a time

locus NOUN
(*Maths*) the path traced by a moving point, or made by points placed in a certain way

locust NOUN
a kind of grasshopper that moves in large swarms, destroying plants

lodge NOUN
1 a small house at the gates of a park
2 a porter's room at the entrance to a building

lodge VERB
1 to live in rented rooms
2 to make a formal complaint
3 to become stuck

lodger NOUN
a person who pays to live in rented rooms

lodgings PLURAL NOUN
rooms rented for living in

loft NOUN
a room or space under a roof

lofty ADJECTIVE **loftier**, **loftiest**
1 tall
2 proud or noble
loftily ADVERB

log NOUN
1 a large piece cut from a fallen tree
2 a record of a voyage or flight

log VERB **logging**, **logged**
to enter facts in a log
log on or **off** to start or finish using a computer

loganberry NOUN **loganberries**
a dark red fruit like a blackberry

logarithm NOUN
one of a series of numbers set out in tables which make it possible to do sums by adding and subtracting instead of multiplying and dividing

logbook NOUN
1 a book in which a log of a voyage is kept
2 the registration document of a motor vehicle

log cabin NOUN
a hut built of logs

loggerheads PLURAL NOUN
at loggerheads disagreeing or quarrelling

logic NOUN
1 the process of reasoning
2 a system or method of reasoning

logical ADJECTIVE
using logic; reasoning or reasoned correctly
logically ADVERB

logo NOUN **logos**
a printed symbol used by a business company etc. as its emblem

loin NOUN
the side and back of the body between the ribs and the hip bone

loiter VERB
to linger or stand about idly

loll VERB
1 to lean lazily against something
2 to hang loosely

lollipop NOUN
a large round hard sweet on a stick

lolly NOUN **lollies** (*informal*)
1 a lollipop
2 money

lone ADJECTIVE
solitary

lonely ADJECTIVE **lonelier**, **loneliest**
1 sad when you are on your own
2 solitary
3 not often visited or used
loneliness NOUN

lonesome ADJECTIVE
feeling lonely

long[1] ADJECTIVE
1 measuring a lot from one end to the other
2 taking a lot of time
3 having a certain length *10 metres long*

long ADVERB
1 for a long time *Have you been waiting long?*
2 at a long time before or after *long ago*
3 throughout a time *all night long*

long[2] VERB
to feel a strong desire

longhand NOUN
ordinary writing, not shorthand

longing NOUN
a strong desire

longitude NOUN
the distance east or west of the Greenwich meridian, measured in degrees

long jump NOUN
an athletic contest of jumping as far as possible along the ground in one leap

long-range ADJECTIVE
covering a long distance or period of time

longship NOUN
a long narrow warship used by the Vikings

long-sighted ADJECTIVE
able to see distant things clearly but not things that are close

long wave NOUN
a radio wave of a wavelength above one kilometre and a frequency less than 300 kilohertz

long-winded ADJECTIVE
talking or writing at great length

loo NOUN **loos**
(*informal*) a toilet

loofah NOUN
a rough sponge made from a dried gourd

look VERB
1 to turn the eyes to see
2 to face in a particular direction
3 to have a certain appearance *to look sad*
look after 1 to protect or take care of 2 to be in charge of **look for** to try to find **look forward to** to be waiting eagerly for **look into** to investigate **look out** to be careful

look NOUN
1 the act of looking; a gaze or glance
2 general appearance

lookout NOUN
1 the act of watching for something *keep a lookout*
2 a place for keeping watch
3 a person who keeps watch
4 (*informal*) a person's own fault or concern *That's his lookout.*

loom[1] NOUN
a machine for weaving cloth

loom[2] VERB
to appear suddenly and threateningly

loop NOUN
1 the shape made by a curve crossing itself
2 a piece of string etc. made into this shape

loop VERB
1 to make into a loop
2 to enclose in a loop

loophole NOUN
a way of avoiding a rule or promise without breaking it

loose ADJECTIVE
1 not tight or firmly fixed
2 not tied up or shut in
3 not packed in a box or packet
4 not exact *a loose translation*
loosely ADVERB

loose VERB
1 to loosen
2 to untie or release
Do not confuse this word with *lose*.

loose-leaf ADJECTIVE
(of a folder) having each sheet of paper separate and able to be removed

loosen VERB
to make or become loose or looser

loot NOUN
stolen things; goods taken from an enemy

loot VERB
to take loot from
looter NOUN

lop VERB **lopping**, **lopped**
to cut away branches or twigs

lope VERB
to run with a long jumping stride

lopsided ADJECTIVE
with one side lower or smaller than the other

lord NOUN
1 a nobleman
2 a master or ruler

lordly ADJECTIVE **lordlier**, **lordliest**
1 to do with a lord
2 proud or haughty

lordship *NOUN*
a title used in speaking to or about a lord

lore *NOUN*
a set of traditional facts or beliefs

lorry *NOUN* **lorries**
a large motor vehicle for carrying heavy loads

lose *VERB* **lost**
1 to be without something you once had
2 to fail to keep or obtain
3 to be defeated in a contest or argument
4 to cause the loss of
5 (of a clock or watch) to become behind the correct time
loser *NOUN*

Do not confuse this word with *loose*.

loss *NOUN*
1 the act of losing something
2 something lost
at a loss unsure

lost *past tense and past participle* of **lose**

lost *ADJECTIVE*
1 not knowing where you are or which way to go
2 missing or strayed

lot *NOUN*
1 a large number or amount *a lot of friends*
lots of time
2 a person's fate or situation in life
3 something for sale at an auction
4 a piece of land
a lot very much *a lot better* **the lot** or **the whole lot** everything

loth *ADJECTIVE*
another spelling of **loath**

lotion *NOUN*
a liquid for putting on the skin

lottery *NOUN* **lotteries**
a way of raising money by selling numbered tickets and giving prizes to winners

lotus *NOUN*
a kind of tropical water lily

loud *ADJECTIVE*
1 producing a lot of noise
2 unpleasantly bright *loud colours*

loudspeaker *NOUN*
a device that changes electrical signals into sound

lounge *NOUN*
a comfortable room

lounge *VERB*
to sit in a lazy and relaxed way

louse *NOUN* **lice**
a small insect that lives as a parasite on animals, people, or plants

lousy *ADJECTIVE* **lousier, lousiest**
(*informal*) very bad or unpleasant

lout *NOUN*
a bad-mannered man

lovable *ADJECTIVE*
easy to love

love *NOUN*
1 great liking or affection
2 sexual affection
3 a loved person
4 no score in tennis
in love feeling strong love

love *VERB*
to feel love for

lovely *ADJECTIVE* **lovelier, loveliest**
1 beautiful
2 very pleasant or enjoyable
loveliness *NOUN*

lover *NOUN*
1 someone who loves something
a music lover
2 an unmarried person having a sexual relationship

lovesick *ADJECTIVE*
longing for someone you love

low[1] *ADJECTIVE*
1 only reaching a short way up
2 below average in importance, quality, amount, etc.
3 unhappy
4 not high-pitched *low notes*

low[2] *VERB*
to moo like a cow

lower *ADJECTIVE, ADVERB*
less high

lower *VERB*
to make or become lower

lowlands *PLURAL NOUN*
flat low-lying country
lowland *ADJECTIVE*

lowly *ADJECTIVE* **lowlier, lowliest**
humble
lowliness *NOUN*

loyal *ADJECTIVE*
firmly supporting your friends or country etc.
loyally *ADVERB* **loyalty** *NOUN*

loyalist *NOUN*
a person who is loyal to the government during a revolt

lozenge *NOUN*
1 a small flavoured tablet containing medicine
2 a diamond shape

lubricant *NOUN*
a lubricating substance

lubricate *VERB*
to oil or grease something so that it moves smoothly
lubrication *NOUN*

lucid *ADJECTIVE*
1 clear and easy to understand
2 thinking clearly
lucidly *ADVERB*

luck *NOUN*
1 the way things happen
2 good fortune

luckless *ADJECTIVE*
unlucky or unfortunate

lucky *ADJECTIVE* **luckier**, **luckiest**
bringing or resulting from good luck
luckily *ADVERB*

lucrative (loo-kruh-tiv) *ADJECTIVE*
profitable

ludicrous *ADJECTIVE*
ridiculous or laughable
ludicrously *ADVERB*

ludo *NOUN*
a game played with counters on a board

lug *VERB* **lugging**, **lugged**
to drag or carry something heavy

lug *NOUN*
1 an ear-like part on an object, for carrying or fixing it
2 (*informal*) an ear

luggage *NOUN*
suitcases and bags taken on a journey

lugubrious (lug-oo-bree-us) *ADJECTIVE*
gloomy or mournful

lukewarm *ADJECTIVE*
1 slightly warm
2 not enthusiastic *lukewarm applause*

lull *VERB*
1 to soothe or calm
2 to give a false feeling of being safe

lull *NOUN*
a short period of quiet

lullaby *NOUN* **lullabies**
a song to send a baby to sleep

lumbago *NOUN*
pain in the lower back

lumber *NOUN*
unwanted furniture or junk

lumber *VERB*
1 to leave someone with an unpleasant task
2 to move in a clumsy way

lumberjack *NOUN*
a person who fells trees and cuts timber

luminous *ADJECTIVE*
glowing in the dark
luminosity *NOUN*

lump *NOUN*
1 a solid piece of something
2 a swelling

lump *VERB*
to put or treat things together in a group
lump it (*informal*) to put up with something unwelcome

lumpy *ADJECTIVE* **lumpier**, **lumpiest**
containing or covered in lumps

lunacy *NOUN* **lunacies**
insanity or foolishness

lunar *ADJECTIVE*
to do with the moon

lunatic *NOUN*
an insane person
lunatic *ADJECTIVE*

lunch *NOUN*
a meal eaten in the middle of the day

lunch *VERB*
to eat lunch

luncheon *NOUN*
(*formal*) lunch

lung *NOUN*
either of the two parts of the body, in the chest, used in breathing

lunge *VERB*
to thrust the body forward suddenly
lunge *NOUN*

lupin *NOUN*
a garden plant with tall spikes of flowers

lurch[1] *VERB*
to stagger or lean over suddenly
lurch *NOUN*

lurch[2] *NOUN*
leave somebody in the lurch to leave them in difficulties

lure *VERB*
to tempt into a trap
lure *NOUN*

lurid (lewr-id) *ADJECTIVE*
1 very bright or gaudy
2 sensational and shocking

lurk *VERB*
to wait where you cannot be seen

luscious (lush-us) *ADJECTIVE*
delicious

lush *ADJECTIVE*
1 growing thickly and strongly
2 luxurious

lust *NOUN*
powerful sexual desire
lustful *ADJECTIVE*

lust *VERB*
to have a powerful desire

lustre *NOUN*
brightness or brilliance

a b c d e f g h i j k l m n o p q r s t u v w x y z

lustrous ADJECTIVE
bright and shining

lusty ADJECTIVE **lustier, lustiest**
strong and vigorous
lustily ADVERB

lute NOUN
a stringed musical instrument with a pear-shaped body

luxuriant ADJECTIVE
growing abundantly
Do not confuse this word with *luxurious*.

luxuriate VERB
to enjoy something as a luxury

luxurious ADJECTIVE
expensive and comfortable
luxuriously ADVERB
Do not confuse this word with *luxuriant*.

luxury NOUN **luxuries**
1 something expensive but inessential
2 expensive and comfortable surroundings

Lycra NOUN
(*trademark*) a thin stretchy material

lying *present participle of* **lie** [1] *and* **lie** [2]

lymph (limf) NOUN
a colourless fluid from the flesh or organs of the body

lynch VERB
to join together to execute someone without a proper trial

lynx NOUN
a wild animal like a large cat with sharp sight

lyre NOUN
an ancient musical instrument like a small harp

lyric (li-rik) NOUN
1 a short poem that expresses the poet's feelings
2 the words of a song

lyrical ADJECTIVE
1 like a song
2 expressing poetic feelings
lyrically ADVERB

Mm

mac NOUN
(*informal*) a mackintosh

macabre (mak-ahbr) ADJECTIVE
strange and horrible

macaroni NOUN
pasta in the form of short tubes

macaroon NOUN
a small sweet cake or biscuit made with ground almonds

macaw (ma-**kaw**) NOUN
a brightly coloured parrot with a long tail

mace NOUN
an ornamental rod or staff carried by a mayor or other official

machete (mash-**et**-ee) NOUN
a broad heavy knife used as a tool or weapon

machine NOUN
a piece of equipment with parts that together perform a task

machine VERB
to make with a machine

machine gun NOUN
a gun that fires a rapid succession of bullets

machinery NOUN
1 machines
2 the moving parts of a machine
3 an organized system

macho (**mach**-oh) ADJECTIVE
masculine in an aggressive way

mackerel NOUN
a sea fish used as food

mackintosh NOUN
a raincoat

mad ADJECTIVE **madder, maddest**
1 ill in the mind; insane
2 extremely foolish
3 very keen or excited *mad about football*
4 (*informal*) angry
madness NOUN

madam NOUN
a polite way of addressing a woman

madden VERB
to make mad or angry

madly ADVERB
very much *madly in love*

madrigal NOUN
an unaccompanied song for several voices singing different parts together

maelstrom (**mayl**-strom) NOUN
1 a great whirlpool
2 a state of great confusion

maestro (**my**-stroh) NOUN **maestros**
a famous musician

magazine NOUN
1 a regular publication with articles, stories, and features
2 the part of a gun that holds the cartridges
3 a store for weapons and ammunition

maggot NOUN
the larva of some kinds of fly

magic *NOUN*
1 the art of making things happen by a mysterious power
2 mysterious tricks performed for entertainment
3 an enchanting quality
magic *ADJECTIVE*

magical *ADJECTIVE*
1 using magic
2 wonderful or marvellous
magically *ADVERB*

magician *NOUN*
1 a person who does magic tricks
2 a wizard

magistrate *NOUN*
an official who hears and judges minor legal cases

magma *NOUN*
a molten substance beneath the earth's crust

magnanimous (mag-**nan**-im-us) *ADJECTIVE*
generous and forgiving

magnate *NOUN*
a wealthy influential person, especially in business

magnesia *NOUN*
a white powder that is a compound of magnesium, used in medicine

magnesium *NOUN*
a silvery-white metal that burns with a very bright flame

magnet *NOUN*
a piece of iron or steel that can attract metal

magnetic *ADJECTIVE*
1 having or using the powers of a magnet
2 having the power to attract people
a magnetic personality

magnetism *NOUN*
1 the properties and effects of magnetic substances
2 great personal charm and attraction

magnetize *VERB*
to make into a magnet

magnificent *ADJECTIVE*
1 grand or splendid in appearance
2 excellent
magnificence *NOUN*

magnify *VERB* **magnifies**, **magnified**
1 to make something look bigger than it really is
2 to exaggerate
magnification *NOUN*

magnitude *NOUN*
1 size or extent
2 importance

magnolia *NOUN*
a tree with large white or pale-pink flowers

magpie *NOUN*
a large black and white bird related to the crow

mahogany *NOUN*
a hard brown wood

maid *NOUN*
a female servant

maiden *NOUN*
(*old use*) an unmarried girl

maiden *ADJECTIVE*
1 not married *a maiden aunt*
2 first *a maiden voyage*

mail [1] *NOUN*
letters and parcels sent by post

mail *VERB*
to send by post

mail [2] *NOUN*
armour made of metal rings joined together

maim *VERB*
to injure or disable

main *ADJECTIVE*
largest or most important

main *NOUN*
the main pipe or cable in a public system carrying water, gas, or electricity

mainland *NOUN*
the main part of a country or continent

mainly *ADVERB*
1 chiefly
2 almost completely
3 usually

mainstay *NOUN*
the chief support or main part

maintain *VERB*
1 to cause to continue or exist
2 to keep in good condition
3 to provide money for
4 to state that something is true

maintenance *NOUN*
1 the process of keeping something in good condition
2 money for food and clothing

maize *NOUN*
a tall kind of corn with large seeds on cobs

majestic *ADJECTIVE*
1 stately and dignified
2 imposing
majestically *ADVERB*

majesty *NOUN* **majesties**
1 the title of a king or queen
2 the state of being majestic

major *ADJECTIVE*
1 very important
2 of the musical scale with a semitone after the 3rd and 7th notes

major *NOUN*
an army officer ranking next above a captain

majority NOUN **majorities**
1 the greatest part of a group of people or things
2 the amount by which the winner in an election beats the loser
3 the age at which a person legally becomes an adult

make VERB **made**
1 to bring into existence by putting things together
2 to cause or compel
3 to gain or earn
4 to achieve or reach
5 to reckon *What do you make the time?*
6 to result in or add up to *4 and 6 make 10.*
7 to perform an action etc. *to make an effort*
8 to arrange a bed for use
make out to manage to see, hear, or understand something **make up 1** to invent a story or excuse **2** to be friendly again
maker NOUN

make NOUN
a brand of goods

make-believe NOUN
pretending or in fantasy

makeshift ADJECTIVE
used when there is nothing better

make-up NOUN
1 cosmetics
2 the way something is made up

malady NOUN **maladies**
an illness or disease

malaria NOUN
a feverish disease spread by mosquitoes
malarial ADJECTIVE

male ADJECTIVE
belonging to the sex that reproduces by fertilizing egg cells produced by the female

male NOUN
a male person, animal, or plant

malevolent (ma-**lev**-ol-ent) ADJECTIVE
wishing to harm people
malevolence NOUN

malfunction NOUN
a fault or failure in a machine

malfunction VERB
to fail to work properly

malice NOUN
a desire to harm other people

malicious ADJECTIVE
wishing to do harm

malign (mal-**yn**) ADJECTIVE
1 harmful
2 showing malice

malign VERB
to say unpleasant and untrue things about someone

malignant ADJECTIVE
1 (of a tumour) growing uncontrollably
2 full of malice

malinger VERB
to pretend to be ill in order to avoid work
malingerer NOUN

mall (mal or mawl) NOUN
a shopping area

mallard NOUN
a wild duck

malleable ADJECTIVE
1 able to be pressed or hammered into shape
2 easy to influence
malleability NOUN

mallet NOUN
a heavy wooden hammer

malnutrition NOUN
bad health from lack of good food

malpractice NOUN
wrongdoing by a professional person

malt NOUN
dried barley used in brewing, making vinegar, etc.

maltreat VERB
to treat badly
maltreatment NOUN

mammal NOUN
an animal of which the female gives birth to live young

mammoth NOUN
an extinct elephant with curved tusks

mammoth ADJECTIVE
huge

man NOUN **men**
1 a grown-up male human being
2 an individual person
3 human beings in general
4 a piece used in board games

man VERB **manning, manned**
to supply with people to work something

manacle NOUN
a fetter or handcuff

manacle VERB
to fasten with manacles

manage VERB
1 to be in charge of a business or a group of people
2 to cope with something difficult
manageable ADJECTIVE

m

management NOUN
1 the process of managing
2 people in charge

manager NOUN
a person who manages something
managerial (man-a-**jeer**-ee-al) ADJECTIVE

mandarin NOUN
1 an important official
2 a kind of small orange

mandate NOUN
authority given to someone to carry out a
certain task or policy

mandatory ADJECTIVE
obligatory or compulsory

mandible NOUN
the lower jaw

mandolin NOUN
a musical instrument like a lute

mane NOUN
the long hair on a horse's or lion's neck

manganese NOUN
a hard brittle metal

mange NOUN
a skin disease of dogs, cats, etc.

manger NOUN
a trough in a stable for animals to feed from

mangle VERB
to damage by crushing or cutting roughly

mango NOUN **mangoes**
a tropical fruit with yellow pulp

mangy ADJECTIVE **mangier, mangiest**
1 scruffy or dirty
2 suffering from mange

manhandle VERB
to treat or push roughly

manhole NOUN
an opening large enough to let a person
through

manhood NOUN
the condition of being a man

mania NOUN
1 violent madness
2 great enthusiasm *a mania for sport*

maniac NOUN
a person with mania

manic ADJECTIVE
suffering from mania

manicure NOUN
care and treatment of the hands and nails
manicurist NOUN

manifest ADJECTIVE
clear and obvious
manifestly ADVERB

manifest VERB
to show a thing clearly
manifestation NOUN

manifesto NOUN **manifestos**
a public statement of policies

manifold ADJECTIVE
of many kinds

manipulate VERB
1 to handle or arrange skilfully
2 to get someone to do what you want
manipulation NOUN

mankind NOUN
human beings in general

manly ADJECTIVE **manlier, manliest**
1 suitable for a man
2 brave and strong
manliness NOUN

manner NOUN
1 the way something happens or is done
2 a person's way of behaving
3 sort *all manner of things*

mannerism NOUN
a person's particular gesture or way of
speaking

manners PLURAL NOUN
how a person behaves with other people

mannish ADJECTIVE
(of a woman) like a man

manoeuvre (man-**oo**-ver) NOUN
a difficult or skilful or cunning action

manoeuvre VERB
to move carefully and skilfully
manoeuvrable ADJECTIVE

manor NOUN
a large country house and its land

manpower NOUN
the number of people available for work

manse NOUN
a church minister's house, especially in
Scotland

mansion NOUN
a large stately house

manslaughter NOUN
the unlawful but unintentional killing of
a person

mantle NOUN
1 a cloak
2 a covering *a mantle of snow*

mantra NOUN
a word or phrase that is constantly repeated
in meditation

manual ADJECTIVE
worked by or done with the hands
manually ADVERB

a b c d e f g h i j k l **m** n o p q r s t u v w x y z

manual NOUN
a handbook giving instructions

manufacture VERB
to make things in large numbers
manufacture NOUN **manufacturer** NOUN

manure NOUN
fertilizer made from animal dung

manuscript NOUN
a written or typed document

many ADJECTIVE **more**, **most**
great in number

many NOUN
a large number of people or things *Many were found.*

map NOUN
a diagram of part or all of the earth's surface or of the sky

map VERB **mapping**, **mapped**
1 to make a map of an area
2 to plan

maple NOUN
a tree with broad leaves

mar VERB **marring**, **marred**
to spoil

marathon NOUN
a long-distance running race, especially one covering 26 miles 385 yards (42.195 km)

marauding ADJECTIVE
going in search of plunder
marauder NOUN

marble NOUN
1 a small glass ball used in games
2 limestone polished and used in sculpture or building

March NOUN
the third month of the year

march VERB
to walk with regular steps
marcher NOUN

march NOUN
1 a spell of marching
2 music suitable for marching to

mare NOUN
a female horse or donkey

margarine NOUN
a substance like butter, made from animal or vegetable fats

margin NOUN
1 an edge or border
2 the blank space at the edge of a page
3 the difference between two scores etc.

marginal ADJECTIVE
very slight
marginally ADVERB

marigold NOUN
a yellow or orange garden flower

marijuana (ma-ri-**hwah**-na) NOUN
a drug made from the hemp plant

marine (ma-**reen**) ADJECTIVE
to do with the sea

marine NOUN
a member of troops trained to serve at sea and on land

mariner (**ma**-rin-er) NOUN
a sailor

marionette NOUN
a puppet worked by strings

marital ADJECTIVE
to do with marriage

maritime ADJECTIVE
to do with the sea or ships

marjoram NOUN
a herb used in cooking

mark NOUN
1 a spot or stain etc. on something
2 a number or letter put as a grade on a piece of work
3 a distinguishing feature
4 a sign or symbol *a mark of respect*
5 a target

mark VERB
1 to make a mark on something
2 to give a mark to a piece of work
3 to pay attention to
4 to keep close to an opposing player in football etc.
marker NOUN

marked ADJECTIVE
distinct; noticeable *a marked improvement*
markedly ADVERB

market NOUN
1 a place where items are bought and sold from stalls
2 a demand for a product

market VERB
to offer for sale

marksman NOUN **marksmen**
an expert in shooting at a target

marmalade NOUN
jam made from oranges, lemons, etc.

marmoset NOUN
a kind of small monkey

maroon[1] VERB
to abandon or isolate in a deserted place

maroon[2] NOUN
a dark red colour

marquee (mar-**kee**) NOUN
a large tent used for a party, etc.

m

marquis NOUN
a nobleman ranking above an earl

marriage NOUN
1 the state of being married
2 a wedding

marrow NOUN
1 a long vegetable with a thick green skin
2 the soft substance inside bones

marry VERB **marries**, **married**
1 to become a person's husband or wife
2 to join two people as husband and wife

marsh NOUN
a low-lying area of wet ground
marshy ADJECTIVE

marshal NOUN
1 an official who supervises a contest or ceremony etc.
2 an officer of very high rank *a Field Marshal*
marshal VERB **marshalling**, **marshalled**
1 to arrange neatly
2 to usher or escort

marshmallow NOUN
a soft spongy sweet, usually pink or white

marsupial (mar-**soo**-pee-al) NOUN
an animal that carries its young in a pouch on the front of its body, e.g. a kangaroo

martial ADJECTIVE
to do with war

martin NOUN
a bird similar to a swallow

martinet NOUN
a very strict person

martyr NOUN
a person who is killed or made to suffer because of their beliefs
martyrdom NOUN
martyr VERB
to kill or torment someone as a martyr

marvel NOUN
a wonderful thing
marvel VERB **marvelling**, **marvelled**
to be filled with wonder

marvellous ADJECTIVE
wonderful

marzipan NOUN
a soft sweet food made with ground almonds

mascara NOUN
a cosmetic for darkening the eyelashes

mascot NOUN
a person, animal, or thing that is believed to bring good luck

masculine ADJECTIVE
1 to do with men
2 typical of or suitable for men
3 (in some languages) belonging to the class of words which includes words referring to men
masculinity NOUN

mash VERB
to crush into a soft mass

mash NOUN
(*informal*) mashed potato

mask NOUN
a covering disguising or protecting the face

mask VERB
1 to cover with a mask
2 to disguise or conceal

masochist (mas-ok-ist) NOUN
a person who gets pleasure from pain or humiliation
masochism NOUN

mason NOUN
a person who builds or works with stone

masonry NOUN
1 the stone parts of a building; stonework
2 a mason's work

masquerade NOUN
a pretence
masquerade VERB
to pretend to be something *masqueraded as a police officer*

Mass NOUN
the Communion service in the Roman Catholic Church

mass NOUN
1 a large amount
2 a heap or other collection of matter
3 (*Science*) the quantity of physical matter that a thing contains
mass ADJECTIVE
involving a large number of people
mass murder
mass VERB
to collect into a mass

massacre NOUN
the killing of a large number of people
massacre VERB
to kill a large number of people

massage (mas-ah*z*h) VERB
to rub and press the body to make it less stiff or less painful
massage NOUN

massive ADJECTIVE
large and heavy

mast NOUN
a tall pole holding up a ship's sails or a flag or aerial

master NOUN
1 a man in charge of something
2 a great artist, composer, etc.

master VERB
1 to learn a subject or a skill thoroughly
2 to bring under control

masterful ADJECTIVE
1 domineering
2 very skilful

masterly ADJECTIVE
very skilful

mastermind NOUN
1 a very clever person
2 the person who plans and organizes a scheme or crime

mastermind VERB
to plan and organize a scheme or crime

masterpiece NOUN
a very fine piece of work

mastery NOUN
full control or knowledge

mastiff NOUN
a large kind of dog

masturbate VERB
to get sexual pleasure by rubbing the genitals
masturbation NOUN

mat NOUN
1 a small carpet
2 a small piece of material put on a table to protect the surface

matador NOUN
a bullfighter who fights on foot

match 1 NOUN
a small thin stick with a head that gives a flame when rubbed

match 2 NOUN
1 a game or contest between two teams or players
2 one person or thing that matches another
3 a marriage

match VERB
1 to be equal or similar to
2 to put teams or players to compete against each other
3 to find something similar or corresponding

matchbox NOUN
a box containing matches

matchstick NOUN
the stem of a match

mate NOUN
1 (informal) a companion or friend
2 each of a mated pair of birds or animals
3 an officer on a merchant ship

mate VERB
1 to come or bring two together to breed
2 to put things together as a pair

material NOUN
1 anything used for making something else
2 cloth or fabric

material ADJECTIVE
1 to do with possessions, money, etc.
2 important a material difference

materialism NOUN
the belief that possessions are important
materialistic ADJECTIVE

materialize VERB
1 to appear or become visible
2 to happen

maternal ADJECTIVE
1 to do with a mother
2 motherly
maternally ADVERB

maternity NOUN
motherhood

matey ADJECTIVE
(informal) friendly and sociable

mathematician NOUN
an expert in mathematics

mathematics NOUN
the study of numbers, measurements, and shapes
mathematical ADJECTIVE

maths NOUN
mathematics

matinée NOUN
an afternoon performance at a theatre or cinema

matins NOUN
a morning church service

matriarch (may-tree-ark) NOUN
a woman who is head of a family or tribe
matriarchal ADJECTIVE **matriarchy** NOUN

matrimony NOUN
marriage
matrimonial ADJECTIVE

matrix (may-triks) NOUN **matrices**
1 (Maths) a set of quantities arranged in rows and columns
2 a mould or framework

matron NOUN
1 a mature married woman
2 a woman in charge of nursing in a school, hospital, etc.
matronly ADJECTIVE

matt ADJECTIVE
having a dull surface

matted ADJECTIVE
tangled into a mass

matter NOUN
1 something you can touch or see
2 a substance
3 things of a certain kind printed matter
4 something to be thought about or done a serious matter
5 a quantity in a matter of minutes

matter VERB
to be important

matter-of-fact *ADJECTIVE*
keeping to facts; not imaginative or emotional

matting *NOUN*
rough material for covering floors

mattress *NOUN*
a thick layer of soft material in a covering, used on a bed

mature *ADJECTIVE*
1 fully grown or developed
2 grown-up
maturity *NOUN*

mature *VERB*
to make or become mature

maudlin *ADJECTIVE*
feebly sentimental

maul *VERB*
to injure by handling or clawing

mausoleum (maw-sol-**ee**-um) *NOUN*
a magnificent tomb

mauve (mohv) *NOUN*
a pale purple colour

maverick *NOUN*
an independent or eccentric person

maxim *NOUN*
a short saying giving a general truth

maximize *VERB*
to make as great or large as possible

maximum *NOUN* **maxima** or **maximums**
the greatest possible number or amount

maximum *ADJECTIVE*
greatest or most

May *NOUN*
the fifth month of the year

may *AUXILIARY VERB* **may**, **might**
1 used to express permission *You may go now.*
2 used to express possibility *It may be true.*
3 used to express wish *Long may it last.*
4 used to express uncertainty *whoever it may be*

maybe *ADVERB*
perhaps; possibly

mayday *NOUN*
an international radio signal calling for help

mayfly *NOUN* **mayflies**
an insect that lives for a short time in spring

mayhem *NOUN*
violent confusion or damage

mayonnaise *NOUN*
a savoury sauce used with salads

mayor *NOUN*
the person in charge of the council in a town or city

mayoress *NOUN*
the wife of a mayor

maypole *NOUN*
a decorated pole round which people dance on 1 May

maze *NOUN*
a complicated network of paths designed as a puzzle

Mb *ABBREVIATION*
megabyte(s)

me *PRONOUN*
the form of **I** used as the object of a verb or after a preposition

mead *NOUN*
an alcoholic drink made from honey and water

meadow *NOUN*
a field of grass

meagre *ADJECTIVE*
barely enough *a meagre diet*

meal [1] *NOUN*
food served and eaten at one sitting

meal [2] *NOUN*
coarsely-ground grain
mealy *ADJECTIVE*

mean [1] *VERB* **meant** (ment)
1 to have as an equivalent or explanation
2 to intend
3 to indicate or have as a result

mean [2] *ADJECTIVE* **meaner**, **meanest**
1 not generous; miserly
2 unkind or spiteful
3 poor in quality or appearance
meanness *NOUN*

mean [3] *NOUN*
a point or number midway between two extremes

mean *ADJECTIVE*
midway between two points

meander (mee-an-der) *VERB*
to take a winding course

meaning *NOUN*
what something means
meaningful *ADJECTIVE* **meaningless** *ADJECTIVE*

means *NOUN*
a way of achieving something
by all means certainly

means *PLURAL NOUN*
money or other wealth

meantime *NOUN*
in the meantime meanwhile

meanwhile *ADVERB*
in the time between two events

measles *NOUN*
an infectious disease with red spots

measly *ADJECTIVE*
(*informal*) not adequate or generous

measure *VERB*
1 to find the size, amount, or extent of
2 to be a certain size
measurable *ADJECTIVE*

measure *NOUN*
1 a unit used for measuring
2 a device used in measuring
3 the size or quantity of something
4 something done for a particular purpose
measures to stop vandalism

measurement *NOUN*
1 the process of measuring something
2 a size or amount found by measuring

meat *NOUN*
animal flesh used as food
meaty *ADJECTIVE*

mechanic *NOUN*
a person who maintains or repairs machinery

mechanical *ADJECTIVE*
1 to do with machines
2 done or doing things without thought
mechanically *ADVERB*

mechanics *NOUN*
1 the study of movement and force
2 the study or use of machines

mechanism *NOUN*
1 the moving parts of a machine
2 a process

mechanized *ADJECTIVE*
equipped with machines
mechanization *NOUN*

medal *NOUN*
a metal disc, star, or cross given for bravery or an achievement

medallion *NOUN*
a large medal worn as an ornament

medallist *NOUN*
a winner of a medal

meddle *VERB*
to interfere or tinker
meddler *NOUN*

meddlesome *ADJECTIVE*
liking to meddle

media *plural* of **medium** *NOUN*
the media newspapers, radio, and television

medial *ADJECTIVE*
1 in the middle
2 average

median *ADJECTIVE*
in the middle

median *NOUN*
1 a median point or line
2 (*Maths*) the middle number in a set of numbers
3 a straight line passing from a point of a triangle to the centre of the opposite side

mediate *VERB*
to negotiate between sides in a dispute
mediation *NOUN* **mediator** *NOUN*

medical *ADJECTIVE*
to do with the treatment of disease
medically *ADVERB*

medicated *ADJECTIVE*
containing a medicine

medication *NOUN*
1 a medicine
2 treatment using medicine

medicine *NOUN*
1 a substance taken to cure a disease
2 the study and treatment of diseases
medicinal (med-**iss**-in-al) *ADJECTIVE*

medieval *ADJECTIVE*
of Europe from about 1000 to 1453

mediocre *ADJECTIVE*
not very good; ordinary
mediocrity *NOUN*

meditate *VERB*
to think deeply and quietly
meditation *NOUN*

medium *ADJECTIVE*
neither large nor small; moderate

medium *NOUN* **mediums** or **media**
1 a thing in which something exists or moves
2 a person who claims to communicate with the dead

medium wave *NOUN*
a radio wave of a frequency between 300 kilohertz and 3 megahertz

medley *NOUN* **medleys**
1 an assortment
2 a collection of tunes

meek *ADJECTIVE* **meeker**, **meekest**
quiet and obedient
meekly *ADVERB*

meet *VERB* **met**
1 to come together or into contact
2 to go to receive an arrival
3 to pay a bill or cost
4 to satisfy or fulfil *to meet your needs*

meet *NOUN*
a gathering of riders and hounds for a hunt

meeting *NOUN*
1 the act of coming together
2 a number of people who have come together

megabyte NOUN
(*ICT*) a unit of information roughly equal to one million bytes

megahertz NOUN
a unit of frequency equal to one million hertz

megaphone NOUN
a funnel-shaped device for amplifying the voice

melancholy ADJECTIVE
sad; gloomy

melancholy NOUN
sadness or depression

melee (mel-ay) NOUN
1 a confused fight
2 a muddle

mellow ADJECTIVE **mellower, mellowest**
1 soft and rich in flavour, colour, or sound
2 more kindly with age

mellow VERB
to make or become mellow

melodic ADJECTIVE
to do with melody

melodious ADJECTIVE
pleasant to listen to

melodrama NOUN
a play full of excitement and exaggerated emotion
melodramatic ADJECTIVE

melody NOUN **melodies**
a pleasing tune

melon NOUN
a large sweet fruit with a yellow or green skin

melt VERB
1 to make or become liquid by heating
2 to disappear slowly

member NOUN
a person belonging to a particular society or group
membership NOUN

membrane NOUN
a thin skin or similar covering

memento NOUN **mementoes**
a souvenir

memo (mem-oh) NOUN **memos**
a note from one person to another in an office

memoir (mem-wahr) NOUN
a biography written by someone who knew the person

memoirs (mem-wahrz) PLURAL NOUN
an account of a person's life written by that person

memorable ADJECTIVE
1 worth remembering
2 easy to remember
memorably ADVERB

memorandum NOUN **memoranda** or **memorandums**
a note to remind yourself of something

memorial NOUN
something to remind people of a person or event
memorial ADJECTIVE

memorize VERB
to get into your memory

memory NOUN **memories**
1 the ability to remember
2 something you remember
3 (*ICT*) the part of a computer where information is stored

menace NOUN
1 a threat or danger
2 a troublesome person or thing

menace VERB
to threaten with harm or danger

menagerie NOUN
a small zoo

mend VERB
1 to repair
2 to make or become better
mender NOUN

menial (meen-ee-al) ADJECTIVE
needing little or no skill or thought
menially ADVERB

menial NOUN
a person who does menial work

meningitis NOUN
a disease causing inflammation of the membranes (*meninges*) round the brain and spinal cord

menopause NOUN
the time of life when a woman stops menstruating

menstruate VERB
to bleed from the womb about once a month
menstruation NOUN **menstrual** ADJECTIVE

mental ADJECTIVE
to do with the mind
mentally ADVERB

mentality NOUN **mentalities**
a person's mental ability or attitude

menthol NOUN
a solid white peppermint-flavoured substance

mention VERB
to speak or write about briefly
mention NOUN

mentor NOUN
an experienced and trusted adviser

menu NOUN **menus**
1 a list of food available
2 (*ICT*) a list of options shown on a computer screen

mercantile ADJECTIVE
to do with trade or trading

mercenary ADJECTIVE
working only for money or some other reward

mercenary NOUN **mercenaries**
a soldier hired to serve in a foreign army

merchandise NOUN
goods for sale

merchant NOUN
a person involved in trade

merchant navy NOUN
the ships and sailors that carry goods for trade

merciful ADJECTIVE
showing mercy
mercifully ADVERB

merciless ADJECTIVE
showing no mercy; cruel
mercilessly ADVERB

mercury NOUN
a heavy silvery liquid metal used in
thermometers

mercy NOUN **mercies**
1 kindness or pity shown to a wrongdoer or
enemy etc.
2 something to be thankful for

mere ADJECTIVE
not more than *a mere child*

merely ADVERB
only; simply

merge VERB
to combine or blend

merger NOUN
the combining of two business companies

meridian NOUN
a line on a map or globe from the North Pole
to the South Pole

meringue (mer-**ang**) NOUN
a crisp cake made from egg white and sugar

merit NOUN
1 a quality that deserves praise
2 excellence

merit VERB
to deserve

meritorious ADJECTIVE
deserving praise

mermaid NOUN
a mythical sea creature with a woman's body
and a fish's tail

merriment NOUN
cheerful behaviour

merry ADJECTIVE **merrier, merriest**
cheerful and lively
merrily ADVERB

merry-go-round NOUN
a roundabout at a fair

mesh NOUN
1 the open spaces in a net or sieve
2 material made like a net

mesh VERB
(of gears) to engage

mesmerize VERB
to fascinate or hold a person's attention
completely

mess NOUN
1 a dirty or untidy state
2 a difficult or confused situation
3 (in the armed forces) a dining room

mess VERB
mess about to behave stupidly or
idly **mess up** to do something badly

message NOUN
1 a piece of information sent from one person
to another
2 the main theme of a book, film, etc.

messenger NOUN
a person who carries a message

Messiah (mis-**I**-a) NOUN
1 a promised saviour
2 Christ

messy ADJECTIVE **messier, messiest**
dirty and untidy

metabolism (mit-**ab**-ol-izm) NOUN
the process by which food is built up into
living material in a plant or animal
metabolic ADJECTIVE

metal NOUN
a chemical substance that conducts heat and
electricity and melts when it is heated
metallic ADJECTIVE

metallurgy (mit-**al**-er-jee) NOUN
the study of metals
metallurgist NOUN

metamorphosis (met-a-**mor**-fo-sis) NOUN
metamorphoses
a complete change by a living thing

metaphor NOUN
the use of a word or phrase in a way that is not
literal, e.g. *to break your heart*
metaphorical ADJECTIVE

mete VERB
mete out to deal out something unpleasant

meteor NOUN
a piece of rock or metal in space that
burns up when it enters the earth's
atmosphere

m

meteoric *ADJECTIVE*
rapid and brilliant *a meteoric career*

meteorite *NOUN*
the remains of a meteor that has landed on the earth

meteorology *NOUN*
the study of the conditions of the climate and weather
meteorological *ADJECTIVE* **meteorologist** *NOUN*

meter *NOUN*
a device for measuring how much of something has been used

meter *VERB*
to measure with a meter
Do not confuse this word with *metre*.

methane (mee-thayn) *NOUN*
an inflammable gas produced by decaying matter

method *NOUN*
1 a way of doing something
2 methodical behaviour

methodical *ADJECTIVE*
doing things in a systematic way
methodically *ADVERB*

meths *NOUN*
(*informal*) methylated spirits, a liquid fuel made from alcohol

meticulous *ADJECTIVE*
careful and precise

metre *NOUN*
1 a unit of length in the metric system, about 39½ inches
2 rhythm in poetry
Do not confuse this word with *meter*.

metric *ADJECTIVE*
to do with a measuring system based on decimal units (metre, litre, and gram)

metrical *ADJECTIVE*
in rhythmic metre, not prose

metronome *NOUN*
a device that marks the beat in music

metropolis *NOUN*
the chief city of a country or region
metropolitan *ADJECTIVE*

mettle *NOUN*
courage or strength of character

mew *VERB*
to make a cat's cry
mew *NOUN*

mews *NOUN*
a row of houses in a small street or square, originally stables

miasma (mee-**az**-ma) *NOUN*
unpleasant or unhealthy air

mica *NOUN*
a mineral used to make electrical insulators

mice *plural* of **mouse**

microbe *NOUN*
a micro-organism

microchip *NOUN*
a tiny piece of silicon designed to work like an electric circuit

microcosm *NOUN*
a world in miniature; something regarded as resembling something else on a very small scale

microfiche *NOUN*
a piece of film on which pages of information are photographed in reduced size

microfilm *NOUN*
a length of film on which written or printed material is photographed in reduced size

microorganism *NOUN*
a microscopic creature, e.g. a bacterium or virus

microphone *NOUN*
an electrical device that picks up sound waves for recording, amplifying, or broadcasting

microprocessor *NOUN*
the central processing unit of a computer, consisting of one or more microchips

microscope *NOUN*
an instrument with lenses that magnify tiny objects or details

microscopic *ADJECTIVE*
extremely small

microwave *NOUN*
1 a very short electromagnetic wave
2 an oven that uses microwaves to heat or cook food

microwave *VERB*
to cook in a microwave oven

mid *ADJECTIVE*
1 in the middle of *mid-July*
2 middle *in his mid thirties*

midday *NOUN*
the middle of the day; noon

middle *NOUN*
the point that is at the same distance from all sides or edges or ends

middle *ADJECTIVE*
1 placed or happening in the middle
2 moderate in size or rank etc.

middle-aged *ADJECTIVE*
aged between about 40 and 60
middle age *NOUN*

middle class or **classes** *NOUN*
the class of people including business and

professional people
middle-class ADJECTIVE

middling ADJECTIVE
of medium size or quality

midge NOUN
a small insect like a gnat

midget NOUN
an extremely small person or thing
midget ADJECTIVE

midland ADJECTIVE
1 to do with the middle part of a country
2 to do with the Midlands

midnight NOUN
twelve o'clock at night

midriff NOUN
the front part of the body above the waist

midst NOUN
the middle

midway ADVERB
halfway

midwife NOUN **midwives**
a person trained to look after a woman during childbirth

might[1] NOUN
great strength or power

might[2] AUXILIARY VERB
(*the past tense* of **may**) used to express possibility *It might be true.*

mighty ADJECTIVE
strong or powerful
mightily ADVERB

migraine NOUN
a severe kind of headache

migrant NOUN
a person or animal that migrates or has migrated

migrate VERB
to leave one country or place and settle in another
migration NOUN

mike NOUN
(*informal*) a microphone

mild ADJECTIVE **milder**, **mildest**
1 gentle
2 not strongly flavoured
3 warm and pleasant
mildly ADVERB

mildew NOUN
a white coating of fungus on damp surfaces
mildewed ADJECTIVE

mile NOUN
a measure of distance equal to 1,760 yards (about 1.6 kilometres)

mileage NOUN
1 the number of miles travelled
2 benefit or advantage

milestone NOUN
an important event

milieu (meel-yer) NOUN **milieus** or **milieux**
surroundings

militant ADJECTIVE
1 eager to fight
2 forceful or aggressive
militancy NOUN

military ADJECTIVE
to do with soldiers or the armed forces

militate VERB
to be a strong influence against something
Do not confuse this word with *mitigate*.

militia (mil-**ish**-a) NOUN **militias**
a military force of civilians

milk NOUN
a white liquid produced by female mammals to feed their young
milky ADJECTIVE

milk VERB
to take the milk from a cow or other animal

milkshake NOUN
a drink made from milk whisked with sweet fruit flavouring

milk tooth NOUN **milk teeth**
one of the first set of teeth of a child or animal

mill NOUN
1 a place or machine for grinding corn
2 a grinding machine *a pepper mill*
3 a factory *a paper mill*

mill VERB
1 to grind or crush in a mill
2 to move in a confused crowd
miller NOUN

millennium NOUN **millennia** or **millenniums**
a period of 1,000 years

millet NOUN
a kind of cereal with tiny seeds

milligram NOUN
one thousandth of a gram

millilitre NOUN
one thousandth of a litre

millimetre NOUN
one thousandth of a metre

milliner NOUN
a person who makes and sells women's hats
millinery NOUN

million NOUN **millions** or **million**
one thousand thousand (1,000,000)
millionth ADJECTIVE, NOUN

millionaire NOUN
a person who has a million pounds or dollars

millipede NOUN
an insect with many legs

millstone NOUN
a heavy responsibility

mime NOUN
acting without words

mime VERB
to perform a mime

mimic VERB **mimicking, mimicked**
to imitate someone in an amusing or mocking way
mimicry NOUN

mimic NOUN
a person who mimics others

mimosa NOUN
a tree with small yellow flowers

minaret NOUN
the tall tower of a mosque

mince VERB
to chop into small pieces
mincer NOUN

mince NOUN
minced meat

mincemeat NOUN
a sweet mixture of currants, raisins, apple, etc. used in pies

mince pie NOUN
a pie filled with mincemeat

mind NOUN
1 the ability to think, feel, and remember
2 a person's opinion or intention *changed my mind*

mind VERB
1 to look after
2 to be careful about
3 to object to
minder NOUN

mindful ADJECTIVE
taking thought or care

mindless ADJECTIVE
done without thinking

mine[1] POSSESSIVE PRONOUN
belonging to me

mine[2] NOUN
1 a place where minerals are dug from the ground
2 an explosive device in the ground or sea

mine VERB
1 to dig from a mine
2 to lay explosive mines in

minefield NOUN
1 an area of explosive mines
2 something with hidden dangers or problems

miner NOUN
a person who works in a mine

mineral NOUN
1 a hard inorganic substance found in the ground
2 a cold non-alcoholic drink

mineralogy (min-er-**al**-o-jee) NOUN
the study of minerals
mineralogist NOUN

mineral water NOUN
water containing mineral salts or gases

minestrone (mini-**stroh**-nee) NOUN
a soup containing vegetables and pasta

mingle VERB
to mix or blend

miniature ADJECTIVE
1 very small
2 on a small scale

minim NOUN
a note in music, lasting twice as long as a crotchet (♩)

minimal ADJECTIVE
very little; as little as possible

minimize VERB
to make as small as possible

minimum NOUN **minima** or **minimums**
the lowest possible number or amount

minimum ADJECTIVE
least or smallest

minion NOUN
a humble assistant

minister NOUN
1 a person in charge of a government department
2 a member of the clergy
ministerial ADJECTIVE

minister VERB
to attend to people's needs

ministry NOUN **ministries**
1 a government department
2 the work of the clergy

mink NOUN
1 an animal like a stoat
2 its brown fur

minnow NOUN
a tiny freshwater fish

minor ADJECTIVE
1 of less importance
2 of the musical scale with a semitone after the second note

minor NOUN
a person under the age of legal responsibility

minority NOUN **minorities**
1 the smallest part of a group
2 a small group that is different

a b c d e f g h i j k l **m** n o p q r s t u v w x y z

minstrel NOUN
a travelling musician in medieval times

mint [1] NOUN
1 a plant with fragrant leaves used as flavouring
2 peppermint or a sweet flavoured with this

mint [2] NOUN
the place where coins are made
in mint condition like new

mint VERB
to make coins

minuet NOUN
a slow stately dance

minus PREPOSITION
with the next number or thing subtracted

minus ADJECTIVE
less than zero *minus ten degrees* (-10°)

minuscule ADJECTIVE
extremely small

minute [1] (**min**-it) NOUN
1 one sixtieth of an hour
2 a very short time
3 one sixtieth of a degree (used in measuring angles)

minute [2] (my-**newt**) ADJECTIVE
very small or detailed

minutes PLURAL NOUN
a summary of things said at a meeting

minx NOUN
a cheeky or mischievous girl

miracle NOUN
something wonderful, believed to have a supernatural cause
miraculous ADJECTIVE

mirage (mi-**rahzh**) NOUN
something that seems to be there but is not

mire NOUN
1 a swamp
2 deep mud

mirror NOUN
a surface of reflecting material

mirror VERB
to reflect in or like a mirror

mirth NOUN
merriment or laughter
mirthful ADJECTIVE

misadventure NOUN
a piece of bad luck

misappropriate VERB
to take dishonestly
misappropriation NOUN

misbehave VERB
to behave badly
misbehaviour NOUN

miscalculate VERB
to calculate incorrectly
miscalculation NOUN

miscarriage NOUN
1 the birth of a baby before it has developed
2 a failure of justice

miscellaneous (mis-el-**ay**-nee-us) ADJECTIVE
of various kinds; mixed

miscellany (mis-**el**-an-ee) NOUN
miscellanies
a collection or mixture of different things

mischance NOUN
misfortune

mischief NOUN
1 naughty or troublesome behaviour
2 trouble caused by this

mischievous ADJECTIVE
naughty or troublesome

misconception NOUN
a mistaken idea

misconduct NOUN
bad behaviour by someone in authority

misdemeanour NOUN
a minor offence or crime

miser NOUN
a person who hoards money and spends little
miserly ADJECTIVE

miserable ADJECTIVE
1 very unhappy or uncomfortable
2 unpleasant *miserable weather*

misery NOUN **miseries**
great unhappiness

misfire VERB
to fail to fire or have the right effect

misfit NOUN
a person who does not fit in well with other people

misfortune NOUN
1 bad luck
2 an unlucky event or accident

misgiving NOUN
a feeling of doubt or slight mistrust

misguided ADJECTIVE
guided by mistaken ideas or beliefs

mishap (mis-hap) NOUN
an unlucky accident

misjudge VERB
to judge wrongly
misjudgement NOUN

mislay VERB **mislaid**
to lose for a short time

mislead VERB **misled**
to give somebody a wrong idea deliberately

misnomer NOUN
an unsuitable name for something

misprint NOUN
a mistake in printing

misrule NOUN
bad government

Miss NOUN
a title put before a girl's or unmarried woman's name

miss VERB
1 to fail to hit, reach, catch, see, hear, or find something
2 to feel the loss or absence of
3 to notice that something has gone

miss NOUN
a failure to hit something

misshapen ADJECTIVE
badly shaped

missile NOUN
a weapon or other object fired or thrown at a target

missing ADJECTIVE
lost or asbent

mission NOUN
1 an important task to be done
2 a military or scientific expedition

missionary NOUN **missionaries**
a person sent to another country to spread a religion

misspell VERB **misspelt** or **misspelled**
to spell wrongly

mist NOUN
1 damp cloudy air
2 condensed water vapour
misty ADJECTIVE

mist VERB
to become covered in mist

mistake NOUN
something wrong

mistake VERB **mistook**, **mistaken**
1 to misunderstand
2 to choose or identify wrongly

mistaken ADJECTIVE
wrong or incorrect

mister NOUN
(*informal*) a form of address to a man

mistletoe NOUN
a plant with white berries

mistreat VERB
to treat badly

mistress NOUN
1 a woman in charge of something
2 a man's lover who is not his wife

mistrust VERB
to have no trust in
mistrust NOUN

misunderstand VERB **misunderstood**
to get a wrong idea or impression of
misunderstanding NOUN

misuse (mis-**yooz**) VERB
1 to use incorrectly
2 to treat badly
misuse (mis-**yooss**) NOUN

mite NOUN
1 a tiny creature
2 a small child

mitigate VERB
to make less severe
mitigation NOUN
Do not confuse this word with *militate*.

mitre NOUN
1 a tall pointed bishop's hat
2 a joint in wood

mitten NOUN
a glove with a combined part for the fingers

mix VERB
1 to blend or unite things into one
2 to socialize
mix up to confuse

mix NOUN
a mixture

mixed ADJECTIVE
containing two or more kinds

mixture NOUN
something made of different things mixed together

mix-up NOUN
a state of confusion

mnemonic (nim-**on**-ik) NOUN
words that help you to remember something

moan VERB
1 to make a long low sound of pain
2 to grumble
moan NOUN

moat NOUN
a deep wide ditch round a castle, filled with water

mob NOUN
a large noisy crowd

mob VERB **mobbing**, **mobbed**
to crowd round

mobile ADJECTIVE
able to be moved or carried easily
mobility NOUN

mobile NOUN
1 a hanging decoration that moves in air currents
2 a mobile phone

mobilize VERB
to bring together for war or other activity
mobilization NOUN

moccasin NOUN
a soft leather shoe

mock VERB
to make fun of
mock ADJECTIVE
imitation; not real

mockery NOUN **mockeries**
ridicule or contempt

mode NOUN
1 the way a thing is done
2 what is fashionable

model NOUN
1 a small-scale copy
2 a particular design
3 a person who poses for an artist or displays
clothes
4 a person or thing worth copying
model VERB **modelling, modelled**
1 to make a model of
2 to design or plan using another thing as an
example
3 to work as a model

modem (moh-dem) NOUN
(ICT) a device linking a computer to a
telephone line

moderate (mod-er-at) ADJECTIVE
1 not extremely small or great or hot etc.
2 not extreme moderate opinions
moderately ADVERB
moderate (mod-er-ayt) VERB
to make or become moderate
moderation NOUN

modern ADJECTIVE
1 belonging to recent times
2 fashionable
modernity NOUN

modernize VERB
to make more modern

modest ADJECTIVE
1 not vain or boastful
2 moderate in size or appearance
modesty NOUN

modicum NOUN
a small amount

modify VERB **modifies, modified**
to change something slightly
modification NOUN

module NOUN
1 a self-contained component
2 a unit of study
modular ADJECTIVE

mogul (moh-gul) NOUN
an influential person

mohair NOUN
fine silky wool from an angora goat

moist ADJECTIVE
slightly wet

moisten VERB
to make slightly wet

moisture NOUN
water in tiny drops

molar NOUN
a wide tooth at the back of the jaw

molasses NOUN
dark syrup from raw sugar

mole[1] NOUN
a small furry animal that burrows

mole[2] NOUN
a small dark spot on skin

molecule NOUN
the smallest part into which a substance can
be divided without changing its chemical
nature
molecular ADJECTIVE

molest VERB
to annoy or pester
molestation NOUN

mollify VERB **mollifies, mollified**
to make less angry

mollusc NOUN
an animal with a soft body, e.g. a snail

molten ADJECTIVE
(of metal) made liquid by great heat

moment NOUN
1 a very short time
2 a particular time

momentary ADJECTIVE
lasting only a moment
momentarily ADVERB

momentous ADJECTIVE
very important

momentum NOUN
the ability to keep moving or developing

monarch NOUN
a king, queen, emperor, or empress

monarchy NOUN **monarchies**
a place or government with a monarch

monastery NOUN **monasteries**
a place where monks live
monastic ADJECTIVE

Monday NOUN
the day of the week following Sunday

money NOUN
coins and banknotes
monetary ADJECTIVE

mongoose NOUN **mongooses**
a small tropical animal

mongrel (mung-rel) NOUN
a dog of mixed breeds

monitor NOUN
1 a device for watching or testing
2 a screen that displays computer data
3 a school pupil with special responsibility

monitor VERB
to watch or test work being done or the person doing it

monk NOUN
one of a community of religious men living according to rules

monkey NOUN **monkeys**
1 an animal with long arms, hands with thumbs, and often a tail
2 a mischievous child

monochrome ADJECTIVE
in one colour

monocle NOUN
a lens for one eye

monogamy NOUN
marriage to only one person at a time

monogram NOUN
a design made of letters

monolithic ADJECTIVE
(of an organization) huge and difficult to change

monologue NOUN
a speech by one person

monopolize VERB
to take or dominate the whole of

monopoly NOUN **monopolies**
1 the exclusive right to sell something
2 complete possession or use of something by one group

monotonous ADJECTIVE
dull because it does not change

monotony NOUN
lack of change or variety

monsoon NOUN
a strong wind with rain in the Indian Ocean

monster NOUN
1 a large frightening creature
2 a cruel person

monster ADJECTIVE
(informal) huge

monstrosity NOUN **monstrosities**
a monstrous thing

monstrous ADJECTIVE
1 like a monster; huge and ugly
2 shocking or outrageous

month NOUN
each of the twelve parts into which a year is divided

monthly ADJECTIVE, ADVERB
happening or done once a month

monument NOUN
a statue or building put up as a memorial
monumental ADJECTIVE

moo VERB **moos, mooing, mooed**
to make the low deep sound of a cow
moo NOUN

mood NOUN
the way someone feels

moody ADJECTIVE **moodier, moodiest**
gloomy or sullen
moodily ADVERB

moon NOUN
1 the natural satellite of the earth seen at night
2 a satellite of any planet

moon VERB
to go about in a dreamy way

moonlight NOUN
light from the moon
moonlit ADJECTIVE

moor[1] NOUN
an area of rough land

moor[2] VERB
to fasten a boat

moorhen NOUN
a small waterbird

mooring NOUN
a place where a boat can be moored

moose NOUN
a North American elk

moot ADJECTIVE
open to debate

mop NOUN
1 a soft pad on a stick, used for cleaning floors etc.
2 a thick mass of hair

mop VERB **mopping, mopped**
to clean or wipe with a mop etc.

mope VERB
to be sad and gloomy

moped (moh-ped) NOUN
a small motorcycle with pedals

moral ADJECTIVE
1 to do with right and wrong
2 virtuous

moral NOUN
a lesson in right behaviour taught by a story or event

morale (mor-ahl) NOUN
the level of confidence of people

morality NOUN
standards of behaviour

moralize VERB
to speak about right and wrong behaviour

morals PLURAL NOUN
standards of behaviour

morass (mo-rass) NOUN
1 a marsh or bog
2 a confused mass

moratorium NOUN **moratoriums**
a temporary ban

morbid ADJECTIVE
thinking about gloomy things

more ADJECTIVE (comparative of **much** and **many**)
greater in amount or degree

more NOUN
a greater amount

more ADVERB
1 to a greater extent   *more beautiful*
2 again   *once more*

moreover ADVERB
besides; in addition

morning NOUN
the early part of the day before noon

moron NOUN
(*informal*) a stupid person
moronic ADJECTIVE

morose ADJECTIVE
bad-tempered

morphine NOUN
a drug made from opium, used to lessen pain

Morse code NOUN
a signalling code using short and long sounds
or flashes of light (dots and dashes) to
represent letters

morsel NOUN
a small piece of food

mortal ADJECTIVE
1 not living for ever
2 causing death
mortally ADVERB

mortal NOUN
a human being

mortality NOUN
1 the state of being mortal
2 the number of people who die over a period

mortar NOUN
1 a mixture of sand, cement, and water used
in fixing bricks etc.
2 a hard bowl for pounding substances with a
pestle
3 a short cannon for firing shells at a high
angle

mortarboard NOUN
an academic cap with a stiff square top

mortgage (mor-gij) NOUN
a loan to buy a house, with the house as
security

mortgage VERB
to offer as security

mortify VERB **mortifies**, **mortified**
to humiliate

mortuary NOUN **mortuaries**
a place where dead bodies are kept before
being buried or cremated

mosaic (mo-zay-ik) NOUN
a picture or design made from small coloured
pieces of stone or glass

mosque (mosk) NOUN
a Muslim place of worship

mosquito NOUN **mosquitoes**
a kind of gnat that sucks blood

moss NOUN
a plant growing in clumps in damp places
mossy ADJECTIVE

most ADJECTIVE (superlative of **much** and
many)
greatest in amount or degree

most NOUN
the greatest amount

most ADVERB
1 to the greatest extent
2 very or extremely

mostly ADVERB
mainly

motel NOUN
a roadside hotel for motorists

moth NOUN
an insect like a butterfly, which flies at night

mother NOUN
a female parent
motherhood NOUN **motherly** ADJECTIVE

mother VERB
to look after in a caring way

mother-in-law NOUN **mothers-in-law**
the mother of a person's husband or wife

mother-of-pearl NOUN
a pearly substance lining the shells of
mussels etc.

motif (moh-**teef**) NOUN
a repeated design or theme

motion NOUN
1 a way of moving
2 a proposal at a meeting

motion VERB
to signal by a gesture

motivate VERB
to give a motive or reason to
motivation NOUN

motive NOUN
what makes a person do something

motive ADJECTIVE
producing movement

motley ADJECTIVE
having many colours or kinds

motor NOUN
a machine providing power to drive machinery etc.

motor VERB
to travel in a car

motorbike NOUN
a motorcycle

motorcade NOUN
a procession of cars

motorcycle NOUN
a two-wheeled road vehicle with an engine
motorcyclist NOUN

motorist NOUN
a person who drives a car

motorway NOUN
a major road with several lanes for fast traffic

mottled ADJECTIVE
marked with spots or patches of colour

motto NOUN **mottoes**
a short saying

mould [1] NOUN
a hollow container for setting liquid in a special shape

mould VERB
to give a particular shape or character to

mould [2] NOUN
a furry growth of tiny fungi

moulder VERB
to decay into dust

mouldy ADJECTIVE **mouldier, mouldiest**
covered with mould

moult VERB
(of an animal) to shed feathers, hair, or skin

mound NOUN
1 a pile of earth or stones etc.
2 a small hill

mount VERB
1 to climb or go up
2 to get on a horse, bicycle, etc.
3 to increase in amount
4 to place or fix in position
5 to organize

mount NOUN
1 a mountain
2 something on which an object is mounted
3 a horse for riding

mountain NOUN
1 a very high hill
2 a large heap or amount

mountaineer NOUN
a person who climbs mountains
mountaineering NOUN

mountainous ADJECTIVE
1 having many mountains
2 huge

mourn VERB
to be sad when someone has died
mourner NOUN **mournful** ADJECTIVE

mouse NOUN **mice**
1 a small furry animal with a long thin tail
2 (*ICT*) a device moved around by hand to control the movements of a cursor on a computer screen

mousse (mooss) NOUN
a creamy flavoured pudding

moustache (mus-tahsh) NOUN
hair growing on a man's upper lip

mousy ADJECTIVE **mousier, mousiest**
1 a light brown colour
2 dull and timid

mouth NOUN
1 the opening through which food is taken into the body
2 the place where a river enters the sea
3 an opening or outlet

mouth VERB
to form words without saying them

mouthful NOUN **mouthfuls**
an amount of food that can be put in the mouth

mouthpiece NOUN
the part of a musical instrument etc. put to the mouth

move VERB
1 to take or go from one place to another
2 to affect a person's feelings
3 to put forward a formal statement for discussion
movable ADJECTIVE **mover** NOUN

move NOUN
1 a movement or action
2 a player's turn in a game

movement NOUN
1 the act of moving or being moved
2 a group of people working together for a cause
3 (*Music*) a main division of a work

movie NOUN
(*American*) (*informal*) a cinema film

moving ADJECTIVE
causing strong emotion

mow VERB **mowed, mown**
to cut grass etc. with a machine or scythe
mow down to knock down and kill
mower NOUN

MP *ABBREVIATION* **MPs**
Member of Parliament

m.p.h. *ABBREVIATION*
miles per hour

MP3 *NOUN*
(*ICT*) a system of compressing audio files so that they can be downloaded from the Internet

Mr (**mist**-er) *NOUN*
a title put before a man's name

Mrs (**mis**-iz) *NOUN*
a title put before a married woman's name

Ms (miz) *NOUN*
a title put before a married or unmarried woman's name

much *ADJECTIVE* **more**, **most**
existing in a large amount

much *NOUN*
a large amount

much *ADVERB*
1 greatly or considerably *much to my surprise*
2 approximately *much the same*

muck *NOUN*
1 farmyard manure
2 dirt or filth
mucky *ADJECTIVE*

mucous (**mew**-kus) *ADJECTIVE*
like or covered with mucus

mucus (**mew**-kus) *NOUN*
the moist sticky substance in the throat etc.

mud *NOUN*
wet soft earth

muddle *VERB*
1 to jumble or mix things up
2 to confuse

muddle *NOUN*
a muddled state

muddy *ADJECTIVE* **muddier**, **muddiest**
1 covered in mud
2 vague and unclear

muesli (**mooz**-lee) *NOUN*
a breakfast food made of mixed cereals, dried fruit, and nuts

muff *NOUN*
a tube-shaped piece of warm material for keeping the hands warm

muffin *NOUN*
1 a flat toasted bun
2 a small sponge cake

muffle *VERB*
1 to cover or wrap for protection or warmth
2 to deaden the sound of

muffler *NOUN*
a scarf

mug *NOUN*
1 a large straight-sided cup
2 (*informal*) a person who is easily deceived
3 (*informal*) the face

mug *VERB* **mugging**, **mugged**
to attack and rob in the street
mugger *NOUN*

muggy *ADJECTIVE* **muggier**, **muggiest**
unpleasantly warm and damp

mulberry *NOUN* **mulberries**
a purple or white fruit like a blackberry

mule *NOUN*
an animal that is the offspring of a donkey and a mare

mull *VERB*
mull over to think about carefully

mullet *NOUN*
a kind of fish used as food

multiple *ADJECTIVE*
having many parts or elements

multiple *NOUN*
a number that contains another number an exact number of times

multiply *VERB* **multiplies**, **multiplied**
1 to take a number a given quantity of times
2 to make or become many
multiplication *NOUN*

multitude *NOUN*
a great number of people or things

mum[1] *NOUN*
(*informal*) mother

mum[2] *ADJECTIVE*
(*informal*) silent *keep mum*

mumble *VERB*
to speak indistinctly
mumble *NOUN*

mummy[1] *NOUN* **mummies**
(*informal*) mother

mummy[2] *NOUN* **mummies**
an embalmed dead body in ancient Egypt

mumps *NOUN*
an infectious disease that makes the neck swell painfully

munch *VERB*
to chew steadily and noisily

mundane *ADJECTIVE*
ordinary; not exciting

municipal *ADJECTIVE*
to do with a town or city

municipality *NOUN* **municipalities**
a town or city with local government

mural *NOUN*
a picture painted on a wall

murder *VERB*
to kill a person unlawfully and deliberately

murder NOUN
the act of murdering a person
murderous ADJECTIVE

murderer NOUN
a person who commits murder

murky ADJECTIVE **murkier**, **murkiest**
dark and gloomy

murmur VERB
1 to make a low continuous sound
2 to speak in a soft voice
murmur NOUN

muscle NOUN
1 body tissue which contracts and relaxes to
produce movement
2 physical strength
muscular ADJECTIVE

muse VERB
to think deeply

museum NOUN
a place where historical or scientific objects
are displayed

mush NOUN
soft pulp

mushroom NOUN
an edible fungus with a dome-shaped top

mushroom VERB
to appear suddenly in large numbers

mushy ADJECTIVE **mushier**, **mushiest**
1 soft and wet
2 sentimental

music NOUN
pleasant or interesting sounds made by
instruments or by the voice

musical ADJECTIVE
1 to do with music
2 talented in music

musical NOUN
a play or film with songs

musician NOUN
someone who plays a musical instrument

musk NOUN
a strong-smelling substance used in
perfumes
musky ADJECTIVE

musket NOUN
a gun with a long barrel, formerly used by
soldiers

musketeer NOUN
a soldier armed with a musket

Muslim NOUN
a person who follows the religious teachings
of Muhammad (570–632)

muslin NOUN
thin soft cotton cloth

mussel NOUN
a black shellfish

must AUXILIARY VERB
1 used to express necessity *We must go.*
2 used to express certainty *You must be
joking!*

mustang NOUN
a wild horse of North America

mustard NOUN
a hot yellow paste used to flavour food

muster VERB
to assemble or gather together

mustn't
must not

musty ADJECTIVE **mustier**, **mustiest**
smelling or tasting mouldy

mutate VERB
to undergo a change in form
mutation NOUN

mute ADJECTIVE
1 not able to speak
2 (of a letter) not pronounced

muted ADJECTIVE
made quiet or less intense

mutilate VERB
to damage by breaking or cutting off a part
mutilation NOUN

mutiny NOUN **mutinies**
a rebellion by members of the armed forces
mutinous ADJECTIVE

mutiny VERB **mutinies**, **mutinied**
to take part in a mutiny

mutter VERB
1 to speak in a low voice
2 to grumble
mutter NOUN

mutton NOUN
meat from a sheep

mutual ADJECTIVE
1 given or done to each other *mutual respect*
2 shared *a mutual friend*
mutually ADVERB

muzzle NOUN
1 an animal's nose and mouth
2 a cover put over an animal's nose and
mouth to prevent it biting
3 the open end of a gun

muzzle VERB
to put a muzzle on

my ADJECTIVE
belonging to me

myriad (mi**rri**-ad) ADJECTIVE
very many
myriad NOUN

a b c d e f g h i j k l **m** n o p q r s t u v w x y z

myrrh (mer) *NOUN*
a substance used in perfumes and medicine

myself *PRONOUN*
I or me and nobody else *I cut myself. I myself have said it.*
by myself alone; on my own

mysterious *ADJECTIVE*
full of mystery

mystery *NOUN* **mysteries**
something that cannot be explained

mystic *ADJECTIVE*
1 having a spiritual meaning
2 filling people with wonder

mystical *ADJECTIVE*
having a special spiritual meaning
mysticism *NOUN*

mystify *VERB* **mystifies**, **mystified**
to puzzle or bewilder
mystification *NOUN*

mystique (mis-**teek**) *NOUN*
an air of mystery or secret power

myth *NOUN*
1 an ancient story about gods and heroes
2 an untrue story or belief

mythical *ADJECTIVE*
1 imaginary; found only in myths
2 to do with myths

mythology *NOUN* **mythologies**
a collection of myths
mythological *ADJECTIVE*

myxomatosis (miks-om-at-**oh**-sis) *NOUN*
a disease that kills rabbits

Nn

nab *VERB* **nabbing**, **nabbed** (*informal*)
1 to catch or arrest
2 to seize or grab

nag^1 *VERB* **nagging**, **nagged**
1 to pester or criticize about minor things
2 (of a pain) to hurt constantly

nag^2 *NOUN*
(*informal*) a horse

nail *NOUN*
1 the hard covering over the end of a finger or toe
2 a thin pointed piece of metal for fastening wood etc.

nail *VERB*
1 to fasten with nails
2 to catch or arrest

naive (nah-**eev**) *ADJECTIVE*
innocent and trusting
naivety *NOUN*

naked *ADJECTIVE*
1 without any clothes or covering
2 obvious *the naked truth*

name *NOUN*
1 the word or words by which a person, place, or thing is known
2 a person's reputation

name *VERB*
1 to give a name to
2 to state the name of
3 to specify

nameless *ADJECTIVE*
not having a name

namely *ADVERB*
that is to say

namesake *NOUN*
a person or thing with the same name as another

nanny *NOUN* **nannies**
a woman who looks after young children

nanny goat *NOUN*
a female goat

nap^1 *NOUN*
a short sleep

nap^2 *NOUN*
short raised fibres on cloth

nape *NOUN*
the back of the neck

napkin *NOUN*
a piece of cloth or paper used for wiping the lips or fingers

nappy *NOUN* **nappies**
a piece of cloth or padding put round a baby's bottom to absorb the urine and faeces

narcissus *NOUN* **narcissi** or **narcissuses**
a garden flower like a daffodil

narcotic *NOUN*
a drug that makes a person sleepy or unconscious
narcotic *ADJECTIVE*

narrate *VERB*
to tell a story
narration *NOUN* **narrator** *NOUN*

narrative *NOUN*
a spoken or written account of something

narrow *ADJECTIVE*
1 not wide or broad
2 uncomfortably close
narrowly *ADVERB*

narrow *VERB*
to make or become narrower

narrow-minded *ADJECTIVE*
not tolerant of other beliefs and ways

nasal *ADJECTIVE*
1 to do with the nose
2 sounding through the nose

nasturtium (na-ster-shum) *NOUN*
a garden plant with round leaves and bright flowers

nasty *ADJECTIVE* **nastier**, **nastiest**
unpleasant or unkind

nation *NOUN*
a community of people living under one government
national *ADJECTIVE*

nationalism *NOUN*
the desire for a country to be independent
nationalist *NOUN* **nationalistic** *ADJECTIVE*

nationality *NOUN* **nationalities**
the condition of belonging to a nation

nationalize *VERB*
to put an industry or business under state ownership
nationalization *NOUN*

nationwide *ADJECTIVE, ADVERB*
over the whole of a country

native *NOUN*
a person born in a particular place

native *ADJECTIVE*
originating in or belonging to a particular place

nativity *NOUN* **nativities**
a person's birth

natty *ADJECTIVE* **nattier**, **nattiest**
(*informal*) neat and smart
nattily *ADVERB*

natural *ADJECTIVE*
1 produced by nature
2 normal
3 having an ability from birth
4 (of a note in music) neither sharp nor flat
naturally *ADVERB*

natural *NOUN*
a natural note in music; a sign (♮) that shows this

natural history *NOUN*
the study of plants and animals

naturalist *NOUN*
an expert in natural history

naturalize *VERB*
to give a person full rights as a citizen
naturalization *NOUN*

nature *NOUN*
1 everything in the world that was not made by people
2 the qualities and characteristics of a person or thing *a loving nature*
3 a kind or sort *things of that nature*

naturist *NOUN*
a person who practises nudism
naturism *NOUN*

naught *NOUN*
(*old use*) nothing

naughty *ADJECTIVE* **naughtier**, **naughtiest**
1 badly behaved or disobedient
2 slightly indecent
naughtiness *NOUN*

nausea (naw-zee-a) *NOUN*
a feeling of sickness or disgust
nauseating *ADJECTIVE*

nauseous *ADJECTIVE*
sickening; disgusting

nautical *ADJECTIVE*
to do with ships or sailors

naval *ADJECTIVE*
to do with a navy

nave *NOUN*
the main central part of a church

navel *NOUN*
the hollow in the abdomen where the umbilical cord was attached

navigable *ADJECTIVE*
suitable for ships to sail in
navigability *NOUN*

navigate *VERB*
1 to sail on a river or sea
2 to calculate the route of a ship, aircraft, or vehicle
navigation *NOUN* **navigator** *NOUN*

navvy *NOUN* **navvies**
a labourer working on a road, railway, canal, etc.

navy *NOUN* **navies**
a country's warships and crews

navy blue *NOUN*
a dark blue colour, the colour of naval uniform

nay *ADVERB*
(*old use*) no

Nazi (nah-tsee) *NOUN* **Nazis**
a member of the National Socialist Party in Germany in 1933–45
Nazism *NOUN*

NB *ABBREVIATION*
note well

near *ADVERB, ADJECTIVE*
not far away

near *PREPOSITION*
not far away from

near *VERB*
to come near to

nearby *ADJECTIVE*
near

a b c d e f g h i j k l m **n** o p q r s t u v w x y z

nearly *ADVERB*
almost

neat *ADJECTIVE* **neater, neatest**
1 simple and tidy
2 not diluted

neaten *VERB*
to make something neat

nebula *NOUN* **nebulae** or **nebulas**
a bright or dark patch in the sky

nebulous *ADJECTIVE*
indistinct or vague

necessary *ADJECTIVE*
needed; essential
necessarily *ADVERB*

necessitate *VERB*
to make necessary

necessity *NOUN* **necessities**
1 need
2 something needed

neck *NOUN*
1 the part of the body that joins the head to the shoulders
2 a narrow part of something

necklace *NOUN*
an ornament worn round the neck

nectar *NOUN*
1 a sweet liquid collected by bees from flowers
2 a delicious drink

nectarine *NOUN*
a kind of peach with a thin smooth skin

need *VERB*
1 to be without something you should have
2 to have to do something *You need to answer.*

need *NOUN*
1 something needed
2 a situation where something is necessary *no need to cry*
3 great poverty or hardship

needful *ADJECTIVE*
necessary

needle *NOUN*
1 a thin pointed piece of steel used in sewing
2 something thin and pointed
3 a pointer

needle *VERB*
to provoke

needless *ADJECTIVE*
not necessary

needlework *NOUN*
sewing or embroidery

needy *ADJECTIVE* **needier, neediest**
very poor

nefarious (nif-**air**-ee-us) *ADJECTIVE*
wicked

negate *VERB*
1 to make ineffective
2 to disprove or deny
negation *NOUN*

negative *ADJECTIVE*
1 that says 'no' *a negative answer*
2 looking only at the bad aspects
3 (of a test) showing no sign of what is being tested
4 less than nought; minus
5 to do with the kind of electric charge carried by electrons
negatively *ADVERB*

negative *NOUN*
1 a negative statement
2 a film with the dark and light parts reversed

neglect *VERB*
to fail to do something or attend to something

neglect *NOUN*
the state of being neglected

negligent *ADJECTIVE*
showing a lack of care
negligence *NOUN*

negligible *ADJECTIVE*
not big or important enough to bother about

negotiable *ADJECTIVE*
able to be changed after being discussed

negotiate *VERB*
1 to discuss with others to reach an agreement
2 to arrange after discussion
3 to get over an obstacle
negotiation *NOUN* **negotiator** *NOUN*

neigh *VERB*
to make the cry of a horse
neigh *NOUN*

neighbour *NOUN*
a person who lives near another
neighbouring *ADJECTIVE*

neighbourhood *NOUN*
1 the surrounding district or area
2 a district

neighbourly *ADVERB*
helpful to local people

neither *ADJECTIVE, PRONOUN*
not one or the other of two

neither *ADVERB* (used with **nor**)
not either of two possibilities

neolithic *ADJECTIVE*
of the later part of the Stone Age

neon *NOUN*
a gas that glows when electricity passes through it

nephew *NOUN*
the son of a person's brother or sister

nerve *NOUN*
1 any of the fibres in the body that carry messages to and from the brain
2 courage; calmness
3 impudence

nerve-racking *ADJECTIVE*
causing anxiety or stress

nervous *ADJECTIVE*
1 easily upset or scared
2 to do with the nerves *a nervous illness*

nervy *ADJECTIVE* **nervier**, **nerviest**
nervous

nest *NOUN*
1 a structure in which birds rear their young
2 a set of similar things

nestle *VERB*
to curl up comfortably

nestling *NOUN*
a bird that is too young to leave the nest

net[1] *NOUN*
material made of pieces of thread, cord, or wire, etc. joined together in a criss-cross pattern with holes between
the Net the Internet

net *VERB* **netting**, **netted**
to cover or catch with a net

net[2] *ADJECTIVE*
remaining after items have been deducted
income net of tax

netball *NOUN*
a game in which two teams try to throw a ball into a high net hanging from a ring

nether *ADJECTIVE*
lower

netting *NOUN*
a piece of net

nettle *NOUN*
a wild plant with leaves that sting when they are touched

nettle *VERB*
to annoy or provoke

network *NOUN*
an organization with parts that work together

neuralgia *NOUN*
pain along a nerve

neuron or **neurone** *NOUN*
a cell that is part of the nervous system

neurotic *ADJECTIVE*
nervously and obsessively anxious

neuter *ADJECTIVE*
neither masculine nor feminine

neutral *ADJECTIVE*
1 not supporting either side in a war
2 not distinctive
neutrality *NOUN*

neutral *NOUN*
a gear that disconnects the engine

neutralize *VERB*
to stop from having any effect
neutralization *NOUN*

neutron *NOUN*
a particle of matter with no electric charge

never *ADVERB*
1 at no time; not ever
2 not at all

nevertheless *ADVERB*
in spite of this; although this is a fact

new *ADJECTIVE*
1 not existing before
2 just made, bought, etc.
newly *ADVERB*

newcomer *NOUN*
a person who has arrived recently

newfangled *ADJECTIVE*
new and unfamiliar in method or style

new moon *NOUN*
the moon at the beginning of its cycle, visible as a thin crescent

news *NOUN*
information about recent events

newsagent *NOUN*
a shopkeeper who sells newspapers

newspaper *NOUN*
a daily or weekly publication containing news reports, articles, etc.

newt *NOUN*
a small animal like a lizard, living near or in water

newton *NOUN*
a unit for measuring force

next *ADJECTIVE, ADVERB*
nearest; coming immediately after

next door *ADVERB, ADJECTIVE*
in the next house or room

next of kin *NOUN*
a person's closest relative

nib *NOUN*
the pointed metal part of a pen

nibble *VERB*
to take quick small bites

nice *ADJECTIVE* **nicer**, **nicest**
1 pleasant or kind
2 precise or careful
nicely *ADVERB*

nicety (ny-sit-ee) *NOUN* **niceties**
1 precision
2 a small detail

niche (neesh) *NOUN*
1 a recess in a wall
2 a suitable place

nick *NOUN*
a small cut or notch

nick *VERB*
1 to make a nick in
2 (*informal*) to steal
3 (*informal*) to arrest

nickel *NOUN*
a silvery white metal

nickname *NOUN*
a name used instead of a person's real name

nicotine *NOUN*
an oily substance found in tobacco

niece *NOUN*
the daughter of a person's brother or sister

niggardly *ADJECTIVE*
mean or stingy

niggle *VERB*
1 to fuss over details
2 to be a small but constant worry

nigh *ADVERB, PREPOSITION*
(*old use*) near

night *NOUN*
1 the dark hours between sunset and sunrise
2 a particular night or evening

nightfall *NOUN*
the beginning of night

nightie *NOUN*
(*informal*) a nightdress

nightingale *NOUN*
a small brown bird that sings sweetly

nightly *ADJECTIVE, ADVERB*
happening every night

nightmare *NOUN*
1 a frightening dream
2 an unpleasant experience
nightmarish *ADJECTIVE*

nil *NOUN*
nothing or nought

nimble *ADJECTIVE*
able to move quickly
nimbly *ADVERB*

nine *NOUN, ADJECTIVE*
the number 9
ninth *ADJECTIVE, NOUN*

nineteen *NOUN, ADJECTIVE*
the number 19
nineteenth *ADJECTIVE, NOUN*

ninety *NOUN, ADJECTIVE* **nineties**
the number 90
ninetieth *ADJECTIVE, NOUN*

nip *VERB* **nipping, nipped**
1 to pinch or bite quickly
2 (*informal*) to go quickly

nip *NOUN*
1 a quick pinch or bite
2 sharp coldness *a nip in the air*
3 a small amount *a nip of brandy*

nipper *NOUN*
(*informal*) a young child

nipple *NOUN*
the part of a mother's breast from which a
baby sucks milk

nippy *ADJECTIVE* **nippier, nippiest** (*informal*)
1 quick or nimble
2 cold

nit *NOUN*
a parasitic insect or its egg

nit-picking *NOUN*
the pointing out of small faults

nitrate *NOUN*
a substance from nitric acid, used as a fertilizer

nitric acid (ny-trik) *NOUN*
a strong acid containing nitrogen

nitrogen (ny-tro-jen) *NOUN*
a gas that makes up about four-fifths of air

no *ADJECTIVE*
not any *no money*

no *ADVERB*
1 used to deny or refuse something
2 not at all *no better*

No. or **no.** *ABBREVIATION*
number

nobility *NOUN* **nobilities**
1 a noble state
2 the aristocracy

noble *ADJECTIVE* **nobler, noblest**
1 of high social rank
2 good or impressive
nobly *ADVERB*

noble *NOUN*
a person of high social rank
nobleman *NOUN* **noblewoman** *NOUN*

nobody *PRONOUN*
no person; no one

nocturnal *ADJECTIVE*
active at night

nod *VERB* **nodding, nodded**
to move the head up and down
nod *NOUN*

node *NOUN*
a swelling like a small knob

nodule *NOUN*
a small knob or lump

noise *NOUN*
a sound, especially a loud or unpleasant one
noisy *ADJECTIVE*

nomad *NOUN*
a member of a tribe that moves from place to place
nomadic *ADJECTIVE*

no man's land *NOUN*
an area that does not belong to anybody

nominal *ADJECTIVE*
1 in name only *the nominal ruler*
2 small *a nominal fee*
nominally *ADVERB*

nominate *VERB*
to propose as a candidate in an election
nomination *NOUN*
nominee *NOUN*

nonchalant (non-shal-ant) *ADJECTIVE*
calm and casual
nonchalance *NOUN*

nondescript *ADJECTIVE*
having no special qualities

none *PRONOUN*
1 not any
2 no one

none *ADVERB*
not at all *none too sure*

nonentity *NOUN* **nonentities**
an unimportant person

non-existent *ADJECTIVE*
not existing or unreal

non-fiction *NOUN*
books and writing about real people and events

non-flammable *ADJECTIVE*
not able to be set on fire

nonplussed *ADJECTIVE*
puzzled or confused

nonsense *NOUN*
1 meaningless words
2 foolish ideas
nonsensical (non-**sens**-ik-al) *ADJECTIVE*

non-stop *ADJECTIVE, ADVERB*
without stopping

noodles *PLURAL NOUN*
pasta in long narrow strips

nook *NOUN*
a sheltered corner

noon *NOUN*
twelve o'clock midday

no one *NOUN*
no person; nobody

noose *NOUN*
a loop in a rope that tightens when the rope is pulled

nor *CONJUNCTION*
and not

norm *NOUN*
1 a standard or average type, amount, etc.
2 normal or expected behaviour

normal *ADJECTIVE*
1 usual or ordinary
2 natural and healthy
normality *NOUN* **normally** *ADVERB*

north *NOUN*
1 the direction to the left of a person who faces east
2 the northern part of a country, city, etc.

north *ADJECTIVE, ADVERB*
towards or in the north; coming from the north

north-east *NOUN, ADJECTIVE, ADVERB*
midway between north and east
north-easterly *ADJECTIVE*
north-eastern *ADJECTIVE*

northerly *ADJECTIVE*
1 coming from the north
2 facing the north

northern *ADJECTIVE*
of or in the north

northerner *NOUN*
a person from the north of a country

northward *ADJECTIVE, ADVERB*
towards the north
northwards *ADVERB*

north-west *NOUN, ADJECTIVE, ADVERB*
midway between north and west
north-westerly *ADJECTIVE*
north-western *ADJECTIVE*

nose *NOUN*
1 the part of the face that is used for breathing and smelling
2 the front end or part

nose *VERB*
to go forward cautiously

nosedive *NOUN*
a steep downward dive by an aircraft

nostalgia (nos-tal-ja) *NOUN*
longing for the past
nostalgic *ADJECTIVE*

nostril *NOUN*
either of the two openings of the nose

nosy *ADJECTIVE* **nosier, nosiest**
(*informal*) inquisitive or prying

not *ADVERB*
used to express a negative

notable *ADJECTIVE*
worth noticing
notably *ADVERB*

notation NOUN
a system of symbols representing numbers, quantities, etc.

notch NOUN
a small V-shape cut into a surface

notch VERB
to cut a notch in
notch up to score or achieve

note NOUN
1 something written down as a reminder
2 a short letter
3 a banknote
4 a single sound in music
5 a sound or quality that indicates something *a note of warning*
6 notice or attention *take note*

note VERB
1 to write down
2 to pay attention to

noted ADJECTIVE
famous for a particular reason *an area noted for its beaches*

notepaper NOUN
paper for writing letters

noteworthy ADJECTIVE
important or remarkable

nothing NOUN
1 no thing; not anything
2 no amount; nought

nothing ADVERB
1 not at all
2 in no way *nothing like as good*

notice NOUN
1 a printed announcement
2 attention *escaped my notice*
3 a formal announcement of leaving a job or dismissing an employee

notice VERB
to see or become aware of

noticeable ADJECTIVE
easily seen or noticed
noticeably ADVERB

notify VERB **notifies**, **notified**
to tell someone formally or officially
notifiable ADJECTIVE **notification** NOUN

notion NOUN
a vague idea

notional ADJECTIVE
guessed and not definite

notorious ADJECTIVE
well-known for something bad
notoriety (noh-ter-I-it-ee) NOUN

notwithstanding PREPOSITION
in spite of

nougat (noo-gah) NOUN
a chewy sweet made from nuts and sugar or honey

nought NOUN
1 the figure 0
2 nothing

noun NOUN
a word that stands for a person, place, or thing

nourish VERB
to keep a person, animal, or plant alive with food

nourishment NOUN
1 the process of nourishing
2 food

nova (noh-va) NOUN **novae**
a star that suddenly brightens for a time

novel NOUN
a story that fills a whole book
novelist NOUN

novel ADJECTIVE
new and unusual

novelty NOUN **novelties**
1 newness and originality
2 something new and unusual
3 a cheap toy

November NOUN
the eleventh month of the year

novice NOUN
1 a beginner
2 a person preparing to be a monk or nun

now ADVERB
1 at this time
2 by this time
3 immediately

now CONJUNCTION
as a result of or at the same time as *Now that you have come, we'll start.*

nowadays ADVERB
at the present time

nowhere ADVERB
not anywhere

noxious ADJECTIVE
unpleasant and harmful

nozzle NOUN
the spout of a hose, pipe, or tube

nuance NOUN
a slight difference

nub NOUN
1 a small knob or lump
2 the central point of a problem

nuclear ADJECTIVE
1 to do with a nucleus
2 using the energy created by the nuclei of atoms

nucleus *NOUN* **nuclei**
1 a central part
2 the central part of an atom or of a seed

nude *ADJECTIVE*
not wearing any clothes; naked
nudity *NOUN*

nudge *VERB*
1 to poke a person gently
2 to push slightly
nudge *NOUN*

nudism *NOUN*
the belief that going naked is beneficial
nudist *NOUN*

nugget *NOUN*
1 a rough lump of gold
2 a valuable fact

nuisance *NOUN*
an annoying person or thing

null *ADJECTIVE*
not legally valid

nullify *VERB* **nullifies**, **nullified**
to make invalid

numb *ADJECTIVE*
unable to feel or move

numb *VERB*
to make numb

number *NOUN*
1 a symbol or word indicating how many or identifying something
2 a quantity of people or things
3 one issue of a magazine or newspaper
4 a song

number *VERB*
1 to mark with numbers
2 to count
3 to amount to

numeral *NOUN*
a symbol that represents a certain number

numerate (**new**-mer-at) *ADJECTIVE*
having a good understanding of numbers
numeracy *NOUN*

numerator *NOUN*
the number above the line in a fraction, e.g. 3 in ¾

numerical *ADJECTIVE*
to do with or consisting of numbers
numerically *ADVERB*

numerous *ADJECTIVE*
many

nun *NOUN*
one of a community of religious women living according to rules

nunnery *NOUN* **nunneries**
a convent

nuptial *ADJECTIVE*
to do with marriage

nurse *NOUN*
a person trained to look after sick or injured people

nurse *VERB*
1 to look after someone who is ill or injured
2 to feed a baby at the breast
3 to hold carefully

nursery *NOUN* **nurseries**
1 a place where young children are looked after
2 a place where plants are grown

nursery rhyme *NOUN*
a simple rhyme or song of the kind that young children like

nurture *VERB*
1 to train and educate
2 to nourish

nut *NOUN*
1 a fruit with a hard shell containing a kernel
2 a small piece of metal with a hole in the middle, for screwing on a bolt
nutty *ADJECTIVE*

nutmeg *NOUN*
the hard seed of a tropical tree, grated and used in cooking

nutrient (**new**-tree-ent) *NOUN*
a nourishing substance

nutrition *NOUN*
1 nourishment
2 the study of what nourishes people
nutritious *ADJECTIVE*

nutshell *NOUN*
in a nutshell stated very briefly

nuzzle *VERB*
to rub gently with the nose

nylon *NOUN*
a strong synthetic cloth or fibre

nymph *NOUN*
a female spirit in myths

Oo

O *INTERJECTION*
oh

oaf *NOUN*
a stupid or clumsy person

oak *NOUN*
a large tree with seeds called acorns

OAP *ABBREVIATION*
old-age pensioner

oar *NOUN*
a pole with a flat blade at one end, used for rowing a boat

oasis (oh-**ay**-sis) *NOUN*
a fertile place in a desert, with a spring or well of water

oath *NOUN*
a solemn promise

oatmeal *NOUN*
a food of ground oats

oats *PLURAL NOUN*
a plant used to make food

obedient *ADJECTIVE*
doing what you are told; willing to obey
obedience *NOUN*

obelisk *NOUN*
a tall pillar as a monument

obese (o-**beess**) *ADJECTIVE*
very fat
obesity *NOUN*

obey *VERB*
to do what you are told to do

obituary *NOUN* **obituaries**
a newspaper announcement of a person's death

object (ob-**jikt**) *NOUN*
1 something that can be seen or touched
2 an aim or purpose
3 a person or thing to which an action or feeling is directed *an object of pity*
4 (*Grammar*) the word or words naming who or what is acted on by a verb or preposition, e.g. *him* in *The dog bit him* and *against him*

object (ob-**jekt**) *VERB*
to say that you do not approve of something or do not agree
objector *NOUN*

objection *NOUN*
a reason for not approving of something

objectionable *ADJECTIVE*
unpleasant or nasty

objective *NOUN*
an aim or intention

objective *ADJECTIVE*
not influenced by personal opinions
objectivity *NOUN*

obligation *NOUN*
a promise or duty you have to fulfil

obligatory *ADJECTIVE*
compulsory; not optional

oblige *VERB*
1 to force or compel
2 to help and please someone
be obliged to to feel gratitude towards

obliging *ADJECTIVE*
polite and helpful

oblique (ob-**leek**) *ADJECTIVE*
1 slanting
2 not saying something in a direct way

obliterate *VERB*
to blot out or remove all traces of
obliteration *NOUN*

oblivion *NOUN*
1 the state of being forgotten
2 the state of being unconscious

oblivious *ADJECTIVE*
completely unaware of something

oblong *ADJECTIVE*
rectangular in shape and longer than it is wide
oblong *NOUN*

obnoxious *ADJECTIVE*
very unpleasant; objectionable

oboe *NOUN*
a high-pitched woodwind instrument
oboist *NOUN*

obscene (ob-**seen**) *ADJECTIVE*
indecent in an offensive way
obscenity *NOUN*

obscure *ADJECTIVE*
1 difficult to see or understand
2 not well-known

obscure *VERB*
to make obscure; to darken or conceal

obscurity *NOUN*
the state of being obscure or unknown

obsequious (ob-**seek**-wee-us) *ADJECTIVE*
too willing to obey or serve someone

observance *NOUN*
the practice of obeying a law or custom

observant *ADJECTIVE*
quick at observing or noticing things

observation *NOUN*
1 the act of observing or watching
2 a comment or remark

observatory *NOUN* **observatories**
a building with equipment for observing the stars or weather

observe *VERB*
1 to see and notice
2 to obey a law or rule
3 to keep a custom or religious festival
4 to make a remark
observer *NOUN*

obsess *VERB*
to occupy a person's thoughts constantly
obsessive *ADJECTIVE*

obsession *NOUN*
an idea or feeling that dominates a person's mind

obsolescent *ADJECTIVE*
going out of use or fashion
obsolescence *NOUN*

obsolete *ADJECTIVE*
not used any more; out of date

obstacle *NOUN*
something that stands in the way

obstetrics *NOUN*
the branch of medicine and surgery that deals with childbirth

obstinate *ADJECTIVE*
1 keeping firmly to your own ideas or ways, even though they may be wrong
2 difficult to overcome or deal with
obstinacy *NOUN*

obstreperous (ob-**strep**-er-us) *ADJECTIVE*
noisy and unruly

obstruct *VERB*
to stop a person or thing from getting past
obstruction *NOUN*

obtain *VERB*
to get or be given something

obtrusive *ADJECTIVE*
unpleasantly noticeable

obtuse *ADJECTIVE*
slow to understand

obtuse angle *NOUN*
an angle of between 90° and 180°

obverse *NOUN*
the side of a coin or medal showing the head or chief design

obvious *ADJECTIVE*
easy to see or understand
obviously *ADVERB*

occasion *NOUN*
1 the time when something happens
2 a special event
3 a suitable time
occasion *VERB*
(*formal*) to cause

occasional *ADJECTIVE*
1 happening from time to time but not frequently
2 for special occasions
occasionally *ADVERB*

occult *ADJECTIVE*
to do with supernatural or magic things

occupant *NOUN*
someone who occupies a place
occupancy *NOUN*

occupation *NOUN*
1 a person's job or profession
2 something done to pass the time
3 the act of capturing a country by force

occupational *ADJECTIVE*
caused by an occupation *an occupational disease*

occupy *VERB* **occupies**, **occupied**
1 to live in a place
2 to fill a space or position
3 to capture a country and place troops in it
4 to keep someone busy
occupier *NOUN*

occur *VERB* **occurring**, **occurred**
1 to happen or exist
2 to be found
3 to come into a person's mind

occurrence *NOUN*
something that happens

ocean *NOUN*
the water that surround the continents of the earth
oceanic *ADJECTIVE*

ochre (oh-ker) *NOUN*
1 a mineral used as a pigment
2 a pale brownish yellow

o'clock *ADVERB*
used after a number to give the time
one o'clock

octagon *NOUN*
a flat shape with eight sides and eight angles
octagonal *ADJECTIVE*

octave *NOUN*
the interval of eight steps between one musical note and the next note of the same name

octet *NOUN*
1 a group of eight musicians
2 a piece of music for eight musicians

October *NOUN*
the tenth month of the year

octopus *NOUN* **octopuses**
a sea creature with eight long tentacles

odd *ADJECTIVE*
1 strange or unusual
2 (of a number) not able to be divided exactly by 2, e.g. 3, 5, 7, etc.
3 left over from a pair or set *an odd sock*
4 of various kinds *odd jobs*
oddly *ADVERB*

oddity *NOUN* **oddities**
a strange person or thing

oddments *PLURAL NOUN*
scraps or pieces left over

odds *PLURAL NOUN*
the chances that a certain thing will happen
at odds with in conflict with **odds and ends** small things of various kinds

ode *NOUN*
a poem addressed to a person or thing

odious (oh-dee-us) *ADJECTIVE*
extremely unpleasant; hateful

odium (oh-dee-um) *NOUN*
general hatred or disgust

odour *NOUN*
an unpleasant smell
odorous *ADJECTIVE*

odyssey (od-iss-ee) *NOUN* **odysseys**
a long adventurous journey

oesophagus (ee-sof-a-gus) *NOUN*
oesophagi
the gullet

oestrogen (ees-tro-jen) *NOUN*
a hormone which develops female physical
characteristics

of *PREPOSITION*
1 belonging to
2 concerning; about
3 made from
4 in relation to

off *PREPOSITION*
1 away or down from
2 not taking or wanting *off your food*
3 deducted from

off *ADVERB*
1 away or down
2 not working or happening
3 completely *Finish it off.*
4 (of food) beginning to go bad

offal *NOUN*
the organs of an animal (e.g. liver and
kidneys) used as food

off-colour *ADJECTIVE*
slightly unwell

offence *NOUN*
1 an illegal action
2 a feeling of resentment

offend *VERB*
1 to cause offence to
2 to do wrong

offensive *ADJECTIVE*
1 causing offence
2 disgusting
3 used in attacking *offensive weapons*
offensive *NOUN*
an attack

offer *VERB*
1 to present something for someone to
accept
2 to say you are willing to do or pay
something
offer *NOUN*
1 the act of offering

2 an amount offered
3 a reduced price

offering *NOUN*
something offered

offhand *ADJECTIVE*
1 said or done without preparation
2 casual and rude

office *NOUN*
1 a room or building used for business work
2 a government department
3 an important job or position

officer *NOUN*
1 a person in charge of others, especially in
the armed forces
2 an official
3 a member of the police force

official *ADJECTIVE*
1 done or said by someone with authority
2 done as part of a job or position
official duties
officially *ADVERB*
Do not confuse this word with *officious*.

official *NOUN*
a person who holds a position of authority

officiate *VERB*
to be in charge of a meeting, event, etc.

officious *ADJECTIVE*
too ready to give orders; bossy
officiously *ADVERB*
Do not confuse this word with *official*.

offing *NOUN*
in the offing about to arrive or happen

off-licence *NOUN*
a shop selling alcoholic drinks to be drunk
away from the shop

off-putting *ADJECTIVE*
making you less keen on something

offset *VERB* **offsetting**, **offset**
to cancel out or make up for something

offshoot *NOUN*
something developed from something else

offshore *ADJECTIVE*
1 from the land towards the sea
2 in the sea some distance from the shore

offside *ADJECTIVE, ADVERB*
(of a player in football etc.) in a position not
allowed by the rules of the game

offspring *NOUN* **offspring**
1 a person's child or children
2 the young of an animal

often *ADVERB*
many times; in many cases

ogle *VERB*
to stare at someone attractive

ogre NOUN
1 a cruel giant in fairy tales
2 a terrifying person

oh EXCLAMATION
an exclamation of pain, surprise, delight, etc.

ohm NOUN
(*Science*) a unit of electrical resistance

oil NOUN
1 a thick slippery liquid that will not dissolve in water
2 a kind of petroleum used as fuel
3 oil paint
oily ADJECTIVE

oil VERB
to put oil on machinery to make it work smoothly

oil rig NOUN
a structure with equipment for drilling for oil

oilskin NOUN
cloth made waterproof by treatment with oil

ointment NOUN
a cream or slippery paste for putting on sore skin and cuts

OK or **okay** ADVERB, ADJECTIVE
(*informal*) all right

old ADJECTIVE
1 not new; born or made or existing from a long time ago
2 of a particular age *ten years old*
3 former or original *our old house*
of old long ago; in the distant past

old age NOUN
the time when a person is old

olden ADJECTIVE
of former times

old-fashioned ADJECTIVE
old in style; no longer fashionable

olive NOUN
1 a small green or black bitter fruit
2 the tree from which this comes

olive branch NOUN
an offer of peace or friendship after a quarrel

Olympic Games or
Olympics PLURAL NOUN
a series of international sports contests held every four years in a different part of the world
Olympic ADJECTIVE

ombudsman NOUN **ombudsmen**
an official who investigates complaints against government organizations

omega (oh-meg-a) NOUN
the last letter of the Greek alphabet, equivalent to a long Roman *o*

omelette NOUN
eggs beaten and cooked in a pan

omen NOUN
a sign of what is going to happen

ominous ADJECTIVE
suggesting trouble soon or in the future

omission NOUN
something that has been omitted or not done

omit VERB **omitting**, **omitted**
1 to miss something out
2 to fail to do something

omnibus NOUN
a book or radio or television programme containing several stories or episodes that were previously published or broadcast separately

omnipotent ADJECTIVE
having unlimited power

omniscient (om-**niss**-ee-ent) ADJECTIVE
knowing everything
omniscience NOUN

omnivorous (om-**niv**-er-us) ADJECTIVE
eating all kinds of food
omnivore NOUN

on PREPOSITION
1 supported by; covering; added or attached to *the sign on the door*
2 close to; towards
3 during; at the time of *on my birthday*
4 concerning *a book on butterflies*

on ADVERB
1 so as to be on something *Put it on.*
2 further forward *Move on!*
3 working; in action

once ADVERB
1 for one time or on one occasion
2 formerly

once NOUN
one time *just this once*

once CONJUNCTION
as soon as

oncoming ADJECTIVE
approaching; coming towards you

one ADJECTIVE
1 single
2 individual or united

one NOUN
1 the smallest whole number, 1
2 a person or thing alone

one PRONOUN
1 a person or thing previously mentioned
2 a person; any person *One likes to help.*
oneself PRONOUN

onerous (**ohn**-er-us or **on**-er-us) ADJECTIVE
difficult to bear or do

one-sided *ADJECTIVE*
1 with one side much stronger or active than the other
2 unfair *a one-sided account*

ongoing *ADJECTIVE*
continuing to exist or be in progress

onion *NOUN*
a round vegetable with a strong flavour

online *ADJECTIVE, ADVERB*
connected to a computer, the Internet, etc.

onlooker *NOUN*
a spectator

only *ADJECTIVE*
being the one person or thing of a kind
my only wish

only *ADVERB*
no more than; and that is all *only three left*

onset *NOUN*
1 a beginning *the onset of winter*
2 an attack

onslaught *NOUN*
a fierce attack

onto *PREPOSITION*
to a position on

onus (oh-nus) *NOUN*
the duty or responsibility

onward *ADVERB, ADJECTIVE*
going forward; further on
onwards *ADVERB*

onyx *NOUN*
a stone like marble, with different colours in layers

ooze *VERB*
1 to flow out or trickle slowly
2 to allow to flow out slowly

opal *NOUN*
a kind of stone with a rainbow sheen

opaque (o-payk) *ADJECTIVE*
not able to be seen through

open *ADJECTIVE*
1 not closed or fastened
2 not covered or blocked up
3 spread out; unfolded
4 not restricted *open access*
5 letting in visitors or customers
6 with wide empty spaces *open country*
7 honest and frank
8 not decided *an open mind*
9 willing or likely to receive *open to suggestions*

open *VERB*
1 to make or become open
2 to begin
opener *NOUN*

open-air *ADJECTIVE*
happening out of doors

opening *NOUN*
1 a space or gap; a place where something opens
2 a beginning
3 an opportunity

openly *ADVERB*
without secrecy

opera *NOUN*
a stage drama in which all or most of the words are sung
operatic *ADJECTIVE*

operate *VERB*
1 to make a machine work
2 to be in action
3 to perform a surgical operation

operation *NOUN*
1 a piece of work or method of working
2 surgery on the body to take away or repair a part of it
3 a planned military activity
operational *ADJECTIVE*

operative *ADJECTIVE*
working or functioning

operator *NOUN*
a person who works something, especially a telephone switchboard

operetta *NOUN*
a short light opera

opinion *NOUN*
what you think of something; a belief or judgement

opinionated *ADJECTIVE*
having and expressing strong opinions regardless of others

opium *NOUN*
a drug made from the juice of certain poppies

opponent *NOUN*
a person or group opposing another in a contest or war

opportune *ADJECTIVE*
1 (of a time) suitable for a purpose
2 happening at a suitable time
opportunely *ADVERB*

opportunist *NOUN*
a person who is quick to seize opportunities
opportunism *NOUN*

opportunity *NOUN* **opportunities**
a good chance to do a particular thing

oppose *VERB*
1 to argue or fight against
2 to contrast
be opposed to to be strongly against

opposite *ADJECTIVE*
1 placed on the other or further side
2 moving away from or towards each other
3 completely different

opposite *NOUN*
an opposite person or thing

opposite *PREPOSITION*
opposite to; facing

opposition *NOUN*
1 the act of opposing; resistance
2 the people who oppose something
the Opposition the chief political party
opposing the one that is in power

oppress *VERB*
1 to govern or treat people cruelly or unjustly
2 to worry someone or make them very sad
oppression *NOUN* **oppressor** *NOUN*

oppressive *ADJECTIVE*
1 cruel or harsh
2 worrying and difficult to bear
3 (of the weather) humid

opt *VERB*
to choose
opt out to decide not to take part

optic *ADJECTIVE*
to do with the eye or sight

optical *ADJECTIVE*
to do with sight

optician *NOUN*
a person who tests the eyesight and provides
glasses and contact lenses

optics *NOUN*
the study of sight and of light

optimist *NOUN*
a person who expects that things will turn
out well
optimism *NOUN* **optimistic** *ADJECTIVE*

optimum *ADJECTIVE*
best; most favourable
optimal *ADJECTIVE*

option *NOUN*
1 the right or power to choose
2 something that may be chosen

optional *ADJECTIVE*
that you can choose to do

opulent *ADJECTIVE*
wealthy or luxurious
opulence *NOUN*

or *CONJUNCTION*
used to show a choice

oracle *NOUN*
(in the ancient world) a shrine of a god where
people sought advice about the future

oral *ADJECTIVE*
1 spoken, not written
2 to do with or using the mouth
orally *ADVERB*

oral *NOUN*
a spoken exam or test

orange *NOUN*
1 a citrus fruit with reddish-yellow peel
2 a reddish-yellow colour

orangeade *NOUN*
an orange-flavoured drink

orang-utan *NOUN*
a large reddish-brown ape with long arms

oration *NOUN*
a long formal speech

orator *NOUN*
a public speaker
oratorical *ADJECTIVE*

oratorio *NOUN* **oratorios**
a long piece of choral music on a religious
theme

oratory *NOUN*
the art or practice of making speeches

orb *NOUN*
a sphere or globe

orbit *NOUN*
1 the curved path of an object moving round
a planet
2 a range of control
orbital *ADJECTIVE*

orbit *VERB*
to move in an orbit

orchard *NOUN*
a piece of ground with fruit trees

orchestra *NOUN*
a group of musicians playing together under a
conductor
orchestral *ADJECTIVE*

orchestrate *VERB*
1 to arrange music for an orchestra
2 to coordinate carefully
orchestration *NOUN*

orchid *NOUN*
a plant with brightly coloured flowers in
unusual shapes

ordain *VERB*
1 to make a person a member of the Christian
clergy
2 to declare or order by law

ordeal *NOUN*
a difficult or unpleasant experience

order *NOUN*
1 a command
2 a request for goods to be supplied
3 the way things are arranged
alphabetical order
4 a satisfactory condition *working order*
5 obedience to laws
6 a kind or sort *bravery of the highest order*
7 a group of monks or nuns who live by
religious rules
in order that or **in order to** for the
purpose of

order *VERB*
1 to command
2 to ask for goods to be supplied
3 to put into order

orderly *ADJECTIVE*
1 arranged neatly or well
2 well-behaved and obedient

orderly *NOUN* **orderlies**
1 a soldier who assists an officer
2 an assistant in a hospital

ordinal number *NOUN*
a number that shows a thing's position in a series, e.g. first, second, third, etc.

ordinance *NOUN*
a command or decree

ordinary *ADJECTIVE*
normal or usual; not special
out of the ordinary unusual
ordinarily *ADVERB*

ordination *NOUN*
the act of ordaining someone as a member of the clergy

ordnance *NOUN*
weapons and other military equipment

ore *NOUN*
rock with a valuable mineral in it

oregano (o-ri-**gah**-noh) *NOUN*
a wild herb used in cooking

organ *NOUN*
1 a keyboard instrument with sound produced by air forced through pipes
2 a part of the body with a particular function

organic *ADJECTIVE*
1 to do with the organs of the body
2 to do with living things
3 grown without the use of chemical fertilizers and pesticides

organism *NOUN*
a living thing

organist *NOUN*
a person who plays the organ

organization *NOUN*
1 a group of people working together in business, government, etc.
2 the process of organizing

organize *VERB*
1 to plan and prepare
2 to form people into a group to work together
3 to put in order

orgasm *NOUN*
the climax of sexual excitement

Orient *NOUN*
the East

oriental *ADJECTIVE*
to do with eastern countries

orientate *VERB*
1 to face or place something in a certain direction
2 to get your bearings
orientation *NOUN*

orienteering *NOUN*
the sport of finding your way across rough country

orifice *NOUN*
an opening in the body

origami (o-rig-ah-mee) *NOUN*
the art of folding paper into special shapes

origin *NOUN*
1 the point or cause from which something began
2 a person's family background

original *ADJECTIVE*
1 existing from the start
2 new in its design etc.
3 producing new ideas
originality *NOUN* **originally** *ADVERB*

originate *VERB*
1 to cause to begin; to create
2 to have as an origin

ornament *NOUN*
an object displayed or worn as a decoration

ornamental *ADJECTIVE*
decorative rather than useful

ornamentation *NOUN*
artistic decoration

ornate *ADJECTIVE*
elaborately decorated

ornithology *NOUN*
the study of birds
ornithologist *NOUN*

orphan *NOUN*
a child whose parents have died

orphanage *NOUN*
a home for orphans

orthodox *ADJECTIVE*
1 holding accepted beliefs
2 conventional or normal
orthodoxy *NOUN*

orthopaedic (orth-o-**pee**-dik) *ADJECTIVE*
to do with diseases and injuries of the bones and muscles

oscillate *VERB*
1 to move to and fro
2 to waver or vary
oscillation *NOUN*

osmosis NOUN
the passing of fluid through a porous partition into another more concentrated fluid

ostensible ADJECTIVE
apparent, but not necessarily true or genuine *ostensible reasons*
ostensibly ADVERB

ostentatious ADJECTIVE
making a showy display
ostentation NOUN

osteopath NOUN
a person who treats diseases and abnormalities by manipulating the bones and muscles
osteopathy NOUN

ostracize VERB
to exclude a person from a group
ostracism NOUN

ostrich NOUN
a large long-legged bird that cannot fly

other ADJECTIVE
1 different
2 additional or remaining
3 just recent or past *the other day*
other NOUN, PRONOUN
the other person or thing

otherwise ADVERB
1 if things happen differently
2 in other ways
3 differently *cannot do otherwise*

otter NOUN
a fish-eating river animal with webbed feet and a flat tail

ought AUXILIARY VERB
1 expressing duty or need *We ought to stay.*
2 expressing probability *They ought to be home soon.*

oughtn't
ought not

ounce NOUN
a unit of weight equal to $1/16$ of a pound (about 28 grams)

our ADJECTIVE
belonging to us

ours POSSESSIVE PRONOUN
something belonging to us *These seats are ours.*
It is incorrect to write *our's*.

ourselves PRONOUN
we and nobody else *We hurt ourselves. We ourselves have said it.*
by ourselves alone; on our own

oust VERB
to drive a person out from a position or office

out ADVERB
1 away from a particular place or position
2 into the open or into existence
3 no longer burning or shining
4 in error *out by 10%*
5 to or at an end; completely *sold out*
6 strongly or openly *to speak out*
7 (in cricket) no longer batting
out of doors in the open air

out-and-out ADJECTIVE
thorough or complete

outback NOUN
the remote inland districts of Australia

outbreak NOUN
the beginning of something unpleasant or violent, e.g. disease or war

outburst NOUN
a sudden bursting out of anger or laughter etc.

outcast NOUN
a person who has been rejected by family or society

outcome NOUN
a result of events

outcry NOUN **outcries**
a strong protest

outdated ADJECTIVE
out of date

outdo VERB **outdoes, outdid, outdone**
to do better than

outdoor ADJECTIVE
done or used in the open air

outdoors ADVERB
in the open air

outer ADJECTIVE
nearer to the outside
outermost ADJECTIVE

outfit NOUN
1 a set of clothes or equipment
2 (*informal*) a team or organization

outgoings PLURAL NOUN
expenditure

outgrow VERB **outgrew, outgrown**
1 to become too old or big for
2 to grow faster or larger than

outhouse NOUN
a small building separate from the main one

outing NOUN
a journey for pleasure

outlandish ADJECTIVE
looking or sounding strange

outlast VERB
to last longer than

outlaw NOUN
a person who is excluded from legal rights and protection

a b c d e f g h i j k l m n **o** p q r s t u v w x y z

outlaw VERB
1 to make a person an outlaw
2 to forbid or ban

outlay NOUN
an amount of money spent

outlet NOUN
1 a way for something to get out
2 a way of expressing feelings
3 a place from which goods are sold

outline NOUN
1 a line showing a boundary or shape
2 a summary

outline VERB
1 to make an outline of
2 to summarize

outlive VERB
to live or last longer than

outlook NOUN
1 a view from a window
2 a mental attitude
3 future prospects

outlying ADJECTIVE
remote

outmoded ADJECTIVE
no longer useful or fashionable

outnumber VERB
to be more in number than

out of date ADJECTIVE
no longer valid or fashionable

outpatient NOUN
a person who visits a hospital for treatment
but does not stay there

outpost NOUN
a distant settlement

output NOUN
1 the amount of goods etc. produced
2 the information or results from a computer

outrage NOUN
something wicked or cruel that shocks
people

outrage VERB
to shock and anger people

outrageous ADJECTIVE
1 very wicked
2 very extravagant

outright ADVERB
1 completely
2 frankly *Tell him outright.*

outright ADJECTIVE
thorough or complete *an outright lie*

outrun VERB **outrunning, outran, outrun**
to run faster or further than

outset NOUN
the beginning of something

outside NOUN
the outer side, surface, or part

outside ADJECTIVE
1 on or coming from the outside
2 remote or slight

outside ADVERB
on or to the outside; outdoors

outside PREPOSITION
on or to the outside of *outside the door*

outsider NOUN
1 a person who does not belong
2 a contestant with little chance of winning

outsize ADJECTIVE
much larger than average

outskirts PLURAL NOUN
the outer districts of a town

outspoken ADJECTIVE
speaking or spoken frankly

outstanding ADJECTIVE
1 extremely good or distinguished
2 not yet paid or dealt with

outstrip VERB **outstripping, outstripped**
1 to run faster or further than
2 to be or do better than

outward ADJECTIVE
1 on the outside
2 going or facing outwards

outward ADVERB
outwards

outwardly ADVERB
on the outside; as it appears

outwards ADVERB
towards the outside

outweigh VERB
be be more important than

outwit VERB **outwitting, outwitted**
to deceive with cunning

ova NOUN *plural* of **ovum**

oval ADJECTIVE
shaped like an egg
oval NOUN

ovary NOUN **ovaries**
either of the two female organs in which egg
cells are produced

ovation NOUN
a round of applause

oven NOUN
a closed space for cooking or heating food or
for baking clay

over PREPOSITION
1 above
2 more than
3 concerning *quarrelled over money*
4 across the top of; on or to the other side of
5 in superiority or preference to *a victory over
their enemy*

over ADVERB
1 from an upright position *fall over*
2 so that a different side shows *Turn it over.*
3 at or to a place *Walk over to our house.*
4 remaining *nothing left over*
5 all through *Think it over.*
6 at an end *The lesson is over.*

over NOUN
a series of six balls bowled in cricket

overall ADJECTIVE
including everything *the overall cost*

overall ADVERB
in general *has improved overall*

overall NOUN
a light coat worn to protect other clothes when working

overalls PLURAL NOUN
a combined bib and trousers worn over other clothes to protect them

overarm ADJECTIVE, ADVERB
with the arm lifted above shoulder level and coming down in front of the body

overawe VERB
to overcome a person with awe

overbearing ADJECTIVE
domineering

overboard ADVERB
into the water from a ship

overcast ADJECTIVE
covered with cloud

overcoat NOUN
a warm outdoor coat

overcome VERB **overcame**, **overcome**
1 to win a victory over
2 to have a strong physical or emotional effect on
3 to find a way of dealing with

overcrowded ADJECTIVE
having too many people

overdo VERB **overdid**, **overdone**
1 to do something too much
2 to cook food for too long

overdose NOUN
too large a dose of a drug

overdraft NOUN
the amount by which a bank account is overdrawn

overdraw VERB **overdrew**, **overdrawn**
to draw more money from a bank account than you have in it

overdue ADJECTIVE
not paid or arrived by the proper time

overestimate VERB
to estimate too highly

overflow VERB
to flow over the edge
overflow NOUN

overgrown ADJECTIVE
covered with weeds or unwanted plants

overhang VERB **overhung**
to jut out over something

overhaul VERB
to examine and repair
overhaul NOUN

overhead ADJECTIVE, ADVERB
1 directly above
2 in the sky

overheads PLURAL NOUN
the expenses of running a business

overhear VERB **overheard**
to hear something you were not meant to hear

overjoyed ADJECTIVE
filled with great joy

overland ADJECTIVE, ADVERB
travelling over the land

overlap VERB **overlapping**, **overlapped**
1 to lie across part of
2 to happen partly at the same time
overlap NOUN

overleaf ADVERB
on the other side of the page

overload VERB
to put too great a load on

overlook VERB
1 not to notice or consider something
2 to ignore a wrong deliberately
3 to have a view over something

overlord NOUN
a supreme lord

overnight ADJECTIVE, ADVERB
1 of or during a night *an overnight stop*
2 very quick or quickly

overpower VERB
to defeat by greater strength

overpowering ADJECTIVE
very strong

overrate VERB
to have too high an opinion of
overrated ADJECTIVE

override VERB **overrode**, **overridden**
1 to overrule
2 to be more important than
overriding ADJECTIVE

overrule VERB
to reject a suggestion etc. by using your authority

overrun *VERB* **overrunning, overran, overrun**
to grow or spread over

overseas *ADVERB*
across or beyond the sea; abroad

oversee *VERB* **oversaw, overseen**
to watch over or supervise
overseer *NOUN*

overshadow *VERB*
1 to cast a shadow over
2 to make a person or thing seem unimportant

oversight *NOUN*
a mistake made by not noticing something

overt *ADJECTIVE*
done or shown openly

overtake *VERB* **overtook, overtaken**
to catch up with or pass someone ahead

overthrow *VERB* **overthrew, overthrown**
to remove from power by force
overthrow *NOUN*

overtime *NOUN*
1 time spent working outside the normal hours
2 payment for this

overtone *NOUN*
a feeling or quality suggested but not expressed

overture *NOUN*
1 an orchestral introduction
2 an attempt to start a discussion

overturn *VERB*
1 to turn over or upside down
2 to reverse a legal decision

overweight *ADJECTIVE*
too heavy

overwhelm *VERB*
1 to bury or drown beneath a huge mass
2 to overcome completely
overwhelming *ADJECTIVE*

overwrought *ADJECTIVE*
upset and anxious

ovulate *VERB*
to produce an egg cell from an ovary

ovum (oh-vum) *NOUN* **ova**
a female cell that can develop into a new individual when it is fertilized

owe *VERB*
1 to have a duty to pay or give something to someone
2 to have something thanks to another person or thing *owed their lives to the pilot's skill*
owing to because of; caused by

owl *NOUN*
a bird of prey with large eyes, flying at night

own *ADJECTIVE*
belonging to yourself or itself
on your own alone

own *VERB*
1 to have as your property
2 to acknowledge or admit
own up to confess

owner *NOUN*
the person who owns something
ownership *NOUN*

ox *NOUN* **oxen**
a large animal kept for its meat and for pulling carts

oxide *NOUN*
a compound of oxygen and one other element

oxygen *NOUN*
a gas that exists in the air and is essential to life

oyster *NOUN*
a kind of shellfish with a shell that can contain a pearl

ozone *NOUN*
a form of oxygen with a sharp smell

Pp

p. *ABBREVIATION*
page

pace *NOUN*
1 one step in walking or running
2 speed of walking or running *a slow pace*

pace *VERB*
to walk with slow or regular steps

pacemaker *NOUN*
1 a person who sets the pace for another in a race
2 an electronic device put into the body by surgery to keep the heart beating

pacifist (pas-if-ist) *NOUN*
a person who refuses to support violent means
pacifism *NOUN*

pacify *VERB* **pacifies, pacified**
1 to calm a person
2 to bring peace to a country

pack NOUN
1 a collection of things wrapped or tied together
2 a set of playing cards
3 a bag carried on your back
4 a large amount *a pack of lies*
5 a group of hounds or wolves etc.

pack VERB
1 to put things into a suitcase, bag, box, etc.
2 to crowd together

package NOUN
1 a parcel or packet
2 a number of things offered together
packaging NOUN

packet NOUN
a small parcel

pact NOUN
an agreement or treaty

pad [1] NOUN
1 a soft thick mass of material
2 a piece of soft material worn for protection
3 a set of sheets of paper fastened together
4 the soft fleshy part under an animal's foot or the end of a finger or toe
5 a platform for launching a rocket

pad VERB **padding**, **padded**
to put a pad on or in
pad out to make something last longer

pad [2] VERB **padding**, **padded**
to walk softly

padding NOUN
material used to pad things

paddle VERB
1 to move a boat along with a paddle
2 to walk about with bare feet in shallow water

paddle NOUN
1 a short oar with a broad blade
2 a spell of paddling

paddock NOUN
a small field for keeping horses

paddy field NOUN
a field where rice is grown

padlock NOUN
a detachable lock with a hinged metal loop that passes through a ring or chain

padlock VERB
to lock with a padlock

paediatrics (peed-ee-**at**-riks) NOUN
the study of children's diseases
paediatric ADJECTIVE **paediatrician** NOUN

pagan (**pay**-gan) NOUN
a person who does not believe in one of the chief religions
pagan ADJECTIVE **paganism** NOUN

page [1] NOUN
a piece of paper that is part of a book or newspaper etc.; one side of this

page [2] NOUN
1 a boy or man employed as an attendant
2 a young boy attending a bride at a wedding

pageant NOUN
1 a play or entertainment on a historical subject
2 a procession of people in costume as an entertainment
pageantry NOUN

pager NOUN
a small radio device that can receive messages

pagoda (pag-**oh**-da) NOUN
a tower or temple in Asia, shaped like a tall pyramid

paid *past tense* of **pay**
put paid to (*informal*) to put an end to

pail NOUN
a bucket

pain NOUN
1 an unpleasant feeling caused by injury or disease
2 suffering in the mind

pain VERB
to cause suffering or distress to

painful ADJECTIVE
causing pain or distress
painfully ADVERB

painless ADJECTIVE
not causing any pain or distress

painstaking ADJECTIVE
very careful and thorough

paint NOUN
a liquid substance put on a surface to colour it

paint VERB
1 to put paint on a surface
2 to make a picture with paints

paintbrush NOUN
a brush for putting paint on a surface

painter NOUN
a person who paints

painting NOUN
1 a painted picture
2 the use of paints to make a picture

pair NOUN
1 a set of two things or people
2 something made of two joined parts *a pair of scissors*

pair VERB
to put two things together as a pair
pair off to form a couple

pal NOUN
(*informal*) a friend

palace NOUN
a large house where a king, queen, or other important person lives

palatable ADJECTIVE
pleasant to eat

palate NOUN
1 the roof of the mouth
2 a person's sense of taste
Do not confuse this word with *palette* and *pallet*.

palatial (pa-lay-shal) ADJECTIVE
like a palace; large and splendid

pale[1] ADJECTIVE
1 almost white *a pale face*
2 not bright in colour or light *pale green*

pale[2] NOUN
a boundary
beyond the pale beyond what is acceptable

palette NOUN
a board on which an artist mixes paints
Do not confuse this word with *palate* and *pallet*.

palindrome NOUN
a word or phrase that reads the same backwards as forwards, e.g. *radar* or *Madam, I'm Adam*

paling NOUN
a fence made of wooden posts or railings

palisade NOUN
a fence of pointed sticks or boards

pall[1] (pawl) NOUN
1 a cloth spread over a coffin
2 a dark covering *a pall of smoke*

pall[2] (pawl) VERB
to seem dull or uninteresting after a while

pallet NOUN
1 a mattress stuffed with straw
2 a hard narrow bed
3 a large platform for stacking and transporting goods
Do not confuse this word with *palate* and *palette*.

palliative NOUN
something that lessens pain or suffering

pallid ADJECTIVE
pale from illness

pallor NOUN
paleness of a person's face

palm NOUN
1 the flat inner part of the hand
2 a tropical tree with large leaves and no branches

palm VERB
palm off to fool a person into accepting something

palpable ADJECTIVE
1 able to be touched or felt
2 obvious *a palpable lie*
palpably ADVERB

palpitate VERB
(of the heart) to beat hard and quickly
palpitation NOUN

palsy (pawl-zee) NOUN
(*old use*) paralysis

paltry (pol-tree) ADJECTIVE
small and almost worthless *a paltry amount*

pampas NOUN
wide grassy plains in South America

pampas grass NOUN
a tall grass with long feathery flowers

pamper VERB
to treat or look after someone very kindly and indulgently

pamphlet NOUN
a leaflet or booklet giving information on a subject

pan NOUN
1 a wide container with a flat base, used in cooking
2 something shaped like this
3 the bowl of a lavatory

panacea (pan-a-see-a) NOUN
a cure for all kinds of diseases or troubles

panache (pan-ash) NOUN
a confident stylish manner

pancake NOUN
a thin round cake of batter fried on both sides

pancreas (pan-kree-as) NOUN
a gland near the stomach, producing insulin and digestive juices

panda NOUN
a large bear-like black-and-white animal found in China

pandemonium NOUN
uproar and confusion

pander VERB
pander to to give someone whatever they want

pane NOUN
a sheet of glass in a window

panel NOUN
1 a long flat piece of wood, metal, etc. that is part of a door, wall, piece of furniture, etc.
2 a flat board with controls or instruments on it
3 a group of people chosen to discuss or decide something
panelled ADJECTIVE **panelling** NOUN

pang NOUN
a sudden sharp pain

panic NOUN
sudden uncontrollable fear
panicky ADJECTIVE

panic VERB **panicking**, **panicked**
to fill or be filled with panic

pannier NOUN
a bag or basket hung on one side of a bicycle, motorcycle, or horse

panorama NOUN
a view or picture of a wide area
panoramic ADJECTIVE

pansy NOUN **pansies**
a small brightly coloured garden flower

pant VERB
to take short quick breaths after running or working hard

panther NOUN
a large black leopard

panties PLURAL NOUN
(*informal*) short knickers

pantile NOUN
a curved tile for a roof

pantomime NOUN
1 a Christmas entertainment, usually based on a fairy tale
2 mime

pantry NOUN **pantries**
a small room for storing food; a larder

pants PLURAL NOUN
1 underpants or knickers
2 (*American*) trousers

pap NOUN
1 soft food suitable for babies
2 trivial entertainment; nonsense

papacy (pay-pa-see) NOUN
the position of Pope

papal (pay-pal) ADJECTIVE
to do with the Pope

paper NOUN
1 a substance made in thin sheets from wood, rags, etc., used for writing or printing or drawing on or for wrapping
2 a newspaper
3 wallpaper
4 a document
5 a set of examination questions

paper VERB
to cover a wall or room with wallpaper

paperback NOUN
a book with a thin flexible cover

papier mâché (pap-yay **mash**-ay) NOUN
paper made into pulp and moulded to make models, ornaments, etc.

paprika (pap-rik-a) NOUN
a powdered spice made from red pepper

papyrus (pap-y-rus) NOUN
paper made from the stems of a plant like a reed, used in ancient Egypt

par NOUN
1 an average or normal amount or condition
2 (in golf) the number of strokes that a good player should normally take for a hole or course

parable NOUN
a story told to teach people a moral

parabola (pa-rab-ol-a) NOUN
a curve like the path of an object thrown into the air and falling down again
parabolic ADJECTIVE

parachute NOUN
an umbrella-like device on which people or things can float to the ground from an aircraft

parade NOUN
1 a procession of people or things
2 an assembly of troops for inspection or drill
3 a public square or promenade

parade VERB
1 to move in a parade
2 to assemble for a parade
3 to display in an obvious way

paradise NOUN
1 heaven
2 a place of great happiness

paradox NOUN
a statement that seems to contradict itself but which contains a truth, e.g. 'More haste, less speed'
paradoxical ADJECTIVE

paraffin NOUN
a kind of oil used as fuel

paragon NOUN
a person or thing that seems perfect

paragraph NOUN
one or more sentences on a single subject, forming a section of a piece of writing and beginning on a new line

parakeet NOUN
a kind of small parrot

parallel ADJECTIVE
(of lines etc.) side by side and the same distance apart from each other for their whole length

parallel NOUN
1 something similar or corresponding
2 a comparison
3 a line that is parallel to another
4 a line of latitude

parallel VERB **paralleling**, **paralleled**
to be similar to or correspond to

a b c d e f g h i j k l m n o **p** q r s t u v w x y z

parallelogram NOUN
a four-sided figure with opposite sides equal and parallel

paralyse VERB **paralysing**, **paralysed**
1 to cause paralysis in
2 to make unable to move *be paralysed with fear*

paralysis NOUN
a state of being unable to move a muscle or muscles, especially because of disease or injury

paramedic NOUN
a member of an ambulance crew or other person trained to assist medical staff

parameter NOUN
a quantity or factor that is variable and affects other things by its changes

paramilitary ADJECTIVE
organized like a military force but not part of the armed services

paramount ADJECTIVE
more important than anything else

paranoia NOUN
1 a mental illness in which a person wrongly believes that other people want to hurt them
2 an unjustified suspicion and mistrust of others
paranoid ADJECTIVE

paranormal ADJECTIVE
beyond what is normal and can be rationally explained

parapet NOUN
a low wall along the edge of a balcony, bridge, roof, etc.

paraphernalia NOUN
numerous pieces of equipment, belongings, etc.

paraphrase VERB
to express the meaning of something in different words
paraphrase NOUN

paraplegia NOUN
paralysis of the lower half of the body
paraplegic NOUN

parasite NOUN
an animal or plant that lives in or on another, from which it gets its food
parasitic ADJECTIVE

parasol NOUN
a light umbrella used to give shade from the sun

paratroops PLURAL NOUN
troops trained to be dropped from aircraft by parachute
paratrooper NOUN

parcel NOUN
an item wrapped up for sending by post

parcel VERB **parcelling**, **parcelled**
1 to wrap something up as a parcel
2 to divide into shares

parched ADJECTIVE
1 very dry
2 very thirsty

parchment NOUN
a kind of heavy paper, originally made from animal skins

pardon NOUN
1 forgiveness
2 the cancelling of a punishment

pardon VERB
1 to forgive or excuse someone
2 to cancel a person's punishment

pare (*say as* pair) VERB
1 to trim by cutting away the edges
2 to reduce gradually

parent NOUN
1 a mother or father; a living thing that has produced young
2 a source from which others are derived *the parent company*
parental (pa-**rent**-al) ADJECTIVE

parentage NOUN
the identity of a person's parents

parenthesis (pa-**ren**-thi-sis) NOUN
parentheses
1 extra words put into a sentence, usually between brackets or dashes
2 either of a pair of brackets in writing

pariah (pa-**ry**-a) NOUN
an outcast

parish NOUN
a district with its own church

parishioner NOUN
someone who lives in a particular parish

parity NOUN
equality

park NOUN
a large public area with grass and trees

park VERB
to leave a vehicle in a place for a time

parka NOUN
a warm jacket with a hood attached

Parkinson's disease NOUN
a disease that causes trembling of the arms and legs and stiff muscles

parley VERB
to hold a discussion with someone
parley NOUN

parliament NOUN
the assembly that makes a country's laws
parliamentary ADJECTIVE

parlour NOUN
(old use) a sitting room

parochial ADJECTIVE
1 to do with a church parish
2 interested only in your own area

parody NOUN **parodies**
an amusing imitation of the style of a writer, composer, literary work, etc.

parody VERB **parodies**, **parodied**
to make or be a parody of

parole NOUN
the release of a prisoner before the end of a sentence on condition of good behaviour
on parole

parole VERB
to release on parole

paroxysm (pa-roks-izm) NOUN
an outburst of rage, jealousy, laughter, etc.

parrot NOUN
a brightly coloured tropical bird that can imitate human speech

parry VERB **parries**, **parried**
1 to turn aside an opponent's weapon or blow
2 to avoid an awkward question

parsimonious ADJECTIVE
sparing in the use of something
parsimony NOUN

parsley NOUN
a plant with crinkled green leaves used to flavour and decorate food

parsnip NOUN
a plant with a yellow root used as a vegetable

parson NOUN
a member of the clergy, especially a rector or vicar

parsonage NOUN
a parson's house

part NOUN
1 some but not all of a thing or number of things
2 the character played by an actor
3 the words spoken by a character in a play
4 a contribution to an activity played an important part in the project
5 one side in an agreement or dispute
take part to join in an activity

part VERB
to separate or divide
part with to give away or get rid of

partake VERB **partook**, **partaken**
partake of 1 to eat or drink 2 to take part in

partial ADJECTIVE
1 not complete or total a partial eclipse
2 favouring one side
be partial to to be fond of
partially ADVERB

partiality NOUN
1 a preference for one side over another
2 a liking

participant NOUN
someone who takes part in something

participate VERB
to take part in something
participation NOUN **participator** NOUN

participle NOUN
a word formed from a verb and used to form certain tenses (e.g. It has gone, It is going) or the passive (e.g. We were guided to our seats), or as an adjective (e.g. a guided missile, a guiding light)

particle NOUN
a very small piece or amount

particular ADJECTIVE
1 of this one and no other This particular stamp is very rare.
2 special take particular care
3 fussy; choosing carefully very particular about his clothes
in particular especially
particularly ADVERB

particulars PLURAL NOUN
details or facts

parting NOUN
1 leaving or separation
2 a line where hair is combed in different directions

partisan NOUN
1 a strong supporter of a party or group etc.
2 a member of an organization resisting the authorities in a conquered country

partisan ADJECTIVE
strongly supporting a particular cause

partition NOUN
1 a thin wall dividing a room or space
2 the act of dividing a country into separate parts

partition VERB
1 to divide something into separate parts
2 to divide a room or space with a partition

partly ADVERB
to some extent but not completely

partner NOUN
1 one of a pair of people who do something together
2 a person who jointly owns a business with others
3 a husband, wife, or lover
partnership NOUN

partner VERB
to be a person's partner

part of speech NOUN
any of the groups into which words are divided in grammar (noun, pronoun, adjective, verb, adverb, preposition, conjunction, exclamation)

partook *past tense* of **partake**

partridge NOUN
a game bird with brown feathers

part-time ADJECTIVE, ADVERB
working for only some of the normal hours

party NOUN **parties**
1 a gathering of people for enjoyment
2 a group working or travelling together
3 an organized group of people with similar political beliefs
4 a person who is involved in an action or lawsuit etc. *the guilty party*

pass VERB
1 to go past; to go or move in a certain direction
2 to move something in a certain direction
3 to give or transfer something to another person
4 (in ball games) to kick or throw the ball to another player
5 to be successful in a test or exam
6 to approve or accept
7 to occupy time
8 to happen
9 to come to an end
10 to utter a remark
11 (in a game, quiz, etc.) to choose not to answer or make a move
pass out to faint

pass NOUN
1 the act of passing something
2 success in an examination
3 (in ball games) a kick or throw of the ball to another player
4 a permit to go in or out of a place
5 a route through a gap in a range of mountains
6 a critical state of affairs *come to a pretty pass*

passable ADJECTIVE
1 able to be passed
2 acceptable but not very good
passably ADVERB

passage NOUN
1 a way through something
2 a journey by sea or air
3 a section of a piece of writing or music
4 passing *the passage of time*

passageway NOUN
a passage or way through

passenger NOUN
a person who is driven or carried in a car, train, ship, or aircraft etc.

passion NOUN
1 strong emotion
2 great enthusiasm

passionate ADJECTIVE
full of passion

passive ADJECTIVE
1 not resisting or fighting
2 acted upon and not active
3 (of a verb) in the form used when the subject of the sentence receives the action, e.g. *is sold* in *Milk is sold here.*

Passover NOUN
a Jewish religious festival commemorating the freeing of the Jews from slavery in Egypt

passport NOUN
an official document entitling the holder to travel abroad

password NOUN
1 a secret word or phrase used to distinguish friends from enemies
2 (*ICT*) a word keyed in to gain access to certain computer files

past ADJECTIVE
of the time gone by *the past week*

past NOUN
the time gone by

past PREPOSITION
1 beyond *past the school*
2 after *past midnight*

pasta NOUN
an Italian food consisting of a dried paste made from flour and shaped into macaroni, spaghetti, etc.

paste NOUN
1 a soft, moist, and sticky substance
2 a thick glue for sticking paper
3 a soft edible mixture

paste VERB
1 to stick something on a surface with paste
2 to coat with paste
3 (*ICT*) to insert text cut or copied from another place

pastel NOUN
1 a crayon that is like chalk
2 a light delicate colour

pasteurize VERB
to purify milk by heating and then cooling it

pastille NOUN
a small flavoured sweet for sucking

pastime NOUN
a hobby or interest that a person follows in their spare time

pastor NOUN
a member of the clergy in charge of a church

pastoral ADJECTIVE
1 to do with country life
2 to do with a pastor or a pastor's duties

pastry NOUN **pastries**
1 dough made with flour, fat, and water, rolled flat and baked
2 a small cake with pastry

pasture NOUN
land covered with grass etc. for cattle to graze on

pasty[1] (pas-tee) NOUN **pasties**
pastry with a filling of meat and vegetables

pasty[2] (pay-stee) ADJECTIVE **pastier, pastiest**
looking pale and unhealthy

pat VERB **patting, patted**
to tap gently with the open hand

pat NOUN
1 a patting movement or sound
2 a small piece of butter or other soft substance

patch NOUN
1 a piece of material or metal etc. put over a hole or damaged place
2 an area that is different from its surroundings
3 a piece of ground
4 a small area or piece of something *patches of fog*

patch VERB
to put a patch on

patchwork NOUN
needlework in which small pieces of different cloth are sewn edge to edge

patchy ADJECTIVE **patchier, patchiest**
occurring in patches; uneven
patchily ADVERB

pâté (pat-ay) NOUN
paste made of meat, fish, or vegetables

patent NOUN
an official statement giving an inventor the sole right to make or sell an invention

patent ADJECTIVE
1 protected by a patent *patent medicines*
2 obvious

patent VERB
to be given a patent for something

patent leather NOUN
glossy leather

patently ADVERB
clearly or obviously *is patently untrue*

paternal ADJECTIVE
1 to do with a father
2 fatherly

paternity NOUN
1 fatherhood
2 the state of being the father of a particular baby

path NOUN
1 a narrow way for walking along
2 a line along which a person or thing moves
3 a course of action

pathetic ADJECTIVE
1 making you feel pity or sympathy
2 completely inadequate or useless
pathetically ADVERB

pathological ADJECTIVE
1 to do with pathology or disease
2 (informal) compulsive *a pathological liar*

pathology NOUN
the study of diseases of the body
pathologist NOUN

pathos (pay-thoss) NOUN
a quality of making people feel pity or sympathy

patience NOUN
1 the state of being patient
2 a card game for one person

patient ADJECTIVE
able to wait for a long time or put up with trouble or inconvenience without getting anxious or angry
patiently ADVERB

patient NOUN
a person receiving treatment from a doctor or dentist

patio NOUN **patios**
a paved area beside a house

patriarch NOUN
1 the male head of a family or tribe
2 a bishop of high rank in the Orthodox Christian Church
patriarchal ADJECTIVE

patrician NOUN
an ancient Roman noble

patrician ADJECTIVE
aristocratic

patriot NOUN
someone who loves their country and supports it loyally

patriotic ADJECTIVE
loyal to your country
patriotism NOUN

patrol VERB **patrolling, patrolled**
to walk or travel regularly over an area to guard it

patrol NOUN
1 a patrolling group of people, ships, aircraft, etc.
2 a group of Scouts or Guides

a
b
c
d
e
f
g
h
i
j
k
l
m
n
o
p
q
r
s
t
u
v
w
x
y
z

patron NOUN
1 someone who supports a person or cause
2 a regular customer

patronage NOUN
support given by a patron

patronize VERB
1 to be a regular customer of a particular shop, restaurant, etc.
2 to talk to someone in a way that shows you think them inferior

patron saint NOUN
a saint who is thought to protect a particular place or activity

patter[1] NOUN
a series of light tapping sounds

patter VERB
to make light tapping sounds

patter[2] NOUN
the quick talk of a comedian, salesperson, etc.

pattern NOUN
1 a repeated arrangement of lines, shapes, or colours etc.
2 a thing to be copied to make something
3 the regular way in which something happens
4 an excellent example or model

patty NOUN **patties**
a small pie or pasty

paucity NOUN
(formal) smallness of number or quantity

paunch NOUN
a large belly

pauper NOUN
a person who is very poor

pause NOUN
a temporary stop in speaking or doing something

pause VERB
to stop something for a short time

pave VERB
to lay a hard surface on a road or path etc.

pavement NOUN
a paved path along the side of a street

pavilion NOUN
1 a building for use by players and spectators at a sports ground
2 a large ornamental building

paw NOUN
the foot of an animal that has claws

paw VERB
to touch or scrape something with a hand or foot

pawn[1] NOUN
1 the least valuable piece in chess
2 a person whose actions are controlled by somebody else

pawn[2] VERB
to leave something with a pawnbroker as security for a loan

pawnbroker NOUN
a shopkeeper who lends money to people in return for objects that they leave as security

pawpaw NOUN
an orange-coloured tropical fruit used as food

pay VERB **paid**
1 to give money in return for goods or services
2 to give what is owed *pay your debts*
3 to be profitable or worthwhile *It pays to advertise.*
4 to give or express *to pay a compliment*
5 to suffer a penalty

pay NOUN
salary or wages

payable ADJECTIVE
that must be paid

payee NOUN
a person to whom money is paid or is to be paid

payment NOUN
1 the act of paying
2 money paid

payphone NOUN
a public telephone operated by coins or a card

payroll NOUN
a list of employees entitled to be paid

PC ABBREVIATION
1 personal computer
2 police constable

PE ABBREVIATION
physical education

pea NOUN
1 the small round green seed of a climbing plant, growing inside a pod and used as a vegetable
2 the plant bearing these pods

peace NOUN
1 a time when there is no war or disorder
2 quietness and calm

peaceable ADJECTIVE
fond of peace; not quarrelsome or warlike
peaceably ADVERB

peaceful ADJECTIVE
quiet and calm
peacefully ADVERB

peach NOUN
a round soft juicy fruit with a pinkish or yellowish skin and a large stone

peacock NOUN
a large bird with a long brightly coloured tail that it can spread out like a fan

peahen NOUN
a female peacock

peak NOUN
1 a pointed top, especially of a mountain
2 the highest or most intense part of something
3 the part of a cap that sticks out in front
peaked ADJECTIVE

peak VERB
to reach a highest point or value

peaky ADJECTIVE **peakier**, **peakiest**
pale and unwell

peal NOUN
1 the loud ringing of a bell or bells
2 a loud burst of thunder or laughter

peal VERB
(of bells) to ring loudly

peanut NOUN
a small round nut that grows in a pod in the ground

peanut butter NOUN
roasted peanuts crushed into a paste

pear NOUN
a juicy fruit that narrows near the stalk

pearl NOUN
a small shiny white ball found in the shells of some oysters and used as a jewel
pearly ADJECTIVE

peasant NOUN
a person who belongs to a farming community, especially in poor areas
peasantry NOUN

peat NOUN
rotted plant material dug out of the ground and used as fuel

pebble NOUN
a small round stone
pebbly ADJECTIVE

peck VERB
1 to bite at something quickly with the beak
2 to kiss someone lightly

peck NOUN
1 a quick bite by a bird
2 a light kiss

peckish ADJECTIVE
(informal) slightly hungry

peculiar ADJECTIVE
1 strange or unusual
2 belonging to a particular person, place, or thing

peculiarity NOUN **peculiarities**
a distinctive feature

pedal NOUN
a lever pressed by the foot to operate a bicycle, car, machine, etc.

pedal VERB **pedalling**, **pedalled**
to move or work something, especially a bicycle, by means of pedals

pedant NOUN
a pedantic person

pedantic ADJECTIVE
too concerned with minor details or formalities
pedantically ADVERB

peddle VERB
1 to go from house to house selling small goods
2 to sell illegal drugs

pedestal NOUN
the base for a statue or pillar etc.

pedestrian NOUN
a person who is walking

pedestrian ADJECTIVE
ordinary and dull

pedestrian crossing NOUN
a place where traffic has to stop to allow pedestrians to cross the road

pedigree NOUN
a list of a person's or animal's ancestors

pediment NOUN
a wide triangular part decorating the top of a building

pedlar NOUN
a person who goes from house to house selling small things

peek VERB
to have a quick look at something
peek NOUN

peel NOUN
the skin of certain fruits and vegetables

peel VERB
1 to remove the peel or covering from
2 to come off in strips
3 to lose a covering or layer of skin

peelings PLURAL NOUN
strips of skin peeled from potatoes etc.

peep VERB
1 to look quickly or secretly
2 to look through a narrow opening
3 to come briefly into view
peep NOUN

peer [1] VERB
to look at something closely or with difficulty

peer [2] NOUN
1 a member of the nobility
2 someone who is equal to another in rank, merit, or age etc.

peerage NOUN
1 peers collectively
2 the rank of a peer

peer group NOUN
a group of people of roughly the same age or status

peerless ADJECTIVE
without an equal; better than the others

peeved ADJECTIVE
(informal) annoyed

peevish ADJECTIVE
irritable

peewit NOUN
a lapwing

peg NOUN
a piece of wood, plastic, etc. for fastening things together or hanging things on

peg VERB **pegging, pegged**
1 to fix with pegs
2 to keep wages or prices at a fixed level

pejorative (pij-orra-tiv) ADJECTIVE
showing disapproval; derogatory

Pekinese NOUN
a small dog with short legs, a flat face, and long silky hair

pelican NOUN
a large bird with a pouch in its long beak for storing fish

pelican crossing NOUN
a pedestrian crossing controlled by lights

pellet NOUN
a tiny ball of metal, food, paper, etc.

pell-mell ADVERB, ADJECTIVE
in a hasty untidy way

pelmet NOUN
an ornamental strip of wood etc. above a window, used to conceal a curtain rail

pelt [1] VERB
1 to throw a lot of things at
2 to run fast
3 to rain very hard

pelt [2] NOUN
an animal skin

pelvis NOUN
the round framework of bones at the lower end of the spine
pelvic ADJECTIVE

pen [1] NOUN
an instrument with a point for writing with ink

pen [2] NOUN
an enclosure for cattle, sheep, etc.
pen VERB **penning, penned**
to shut animals etc. into a pen

penal (peen-al) ADJECTIVE
to do with the punishment of criminals

penalize VERB
to punish

penalty NOUN **penalties**
1 a punishment
2 a point or advantage given to one side in a game when the other side has broken a rule

penance NOUN
a punishment willingly suffered to show regret for a wrong

pence PLURAL NOUN
SEE **penny**

penchant NOUN
a liking or inclination

pencil NOUN
an instrument for drawing or writing, made of a stick of graphite in a cylinder of wood or metal

pencil VERB **pencilling, pencilled**
to write or mark with a pencil

pendant NOUN
an ornament worn on a chain round the neck

pending ADJECTIVE
1 waiting to be decided or settled
2 about to happen

pending PREPOSITION
while waiting for; until *pending approval*

pendulum NOUN
a weight hung to swing to and fro, especially in the works of a clock

penetrable ADJECTIVE
able to be penetrated

penetrate VERB
to make or find a way through or into something
penetration NOUN

penetrating ADJECTIVE
1 showing great insight
2 clearly heard

penfriend NOUN
a friend with whom you exchange letters without meeting

penguin NOUN
a seabird that cannot fly

penicillin NOUN
an antibiotic obtained from mould

peninsula NOUN
a piece of land almost surrounded by water
peninsular ADJECTIVE

penis (peen-iss) NOUN
the part of the body with which a male urinates and has sexual intercourse

penitence NOUN
regret for having done wrong
penitent ADJECTIVE

penknife NOUN **penknives**
a small folding knife

pen-name NOUN
a name used by an author instead of their real name

pennant NOUN
a long pointed flag

penniless ADJECTIVE
having no money

penny NOUN **pennies** or **pence**
1 a British coin worth $1/10$ of a pound
2 a former coin worth $1/12$ of a shilling

pension NOUN
an income of regular payments made to someone who is retired, widowed, or disabled

pension VERB
pension off to make someone retire early

pensioner NOUN
a person who receives a pension

pensive ADJECTIVE
deep in thought

pentagon NOUN
a flat shape with five sides
pentagonal ADJECTIVE

pentathlon NOUN
an athletic contest consisting of five events

Pentecost NOUN
1 the Jewish harvest festival, fifty days after Passover
2 Whit Sunday

penthouse NOUN
a flat at the top of a tall building

pent-up ADJECTIVE
shut in *pent-up feelings*

penultimate ADJECTIVE
last but one

penumbra NOUN
an area that is partly shaded, e.g. during an eclipse

penury NOUN
(*formal*) great poverty

peony NOUN **peonies**
a plant with large round red, pink, or white flowers

people PLURAL NOUN
1 human beings
2 men, women, and children belonging to a particular country, area, etc.

people NOUN
a community or nation *a warlike people the English-speaking peoples*

people VERB
to fill a place with people

pep NOUN
(*informal*) vigour or energy

pepper NOUN
1 a hot-tasting powder used to flavour food
2 a bright green, red, or yellow vegetable
peppery ADJECTIVE

pepper VERB
1 to sprinkle with pepper
2 to pelt with small objects

peppercorn NOUN
the dried black berry from which pepper is made

peppermint NOUN
1 a kind of mint used for flavouring
2 a sweet flavoured with this mint

pepperoni NOUN
beef and pork sausage seasoned with pepper

pep talk NOUN
(*informal*) a talk given to encourage people

per PREPOSITION
for each *£5 per person*

per annum ADVERB
for each year; yearly

perceive VERB
to see, hear, or understand clearly

per cent ADVERB
for or in every hundred *three per cent (3%)*

percentage NOUN
an amount or rate expressed as a proportion of 100

perceptible ADJECTIVE
able to be seen or heard or noticed
perceptibly ADVERB

perception NOUN
1 the ability to see or hear or understand something
2 the receiving of information through the senses

perceptive ADJECTIVE
quick to see or understand things

perch [1] NOUN
1 a place where a bird sits or rests
2 a seat high up

perch VERB
to rest or place on a perch

perch [2] NOUN **perch**
an edible freshwater fish

percolate VERB
to flow or force through small holes or spaces
percolation NOUN

percolator NOUN
a pot for making coffee

percussion NOUN
musical instruments (e.g. drums and cymbals) played by being struck or shaken

peregrine NOUN
a kind of falcon

perennial ADJECTIVE
lasting for many years
perennially ADVERB

perennial NOUN
a plant that lives for many years

perfect (per-fikt) ADJECTIVE
1 so good that it cannot be made any better
2 complete *perfect strangers*
3 (of a verb) showing a completed action,
e.g. *He has arrived.*
perfectly ADVERB

perfect (per-fekt) VERB
to make perfect

perfection NOUN
a perfect state

perfectionist NOUN
a person who is only satisfied if something is
done perfectly

perforate VERB
1 to make tiny holes in something
2 to pierce
perforated ADJECTIVE **perforation** NOUN

perform VERB
1 to do something in front of an audience
2 to do or carry out a process
performer NOUN

performance NOUN
1 the act of performing
2 an entertainment in a theatre, on
television, etc.

perfume NOUN
1 a pleasant smell
2 a liquid with a pleasant smell

perfume VERB
to give a pleasant smell to

perfunctory ADJECTIVE
done without much care or interest
perfunctorily ADVERB

perhaps ADVERB
it may be; possibly

peril NOUN
an immediate danger

perilous ADJECTIVE
immediately dangerous
perilously ADVERB

perimeter NOUN
1 an outer edge or boundary
2 the distance round the edge
Do not confuse this word with *parameter*.

period NOUN
1 a length of time
2 the time allowed for a lesson in school
3 the time when a woman menstruates
4 (in punctuation) a full stop

periodic ADJECTIVE
occurring at regular intervals
periodically ADVERB

periodical NOUN
a magazine published at regular intervals

periodic table NOUN
(*Science*) a table in which the chemical
elements are arranged in order of increasing
atomic number

peripatetic ADJECTIVE
going from place to place

peripheral ADJECTIVE
1 of minor importance
2 at the edge or boundary

periphery NOUN **peripheries**
the part at the edge or boundary

periscope NOUN
a tube and mirrors allowing a viewer to see
things that are otherwise out of sight

perish VERB
1 to die or be destroyed
2 to rot
perishable ADJECTIVE

perished ADJECTIVE
(*informal*) feeling very cold

perishing ADJECTIVE
(*informal*) freezing cold *It's perishing outside!*

periwinkle NOUN
1 a trailing plant with blue or white flowers
2 a winkle

perjure VERB
perjure yourself to lie under oath

perjury NOUN
the crime of telling a lie when under oath in a
lawcourt

perk [1] VERB
perk up to become more cheerful

perk [2] NOUN
(*informal*) something extra given to a worker

perky ADJECTIVE **perkier**, **perkiest**
lively and cheerful

perm NOUN
treatment of hair to give it long-lasting waves
or curls

perm VERB
to give a perm to hair

permafrost NOUN
a permanently frozen layer of soil in polar
regions

permanent ADJECTIVE
lasting for always or for a very long time
permanence NOUN **permanently** ADVERB

permeable ADJECTIVE
able to be permeated by fluids etc.
permeability NOUN

permeate VERB
to spread into every part of

permissible ADJECTIVE
permitted

permission NOUN
the right to do something given by someone
in authority

permissive ADJECTIVE
letting people do what they wish; too tolerant
or liberal

permit (per-mit) VERB **permitting,
permitted**
to give permission or a chance to do
something

permit (per-mit) NOUN
written or printed permission to do
something *a fishing permit*

permutation NOUN
1 the changing of the order of a set of things
2 a changed order *3, 1, 2 is a permutation of
1, 2, 3.*

pernicious ADJECTIVE
very harmful

peroxide NOUN
a chemical used for bleaching hair

perpendicular ADJECTIVE
upright; at a right angle to a line or surface

perpetrate VERB
to commit a crime, error, etc.
perpetrator NOUN

perpetual ADJECTIVE
1 lasting for ever or for a long time
2 constant; continual
perpetually ADVERB

perpetuate VERB
to cause to continue or be remembered for a
long time *a statue to perpetuate his memory*

perplex VERB
to bewilder or puzzle
perplexity NOUN

persecute VERB
to be continually cruel to somebody
persecution NOUN

persevere VERB
to go on doing something even though it is
difficult
perseverance NOUN

persist VERB
1 to continue firmly or obstinately
2 to continue to happen or exist

persistent ADJECTIVE
continuing; persisting
persistence NOUN **persistently** ADVERB

person NOUN
1 a human being; a man, woman, or child
2 (*Grammar*) any of the three groups of
personal pronouns and forms taken by verbs,
referring to the person speaking (e.g. *I, we*),
the person addressed (e.g. *you*), or a person
spoken about (e.g. *he* or *she* or *they*)

personable ADJECTIVE
pleasing in appearance and behaviour

personage NOUN
an important or well-known person

personal ADJECTIVE
1 belonging to or concerning a particular
person *personal belongings*
2 private *personal business*
3 criticizing a person's appearance or
character *personal remarks*

personal computer NOUN
a small computer designed for a single user

personality NOUN **personalities**
1 a person's character
2 a famous person

personally ADVERB
1 in person
2 as far as I am concerned

personify VERB **personifies, personified**
to represent a quality or idea as a person
personification NOUN

personnel NOUN
the people employed by a large organization

perspective NOUN
1 the impression of depth and space in a
picture or scene
2 a person's point of view

Perspex NOUN
(*trademark*) a tough transparent plastic

perspicacious ADJECTIVE
quick to notice or understand things
perspicacity NOUN

perspire VERB
to sweat
perspiration NOUN

persuade VERB
to make someone believe or agree to do
something

persuasion NOUN
1 the act of persuading
2 a firm belief

persuasive ADJECTIVE
likely to persuade someone; convincing

pert ADJECTIVE
cheeky
pertly ADVERB

pertain VERB
be relevant to something *evidence pertaining
to the crime*

pertinent *ADJECTIVE*
relevant to a subject being discussed

perturb *VERB*
to worry someone a lot
perturbation *NOUN*

peruse *VERB*
to read something carefully
perusal *NOUN*

pervade *VERB*
to spread all through

perverse *ADJECTIVE*
obstinately doing something unreasonable or unwanted
perversely *ADVERB* **perversity** *NOUN*

pervert (per-**vert**) *VERB*
1 to turn something from the right course of action
2 to make a person behave wickedly or abnormally
perversion *NOUN*

pessimist *NOUN*
a person who expects that things will turn out badly
pessimism *NOUN* **pessimistic** *ADJECTIVE*
pessimistically *ADVERB*

pest *NOUN*
1 a destructive insect or animal, such as a locust or mouse
2 a nuisance

pester *VERB*
to keep annoying someone with questions or requests

pesticide *NOUN*
a substance for killing harmful insects and other pests

pestilence *NOUN*
a deadly epidemic

pestle *NOUN*
a tool with a heavy rounded end for pounding substances in a mortar

pet *NOUN*
1 a tame animal kept in the home
2 a favourite person
pet *ADJECTIVE*
favourite or particular
pet *VERB* **petting**, **petted**
to stroke or pat someone affectionately

petal *NOUN*
each of the separate coloured parts of a flower

peter *VERB*
peter out to become gradually less and cease to exist

petition *NOUN*
a formal written request signed by many people

petition *VERB*
to submit a petition to
petitioner *NOUN*

petrel *NOUN*
a kind of seabird

petrify *VERB* **petrifies**, **petrified**
1 to terrify someone so much they cannot move
2 to turn to stone

petrochemical *NOUN*
a chemical substance obtained from petroleum or natural gas

petrol *NOUN*
a liquid made from petroleum, used as fuel for engines

petroleum *NOUN*
an oil found underground and refined to make fuel

petticoat *NOUN*
a dress-length item of underwear worn by a woman or girl under a skirt or dress

petting *NOUN*
affectionate touching or fondling

pettish *ADJECTIVE*
irritable or bad-tempered; peevish

petty *ADJECTIVE* **pettier**, **pettiest**
1 unimportant or trivial
2 mean and small-minded
pettily *ADVERB* **pettiness** *NOUN*

petty cash *NOUN*
cash kept in an office for small payments

petty officer *NOUN*
a non-commissioned officer in the navy

petulant *ADJECTIVE*
irritable or bad-tempered
petulance *NOUN*

petunia *NOUN*
a garden plant with funnel-shaped flowers

pew *NOUN*
a long wooden seat in a church

pewter *NOUN*
a grey alloy of tin and lead

pH *NOUN*
a measure of the acid or alkaline content of a solution

phantom *NOUN*
1 a ghost
2 something that does not really exist

Pharaoh (**fair**-oh) *NOUN*
the title of a king in ancient Egypt

pharmaceutical *ADJECTIVE*
to do with medicines and drugs

pharmacist *NOUN*
a person who prepares and sells medicines

a
b
c
d
e
f
g
h
i
j
k
l
m
n
o
p
q
r
s
t
u
v
w
x
y
z

pharmacy NOUN **pharmacies**
1 a shop selling medicines
2 the process of preparing medicines

phase NOUN
a stage in the progress or development of something

phase VERB
to do something in planned stages

pheasant NOUN
a game bird with a long tail

phenomenal ADJECTIVE
amazing or remarkable
phenomenally ADVERB

phenomenon NOUN **phenomena**
a remarkable event or fact

phial NOUN
a small glass bottle

philander VERB
(of a man) to have casual affairs with women
philanderer NOUN

philanthropy NOUN
concern for and generosity to fellow human beings
philanthropic ADJECTIVE **philanthropist** NOUN

philately (fil-at-il-ee) NOUN
stamp-collecting
philatelist NOUN

philistine NOUN
a person who dislikes the arts and creative works

philology NOUN
the study of words and their history
philological ADJECTIVE **philologist** NOUN

philosopher NOUN
an expert in philosophy

philosophical ADJECTIVE
1 to do with philosophy
2 calm after a misfortune or disappointment
philosophically ADVERB

philosophy NOUN **philosophies**
1 the study of truths about life, morals, etc.
2 a set of ideas or principles or beliefs

philtre (fil-ter) NOUN
a love potion

phlegm (flem) NOUN
thick mucus that forms in the throat and lungs during a cold

phlegmatic (fleg-mat-ik) ADJECTIVE
not easily excited or worried
phlegmatically ADVERB

phobia (foh-bee-a) NOUN
great or abnormal fear of something

phoenix (feen-iks) NOUN
a mythical bird that was believed to burn itself to death and be born again from the ashes

phone NOUN
a telephone

phone VERB
to telephone

phonecard NOUN
a plastic card used to work some public telephones

phonetic (fon-et-ik) ADJECTIVE
1 to do with speech sounds
2 representing speech sounds
phonetically ADVERB

phoney ADJECTIVE **phonier, phoniest**
(informal) sham; not genuine

phosphorus NOUN
a chemical substance that glows in the dark

photo NOUN
(informal) a photograph

photocopy NOUN **photocopies**
a copy of a document or page etc. made by photographing it on special paper

photocopy VERB **photocopies, photocopied**
to make a photocopy of
photocopier NOUN

photoelectric ADJECTIVE
using the electrical effects of light

photogenic ADJECTIVE
looking attractive in photographs

photograph NOUN
a picture made by the effect of light on film, using a camera

photograph VERB
to take a photograph of
photographer NOUN

photography NOUN
the process of taking photographs
photographic ADJECTIVE

photosynthesis NOUN
the process by which plants convert sunlight into complex substances that give off oxygen

phrase NOUN
1 a group of words that form a unit in a sentence or clause
2 a short section of a tune

phrase VERB
to express in words

phraseology NOUN
the way something is worded

physical ADJECTIVE
1 to do with the body rather than the mind
2 to do with things that can be touched or seen
physically ADVERB

physician NOUN
a doctor, especially one who is not a surgeon

physicist (fiz-i-sist) NOUN
an expert in physics

physics (fiz-iks) NOUN
the study of the properties of matter and
energy (e.g. heat, light, sound, and
movement)

physiognomy (fiz-ee-on-o-mee) NOUN
the features of a person's face

physiology NOUN
the study of the body and its parts and how
they function
physiological ADJECTIVE **physiologist** NOUN

physiotherapy NOUN
the treatment of a disease or injury by
massage, exercises, etc.
physiotherapist NOUN

physique NOUN
a person's build

pi NOUN
the symbol (π) of the ratio of the
circumference of a circle to its diameter,
approximately 3.142

pianist NOUN
a person who plays the piano

piano NOUN **pianos**
a large musical instrument with a keyboard

piccolo NOUN **piccolos**
a small high-pitched flute

pick[1] VERB
1 to separate a flower or fruit from its plant
2 to choose carefully
3 to pull bits off or out of
4 to open a lock with an instrument other
than a key
5 to provoke a fight or quarrel
6 to steal from someone's pocket
pick on to single out for criticism **pick up**
1 to lift 2 to collect 3 to learn or acquire
something 4 to get better or recover

pick NOUN
1 a choice
2 the best of a group

pick[2] NOUN
a pickaxe

pickaxe NOUN
a heavy pointed tool with a long handle, used
for breaking up hard ground etc.

picket NOUN
1 a striker or group of strikers who try to
persuade other people not to go into a place
of work during a strike
2 a pointed post as part of a fence

picket VERB
to put a picket at a place of work

pickle NOUN
1 a strong-tasting food made of preserved
vegetables
2 (informal) a mess

pickle VERB
to preserve food in vinegar or salt water

pickpocket NOUN
a thief who steals from pockets and bags

picnic NOUN
a meal eaten in the open air, e.g. on an outing

picnic VERB **picnicking**, **picnicked**
to have a picnic
picnicker NOUN

pictorial ADJECTIVE
with or using pictures
pictorially ADVERB

picture NOUN
1 a painting, drawing, or photograph of a
person or thing
2 a film at the cinema
3 how something seems; an impression

picture VERB
1 to show in a picture
2 to imagine

picturesque ADJECTIVE
forming an attractive scene

pidgin NOUN
a simplified form of a language used by
people who do not speak the same language

pie NOUN
a baked dish of meat, fish, or fruit covered
with pastry

piebald ADJECTIVE
having patches of black and white

piece NOUN
1 a part or portion of something
2 a separate thing or example
3 a work of writing, music, etc.
4 one of the objects used to play a game on a
board
5 a coin *a 50p piece*

piece VERB
to put pieces together to make something

piecemeal ADJECTIVE, ADVERB
done or made one piece at a time

pie chart NOUN
a circle divided into sectors to show the way in
which something is divided up

pier NOUN
1 a long platform built out into the sea for
walking on
2 a pillar supporting a bridge or arch

pierce VERB
to make a hole through

290

piercing ADJECTIVE
1 very loud and high-pitched
2 penetrating; very strong *a piercing wind*

piety NOUN
a religious and devout state or attitude

piffle NOUN
(*informal*) nonsense

pig NOUN
1 a fat animal with short legs and a blunt
snout, kept for its meat
2 (*informal*) a greedy or dirty person

pigeon NOUN
a bird with a fat body and small head

pigeonhole NOUN
a small compartment for holding letters,
messages, or papers, for collection

piggyback NOUN
a ride on a person's back or shoulders

piggy bank NOUN
a money box in the shape of a pig with a slot
on top

pig-headed ADJECTIVE
stubborn

piglet NOUN
a young pig

pigment NOUN
1 a substance that colours animal and plant
tissue
2 a substance that gives colour to paint, inks,
dyes, etc.
pigmentation NOUN

pigsty NOUN **pigsties**
1 a partly-covered pen for pigs
2 a filthy room or house

pigtail NOUN
a plait of hair at the back of the head

pike NOUN
1 a heavy spear
2 a large freshwater fish

pilchard NOUN
a small sea fish

pile NOUN
1 a number of things on top of one another
2 (*informal*) a large amount
3 a large impressive building
4 a raised surface on fabric, carpet, etc.
pile VERB
to put things in a pile

pile-up NOUN
a road accident involving several vehicles

pilfer VERB
to steal things of little value

pilgrim NOUN
a person who travels to a holy place

pilgrimage NOUN
a journey to a holy place

pill NOUN
a small solid piece of medicine for swallowing

pillage VERB
to carry off goods using force; to plunder
pillage NOUN

pillar NOUN
a tall stone or wooden post

pillar box NOUN
a postbox standing in a street

pillion NOUN
a seat behind the driver on a motorcycle

pillory NOUN **pillories**
a wooden framework with holes for a
person's head and hands, in which offenders
were formerly made to stand as a punishment
pillory VERB **pillories**, **pilloried**
to expose a person to public ridicule or anger

pillow NOUN
a cushion for a person's head to rest on,
especially in bed

pillowcase or **pillowslip** NOUN
a cloth cover for a pillow

pilot NOUN
1 a person who flies an aircraft
2 a person who steers a ship in and out of a
port
3 a guide
pilot VERB
1 to be the pilot of an aircraft or ship
2 to guide or steer
pilot ADJECTIVE
testing something on a small scale *a pilot
scheme*

pilot light NOUN
1 a small flame that lights a larger burner on a
gas cooker etc.
2 an electric indicator light

pimp NOUN
a man who obtains clients for prostitutes

pimple NOUN
a small round raised spot on the skin
pimply ADJECTIVE

PIN ABBREVIATION
personal identification number; a number
used as a password at a cash machine,
computer, etc.

pin NOUN
1 a short thin piece of metal with a sharp
point and a rounded head, used to fasten
pieces of cloth or paper etc.
2 a pointed device for fixing or marking
something
pins and needles a tingling feeling

pin *VERB* **pinning, pinned**
  1 to fasten with a pin or pins
  2 to hold someone firmly so they cannot move
  3 to fix the blame or responsibility on someone

pinafore *NOUN*
  an apron with a bib top

pinball *NOUN*
  a game in which metal balls are shot across a table and score points when they strike targets

pincer *NOUN*
  the claw of a shellfish such as a lobster

pincers *PLURAL NOUN*
  a tool with two parts that are pressed together for gripping

pinch *VERB*
  1 to squeeze something tightly between two things, especially between the finger and thumb
  2 (*informal*) to steal

pinch *NOUN*
  1 a pinching movement
  2 a small amount *a pinch of salt*

pine[1] *NOUN*
  an evergreen tree with needle-shaped leaves

pine[2] *VERB*
  1 to feel an intense longing
  2 to become weak through longing

pineapple *NOUN*
  a large tropical fruit with a tough prickly skin and yellow flesh

ping *VERB*
  to make a short sharp ringing sound
  ping *NOUN*

ping-pong *NOUN*
  table tennis

pink *ADJECTIVE*
  pale red

pink *NOUN*
  1 a pale red colour
  2 a garden plant with fragrant flowers

pinnacle *NOUN*
  1 a pointed ornament on a roof
  2 a high pointed piece of rock
  3 the highest point of something

pinpoint *ADJECTIVE*
  exact or precise *with pinpoint accuracy*

pinpoint *VERB*
  to find or identify precisely

pinprick *NOUN*
  a small annoyance

pinstripe *NOUN*
  one of the very narrow stripes that form a pattern in cloth
  pinstriped *ADJECTIVE*

pint *NOUN*
  a measure for liquids, equal to one-eighth of a gallon

pin-up *NOUN*
  (*informal*) a picture of an attractive or famous person for pinning on a wall

pioneer *NOUN*
  one of the first people to go to a place or to develop an idea

pioneer *VERB*
  to be the first to develop something

pious *ADJECTIVE*
  very religious; devout

pip *NOUN*
  1 a small hard seed of an apple, pear, orange, etc.
  2 one of the stars on the shoulder of an army officer's uniform
  3 a short high-pitched sound

pip *VERB* **pipping, pipped**
  (*informal*) to defeat by a small amount

pipe *NOUN*
  1 a tube through which water or gas etc. can flow
  2 a narrow tube with a bowl at one end for smoking tobacco
  3 a tube forming a musical instrument or part of one

pipe *VERB*
  1 to send something along pipes
  2 to transmit music by wire or cable
  3 to play music on a pipe or the bagpipes

pipe dream *NOUN*
  an impossible wish

pipeline *NOUN*
  a pipe for carrying oil or water etc. a long distance

piper *NOUN*
  a person who plays a pipe or bagpipes

pipette *NOUN*
  a small glass tube used in a laboratory

piping *NOUN*
  1 pipes; a length of pipe
  2 a decorative line of icing etc. on a cake
  3 a long narrow piece of separate fabric on the edge of clothing, upholstery, etc.

piping *ADJECTIVE*
  shrill *a piping voice*
  piping hot very hot

pippin *NOUN*
  a kind of apple

piquant (pee-kant) *ADJECTIVE*
  1 pleasantly sharp and appetizing *a piquant smell*
  2 pleasantly stimulating
  piquancy *NOUN*

pique (peek) NOUN
a feeling of hurt pride

pique VERB
to hurt the pride of

piracy NOUN
the activity of pirates

piranha NOUN
a South American freshwater fish that has sharp teeth and eats flesh

pirate NOUN
a person who attacks and robs ships at sea
piratical ADJECTIVE

pirouette NOUN
a spinning movement of the body while balanced on the point of the toe or on one foot

pirouette VERB
to perform a pirouette

pistachio NOUN **pistachios**
a nut with a green kernel

pistil NOUN
the part of a flower that produces the seed

pistol NOUN
a small gun held in the hand

piston NOUN
a disc or cylinder that fits inside a tube in which it moves up and down as part of an engine or pump etc.

pit NOUN
1 a deep hole
2 a hollow
3 a coal mine
4 the part of a race circuit where cars are refuelled and repaired during a race

pit VERB **pitting, pitted**
1 to make holes or hollows in
2 to put somebody in a competition with somebody else
pitted ADJECTIVE

pitch [1] NOUN
1 a piece of ground marked out for cricket, football, etc.
2 the highness or lowness of a voice or a musical note
3 intensity or strength *at fever pitch*
4 the steepness of a roof or other slope

pitch VERB
1 to throw or fling
2 to set up a tent or camp
3 to fall heavily
4 to move up and down on a rough sea
5 to set something at a particular level
6 (of a bowled ball in cricket) to strike the ground

pitch [2] NOUN
a black sticky substance like tar

pitch-black or **pitch-dark** NOUN
completely black or dark

pitched battle NOUN
a battle between armies in prepared positions

pitcher NOUN
a large jug

pitchfork NOUN
a large fork with two prongs, used for lifting hay

piteous ADJECTIVE
arousing pity
piteously ADVERB

pitfall NOUN
an unsuspected danger or difficulty

pith NOUN
the spongy substance in the stems of certain plants or lining the rind of oranges etc.

pithy ADJECTIVE **pithier, pithiest**
1 like pith; containing pith
2 short and full of meaning *pithy comments*

pitiable ADJECTIVE
arousing pity; pitiful

pitiful ADJECTIVE
arousing pity; pathetic
pitifully ADVERB

pitiless ADJECTIVE
showing no pity
pitilessly ADVERB

pittance NOUN
a small allowance of money

pity NOUN
1 the feeling of being sorry for someone else's pain or trouble
2 a cause for regret *It's a pity you can't come.*

pity VERB **pities, pitied**
to feel pity for

pivot NOUN
a point or part on which something turns or balances

pivot VERB
to turn on a pivot

pivotal ADJECTIVE
1 fixed on a pivot
2 of crucial importance

pixel (piks-el) NOUN
each of the tiny dots on a computer display screen from which the image is formed

pixie NOUN
a small fairy or elf

pizza (peets-a) NOUN
an Italian food of a savoury mixture baked on a flat piece of dough

pizzicato ADJECTIVE, ADVERB
(*Music*) played by plucking the strings instead of using the bow

placard NOUN
a displayed poster or notice

placate VERB
to make someone feel calmer and less angry

place NOUN
1 an area or position
2 a seat
3 a job
4 a person's home *at my place*
5 a duty or function *not my place to interfere*
6 a point in a series of things *in the first place*
in place of instead of **take place** to happen

place VERB
to put in a particular place

placebo (plas-ee-boh) NOUN **placebos**
a substance with no physical effect, given as if it were a medicine

placenta NOUN
a piece of body tissue that provides a fetus with nourishment in the womb

placid ADJECTIVE
calm and peaceful; not easily made anxious or upset
placidly ADVERB **placidity** NOUN

plagiarize VERB
to use someone else's writings or ideas as if they were your own
plagiarism NOUN **plagiarist** NOUN

plague NOUN
1 a dangerous illness that spreads quickly
2 a large number of pests

plague VERB
to pester or annoy

plaice NOUN **plaice**
a flat edible sea fish

plaid (plad) NOUN
cloth with a tartan or similar pattern

plain ADJECTIVE
1 simple; not decorated or elaborate
2 not beautiful
3 easy to see or hear or understand
4 frank and straightforward
plainly ADVERB **plainness** NOUN

plain NOUN
a large area of flat country
Do not confuse this word with *plane*.

plain clothes NOUN
civilian clothes worn instead of a uniform, e.g. by the police

plaintiff NOUN
someone who brings a complaint against another person to a lawcourt

plaintive ADJECTIVE
sounding sad *a plaintive cry*

plait (plat) VERB
to weave several strands of hair or rope into one length

plait NOUN
a length of hair or rope that has been plaited

plan NOUN
1 a way of doing something thought out in advance
2 a drawing showing the parts of something
3 a map of a town or district

plan VERB **planning**, **planned**
to make a plan for something
planner NOUN

plane[1] NOUN
1 an aeroplane
2 a tool for making wood smooth by scraping its surface
3 a flat or level surface

plane VERB
to smooth wood with a plane

plane ADJECTIVE
flat or level *a plane surface*
Do not confuse this word with *plain*.

plane[2] NOUN
a tall tree with broad leaves

planet NOUN
any of the large round masses that move in an orbit round the sun
planetary ADJECTIVE

plank NOUN
a long flat piece of wood

plankton NOUN
microscopic plants and animals floating in the sea, lakes, etc.

plant NOUN
1 a living thing that cannot move, makes its food from chemical substances, and usually has a stem, leaves, and roots
2 a factory or its equipment

plant VERB
1 to put something in soil for growing
2 to fix something firmly in place
planter NOUN

plantation NOUN
1 a large area of land where cotton, tobacco, or tea etc. is planted
2 an area of planted trees

plaque (plak) NOUN
1 a flat piece of metal or porcelain fixed on a wall as an ornament or memorial
2 a film that forms on teeth and gums, containing bacteria

plasma NOUN
the colourless liquid part of blood, carrying the corpuscles

plaster *NOUN*
1 a covering put over the skin to protect a cut
2 a mixture of lime, sand, and water etc. for covering walls and ceilings
3 plaster of Paris, or a cast made of this

plaster *VERB*
1 to cover a surface with plaster
2 to cover something thickly

plaster of Paris *NOUN*
a white paste used for making moulds or for casts round a broken leg or arm

plastic *NOUN*
a light synthetic substance that can be moulded into a special shape

plastic *ADJECTIVE*
1 made of plastic
2 soft and easy to mould
plasticity *NOUN*

plastic surgery *NOUN*
surgery to repair injured parts of the body

plate *NOUN*
1 an almost flat circular object from which food is eaten or served
2 a thin flat sheet of metal, glass, etc.
3 an illustration in a book

plate *VERB*
1 to coat metal with a thin layer of gold, silver, tin, etc.
2 to cover with sheets of metal

plateau (plat-oh) *NOUN* **plateaux** or **plateaus**
a flat area of high land

plateful *NOUN* **platefuls**
an amount that will fill a plate

platform *NOUN*
1 a flat raised area for passengers to stand on at a railway station
2 a raised surface for someone speaking to an audience

platinum *NOUN*
a valuable silver-coloured metal that does not tarnish

platitude *NOUN*
a remark that has been used so often that it is no longer interesting
platitudinous *ADJECTIVE*

platoon *NOUN*
a small group of soldiers

platter *NOUN*
a flat dish or plate

platypus *NOUN*
an Australian animal with a beak like a duck, which lays eggs but is a mammal

plaudits *PLURAL NOUN*
expressions of approval

plausible *ADJECTIVE*
seeming to be genuine but perhaps deceptive *a plausible excuse*
plausibility *NOUN* **plausibly** *ADVERB*

play *VERB*
1 to take part in a game, sport, or amusement
2 to make music or sound with a musical instrument etc.
3 to perform a part in a play or film
play up (*informal*) to tease or annoy someone

play *NOUN*
1 the activity of playing
2 a story acted on a stage or on radio or television

player *NOUN*
1 an actor
2 a member of a sports team
3 someone who plays a musical instrument

playful *ADJECTIVE*
1 wanting to play; full of fun
2 done in fun; not serious
playfully *ADVERB*

playground *NOUN*
a piece of ground for children to play on

playgroup *NOUN*
a supervised group of young children who play together

playing card *NOUN*
each of a set of cards used for playing games

playing field *NOUN*
a field used for outdoor games

playmate *NOUN*
a person a child plays games with

play-off *NOUN*
an extra match to decide a draw or tie

playschool *NOUN*
a nursery school or playgroup

plaything *NOUN*
a toy

playwright *NOUN*
a person who writes plays

plea *NOUN*
1 a request or appeal
2 an excuse
3 a formal statement of guilty or not guilty made in a lawcourt by an accused person

plead *VERB*
1 to beg someone to do something
2 to state formally in a lawcourt that you are guilty or not guilty
3 to give something as an excuse

pleasant *ADJECTIVE*
pleasing; giving pleasure
pleasantly *ADVERB* **pleasantness** *NOUN*

a
b
c
d
e
f
g
h
i
j
k
l
m
n
o
p
q
r
s
t
u
v
w
x
y
z

pleasantry NOUN **pleasantries**
a friendly or good-humoured remark

please VERB
1 to make a person feel satisfied or glad
2 used in polite requests *Please ring the bell.*
3 to think suitable *Do as you please.*

pleased ADJECTIVE
happy or glad

pleasurable ADJECTIVE
causing pleasure

pleasure NOUN
1 a feeling of satisfaction or gladness
2 something that pleases

pleat NOUN
a flat fold made by doubling cloth on itself
pleated ADJECTIVE

plectrum NOUN **plectrums** or **plectra**
a small piece of metal or bone etc. for
plucking the strings of a musical instrument

pledge NOUN
1 a solemn promise
2 something given as security for a loan

pledge VERB
1 to promise solemnly to do or give
something
2 to give as security

plentiful ADJECTIVE
existing in large numbers; abundant
plentifully ADVERB

plenty NOUN
as much as is needed or wanted

plethora NOUN
too large a quantity of something

pleurisy (ploor-i-see) NOUN
inflammation of the membrane round the
lungs

pliable ADJECTIVE
1 easy to bend; flexible
2 easy to influence or control
pliability NOUN

pliant ADJECTIVE
pliable

pliers PLURAL NOUN
a tool with jaws for gripping things

plight NOUN
a difficult situation

plimsoll NOUN
a canvas sports shoe with a rubber sole

Plimsoll line NOUN
a mark on a ship's side showing how deep it
may legally go down in the water when
loaded

plinth NOUN
a block or slab forming the base of a column

plod VERB **plodding, plodded**
1 to walk slowly and heavily
2 to work steadily
plodder NOUN

plonk NOUN
(*informal*) cheap wine

plonk VERB
(*informal*) to put something down clumsily or
heavily

plop VERB **plopping, plopped**
to make the sound of something dropping
into water
plop NOUN

plot NOUN
1 a secret plan
2 the story in a play, novel, or film
3 a small piece of land

plot VERB **plotting, plotted**
1 to make a secret plan
2 to make a chart or graph of something

plough NOUN
a farming implement for turning the soil over

plough VERB
1 to turn over soil with a plough
2 to go through something with great effort
or difficulty

ploughshare NOUN
the cutting blade of a plough

plover (pluv-er) NOUN
a kind of wading bird

ploy NOUN
a clever manoeuvre to gain an advantage

pluck VERB
1 to pick a flower or fruit
2 to pull the feathers off a bird
3 to pull something up or out
4 to pull a string (e.g. on a guitar) and let it go
again

pluck NOUN
courage or spirit

plucky ADJECTIVE **pluckier, pluckiest**
brave or spirited
pluckily ADVERB

plug NOUN
1 something used to stop a hole
2 a device that fits into a socket to connect
wires to an electricity supply
3 (*informal*) a piece of publicity

plug VERB **plugging, plugged**
1 to stop up a hole
2 (*informal*) to publicize something

plum NOUN
1 a soft juicy fruit with a pointed stone
2 a reddish-purple colour

plumage (ploom-ij) NOUN
a bird's feathers

plumb *VERB*
1 to measure the depth of water
2 to fit a room or building with plumbing
3 to solve a mystery

plumb *ADJECTIVE*
exactly upright; vertical

plumb *ADVERB*
(*informal*) exactly *plumb in the middle*

plumber *NOUN*
a person who fits and mends plumbing

plumbing *NOUN*
1 the water pipes, water tanks, and drainage pipes in a building
2 the work of a plumber

plumb line *NOUN*
a cord with a weight on the end, used to measure depth or to see whether a surface is vertical

plume *NOUN*
1 a large feather
2 something shaped like a feather *a plume of smoke*
plumed *ADJECTIVE*

plummet *NOUN*
a plumb line or the weight on its end

plummet *VERB*
1 to drop downwards rapidly
2 to decrease rapidly in value

plump [1] *ADJECTIVE*
slightly fat; rounded
plumpness *NOUN*

plump *VERB*
to make rounded *plump up a cushion*

plump [2] *VERB*
plump for (*informal*) to choose

plunder *VERB*
to rob a person or place using force, especially during a war or riot
plunderer *NOUN*

plunder *NOUN*
1 the act of plundering
2 goods that have been plundered

plunge *VERB*
1 to go or push forcefully into something
2 to fall or go downwards suddenly
3 to go or force into action etc.
plunge *NOUN*

plural *NOUN*
the form of a noun or verb when it stands for more than one person or thing *The plural of 'child' is 'children'.*
plural *ADJECTIVE*

plus *PREPOSITION*
used to show addition *2 plus 2 equals four (2 + 2 = 4).*

plus *ADJECTIVE*
1 (of a grade) slightly higher *B plus*
2 more than zero *a temperature between minus ten and plus ten degrees*

plush *NOUN*
a thick velvety cloth used in furnishings
plushy *ADJECTIVE*

plutonium *NOUN*
a radioactive substance used in nuclear weapons and reactors

ply [1] *NOUN* **plies**
1 a thickness or layer of wood or cloth etc.
2 a strand in yarn *4-ply wool*

ply [2] *VERB* **plies**, **plied**
1 to use or wield a tool or weapon
2 to work at a trade or business
3 to keep supplying someone with something

plywood *NOUN*
strong thin board made of layers of wood glued together

p.m. *ABBREVIATION*
after noon

pneumatic (new-mat-ik) *ADJECTIVE*
filled with or worked by compressed air *a pneumatic drill*
pneumatically *ADVERB*

pneumonia (new-moh-nee-a) *NOUN*
a serious illness caused by inflammation of one or both lungs

PO *ABBREVIATION*
1 Post Office
2 postal order

poach *VERB*
1 to cook slowly in liquid
2 to steal game or fish from someone else's land or water
poacher *NOUN*

pocket *NOUN*
1 a small bag-shaped part, especially in a piece of clothing
2 an isolated part or area *pockets of rain*

pocket *VERB*
1 to put into a pocket
2 to steal

pocket money *NOUN*
money given to a child to spend

pockmark *NOUN*
a scar or mark left on the skin by a disease
pockmarked *ADJECTIVE*

pod *NOUN*
a long seed-container on a pea or bean plant

podcast *NOUN*
a radio broadcast that can be downloaded from the Internet and played on a computer or MP3 player

a
b
c
d
e
f
g
h
i
j
k
l
m
n
o
P
q
r
s
t
u
v
w
x
y
z

podgy ADJECTIVE **podgier**, **podgiest**
short and fat

podium (poh-dee-um) NOUN **podiums** or **podia**
a small platform on which a music conductor or someone making a speech stands

poem NOUN
a piece of poetry

poet NOUN
a person who writes poetry

poetic ADJECTIVE
of or like poetry
poetically ADVERB

poetry NOUN
writing arranged in short lines, usually with a particular rhythm and sometimes with rhymes

pogrom NOUN
an organized massacre of people

poignant (poin-yuhnt) ADJECTIVE
very moving or distressing *poignant memories*
poignancy NOUN

point NOUN
1 the narrow or sharp end of something
2 a dot *a decimal point*
3 a particular place or time
4 a detail or characteristic *has some good points*
5 the important or essential idea *keep to the point*
6 purpose or value *no point in hurrying*
7 an electrical socket
8 a device for changing a train from one track to another

point VERB
1 to show where something is, especially by holding out a finger etc. towards it
2 to aim or direct *to point a gun*
3 to fill in the parts between bricks with mortar or cement
point out to draw attention to

point-blank ADJECTIVE
1 (of a shot) fired from close to the target
2 direct and straightforward *a point-blank refusal*

point-blank ADVERB
in a direct manner *refused point-blank*

pointed ADJECTIVE
1 with a point at the end
2 (of a remark) clearly directed at a person
pointedly ADVERB

pointer NOUN
1 a rod used to point at something
2 a dog that points with its muzzle towards birds that it scents
3 a hint

pointless ADJECTIVE
having no purpose
pointlessly ADVERB

point of view NOUN **points of view**
a way of looking at or thinking about something

poise NOUN
1 a dignified self-confident manner
2 a state of balance

poise VERB
to balance

poised ADJECTIVE
1 dignified and self-confident
2 prepared or ready

poison NOUN
a substance that can harm or kill a living thing if swallowed or absorbed into the body
poisonous ADJECTIVE

poison VERB
1 to give poison to; to kill with poison
2 to put poison in something
3 to corrupt or spoil something *He poisoned their minds.*
poisoner NOUN

poisonous ADJECTIVE
containing poison and causing death or harm

poke VERB
1 to prod or jab
2 to push out or forward

poke NOUN
a prod or poking movement

poker[1] NOUN
a metal rod for poking a fire

poker[2] NOUN
a card game in which players bet on who has the best cards

poky ADJECTIVE **pokier**, **pokiest**
small and cramped

polar ADJECTIVE
1 to do with or near the North Pole or South Pole
2 to do with either pole of a magnet
polarity NOUN

polar bear NOUN
a white bear living in Arctic regions

polarize VERB
1 (*Science*) to keep vibrations of light waves etc. to a single direction
2 to divide into two opposing groups
polarization NOUN

Polaroid NOUN
(*trademark*) a type of plastic which reduces the brightness of light passing through it

Polaroid camera NOUN
(*trademark*) a camera that produces a finished photograph a few seconds after taking it

pole[1] *NOUN*
a long slender rounded piece of wood or metal

pole[2] *NOUN*
1 a point on the earth's surface that is as far north (**North Pole**) or as far south (**South Pole**) as possible
2 each end of a magnet or electric cell

polecat *NOUN*
an animal of the weasel family

polemical *ADJECTIVE*
attacking a person's opinion or actions

pole star *NOUN*
the star above the North Pole

pole vault *NOUN*
an athletic contest in which competitors jump over a high bar with the help of a long flexible pole

police *NOUN*
officials who enforce laws and catch criminals

police *VERB*
to keep order in a place by means of police

policeman *NOUN* **policemen**
a male police officer

police officer *NOUN*
a member of the police

policewoman *NOUN* **policewomen**
a female police officer

policy *NOUN* **policies**
1 the aims or plans of a person or group
2 an insurance agreement

polio *NOUN*
poliomyelitis

poliomyelitis *NOUN*
a disease that can cause paralysis

polish *VERB*
1 to make smooth and shiny by rubbing
2 to make a thing better with small corrections
polish off to finish off

polish *NOUN*
1 a substance used in polishing
2 a shine

polite *ADJECTIVE*
having good manners
politely *ADVERB* **politeness** *NOUN*

politic *ADJECTIVE*
prudent or wise

political *ADJECTIVE*
connected with the governing of a country or region
politically *ADVERB*

politician *NOUN*
a person involved in politics

politics *NOUN*
the business of governing a country or region

polka *NOUN*
a lively dance for couples

poll (*say as* pole) *NOUN*
1 the process of voting at an election
2 the number of votes cast
3 an opinion poll

poll *VERB*
to receive a certain number of votes in an election

pollen *NOUN*
powder produced by the anthers of flowers, containing male cells for fertilizing other flowers

pollinate *VERB*
to fertilize a plant with pollen
pollination *NOUN*

poll tax *NOUN*
a tax that every adult has to pay

pollutant *NOUN*
something that pollutes

pollute *VERB*
to make the air, water, etc. dirty or impure
pollution *NOUN*

polo *NOUN*
a game like hockey, with players on horseback

polo neck *NOUN*
a high round turned-over collar
polo-necked *ADJECTIVE*

poltergeist *NOUN*
a ghost or spirit that throws things about noisily

polyester *NOUN*
a synthetic material used to make clothing

polygamy *NOUN*
the practice of having more than one wife at a time
polygamous *ADJECTIVE*

polyglot *ADJECTIVE*
knowing or using several languages

polygon *NOUN*
a flat shape with many sides
polygonal *ADJECTIVE*

polyhedron *NOUN*
a solid shape with many sides

polymer *NOUN*
a substance whose molecule is formed from a large number of simple molecules combined

polystyrene *NOUN*
a kind of plastic used for insulating or packing

polythene *NOUN*
a lightweight plastic used to make bags, wrappings, etc.

a b c d e f g h i j k l m n o **p** q r s t u v w x y z

polyunsaturated ADJECTIVE
(of fats) not forming cholesterol in the blood

pomegranate NOUN
a tropical fruit with many seeds

pomp NOUN
solemn splendour on public occasions

pompom NOUN
a ball of coloured threads used as a decoration

pompous ADJECTIVE
full of excessive dignity and self-importance
pomposity NOUN

pond NOUN
a small lake

ponder VERB
to think deeply and seriously

ponderous ADJECTIVE
1 heavy and awkward
2 laborious and dull

pong NOUN
(informal) an unpleasant smell

pontiff NOUN
the Pope

pontificate VERB
to give your opinions in a pompous way

pontoon[1] NOUN
a boat or float supporting a bridge over a river

pontoon[2] NOUN
a card game in which players try to get cards whose value totals 21

pony NOUN **ponies**
a small horse

ponytail NOUN
a bunch of long hair tied at the back of the head

pony-trekking NOUN
travelling across country on a pony for pleasure
pony-trekker NOUN

poodle NOUN
a dog with thick curly hair

pool NOUN
1 an area or patch of still water
2 the fund of money staked in a gambling game
3 a group of things shared by several people
4 a game resembling billiards

pool VERB
to put money or things together for sharing

poor ADJECTIVE
1 having little money or other resources
2 not good; inadequate poor work
3 deserving pity

poorly ADVERB
1 in a poor way; badly
2 unwell; slightly ill

pop[1] NOUN
1 a small explosive sound
2 a fizzy drink

pop VERB **popping**, **popped**
1 to make a pop
2 (informal) to go or put something somewhere quickly

pop[2] NOUN
modern popular music

popcorn NOUN
maize heated so that it bursts and forms fluffy balls

Pope NOUN
the head of the Roman Catholic Church

poplar NOUN
a tall slender tree

poplin NOUN
a plain woven cotton material

poppy NOUN **poppies**
a plant with large red flowers

populace NOUN
the general public

popular ADJECTIVE
1 liked or enjoyed by many people
2 held or believed by many people
popular beliefs
3 intended for the general public
popularity NOUN **popularly** ADVERB

popularize VERB
to make generally liked or known
popularization NOUN

populate VERB
to supply with a population; to inhabit

population NOUN
the people who live in a district or country

porcelain NOUN
fine china

porch NOUN
a shelter outside the entrance to a building

porcupine NOUN
an animal covered with long prickles

pore[1] NOUN
a tiny opening in the skin, allowing moisture to pass through

pore[2] VERB
pore over to study closely
Do not confuse this word with pour.

pork NOUN
meat from a pig

pornography NOUN
obscene pictures or writings
pornographic ADJECTIVE

porous ADJECTIVE
allowing liquid or air to pass through

porpoise (por-pus) *NOUN*
a sea animal like a small whale

porridge *NOUN*
a food made by boiling oatmeal to a thick paste

port [1] *NOUN*
1 a harbour
2 a town with a harbour
3 the left-hand side of a ship or aircraft facing forward

port [2] *NOUN*
a strong red Portuguese wine

portable *ADJECTIVE*
able to be carried

portal *NOUN*
a doorway or gateway

portcullis *NOUN*
a heavy grating that can be lowered in grooves to block the gateway to a castle

portend *VERB*
to be a warning of something unwelcome

portent *NOUN*
an omen; a sign that something will happen

portentous *ADJECTIVE*
1 serving as a sign
2 solemn

porter *NOUN*
1 a person who carries luggage or other goods
2 an official at the entrance to a large building

portfolio *NOUN* **portfolios**
1 a case for holding documents or drawings
2 a government minister's special responsibility

porthole *NOUN*
a window in the side of a ship or aircraft

portico *NOUN* **porticoes** or **porticos**
a roof supported on columns, forming a porch of a building

portion *NOUN*
a part or share given to someone

portion *VERB*
to divide something into portions

portly *ADJECTIVE* **portlier**, **portliest**
slightly fat
portliness *NOUN*

portrait *NOUN*
1 a picture of a person or animal
2 a description in words

portray *VERB*
1 to make a picture of a person or scene etc.
2 to describe or show
portrayal *NOUN*

pose *NOUN*
1 a position or posture of the body
2 a way of behaving to make a particular impression

pose *VERB*
1 to take up a pose
2 to pretend
3 to present *poses a problem for us*

poser *NOUN*
1 a puzzling question or problem
2 a person who tries to impress people

posh *ADJECTIVE* (*informal*)
1 very smart; high-class *a posh restaurant*
2 upper-class *a posh accent*

position *NOUN*
1 the place where something is or should be
2 the way a person or thing is placed or arranged *a standing position*
3 a situation or condition *in an awkward position*
4 a job
positional *ADJECTIVE*

position *VERB*
to put in a certain position

positive *ADJECTIVE*
1 definite or certain
2 agreeing or consenting *a positive answer*
3 confident and hopeful
4 (of a test) showing signs of what is being tested
5 greater than nought
6 to do with the kind of electric charge that lacks electrons
7 (of a photograph) with the light and dark parts as normal
positively *ADVERB*

posse (poss-ee) *NOUN*
a group of people helping a sheriff

possess *VERB*
1 to have or own
2 to control someone's thoughts or behaviour
possessor *NOUN*

possessed *ADJECTIVE*
seeming to be controlled by strong emotion or an evil spirit

possession *NOUN*
1 something someone owns
2 the state of owning something

possessive *ADJECTIVE*
1 wanting to possess and keep things for yourself
2 (*Grammar*) (of an adjective or pronoun) showing that someone owns something (e.g. *mine*, *their*)

possibility NOUN **possibilities**
1 the fact of being possible
2 something that may exist or happen etc.

possible ADJECTIVE
able to exist, happen, be done, or be used

possibly ADVERB
1 in any way *can't possibly do it*
2 perhaps

possum NOUN
an opossum

post NOUN
1 an upright piece of wood, concrete, etc. fixed in the ground
2 the collecting and delivering of letters, parcels, etc.
3 letters and parcels
4 a job
5 the place where someone is on duty

post VERB
1 to send a letter or parcel etc. by post
2 to put up a notice or poster etc.
3 to place information on an Internet site
4 to place someone on duty

postage NOUN
the charge for sending something by post

postal ADJECTIVE
of the post; by post

postal order NOUN
a document bought from a post office for sending money by post

postbox NOUN
a box for posting letters

postcard NOUN
a card for sending messages by post

postcode NOUN
a group of letters and numbers included in an address to help in sorting the post

poster NOUN
a large sheet of paper with an announcement or advertisement

posterior ADJECTIVE
1 situated at the back
2 coming after

posterior NOUN
the buttocks

posterity NOUN
future generations of people

postgraduate NOUN
a person who does university study after a first degree

post-haste ADVERB
with great speed

posthumous (poss-tew-mus) ADJECTIVE
coming or happening after a person's death
posthumously ADVERB

postman NOUN **postmen**
someone who delivers letters

postmark NOUN
an official mark put on a postal item to show the place and date of posting

post-mortem NOUN
an examination of a dead body to discover the cause of death

post office NOUN
1 an office for sending letters and parcels
2 the national organization for postal services

postpone VERB
to fix a later time for
postponement NOUN

postscript NOUN
an addition at the end of a letter or book

postulate VERB
to propose that something is true as part of an argument
postulation NOUN

posture NOUN
a particular position of the body

post-war ADJECTIVE
of the time after a war

posy NOUN **posies**
a small bunch of flowers

pot NOUN
1 a deep usually round container
2 (*informal*) a lot of something *pots of money*
pot luck (*informal*) whatever is available

pot VERB **potting**, **potted**
to put into a pot

potash NOUN
potassium carbonate

potassium NOUN
a soft silvery-white metal substance that is essential for living things

potato NOUN **potatoes**
a starchy white tuber growing underground, used as a vegetable

potent ADJECTIVE
powerful; strong
potency NOUN

potentate NOUN
a powerful monarch or ruler

potential (po-**ten**-shal) ADJECTIVE
capable of happening or developing
a potential winner
potentially ADVERB

potential NOUN
the ability of a person or thing to develop in the future

pothole NOUN
1 a deep natural hole in the ground
2 a hole in a road

potion *NOUN*
a liquid for drinking as a medicine etc.

potpourri (poh-poor-ee) *NOUN*
a scented mixture of dried petals and spices

pot shot *NOUN*
a casual shot

potted *ADJECTIVE*
1 shortened or abridged *a potted account*
2 preserved in a pot *potted shrimps*

potter [1] *NOUN*
a person who makes pottery

potter [2] *VERB*
to work or move about in a leisurely way

pottery *NOUN* **potteries**
1 items made of baked clay
2 the craft of making these things
3 a place where a potter works

potty [1] *ADJECTIVE* **pottier**, **pottiest**
(*informal*) eccentric or foolish

potty [2] *NOUN* **potties**
(*informal*) a small bowl used by a young child instead of a toilet

pouch *NOUN*
1 a small bag or pocket
2 a fold of skin in which a kangaroo etc. keeps its young

pouffe (poof) *NOUN*
a low padded stool

poultice *NOUN*
a soft hot dressing put on a sore or inflamed place

poultry *NOUN*
birds (e.g. chickens and geese) kept for their eggs and meat

pounce *VERB*
to jump or swoop down quickly on something
pounce *NOUN*

pound [1] *NOUN*
1 a unit of money (in Britain = 100 pence)
2 a unit of weight equal to 16 ounces or about 454 grams

pound [2] *NOUN*
an enclosure for animals or vehicles

pound [3] *VERB*
1 to hit something hard and often
2 to run or go heavily
3 (of the heart) to beat fast

pour *VERB*
1 to flow or make something flow
2 to rain heavily
3 to arrive in large numbers
Do not confuse this word with *pore*.

pout *VERB*
to push the lips out when annoyed or sulking
pout *NOUN*

poverty *NOUN*
1 the state of being poor
2 a lack or scarcity *a poverty of ideas*

powder *NOUN*
1 a mass of fine dry particles
2 a medicine or cosmetic etc. made as a powder
3 gunpowder

powder *VERB*
1 to put powder on
2 to make into powder

powdery *ADJECTIVE*
1 covered in powder
2 like powder

power *NOUN*
1 strength or energy
2 an ability *the power of speech*
3 political authority or control
4 a powerful country or organization
5 mechanical or electrical energy
6 (*Science*) the rate of doing work, measured in watts or horsepower
7 (*Maths*) the product of a number multiplied by itself *The third power of $2 = 2 \times 2 \times 2 = 8$.*

powerboat *NOUN*
a powerful motor boat

powerful *ADJECTIVE*
having great power or influence
powerfully *ADVERB*

powerless *ADJECTIVE*
having no power or influence

power station *NOUN*
a building where electricity is produced

pp. *ABBREVIATION*
pages

practicable *ADJECTIVE*
able to be done
Do not confuse this word with *practical*.

practical *ADJECTIVE*
1 able to do or make useful things
2 likely to be useful
3 involving activity rather than just theory
Do not confuse this word with *practicable*.

practical *NOUN*
a lesson or examination in which something has to be made or done

practical joke *NOUN*
a trick played on someone

practically *ADVERB*
1 in a practical way
2 almost *I've practically finished.*

practice NOUN
1 the process of doing something repeatedly to become better at it
2 action and not theory *works well in practice*
3 the professional business of a doctor, lawyer, etc.
4 a habit or custom
See the note at **practise**.

practise VERB
1 to do something repeatedly to become better at it
2 to do something habitually *Practise what you preach.*
3 to work as a doctor, lawyer, etc.
Note the spelling: *practice* for the noun, *practise* for the verb.

practised ADJECTIVE
experienced or expert

practitioner NOUN
a professional worker, especially a doctor

pragmatic ADJECTIVE
treating things in a practical way *a pragmatic approach to the problem*
pragmatically ADVERB **pragmatism** NOUN

prairie NOUN
a large area of flat grass-covered land in North America

praise VERB
1 to say good things about a person or thing
2 to honour God in words

praise NOUN
words that praise somebody or something

praiseworthy ADJECTIVE
deserving praise

pram NOUN
a four-wheeled carriage for a baby, pushed by a person walking

prance VERB
to move about in a lively or happy way

prank NOUN
a practical joke or mischievous action

prawn NOUN
an edible shellfish like a large shrimp

pray VERB
1 to talk to God
2 to ask earnestly for something

prayer NOUN
words used in praying

preach VERB
to give a religious or moral talk
preacher NOUN

preamble NOUN
the introduction to a speech or book or document etc.

pre-arranged ADJECTIVE
arranged beforehand

precarious ADJECTIVE
not safe or secure
precariously ADVERB

precaution NOUN
something done to prevent future trouble or danger

precede VERB
to come or go before something else
Do not confuse this word with *proceed*.

precedence (press-i-dens) NOUN
the right to be first or go first

precedent (press-i-dent) NOUN
a previous case used as an example to be followed

precept NOUN
a rule for action or conduct

precinct NOUN
1 a part of a town where traffic is not allowed
2 the area round a cathedral or other large building

precious ADJECTIVE
1 very valuable
2 greatly loved

precious ADVERB
(*informal*) very *precious little*

precipice NOUN
a steep cliff

precipitate VERB
1 to make something happen
2 to throw or send down

precipitate ADJECTIVE
hurried or hasty *a precipitate departure*

precipitation NOUN
rain, snow, or hail falling

precipitous ADJECTIVE
very steep
precipitously ADVERB

precis (pray-see) NOUN **precis**
a summary

precise ADJECTIVE
exact; clearly stated
precisely ADVERB

precision NOUN
accuracy

preclude VERB
to prevent from happening

precocious ADJECTIVE
(of a child) unusually advanced or developed
precociously ADVERB

preconceived ADJECTIVE
(of an idea) formed before full information is available
preconception NOUN

precursor NOUN
an earlier form of a thing

predator (pred-a-ter) NOUN
an animal that hunts or preys on others
predatory ADJECTIVE

predecessor NOUN
an earlier holder of a job or position

predestine VERB
to determine beforehand
predestination NOUN

predicament (prid-ik-a-ment) NOUN
a difficult or unpleasant situation

predicate NOUN
(*Grammar*) the part of a sentence that says
something about the subject, e.g. 'is short' in
Life is short.

predict VERB
to say what will happen in the future
predictable ADJECTIVE

prediction NOUN
something predicted

predispose VERB
to influence in advance
predisposition NOUN

predominant ADJECTIVE
most important or noticeable
predominance NOUN **predominantly** ADVERB

predominate VERB
to be the largest or most important or most
powerful

pre-empt VERB
to take action to prevent or block something
pre-emptive ADJECTIVE

preen VERB
(of a bird) to smooth its feathers with its beak

prefabricated ADJECTIVE
made in sections ready to be assembled
prefabrication NOUN

preface (pref-as) NOUN
an introduction at the beginning of a book or
speech

preface VERB
to add introductory words to

prefect NOUN
1 a senior pupil in a school, given authority to
help to keep order
2 a regional official in some countries

prefer VERB **preferring, preferred**
1 to like one person or thing more than
another
2 (*formal*) to put forward a charge

preferable (pref-er-a-bul) ADJECTIVE
liked better; more desirable
preferably ADVERB

preference (pref-er-ens) NOUN
a greater liking

preferential (pref-er-en-shal) ADJECTIVE
better than for other people *preferential
treatment*

prefix NOUN
(*Grammar*) a word or syllable joined to the
front of a word to change or add to its
meaning, as in *dis*order, *out*stretched,
*un*happy

pregnant ADJECTIVE
having a fetus in the womb
pregnancy NOUN

prehistoric ADJECTIVE
belonging to ancient times before written
records
prehistory NOUN

prejudice NOUN
an unfair opinion or dislike
prejudiced ADJECTIVE

preliminary ADJECTIVE
coming before an important action or event

prelude NOUN
1 a thing that comes before
2 a short piece of music

premature ADJECTIVE
coming before the usual or proper time
prematurely ADVERB

premeditated ADJECTIVE
planned beforehand

premier (prem-ee-er) ADJECTIVE
first in importance, order, or time

premier NOUN
a prime minister or other head of
government

premiere (prem-yair) NOUN
the first public performance of a play or film

premises PLURAL NOUN
a building and its grounds

premiss (prem-iss) NOUN
a statement used as the basis for reasoning

premium NOUN
1 an amount or instalment paid to an
insurance company
2 an extra charge or payment

premonition NOUN
a feeling that something is about to happen

preoccupied ADJECTIVE
thinking mainly about one thing
preoccupation NOUN

preparation NOUN
1 the process of getting something ready
2 something done to get ready for an event or
activity
3 something prepared, e.g. a medicine

preparatory ADJECTIVE
preparing for something

a
b
c
d
e
f
g
h
i
j
k
l
m
n
o
p
q
r
s
t
u
v
w
x
y
z

prepare *VERB*
to get ready; to make something ready

preponderate *VERB*
to be greater or more important than others
preponderance *NOUN*

preposition *NOUN*
a word used with a noun or pronoun to show place, position, time, or means, e.g. *at* home, *in* the hall, *on* Sunday, *by* train

prepossessing *ADJECTIVE*
pleasant or attractive

preposterous *ADJECTIVE*
completely absurd or foolish

prerequisite *NOUN*
something necessary before something else can be done

prerogative *NOUN*
a right or privilege belonging to one person or group

prescribe *VERB*
1 to advise a person to use a particular medicine or treatment
2 to say what should be done
Do not confuse this word with *proscribe*.

prescription *NOUN*
1 a doctor's written order for a medicine
2 the medicine prescribed

prescriptive *ADJECTIVE*
laying down rules

presence *NOUN*
1 the state of being present
2 a person's impressive appearance or manner

present[1] (**prez**-ent) *ADJECTIVE*
1 being in a particular place
2 to do with now; existing now
present (**prez**-ent) *NOUN*
present times or events; the time now

present[2] (**prez**-ent) *NOUN*
something given or received as a gift
present (**priz**-ent) *VERB*
1 to give something formally
2 to introduce someone to another person
3 to put on a play or other entertainment
4 to show
5 to cause or provide something
This presents a problem.
presentation *NOUN* **presenter** *NOUN*

presentable *ADJECTIVE*
fit to be presented to other people; looking good

presentation *NOUN*
1 the act of presenting something
2 something presented
3 a talk or demonstration
4 the way in which something is written or shown

presentiment *NOUN*
a feeling that something bad is about to happen

presently *ADVERB*
1 soon; shortly
2 now

preservative *NOUN*
a substance added to food to preserve it

preserve *VERB*
to keep something safe or in good condition
preserver *NOUN* **preservation** *NOUN*
preserve *NOUN*
1 jam made with fruit boiled with sugar
2 a place or activity associated with a particular person or group

preside *VERB*
to be in charge of a meeting etc.

president *NOUN*
1 the person in charge of a club, society, or council etc.
2 the head of state in a republic
presidency *NOUN* **presidential** *ADJECTIVE*

press *VERB*
1 to put weight or force on something
2 to make something by pressing
3 to make clothes smooth by ironing them
4 to urge
press *NOUN*
1 a device for pressing things
2 a machine for printing things
3 a firm that prints or publishes books etc.
4 newspapers and journalists

press conference *NOUN*
an interview with a group of journalists

pressing *ADJECTIVE*
needing immediate action; urgent

press-up *NOUN*
an exercise performed by lying face down and pressing down with the hands to lift the body

pressure *NOUN*
1 continuous pressing
2 the force with which something presses
3 the force of the atmosphere on the earth's surface
4 strong influence or persuasion

pressurize *VERB*
1 to maintain a compartment at a constant air pressure
2 to influence or persuade someone
pressurization *NOUN*

prestige (**pres-teej**) *NOUN*
good reputation
prestigious *ADJECTIVE*

presumably *ADVERB*
according to what you may presume

presume *VERB*
1 to suppose or assume to be true
2 to be bold enough *I won't presume to advise you.*
presumption *NOUN*

presumptive *ADJECTIVE*
presuming something

presumptuous *ADJECTIVE*
too bold or confident
presumptuously *ADVERB*

presuppose *VERB*
to suppose or assume beforehand
presupposition *NOUN*

pretence *NOUN*
an attempt to pretend that something is true

pretend *VERB*
1 to behave as if something is true or real when you know it is not
2 to put forward a claim

pretender *NOUN*
a person who claims a throne or title

pretension *NOUN*
1 a doubtful claim
2 showy behaviour

pretentious *ADJECTIVE*
1 trying to impress
2 showy or ostentatious
pretentiously *ADVERB*

pretext *NOUN*
a reason put forward to conceal the true reason

pretty *ADJECTIVE* **prettier**, **prettiest**
attractive in a delicate way
prettiness *NOUN*

pretty *ADVERB*
quite *pretty silly*

prevail *VERB*
1 to be the most frequent or general
2 to be victorious

prevalent (prev-a-lent) *ADJECTIVE*
most frequent or common
prevalence *NOUN*

prevaricate *VERB*
to be evasive or misleading
prevarication *NOUN*

prevent *VERB*
1 to stop something from happening
2 to stop a person from doing something
prevention *NOUN*

preventive or **preventative** *ADJECTIVE*
helping to prevent something

preview *NOUN*
a showing of a film or play etc. before its general release

previous *ADJECTIVE*
existing or happening before; preceding
previously *ADVERB*

prey (*say as* pray) *NOUN*
an animal that is hunted or killed by another for food

prey *VERB*
prey on 1 to hunt or take as prey 2 to worry or obsess

price *NOUN*
1 the amount of money to be paid for something
2 something that must be given or done to achieve something

price *VERB*
to decide the price of

priceless *ADJECTIVE*
1 very valuable
2 (*informal*) very amusing

prick *VERB*
1 to make a tiny hole in
2 to hurt somebody with a pin or needle etc.
prick up your ears to start listening closely

prick *NOUN*
1 the act of pricking
2 a feeling of pricking

prickle *NOUN*
1 a small thorn
2 a sharp spine on a hedgehog or cactus etc.
3 a feeling of pricking

prickle *VERB*
to feel or cause a pricking feeling

prickly *ADJECTIVE* **pricklier**, **prickliest**
1 full of prickles
2 stinging or pricking
3 touchy; irritable

pride *NOUN*
1 a feeling of pleasure or satisfaction with what you have achieved
2 something that makes you feel proud
3 dignity or self-respect
4 too high an opinion of yourself
5 a group of lions

pride *VERB*
pride yourself on to be proud of

priest *NOUN*
1 a member of the clergy in certain Christian Churches
2 a person who conducts religious ceremonies in a non-Christian religion
priesthood *NOUN*

priestess *NOUN*
a female priest in a non-Christian religion

prig *NOUN*
a self-righteous person
priggish *ADJECTIVE*

prim *ADJECTIVE* **primmer**, **primmest**
formal and correct in manner

prima donna (preem-uh) *NOUN*
1 the chief female singer in an opera
2 a woman who is temperamental

primary *ADJECTIVE*
first or most important
primarily *ADVERB*

primary colour *NOUN*
one of the colours (red, yellow, and blue)
from which all others can be made by mixing

primary school *NOUN*
a school for the first stage of education

primate *NOUN*
1 an animal of the group that includes human
beings, apes, and monkeys
2 an archbishop

prime *ADJECTIVE*
1 chief; most important
2 excellent; first-rate

prime *NOUN*
the best time or stage of something　*in the
prime of life*

prime *VERB*
1 to prepare something for use or action
2 to put a coat of liquid on a surface to
prepare it for painting
3 to equip a person with information

prime minister *NOUN*
the head of a government

prime number *NOUN*
a number (e.g. 2, 3, 5, 7, 11) that can be
divided exactly only by itself and one

primer *NOUN*
1 a liquid for priming a surface
2 an elementary textbook

primeval *ADJECTIVE*
belonging to the earliest times of the world

primitive *ADJECTIVE*
at an early stage of civilization or
development

primrose *NOUN*
a pale yellow flower that blooms in spring

prince *NOUN*
1 the son of a king or queen
2 a man or boy in a royal family
princely *ADJECTIVE*

princess *NOUN*
1 the daughter of a king or queen
2 a woman or girl in a royal family
3 the wife of a prince

principal *ADJECTIVE*
chief or most important
principally *ADVERB*

principal *NOUN*
the head of a college or school
Do not confuse this word with *principle*.

principality *NOUN* **principalities**
a country ruled by a prince

principle *NOUN*
1 a general truth, belief, or rule
2 a rule of conduct
Do not confuse this word with *principal*.

print *VERB*
1 to put words or pictures on paper by using a
machine or computer
2 to write with letters not joined together
3 to press a mark or design etc. on a surface
4 to make a photograph from a negative

print *NOUN*
1 printed lettering or words
2 a mark made by something pressing on a
surface
3 a printed picture, photograph, or design

printed circuit *NOUN*
an electric circuit made by pressing thin
metal strips on a board

printer *NOUN*
1 someone who prints books or newspapers
2 a machine that prints on paper from
computer data

printout *NOUN*
printed information produced by a computer

prior *ADJECTIVE*
earlier or more important than something
else　*a prior engagement*

prior *NOUN*
the chief monk of a religious order

prioritize *VERB*
to put tasks etc. in order of importance

priority *NOUN* **priorities**
1 the state of being earlier or more important
than something else
2 something considered more important
than other things

priory *NOUN* **priories**
a religious house of certain monks or nuns

prise *VERB*
to lever something out or open

prism (prizm) *NOUN*
1 a solid piece of glass with triangular ends,
which breaks up light into the colours of the
rainbow
2 (*Maths*) a solid shape with ends that are
triangles or polygons which are equal and
parallel

a b c d e f g h i j k l m n o **p** q r s t u v w x y z

prison NOUN
a place where criminals are kept as a
punishment

prisoner NOUN
1 a person kept in a prison
2 a captive

pristine ADJECTIVE
in its original condition; unspoilt

privacy NOUN
a state of being private

private ADJECTIVE
1 belonging to a particular person or group
2 confidential *private talks*
3 quiet and secluded
4 not holding public office *a private citizen*
5 not run by the state *private medicine*

private NOUN
a soldier of the lowest rank

privation NOUN
loss or lack of something needed

privatize VERB
to transfer from the state to private owners
privatization NOUN

privet NOUN
an evergreen shrub used to make hedges

privilege NOUN
a special right or advantage given to one
person or group
privileged ADJECTIVE

privy ADJECTIVE
privy to sharing in a secret

prize NOUN
1 an award given to the winner of a game or
competition etc.
2 something taken from an enemy

prize VERB
to value very much

pro[1] NOUN **pros**
(*informal*) a professional

pro[2] NOUN
pros and cons reasons for and against
something

probability NOUN **probabilities**
1 likelihood
2 something that is probable

probable ADJECTIVE
likely to happen or be true

probably ADVERB
very likely

probation NOUN
1 a period of testing a person's suitability at
the start of a job
2 the release of a prisoner on good behaviour
and under supervision

probe NOUN
1 a long thin instrument used to inspect a
wound
2 an unmanned spacecraft used for
exploring
3 an investigation

probe VERB
1 to explore or look at with a probe
2 to investigate

problem NOUN
1 something difficult to deal with or
understand
2 something that has to be done or answered

problematic or
problematical ADJECTIVE
difficult or uncertain

procedure NOUN
an orderly way of doing something

proceed VERB
1 to go forward or onward
2 to go on to do something *proceeded to
explain the idea*
Do not confuse this word with *precede*.

proceedings PLURAL NOUN
1 things that happen; activities
2 a lawsuit

proceeds PLURAL NOUN
the money made from a sale or event

process NOUN **processes**
a series of actions for making or doing
something

process VERB
to put something through a process

procession NOUN
a number of people or vehicles etc. moving
steadily forward in line

processor NOUN
1 a machine that processes things
2 the part of a computer that controls all its
operations

proclaim VERB
to announce officially or publicly

proclamation NOUN
an official announcement

procrastinate VERB
to put off doing something
procrastination NOUN

procreate VERB
to produce offspring by the natural process of
reproduction
procreation NOUN

procure VERB
to obtain or acquire
procurement NOUN

prod *VERB* **prodding, prodded**
1 to poke
2 to stimulate someone into action
prod *NOUN*

prodigal *ADJECTIVE*
wasteful or extravagant
prodigally *ADVERB* **prodigality** *NOUN*

prodigious *ADJECTIVE*
wonderful or enormous
prodigiously *ADVERB*

prodigy *NOUN* **prodigies**
1 a young person with exceptional abilities
2 a wonderful thing

produce (prod-**yooss**) *VERB*
1 to make or create; to bring something into existence
2 to bring something out so that it can be seen
3 to organize the performance of a play, making of a film, etc.
4 (*Maths*) to extend a line further
producer *NOUN*

produce (prod-**yooss**) *NOUN*
things produced, especially by farmers

producer *NOUN*
a person who produces a play, film, etc.

product *NOUN*
1 something produced
2 the result of multiplying two numbers

production *NOUN*
1 the process of making or creating something
2 the amount produced
3 a version of a play, opera, etc.

productive *ADJECTIVE*
1 producing a lot of things
2 producing good results
productivity *NOUN*

profane *ADJECTIVE*
showing disrespect for holy things

profanity *NOUN* **profanities**
a word or words that show disrespect for holy things

profess *VERB*
1 to declare or express
2 to claim *professed to be an authority*

profession *NOUN*
1 an occupation that needs special training, such as medicine or law
2 a declaration *professions of loyalty*

professional *ADJECTIVE*
1 to do with a profession
2 doing work as a full-time job for payment
3 done with a high standard of skill
professional *NOUN*

professor *NOUN*
a university teacher of the highest rank
professorship *NOUN*

proffer *VERB*
to offer

proficient *ADJECTIVE*
trained to do something with skill
proficiency *NOUN*

profile *NOUN*
1 a side view of a person's face
2 a short description of a person's character or career

profit *NOUN*
1 the extra money obtained by selling something for more than it cost to buy or make
2 an advantage gained
profit *VERB*
to gain an advantage or benefit

profitable *ADJECTIVE*
providing a profit or benefit
profitably *ADVERB*

profligate *ADJECTIVE*
wasteful and extravagant
profligacy *NOUN*

profound *ADJECTIVE*
1 very deep or intense *a profound interest*
2 showing great knowledge or understanding *a profound remark*
profoundly *ADVERB* **profundity** *NOUN*

profuse *ADJECTIVE*
lavish or plentiful
profusion *NOUN*

progeny (proj-in-ee) *NOUN*
offspring or descendants

prognosis *NOUN* **prognoses**
a prediction about how a disease will develop

program *NOUN*
a series of coded instructions for a computer
program *VERB* **programming, programmed**
to put instructions into a computer by means of a program
programmer *NOUN*

programme *NOUN*
1 a list of planned events
2 a pamphlet giving details of a play, concert, football match, etc.
3 a show, play, or talk etc. on radio or television

progress (proh-gress) *NOUN*
1 forward movement; an advance
2 a development or improvement

progress (pro-**gress**) *VERB*
1 to move forward
2 to develop or improve

progression *NOUN*
1 the process of moving forward or developing
2 (*Maths*) a sequence of numbers each having the same relation to the one before

progressive *ADJECTIVE*
1 moving forward or developing
2 in favour of political or social reform
3 (of a disease) becoming more severe

prohibit *VERB*
to forbid or ban
prohibition *NOUN*

prohibitive *ADJECTIVE*
(of prices) too high for most people to afford

project (**proj**-ekt) *NOUN*
1 a plan or scheme
2 a piece of research into a subject

project (pro-**jekt**) *VERB*
1 to stick out
2 to show a picture on a screen
3 to give people a particular impression
projection *NOUN*

projectile *NOUN*
a missile

projector *NOUN*
a machine for showing films or photographs on a screen

proletariat (proh-lit-**air**-ee-at) *NOUN*
the ordinary working people

proliferate *VERB*
to increase in numbers
proliferation *NOUN*

prolific *ADJECTIVE*
producing a lot *a prolific author*

prologue (**proh**-log) *NOUN*
an introduction to a poem or play etc.

prolong *VERB*
to make a thing longer or make it last for a long time

prom *NOUN* (*informal*)
1 a promenade
2 a promenade concert
3 (*American*) a formal school dance

promenade (prom-in-**ahd**) *NOUN*
a place suitable for walking, especially beside the seashore

promenade concert *NOUN*
a concert at which part of the audience stands

prominence *NOUN*
1 conspicuousness
2 fame

prominent *ADJECTIVE*
1 easily seen; conspicuous *in a prominent position*
2 sticking out
3 important
prominently *ADVERB*

promiscuous *ADJECTIVE*
1 having casual sexual relationships
2 indiscriminate
promiscuity *NOUN*

promise *NOUN*
1 a statement that you will do or not do something
2 an indication of future success
promise *VERB*
to make a promise

promising *ADJECTIVE*
likely to be good or successful

promontory *NOUN* **promontories**
a piece of high land jutting into a sea or lake

promote *VERB*
1 to move a person to a higher rank or position
2 to help the progress of
3 to publicize or advertise
promotion *NOUN*

prompt *ADJECTIVE*
immediate; not involving delay
a prompt reply
promptly *ADVERB*
prompt *ADVERB*
exactly *at 7.20 a.m. prompt*
prompt *VERB*
1 to cause or encourage a person to do something
2 to remind an actor or speaker of the words to speak next
prompter *NOUN*

promulgate *VERB*
to make known to the public; to proclaim
promulgation *NOUN*

prone *ADJECTIVE*
lying face downwards
prone to likely to do or suffer from something *is prone to exaggerate*

prong *NOUN*
each of the spikes on a fork
pronged *ADJECTIVE*

pronoun *NOUN*
a word used instead of a noun (e.g. *I*, *we*, *who*, *this*)

pronounce *VERB*
1 to say a sound or word in a particular way
2 to declare formally

pronounced *ADJECTIVE*
noticeable *a pronounced limp*

pronouncement NOUN
a declaration

pronunciation NOUN
the way a word is pronounced
Note the spelling -nunc- and not -nounc-.

proof NOUN
1 evidence that shows something to be true
2 a copy of printed matter made for checking before other copies are printed

proof ADJECTIVE
able to resist something bullet-proof

prop ¹ NOUN
a support made of a long piece of wood or metal

prop VERB **propping, propped**
to support something by leaning it against a surface

prop ² NOUN
an object or piece of furniture used in a play or film

propaganda NOUN
biased or misleading publicity intended to make people believe something

propagate VERB
1 to breed or reproduce
2 to spread an idea or belief

propel VERB **propelling, propelled**
to push something forward

propeller NOUN
a device with blades that spin round to drive an aircraft or ship

propensity NOUN **propensities**
a natural tendency

proper ADJECTIVE
1 suitable or right
2 respectable
3 (informal) complete or thorough a proper nuisance
properly ADVERB

proper noun NOUN
the name of an individual person or thing, e.g. Mary, London, Spain, usually written with a capital first letter

property NOUN **properties**
1 a thing or things that belong to somebody
2 a building or land owned by someone
3 a quality or characteristic

prophecy NOUN **prophecies**
1 a statement that predicts what will happen
2 the action of prophesying

prophesy VERB **prophesies, prophesied**
to say what will happen in the future

prophet NOUN
1 a person who makes prophecies
2 a religious teacher believed to be inspired by God

prophetic ADJECTIVE
saying or showing what will happen in the future

propitious ADJECTIVE
favourable

proponent NOUN
a person who favours something

proportion NOUN
1 a part or share of a whole thing
2 a ratio
3 the correct relation of size, amount, or importance

proportional or **proportionate** ADJECTIVE
in proportion; according to a ratio

proportional representation NOUN
a system in which each political party has a number of Members of Parliament in proportion to the number of votes for all its candidates

proposal NOUN
1 the act of proposing
2 something proposed
3 an offer of marriage

propose VERB
1 to suggest an idea or plan etc.
2 to plan or intend to do something
3 to ask someone to marry you

proposition NOUN
1 a suggestion or offer
2 a statement
3 (informal) an undertaking or problem a difficult proposition

propound VERB
to put forward an idea for consideration

proprietor NOUN
the owner of a shop or business

propriety NOUN **proprieties**
1 the state of being proper
2 correct behaviour

propulsion NOUN
forward movement

prosaic ADJECTIVE
dull and ordinary

proscribe VERB
to forbid by law
Do not confuse this word with prescribe.

prose NOUN
ordinary writing or speech as distinct from verse

prosecute VERB
1 to bring a criminal charge against someone
2 to continue with something
prosecutor NOUN

prosecution NOUN
1 the process of prosecuting
2 the lawyers prosecuting someone in a lawcourt

prospect (pros-pekt) NOUN
1 a possibility or expectation *little prospect of success*
2 a wide view

prospect (pro-spekt) VERB
to explore in search of gold or some other mineral
prospector NOUN

prospective ADJECTIVE
expected to be or to happen *prospective customers*

prospectus NOUN
a booklet describing a school, business, company, etc.

prosper VERB
to be successful

prosperous ADJECTIVE
successful or rich

prosperity NOUN
success and wealth

prostitute NOUN
a person who offers sexual intercourse for payment
prostitution NOUN

prostrate ADJECTIVE
lying face downwards

prostrate VERB
prostrate yourself to lie flat on the ground in submission
prostration NOUN

protagonist NOUN
the main character in a play

protect VERB
to keep safe from harm or injury
protection NOUN

protective ADJECTIVE
giving protection

protector NOUN
a defender or guardian

protectorate NOUN
a country that is under the protection of a stronger country

protégé (prot-ezh-ay) NOUN
a person who is guided and supported by a more experienced person

protein NOUN
a substance found in living things and an essential part of the human and animal diet

protest (proh-test) NOUN
a statement or action showing disapproval

protest (pro-test) VERB
1 to make a protest
2 to declare firmly *protested their innocence*
protester NOUN

Protestant NOUN
a member of any of the western Christian Churches separated from the Roman Catholic Church

protocol NOUN
correct or official procedure

proton NOUN
a particle of matter with a positive electric charge

prototype NOUN
the first model of something, from which others are copied

protract VERB
to make something last longer than usual
protracted ADJECTIVE

protractor NOUN
an instrument for measuring angles

protrude VERB
to stick out from a surface
protrusion NOUN

proud ADJECTIVE
1 pleased with yourself or someone else who has done well
2 causing pride *a proud moment*
3 full of self-respect *too proud to ask for help*
4 having too high an opinion of yourself
proudly ADVERB

prove VERB
1 to show that something is true
2 to turn out *a forecast that proved to be true*
provable ADJECTIVE

proven (proh-ven) ADJECTIVE
proved *of proven ability*

proverb NOUN
a well-known saying that states a truth, e.g. *Many hands make light work.*

proverbial ADJECTIVE
1 referred to in a proverb
2 well-known

provide VERB
1 to supply or make available
2 to prepare for something *to provide for emergencies*
provided or **providing that** on condition that

providence NOUN
wise preparation for the future

provident ADJECTIVE
wisely providing for the future; thrifty

providential ADJECTIVE
happening very luckily
providentially ADVERB

province NOUN
1 a major division of a country
2 a person's area of special knowledge or responsibility

provincial (pro-**vin**-shul) ADJECTIVE
1 to do with the provinces
2 culturally limited or narrow-minded

provision NOUN
1 the providing of something
2 a statement in a legal document

provisional ADJECTIVE
arranged or agreed on for the time being
provisionally ADVERB

provisions PLURAL NOUN
supplies of food and drink

proviso (prov-y-zoh) NOUN **provisos**
a condition insisted on in advance

provocative ADJECTIVE
likely to make someone angry

provoke VERB
1 to make a person angry
2 to cause or give rise to
provocation NOUN

prow NOUN
the front end of a ship

prowess NOUN
great ability or daring

prowl VERB
to move about quietly or cautiously
prowler NOUN

proximity NOUN
nearness

proxy NOUN **proxies**
a person authorized to act for another person

prude NOUN
a person who is easily shocked by things to do with sex
prudish ADJECTIVE

prudent ADJECTIVE
careful and cautious
prudence NOUN **prudently** ADVERB

prune [1] NOUN
a dried plum

prune [2] VERB
to cut off unwanted parts of a tree or bush etc.

pry VERB **pries**, **pried**
to look into or ask about someone else's private business

PS ABBREVIATION
postscript

psalm (sahm) NOUN
a religious song

pseudonym NOUN
a false name used by an author

psychedelic (sy-ker-**del**-ik) ADJECTIVE
having vivid colours and patterns

psychiatrist (sy-**ky**-a-trist) NOUN
a doctor who treats mental illnesses
psychiatric ADJECTIVE **psychiatry** NOUN

psychic (**sy**-kik) ADJECTIVE
1 supernatural
2 having the power to predict the future
3 to do with the mind or soul

psychoanalysis NOUN
investigation of a person's mental processes by psychotherapy
psychoanalyst NOUN

psychology NOUN
the study of the mind
psychological ADJECTIVE **psychologist** NOUN

psychotherapy NOUN
treatment of mental illness by psychological methods
psychotherapist NOUN

ptarmigan (**tar**-mig-an) NOUN
a bird of the grouse family

pterodactyl (te-ro-**dak**-til) NOUN
an extinct flying reptile

PTO ABBREVIATION
please turn over

pub NOUN
a building licensed to serve alcoholic drinks; a public house

puberty NOUN
the time when a young person is developing physically into an adult

pubic ADJECTIVE
to do with the lower front part of the abdomen

public ADJECTIVE
belonging to or known by people in general
publicly ADVERB

public NOUN
people in general

publican NOUN
the person in charge of a pub

publication NOUN
1 the process of publishing
2 a published book or newspaper etc.

public house NOUN
a building licensed to serve alcoholic drinks; a pub

publicity NOUN
advertising and other methods of bringing things to people's attention

publicize VERB
to bring something to people's attention; advertise

public school NOUN
a private school that charges fees

publish VERB
1 to have something printed and sold to the public
2 to announce in public
publisher NOUN

puce ADJECTIVE
of a brownish-purple colour

puck NOUN
a hard rubber disc used in ice hockey

pucker VERB
to wrinkle

pudding NOUN
1 the sweet course of a meal
2 a food made from suet and flour

puddle NOUN
a shallow patch of liquid on the ground

puerile ADJECTIVE
silly and childish

puff NOUN
1 a short blowing of breath, wind, or smoke etc.
2 a soft pad for putting powder on the skin
3 a cake of light pastry filled with cream

puff VERB
1 to blow out puffs of smoke etc.
2 to breathe with difficulty
3 to inflate or swell something

puffin NOUN
a seabird with a large striped beak

puffy ADJECTIVE **puffier, puffiest**
puffed out; swollen

pug NOUN
a small dog with a flat face like a bulldog

pugnacious ADJECTIVE
wanting to fight; aggressive

puke VERB
(informal) to vomit

pull VERB
1 to make a thing come towards you or after you
2 to move by a driving force The car pulled into the road.
pull in to move to the side of the road
pull off to achieve
pull NOUN

pullet NOUN
a young hen

pulley NOUN **pulleys**
a wheel with a rope, chain, or belt over it, used for lifting or moving loads

pullover NOUN
a knitted piece of clothing for the top half of the body

pulp NOUN
1 the soft moist part of fruit
2 any soft moist mass
pulpy ADJECTIVE

pulpit NOUN
a small enclosed platform for the preacher in a church

pulsate VERB
to expand and contract rhythmically
pulsation NOUN

pulse [1] NOUN
1 the rhythmical movement of the arteries as blood is pumped through them by the beating of the heart
2 a throb

pulse VERB
to throb or pulsate

pulse [2] NOUN
the edible seed of peas, beans, lentils, etc.

pulverize VERB
to crush into powder

puma NOUN
a large American brown cat

pumice NOUN
a kind of porous stone used as an abrasive especially for removing hard skin

pummel VERB **pummelling, pummelled**
to hit repeatedly with the fists

pump [1] NOUN
a machine that pushes air or liquid into or out of something, or along pipes

pump VERB
1 to move air or liquid with a pump
2 (informal) to question someone
pump up to inflate

pump [2] NOUN
a canvas sports shoe with a rubber sole

pumpkin NOUN
a large round fruit with a hard orange skin

pun NOUN
a joking use of a word sounding the same as another, e.g. 'When is coffee like earth? When it is ground.'

punch [1] VERB
1 to hit someone with your fist
2 to make a hole in something

punch NOUN
1 a hit with a fist
2 a device for making holes in paper, metal, leather, etc.
3 force or vigour

punch [2] NOUN
a drink made by mixing wine or spirits and fruit juice in a bowl

punchline NOUN
words that give the climax of a joke or story

punctilious *ADJECTIVE*
careful about correct behaviour and detail

punctual *ADJECTIVE*
doing things exactly at the time arranged
punctuality *NOUN* **punctually** *ADVERB*

punctuate *VERB*
1 to put punctuation marks into writing
2 to include or interrupt *a speech punctuated with cheers*

punctuation *NOUN*
marks such as commas, full stops, and brackets put into a piece of writing to make it easier to read

puncture *NOUN*
a small hole made by something sharp, especially in a tyre

puncture *VERB*
to make a puncture in

pundit *NOUN*
a person who is an authority on something

pungent (pun-jent) *ADJECTIVE*
having a strong taste or smell
pungency *NOUN*

punish *VERB*
to make a person suffer for doing wrong

punishment *NOUN*
1 the act of punishing
2 something suffered for doing wrong

punitive (pew-nit-iv) *ADJECTIVE*
inflicting or intended as a punishment

punk *NOUN*
1 a loud aggressive style of rock music
2 a person who listens to this music

punnet *NOUN*
a small container for soft fruit

punt¹ *NOUN*
a flat-bottomed boat, moved by pushing a pole against the bottom of a river

punt *VERB*
to travel in a punt

punt² *VERB*
to kick a football after dropping it from your hands and before it touches the ground

punter *NOUN*
1 a person who bets
2 (*informal*) a customer

puny *ADJECTIVE* **punier**, **puniest**
small and weak

pup *NOUN*
1 a puppy
2 a young seal

pupa *NOUN* **pupae**
a chrysalis

pupil *NOUN*
1 a person being taught, especially at school
2 the opening in the centre of the eyeball

puppet *NOUN*
1 a doll that can be made to move by fitting it over your hand or working it by strings or wires
2 a person whose actions are controlled by someone else

puppy *NOUN* **puppies**
a young dog

purchase *VERB*
to buy
purchaser *NOUN*

purchase *NOUN*
1 something that is bought
2 the act of buying
3 a firm hold or grip

purdah *NOUN*
the Muslim or Hindu custom of keeping women from the sight of men or strangers

pure *ADJECTIVE*
1 not mixed with anything else *pure gold*
2 clean or clear *pure spring water*
3 free from evil or sin
4 mere; nothing but *pure nonsense*
purely *ADVERB*

purgatory *NOUN*
1 (in Roman Catholic belief) a place in which souls are purified by punishment before they can enter heaven
2 a state of temporary suffering

purge *VERB*
to get rid of unwanted people or things

purge *NOUN*
an act of purging

purify *VERB* **purifies**, **purified**
to make pure
purification *NOUN*

purist *NOUN*
a person who insists on correctness, especially in language

Puritan *NOUN*
a Protestant in the 16th and 17th centuries who wanted simpler religious ceremonies and strictly moral behaviour

puritan *NOUN*
a person with strict morals
puritanical *ADJECTIVE*

purity *NOUN*
a pure state

purl *VERB*
to knit with a stitch that makes a ridge towards the person knitting
purl *NOUN*

purloin *VERB*
(*formal*) to steal

purple *ADJECTIVE*
of a deep reddish-blue colour

purport (per-port) *VERB*
to claim *a letter purporting to be from the council*

purpose *NOUN*
1 what you intend to do; a plan or aim
2 determination
on purpose deliberately

purposeful *ADJECTIVE*
determined
purposefully *ADVERB*

purposely *ADVERB*
on purpose

purr *VERB*
to make the low murmuring sound that a cat makes when pleased
purr *NOUN*

purse *NOUN*
1 a small pouch for carrying money
2 (*American*) a handbag

purse *VERB*
to draw your lips tightly together in disapproval

purser *NOUN*
a ship's officer in charge of accounts

pursue *VERB*
1 to chase someone in order to catch them
2 to continue with or work at *to pursue a career*
pursuer *NOUN*

pursuit *NOUN*
1 the act of pursuing
2 a regular activity

purvey *VERB*
(*formal*) to supply food etc. as a trade
purveyor *NOUN*

pus *NOUN*
a thick yellowish substance produced in infected tissue, e.g. in an abscess or boil

push *VERB*
1 to make a thing go away from you
2 to move yourself by using force *pushed in front of us*
3 to try to force someone to do or use something
push *NOUN*
a pushing movement or effort

pushchair *NOUN*
a folding chair on wheels, for a young child to be pushed in

pushy *ADJECTIVE* **pushier**, **pushiest**
unpleasantly assertive and eager

puss or **pussy** *NOUN* **pusses** or **pussies**
(*informal*) a cat

pussyfoot *VERB*
to act too cautiously and timidly

put *VERB* **putting**, **put**
This word has many uses, including
1 to move a person or thing to a place or position
2 to make a person or thing do or experience something or be in a certain condition *put the light on   put me in a good mood*
3 to express in words *Try to put it tactfully.*
put off to postpone   **put up** to construct or build   **put up with** to tolerate

putrid (pew-trid) *ADJECTIVE*
rotting and stinking

putt *VERB*
to hit a golf ball gently towards the hole
putt *NOUN*

putty *NOUN*
a soft paste that sets hard, used for fitting glass into windows

puzzle *NOUN*
1 a difficult question or problem
2 a game or toy that sets a problem to solve

puzzle *VERB*
1 to make someone confused by something that is difficult to understand
2 to think patiently about how to solve something
puzzled *ADJECTIVE* **puzzlement** *NOUN*

PVC *ABBREVIATION*
polyvinyl chloride, a plastic used to make clothing, pipes, flooring, etc.

pygmy (pig-mee) *NOUN* **pygmies**
1 a very small person or thing
2 a member of certain unusually short peoples of equatorial Africa

pyjamas *PLURAL NOUN*
a loose jacket and trousers worn in bed

pylon *NOUN*
a tall steel framework supporting electric cables

pyramid *NOUN*
1 a structure with a square base and with sloping sides that meet in a point at the top
2 an ancient Egyptian tomb shaped like this

pyre *NOUN*
a pile of wood for burning a dead body as part of a funeral ceremony

python *NOUN*
a large snake that kills its prey by crushing it

a b c d e f g h i j k l m n o **p** q r s t u v w x y z

Qq

quack *VERB*
to make the harsh cry of a duck
quack *NOUN*

quad (kwod) *NOUN*
1 a quadrangle
2 a quadruplet

quadrangle *NOUN*
a rectangular courtyard with buildings
round it

quadrant *NOUN*
a quarter of a circle

quadrilateral *NOUN*
a flat geometric shape with four sides

quadruped *NOUN*
an animal with four feet

quadruple *ADJECTIVE*
1 four times as much or as many
2 having four parts

quadruple *VERB*
to make or become four times as much
or as many

quadruplet *NOUN*
each of four children born to the same
mother at one time

quaff (kwof) *VERB*
to drink eagerly

quagmire *NOUN*
a bog or marsh

quail[1] *NOUN*
a bird related to the partridge

quail[2] *VERB*
to feel or show fear

quaint *ADJECTIVE*
attractively odd or old-fashioned

quake *VERB*
to tremble; to shake with fear

quake *NOUN*
an earthquake

Quaker *NOUN*
a member of a religious group called
the Society of Friends, founded in the
17th century

qualification *NOUN*
1 a skill or ability that makes someone
suitable for a job
2 a statement that qualifies

qualify *VERB* **qualifies, qualified**
1 to make or become able to do something
2 to make a remark or statement less extreme
3 (of an adjective) to add meaning to a noun
qualified *ADJECTIVE*

quality *NOUN* **qualities**
1 the degree of goodness or worth
2 something special in a person or thing

qualm (kwahm) *NOUN*
a doubt about whether something you have
done is fair or right

quandary *NOUN* **quandaries**
a difficult situation or decision

quantify *VERB* **quantifies, quantified**
to describe or express as an amount or a
number

quantity *NOUN* **quantities**
1 the amount there is of something
2 a large amount

quantum *NOUN*
a quantity or amount

quantum leap or **quantum jump**
NOUN
a sudden large increase or advance

quarantine *NOUN*
the process of keeping a person or animal
isolated in case they have a disease

quarrel *NOUN*
an angry disagreement

quarrel *VERB* **quarrelling, quarrelled**
to have a quarrel

quarrelsome *ADJECTIVE*
fond of quarrelling

quarry[1] *NOUN* **quarries**
an open place where stone for building is
taken from the ground

quarry *VERB* **quarries, quarried**
to dig from a quarry

quarry[2] *NOUN* **quarries**
a hunted animal

quart *NOUN*
two pints (1.13 litres)

quarter *NOUN*
1 each of four equal parts of a thing
2 three months, one-fourth of a year
3 a district or region
at close quarters very close together

quarter *VERB*
1 to divide into quarters
2 to put soldiers etc. into lodgings

quarter-final *NOUN*
each of the matches or rounds before a
semi-final
quarter-finalist *NOUN*

quarterly *ADJECTIVE, ADVERB*
happening or produced once every three
months

quarterly *NOUN* **quarterlies**
a quarterly magazine

quarters *PLURAL NOUN*
lodgings

quartet *NOUN*
1 a group of four musicians
2 a piece of music for four musicians

quartz *NOUN*
a hard mineral, often in crystal form

quasar *NOUN*
a huge remote star in the sky

quash *VERB*
1 to cancel or annul a previous decision
2 to crush a rebellion

quaver *VERB*
to tremble or quiver

quaver *NOUN*
1 a quavering sound
2 a note in music (♪) lasting half as long as a crotchet

quay (kee) *NOUN*
a landing place for loading and unloading ships

queasy *ADJECTIVE* **queasier, queasiest**
feeling slightly sick
queasiness *NOUN*

queen *NOUN*
1 a country's female ruler who reigns because of her birth
2 the wife of a king
3 a female bee or ant that produces eggs
4 the most powerful piece in chess
5 a playing card with a picture of a queen
queenship *NOUN*

queen mother *NOUN*
a king's widow who is the mother of the present king or queen

queer *ADJECTIVE*
1 strange or eccentric
2 slightly ill or faint
queerly *ADVERB* **queerness** *NOUN*

quell *VERB*
1 to crush a rebellion
2 to resist feeling fear, anger, etc.

quench *VERB*
1 to satisfy your thirst by drinking
2 to put out a fire or flame

query *NOUN* **queries**
1 a question
2 a question mark

query *VERB* **queries, queried**
to question whether something is true or correct

quest *NOUN*
a long search for something

question *NOUN*
1 a sentence that asks something or needs an answer
2 a problem or matter to be discussed
3 a matter that may be doubted *no question of any refund*
out of the question impossible

question *VERB*
1 to ask someone questions
2 to express doubt about something
questioner *NOUN*

questionable *ADJECTIVE*
causing doubt; not certainly true or honest or advisable

question mark *NOUN*
the punctuation mark (?) placed after a question

questionnaire *NOUN*
a written set of questions answered by a number of people to provide information for a survey

queue (kew) *NOUN*
a line of waiting people or vehicles

queue *VERB* **queues, queueing, queued**
to wait in a queue

quibble *NOUN*
a trivial objection

quibble *VERB*
to make trivial objections

quiche (keesh) *NOUN*
an open tart with a savoury filling

quick *ADJECTIVE*
1 taking or needing only a short time
2 done in a short time
3 able to notice or learn or think quickly
quickly *ADVERB*

quicken *VERB*
to make or become quicker

quicksand *NOUN*
an area of loose wet deep sand that sucks in anything resting or falling on top of it

quicksilver *NOUN*
mercury

quid *NOUN*
(*informal*) a pound in money

quiet *ADJECTIVE*
1 not making any sound or noise
2 calm and peaceful
quietly *ADVERB* **quietness** *NOUN*

quiet *NOUN*
quietness

quieten *VERB*
to make or become quiet

quiff *NOUN*
an upright tuft of hair

quill *NOUN*
1 a pen made from a large feather
2 one of the spines of a hedgehog or porcupine

quilt *NOUN*
a padded cover for a bed

quilted ADJECTIVE
having a layer of padding fitted with lines of stitching

quin NOUN
a quintuplet

quince NOUN
a hard pear-shaped fruit used for making jam

quinine (kwin-**een**) NOUN
a bitter-tasting medicine used to cure malaria

quintessential ADJECTIVE
most essential or necessary

quintet NOUN
1 a group of five musicians
2 a piece of music for five musicians

quintuplet NOUN
each of five children born to the same mother at one time

quip NOUN
a witty remark

quirk NOUN
1 a peculiarity of a person's behaviour
2 an odd thing that happens by chance
quirky ADJECTIVE

quit VERB **quitting**, **quitted** or **quit**
1 to leave or abandon
2 (informal) to stop doing something

quite ADVERB
1 completely or entirely
2 somewhat; to some extent

quits ADJECTIVE
even or equal after paying someone back

quiver[1] VERB
to tremble
quiver NOUN

quiver[2] NOUN
a container for arrows

quiz NOUN
a competition in which people answer questions

quiz VERB **quizzes**, **quizzing**, **quizzed**
to question someone closely

quizzical ADJECTIVE
1 in a questioning way
2 gently amused
quizzically ADVERB

quota NOUN
a fixed share that must be given or received by each in a group

quotation NOUN
1 the act of quoting
2 something quoted
3 a statement of a price

quotation marks PLURAL NOUN
inverted commas (' ' or " "), used to mark a quotation

quote VERB
1 to repeat words first written or spoken by someone else
2 to state a price

quote NOUN
a quotation

quotient (**kwoh**-shuhnt) NOUN
the result of dividing one number by another

Rr

rabbi NOUN **rabbis**
a Jewish religious leader

rabbit NOUN
a furry burrowing animal with long ears

rabble NOUN
a disorderly crowd or mob

rabid ADJECTIVE
suffering from rabies

rabies NOUN
a fatal disease that can be passed to humans by the bite of an infected dog or other animal

raccoon NOUN
a furry North American animal with a bushy striped tail

race[1] NOUN
a competition to be the first or fastest

race VERB
1 to compete in a race
2 to move fast
racer NOUN

race[2] NOUN
a large group of people having the same ancestors and physical characteristics

racecourse NOUN
a place where horse races are run

racehorse NOUN
a horse bred or kept for racing

racetrack NOUN
a track for horse or vehicle races

racial (ray-shul) ADJECTIVE
to do with the races of the world
racially ADVERB

racism or **racialism** NOUN
1 belief that a particular race is superior to others
2 discrimination against people because of their race
racist or **racialist** NOUN

rack [1] *NOUN*
1 a framework used as a shelf or container
2 a former device for torturing people by stretching them

rack *VERB*
to torment *was racked with guilt*
rack your brains to think hard to solve a problem

rack [2] *NOUN*
go to rack and ruin to become gradually worse from neglect

racket [1] *NOUN*
a bat with strings stretched across a frame, used in tennis etc.

racket [2] *NOUN*
1 a loud noise or din
2 a dishonest or illegal business

racketeer *NOUN*
a person involved in a dishonest or illegal business
racketeering *NOUN*

racoon *NOUN*
another spelling of **raccoon**

racquet *NOUN*
another spelling of **racket** [1]

racy *ADJECTIVE* **racier, raciest**
lively and slightly shocking in style

radar *NOUN*
a system that uses radio waves to show the position of objects that cannot be seen because of darkness, fog, distance, etc.

radial *ADJECTIVE*
1 to do with rays or radii
2 having spokes or lines that radiate from a central point
radially *ADVERB*

radiant *ADJECTIVE*
1 radiating light or heat etc.
2 (of heat) radiated
3 looking bright and happy
radiance *NOUN* **radiantly** *ADVERB*

radiate *VERB*
1 to send out energy in rays
2 to give out a strong feeling or quality *radiated confidence*
3 to spread out from a central point

radiation *NOUN*
1 light, heat, or other energy radiated
2 the energy or particles sent out by a radioactive substance

radiator *NOUN*
1 a metal case that is heated electrically or by hot water
2 a device that cools the engine of a motor vehicle

radical *ADJECTIVE*
1 basic and thorough *radical changes*
2 wanting to make great reforms *a radical politician*
radically *ADVERB*

radical *NOUN*
a person who wants to make great reforms

radicle *NOUN*
a root that forms in the seed of a plant

radio *NOUN* **radios**
1 the process of sending and receiving sound or pictures by means of electromagnetic waves
2 an apparatus for receiving or transmitting sound in this way
3 the activity of sound broadcasting

radio *VERB* **radios, radioing, radioed**
to send a message to someone by radio

radioactive *ADJECTIVE*
having atoms that send out radiation
radioactivity *NOUN*

radiology *NOUN*
the study of X-rays and similar radiation, especially in treating diseases
radiologist *NOUN*

radiotherapy *NOUN*
the use of radioactive substances in treating diseases

radish *NOUN*
a small hard round red vegetable, eaten raw in salads

radium *NOUN*
a radioactive substance used in radiotherapy

radius *NOUN* **radii** or **radiuses**
1 a straight line from the centre of a circle or sphere to the circumference
2 a range or distance from a central point

radon *NOUN*
a radioactive gas used in radiotherapy

raffia *NOUN*
soft fibre from the leaves of a palm tree

raffle *NOUN*
a kind of lottery, usually to raise money for a charity

raffle *VERB*
to offer something as a prize in a raffle

raft *NOUN*
a row of logs or planks tied together and used as a flat boat

rafter *NOUN*
each of the sloping beams that help to hold up a roof

a b c d e f g h i j k l m n o p q **r** s t u v w x y z

rag NOUN
an old or torn piece of cloth
in rags wearing old and torn clothes

rage NOUN
great or violent anger
all the rage fashionable for a short time

rage VERB
1 to be fiercely angry
2 to continue with great force *A storm was raging.*

ragged ADJECTIVE
1 torn or frayed
2 wearing torn clothes

ragtime NOUN
a kind of jazz music

raid NOUN
1 a sudden attack
2 a surprise visit by police to discover criminal activity

raid VERB
to make a raid on a place
raider NOUN

rail¹ NOUN
1 a bar for hanging things on or forming part of a fence etc.
2 a long metal bar forming part of a railway track
by rail on a train

rail² VERB
to protest angrily or bitterly

railings PLURAL NOUN
a fence made of metal bars

railroad NOUN
(*American*) a railway

railway NOUN
1 a track of parallel metal bars for trains to travel on
2 a system of transport using rails

raiment NOUN
(*old use*) clothing

rain NOUN
drops of water that fall from the sky
rainy ADJECTIVE

rain VERB
1 to fall as rain
2 to send down like rain *rained blows on them*

rainbow NOUN
an arch of all the colours of the spectrum formed in the sky when the sun shines through rain

raincoat NOUN
a waterproof coat

raindrop NOUN
a single drop of rain

rainfall NOUN
the amount of rain that falls in a particular place or time

rainforest NOUN
a dense tropical forest in an area of heavy rainfall

raise VERB
1 to move something to a higher place or an upright position
2 to increase the amount or level of
3 to collect
4 to bring up young children or animals
5 to rouse or cause *raised a laugh with his joke*
6 to put forward *raised objections*

raisin NOUN
a dried grape

raja NOUN
an Indian king or prince

rake NOUN
a gardening tool with a row of short spikes fixed to a long handle, used for gathering leaves or smoothing earth

rake VERB
1 to gather or smooth with a rake
2 to search
rake up 1 collect 2 to remind people of unpleasant or embarrassing events in the past

rally NOUN **rallies**
1 a large meeting to support a cause or share an interest
2 a competition in driving
3 a series of strokes in tennis before a point is scored
4 a recovery

rally VERB **rallies, rallied**
1 to bring or come together for a united effort
2 to recover strength

RAM ABBREVIATION
(*ICT*) random-access memory, with contents that a system can access directly without having to read through a sequence of items

ram NOUN
1 a male sheep
2 a device for ramming things

ram VERB **ramming, rammed**
to push one thing hard against another

Ramadan NOUN
the ninth month of the Muslim year, with strict fasting during the day

ramble NOUN
a long walk in the country

ramble VERB
1 to go for a ramble
2 to speak or write aimlessly
rambler NOUN

ramifications PLURAL NOUN
the many effects of a plan or action

ramp NOUN
a slope joining two different levels

rampage VERB
to rush about or attack violently

rampage NOUN
on the rampage behaving in a wild and violent way

rampant ADJECTIVE
growing or spreading uncontrollably
rampant disease

rampart NOUN
a bank of earth or a wall built as a fortification

ramshackle ADJECTIVE
badly made and rickety

ranch NOUN
a large cattle farm in America

rancid ADJECTIVE
smelling or tasting unpleasantly stale

rancour NOUN
bitter resentment or hatred
rancorous ADJECTIVE

random NOUN
at random using no particular order or method

random ADJECTIVE
done or taken at random *a random sample*
randomly ADVERB

range NOUN
1 a set of different things of the same type
a wide range of backgrounds
2 the limits between which something varies
an age range of 15 to 18
3 the distance that a gun can shoot, an aircraft can travel, a sound can be heard, etc.
4 a place with targets for shooting practice
5 a line or series of mountains or hills
6 a large open area of grazing land or hunting ground
7 a kitchen fireplace with ovens

range VERB
1 to exist between two limits
2 to arrange
3 to move over a wide area

Ranger NOUN
a senior Guide

ranger NOUN
a keeper who patrols a park, forest, etc.

rani or **ranee** (**rah**-nee) NOUN
a rajah's wife or widow

rank [1] NOUN
1 a line of people or things
2 a place where taxis wait
3 a position in a series of different levels
the rank of sergeant

rank VERB
1 to put things in order according to their rank
2 to have a certain rank or place
ranks among the greatest writers

rank [2] ADJECTIVE
1 growing too thickly and coarsely
2 smelling very unpleasant
3 unmistakably bad *rank injustice*

rank and file NOUN
the ordinary people or soldiers, not the leaders

rankle VERB
to cause lasting annoyance or resentment

ransack VERB
1 to search thoroughly or roughly
2 to rob or pillage a place

ransom NOUN
money that has to be paid for a prisoner to be set free

ransom VERB
to free a prisoner by paying a ransom

rant VERB
to speak loudly and violently

rap VERB **rapping**, **rapped**
to knock loudly

rap NOUN
1 a rapping movement or sound
2 (*informal*) blame or punishment
3 rhymes spoken with a backing of rock music
rapper NOUN

rape [1] NOUN
the act of having sexual intercourse with someone by force

rape VERB
to force someone to have sexual intercourse
rapist NOUN

rape [2] NOUN
a plant with bright yellow flowers, grown as food for sheep and for the oil obtained from its seed

rapid ADJECTIVE
moving very quickly; swift
rapidly ADVERB

rapidity NOUN
great speed

rapids PLURAL NOUN
part of a river where the water flows swiftly

rapier NOUN
a thin lightweight sword

rapport (rap-**or**) NOUN
a good relationship between people

rapt ADJECTIVE
intent and absorbed; enraptured
raptly ADVERB

rapture NOUN
very great delight
rapturous ADJECTIVE

rare ADJECTIVE **rarer**, **rarest**
1 not often found or happening
2 (of air) thin and below normal pressure
3 (of meat) only lightly cooked
rarely ADVERB **rareness** NOUN

rarity NOUN **rarities**
1 the state of being rare
2 something unusual or rare

rascal NOUN
a dishonest or mischievous person
rascally ADJECTIVE

rash [1] ADJECTIVE
acting or done regardless of the possible risks
or effects
rashly ADVERB

rash [2] NOUN
1 an outbreak of spots or patches on the skin
2 a number of unwelcome events in a short
time *a rash of accidents*

rasher NOUN
a thin slice of bacon

rasp NOUN
1 a file with sharp points on its surface
2 a rough grating sound

rasp VERB
1 to scrape roughly
2 to make a rough grating sound or effect

raspberry NOUN **raspberries**
a small soft red fruit

rat NOUN
1 an animal like a large mouse
2 an unpleasant or treacherous person

ratchet NOUN
a row of notches on a bar or wheel in which a
device catches to prevent it running
backwards

rate NOUN
1 speed
2 a measure of cost, value, etc. *postage rates*
3 quality or standard *first-rate*
at any rate anyway

rate VERB
1 to put a value on
2 to regard as *rated me among their friends*

rates PLURAL NOUN
a local tax paid by owners of commercial land
and buildings

rather ADVERB
1 slightly or somewhat
2 more willingly *would rather not go*
3 more exactly; instead of *is lazy rather than
stupid*

ratify VERB **ratifies**, **ratified**
to confirm or agree to something officially
ratification NOUN

rating NOUN
1 the way something is rated
2 a sailor who is not an officer

ratio NOUN **ratios**
the relationship between two numbers or
amounts

ration NOUN
an amount allowed to one person

ration VERB
to share out in fixed amounts

rational ADJECTIVE
1 reasonable or sane
2 able to reason
rationally ADVERB

rationale (rash-uhn-**ahl**) NOUN
the reasons which explain a decision,
belief, etc.

rationalize VERB
1 to make logical and consistent
2 to justify something by inventing a
reasonable explanation
3 to reorganize and make more efficient
rationalization NOUN

rations PLURAL NOUN
a fixed daily amount of food issued to
a soldier etc.

rat race NOUN
a continuous struggle for success in a career,
business, etc.

rattle VERB
1 to make a series of short sharp hard sounds
2 to make a person nervous or flustered
rattle off to say or recite rapidly

rattle NOUN
1 a rattling sound
2 a device or toy that rattles

rattlesnake NOUN
a poisonous American snake with a tail that
rattles

ratty ADJECTIVE **rattier**, **rattiest**
(*informal*) irritable

raucous (**raw**-kus) ADJECTIVE
loud and harsh

ravage VERB
to do great damage to an area

ravages PLURAL NOUN
damaging effects

rave VERB
1 to talk wildly or angrily
2 to talk enthusiastically

rave NOUN
(*informal*) a large party or event with dancing
to loud electronic music

raven NOUN
a large black bird, related to the crow

ravenous ADJECTIVE
very hungry
ravenously ADVERB

ravine NOUN
a deep narrow gorge or valley

raving ADJECTIVE
mad; crazy

ravishing ADJECTIVE
very beautiful

raw ADJECTIVE
1 not cooked
2 in the natural state; not yet processed
3 lacking experience　*raw recruits*
4 with the skin removed　*a raw wound*
5 cold and damp　*a raw morning*

raw deal NOUN
unfair treatment

raw material NOUN
natural substances used in industry

ray [1] NOUN
1 a thin line of light, heat, or other radiation
2 each of a set of lines or parts extending from
a centre
3 a trace of something　*a ray of hope*

ray [2] NOUN
a large sea fish with a flat body and a long tail

rayon NOUN
a synthetic fibre or cloth made from cellulose

raze VERB
to destroy a building or town completely

razor NOUN
a device with a sharp blade used for shaving

reach VERB
1 to go as far as; to arrive at a place or thing
2 to stretch out your hand to get or touch
something
3 to succeed in achieving something

reach NOUN
1 the distance a person or thing can reach
2 a distance you can easily travel　*within
reach of the sea*

react VERB
1 to respond to something; to have a reaction
2 to undergo a chemical change

reaction NOUN
1 an effect or feeling produced in one person
or thing by another
2 a chemical change
reactions the ability to move in response to
something　*quick reactions*

reactionary ADJECTIVE
opposed to progress or reform

reactor NOUN
an apparatus for the controlled production of
nuclear power

read VERB　read (*say as* red)
1 to look at something written or printed and
understand it or say it aloud
2 (of a computer) to copy, search, or extract
data
3 to indicate or register　*The thermometer
reads 20°.*
4 to study a subject at university
readable ADJECTIVE

reader NOUN
1 a person who reads
2 a book that helps you learn to read

readily (red-il-ee) ADVERB
1 willingly
2 easily; without any difficulty

reading NOUN
1 the activity of reading books
2 the figure shown on a meter or gauge etc.

ready ADJECTIVE　readier, readiest
1 fully prepared or willing
2 available to be used
3 quick or prompt
at the ready ready for use or action
readiness NOUN

reagent NOUN
a substance used in a chemical reaction

real ADJECTIVE
1 existing or true
2 genuine　*real pearls*

real estate NOUN
(*American*) property consisting of land and
buildings

realism NOUN
the seeing or showing of things as they really
are
realist NOUN

realistic ADJECTIVE
1 true to life
2 seeing things as they really are
realistically ADVERB

reality NOUN　realities
1 what is real　*to face reality*
2 something real　*the realities of the situation*

realize VERB
1 to be fully aware of something
2 to make a hope or plan etc. happen　*realized
her ambition*
realization NOUN

really ADVERB
1 truly or in fact
2 very　*is really clever*

realm (relm) NOUN
1 a kingdom
2 an area of knowledge, interest, etc.

reams PLURAL NOUN
a large quantity of writing

reap VERB
1 to cut down and gather corn when it is ripe
2 to obtain as the result of something done *reaped great benefit*
reaper NOUN

reappear VERB
to appear again

rear[1] NOUN
the back part

rear ADJECTIVE
placed at the rear

rear[2] VERB
1 to bring up children or animals
2 (of an animal) to rise on its hind legs

rearguard NOUN
troops protecting the rear of an army

rearrange VERB
to arrange in a different way or order
rearrangement NOUN

reason NOUN
1 a cause or explanation
2 reasoning or common sense

reason VERB
1 to think and draw conclusions
2 to try to persuade by giving reasons

reasonable ADJECTIVE
1 sensible or logical
2 fair or moderate *reasonable prices*
3 fairly good *a reasonable standard of living*
reasonably ADVERB

reassure VERB
to restore someone's confidence by removing doubts and fears
reassurance NOUN

rebate NOUN
a reduction in the amount to be paid; a partial refund

rebel (rib-el) VERB **rebelling, rebelled**
to fight against the people in power

rebel (reb-el) NOUN
1 someone who rebels against the people in power
2 someone who rejects normal social conventions

rebellion NOUN
1 refusal to obey
2 an organized armed resistance to the people in power

rebellious ADJECTIVE
refusing to obey authority

rebound VERB
to bounce back after hitting something
rebound NOUN

rebuff NOUN
an unkind refusal or snub

rebuff VERB
to snub

rebuild VERB **rebuilt**
to build something again after it has been destroyed

rebuke VERB
to speak severely to a person who has done wrong
rebuke NOUN

rebut VERB **rebutting, rebutted**
to reject an accusation or criticism
rebuttal NOUN

recalcitrant ADJECTIVE
disobedient or uncooperative
recalcitrance NOUN

recall (ri-kawl) VERB
1 to bring back into the mind
2 to ask for something to be returned

recall (ree-kawl) NOUN
1 the ability to remember
2 an order to return something

recap VERB **recapping, recapped**
(*informal*) to recapitulate
recap NOUN

recapitulate VERB
to state again the main points of what has been said
recapitulation NOUN

recapture VERB
1 to capture again
2 to experience again a mood or feeling
recapture NOUN

recede VERB
1 to go back from a certain point
2 (of a man's hair) to stop growing at the front of the head

receipt (ris-eet) NOUN
1 a written statement for money paid or something received
2 the act of receiving something

receive VERB
1 to take or get something that is given or sent to you
2 to experience something
3 to greet someone who comes

receiver NOUN
1 an apparatus for receiving radio and television broadcasts
2 the part of a telephone used for speaking and listening

recent ADJECTIVE
happening or made or done a short time ago
recently ADVERB

receptacle NOUN
something for holding things; a container

reception NOUN
1 the way a person or thing is received
2 a formal party to receive guests
3 a place in a hotel or office where visitors are greeted
4 the quality of television or radio signals

receptionist NOUN
a person who greets and deals with visitors, clients, etc.

receptive ADJECTIVE
quick or willing to consider ideas etc.

recess NOUN
1 an alcove
2 a pause in work or business

recession NOUN
1 a reduction in a country's trade or prosperity
2 the act of moving back

recipe (ress-ip-ee) NOUN
a set of instructions for preparing or cooking food

recipient NOUN
a person who receives something

reciprocal (ris-ip-rok-al) ADJECTIVE
given and received *reciprocal help*

reciprocal NOUN
a reversed fraction *³/₂ is the reciprocal of ²/₃* .

reciprocate VERB
to do or feel the same thing in return

recital NOUN
1 the act of reciting
2 a musical entertainment by one performer or group

recite VERB
to say aloud from memory
recitation NOUN

reckless ADJECTIVE
carelessly ignoring danger
recklessly ADVERB

reckon VERB
1 to calculate or count up
2 to have as an opinion
reckon with to take into account *didn't reckon with a rail strike*

reclaim VERB
1 to claim or get back
2 to make usable again *reclaimed land*
reclamation NOUN

recline VERB
to lean or lie back

recluse NOUN
a person who lives alone and avoids company
reclusive ADJECTIVE

recognition NOUN
1 the act of recognizing
2 acceptance as genuine or lawful

recognize VERB
1 to know a person or thing from before
2 to realize
3 to accept as genuine or lawful
recognizable ADJECTIVE

recoil VERB
1 to move back suddenly in shock or disgust
2 (of a gun) to jerk back when fired

recollect VERB
to remember
recollection NOUN

recommend VERB
1 to speak well of a person or thing
2 to advise a course of action
recommendation NOUN

recompense VERB
to repay or reward
recompense NOUN

reconcile VERB
1 to make people friendly again after a quarrel
2 to make things agree
be reconciled to to be willing to accept an unwelcome situation
reconciliation NOUN

recondition VERB
to overhaul and repair

reconnaissance (rik-on-i-sans) NOUN
a survey of an area to gather information for military purposes

reconnoitre VERB
to make a reconnaissance of an area

reconsider VERB
to consider something again and perhaps change an earlier decision
reconsideration NOUN

reconstitute VERB
to form something again or differently

reconstruct VERB
1 to construct or build again
2 to create or act out past events again
reconstruction NOUN

record (rek-ord) NOUN
1 a written or printed piece of information kept for the future
2 a disc on which sound has been recorded
3 the best performance in a sport etc.
4 facts known about a person's past life or career etc.

record (rik-ord) VERB
1 to put down in writing or other permanent form
2 to store sounds or pictures on a disc or magnetic tape etc. for replaying in the future

recorder *NOUN*
1 a kind of flute held downwards from the player's mouth
2 a person or thing that records something

recount[1] (ri-**kownt**) *VERB*
to give an account of

recount[2] (ree-**kownt**) *VERB*
to count again
recount *NOUN*

recoup (ri-**koop**) *VERB*
to recover the cost of an investment etc. or of a loss

recourse *NOUN*
a source of help
have recourse to to go to a person or thing for help

recover *VERB*
1 to get something back after losing it
2 to get well again after an illness or injury

recovery *NOUN* **recoveries**
1 the act of recovering something
2 a return to normal health or strength

recreation *NOUN*
1 enjoyable activity done in spare time
2 a game or hobby etc.
recreational *ADJECTIVE*

recrimination *NOUN*
an accusation made against a person who has accused you of something

recruit *NOUN*
a new soldier or member
recruit *VERB*
to enlist as a recruit
recruitment *NOUN*

rectangle *NOUN*
a shape with four sides and four right angles, usually longer than it is wide
rectangular *ADJECTIVE*

rectify *VERB* **rectifies**, **rectified**
to correct or put right
rectification *NOUN*

rectitude *NOUN*
moral goodness; honest or straightforward behaviour

rector *NOUN*
a member of the Church of England clergy in charge of a parish

rectum *NOUN*
the last part of the large intestine, ending at the anus

recuperate *VERB*
to recover after an illness
recuperation *NOUN*

recur *VERB* **recurring**, **recurred**
to happen again
recurrence *NOUN*

recurrent *ADJECTIVE*
happening often or regularly

recurring decimal *NOUN*
(*Maths*) a decimal fraction in which a digit or group of digits is repeated indefinitely, e.g. 0.666 ...

recycle *VERB*
to convert waste material into a form in which it can be used again

red *ADJECTIVE* **redder**, **reddest**
of the colour of blood or a colour rather like this
redness *NOUN*
red *NOUN*
a red colour
in the red in debt **see red** to become angry

redden *VERB*
to make or become red

reddish *ADJECTIVE*
rather red

redeem *VERB*
1 to make up for faults
2 to buy something back or pay off a debt
3 to save a person from damnation
redeemer *NOUN* **redemption** *NOUN*

red-handed *ADJECTIVE*
catch red-handed to catch someone in the act of committing a crime

redhead *NOUN*
a person with reddish hair

red herring *NOUN*
something that draws attention away from the main subject; a misleading clue

red-hot *ADJECTIVE*
very hot; so hot that it has turned red

redolent (**red**-ol-ent) *ADJECTIVE*
1 having a strong smell *redolent of onions*
2 strongly reminding you of something *redolent of romance*

redoubtable *ADJECTIVE*
brave; formidable

redress *VERB*
to put right a situation that is wrong or unfair
redress *NOUN*
1 the act of setting right
2 compensation

red tape *NOUN*
use of too many rules and forms in official business

reduce *VERB*
1 to make or become smaller or less
2 to force someone into a condition or situation *was reduced to borrowing*

reduction *NOUN*
1 the process of reducing
2 the amount by which something is reduced

redundant *ADJECTIVE*
not needed, especially for a particular job
redundancy *NOUN*

reed *NOUN*
1 a tall plant that grows in water or marshy ground
2 a thin strip that vibrates to make the sound in a clarinet or other wind instrument

reedy *ADJECTIVE* **reedier**, **reediest**
1 full of reeds
2 (of a voice) having a thin high tone

reef[1] *NOUN*
a ridge of rock, coral, or sand near the surface of the sea

reef[2] *VERB*
to shorten a sail by drawing in a strip (called a **reef**) at the top or bottom to reduce the area exposed to the wind

reef knot *NOUN*
a symmetrical secure double knot

reek *VERB*
to smell strongly or unpleasantly
reek *NOUN*

reel *NOUN*
1 a round device on which cotton, thread, film, etc. is wound
2 a lively Scottish dance

reel *VERB*
1 to wind something on or off a reel
2 to stagger
3 to feel giddy or confused
reel off to say something quickly

ref *NOUN*
(*informal*) a referee

refer *VERB* **referring**, **referred**
to pass a problem etc. to someone else
refer to 1 to mention or speak about 2 to look in a book etc. for information
referral *NOUN*

referee *NOUN*
1 an official who ensures that players obey the rules of a game
2 someone willing to write in support of a candidate for a job

referee *VERB*
to act as a referee

reference *NOUN*
1 the act of referring to something
2 a direction to information in a book
3 a supporting letter from a previous employer
in or **with reference to** concerning or about

reference book *NOUN*
a book (e.g. encyclopedia) that gives information

referendum *NOUN* **referendums** or **referenda**
a vote on a particular question by all the people of a country

refill *VERB*
to fill again

refill *NOUN*
a container of a substance needed to refill something

refine *VERB*
1 to purify
2 to improve something with small changes

refined *ADJECTIVE*
1 purified
2 having good taste or manners

refinement *NOUN*
1 the action of refining
2 good taste or manners
3 an improvement

refinery *NOUN* **refineries**
a factory for refining something *an oil refinery*

reflect *VERB*
1 to send back light, heat, or sound etc. from a surface
2 (of a mirror) to form an image of
3 to think something over
4 to be a sign of something

reflection *NOUN*
1 the process of reflecting
2 an image reflected, e.g. in a mirror

reflective *ADJECTIVE*
thoughtful

reflector *NOUN*
a device or surface that reflects light

reflex *NOUN*
a movement or action done without any conscious thought

reflex angle *NOUN*
an angle of more than 180°

reflexive pronoun *NOUN*
(*Grammar*) any of the pronouns *myself*, *herself*, *himself*, etc., which refer back to the subject of a verb

reform *VERB*
1 to make changes in something to improve it
2 to give up bad habits or practices
reformer *NOUN*

reform *NOUN*
1 the process of reforming
2 a change or improvement

reformation NOUN
the act of reforming
the Reformation a 16th-century religious movement in Europe intended to reform the Roman Catholic Church, from which the Protestant Churches arose

refract VERB
to bend a ray of light at the point where it enters water or glass etc. at an angle
refraction NOUN

refrain[1] VERB
to stop yourself from doing something

refrain[2] NOUN
the chorus of a song

refresh VERB
to make someone feel fresh and strong again
refresh someone's memory to remind someone of facts they may have forgotten

refreshing ADJECTIVE
1 producing new strength
2 pleasantly different or unusual

refreshment NOUN
food and drink

refrigerate VERB
to make and keep food cold to preserve it
refrigeration NOUN

refrigerator NOUN
a cabinet in which food is stored at a very low temperature

refuel VERB **refuelling**, **refuelled**
to supply a ship or aircraft with more fuel

refuge NOUN
a place where a person is safe from pursuit or danger

refugee NOUN
someone who seeks refuge in another country

refund (ri-**fund**) VERB
to pay money back

refund (**ree**-fund) NOUN
money paid back

refurbish VERB
to redecorate and brighten a place

refusal NOUN
an act of refusing

refuse (ri-**fewz**) VERB
to say that you will not do something, when asked to

refuse (**ref**-yooss) NOUN
waste material

refute VERB
to show a person or statement to be wrong
refutation NOUN
This word does not mean simply 'deny' or 'reject'.

regain VERB
1 to get something back after losing it
2 to reach a place again

regal (**ree**-gal) ADJECTIVE
1 to do with a king or queen
2 dignified and splendid

regale VERB
to entertain with conversation

regalia PLURAL NOUN
the emblems of royalty or rank

regard VERB
1 to think of in a certain way *regarded the matter as serious*
2 to look or gaze at

regard NOUN
1 consideration or heed
2 respect
3 a gaze
with or **in regard to** concerning; about

regarding PREPOSITION
concerning; about

regardless ADVERB
without considering something *regardless of the cost*

regards PLURAL NOUN
kind wishes sent in a message

regatta NOUN
a meeting for boat or yacht races

regency NOUN **regencies**
1 being a regent
2 a period when a country is ruled by a regent

regenerate VERB
to give new life or strength to something
regeneration NOUN

regent NOUN
a person appointed to rule in place of a king or queen

reggae (**reg**-ay) NOUN
a West Indian style of music with a strong beat

regime (ray-**zheem**) NOUN
a system of government or organization

regiment NOUN
an army unit, usually divided into battalions or companies
regimental ADJECTIVE

region NOUN
a part of a country or of the world

regional ADJECTIVE
to do with a region or regions
regionally ADVERB

register NOUN
1 an official list
2 a book for recording information about school attendance
3 the range of a voice or musical instrument

register VERB
1 to list in a register
2 (of a gauge) to show a figure or amount
3 to make an impression on the mind
registration NOUN

register office or **registry office** NOUN
an office where marriages are performed and records of births, marriages, and deaths are kept

registrar NOUN
an official whose job is to keep written records or registers

registration number NOUN
a series of letters and numbers identifying a motor vehicle

registry NOUN **registries**
a place where registers are kept

regret NOUN
a feeling of sorrow or disappointment

regret VERB **regretting**, **regretted**
to feel regret about

regretful ADJECTIVE
feeling regret
regretfully ADVERB

regrettable ADJECTIVE
to be regretted; unfortunate
regrettably ADVERB

regular ADJECTIVE
1 happening or done always at certain times
2 even or symmetrical
3 normal or correct
4 belonging to a country's permanent armed forces
regularity NOUN **regularly** ADVERB

regulate VERB
1 to control by rules
2 to make a machine work at a certain speed
regulator NOUN **regulatory** ADJECTIVE

regulation NOUN
1 the process of regulating
2 a rule or law

regurgitate VERB
to bring swallowed food up again into the mouth
regurgitation NOUN

rehabilitate VERB
to restore a person to a normal life after being in prison, ill, etc.
rehabilitation NOUN

rehash VERB
(informal) to reuse old ideas or material without much change or improvement

rehearse VERB
to practise before performing to an audience
rehearsal NOUN

reign VERB
1 to rule a country as king or queen
2 to prevail Silence reigned.

reign NOUN
the time when a king or queen reigns

reimburse VERB
to repay money spent
reimbursement NOUN

rein NOUN
each of a pair of straps used to guide a horse

reincarnation NOUN
the act of being born again into a new body

reindeer NOUN
a kind of deer that lives in Arctic regions

reinforce VERB
to strengthen by adding extra people or supports etc.

reinforcement NOUN
1 the process of reinforcing
2 something that reinforces

reinforcements PLURAL NOUN
extra troops or ships etc. sent to strengthen a force

reinstate VERB
to put a person or thing back into a former position
reinstatement NOUN

reiterate VERB
to say something again
reiteration NOUN

reject (ri-jekt) VERB
1 to refuse to accept a person or thing
2 to throw away or discard
rejection NOUN

reject (ree-jekt) NOUN
a person or thing that is rejected

rejoice VERB
to feel or show great joy

rejoin VERB
to meet with again

rejoinder NOUN
an answer or retort

rejuvenate VERB
to make a person seem young again
rejuvenation NOUN

relapse VERB
to become worse again after improving
relapse NOUN

relate VERB
1 to tell a story
2 to connect one thing with another
3 to understand and get on well with someone

a
b
c
d
e
f
g
h
i
j
k
l
m
n
o
p
q
r
s
t
u
v
w
x
y
z

related *ADJECTIVE*
belonging to the same family

relation *NOUN*
1 a relative
2 the way one thing is related to another

relationship *NOUN*
1 the way in which people or things are related
2 the way in which people behave towards one another
3 an emotional or sexual association between two people

relative *NOUN*
a person who is related to another

relative *ADJECTIVE*
compared with the average *living in relative comfort*
relatively *ADVERB*

relax *VERB*
1 to stop working; to rest
2 to become less anxious or worried
3 to make a rule etc. less strict or severe
4 to make a limb or muscle less stiff or tense
relaxed *ADJECTIVE* **relaxation** *NOUN*

relay *VERB*
to pass on a message or broadcast

relay *NOUN*
1 a fresh group taking the place of another *working in relays*
2 a relay race
3 the process of relaying a broadcast

relay race *NOUN*
a race between teams in which each person covers part of the distance

release *VERB*
1 to set free or unfasten
2 to let a thing fall or fly or go out
3 to make a film or record etc. available to the public

release *NOUN*
1 the act of releasing
2 a new film or record etc.
3 a device that unfastens something

relegate *VERB*
1 to put into a less important place
2 to place a sports team in a lower division of a league
relegation *NOUN*

relent *VERB*
to become less severe or strict

relentless *ADJECTIVE*
not stopping or relenting
relentlessly *ADVERB*

relevant *ADJECTIVE*
connected with what is being discussed or dealt with
relevance *NOUN*

reliable *ADJECTIVE*
able to be relied on; trustworthy
reliability *NOUN* **reliably** *ADVERB*

reliance *NOUN*
dependence or trust
reliant *ADJECTIVE*

relic *NOUN*
something that has survived from an earlier time

relief *NOUN*
1 the ending or lessening of pain, trouble, etc.
2 something that gives relief or help
3 help given to people in need
4 a person who takes over a turn of duty when another finishes
5 a method of making a map or design that stands out from a flat surface

relief map *NOUN*
a map that shows hills and valleys by shading or moulding

relieve *VERB*
to give relief to a person or thing
relieve of to take something from a person

religion *NOUN*
1 belief in and worship of God or gods
2 a particular system of beliefs and worship

religious *ADJECTIVE*
1 to do with religion
2 believing firmly in a religion

religiously *ADVERB*
carefully and regularly

relinquish *VERB*
to give something up

relish *NOUN*
1 great enjoyment
2 a flavouring for food

relish *VERB*
to enjoy very much

relive *VERB*
to remember something vividly, as though it was happening again

relocate *VERB*
to move or be moved to a new place

reluctant *ADJECTIVE*
not willing or eager
reluctance *NOUN* **reluctantly** *ADVERB*

rely *VERB* **relies, relied**
rely on 1 to trust a person or thing to help or support you 2 to be dependent on

remain *VERB*
1 to be left over
2 to stay or not leave

remainder NOUN
1 the remaining people or things
2 the number left after subtraction or division

remains PLURAL NOUN
1 all that is left over
2 ancient ruins or objects; relics
3 a dead body

remand VERB
to send a prisoner back into custody while
further evidence is being gathered
on remand in prison while waiting for a trial

remark NOUN
something said; a comment

remark VERB
1 to make a remark
2 to notice something

remarkable ADJECTIVE
unusual or extraordinary
remarkably ADVERB

remedial ADJECTIVE
1 helping to cure an illness
2 helping children who learn slowly

remedy NOUN **remedies**
something that cures or relieves a disease or
problem

remedy VERB **remedies**, **remedied**
to be a remedy for

remember VERB
1 to keep something in your mind
2 to bring something back into your mind
remembrance NOUN

remind VERB
1 to help a person remember something
2 to make you think of something because of
being similar

reminder NOUN
something which reminds you

reminisce (rem-in-**iss**) VERB
to think or talk about things from the past

reminiscence NOUN
something remembered from the past

reminiscent ADJECTIVE
reminding you of something

remiss ADJECTIVE
careless; not doing your duty properly

remission NOUN
1 a period during which an illness is less
serious
2 reduction of a prison sentence

remit NOUN
an officially given task or area of activity

remittance NOUN
1 the sending of money
2 the money sent

remnant NOUN
a part or piece left over

remonstrate VERB
to make a protest

remorse NOUN
deep regret for having done wrong

remorseful ADJECTIVE
feeling remorse
remorsefully ADVERB

remorseless ADJECTIVE
relentless; cruel

remote ADJECTIVE
1 far away in place or time
2 isolated
3 unlikely or slight *a remote chance*
remotely ADVERB

remote control NOUN
1 the control of something from a distance,
usually by electricity or radio
2 a device for doing this

removal NOUN
the act of removing or moving, especially to a
new home

remove VERB
1 to take something away or off
2 to get rid of

remuneration NOUN
pay or reward for work done

Renaissance (ruhn-**ay**-suhns) NOUN
the revival of classical styles of art and
literature in Europe in the 14th-16th
centuries

renal (reen-uhl) ADJECTIVE
to do with the kidneys

rename VERB
to give a new name to

render VERB
1 to cause to become *rendered us speechless*
2 to give or perform something *quick to
render help*

rendezvous (rond-ay-voo) NOUN
an arranged meeting between two people, or
the meeting place

rendition NOUN
a performance of music, reading of a
poem, etc.

renegade (ren-ig-ayd) NOUN
a person who deserts a group or religion etc.

renew VERB
1 to restore something to its original
condition or replace it with something new
2 to begin or make or give again
renewal NOUN

a
b
c
d
e
f
g
h
i
j
k
l
m
n
o
p
q
r
s
t
u
v
w
x
y
z

renewable ADJECTIVE
1 able to be renewed
2 (of sources of energy, e.g. the sun or wind power) that cannot be used up

renounce VERB
to give up or reject
renunciation NOUN

renovate VERB
to repair a thing and make it look new
renovation NOUN

renowned ADJECTIVE
famous
renown NOUN

rent NOUN
a regular payment for the use of a house, flat, etc.

rent VERB
to have or allow the use of in return for rent

rental NOUN
an amount paid as rent

renunciation NOUN
the renouncing of something

reorganize VERB
to change the way in which something is organized
reorganization NOUN

repair VERB
to put something into good condition after it has been damaged or broken
repairable ADJECTIVE

repair NOUN
1 the process of repairing
2 a mended place
in good repair well maintained

reparation NOUN
(formal) something done or paid to make up for damage or a loss

repartee NOUN
witty replies and remarks

repatriate VERB
to send someone back to their own country
repatriation NOUN

repay VERB **repaid**
1 to pay back
2 to give in return
repayment NOUN

repeal VERB
to cancel a law officially
repeal NOUN

repeat VERB
1 to say or do the same thing again
2 to tell another person about something told to you

repeat NOUN
1 the act of repeating
2 a radio or television programme that is shown again

repeatedly ADVERB
over and over again

repel VERB **repelling**, **repelled**
1 to drive someone back
2 to push something away by means of a physical force
3 to disgust

repellent ADJECTIVE
disgusting; revolting

repent VERB
to be sorry for what you have done

repentance NOUN
regret for what you have done
repentant ADJECTIVE

repercussion NOUN
an indirect result of something that has happened

repertoire (rep-er-twahr) NOUN
a stock of songs or plays etc. that a person or company performs

repertory NOUN **repertories**
a repertoire

repetition NOUN
1 the act of repeating
2 something repeated

repetitive ADJECTIVE
full of repetitions

replace VERB
1 to put a thing back in its place
2 to take the place of
3 to put a new or different thing in place of
replacement NOUN

replay NOUN
1 a sports match played again after a draw
2 the playing or showing again of a recording

replay VERB
to play a game or recording again

replenish VERB
1 to fill again
2 to add a new supply of
replenishment NOUN

replete ADJECTIVE
full or well supplied

replica NOUN
an exact copy

replicate VERB
to make or become an exact copy of

reply NOUN **replies**
something said or written to deal with a question, letter, etc.

reply VERB **replies**, **replied**
to give a reply to

report VERB
1 to give an account of
2 to make a complaint or accusation against somebody
3 to tell someone in authority that you are present

report NOUN
1 a description or account
2 a statement of how someone has worked or behaved
3 an explosive sound

reporter NOUN
a person who reports news for a newspaper, radio, or television

repose NOUN
calm or rest

repository NOUN **repositories**
a place for storing things

reprehensible ADJECTIVE
deserving blame

represent VERB
1 to help someone by speaking or acting on their behalf
2 to symbolize or stand for
3 to be an example or equivalent of
4 to show a person or thing in a picture or play etc.
5 to describe in a particular way
representation NOUN

representative NOUN
a person or thing that represents others

representative ADJECTIVE
1 representing others
2 typical of a group

repress VERB
1 to control by force
2 to restrain or suppress
repression NOUN

repressive ADJECTIVE
harsh or severe

reprieve NOUN
cancellation of a punishment

reprieve VERB
to give a reprieve to

reprimand NOUN
an official rebuke

reprimand VERB
to give someone a reprimand

reprisal NOUN
an act of revenge

reproach VERB
to tell someone you are upset and disappointed by something they have done
reproach NOUN

reproachful ADJECTIVE
upset and resentful
reproachfully ADVERB

reproduce VERB
1 to cause to exist or happen again
2 to make a copy of
3 to produce offspring

reproduction NOUN
1 a copy of a work of art
2 the process of producing offspring

reproductive ADJECTIVE
to do with reproduction *the reproductive system*

reprove VERB
to rebuke or criticize harshly
reproof NOUN

reptile NOUN
a cold-blooded creeping animal, e.g. a snake, lizard, or crocodile

republic NOUN
a country that has an elected president
republican ADJECTIVE

Republican NOUN
a supporter of the Republican Party in the USA

repudiate VERB
to reject or deny
repudiation NOUN

repugnant ADJECTIVE
unpleasant or disgusting
repugnance NOUN

repulse VERB
1 to drive away or repel
2 to reject an offer etc.

repulsion NOUN
1 the act of repelling or repulsing
2 a feeling of disgust

repulsive ADJECTIVE
disgusting

reputable (rep-yoo-ta-bul) ADJECTIVE
having a good reputation
reputably ADVERB

reputation NOUN
the general opinion about a person or thing

repute NOUN
reputation

reputed ADJECTIVE
said or thought to be something *is reputed to be the best*
reputedly ADVERB

request VERB
1 to ask for
2 to ask someone to do something

request NOUN
1 an act of asking
2 a thing asked for

requiem (rek-wee-em) *NOUN*
1 a special Mass for someone who has died
2 music for the words of this

require *VERB*
1 to need
2 to make someone do something

requirement *NOUN*
what is required; a need

requisite (rek-wiz-it) *ADJECTIVE*
required or needed

requisite *NOUN*
a thing needed

requisition *VERB*
to take something over for official use

rescue *VERB*
to save from danger, harm, etc.
rescuer *NOUN*

rescue *NOUN*
the action of rescuing

research *NOUN*
special study or investigation

research *VERB*
to do research into
researcher *NOUN*

resemblance *NOUN*
likeness or similarity

resemble *VERB*
to be like another person or thing

resent *VERB*
to feel indignant about or insulted by
resentment *NOUN*

resentful *ADJECTIVE*
bitter and indignant about something
resentfully *ADVERB*

reservation *NOUN*
1 the act of reserving
2 something reserved *a hotel reservation*
3 an area of land kept for a special purpose
4 a doubt

reserve *VERB*
1 to keep or order something specially
2 to postpone or put aside

reserve *NOUN*
1 a person or thing kept ready for use
2 an extra player chosen for a team
3 an area of land kept for a special purpose
a nature reserve
4 shyness

reserved *ADJECTIVE*
1 kept for special use
2 shy

reservoir (rez-er-vwar) *NOUN*
a place where water is stored

reshuffle *VERB*
to reorganize a group of people
reshuffle *NOUN*

reside *VERB*
to live in a particular place

residence *NOUN*
1 a place where a person lives
2 the state or time of living in a place

resident *NOUN*
a person living in a particular place
resident *ADJECTIVE*

residential *ADJECTIVE*
1 containing homes
2 providing accommodation *a residential course*

residue *NOUN*
what is left over
residual *ADJECTIVE*

resign *VERB*
to give up your job or position
be resigned to to accept something unwelcome

resignation *NOUN*
1 acceptance of a difficulty without complaining
2 the act of resigning a job or position

resilient *ADJECTIVE*
recovering quickly from illness or difficulty
resilience *NOUN*

resin *NOUN*
a sticky substance produced by plants or made artificially
resinous *ADJECTIVE*

resist *VERB*
to fight or act against

resistance *NOUN*
1 the act of resisting *armed resistance*
2 the ability of a substance to hinder the flow of electricity
resistant *ADJECTIVE*

resistor *NOUN*
a device that increases the resistance to an electric current

resit *VERB* **resitting, resat**
to sit an examination again
resit *NOUN*

resolute *ADJECTIVE*
showing great determination
resolutely *ADVERB*

resolution *NOUN*
1 a resolute manner
2 something you have resolved to do
3 a formal decision
4 the solving of a problem etc.

resolve *VERB*
1 to decide firmly or formally
2 to solve a problem etc.
3 to overcome disagreements

a b c d e f g h i j k l m n o p q r s t u v w x y z

resolve NOUN
1 something you have decided to do
2 great determination

resonant ADJECTIVE
1 resounding or echoing
2 suggesting a feeling, memory, etc.
resonance NOUN

resonate VERB
to resound or echo

resort VERB
resort to to turn to or make use of

resort NOUN
1 a place where people go for relaxation or holidays
2 the act of resorting
the last resort something tried when everything else has failed

resound VERB
to fill a place with sound; to echo

resounding ADJECTIVE
1 loud and echoing
2 very great

resource NOUN
1 something that can be used
2 an ability

resourceful ADJECTIVE
good at finding ways of doing things

respect NOUN
1 admiration for the good qualities of someone or something
2 politeness or consideration
3 a detail or aspect in every respect
with respect to concerning; to do with

respect VERB
to have respect for

respectable ADJECTIVE
1 having good manners and character etc.
2 fairly good
respectability NOUN **respectably** ADVERB

respectful ADJECTIVE
showing respect
respectfully ADVERB

respecting PREPOSITION
concerning; to do with

respective ADJECTIVE
belonging to each one of several went to their respective rooms

respectively ADVERB
in the same order as the people or things already mentioned The American and British teams finished first and second respectively

respiration NOUN
the action of breathing
respiratory ADJECTIVE

respirator NOUN
a device that fits over a person's face to purify air before it is breathed

respite NOUN
an interval of rest or relief

resplendent ADJECTIVE
brilliant with colour or decoration

respond VERB
1 to reply
2 to act in answer to an event etc.

respondent NOUN
the person answering

response NOUN
1 a reply
2 a reaction

responsibility NOUN **responsibilities**
1 the state of being responsible
2 something for which a person is responsible

responsible ADJECTIVE
1 looking after a person or thing and having to take any blame
2 reliable and trustworthy
3 with important duties a responsible job
responsible for causing or bringing about
responsibly ADVERB

responsive ADJECTIVE
quick to respond

rest NOUN
1 a time of sleep or freedom from work
2 a support
3 an interval of silence between notes in music
the rest the remaining part; the others

rest VERB
1 to have a rest
2 to be still
3 to allow to rest sit and rest your feet
4 to lean or place something so it is supported
5 to be left without further investigation etc.
let the matter rest

restaurant NOUN
a place where meals can be bought and eaten

restful ADJECTIVE
giving a feeling of rest

restitution NOUN
1 the act of restoring something
2 compensation

restive ADJECTIVE
restless or impatient

restless ADJECTIVE
unable to rest or keep still

restore VERB
1 to put something back to its original place or condition
2 to clean and repair a work of art or building etc.
restoration NOUN

a b c d e f g h i j k l m n o p q r s t u v w x y z

restrain VERB
to hold a person or thing back
restraint NOUN

restrict VERB
to keep within certain limits
restrictive ADJECTIVE

restriction NOUN
a rule or limit that restricts action

result NOUN
1 something produced by an action or condition etc.
2 the score or situation at the end of a game
3 the answer to a sum or calculation

result VERB
1 to happen as a result
2 to have a particular result *a game that resulted in a draw*

resultant ADJECTIVE
happening as a result

resume VERB
1 to begin again after stopping
2 to take or occupy again *resumed our seats*
resumption NOUN

résumé (rez-yoo-may) NOUN
a summary

resurgence NOUN
a rise or revival of something *a resurgence of interest*

resurrect VERB
to bring back into use or existence

resurrection NOUN
1 the act of coming back to life after being dead
2 a revival
the Resurrection in the Christian religion, the resurrection of Christ three days after his death

resuscitate VERB
to revive an unconscious person
resuscitation NOUN

retail VERB
1 to sell goods to the general public
2 to tell what happened
retailer NOUN

retail NOUN
the selling of goods to the general public

retain VERB
1 to continue to have
2 to hold in place

retake VERB **retook**, **retaken**
to take a test or examination again

retaliate VERB **retaliates**, **retaliating**, **retaliated**
to attack or insult someone in return
retaliation NOUN

retarded ADJECTIVE
not well developed, especially mentally

retch VERB
to strain your throat as if vomiting

retention NOUN
the act of retaining or keeping

retentive ADJECTIVE
(of the memory) able to remember well

reticent ADJECTIVE
reserved and discreet
reticence NOUN

retina NOUN
a layer of membrane at the back of the eyeball, sensitive to light

retinue NOUN
a group of people accompanying an important person

retire VERB
1 to give up regular work at a certain age
2 to retreat or withdraw
3 to go to bed for the night
retirement NOUN

retiring ADJECTIVE
shy; avoiding company

retort NOUN
a witty or angry reply

retort VERB
to make a retort

retrace VERB
to go back over *retraced our steps*

retract VERB
1 to pull back or in
2 to withdraw an offer or statement
retraction NOUN

retreat VERB
to draw back after being defeated or to avoid danger

retreat NOUN
1 an act of retreating
2 a quiet place

retribution NOUN
a deserved punishment

retrieve VERB
1 to bring or get back
2 to rescue
retrieval NOUN

retriever NOUN
a breed of dog trained to retrieve game

retrograde ADJECTIVE
1 going backwards
2 becoming less good

retrospect NOUN
in retrospect when looking back on the past

retrospective ADJECTIVE
1 looking back on the past
2 applying to the past as well as the future
a retrospective law

return VERB
1 to come or go back
2 to give or send back
3 to elect to parliament

return NOUN
1 the act of returning
2 something returned
3 profit *a good return on savings*
4 a return ticket

return match NOUN
a second match played between the same teams

return ticket NOUN
a ticket for a journey to a place and back again

reunify VERB **reunifies**, **reunified**
to make a divided country into one again
reunification NOUN

reunion NOUN
1 the act of reuniting
2 a meeting of people after a long interval of time

reunite VERB
to unite again after being separated

rev VERB **revving**, **revved**
(*informal*) to make an engine run quickly

rev NOUN
(*informal*) a revolution of an engine

Revd ABBREVIATION
Reverend

reveal VERB
to let something be seen or known

reveille (riv-al-ee) NOUN
a military waking signal on a bugle

revel VERB **revelling**, **revelled**
1 to take great delight in something
2 to enjoy yourself in a lively and noisy way
reveller NOUN

revelation NOUN
1 the act of revealing
2 something surprising that is revealed

revelry NOUN
lively enjoyment

revels PLURAL NOUN
lively and noisy festivities

revenge NOUN
the act of harming somebody in return for harm they have done

revenge VERB
to take revenge for harm done

revenue NOUN
1 a country's income from taxes etc.
2 a company's income

reverberate VERB
to be repeated as an echo
reverberation NOUN

revere (riv-eer) VERB
to respect deeply

reverence NOUN
a feeling of awe and deep or religious respect

Reverend NOUN
the title of a member of the clergy

reverent ADJECTIVE
feeling or showing reverence

reverie (rev-er-ee) NOUN
a daydream

reversal NOUN
1 the act of reversing or being reversed
2 a piece of bad luck

reverse ADJECTIVE
opposite in direction, order, or manner etc.

reverse NOUN
1 the reverse side, order, manner, etc.
2 a piece of misfortune
in reverse the opposite way round

reverse VERB
1 to turn in the opposite direction or order etc.
2 to move backwards
3 to cancel a decision
reversible ADJECTIVE

reverse gear NOUN
a gear that allows a vehicle to move backwards

revert VERB
to return to a former condition, subject, etc.
reversion NOUN

review NOUN
1 an inspection or survey
2 a published opinion of a book, film, play, etc.

review VERB
1 to write a review of a book, film, play, etc.
2 to reconsider
3 to inspect or survey
reviewer NOUN
Do not confuse this word with *revue*.

revile VERB
to criticize angrily
revilement NOUN

revise VERB
1 to go over work in preparing for an examination
2 to alter or correct something
revision NOUN

revitalize VERB
to put new strength or vitality into something

a b c d e f g h i j k l m n o p q r s t u v w x y z

revive *VERB*
to come or bring back to life, strength, use, etc.
revival *NOUN*

revoke *VERB*
to withdraw or cancel a decree or licence etc.

revolt *VERB*
1 to rebel
2 to disgust
revolt *NOUN*
1 a rebellion
2 a feeling of disgust

revolting *ADJECTIVE*
disgusting

revolution *NOUN*
1 a rebellion that overthrows the government
2 a complete change
3 the process of revolving; one complete turn

revolutionary *ADJECTIVE*
1 involving a great change
2 to do with a political revolution

revolutionize *VERB*
to make a great change in something

revolve *VERB*
1 to turn in a circle
2 to have as the most important element
a life that revolves around work

revolver *NOUN*
a pistol with a revolving mechanism

revue *NOUN*
an entertainment of songs, sketches, etc.
Do not confuse this word with *review*.

revulsion *NOUN*
1 strong disgust
2 a violent change of feeling

reward *NOUN*
1 something given in return for an achievement or service
2 a sum of money offered for help in catching a criminal or finding lost property
reward *VERB*
to give a reward to

rewarding *ADJECTIVE*
satisfying; worthwhile

rewind *VERB*
to wind a cassette or videotape back to the beginning

rewrite *VERB* **rewrote, rewritten**
to write something again or differently

rhapsody (rap-so-dee) *NOUN* **rhapsodies**
1 a statement of great delight about something
2 a romantic piece of music

rhetoric *NOUN*
the effective use of words in public speaking
rhetorical *ADJECTIVE*

rheumatism *NOUN*
a disease that causes pain and stiffness in joints and muscles
rheumatic *ADJECTIVE*

rhino *NOUN* **rhino** or **rhinos**
(*informal*) a rhinoceros

rhinoceros *NOUN*
a large animal with a horn or two horns on its nose

rhododendron *NOUN*
an evergreen shrub with large trumpet-shaped flowers

rhombus *NOUN*
a shape with four equal sides but no right angles

rhubarb *NOUN*
a plant with thick reddish stalks used as fruit

rhyme *NOUN*
1 a similar sound in the endings of words
2 a poem with rhymes
3 a word that rhymes with another
rhyme *VERB*
1 to form a rhyme
2 to have rhymes

rhythm *NOUN*
a regular pattern of beats, sounds, or movements

rhythmic or **rhythmical** *ADJECTIVE*
having a rhythm
rhythmically *ADVERB*

rib *NOUN*
1 each of the curved bones round the chest
2 a curved part or support
ribbed *ADJECTIVE*

ribald (rib-ald) *ADJECTIVE*
funny in a coarse way
ribaldry *NOUN*

riband *NOUN*
a ribbon

ribbon *NOUN*
a narrow strip of material used for decoration or for tying

rice *NOUN*
the seeds of a cereal plant grown in flooded fields in hot countries

rich *ADJECTIVE*
1 having a lot of money or property
2 having a large supply of something
3 (of colour, sound, or smell) pleasantly deep or strong
4 (of food) containing a lot of fat, butter, eggs, etc.
5 expensive or luxurious
richness *NOUN*

riches *PLURAL NOUN*
wealth

richly *ADVERB*
1 in a rich or luxurious way
2 fully or thoroughly *an award that is richly deserved*

Richter scale *NOUN*
a scale (from 0 to 10) used to show the force of an earthquake

rick [1] *NOUN*
a large neat stack of hay or straw

rick [2] *VERB*
to sprain or wrench

rickets *NOUN*
a disease caused by lack of vitamin D, causing deformed bones

rickety *ADJECTIVE*
likely to break or fall down

rickshaw *NOUN*
a two-wheeled carriage pulled by a person, used in the Far East

ricochet (rik-osh-ay) *VERB* **ricocheting, ricocheted**
to bounce off something
ricochet *NOUN*

rid *VERB* **ridding, rid**
to make a person or place free from something unwanted
get rid of to remove or throw away

riddle *NOUN*
a puzzling question to be solved

riddled *ADJECTIVE*
pierced with many holes *riddled with holes*

ride *NOUN*
a journey on a horse, bicycle, etc. or in a vehicle

ride *VERB* **rode, ridden**
1 to sit on a horse, bicycle, etc. and be carried along on it
2 to travel in a car, bus, train, etc.
3 to float or be supported on something *to ride the waves*

rider *NOUN*
1 someone who rides
2 an extra comment or statement

ridge *NOUN*
1 a long narrow higher part
2 a long narrow range of hills or mountains
ridged *ADJECTIVE*

ridicule *VERB*
to make fun of
ridicule *NOUN*

ridiculous *ADJECTIVE*
silly enough to laugh at
ridiculously *ADVERB*

rife *ADJECTIVE*
happening frequently

riff-raff *NOUN*
disreputable people

rifle *NOUN*
a gun with a long barrel, held against the shoulder

rifle *VERB*
to search through something in order to find or steal something

rift *NOUN*
1 a crack or split
2 a disagreement between friends

rig [1] *VERB* **rigging, rigged**
to provide a ship with ropes, spars, sails, etc.
rig out to provide with clothes or equipment **rig up** to set up in a makeshift way

rig *NOUN*
1 a framework supporting the machinery for drilling an oil well
2 the arrangement of a ship's masts and sails etc.

rig [2] *VERB* **rigging, rigged**
to arrange the result of an election dishonestly

rigging *NOUN*
the ropes etc. that support a ship's mast and sails

right *ADJECTIVE*
1 on or towards the east if you are facing north
2 correct or true
3 fair or just
4 (of political groups) conservative
right-hand *ADJECTIVE*

right *ADVERB*
1 on or towards the right *Turn right here.*
2 straight *Go right on.*
3 completely *Turn right round.*
4 exactly *right in the middle*
5 correctly or appropriately *Did I do that right?*
right away immediately

right *NOUN*
1 the right-hand side or part etc.
2 what is morally good or fair or just
3 something that people are allowed to do or have *the right to vote in elections*

right *VERB*
1 to make a thing upright
2 to put right

right angle *NOUN*
an angle of 90°

righteous *ADJECTIVE*
doing what is right; virtuous
righteousness *NOUN*

rightful *ADJECTIVE*
deserved or proper *in her rightful place*
rightfully *ADVERB*

right-handed *ADJECTIVE*
using the right hand in preference to the left hand

rightly *ADVERB*
correctly or justifiably

rigid *ADJECTIVE*
1 stiff or firm *a rigid support*
2 strict
rigidity *NOUN*

rigmarole *NOUN*
a long rambling statement

rigorous *ADJECTIVE*
1 strict or severe
2 careful and thorough
rigorously *ADVERB*

rigour *NOUN*
strictness or severity

rile *VERB*
(*informal*) to annoy

rim *NOUN*
the outer edge of a cup, wheel, or other round object

rind *NOUN*
the tough skin on bacon, cheese, or fruit

ring [^1] *NOUN*
1 a circle
2 a thin circular piece of metal worn on a finger
3 the space where a circus performs
4 a square area for boxing or wrestling
5 a group of people
ring *VERB* **ringed**
to put a ring round

ring [^2] *VERB* **rang, rung**
1 to cause a bell to sound
2 to make a loud clear sound
3 to be filled with sound
4 to telephone

ring *NOUN*
the act or sound of ringing

ringleader *NOUN*
a person who leads others in rebellion, crime, etc.

ringlet *NOUN*
a curl of hair

ringmaster *NOUN*
the person in charge of a performance in a circus ring

ring road *NOUN*
a road that goes round a town avoiding the centre

rink *NOUN*
an enclosed area of ice for skating

rinse *VERB*
to wash lightly in clear water
rinse *NOUN*
1 an act of rinsing
2 a liquid for colouring the hair

riot *NOUN*
wild or violent behaviour by a crowd
run riot to behave or spread in an uncontrolled way

riot *VERB*
to take part in a riot

riotous *ADJECTIVE*
1 disorderly or unruly
2 boisterous *riotous laughter*

rip *VERB* **ripping, ripped**
to tear roughly
rip off (*informal*) to swindle or overcharge

rip *NOUN*
a torn place

ripe *ADJECTIVE* **riper, ripest**
1 ready to be harvested or eaten
2 ready and suitable

ripen *VERB*
to make or become ripe

rip-off *NOUN*
(*informal*) a fraud or swindle

riposte (rip-ost) *NOUN*
a quick clever reply

ripple *NOUN*
a small wave or series of waves
ripple *VERB*
to form ripples

rise *VERB* **rose, risen**
1 go upwards
2 to increase *Prices will rise.*
3 to get up from lying, sitting, or kneeling
4 to get out of bed
5 to rebel *They rose in revolt against the tyrant.*
6 (of bread, cake, etc.) to swell by the action of yeast
7 (of a river) to begin its course

rise *NOUN*
1 the action of rising; an upward movement
2 an increase in wages, prices, etc.
3 an upward slope
give rise to to cause

rising *NOUN*
a rebellion

risk *NOUN*
a chance of harm or loss

risk VERB
1 to take the chance of harming or losing *They risked their lives.*
2 to accept the chance of harm or loss *risks injury each time he climbs*

risky ADJECTIVE **riskier, riskiest**
full of risk

rite NOUN
a solemn or religious ceremony

ritual NOUN
the series of actions used in a religious or other ceremony
ritual ADJECTIVE **ritually** ADVERB

rival NOUN
a person or thing that competes with another
rivalry NOUN

rival VERB **rivalling, rivalled**
to be a rival of

river NOUN
a large natural stream of water flowing through land

rivet NOUN
a strong nail or bolt for holding pieces of metal together

rivet VERB
1 to fasten with rivets
2 to hold firmly *was riveted to the spot*
3 to fascinate *a riveting performance*

roach [1] NOUN **roach**
a small freshwater fish

roach [2] NOUN
(*informal*) (*American*) a cockroach

road NOUN
1 a level way with a hard surface for traffic to travel on
2 a way or course *the road to success*

road rage NOUN
aggressive behaviour by motorists

roadway NOUN
the part of the road used by traffic

roadworthy ADJECTIVE
(of a vehicle) safe to be used on roads

roam VERB
to wander
roam NOUN

roan ADJECTIVE
(of a horse) brown or black with many white hairs

roar NOUN
a loud deep sound like that made by a lion

roar VERB
1 to make a roar
2 to laugh loudly

roast VERB
to cook meat etc. in an oven or by exposing it to heat

roast ADJECTIVE
roasted *roast beef*

roast NOUN
1 meat for roasting
2 roast meat

rob VERB **robbing, robbed**
to take or steal from *robbed me of my watch*

robber NOUN
a person who robs

robbery NOUN **robberies**
an act of robbing

robe NOUN
a long loose piece of clothing

robin NOUN
a small brown bird with a red breast

robot NOUN
1 a machine that looks or acts like a person
2 a machine operated by remote control
robotic ADJECTIVE

robust ADJECTIVE
strong and vigorous
robustly ADVERB

rock [1] NOUN
1 a large stone or boulder
2 the hard part of the earth's crust
3 a hard stick-shaped sweet

rock [2] VERB
to move gently backwards and forwards

rock NOUN
1 a rocking movement
2 rock music

rock and roll or **rock 'n' roll** NOUN
a kind of popular dance music with a strong beat

rocker NOUN
1 a thing that rocks something or is rocked
2 a rocking chair

rockery NOUN **rockeries**
a mound or bank in a garden, with plants growing among stones

rocket NOUN
1 a device propelled into the air by burning gases, used to send up a missile or a spacecraft
2 a firework that shoots into the air

rocket VERB
1 to move quickly upwards
2 to increase rapidly

rocking chair NOUN
a chair that can be rocked by a person sitting in it

rocking horse NOUN
a model of a horse that can be rocked by a child sitting on it

rock music NOUN
popular music with a heavy beat

rocky[1] ADJECTIVE **rockier**, **rockiest**
1 like rock
2 full of rocks

rocky[2] ADJECTIVE **rockier**, **rockiest**
unsteady

rod NOUN
1 a long thin stick or bar
2 a stick with a line attached for fishing

rodent NOUN
an animal with large front teeth for gnawing,
e.g. a rat or mouse

rodeo NOUN **rodeos**
a show of riding skills by cowboys

roe[1] NOUN
a mass of eggs or reproductive cells in a fish's
body

roe[2] NOUN
a kind of small deer

rogue NOUN
a dishonest or mischievous person
roguery NOUN

roguish ADJECTIVE
playful and mischievous

role NOUN
1 a performer's part in a play or film etc.
2 a purpose or function

roll VERB
1 to move along by turning over and over
2 to form into the shape of a cylinder or ball
3 to flatten something by rolling a rounded
object over it
4 to rock from side to side
5 to pass steadily *The years rolled on.*
6 (of thunder) to make a rumbling sound

roll NOUN
1 something rolled into a cylinder
2 a small portion of baked bread
3 an official list of names
4 a long vibrating sound *a drum roll*

roll-call NOUN
the calling of names from a list

roller NOUN
1 a cylinder used for flattening or spreading
things, or on which something is wound
2 a long swelling sea wave

Rollerblade NOUN
(*trademark*) a skating boot with a line of
wheels for rolling over the ground

roller coaster NOUN
a fairground ride with a series of alternate
steep descents and ascents

roller skate NOUN
a shoe with wheels for rolling over the ground

rollicking ADJECTIVE
boisterous and full of fun

rolling pin NOUN
a heavy cylinder for rolling out pastry

rolling stock NOUN
railway engines and carriages etc.

Roman ADJECTIVE
to do with ancient or modern Rome or its
people
Roman NOUN

Roman alphabet NOUN
the alphabet in which most European
languages are written

Roman Catholic ADJECTIVE
belonging to or to do with the Christian
Church that has the Pope as its leader
Roman Catholicism NOUN

Roman Catholic NOUN
a member of this Church

romance NOUN
1 tender feelings and experiences connected
with love
2 a love affair or story
3 an imaginative story about heroes

Roman numerals PLURAL NOUN
letters that represent numbers (I = 1, V = 5,
X = 10, etc.), used by the ancient Romans

romantic ADJECTIVE
1 to do with love or romance
2 sentimental or unrealistic
romantically ADVERB

Romany NOUN **Romanies**
1 a Gypsy
2 the language of Gypsies

romp VERB
to play in a lively way
romp NOUN

rompers PLURAL NOUN
a one-piece suit of clothing for a baby or
young child

rondo NOUN **rondos**
a piece of music with a recurring theme

roof NOUN
1 the covering on top of a building, shelter,
or vehicle
2 the top inside surface of the mouth

rook NOUN
1 a black crow that nests in groups
2 a chess piece shaped like a castle

rook VERB
(*informal*) to swindle or overcharge

room NOUN
1 a part of a building with its own walls and
ceiling
2 available space *plenty of room*

344

roomy *ADJECTIVE* **roomier**, **roomiest**
having plenty of space

roost *VERB*
(of birds) to perch or settle for sleep

roost *NOUN*
a place where birds roost

rooster *NOUN*
(*American*) a cockerel

root[1] *NOUN*
1 the part of a plant that grows under the ground and absorbs nourishment from the soil
2 a source or basis
3 a number in relation to the number it produces when multiplied by itself *9 is the square root of 81* (9 x 9 = 81).

root *VERB*
1 to grow roots
2 to fix firmly
root out to find and get rid of

root[2] *VERB*
1 (of an animal) to turn up ground in search of food
2 to find by rummaging

rope *NOUN*
a strong thick cord made of twisted strands of fibre

rope *VERB*
to fasten with a rope
rope in to persuade someone to take part

rosary *NOUN* **rosaries**
a string of beads for keeping count of prayers said

rose[1] *NOUN*
1 a shrub that has showy flowers often with thorny stems
2 a deep pink colour

rose[2] *past tense of* **rise**

rosemary *NOUN*
an evergreen shrub with fragrant leaves, used in cooking

rosette *NOUN*
a large circular badge made of ribbon

Rosh Hashana or **Rosh Hashanah**
NOUN
the Jewish New Year

roster *NOUN*
a list showing people's turns to be on duty etc.

rostrum *NOUN*
a platform for one person

rosy *ADJECTIVE* **rosier**, **rosiest**
1 deep pink
2 hopeful or cheerful *a rosy future*
rosiness *NOUN*

rot *VERB* **rotting**, **rotted**
to decay or go soft

rot *NOUN*
1 the process of rotting
2 (*informal*) nonsense

rota (roh-ta) *NOUN*
a list of duties and the people who must do them

rotary *ADJECTIVE*
going round like a wheel

rotate *VERB*
1 to go round like a wheel
2 to arrange or happen in a series
rotation *NOUN*

rote *NOUN*
by rote from memory or by routine

rotor *NOUN*
a rotating part of a machine or helicopter

rotten *ADJECTIVE*
1 rotted *rotten wood*
2 (*informal*) very bad or unpleasant

rotund *ADJECTIVE*
rounded or plump
rotundity *NOUN*

rouble (roo-bul) *NOUN*
the unit of money in Russia

rouge (roozh) *NOUN*
a reddish cosmetic for colouring the cheeks
rouge *VERB*

rough *ADJECTIVE*
1 not smooth; uneven
2 not gentle or careful; violent *a rough push*
3 not exact *a rough guess*
4 (of the weather or the sea) wild and stormy
roughly *ADVERB*

rough *VERB*
rough it to do without basic comforts **rough out** to draw or plan something roughly

roughage *NOUN*
fibre in food, which helps digestion

roughen *VERB*
to make or become rough

roughshod *ADJECTIVE*
ride roughshod over to treat someone badly or unkindly

roulette (roo-let) *NOUN*
a gambling game with bets placed on where the ball in a rotating disc will come to rest

round *ADJECTIVE*
1 shaped like a circle or ball
2 full or complete *a round dozen*
3 returning to the start *a round trip*
in round figures or **numbers**
approximately, without giving exact units

round ADVERB
1 in a circle or curve *Go round to the back.*
2 to every person *Hand the cakes round.*
3 in a new direction *Turn your chair round.*
4 to someone's house or place of work *Come round after lunch.*
come round to become conscious again **round about** 1 near by
2 approximately

round PREPOSITION
1 on all sides of *a fence round the field*
2 in a curve or circle at an even distance from *The earth moves round the sun.*
3 to all parts of *Show them round the house.*
4 on the further side of *is round the corner*

round NOUN
1 the usual route of a postman etc.
2 one stage in a competition
3 a volley of shots from a gun
4 a whole slice of bread
5 a number of drinks bought together

round VERB
1 to make or become round
2 to travel round
round off to complete the last stages of
round up to gather together

roundabout NOUN
1 a circular structure at a junction of roads, which traffic goes round
2 a circular revolving ride at a fair

roundabout ADJECTIVE
indirect; not straight

rounders NOUN
a game in which players try to hit a ball and run round a circuit

Roundhead NOUN
an opponent of King Charles I in the English Civil War (1642–9)

roundly ADVERB
severely *were roundly criticized*

round trip NOUN
a trip to one or more places and back again

rouse VERB
1 to make or become awake
2 to cause to become active or excited

rousing ADJECTIVE
loud or exciting *a rousing speech*

rout VERB
to defeat completely
rout NOUN

route (*say as* root) NOUN
the way taken to get to a place

routine (roo-teen) NOUN
a regular way of doing things
routinely ADVERB

rove VERB
to roam or wander
rover NOUN

row[1] (rhymes with *go*) NOUN
a line of people or things

row[2] (rhymes with *go*) VERB
to make a boat move with oars
rower NOUN

row[3] (rhymes with *cow*) NOUN
1 a loud noise
2 a quarrel

rowan (roh-an) NOUN
a tree that bears hanging bunches of red berries

rowdy ADJECTIVE **rowdier**, **rowdiest**
noisy and disorderly
rowdiness NOUN

rowing boat NOUN
a boat that is rowed with oars

royal ADJECTIVE
to do with a king or queen

royalty NOUN **royalties**
1 being royal
2 a royal person or persons *in the presence of royalty*
3 a payment made to an author or composer etc. for each copy of a work sold or for each performance

rub VERB **rubbing**, **rubbed**
to move something backwards and forwards while pressing it on something else
rub out to remove by rubbing
rub NOUN

rubber NOUN
1 a strong elastic substance used for making tyres, balls, hoses, etc.
2 a piece of rubber for erasing pencil marks
rubbery ADJECTIVE

rubbish NOUN
1 things that are worthless or not wanted
2 nonsense

rubble NOUN
broken pieces of brick or stone

rubella NOUN
an infectious disease which causes a red rash

ruby NOUN **rubies**
a red jewel

ruck VERB
to crease or wrinkle
ruck NOUN

rucksack NOUN
a bag carried on the back

ructions PLURAL NOUN
protests and noisy argument

rudder NOUN
a hinged upright piece at the back of a ship or aircraft, used for steering

ruddy *ADJECTIVE* **ruddier, ruddiest**
red and healthy-looking

rude *ADJECTIVE* **ruder, rudest**
1 impolite
2 indecent or improper
3 roughly made; crude
4 vigorous and hearty *in rude health*
rudely *ADVERB* **rudeness** *NOUN*

rudimentary *ADJECTIVE*
1 basic or elementary
2 not fully developed *rudimentary wings*

rudiments *PLURAL NOUN*
the basic principles of a subject

rueful *ADJECTIVE*
regretful
ruefully *ADVERB*

ruff *NOUN*
1 a starched pleated frill worn round the neck
2 a ring of feathers round a bird's neck

ruffian *NOUN*
a violent lawless person

ruffle *VERB*
1 to disturb the smoothness of a thing
2 to upset or annoy someone

rug *NOUN*
1 a thick mat
2 a thick blanket

rugby or **rugby football** *NOUN*
a kind of football game using an oval ball that players carry or kick

rugged *ADJECTIVE*
1 having an uneven surface or outline; craggy
2 strong or sturdy

ruin *NOUN*
1 severe damage or destruction
2 a building that has fallen down

ruin *VERB*
to damage or spoil completely
ruination *NOUN*

ruinous *ADJECTIVE*
1 causing ruin
2 in ruins; ruined

rule *NOUN*
1 something that people should obey
2 ruling; governing *foreign rule*
3 a carpenter's ruler
as a rule usually

rule *VERB*
1 to govern or reign
2 to make a decision
3 to draw a straight line with a ruler

ruler *NOUN*
1 a person who governs
2 a strip of wood, metal, or plastic with straight edges, used for measuring and drawing straight lines

ruling *NOUN*
a decision or judgement

rum *NOUN*
a strong alcoholic drink made from sugar

rumble *VERB*
to make a deep heavy continuous sound
rumble *NOUN*

ruminate *VERB*
1 (of an animal) to chew the cud
2 to think hard about something

rummage *VERB*
to turn things over or move them about while looking for something
rummage *NOUN*

rummy *NOUN*
a card game in which players try to form sets of cards

rumour *NOUN*
information that spreads to a lot of people but may not be true

rumour *VERB*
be rumoured to be spread as a rumour

rump *NOUN*
the hind part of an animal

rumple *VERB*
1 to crumple
2 to make untidy

rump steak *NOUN*
a piece of meat from the rump of a cow

rumpus *NOUN*
(*informal*) an uproar or angry protest

run *VERB* **running, ran, run**
1 to move with quick steps and both feet off the ground at each stride
2 to flow
3 to produce a flow of liquid
4 to work or function
5 to manage or organize
6 to compete in a contest
7 to extend
8 to go or take in a vehicle
run away to leave a place secretly or quickly **run down 1** to run over **2** to stop gradually **3** (*informal*) to speak unkindly about **run into 1** to collide with **2** to happen to meet **run out** to have used up a supply **run over** to knock down with a moving vehicle

run *NOUN*
1 the action of running
2 a point scored in cricket or baseball
3 a continuous series of events etc.
4 an enclosure for animals
5 a series of damaged stitches
6 a track *a ski run*
on the run escaping from the police

runaway NOUN
someone who has run away

runaway ADJECTIVE
1 having run away or out of control
2 won easily *a runaway victory*

rundown ADJECTIVE
1 tired and in bad health
2 in bad condition

rung [1] NOUN
each of the steps on a ladder

rung [2] *past participle* of **ring** [2]

runner NOUN
1 a person or animal that runs in a race
2 a groove, rod, or roller for a thing to move on

runner-up NOUN **runners-up**
someone who comes second in a competition

running *present participle* of **run**
in the running having a chance of success

running ADJECTIVE
continuous; without an interval *four days running*

runny ADJECTIVE **runnier**, **runniest**
1 flowing like liquid *runny honey*
2 producing a flow of liquid *a runny nose*

run-of-the-mill ADJECTIVE
ordinary, not special

runway NOUN
a long hard surface for aircraft to take off and land

rupee NOUN
the unit of money in India and Pakistan

rupture VERB
to break or burst
rupture NOUN

rural ADJECTIVE
to do with the countryside

ruse NOUN
a deception or trick

rush [1] VERB
1 to move or act quickly
2 to make someone hurry
3 to attack or capture by dashing forward

rush NOUN
1 a hurry
2 a sudden movement
3 a sudden great demand

rush [2] NOUN
a plant with a thin stem that grows near water

rush hour NOUN
the time when traffic is busiest

rusk NOUN
a kind of hard dry biscuit for babies

russet NOUN
a reddish-brown colour

rust NOUN
1 a red or brown coating that forms on iron or steel exposed to damp
2 a reddish-brown colour

rust VERB
to make or become rusty

rustic ADJECTIVE
1 rural
2 made of rough timber or branches

rustle VERB
1 to make a sound like paper being crumpled
2 to steal horses or cattle
rustle up (*informal*) to produce quickly *rustle up a meal*
rustle NOUN

rustler NOUN
someone who rustles horses or cattle

rusty ADJECTIVE **rustier**, **rustiest**
1 coated with rust
2 less skilful from lack of practice

rut NOUN
a deep track made by a wheel in soft ground
in a rut following a dull routine

ruthless ADJECTIVE
merciless or cruel
ruthlessly ADVERB

rye NOUN
a cereal used to make bread, biscuits, etc.

Ss

S. ABBREVIATION
1 south
2 southern

sabbath NOUN
a weekly day for rest and prayer, Saturday for Jews, Sunday for Christians

sabbatical (sa-**bat**-ikal) NOUN
a period of paid leave granted to a university teacher for study or travel

sable NOUN
1 a kind of dark fur
2 (*poetical use*) black

sabotage NOUN
deliberate damage or disruption to hinder an enemy, organization, etc.

sabotage VERB
to damage or destroy by sabotage

saboteur *NOUN*
a person who commits sabotage

sabre *NOUN*
1 a heavy sword with a curved blade
2 a light fencing sword

sac *NOUN*
a bag-shaped part in an animal or plant

saccharin (sak-er-in) *NOUN*
a sweet substance used as a substitute for sugar

sachet (sash-ay) *NOUN*
a small sealed packet containing shampoo, sugar, etc.

sack¹ *NOUN*
a large bag made of strong material
the sack (*informal*) dismissal from a job

sack *VERB*
(*informal*) to dismiss someone from a job

sack² *VERB*
(*old use*) to plunder a captured town in a violent destructive way
sack *NOUN*

sacrament *NOUN*
a Christian religious ceremony such as baptism or Holy Communion

sacred *ADJECTIVE*
holy; to do with God or a god

sacrifice *NOUN*
1 the offering of something to please a god, e.g. a killed animal
2 the act of giving up something valuable to benefit someone else
3 something sacrificed
sacrificial *ADJECTIVE*

sacrifice *VERB*
to offer something or give it up as a sacrifice

sacrilege (sak-ril-ij) *NOUN*
disrespect for something sacred
sacrilegious *ADJECTIVE*

sacrosanct *ADJECTIVE*
sacred or respected and therefore not to be harmed

sad *ADJECTIVE* **sadder, saddest**
unhappy; showing or causing sorrow
sadly *ADVERB* **sadness** *NOUN*

sadden *VERB*
to make a person sad

saddle *NOUN*
1 a seat put on the back of a horse or other animal
2 the seat of a bicycle
3 a ridge of high land between two peaks

saddle *VERB*
1 to put a saddle on a horse etc.
2 to burden someone with a task or problem

sadist (say-dist) *NOUN*
a person who enjoys hurting or humiliating other people
sadism *NOUN* **sadistic** *ADJECTIVE*

safari *NOUN*
an expedition to see or hunt wild animals

safari park *NOUN*
a park where wild animals are kept in enclosures to be seen by visitors

safe *ADJECTIVE*
1 not in danger
2 not dangerous
safely *ADVERB*

safe *NOUN*
a strong cupboard or box for keeping valuables

safeguard *NOUN*
a protection

safeguard *VERB*
to protect

safety *NOUN*
freedom from harm or danger

safety pin *NOUN*
a U-shaped pin with a clip fastening over the point

saffron *NOUN*
1 a deep yellow colour
2 a kind of crocus with orange-coloured stigmas which are dried and used as flavouring for food

sag *VERB* **sagging, sagged**
1 to sink in the middle from pressure
2 to hang down loosely
sag *NOUN*

saga (sah-ga) *NOUN*
a long story with many episodes or adventures

sagacious (sa-gay-shus) *ADJECTIVE*
shrewd and wise
sagacity *NOUN*

sage¹ *NOUN*
a kind of herb used in cooking

sage² *ADJECTIVE*
wise

sage *NOUN*
a wise person

sago *NOUN*
a starchy white food used to make puddings

said *past tense* of **say**

sail NOUN
1 a large piece of strong cloth attached to a mast etc. to catch the wind and make a ship or boat move
2 a short voyage
3 an arm of a windmill
set sail to begin a voyage by sea
sail VERB
1 to travel in a ship or boat
2 to start a voyage
3 to control a ship or boat
4 to move quickly and smoothly

sailor NOUN
1 a person who sails
2 a member of a ship's crew or of a navy

saint NOUN
a holy or very good person
saintly ADJECTIVE

sake NOUN
for the sake of in order to get or achieve something **for someone's sake** to help or please them

salad NOUN
a mixture of vegetables eaten raw or cold

salamander NOUN
a small lizard-like animal

salami NOUN
a spiced sausage eaten cold

salary NOUN **salaries**
a regular monthly wage

sale NOUN
1 the act of selling
2 a period of selling goods at reduced prices
for sale or **on sale** available to be bought

salesperson NOUN
a person employed to sell goods

salient (say-lee-ent) ADJECTIVE
most noticeable or important　*the salient features*

saline ADJECTIVE
containing salt

saliva NOUN
the natural liquid in a person's or animal's mouth

salivate (sal-iv-ayt) VERB
to form a lot of saliva
salivation NOUN

sallow ADJECTIVE
(of the skin) slightly yellow

sally NOUN **sallies**
1 a sudden rush forward
2 an excursion
3 a lively or witty remark
sally VERB **sallies**, **sallied**
to make a sudden attack

salmon (sam-on) NOUN **salmon**
a large edible fish with pink flesh

salmonella (sal-mon-el-a) NOUN
a bacterium that can cause food poisoning

salon NOUN
1 a large elegant room
2 a room or shop where a hairdresser etc. receives customers

saloon NOUN
1 a car with a hard roof and a separate boot
2 a more comfortable bar in a pub

salsa NOUN
1 a hot spicy sauce
2 a modern Latin American dance

salt NOUN
1 sodium chloride, the white substance that gives sea water its taste and is used for flavouring food
2 a chemical compound of a metal and an acid
salty ADJECTIVE
salt VERB
to flavour or preserve food with salt

salubrious ADJECTIVE
good for people's health

salutary ADJECTIVE
having a good effect　*salutary advice*

salutation NOUN
a greeting

salute VERB
1 to raise the right hand to your head as a sign of respect
2 to greet
3 to admire something openly
salute NOUN
1 the act of saluting
2 the firing of guns as a sign of greeting or respect

salvage VERB
to save or rescue damaged goods or cargo
salvage NOUN

salvation NOUN
1 the act of saving from loss or damage
2 (in Christianity) saving the soul from sin

salve NOUN
1 a soothing ointment
2 something that soothes a person's conscience or pride
salve VERB
to soothe a person's conscience or pride

salvo NOUN **salvoes** or **salvos**
a volley of shots

same ADJECTIVE
1 of one kind; exactly alike or equal
2 not changing; not different

sample NOUN
a small amount that shows what something is like

sample VERB
1 to take a sample of
2 to try part of

sanatorium NOUN **sanatoriums** or **sanatoria**
a hospital for people recovering from illnesses or with illnesses that cannot be cured

sanctify VERB **sanctifies**, **sanctified**
to make holy or sacred

sanctimonious ADJECTIVE
making a show of being virtuous or pious

sanction NOUN
1 action taken against a country
2 a penalty for disobeying a law
3 permission or authorization

sanction VERB
to permit or authorize

sanctity NOUN
a holy or sacred state

sanctuary NOUN **sanctuaries**
1 a safe place or refuge
2 an area where wildlife is protected
3 the part of a church where the altar stands

sand NOUN
the tiny particles that cover the ground in deserts, beaches, etc.

sand VERB
to smooth or polish with sandpaper
sander NOUN

sandal NOUN
a lightweight shoe with straps over the foot

sandalwood NOUN
a scented wood from a tropical tree

sandbag NOUN
a bag filled with sand, used to build defences

sandpaper NOUN
paper coated with sand for smoothing rough surfaces

sands PLURAL NOUN
a beach or sandy area

sandstone NOUN
rock made of compressed sand

sandwich NOUN
slices of bread with a filling between them

sandwich VERB
to put a thing between two others

sandy ADJECTIVE **sandier**, **sandiest**
1 like sand
2 covered with sand
3 a yellowish-red colour

sane ADJECTIVE
1 having a healthy mind; not mad
2 sensible
sanity NOUN

sanguine (sang-gwin) ADJECTIVE
cheerful and optimistic

sanitary ADJECTIVE
1 free from germs and dirt; hygienic
2 to do with sanitation

sanitation NOUN
arrangements for drainage and the disposal of sewage

sanitize VERB
to clean and disinfect

sanity NOUN
a sane state

sap NOUN
the juice inside a plant or tree

sap VERB **sapping**, **sapped**
to take away strength gradually

sapling NOUN
a young tree

sapphire NOUN
a bright-blue jewel

sarcasm NOUN
use of irony or humour to mock someone

sarcastic ADJECTIVE
using sarcasm
sarcastically ADVERB

sardine NOUN
a small sea fish, often sold packed tightly in oil

sardonic ADJECTIVE
grimly amusing
sardonically ADVERB

sari NOUN **saris**
a length of cloth worn wrapped round the body by Indian women and girls

sarong NOUN
a strip of cloth worn tucked round the waist or under the armpits by men and women in south-east Asia

sartorial ADJECTIVE
to do with clothes

sash NOUN
a strip of cloth worn round the waist or over one shoulder

sash window NOUN
a window that slides up and down

SAT ABBREVIATION
standard assessment task

satanic (suh-tan-ik) ADJECTIVE
to do with or like Satan, the Devil in Jewish and Christian teaching

satchel NOUN
a bag worn on the shoulder for carrying school books

satellite NOUN
1 a spacecraft put in orbit round a planet
2 a moon moving in an orbit round a planet
3 a country controlled by a more powerful neighbour

satellite television NOUN
television broadcasting in which the signals are transmitted by a satellite

satiated ADJECTIVE
having as much as or more than you want

satin NOUN
a silky material that is shiny on one side

satire NOUN
1 use of humour or exaggeration to ridicule people in power
2 a play or poem etc. that does this
satirical ADJECTIVE

satisfaction NOUN
1 the act of satisfying
2 the state of being satisfied
3 something that satisfies a desire etc.

satisfactory ADJECTIVE
good enough; adequate
satisfactorily ADVERB

satisfy VERB **satisfies**, **satisfied**
1 to give someone what they need or want
2 to convince
3 to fulfil needs etc.

satsuma NOUN
a kind of mandarin orange originally grown in Japan

saturate VERB
1 to make very wet
2 to make something take in as much as possible of something
saturation NOUN

Saturday NOUN
the day of the week following Friday

sauce NOUN
1 a thick liquid served with food to add flavour
2 (informal) cheek or impudence

saucepan NOUN
a metal cooking pan with a handle at the side

saucer NOUN
a shallow dish on which a cup is placed

saucy ADJECTIVE **saucier**, **sauciest**
cheeky or impudent
saucily ADVERB

sauna NOUN
a room or compartment filled with steam, used as a kind of bath

saunter VERB
to walk slowly and casually
saunter NOUN

sausage NOUN
a tube-shaped skin filled with seasoned minced meat

savage ADJECTIVE
wild and fierce; cruel
savagery NOUN

savage NOUN
a savage or primitive person

savage VERB
to attack fiercely

savannah or **savanna** NOUN
a grassy plain with no trees

save VERB
1 to keep safe or free from harm
2 to keep for later use
3 to avoid wasting something
4 (ICT) to store data in a file
5 (in sports) to prevent an opponent from scoring
save NOUN

save PREPOSITION
except

savings PLURAL NOUN
money saved

saviour NOUN
a person who saves someone

savour NOUN
the taste or smell of something

savour VERB
1 to enjoy the taste or smell of
2 to have a certain taste or smell

savoury ADJECTIVE
1 tasty but not sweet
2 having an appetizing taste or smell

savoury NOUN **savouries**
a savoury dish

saw [1] NOUN
a tool with a jagged edge for cutting wood or metal etc.

saw VERB **sawed**, **sawn**
to cut with a saw

saw [2] past tense of **see** [1]

sawdust NOUN
powder made when wood is cut by a saw

saxophone NOUN
a brass wind instrument with a curved flared opening
saxophonist NOUN

say VERB **said**
1 to speak or express in words
2 to give an opinion

say NOUN
the power to decide something

saying NOUN
a well-known phrase or proverb

scab NOUN
a hard crust that forms over a wound
scabby ADJECTIVE

scabbard NOUN
the sheath of a sword or dagger

scabies (skay-beez) *NOUN*
a contagious skin disease caused by a parasite

scaffold *NOUN*
a platform on which criminals are executed

scaffolding *NOUN*
a structure of poles and platforms for workers to stand on while building or repairing a house etc.

scald *VERB*
to burn yourself with hot liquid or steam
scald *NOUN*

scale[1] *NOUN*
1 a series of units or degrees for measuring
2 a series of musical notes in a fixed pattern
3 proportion or ratio
4 the relative size or importance of something
scale *VERB*
to climb

scale[2] *NOUN*
1 each of the thin overlapping parts on the outside of a fish, snake, etc.
2 a hard substance formed by hard water or on teeth

scalene (skay-leen) *ADJECTIVE*
(of a triangle) having unequal sides

scales *PLURAL NOUN*
a device for weighing

scallop *NOUN*
a shellfish with two hinged fan-shaped shells
scalloped *ADJECTIVE*

scalp *NOUN*
the skin on the top of the head
scalp *VERB*
to cut or tear the scalp from

scalpel *NOUN*
a small knife with a thin sharp blade, used in surgery

scaly *ADJECTIVE* **scalier**, **scaliest**
covered in scales or scale

scam *NOUN*
(*informal*) a dishonest scheme or swindle

scamp *NOUN*
a rascal

scamper *VERB*
to run quickly or playfully
scamper *NOUN*

scampi *PLURAL NOUN*
large prawns

scan *VERB* **scanning**, **scanned**
1 to look at every part of
2 to glance at
3 (of poetry) to be rhythmically correct
4 to sweep a radar or electronic beam over an area

scan *NOUN*
1 an act of scanning
2 an examination using a scanner

scandal *NOUN*
1 something shameful or disgraceful
2 gossip about people's faults and wrongdoings
scandalous *ADJECTIVE*

scandalize *VERB*
to shock by doing or saying something shameful or disgraceful

scanner *NOUN*
1 a machine that examines things by means of light or other rays
2 a machine that converts printed text, pictures, etc. into machine-readable form

scansion *NOUN*
the scanning of verse

scant *ADJECTIVE*
barely enough or adequate

scanty *ADJECTIVE* **scantier**, **scantiest**
small in amount or extent
scantily *ADVERB*

scapegoat *NOUN*
a person who bears the blame or punishment for others

scar *NOUN*
1 the mark left by a cut or burn etc.
2 psychological harm caused by an unpleasant experience
scar *VERB* **scarring**, **scarred**
to make a scar or scars on

scarab *NOUN*
an ornament or symbol carved in the shape of a beetle

scarce *ADJECTIVE* **scarcer**, **scarcest**
1 not plentiful or enough
2 rare

scarcely *ADVERB*
only just; only with difficulty

scarcity *NOUN* **scarcities**
a shortage

scare *VERB*
to frighten
scare *NOUN*
1 a fright
2 a sudden sense of alarm

scarecrow *NOUN*
a figure dressed in old clothes, set up to frighten birds away

scarf *NOUN* **scarves**
a strip of material worn round the neck or head

a
b
c
d
e
f
g
h
i
j
k
l
m
n
o
p
q
r
s
t
u
v
w
x
y
z

scarlet ADJECTIVE, NOUN
a bright red colour

scarp NOUN
a steep slope on a hill

scary ADJECTIVE **scarier**, **scariest**
(*informal*) frightening

scathing ADJECTIVE
severely critical

scatter VERB
1 to throw or send in all directions
2 to leave quickly in all directions

scatterbrain NOUN
a careless forgetful person

scavenge VERB
to search for useful things among rubbish
scavenger NOUN

scenario NOUN **scenarios**
1 a summary of the plot of a play etc.
2 an imagined series of events or set of
circumstances

scene NOUN
1 the place where something has happened
2 a part of a play or film
3 a view as seen by a spectator
4 an angry or noisy outburst
5 an area of activity

scenery NOUN
1 the natural features of a landscape
2 things put on a stage to make it look like a
place

scenic ADJECTIVE
having fine natural scenery

scent NOUN
1 a pleasant smell
2 a liquid perfume
3 an animal's smell that other animals can
detect

scent VERB
1 to discover something by its scent
2 to put scent on or in

sceptic (**skep**-tik) NOUN
a sceptical person

sceptical (**skep**-tik-al) ADJECTIVE
inclined to question things
sceptically ADVERB **scepticism** NOUN

sceptre NOUN
a rod carried by a king or queen as a symbol of
power

schedule (**shed**-yool) NOUN
a programme or timetable of planned events
or work

schedule VERB
1 to put into a schedule
2 to arrange for a certain time

schematic (skee-**mat**-ik) ADJECTIVE
in the form of a diagram or chart

scheme NOUN
a plan of action

scheme VERB
to make plans; to plot

schism (sizm) NOUN
the splitting of a group into two opposing
sections

schizophrenia (skid-zo-**free**-nee-a) NOUN
a kind of mental illness in which people
affected cannot relate their thoughts and
feelings to reality
schizophrenic ADJECTIVE, NOUN

scholar NOUN
1 a person who has studied a subject
thoroughly
2 a person who has been awarded a
scholarship
scholarly ADJECTIVE

scholarship NOUN
1 a grant of money given to a student to pay
for their education
2 the knowledge and methods of scholars

scholastic ADJECTIVE
to do with schools or education

school[1] NOUN
1 a place where children are taught
2 the pupils in a school
3 a group of people who have the same
beliefs or style of work etc.

school VERB
to teach or train

school[2] NOUN
a shoal of fish or whales etc.

schooling NOUN
1 education in a school
2 training

schoolteacher NOUN
a person who teaches in a school

schooner (**skoon**-er) NOUN
a sailing ship with two masts

science NOUN
1 the study of the physical world by means of
observation and experiment
2 a branch of this, such as chemistry, physics,
or biology

science fiction NOUN
stories about imaginary scientific discoveries
or space travel and life on other planets

scientific ADJECTIVE
1 to do with science or scientists
2 studying things systematically
scientifically ADVERB

scientist NOUN
an expert in science

scintillating ADJECTIVE
lively and witty

scissors *PLURAL NOUN*
a cutting instrument with two blades that close against each other

scoff[1] *VERB*
to speak contemptuously

scoff[2] *VERB*
(*informal*) to eat greedily

scold *VERB*
to speak angrily to

scone *NOUN*
a soft flat plain cake

scoop *NOUN*
1 a deep spoon for serving ice cream etc.
2 a news story published exclusively by one newspaper

scoop *VERB*
to lift or hollow out with a scoop

scooter *NOUN*
1 a kind of motorcycle with small wheels
2 a board with wheels and a long handle, pushed along by foot

scope *NOUN*
1 opportunity or possibility
2 the range or extent of a subject

scorch *VERB*
to burn slightly

scorching *ADJECTIVE*
(*informal*) very hot

score *NOUN*
1 the number of points or goals made in a game
2 (*old use*) a group of twenty
3 written or printed music

score *VERB*
1 to get a point or goal in a game
2 to keep a count of the score
3 to mark with lines or cuts
4 to write out a musical score
scorer *NOUN*

scores *PLURAL NOUN*
very many

scorn *NOUN*
contempt

scorn *VERB*
1 to treat with contempt
2 to refuse indignantly

scornful *ADJECTIVE*
contemptuous
scornfully *ADVERB*

scorpion *NOUN*
an animal with eight legs and a poisonous sting

scotch[1] *NOUN*
whisky made in Scotland

scotch[2] *VERB*
to put an end to an idea or rumour etc.

scot-free *ADJECTIVE*
without harm or punishment

scoundrel *NOUN*
a wicked or dishonest person

scour[1] *VERB*
to rub something until it is clean and bright
scourer *NOUN*

scour[2] *VERB*
to search thoroughly

scourge (skerj) *NOUN*
something that causes suffering

Scout *NOUN*
a member of the Scout Association, an organization for boys

scout *NOUN*
someone sent out to collect information

scout *VERB*
1 to act as a scout
2 to search an area thoroughly

scowl *NOUN*
an angry frown

scowl *VERB*
to frown angrily

scrabble *VERB*
to grope or struggle to reach or get something

scraggy *ADJECTIVE* **scraggier**, **scraggiest**
thin and bony

scram *EXCLAMATION*
(*informal*) go away!

scramble *VERB*
1 to move quickly and awkwardly
2 to struggle to do or get something
3 to cook eggs by beating them and heating them in a pan
4 to mix things together
5 to alter a radio or telephone signal so that it has to be decoded

scramble *NOUN*
1 a climb or walk over rough ground
2 a struggle to do or get something
3 a motorcycle race over rough country

scrap[1] *NOUN*
1 a small piece
2 rubbish or waste material

scrap *VERB* **scrapping**, **scrapped**
to get rid of something useless or unwanted

scrap[2] *NOUN*
(*informal*) a fight

scrap *VERB* **scrapping**, **scrapped**
(*informal*) to fight

scrape *VERB*
1 to rub or damage something by passing something hard over it
2 to make a harsh sound by rubbing against a rough or hard surface
3 to remove by scraping
4 to get something by great effort or care
scrape through to succeed by a small margin

scrape *NOUN*
1 a scraping movement or sound
2 a mark etc. made by scraping
3 (*informal*) an awkward situation

scrappy *ADJECTIVE* **scrappier**, **scrappiest**
untidy or carelessly done

scratch *VERB*
1 to mark or cut the surface of a thing with something sharp
2 to rub the skin with fingernails or claws
3 to withdraw from a race or competition

scratch *NOUN*
1 a mark made by scratching
2 the action of scratching
from scratch from the start **up to scratch** good enough
scratchy *ADJECTIVE*

scrawl *NOUN*
untidy handwriting

scrawl *VERB*
to write in a scrawl

scrawny *ADJECTIVE* **scrawnier**, **scrawniest**
thin and bony

scream *NOUN*
1 a loud cry of pain, fear, anger, or excitement
2 a loud piercing sound
3 (*informal*) an amusing person or thing

scream *VERB*
to make a scream

screech *VERB*
to make a harsh high-pitched sound
screech *NOUN*

screen *NOUN*
1 a surface for showing films
2 a device for displaying television pictures or computer data
3 a vehicle's windscreen
4 a movable panel used to hide, protect, or divide something

screen *VERB*
1 to protect, hide, or divide with a screen
2 to show a film or television pictures on a screen
3 to check someone for the presence of a disease
4 to check whether a person is suitable for a job

screenplay *NOUN*
the script of a film, with instructions to the actors

screw *NOUN*
1 a metal pin with a spiral thread round it, holding things together by being twisted in
2 something twisted
3 a propeller on a ship or motor boat

screw *VERB*
1 to fasten with a screw or screws
2 to fit or turn by twisting

screwdriver *NOUN*
a tool for turning screws

scribble *VERB*
1 to write quickly or untidily
2 to make meaningless marks
scribble *NOUN*

scribe *NOUN*
1 a person who made copies of manuscripts
2 (in biblical times) a professional religious scholar
scribal *ADJECTIVE*

scrimp *VERB*
to use money very carefully

script *NOUN*
1 handwriting
2 the text of a play, film, broadcast talk, etc.

scripture *NOUN*
1 sacred writings
2 (in Christianity) the Bible

scroll *NOUN*
1 a roll of paper or parchment used for writing
2 a spiral design

scroll *VERB*
to move the display on a computer screen up or down

scrotum (skroh-tuhm) *NOUN*
the pouch of skin containing the testicles

scrounge *VERB*
to get something without paying for it
scrounger *NOUN*

scrub [1] *VERB* **scrubbing**, **scrubbed**
1 to rub or clean with a hard brush
2 (*informal*) to cancel
scrub *NOUN*

scrub [2] *NOUN*
land covered with low trees and bushes

scruff *NOUN*
the back of the neck

scruffy *ADJECTIVE* **scruffier**, **scruffiest**
shabby and untidy
scruffily *ADVERB*

scrum *NOUN*
a group of forwards from each side in rugby football who push against each other to get possession of the ball

scrumptious ADJECTIVE
(*informal*) delicious

scrunch VERB
1 to crunch
2 to crush or crumple

scruple NOUN
a feeling of doubt about whether something is morally right

scrupulous ADJECTIVE
1 careful and conscientious
2 strictly honest or honourable

scrutinize VERB
to look at carefully

scrutiny NOUN **scrutinies**
a careful examination of something

scuba diving NOUN
swimming underwater using a tank of air strapped to your back

scuff VERB
1 to drag your feet while walking
2 to scrape with your foot

scuffle NOUN
a confused fight or struggle

scuffle VERB
to take part in a scuffle

scullery NOUN **sculleries**
a small room next to a kitchen, used for washing and cleaning

sculpt VERB
to make sculptures

sculptor NOUN
a person who makes sculptures

sculpture NOUN
1 the art of making shapes by carving wood or stone or casting metal
2 a shape made in this way

scum NOUN
froth or dirt on top of a liquid

scupper VERB
to wreck plans or chances

scurf NOUN
flakes of dry skin
scurfy ADJECTIVE

scurrilous ADJECTIVE
rude, insulting, and probably untrue

scurry VERB **scurries**, **scurried**
to run with quick short steps

scurvy NOUN
a disease caused by lack of vitamin C

scuttle[1] NOUN
a container for coal in a house

scuttle[2] VERB
1 to hurry away
2 to sink a ship deliberately

scythe NOUN
a tool with a long curved blade for cutting grass or corn

scythe VERB
to cut with a scythe

sea NOUN
1 the salt water that covers most of the earth's surface
2 a large lake
3 a large area of something *a sea of faces*

seaboard NOUN
a coastline or coastal region

seafaring ADJECTIVE, NOUN
working or travelling on the sea
seafarer NOUN

seafood NOUN
fish or shellfish from the sea used as food

seagull NOUN
a seabird with long wings

sea horse NOUN
a small fish that swims upright, with a head like a horse's head

seal[1] NOUN
a sea mammal with thick fur or bristles

seal[2] NOUN
1 a piece of metal with an engraved design for pressing on a soft substance to leave an impression
2 this impression made on a piece of wax
3 something designed to close an opening
4 a small decorative sticker

seal VERB
1 to close something by sticking two parts together
2 to close securely
3 to press a seal on
4 to settle or decide
seal off to prevent people getting to an area

sea level NOUN
the level of the sea halfway between high and low tide

sealing wax NOUN
a substance that is soft when heated but hardens when cooled, used for sealing documents

sea lion NOUN
a kind of large seal

seam NOUN
1 the line where two edges of cloth or wood etc. join
2 a layer of coal in the ground

seaman NOUN
a sailor

seamanship NOUN
skill in seafaring

seamy ADJECTIVE **seamier**, **seamiest**
sordid or unattractive

seance (say-ahns) *NOUN*
a meeting at which people try to make contact with the dead

sear *VERB*
to scorch or burn

search *VERB*
to look carefully to find something
search *NOUN*

search engine *NOUN*
(ICT) a computer program that searches the Internet

searching *ADJECTIVE*
examining closely and thoroughly

searchlight *NOUN*
a light with a strong beam that can be turned in any direction

searing *ADJECTIVE*
(of a pain) sharp and burning

seasick *ADJECTIVE*
sick because of the movement of a ship

seaside *NOUN*
a place by the sea where people go for holidays

season *NOUN*
1 each of the four main parts of the year (spring, summer, autumn, winter)
2 the time of year when an activity takes place

season *VERB*
1 to give extra flavour to food
2 to dry and treat timber etc. for use

seasonal *ADJECTIVE*
1 for or to do with a season
2 happening in a particular season

seasoning *NOUN*
a substance used to season food

season ticket *NOUN*
a ticket that can be used repeatedly for a period of time

seat *NOUN*
1 a thing made or used for sitting on
2 a place on a council or committee, in parliament, etc.
3 the buttocks
4 the place where something is based or located

seat *VERB*
1 to place in or on a seat
2 to have enough seats for

seat belt *NOUN*
a strap to hold a person securely in a seat

seating *NOUN*
1 the seats in a place
2 the arrangement of seats

seaweed *NOUN*
a plant or plants that grow in the sea

seaworthy *ADJECTIVE*
(of a ship) fit for a sea voyage
seaworthiness *NOUN*

secateurs *PLURAL NOUN*
clippers held in the hand for pruning plants

secede *VERB*
to withdraw from being a member of an organization
secession *NOUN*

secluded *ADJECTIVE*
quiet and sheltered from view
seclusion *NOUN*

second[1] *ADJECTIVE*
1 next after the first
2 another *a second chance*
3 less good *second quality*
second thoughts doubts about a decision

second *NOUN*
1 a person or thing that is second
2 an attendant of a fighter in a boxing match, duel, etc.
3 one-sixtieth of a minute of time or of a degree used in measuring angles

second *VERB*
1 to assist someone
2 to support a proposal

second[2] (sik-ond) *VERB*
to transfer a person temporarily to other work
secondment *NOUN*

secondary *ADJECTIVE*
1 coming after or from something
2 less important

secondary colour *NOUN*
a colour made by mixing two primary colours

secondary school *NOUN*
a school for pupils of more than about 11 years old

second-hand *ADJECTIVE*
bought from or used by a previous owner

secondly *ADVERB*
in the second place; as the second one

second nature *NOUN*
behaviour that has become automatic or habitual

second-rate *ADJECTIVE*
inferior; not very good

second sight *NOUN*
the ability to foresee the future

secrecy *NOUN*
the state of keeping things secret

secret *ADJECTIVE*
1 that must not be told or shown to other people
2 not known by everybody
secretly *ADVERB*

secret NOUN
something secret

secretary (sek-rit-ree) NOUN **secretaries**
1 a person who helps with letters, answers the telephone, etc. in an office
2 the chief assistant of a government minister or ambassador
secretarial ADJECTIVE

secrete VERB
1 to hide something
2 to produce a substance in the body
secretion NOUN

secretive (seek-rit-iv) ADJECTIVE
liking or trying to keep things secret

sect NOUN
a group of people whose beliefs differ from those of others in the same religion

sectarian (sekt-**air**-ee-an) ADJECTIVE
belonging to or supporting a sect

section NOUN
1 a part of something
2 a cross-section

sector NOUN
1 one part of an area
2 a part of something *the private sector*
3 (*Maths*) a section of a circle between two lines drawn from its centre to its circumference

secular ADJECTIVE
to do with worldly affairs, not with religion

secure ADJECTIVE
1 safe against attack
2 certain not to slip or fail
3 reliable
securely ADVERB

secure VERB
1 to make secure
2 to fasten firmly
3 to obtain

security NOUN **securities**
1 a secure state; safety
2 precautions against theft or spying etc.
3 something given as a guarantee for a debt

sedate ADJECTIVE
calm and dignified

sedate VERB
to give a sedative to
sedation NOUN

sedative NOUN
a medicine that makes a person calm

sedge NOUN
a grass-like plant growing in marshes or near water

sediment NOUN
fine particles of solid matter at the bottom of liquid

sedimentary ADJECTIVE
(of rock) formed from particles that have settled on a surface

sedition NOUN
speeches or actions intended to make people rebel
seditious ADJECTIVE

seduce VERB
1 to persuade a person to have sexual intercourse
2 to lead astray with temptations
seduction NOUN

seductive ADJECTIVE
1 sexually attractive
2 tempting

see VERB **saw, seen**
1 to perceive with the eyes
2 to meet or visit
3 to understand
4 to imagine
5 to consider *shall see what we can do*
6 to make sure
7 to discover *see who it is*
8 to escort
see to attend to

seed NOUN
1 a fertilized part of a plant, capable of growing into a new plant
2 a seeded player in a competition

seed VERB
1 to plant or sprinkle seeds in
2 to name the best players and arrange for them not to play against each other in the early rounds of a tournament

seedling NOUN
a young plant growing from a seed

seedy ADJECTIVE **seedier, seediest**
1 full of seeds
2 shabby and disreputable

seeing CONJUNCTION
considering

seek VERB **sought**
1 to search for
2 to try to do or obtain something

seem VERB
to give the impression of being something

seemly ADJECTIVE
(*old use*) (of behaviour etc.) proper or suitable

seep VERB
to ooze slowly out or through something
seepage NOUN

seer NOUN
a prophet

see-saw NOUN
a plank balanced in the middle so that two people can sit, one on each end, and make it go up and down

seethe *VERB*
1 to be angry or excited
2 to bubble and surge like water boiling

segment *NOUN*
a part that is separated from other parts

segregate *VERB*
1 to separate people of different religions,
races, etc.
2 to isolate a person or thing
segregation *NOUN*

seismic (sy-zmik) *ADJECTIVE*
to do with earthquakes

seize *VERB*
1 to take hold of suddenly or forcibly
2 to take possession of by force or by legal
authority
3 to take eagerly
4 to have a sudden effect on *Panic seized us.*
seize up to become jammed

seizure *NOUN*
1 the act of seizing
2 a sudden fit, as in epilepsy or a heart attack

seldom *ADVERB*
rarely; not often

select *VERB*
to choose a person or thing

select *ADJECTIVE*
1 carefully chosen
2 (of a club etc.) choosing its members
carefully

selection *NOUN*
1 the process of selecting
2 a person or thing selected
3 a group selected from a larger group
4 a range of goods from which to choose

selective *ADJECTIVE*
choosing or chosen carefully
selectively *ADVERB*

self *NOUN* **selves**
1 a person as an individual
2 a person's particular nature *is her old self
again*

self-centred *ADJECTIVE*
concerned only with yourself; selfish

self-confident *ADJECTIVE*
confident of your own abilities

self-conscious *ADJECTIVE*
embarrassed or awkward in the presence of
other people

self-contained *ADJECTIVE*
(of accommodation) complete in itself

self-control *NOUN*
the ability to control your own behaviour
self-controlled *ADJECTIVE*

self-defence *NOUN*
1 the process of defending yourself
2 techniques for doing this

self-employed *ADJECTIVE*
working independently, not for an employer

self-evident *ADJECTIVE*
obvious and not needing proof

self-important *ADJECTIVE*
having a high opinion of yourself; pompous

selfish *ADJECTIVE*
doing what you want and not thinking of
other people
selfishly *ADVERB*

selfless *ADJECTIVE*
thinking of other people; considerate

self-made *ADJECTIVE*
rich or successful from your own efforts

self-raising *ADJECTIVE*
(of flour) making cakes rise without needing
to have baking powder etc. added

self-respect *NOUN*
respect for yourself

self-righteous *ADJECTIVE*
smugly sure that you are behaving virtuously

selfsame *ADJECTIVE*
the very same

self-satisfied *ADJECTIVE*
very pleased with yourself

self-service *ADJECTIVE*
at which customers serve themselves

sell *VERB* **sold**
1 to exchange something for money
2 to have something available for people
to buy
3 to be on sale at a certain price *It sells
for £5.99.*
seller *NOUN*

sell-by date *NOUN*
a date marked on a product, after which it
should not be sold

sell-out *NOUN*
an entertainment etc. for which all the tickets
have been sold

selves *plural* of **self**

semantic (sim-an-tik) *ADJECTIVE*
to do with the meanings of words
semantically *ADVERB*

semaphore *NOUN*
a system of signalling by holding flags out
with the arms in positions indicating letters of
the alphabet

semblance *NOUN*
an outward appearance or apparent likeness

semen (seem-en) *NOUN*
a white liquid produced by males and
containing sperm

semibreve *NOUN*
the longest musical note normally used (o),
lasting four times as long as a crotchet

semicircle *NOUN*
half a circle
semicircular *ADJECTIVE*

semicolon *NOUN*
a punctuation mark (;) used to mark a break
that is stronger than a comma

semiconductor *NOUN*
a substance that can conduct electricity but
not as well as most metals do

semi-detached *ADJECTIVE*
(of a house) joined to another house on one
side only

semifinal *NOUN*
a match or round whose winner will take part
in the final

seminar *NOUN*
a meeting for advanced discussion and
research on a subject

semiquaver *NOUN*
a note in music (♪), equal in length to one
quarter of a crotchet

semi-skimmed *ADJECTIVE*
(of milk) having had some of the cream taken
out

Semitic (sim-it-ik) *ADJECTIVE*
to do with the Semites, the group of people
that includes the Jews and Arabs

semitone *NOUN*
half a tone in music

semolina *NOUN*
hard round grains of wheat used to make milk
puddings and pasta

senate *NOUN*
1 the governing council in ancient Rome
2 the upper house of the parliament of the
United States, France, and other countries
senator *NOUN*

send *VERB* **sent**
1 to make a person or thing go or be taken
somewhere
2 to cause to become *was sending me crazy*
send for to order to come or be brought
sender *NOUN*

senile *ADJECTIVE*
weak and forgetful because of old age
senility *NOUN*

senior *ADJECTIVE*
1 older than someone else
2 higher in rank

3 for older children *a senior school*
seniority *NOUN*

senior *NOUN*
1 a person who is older or higher in rank
2 a member of a senior school

senior citizen *NOUN*
an elderly person, especially a pensioner

senna *NOUN*
the dried pods or leaves of a tropical tree,
used as a laxative

sensation *NOUN*
1 a feeling
2 an excited condition or a cause of this

sensational *ADJECTIVE*
causing great excitement or interest
sensationally *ADVERB*

sense *NOUN*
1 the ability to see, hear, smell, touch, or taste
2 the ability to feel or appreciate something
3 the power to think or make decisions
4 meaning

sense *VERB*
1 to feel; to get an impression
2 to detect

senseless *ADJECTIVE*
1 not showing good sense
2 unconscious

sensibility *NOUN* **sensibilities**
sensitiveness or delicate feeling

sensible *ADJECTIVE*
having or showing good sense
sensibly *ADVERB*

sensitive *ADJECTIVE*
1 strongly affected by something
sensitive to light
2 receiving impressions quickly and easily
sensitive fingers
3 easily hurt or offended
4 considerate about other people's feelings
5 needing to be dealt with tactfully *a sensitive
subject*
sensitively *ADVERB* **sensitivity** *NOUN*

sensitize *VERB*
to make a thing sensitive to something

sensor *NOUN*
a device or instrument for detecting a
physical property such as light, heat, or sound

sensory *ADJECTIVE*
1 to do with the senses
2 receiving sensations

sensual *ADJECTIVE*
1 to do with physical pleasure
2 liking or suggesting physical or sexual
pleasures

a
b
c
d
e
f
g
h
i
j
k
l
m
n
o
p
q
r
s
t
u
v
w
x
y
z

sensuous ADJECTIVE
giving pleasure to the senses, especially by being beautiful or delicate

sentence NOUN
1 a group of words that express a complete thought and form a statement, question, exclamation, or command
2 the punishment announced to a convicted person in a lawcourt

sentence VERB
to give someone a sentence in a lawcourt

sentiment NOUN
1 an opinion
2 sentimentality

sentimental ADJECTIVE
showing or arousing excessive feelings of sadness, pity, etc.
sentimentality NOUN

sentinel NOUN
a guard or sentry

sentry NOUN **sentries**
a soldier on guard duty

sepal NOUN
each of the leaves forming the calyx of a bud

separable ADJECTIVE
able to be separated

separate (sep-er-at) ADJECTIVE
1 not joined to anything
2 not shared
separately ADVERB

separate (sep-er-ayt) VERB
1 to make or keep separate
2 to become separate
3 to stop living together as a couple
separation NOUN

September NOUN
the ninth month of the year

septet NOUN
1 a group of seven musicians
2 a piece of music for seven musicians

septic ADJECTIVE
infected with harmful bacteria that cause pus to form

sequel NOUN
1 a book or film etc. that continues the story of an earlier one
2 something that follows or results from an earlier event

sequence NOUN
1 the order in which things happen
2 a series of things

sequin NOUN
a tiny bright disc sewn on clothes etc. to decorate them

serenade NOUN
a song or tune of a kind played by a man under his lover's window

serenade VERB
to sing or play a serenade to

serene ADJECTIVE
calm and peaceful
serenity (ser-en-iti) NOUN

serf NOUN
a farm labourer who worked for a landowner in the Middle Ages, and who was not allowed to leave
serfdom NOUN

sergeant (sar-jent) NOUN
a soldier or policeman in charge of others

sergeant major NOUN
a soldier who is one rank higher than a sergeant

serial NOUN
a story or film etc. that is presented in separate parts
Do not confuse this word with *cereal*.

series NOUN **series**
1 a number of things following or connected with each other
2 a number of separate radio or television programmes with the same characters or on the same subject

serious ADJECTIVE
1 solemn and thoughtful
2 needing careful thought
3 sincere *a serious attempt*
4 causing anxiety *a serious accident*
seriously ADVERB

sermon NOUN
a talk given by a preacher as part of a religious service

serpent NOUN
a snake

serrated ADJECTIVE
having a notched edge

serum (seer-um) NOUN
the thin pale yellow liquid that remains from blood when the rest has clotted and that contains antibodies

servant NOUN
a person who works or serves in someone else's house

serve VERB
1 to work for a person or organization or country etc.
2 to sell things to people in a shop
3 to give out food at a meal
4 to spend time doing something
5 to be suitable for something *will serve our purpose*
6 to start play in tennis etc. by hitting the ball
it serves you right you deserve it

serve NOUN
a service in tennis etc.

server NOUN
1 a person or thing that serves
2 (*ICT*) a computer or program that controls or supplies information to several computers in a network

service NOUN
1 the activity of working for a person or organization or country etc.
2 something that supplies a need *a bus service*
3 the army, navy, or air force *the armed services*
4 a religious ceremony
5 provision of goods, food, etc.
6 a set of dishes and plates etc. for a meal
7 maintenance of a vehicle or machine etc.
8 the action of serving in tennis etc.

service VERB
1 to repair or keep a vehicle or machine etc. in working order
2 to supply with services

serviceable ADJECTIVE
suitable for ordinary use or wear

service station NOUN
a place beside a road, where petrol and various services are available

serviette NOUN
a piece of cloth or paper used to keep your clothes or hands clean at a meal

servile ADJECTIVE
too willing to serve or obey others
servility NOUN

serving NOUN
a helping of food

sesame NOUN
an African plant with seeds that can be eaten or used to make an edible oil

session NOUN
1 a meeting or series of meetings
2 a time spent doing one thing *a recording session*

set VERB **set**
1 to put or fix
2 to make ready to work *to set the alarm*
3 to make or become firm or hard
4 to give someone a task
5 to put into a condition *set them free*
6 (of the sun) to go down below the horizon
set off or **out** to begin a journey **set up** to arrange or organize

set NOUN
1 a group of people or things that belong together
2 a radio or television receiver

3 (*Maths*) a collection of things that have a common property
4 the scenery or stage for a play or film
5 a group of games in a tennis match
6 a badger's burrow

set ADJECTIVE
1 fixed or arranged in advance
2 ready or prepared to do something
set on determined about

setback NOUN
something that stops progress or slows it down

set square NOUN
a device shaped like a right-angled triangle, used in drawing parallel lines etc.

settee NOUN
a long soft seat with a back and arms

setter NOUN
a dog of a long-haired breed that can be trained to stand rigid when it scents game

setting NOUN
1 the way or place in which something is set
2 music for the words of a song etc.
3 a set of cutlery or crockery for one person at a meal

settle VERB
1 to arrange or decide
2 to make or become calm or comfortable or orderly
3 to go and live somewhere
4 to come to rest on something
5 to pay a bill or debt

settlement NOUN
1 the act of settling something
2 the way something is settled
3 a small number of people or houses in a new area

settler NOUN
one of the first people to settle in a new country

set-up NOUN
(*informal*) the way something is organized or arranged

seven NOUN, ADJECTIVE
the number 7
seventh ADJECTIVE, NOUN

seventeen NOUN, ADJECTIVE
the number 17
seventeenth ADJECTIVE, NOUN

seventy NOUN, ADJECTIVE **seventies**
the number 70
seventieth ADJECTIVE, NOUN

sever VERB
to cut or break off
severance NOUN

several ADJECTIVE, NOUN
more than two but not many

a
b
c
d
e
f
g
h
i
j
k
l
m
n
o
p
q
r
s
t
u
v
w
x
y
z

severally *ADVERB*
separately

severe *ADJECTIVE*
1 strict; not gentle or kind
2 intense or forceful *severe weather*
3 very plain
severely *ADVERB* **severity** *NOUN*

sew *VERB* **sewn** or **sewed**
1 to join things together by using a needle and thread
2 to work with a needle and thread or with a sewing machine
Do not confuse this word with *sow*.

sewage (soo-ij) *NOUN*
liquid waste matter carried away in drains

sewer (soo-er) *NOUN*
a large underground drain for carrying away sewage

sex *NOUN*
1 each of the two groups (*male* and *female*) into which living things are placed according to their functions in the process of reproduction
2 sex is to come together in order to have offspring

sexism *NOUN*
discrimination against people of a particular sex
sexist *ADJECTIVE, NOUN*

sextant *NOUN*
an instrument for measuring the angle of the sun and stars, used for finding a position when navigating

sextet *NOUN*
1 a group of six musicians
2 a piece of music for six musicians

sexual *ADJECTIVE*
1 to do with sex or the sexes
2 (of reproduction) happening by the fusion of male and female cells
sexuality *NOUN* **sexually** *ADVERB*

sexy *ADJECTIVE* **sexier**, **sexiest**
(*informal*) sexually attractive or exciting

shabby *ADJECTIVE* **shabbier**, **shabbiest**
1 in a poor or worn-out condition
2 poorly dressed
3 unfair or dishonourable *a shabby trick*
shabbily *ADVERB*

shack *NOUN*
a roughly built hut

shackle *NOUN*
an iron ring for fastening a prisoner's wrist or ankle

shackle *VERB*
1 to put shackles on a prisoner
2 to restrict or limit someone

shade *NOUN*
1 slight darkness when light is blocked
2 a device that reduces or shuts out bright light
3 a colour; the strength of a colour
4 a slight difference

shade *VERB*
1 to shelter something from bright light
2 to make part of a drawing darker
3 to move gradually from one state or quality to another *evening shading into night*
shading *NOUN*

shadow *NOUN*
1 the dark shape that falls on a surface when something is between the surface and a light
2 an area of shade
3 a slight trace
shadowy *ADJECTIVE*

shadow *VERB*
1 to cast a shadow on something
2 to follow a person secretly

shady *ADJECTIVE* **shadier**, **shadiest**
1 giving shade *a shady tree*
2 in the shade *a shady place*
3 (*informal*) not completely honest *a shady deal*

shaft *NOUN*
1 a long slender rod or straight part
2 a ray of light
3 a deep narrow hole

shaggy *ADJECTIVE* **shaggier**, **shaggiest**
1 having long rough hair or fibre
2 (of hair) thick and untidy

shah *NOUN*
the title of the former ruler of Iran

shake *VERB* **shook**, **shaken**
1 to move quickly up and down or from side to side
2 to shock or upset
3 (of the voice) to tremble

shake *NOUN*
1 a shaking movement
2 (*informal*) a milkshake

shaky *ADJECTIVE* **shakier**, **shakiest**
unsteady or wobbly
shakily *ADVERB*

shale *NOUN*
a kind of stone that splits easily into layers

shall *AUXILIARY VERB*
1 used with *I* and *we* to refer to the future *I shall arrive tomorrow.*
2 used with *I* and *we* in questions or suggestions *Shall I shut the door?*
3 used for emphasis *You shall go.*

shallot NOUN
a kind of small onion

shallow ADJECTIVE **shallower**, **shallowest**
1 not deep *shallow water*
2 not capable of deep feelings *a shallow character*

shallows PLURAL NOUN
a shallow part of a stretch of water

sham NOUN
something that is not genuine; a pretence
sham ADJECTIVE

sham VERB **shamming**, **shammed**
to pretend

shamble VERB
to walk or run in a lazy or awkward way

shambles NOUN
a scene of great disorder or bloodshed

shambolic ADJECTIVE
(*informal*) chaotic or disorganized

shame NOUN
1 a feeling of sorrow or guilt for an action
2 dishonour or disgrace
3 something you regret

shame VERB
make a person feel ashamed

shamefaced ADJECTIVE
looking ashamed

shameful ADJECTIVE
disgraceful
shamefully ADVERB

shameless ADJECTIVE
not showing any shame
shamelessly ADVERB

shampoo NOUN **shampoos**
1 a liquid for washing the hair
2 a substance for cleaning a carpet etc.
3 a wash with shampoo

shampoo VERB **shampoos**, **shampooed**
to wash or clean with a shampoo

shamrock NOUN
a plant like clover, the national emblem of Ireland

shank NOUN
1 the leg from the knee to the ankle
2 a long narrow part

shan't
shall not

shanty NOUN **shanties**
1 a crude dwelling or shack
2 a sailors' song with a chorus

shanty town NOUN
a settlement consisting of shanties

shape NOUN
1 a thing's outline; the appearance an outline produces
2 proper form or condition
3 the general form or condition of something

shape VERB
1 to make into a particular shape
2 to develop

shapeless ADJECTIVE
having no definite shape

shapely ADJECTIVE **shapelier**, **shapeliest**
having an attractive shape

share NOUN
1 a part given to one person or thing out of something that is divided
2 each of the equal parts forming a business company's capital

share VERB
1 to give portions of something to two or more people
2 to have or use or experience something jointly with others

shareholder NOUN
a person who owns shares in a company

shark NOUN
1 a large sea fish with sharp teeth
2 a person who exploits or cheats people

sharp ADJECTIVE
1 with an edge or point that can cut or make holes
2 quick at noticing or learning things
3 clear or distinct
4 steep or pointed *a sharp bend*
5 forceful or severe *a sharp pain*
6 loud and shrill *a sharp cry*
7 slightly sour
8 (*Music*) one semitone higher than the natural note *C sharp*

sharp ADVERB
1 sharply *Turn sharp right.*
2 punctually or precisely *at six o'clock sharp*

sharp NOUN
(*Music*) a note one semitone higher than the natural note; the sign (#) that indicates this

sharpen VERB
to make or become sharp
sharpener NOUN

sharp practice NOUN
dishonest or barely honest dealings

shatter VERB
1 to break violently into small pieces
2 to destroy hopes etc.
3 to upset greatly

shave VERB
1 to cut growing hair off the skin with a razor
2 to cut or scrape a thin slice off something
shaver NOUN

shave *NOUN*
the act of shaving the face
a close shave (*informal*) a narrow escape

shaven *ADJECTIVE*
shaved

shavings *PLURAL NOUN*
thin strips shaved off a piece of wood or metal

shawl *NOUN*
a piece of material worn round the shoulders or head or wrapped round a baby

she *PRONOUN*
the female person or animal being talked about

sheaf *NOUN*
1 a bundle of cornstalks tied together
2 a bundle of arrows, papers, etc. held together

shear *VERB* **sheared** or, in sense 1, **shorn**
1 to cut or trim, especially wool from a sheep
2 to break because of a sideways force
shearer *NOUN*
Do not confuse this word with *sheer*.

shears *PLURAL NOUN*
a large pair of scissors used for cutting grass etc.

sheath *NOUN*
1 a cover for the blade of a knife or sword etc.
2 a close-fitting cover
3 a condom

sheathe *VERB*
to put into a sheath or cover

shed[1] *NOUN*
a simple building used for storing things or as a workshop

shed[2] *VERB* **shedding, shed**
1 to let something fall or flow
2 to get rid of

sheen *NOUN*
a shine or gloss

sheep *NOUN* **sheep**
an animal that eats grass and has a thick fleecy coat, kept in flocks for its wool and its meat

sheepdog *NOUN*
a dog trained to guard and herd sheep

sheepish *ADJECTIVE*
embarrassed or ashamed

sheer *ADJECTIVE*
1 complete or thorough *sheer stupidity*
2 vertical *a sheer drop*
3 (of material) thin and transparent

sheer *VERB*
to swerve or move sharply away
Do not confuse this word with *shear*.

sheet *NOUN*
1 a large piece of lightweight material used on a bed
2 a whole flat piece of paper, glass, or metal
3 a wide area of water, ice, flame, etc.

sheikh (shayk) *NOUN*
an Arab chief

shelf *NOUN* **shelves**
1 a flat piece of hard material fixed to a wall or in a piece of furniture for placing things on
2 a flat level surface that sticks out

shell *NOUN*
1 the hard outer covering of an egg, nut, etc., or of an animal such as a snail, crab, or tortoise
2 the walls or framework of a building, ship, etc.
3 a metal case filled with explosive, fired from a large gun

shell *VERB*
1 to take something out of its shell
2 to fire explosive shells at

shellfish *NOUN* **shellfish**
a sea animal that has a shell

shelter *NOUN*
1 a structure that protects people from rain, wind, danger, etc.
2 protection

shelter *VERB*
1 to provide with shelter
2 to protect
3 to find a shelter

shelve *VERB*
1 to put things on shelves
2 to postpone or reject a plan etc.
3 to slope

shepherd *NOUN*
a person who looks after sheep

shepherd *VERB*
to guide or direct people

shepherd's pie *NOUN*
a dish of minced beef or lamb covered with mashed potato

sherbet *NOUN*
a fizzy sweet powder or drink

sheriff *NOUN*
the chief law officer of a county

sherry *NOUN* **sherries**
a kind of strong wine

shield *NOUN*
1 a large piece of metal, wood, etc. carried to protect the body in fighting
2 a model of a triangular shield used as a trophy
3 a protection

shield VERB
to protect from harm or discovery

shift VERB
1 to move or cause to move
2 (of an opinion or situation) to change slightly

shift NOUN
1 a change of position or condition
2 a group of workers who start work as another group finishes
3 a straight dress with no waist

shifty ADJECTIVE
evasive; untrustworthy
shiftily ADVERB

shilling NOUN
a former British coin, equal to 5p

shilly-shally VERB **shilly-shallies**, **shilly-shallied**
to be indecisive

shimmer VERB
to shine with a quivering light
shimmer NOUN

shin NOUN
the front of the leg between the knee and the ankle

shin VERB **shinning**, **shinned**
to climb by using the arms and legs

shine VERB **shone** or, in sense 4, **shined**
1 to give out or reflect light; be bright
2 to be excellent
3 to aim a light
4 to polish *Have you shined your shoes?*

shine NOUN
1 brightness
2 a polish

shingle NOUN
pebbles on a beach

shingles NOUN
an infectious disease producing a painful rash

shiny ADJECTIVE **shinier**, **shiniest**
shining or glossy

ship NOUN
a large boat for journeys at sea

ship VERB **shipping**, **shipped**
to transport goods etc., especially by ship

shipment NOUN
1 the process of shipping goods
2 an amount shipped

shipping NOUN
1 ships *a danger to shipping*
2 the transporting of goods by ship

shipshape ADJECTIVE
in good order; tidy

shipwreck NOUN
1 the wrecking of a ship by storm or accident
2 a wrecked ship
shipwrecked ADJECTIVE

shipyard NOUN
a place where ships are built or repaired

shire NOUN
a county

shirk VERB
to avoid work or a duty
shirker NOUN

shirt NOUN
a piece of light clothing for the top half of the body, with a collar and sleeves

shirty ADJECTIVE **shirtier**, **shirtiest**
(*informal*) annoyed; irritable

shiver VERB
to tremble with cold or fear
shiver NOUN **shivery** ADJECTIVE

shoal NOUN
a large number of fish swimming together

shock NOUN
1 a sudden unpleasant surprise
2 great weakness caused by pain or injury etc.
3 the effect of a violent shake or knock
4 an effect caused by electric current passing through the body
5 a bushy mass of hair

shock VERB
1 to give someone a shock
2 to seem improper or scandalous to

shock absorber NOUN
a device for absorbing jolts and vibrations in a vehicle

shocking ADJECTIVE
1 causing indignation or disgust
2 (*informal*) very bad *shocking weather*

shock wave NOUN
a sharp change in pressure in the air around an explosion or an object moving very quickly

shod *past tense* of **shoe** VERB

shoddy ADJECTIVE **shoddier**, **shoddiest**
badly made or done *shoddy work*

shoe NOUN
1 a stiff covering for the foot
2 a horseshoe
3 something shaped or used like a shoe

shoe VERB **shoes**, **shoeing**, **shod**
to fit with a shoe or shoes

shoehorn NOUN
a curved piece of stiff material for easing on a shoe

shoelace NOUN
a cord for lacing up and fastening a shoe

shoo VERB **shoos**, **shooed**
to frighten or drive away

shoot VERB shot
1 to fire a gun or missile etc.
2 to hurt or kill by shooting
3 to move or send very quickly
4 to kick or hit a ball at a goal
5 to film or photograph

shoot NOUN
a new growth on a plant

shooting star NOUN
a meteor

shop NOUN
1 a building where goods are sold
2 a workshop

shop VERB shopping, shopped
to buy things in shops
shopper NOUN

shop floor NOUN
the workers in a factory

shopkeeper NOUN
a person who owns or manages a shop

shoplifter NOUN
a person who steals from a shop
shoplifting NOUN

shopping NOUN
1 the activity of buying goods in shops
2 goods bought

shop steward NOUN
a trade-union official who represents fellow
workers

shore[1] NOUN
the land along the edge of a sea or of a lake

shore[2] VERB
to prop up with beams etc.

shorn past participle of **shear**

short ADJECTIVE
1 not long in distance or time
2 not tall
3 not having enough of something
4 bad-tempered; curt
5 (of pastry) rich and crumbly because it
contains a lot of fat

short ADVERB
abruptly; suddenly stopped short

shortage NOUN
a lack or scarcity

shortbread NOUN
a rich sweet biscuit, made with butter

short circuit NOUN
a fault in an electrical circuit in which
current flows along a shorter route than
the normal one

short-circuit VERB
to cause a short circuit

shortcoming NOUN
a fault or failure to reach a good standard

short cut NOUN
a route or method that is quicker than the
usual one

shorten VERB
to make or become shorter

shortfall NOUN
an amount less than needed or expected

shorthand NOUN
a set of special signs for writing words down
as quickly as people say them

shortlist NOUN
a list of the most suitable people or things,
from which a final choice will be made

shortlist VERB
to put on a shortlist

shortly ADVERB
1 in a short time; soon
2 in a few words
3 curtly

shorts PLURAL NOUN
trousers with legs that stop at or above the
knee

short-sighted ADJECTIVE
1 unable to see things at a distance clearly
2 lacking imagination or foresight

short-tempered ADJECTIVE
irritable

short-term ADJECTIVE
to do with a short period of time

short wave NOUN
a radio wave of a wavelength between 10 and
100 metres and a frequency of about 3 to 30
megahertz

shot[1] past tense of **shoot**

shot[2] NOUN
1 the firing of a gun or missile etc.
2 something fired from a gun
3 a person judged by skill in shooting a good
shot
4 a heavy metal ball thrown as a sport
5 a stroke in tennis, cricket, billiards, etc.
6 a photograph or filmed scene
7 (informal) an attempt
8 an injection of a drug or vaccine

shotgun NOUN
a gun for firing small shot at close range

should AUXILIARY VERB
1 used to say what someone ought to do You
should have told me
2 used to say what someone expects They
should be here soon.
3 used with I and we to make a polite
statement I should like to come.

shoulder NOUN
the part of the body between the neck and the arm

shoulder VERB
1 to take on your shoulder
2 to accept responsibility or blame

shoulder blade NOUN
either of the two large flat bones at the top of your back

shouldn't
should not

shout NOUN
a loud cry or call

shout VERB
to give a shout

shove VERB
to push roughly
shove NOUN

shovel NOUN
a tool like a spade with the sides turned up, used for lifting

shovel VERB **shovelling**, **shovelled**
1 to move or clear with a shovel
2 (*informal*) to scoop or push quickly and in large amounts *He shovelled the pasta into his mouth.*

show VERB **showed**, **shown**
1 to allow or cause to be seen
2 to make a person understand *Show me how to use it.*
3 to guide *Show him in.*
4 to treat in a certain way *showed us kindness*
5 to be visible
show off to try to impress people **show up** to make or be clearly visible

show NOUN
1 a display or exhibition
2 an entertainment

showdown NOUN
a final test or confrontation

shower NOUN
1 a brief fall of rain or snow
2 a lot of small things coming or falling like rain
3 a device for spraying water to wash a person's body

shower VERB
1 to fall or send things in a shower
2 to wash under a shower

showjumping NOUN
a competition in which riders ride horses over fences and other obstacles

showman NOUN **showmen**
someone who is good at entertaining
showmanship NOUN

show-off NOUN
a person who tries to impress people boastfully

showroom NOUN
a large room where goods are displayed

showy ADJECTIVE **showier**, **showiest**
brightly or highly decorated

shrapnel NOUN
pieces of metal scattered from an exploding shell

shred NOUN
1 a tiny piece torn or cut off something
2 a small amount *not a shred of evidence*

shred VERB **shredding**, **shredded**
to cut into shreds
shredder NOUN

shrew NOUN
a small mouse-like animal

shrewd ADJECTIVE
having good sense and judgement
shrewdly ADVERB

shriek NOUN
a shrill cry or scream

shriek VERB
to give a shriek

shrift NOUN
short shrift curt treatment

shrill ADJECTIVE
sounding very high and piercing
shrilly ADVERB

shrimp NOUN
a small shellfish, pink when boiled

shrine NOUN
an altar, chapel, or other sacred place

shrink VERB **shrank**, **shrunk**
1 to make or become smaller
2 to move back to avoid something
3 to avoid doing something from fear, embarrassment, etc.

shrinkage NOUN
the amount by which something shrinks

shrivel VERB **shrivelling**, **shrivelled**
to make or become dry and wrinkled

shroud NOUN
1 a cloth in which a dead body is wrapped
2 a covering

shroud VERB
1 to wrap in a shroud
2 to cover or conceal *was shrouded in mist*

Shrove Tuesday NOUN
the day before Lent, when pancakes are eaten

shrub NOUN
a woody plant smaller than a tree; a bush
shrubby ADJECTIVE

a
b
c
d
e
f
g
h
i
j
k
l
m
n
o
p
q
r
s
t
u
v
w
x
y
z

shrubbery *NOUN* **shrubberies**
an area planted with shrubs

shrug *VERB* **shrugging**, **shrugged**
to raise your shoulders to show uncertainty or lack of interest
shrug *NOUN*

shrunken *ADJECTIVE*
having shrunk

shudder *VERB*
1 to shiver violently with horror, fear, or cold
2 to make a strong shaking movement
shudder *NOUN*

shuffle *VERB*
1 to walk without lifting the feet
2 to rearrange playing cards by sliding them over each other to get them into random order
3 to shift or rearrange
shuffle *NOUN*

shun *VERB* **shunning**, **shunned**
to avoid; to keep away from something

shunt *VERB*
to move things to a different position

shut *VERB* **shutting**, **shut**
1 to move a door, lid, or cover etc. so that it blocks an opening
2 to bring or fold parts together
shut down 1 to stop something working
2 to stop business **shut up 1** to shut securely
2 (*informal*) to stop talking or making a noise

shutter *NOUN*
1 a panel that can be closed over a window
2 the device in a camera that opens and closes to let in light
shuttered *ADJECTIVE*

shuttle *NOUN*
1 a holder carrying the weft thread across a loom in weaving
2 a train, bus, or aircraft that makes short journeys between two points

shuttle *VERB*
to move, travel, or send backwards and forwards

shuttlecock *NOUN*
a small rounded piece of cork or plastic with a crown of feathers, used in badminton

shy *ADJECTIVE* **shyer**, **shyest**
afraid to meet or talk to other people; timid
shyly *ADVERB*

shy *VERB* **shies**, **shied**
to jump or move suddenly in alarm

SI *NOUN*
an internationally recognized system of metric units of measurement, including the metre and kilogram

Siamese cat *NOUN*
a breed of cat with short pale fur and darker face, ears, tail, and feet

sibling *NOUN*
a brother or sister

sick *ADJECTIVE*
1 physically or mentally unwell
2 vomiting or likely to vomit
3 distressed or disgusted
4 (of humour) dealing with serious subjects in an unpleasant or upsetting way
sick of tired of

sicken *VERB*
1 to begin to be ill
2 to distress or disgust
sickening *ADJECTIVE*

sickle *NOUN*
a tool with a narrow curved blade, used for cutting corn etc.

sickly *ADJECTIVE*
1 often ill; unhealthy
2 making people feel sick *a sickly smell*
3 weak *a sickly smile*

sickness *NOUN*
1 illness
2 a disease
3 vomiting

side *NOUN*
1 a surface, especially one joining the top and bottom of something
2 a line that forms part of the boundary of a triangle, square, etc.
3 the part near the edge and away from the centre
4 the place next to a person or thing *stood at my side*
5 one aspect or view *all sides of the problem*
6 one of two groups or teams etc. who oppose each other
on the side as a sideline

side *ADJECTIVE*
at or on a side *the side door*

side *VERB*
side with to support a person in an argument

sideboard *NOUN*
a long piece of furniture with drawers and cupboards and a flat top

sideburns *PLURAL NOUN*
strips of hair growing on each side of a man's face

side effect *NOUN*
an extra (usually bad) effect that a medicine has on a person

sideline *NOUN*
1 something done in addition to your main job
2 each of the lines on the two long sides of a sports pitch

sidelong *ADJECTIVE*
towards one side; sideways

sideshow *NOUN*
a small entertainment forming part of a large one, e.g. at a fair

sidetrack *VERB*
to take someone's attention away from the main subject

sidewalk *NOUN*
(*American*) a pavement

sideways *ADVERB, ADJECTIVE*
1 to or from one side
2 with one side facing forwards

siding *NOUN*
a short railway line by the side of a main line

sidle *VERB*
to walk in a shy or nervous manner

siege *NOUN*
the surrounding of a place in order to capture it or force someone to surrender

sierra *NOUN*
a range of mountains with sharp peaks, in Spain or parts of America

siesta (see-**est**-a) *NOUN*
an afternoon rest

sieve (siv) *NOUN*
a device with a fine mesh, used to separate the smaller or soft parts of something from the larger or hard parts

sieve *VERB*
to put through a sieve

sift *VERB*
1 to sieve
2 to analyse facts or information carefully

sigh *NOUN*
a sound made by breathing out heavily from tiredness, sadness, relief, etc.

sigh *VERB*
to make a sigh

sight *NOUN*
1 the ability to see
2 a view or glimpse *caught sight of them*
3 a thing that can be seen or is worth seeing
a lovely sight
4 an unsightly thing *I must look a sight.*
5 a device for aiming a gun or telescope etc.
Do not confuse this word with *site*.

sight *VERB*
1 to see or observe something
2 to aim a gun or telescope etc.

sighted *ADJECTIVE*
able to see

sight-reading *NOUN*
playing or singing music at sight, without preparation

sightseeing *NOUN*
visiting interesting places in a town etc.
sightseer *NOUN*

sign *NOUN*
1 something that shows that a thing exists
signs of decay
2 a mark, notice, etc. having a special meaning
3 an action or movement giving an instruction
4 any of the twelve divisions of the zodiac, represented by a symbol

sign *VERB*
1 to make a sign or signal
2 to write your signature on a letter or document
3 to use signing

signal *NOUN*
1 a gesture, sound, etc. that gives information or an instruction
2 a message made up of such things
3 a sequence of electrical impulses or radio waves

signal *VERB* **signalling**, **signalled**
to make a signal to

signal box *NOUN*
a building from which railway signals, points, etc. are controlled

signalman *NOUN*
a person who controls railway signals

signatory *NOUN* **signatories**
a person who signs an agreement etc.

signature *NOUN*
1 a person's name written by himself or herself
2 (*Music*) a set of signs after the clef in a score, showing the key the music is written in

signature tune *NOUN*
a special tune used to introduce a particular programme, performer, etc.

signet ring *NOUN*
a ring with a person's initials or a design engraved on it

significance *NOUN*
meaning or importance

significant *ADJECTIVE*
1 having a meaning; full of meaning
2 important
significantly *ADVERB*

signify *VERB* **signifies**, **signified**
1 to be a sign or symbol of
2 to indicate
3 to be important

a b c d e f g h i j k l m n o p q r s t u v w x y z

signing or **sign language** NOUN
a way of communicating by using gestures etc. instead of sounds, used mainly by deaf people

signpost NOUN
a sign at a road junction etc. showing the names and distances of places down each road

Sikh (seek) NOUN
a member of a religion founded in northern India, believing in one God and accepting some Hindu and some Islamic beliefs
Sikhism NOUN

silage NOUN
fodder made from green crops stored in a silo

silence NOUN
absence of sound or speaking

silence VERB
to make a person or thing silent

silencer NOUN
a device for reducing the sound made by a gun or a vehicle's exhaust system etc.

silent ADJECTIVE
1 without any sound
2 not speaking
silently ADVERB

silhouette (sil-oo-**et**) NOUN
1 a dark shadow seen against a light background
2 a portrait of a person in profile, showing the outline only in solid black

silicon NOUN
a substance found in many rocks, used in making transistors, chips for microprocessors, etc.

silk NOUN
1 a fine soft thread or cloth made from the fibre produced by silkworms
2 a length of silk thread used for embroidery
silken ADJECTIVE **silky** ADJECTIVE

silkworm NOUN
the caterpillar of a kind of moth, which spins a cocoon

sill NOUN
a strip of stone, wood, or metal below a window or door

silly ADJECTIVE **sillier**, **silliest**
foolish or unwise
silliness NOUN

silo (sy-loh) NOUN **silos**
1 a pit or tower for storing green crops or corn or cement etc.
2 an underground place for storing a missile

silt NOUN
sediment laid down by a river or sea etc.

silt VERB
silt up to become blocked with silt

silver NOUN
1 a shiny white precious metal
2 the colour of silver
3 coins or objects made of silver or silver-coloured metal
silvery ADJECTIVE

silver ADJECTIVE
1 made of silver
2 coloured like silver

silver VERB
to make or become silvery

silver medal NOUN
a medal awarded for second place in a competition

silver wedding NOUN
a 25th wedding anniversary

SIM card NOUN
a card in a mobile phone, storing its number and other information

similar ADJECTIVE
nearly the same; of the same kind
similarly ADVERB

similarity NOUN **similarities**
1 a close resemblance
2 a similar feature

simile (sim-il-ee) NOUN
a comparison of one thing with another, e.g. *as brave as a lion*

simmer VERB
to boil very gently
simmer down to calm down

simper VERB
to smile in a silly affected way
simper NOUN

simple ADJECTIVE **simpler**, **simplest**
1 easy; not complicated or elaborate
2 plain or ordinary *a simple cottage*
3 lacking sense or intelligence
simplicity NOUN

simple-minded ADJECTIVE
naive or foolish

simpleton NOUN
a foolish person

simplify VERB **simplifies**, **simplified**
to make simple or easy to understand
simplification NOUN

simply ADVERB
1 in a simple way *Explain it simply.*
2 without doubt; completely *was simply marvellous*
3 only or merely *is simply a question of time*

simulate VERB
1 to reproduce the appearance or conditions of
2 to pretend to have a feeling
simulation NOUN

simulator NOUN
a device for simulating actual conditions or events

simultaneous ADJECTIVE
happening at the same time
simultaneously ADVERB

sin NOUN
1 the breaking of a religious or moral law
2 a very bad action
sin VERB **sinning**, **sinned**
to commit a sin
sinner NOUN

since CONJUNCTION
1 from the time when
2 because
since PREPOSITION
from a certain time *nothing since January*
since ADVERB
between then and now *hasn't been seen since*

sincere ADJECTIVE
truly felt or meant *sincere thanks*
sincerely ADVERB **sincerity** NOUN

sine NOUN
(in a right-angled triangle) the ratio of the length of a side opposite one of the acute angles to the length of the hypotenuse

sinew NOUN
strong tissue that connects a muscle to a bone

sinewy ADJECTIVE
slim, muscular, and strong

sinful ADJECTIVE
1 guilty of sin
2 wicked
sinfully ADVERB

sing VERB **sang**, **sung**
1 to make musical sounds with the voice
2 to perform a song
singer NOUN

singe (sinj) VERB **singeing**
to burn slightly

single ADJECTIVE
1 one only; not double or multiple
2 suitable for one person *a single bed*
3 separate *every single thing*
4 not married
single VERB
single out to pick out or distinguish

single file NOUN
a line of people one behind the other

single-handed ADJECTIVE
without help

single-minded ADJECTIVE
having one purpose only

single ticket NOUN
a ticket for a journey to a place but not back

singly ADVERB
in ones; one by one

sing-song ADJECTIVE
having a repeated rising and falling rhythm

sing-song NOUN
informal singing by a gathering of people

singular NOUN
the form of a noun or verb used when it stands for only one person or thing *The singular is 'child', the plural is 'children'.*

singular ADJECTIVE
uncommon or extraordinary *a person of singular courage*
singularly ADVERB

sinister ADJECTIVE
1 looking evil or harmful
2 wicked *a sinister motive*

sink VERB **sank**, **sunk**
1 to go or cause to go under the surface or to the bottom of the sea etc.
2 to go or fall slowly downwards *sank to their knees*
3 to push something sharp deeply into something *sank its teeth into a bone*
4 to drill a well
5 to invest money
sink in to be understood
sink NOUN
a fixed basin with a drainpipe and taps

sinuous ADJECTIVE
bending or curving

sinus (sy-nus) NOUN
a hollow part in the bones of the skull, connected with the nose

sip VERB **sipping**, **sipped**
to drink in small mouthfuls
sip NOUN

siphon NOUN
1 a pipe or tube in the form of an upside-down U, arranged so that liquid is forced up it and down to a lower level
2 a bottle containing soda water which is released through a tube
siphon VERB
to flow or draw out through a siphon

sir NOUN
1 a word used when speaking politely to a man
2 Sir the title given to a knight or baronet

sire NOUN
the male parent of a horse or dog etc.

sire *VERB*
to be the sire of

siren *NOUN*
1 a device that makes a loud wailing sound as a signal
2 a dangerously attractive woman

sirloin *NOUN*
beef from the upper part of the loin

sissy *NOUN* **sissies**
a timid or cowardly person

sister *NOUN*
1 a daughter of the same parents as another person
2 a woman who is a fellow member or worker
3 a nun
4 a senior hospital nurse
sisterly *ADJECTIVE*

sisterhood *NOUN*
1 companionship between women
2 a society or association of women

sister-in-law *NOUN* **sisters-in-law**
1 the sister of a person's husband or wife
2 the wife of a person's brother

sit *VERB* **sitting, sat**
1 to rest with your body supported on the buttocks
2 to cause someone to sit
3 (of birds) to stay on the nest to hatch eggs
4 to be a candidate in an examination
5 to be situated; to stay
6 (of a lawcourt etc.) to be assembled for business

sitcom *NOUN*
(*informal*) a television comedy with a continuing storyline

site *NOUN*
the place where something happens or happened or is built etc. *a camping site*
Do not confuse this word with *sight*.

site *VERB*
to provide with a site; to locate

sit-in *NOUN*
a protest in which demonstrators sit down in a public place

sitter *NOUN*
1 a person posing for a portrait
2 a person who babysits

sitting *NOUN*
1 the time when people are served a meal
2 the time when a parliament etc. is conducting business

sitting room *NOUN*
a room with comfortable chairs for sitting in

situated *ADJECTIVE*
in a particular place or situation

situation *NOUN*
1 a position with its surroundings
2 a state of affairs at a certain time
3 a job

six *NOUN, ADJECTIVE*
the number 6
at sixes and sevens in a muddle
sixth *ADJECTIVE, NOUN*

sixth form *NOUN*
a form for students aged 16–18 in a secondary school

sixth sense *NOUN*
the ability to know something by instinct or intuition

sixteen *NOUN, ADJECTIVE*
the number 16
sixteenth *ADJECTIVE, NOUN*

sixty *NOUN, ADJECTIVE* **sixties**
the number 60
sixtieth *ADJECTIVE, NOUN*

size *NOUN*
1 the measurements or extent of something
2 any of the series of standard measurements in which certain things are made

size *VERB*
to arrange according to size
size up to form an opinion about

sizeable *ADJECTIVE*
fairly large

sizzle *VERB*
to make a crackling or hissing sound

skate [1] *NOUN*
1 a boot with a steel blade on the sole, used for sliding on ice
2 a roller skate

skate *VERB*
to move on skates
skater *NOUN*

skate [2] *NOUN* **skate**
a large flat sea fish

skateboard *NOUN*
a small board with wheels, used for riding on as a sport
skateboarding *NOUN*

skeleton *NOUN*
1 the framework of bones of the body
2 the shell or other hard part of a crab etc.
3 a framework of a building etc.
skeletal *ADJECTIVE*

sketch *NOUN*
1 a rough drawing or painting
2 a short account of something
3 a short amusing play

sketch *VERB*
to make a sketch of

sketchy ADJECTIVE **sketchier**, **sketchiest**
rough and not detailed or careful

skew ADJECTIVE
askew or slanting

skew VERB
1 to make a thing askew
2 to make something biased or distorted

skewer NOUN
a long pin pushed through meat to hold it
together during cooking

skewer VERB
to pierce with a skewer

ski (skee) NOUN **skis**
each of a pair of long narrow strips fixed under
the feet for moving quickly over snow

ski VERB **skies**, **skiing**, **skied**
to travel on skis
skier NOUN

skid VERB **skidding**, **skidded**
to slide accidentally without control
skid NOUN

skilful ADJECTIVE
having or showing great skill
skilfully ADVERB

skill NOUN
the ability to do something well
skilled ADJECTIVE

skilled ADJECTIVE
1 highly trained or experienced
2 (of work) needing skill

skim VERB **skimming**, **skimmed**
1 to remove something from the surface of
a liquid
2 to move quickly over a surface or through
the air
3 to read something quickly

skimp VERB
to supply or use less than is needed

skimpy ADJECTIVE **skimpier**, **skimpiest**
scanty or too small

skin NOUN
1 the outer covering of a person's or animal's
body
2 the outer layer of a fruit
3 a film formed on the surface of a liquid

skin VERB **skinning**, **skinned**
to take the skin off

skin diving NOUN
swimming under water with breathing
apparatus but without a diving suit
skin diver NOUN

skinflint NOUN
a miserly person

skinny ADJECTIVE **skinnier**, **skinniest**
very thin

skip VERB **skipping**, **skipped**
1 to move along lightly with a hop on each leg
2 to jump with a skipping rope
3 to go quickly from one subject to another
4 to miss out

skip NOUN
1 a skipping movement
2 a large container for builders' rubbish

skipper NOUN
(informal) a captain

skipping rope NOUN
a rope that is swung over the head and under
the feet while jumping

skirmish NOUN
(informal) a minor fight or conflict

skirt NOUN
1 a piece of clothing for a woman or girl that
hangs from the waist
2 the lower part of a dress

skirt VERB
to go round the edge of

skirting NOUN
a narrow board round the wall of a room,
close to the floor

skit NOUN
a satirical sketch or parody

skittish ADJECTIVE
lively and excitable

skittle NOUN
a bottle-shaped object that people try to
knock down by bowling a ball in the game
called *skittles*

skive VERB
(informal) to dodge work
skiver NOUN

skulk VERB
to loiter stealthily

skull NOUN
the framework of bones of the head

skunk NOUN
a furry North American animal that sprays a
bad-smelling fluid to defend itself

sky NOUN **skies**
the space above the earth

skylark NOUN
a lark that sings while it hovers high in the air

skylight NOUN
a window in a roof

skyline NOUN
the outline of land or buildings seen against
the sky

skyscraper NOUN
a very tall building

slab NOUN
a thick flat piece

slack *ADJECTIVE*
1 not pulled tight
2 not busy or working hard

slack *NOUN*
the slack part of a rope etc.

slack *VERB*
to avoid work; to be lazy
slacker *NOUN*

slacken *VERB*
to make or become slack

slacks *PLURAL NOUN*
loose casual trousers

slag *NOUN*
waste material separated from metal in smelting

slain *past participle* of **slay**

slalom *NOUN*
a ski race down a zigzag course

slam *VERB* **slamming**, **slammed**
1 to shut loudly
2 to hit violently
slam *NOUN*

slander *NOUN*
a spoken untrue statement that damages a person's reputation
slanderous *ADJECTIVE*

slander *VERB*
to make a slander against
slanderer *NOUN*

slang *NOUN*
very informal words used by a particular group of people
slangy *ADJECTIVE*

slant *VERB*
1 to slope
2 to present news or information from a particular point of view

slant *NOUN*
a slope

slap *VERB* **slapping**, **slapped**
1 to hit with the palm of the hand or with something flat
2 to apply roughly *slapped paint on the walls*
slap *NOUN*

slapdash *ADJECTIVE*
hasty and careless

slapstick *NOUN*
comedy with people hitting each other, falling over, etc.

slash *VERB*
1 to cut or strike with a long sweeping movement
2 to reduce prices greatly

slash *NOUN*
1 a slashing cut
2 a slanting line (/) used in writing and printing

slat *NOUN*
a thin strip of wood etc. overlapping with others to form a screen

slate *NOUN*
a piece of flat grey rock used in covering a roof or (formerly) for writing on

slate *VERB*
1 to cover a roof with slates
2 (*informal*) to criticize harshly

slaughter *VERB*
1 to kill an animal for food
2 to kill people or animals in large numbers

slaughter *NOUN*
the killing of large numbers of people or animals

slaughterhouse *NOUN*
a place where animals are killed for food

slave *NOUN*
a person who is owned by another and has to work for the owner
slavery *NOUN*

slave *VERB*
to work very hard

slavery *NOUN*
1 the state of being a slave
2 the system of having slaves

slavish *ADJECTIVE*
1 like a slave
2 showing no independence or originality

slay *VERB* **slew**, **slain**
(*literary*) to kill

sled *NOUN*
a sledge

sledge *NOUN*
a vehicle with runners for travelling over snow
sledging *NOUN*

sledgehammer *NOUN*
a large heavy hammer

sleek *ADJECTIVE*
smooth and shiny

sleep *NOUN*
the state in which the eyes are closed, the body relaxed, and the mind unconscious

sleep *VERB* **slept**
to have a sleep

sleeper *NOUN*
1 someone who is asleep
2 each of the wooden or concrete beams on which the railway lines rest
3 a railway carriage fitted for sleeping in

sleeping bag *NOUN*
a padded bag to sleep in, especially when camping

sleepless ADJECTIVE
unable to sleep

sleepwalker NOUN
a person who walks while asleep
sleepwalking NOUN

sleepy ADJECTIVE **sleepier, sleepiest**
1 feeling a need to sleep
2 quiet and lacking activity
sleepily ADVERB

sleet NOUN
a mixture of rain and snow or hail

sleeve NOUN
1 the part of an item of clothing that covers the arm
2 a record cover

sleeveless ADJECTIVE
without sleeves

sleigh (say as slay) NOUN
a large sledge pulled by horses

sleight (say as slight) NOUN
sleight of hand skill in using the hands to do conjuring tricks etc.

slender ADJECTIVE
1 slim and graceful
2 slight or small *a slender chance*

sleuth (slooth) NOUN
a detective

slew *past tense* of **slay**

slice NOUN
1 a thin piece cut off something
2 a portion

slice VERB
1 to cut into slices
2 to cut from a larger piece
3 to cut cleanly

slick ADJECTIVE
1 done or doing things quickly and cleverly
2 slippery

slick NOUN
1 a large patch of oil floating on water
2 a slippery place

slide VERB **slid**
1 to move or cause to move smoothly on a surface
2 to move quietly or secretly

slide NOUN
1 a sliding movement
2 a smooth surface on which people or things can slide
3 a photograph for projecting on a screen
4 a small glass plate on which objects are viewed under a microscope
5 a fastener to keep hair tidy

slight ADJECTIVE
very small; not serious or important

slight VERB
to insult by treating as unimportant
slight NOUN

slightly ADVERB
rather; a little

slim ADJECTIVE **slimmer, slimmest**
1 thin and graceful
2 small; hardly enough *a slim chance*

slim VERB **slimming, slimmed**
to become thinner by dieting
slimmer NOUN

slime NOUN
an unpleasant wet slippery substance

slimy ADJECTIVE **slimier, slimiest**
1 covered in slime
2 wet and slippery

sling NOUN
1 a band placed round the neck and supporting an injured arm
2 a looped strap used to throw a stone etc.

sling VERB **slung**
1 to hang loosely
2 (*informal*) to throw carelessly

slink VERB **slunk**
to move in a stealthy or guilty way

slinky ADJECTIVE **slinkier, slinkiest**
sleek and smooth in appearance or movement

slip VERB **slipping, slipped**
1 to slide accidentally or lose balance
2 to move or put quickly and quietly
3 to escape from *It slipped my mind.*
slip up to make a mistake

slip NOUN
1 an accidental slide or fall
2 a mistake
3 a small piece of paper
4 a petticoat
5 a pillowcase

slipper NOUN
a soft comfortable shoe for wearing indoors

slippery ADJECTIVE
smooth or wet and difficult to stand on or hold

slip road NOUN
a road for entering or leaving a motorway

slipshod ADJECTIVE
careless or untidy

slipstream NOUN
a current of air driven backward as an aircraft or vehicle moves forward

slit NOUN
a narrow straight cut or opening

slit VERB **slitting, slit**
to make a slit

slither _VERB_
to slip or slide unsteadily

sliver _NOUN_
a thin strip of wood or glass etc.

slob _NOUN_
(_informal_) an untidy or lazy person

slobber _VERB_
to dribble from the mouth

sloe _NOUN_
a small dark plum-like fruit

slog _VERB_ **slogging, slogged** (_informal_)
1 to hit hard
2 to work or walk hard and steadily
slog _NOUN_

slogan _NOUN_
a phrase used to advertise a product or idea

sloop _NOUN_
a small sailing ship with one mast

slop _VERB_ **slopping, slopped**
to spill liquid over the edge of its container

slope _VERB_
to lie or turn at an angle; to slant

slope _NOUN_
1 a sloping surface
2 the amount by which something slopes

sloppy _ADJECTIVE_ **sloppier, sloppiest**
1 liquid and splashing easily
2 careless and untidy
3 weakly sentimental

slops _PLURAL NOUN_
1 slopped liquid
2 liquid waste matter

slosh _VERB_ (_informal_)
1 to splash or slop
2 to pour liquid carelessly

slot _NOUN_
a narrow opening to put flat things in
slotted _ADJECTIVE_

slot _VERB_ **slotting, slotted**
to put something into a place where it fits

sloth (rhymes with _both_) _NOUN_
1 laziness
2 a slow-moving South American animal that
lives in trees

slothful _ADJECTIVE_
lazy

slot machine _NOUN_
a machine worked by putting a coin in a slot

slouch _VERB_
to stand or move in a lazy awkward way
slouch _NOUN_

slovenly _ADJECTIVE_
careless or untidy

slow _ADJECTIVE_
1 not quick; taking more time than is usual
2 showing a time earlier than the correct time
Your watch is slow.
3 not able to understand quickly
slowly _ADVERB_

slow _VERB_
to go or cause to go more slowly

slow motion _NOUN_
movement in a film or on television which has
been slowed down

sludge _NOUN_
thick mud

slug _NOUN_
1 a small slimy animal like a snail without a shell
2 a pellet for firing from a gun

sluggish _ADJECTIVE_
slow-moving; not alert

sluice (slooss) _NOUN_
1 a sluice gate
2 a channel carrying off water

sluice _VERB_
to wash with a flow of water

sluice gate _NOUN_
a sliding barrier for controlling a flow of water

slum _NOUN_
an area of dirty overcrowded houses

slumber _VERB_
to sleep
slumber _NOUN_

slump _VERB_
to fall heavily or suddenly

slump _NOUN_
a sudden fall in prices or trade

slur _VERB_ **slurring, slurred**
1 to pronounce words indistinctly
2 (_Music_) to mark with a slur in music

slur _NOUN_
1 a slurred sound
2 something that harms a person's reputation
3 (_Music_) a curved line placed over notes that
are to be played smoothly without a break

slurp _VERB_
to eat or drink with a loud sucking sound
slurp _NOUN_

slurry _NOUN_ **slurries**
a semi-liquid mixture of water and cement, etc.

slush _NOUN_
1 partly melted snow
2 (_informal_) sentimental talk or writing
slushy _ADJECTIVE_

sly _ADJECTIVE_ **slyer, slyest**
1 unpleasantly cunning or secret
2 mischievous and knowing
slyly _ADVERB_

smack[1] *NOUN*
1 a slap
2 a loud sharp sound *hit the wall with a smack*
3 a loud kiss
4 a slight flavour or trace

smack *VERB*
to slap or hit hard
smack of to suggest *a decision that smacks of favouritism*

smack *ADVERB*
(*informal*) forcefully or directly *went smack through the window*

smack[2] *NOUN*
a small fishing boat

small *ADJECTIVE*
1 not large; less than the usual size
2 not important or significant

smallholding *NOUN*
a small farm
smallholder *NOUN*

small hours *PLURAL NOUN*
the hours after midnight

small-minded *ADJECTIVE*
selfish; petty

smallpox *NOUN*
a serious contagious disease that causes a fever and produces spots that leave permanent scars on the skin

small print *NOUN*
the details of a contract, especially if in very small letters or difficult to understand

small talk *NOUN*
conversation about unimportant things

smarmy *ADJECTIVE* **smarmier**, **smarmiest**
(*informal*) polite and flattering in an exaggerated way

smart *ADJECTIVE*
1 neat and elegant; dressed well
2 clever
3 forceful; brisk *a smart pace*
smartly *ADVERB*

smart *VERB*
to feel a stinging pain
smart *NOUN*

smart card *NOUN*
a plastic card which stores information in electronic form

smarten *VERB*
to make or become smarter

smash *VERB*
1 to break noisily into pieces
2 to hit or move with great force
3 to destroy or defeat completely

smash *NOUN*
1 the action or sound of smashing
2 a collision between vehicles
3 (*informal*) a smash hit

smash hit *NOUN*
(*informal*) a very successful song, show, etc.

smashing *ADJECTIVE*
(*informal*) very good or attractive

smattering *NOUN*
a slight knowledge of a subject

smear *VERB*
1 to rub something greasy or sticky on a surface
2 to try to damage someone's reputation
smeary *ADJECTIVE*

smear *NOUN*
1 something smeared
2 a sample of tissue taken to check for faulty cells which may cause cancer
3 a malicious rumour

smell *VERB* **smelt** or **smelled**
1 to be aware of something from the sense organs of the nose
2 to give out a smell

smell *NOUN*
1 the act of smelling
2 the ability to smell things
3 something that can be smelt

smelly *ADJECTIVE* **smellier**, **smelliest**
having a bad smell

smelt *VERB*
to melt ore for its metal

smile *NOUN*
an expression on the face that shows pleasure or amusement, with the lips stretched and turning upwards at the ends

smile *VERB*
to give a smile

smirk *NOUN*
a self-satisfied smile

smirk *VERB*
to give a smirk

smith *NOUN*
1 a person who makes things out of metal
2 a blacksmith

smithy *NOUN* **smithies**
a blacksmith's workshop

smitten *ADJECTIVE*
1 suddenly affected by a disease
2 having a sudden fondness or attraction

smock *NOUN*
a long loose shirt worn over other clothes

smog *NOUN*
thick smoky fog

smoke *NOUN*
1 the mixture of gas and solid particles given off by a burning substance
2 a period of smoking tobacco
smoky *ADJECTIVE*

a
b
c
d
e
f
g
h
i
j
k
l
m
n
o
p
q
r
s
t
u
v
w
x
y
z

smoke *VERB*
1 to give out smoke
2 to inhale and exhale smoke from a cigarette, cigar, etc.
3 to preserve meat or fish by treating it with smoke
smoker *NOUN*

smokeless *ADJECTIVE*
without producing smoke

smokescreen *NOUN*
something that conceals what is happening

smooth *ADJECTIVE*
1 having an even surface without lumps, etc.
2 moving without bumps or jolts
3 not harsh
4 without problems or difficulties
smoothly *ADVERB*

smooth *VERB*
to make smooth

smother *VERB*
1 to suffocate
2 to put out a fire by covering it
3 to cover thickly

smoulder *VERB*
1 to burn slowly without a flame
2 to feel a hidden emotion

smudge *NOUN*
a dirty mark made by rubbing
smudgy *ADJECTIVE*

smudge *VERB*
to make a smudge on

smug *ADJECTIVE*
self-satisfied
smugly *ADVERB*

smuggle *VERB*
to bring goods into a country etc. secretly or illegally
smuggler *NOUN*

smut *NOUN*
a small piece of soot or dirt
smutty *ADJECTIVE*

snack *NOUN*
1 a small meal
2 food eaten between meals

snag *NOUN*
1 an unexpected difficulty
2 a tear in material

snail *NOUN*
a small animal with a soft body and a shell

snake *NOUN*
a reptile with a long narrow body and no legs

snap *VERB* **snapping, snapped**
1 to break suddenly or with a sharp sound
2 to bite suddenly or quickly
3 to speak quickly and angrily
4 to take a quick photograph of
snap up to grab something offered

snap *NOUN*
1 the action or sound of snapping
2 a photograph
3 a card game in which players shout 'Snap!' when they see two similar cards

snap *ADJECTIVE*
sudden *a snap decision*

snappy *ADJECTIVE* **snappier, snappiest**
1 quick and lively
2 irritable

snapshot *NOUN*
a quickly taken photograph

snare *NOUN*
1 a trap for catching birds or animals
2 something attractive but dangerous

snare *VERB*
to catch in a snare

snarl[1] *VERB*
1 to growl angrily
2 to speak in a bad-tempered way
snarl *NOUN*

snarl[2] *VERB*
to make or become tangled or jammed

snatch *VERB*
to take quickly, eagerly, or by force

snatch *NOUN*
1 the act of snatching
2 a short part of a song, conversation, etc.

sneak *VERB*
1 to move quietly and secretly
2 to tell tales

sneak *NOUN*
someone who tells tales

sneaky *ADJECTIVE* **sneakier, sneakiest**
dishonest or deceitful
sneakily *ADVERB*

sneer *VERB*
to speak or behave in a scornful way
sneer *NOUN*

sneeze *VERB*
to send out air suddenly and uncontrollably through the nose and mouth to get rid of something irritating the nostrils
sneeze *NOUN*

snide *ADJECTIVE*
sneering in a sly way

sniff *VERB*
1 to draw in air through the nose
2 to smell something
sniff *NOUN*

sniffle *VERB*
to sniff slightly
sniffle *NOUN*

snigger VERB
to giggle in a sly way
snigger NOUN

snip VERB **snipping, snipped**
to cut in small quick cuts
snip NOUN

snipe NOUN
a marsh bird with a long beak

snipe VERB
1 to shoot at people from a hiding place
2 to criticize in a sly way
sniper NOUN

snippet NOUN
a small piece of news, information, etc.

snivel VERB **snivelling, snivelled**
to cry or complain in a whining way

snob NOUN
a person who despises those who have not
got wealth, power, or particular tastes
snobbery NOUN **snobbish** ADJECTIVE

snooker NOUN
a game played with cues and 21 balls on a
cloth-covered table

snoop VERB
to ask or look around secretly
snooper NOUN

snooty ADJECTIVE **snootier, snootiest**
(informal) haughty and contemptuous

snooze VERB
(informal) to have a short sleep
snooze NOUN

snore VERB
to breathe noisily while sleeping
snore NOUN

snorkel NOUN
a tube through which a swimmer under water
can breathe under water
snorkelling NOUN

snort VERB
to make a rough sound through the nose
snort NOUN

snout NOUN
an animal's projecting nose and jaws

snow NOUN
frozen drops of water that fall from the sky in
small white flakes

snow VERB
to come down as snow

snowball NOUN
snow pressed into a ball for throwing

snowball VERB
to grow quickly in size or intensity

snowdrift NOUN
a bank of snow piled up by the wind

snowdrop NOUN
a small white flower that blooms in early
spring

snowflake NOUN
a flake of snow

snowman NOUN **snowmen**
a figure made of snow

snowplough NOUN
a vehicle for clearing a road or railway of snow

snowshoe NOUN
a frame like a tennis racket for walking on soft
snow

snowy ADJECTIVE **snowier, snowiest**
1 with snow falling
2 covered with snow
3 pure white

snub VERB **snubbing, snubbed**
to treat in a scornful or unfriendly way

snub NOUN
an act of snubbing

snub-nosed ADJECTIVE
having a short turned-up nose

snuff[1] NOUN
powdered tobacco for taking into the nose by
sniffing

snuff[2] VERB
to put out a candle

snuffle VERB
to sniff in a noisy way
snuffle NOUN

snug ADJECTIVE **snugger, snuggest**
1 cosy
2 fitting closely
snugly ADVERB

snuggle VERB
to curl up comfortably

so ADVERB
1 to such an extent *Why are you so cross?*
2 very *The film is so boring.*
3 also *I was wrong but so were you.*
and so on and other similar things

so CONJUNCTION
for that reason

soak VERB
to make very wet
soak up to take in a liquid like a sponge
soak NOUN

so-and-so NOUN **so-and-sos**
a person or thing that need not be named

soap NOUN
1 a substance used with water for washing
and cleaning things
2 a soap opera
soapy ADJECTIVE

soap VERB
to put soap on

a
b
c
d
e
f
g
h
i
j
k
l
m
n
o
p
q
r
s
t
u
v
w
x
y
z

soap opera NOUN
a television serial about the everyday lives of a group of people

soar VERB
1 to rise high in the air
2 to increase rapidly

sob VERB **sobbing, sobbed**
to make a gasping sound when crying
sob NOUN

sober ADJECTIVE
1 not drunk
2 serious and calm
3 not bright or showy

sober VERB
to make or become sober

so-called ADJECTIVE
named in what may be the wrong way

soccer NOUN
football

sociable ADJECTIVE
liking to be with other people

social ADJECTIVE
1 living in a community, not alone
2 to do with life in a community
3 concerned with people's welfare
a social worker
4 helping people to meet each other
a social club
5 sociable
socially ADVERB

socialism NOUN
a political system in which wealth is shared equally between people, and the main industries and trade etc. are controlled by the state

socialist NOUN
a person who believes in socialism

socialize VERB
to meet other people socially

social security NOUN
money and other assistance provided by the state to those in need

social services PLURAL NOUN
welfare services provided by the state, including schools, hospitals, and pensions

society NOUN **societies**
1 people living together in a group or nation
2 a group of people organized for a particular purpose
3 company or companionship

sociology NOUN
the study of human society and social behaviour
sociologist NOUN

sock[1] NOUN
a piece of clothing covering the foot and the lower part of the leg

sock[2] VERB
(*informal*) to hit hard
sock NOUN

socket NOUN
1 a hollow into which something fits
2 a device into which an electric plug or bulb is put

sod NOUN
a piece of turf

soda NOUN
1 a substance made from sodium, such as baking soda
2 soda water

soda water NOUN
water made fizzy with carbon dioxide

sodden ADJECTIVE
made very wet

sodium NOUN
a soft white metallic element from which salt and other substances are formed

sofa NOUN
a long soft seat with a back and arms

soft ADJECTIVE
1 not hard or firm; easily pressed
2 smooth, not rough or stiff
3 gentle; not loud
4 (of a drink) not alcoholic
5 (of a drug) not likely to be addictive
6 (of water) free of minerals that reduce lathering
7 lenient
softly ADVERB

soften VERB
to make or become soft or softer

soft-hearted ADJECTIVE
sympathetic and easily moved

software NOUN
computer programs and data, which are not part of the machinery of a computer

soggy ADJECTIVE **soggier, soggiest**
wet and soft

soil NOUN
1 loose earth in which plants grow
2 territory

soil VERB
to make dirty

solace NOUN
a comfort for someone who is unhappy or disappointed

solar ADJECTIVE
from or to do with the sun

solar panel *NOUN*
a panel designed to produce energy from the sun's rays

solar system *NOUN*
the sun and the planets that revolve round it

solder *NOUN*
a soft alloy that is melted to join metal
solder *VERB*
to join with solder

soldier *NOUN*
a member of an army

sole[1] *NOUN* **soles** or, in sense 2, **sole**
1 the bottom surface of a foot or shoe
2 a flat edible sea fish
sole *VERB*
put a sole on a shoe

sole[2] *ADJECTIVE*
single; only *the sole survivor*
solely *ADVERB*

solemn *ADJECTIVE*
1 serious
2 dignified or formal

sol-fa *NOUN*
a system of syllables (*doh, ray, me, fah, so, la, te*) used to represent the notes of the musical scale

solicit *VERB*
to ask for or try to obtain
solicitation *NOUN*

solicitor *NOUN*
a lawyer who advises clients

solid *ADJECTIVE*
1 not hollow; having no space inside
2 keeping its shape; not liquid or gas
3 continuous *for two solid hours*
4 firm or strongly made *a solid foundation*
5 showing solidarity; unanimous
solidly *ADVERB*
solid *NOUN*
1 a solid thing
2 a shape that has three dimensions

solidarity *NOUN*
unity and support between people

solidify *VERB* **solidifies**, **solidified**
to make or become solid

solidity *NOUN*
the state of being solid

solids *PLURAL NOUN*
food that is not liquid

soliloquy (sol-**il**-ok-wee) *NOUN* **soliloquies**
a speech in a play in which a character expresses thoughts alone, without other characters hearing

solitaire *NOUN*
a game of cards or marbles for one person

solitary *ADJECTIVE*
1 alone or lonely
2 single; by itself

solitude *NOUN*
a solitary state

solo *NOUN* **solos**
something sung, played, danced, or done by one person
solo *ADJECTIVE*

soloist *NOUN*
a musician or singer who performs a solo

solstice (sol-stiss) *NOUN*
either of the two times in each year when the sun is at its furthest point north or south of the equator, 21 June and 22 December

soluble *ADJECTIVE*
able to be dissolved

solution *NOUN*
1 a liquid in which something is dissolved
2 the answer to a problem or puzzle

solve *VERB*
to find the answer to a problem or puzzle

solvent *ADJECTIVE*
having enough money to pay debts
solvency *NOUN*
solvent *NOUN*
a liquid used for dissolving something

sombre *ADJECTIVE*
dark and gloomy

some *ADJECTIVE*
1 a few; a little *some apples some sugar*
2 unknown or not identified *some person*
3 about *some 30 minutes*
some *PRONOUN*
a certain number or amount *Some of them were late.*

somebody or **someone** *NOUN*
1 some person
2 an important person

somehow *ADVERB*
in some way

somersault *NOUN*
a movement in which you turn head over heels before landing on your feet
somersault *VERB*
to perform a somersault

something *NOUN*
a thing which you cannot or do not want to name

sometime *ADVERB*
at some time not specified
sometime *ADJECTIVE*
former *her sometime friend*

sometimes *ADVERB*
at some times but not always

somewhat ADVERB
to some extent

somewhere ADVERB
in or to some place

son NOUN
a male child

sonar NOUN
a device using reflected sound waves to locate objects under water

sonata NOUN
a piece of music for one instrument or two, in several movements

song NOUN
1 a tune for singing
2 singing *burst into song*

songbird NOUN
a bird that sings sweetly

sonic ADJECTIVE
to do with sound waves

son-in-law NOUN **sons-in-law**
a daughter's husband

sonnet NOUN
a poem of 14 lines

soon ADVERB
1 in a short time from now
2 not long after something

sooner ADVERB
rather; in preference *I'd sooner wait.*

soot NOUN
black powder left by smoke
sooty ADJECTIVE

soothe VERB
1 to calm or comfort
2 to ease pain or distress
soothing ADJECTIVE

sop NOUN
something unimportant given to pacify or persuade someone

sophisticated ADJECTIVE
1 having refined or cultured tastes or experience
2 complicated
sophistication NOUN

soporific ADJECTIVE
causing sleep or drowsiness

sopping ADJECTIVE
very wet; drenched

soppy ADJECTIVE **soppier**, **soppiest**
silly and sentimental

soprano NOUN **sopranos**
a woman or boy with a high singing voice

sorcerer NOUN
a magician
sorceress NOUN

sorcery NOUN
magic or witchcraft

sordid ADJECTIVE
1 dirty and nasty
2 dishonourable and selfish *sordid motives*

sore ADJECTIVE
1 painful or smarting
2 (*informal*) annoyed or offended
3 urgent *in sore need*

sore NOUN
a sore place

sorely ADVERB
seriously; very *was sorely tempted to leave*

sorrel[1] NOUN
a herb with sharp-tasting leaves

sorrel[2] NOUN
a reddish-brown horse

sorrow NOUN
1 unhappiness or regret caused by loss or disappointment
2 a cause of this

sorrow VERB
to feel sorrow

sorrowful ADJECTIVE
feeling sorrow
sorrowfully ADVERB

sorry ADJECTIVE **sorrier**, **sorriest**
1 feeling regret
2 feeling pity or sympathy
3 wretched *in a sorry state*

sort NOUN
a group of things or people that are similar

sort VERB
to arrange things in groups according to their size, kind, etc.
sort out to resolve a problem or difficulty

SOS NOUN
an urgent appeal for help

sought *past tense* of **seek**

soul NOUN
1 the spiritual part of a person that is believed by some to be immortal
2 a person's mind and emotions etc.
3 a person *not a soul anywhere*
4 a perfect example of something *the soul of discretion*

soulful ADJECTIVE
having or showing deep feeling
soulfully ADVERB

sound [1] *NOUN*
1 vibrations that travel through the air and can be detected by the ear
2 sound reproduced in a film etc.
3 a mental impression *don't like the sound of it*

sound *VERB*
1 to produce or cause to produce a sound
2 to give an impression *They sound angry.*
3 to test by noting the sounds heard

sound [2] *VERB*
to test the depth of water beneath a ship
sound out to try to find out a person's opinion about something

sound [3] *ADJECTIVE*
1 in good condition; not damaged
2 healthy; not diseased
3 reasonable or correct *sound ideas*
4 reliable or secure *a sound investment*
5 thorough or deep *a sound sleep*
soundly *ADVERB*

sound [4] *NOUN*
a narrow stretch of water

sound barrier *NOUN*
the resistance of the air to objects moving at speeds near the speed of sound

sound bite *NOUN*
a short memorable extract from a speech or statement by a politician etc.

sound effects *PLURAL NOUN*
sounds produced artificially to make a play, film, etc. more realistic

soundtrack *NOUN*
the sound that goes with a cinema film

soup *NOUN*
liquid food made from stewed bones, meat, fish, vegetables, etc.

sour *ADJECTIVE*
1 tasting sharp like unripe fruit
2 stale and unpleasant *sour milk*
3 bad-tempered

sour *VERB*
to make or become sour

source *NOUN*
1 the place from which something comes
2 the starting point of a river

south *NOUN*
1 the direction to the right of a person who faces east
2 the southern part of a country, city, etc.

south *ADJECTIVE, ADVERB*
towards or in the south; coming from the south

south-east *NOUN, ADJECTIVE, ADVERB*
midway between south and east
south-easterly *ADJECTIVE*
south-eastern *ADJECTIVE*

southerly *ADJECTIVE*
1 coming from the south
2 facing the south

southern *ADJECTIVE*
of or in the south

southerner *NOUN*
a person from the south of a country

southward *ADJECTIVE, ADVERB*
towards the south
southwards *ADVERB*

south-west *NOUN, ADJECTIVE, ADVERB*
midway between south and west
south-westerly *ADJECTIVE*
south-western *ADJECTIVE*

souvenir (soo-ven-**eer**) *NOUN*
something given or kept as a reminder of a person, place, or event

sou'wester *NOUN*
a waterproof hat with a wide flap at the back

sovereign *NOUN*
1 a king or queen who is the ruler of a country
2 an old British gold coin worth £1

sovereign *ADJECTIVE*
1 supreme *sovereign power*
2 having sovereignty *sovereign states*

sovereignty *NOUN*
the power a country has to govern itself

sow [1] (rhymes with *go*) *VERB* **sown** or **sowed**
1 to put seeds into the ground to grow
2 to cause feelings or ideas to develop
sower *NOUN*

　Do not confuse this word with *sew*.

sow [2] (rhymes with *cow*) *NOUN*
a female pig

soya bean *NOUN*
a kind of bean from which edible oil and flour are made

soy sauce or **soya sauce** *NOUN*
a Chinese or Japanese sauce made from fermented soya beans

spa *NOUN*
a health resort where there is a spring of water containing mineral salts

space *NOUN*
1 the whole area outside the earth, where the stars and planets are
2 an area or volume
3 an empty area; a gap
4 an interval of time

space *VERB*
to arrange things with spaces between

spacecraft *NOUN* **spacecraft**
a vehicle for travelling in space

spaceman *NOUN* **spacemen**
a traveller in space, especially in stories

spaceship NOUN
a manned spacecraft

spacious ADJECTIVE
providing a lot of space

spade [1] NOUN
a tool with a long handle and a wide blade for digging

spade [2] NOUN
a playing card with black heart-like shapes on it

spaghetti NOUN
pasta made in long thin strands

span NOUN
1 the length from end to end or across something
2 the part between two uprights of an arch or bridge
3 the length of a period of time
4 the distance from the tip of the thumb to the tip of the little finger when the hand is spread out

span VERB **spanning**, **spanned**
to reach from one side or end to the other

spangle NOUN
a small piece of glittering material

spaniel NOUN
a kind of dog with long ears and silky fur

spank VERB
to smack a person on the bottom as a punishment

spanner NOUN
a tool for gripping and turning the nut on a bolt etc.

spar [1] NOUN
a strong pole used for a mast or boom etc. on a ship

spar [2] VERB **sparring**, **sparred**
1 to practise boxing
2 to quarrel or argue

spare VERB
1 to afford to give or do without
2 to be merciful towards someone
3 to avoid making a person suffer something *Spare me the details.*
4 to use or treat economically *No expense will be spared.*

spare ADJECTIVE
1 not used but kept ready in case it is needed
2 thin or lean

spark NOUN
1 a tiny glowing particle
2 a flash produced electrically
3 a trace *a spark of hope*

spark VERB
to give off a spark or sparks

sparkle VERB
1 to shine with tiny flashes of light
2 to be lively and witty
sparkle NOUN

sparkler NOUN
a hand-held firework that gives off sparks

sparrow NOUN
a small brown bird

sparse ADJECTIVE
thinly scattered
sparsely ADVERB

spartan ADJECTIVE
simple and without comfort

spasm NOUN
1 a sudden involuntary movement of a muscle
2 a sudden brief spell of activity

spasmodic ADJECTIVE
1 happening or done at irregular intervals
2 to do with or caused by a spasm
spasmodically ADVERB

spastic NOUN
a person suffering from spasms of the muscles and jerky movements, especially caused by cerebral palsy
spastic ADJECTIVE
This word can be offensive to some people. Use *person with cerebral palsy* instead.

spat *past tense* of **spit** [1]

spate NOUN
a sudden flood or rush

spathe (rhymes with *bathe*) NOUN
a large petal-like part of a flower, round a central spike

spatial ADJECTIVE
to do with space

spatter VERB
1 to scatter in small drops
2 to splash *spattered with mud*

spatula NOUN
a tool with a broad flexible blade, used for spreading or mixing

spawn NOUN
the eggs of fish, frogs, toads, or shellfish

spawn VERB
1 to produce spawn
2 to produce in great quantities

spay VERB
sterilize a female animal by removing the ovaries

speak VERB **spoke**, **spoken**
1 to say something; to talk
2 to be able to talk in a specified foreign language
3 to give a speech

speaker NOUN
1 a person who is speaking
2 someone who makes a speech
3 a loudspeaker
the Speaker an official who controls the debates in Parliament

spear NOUN
a long pointed weapon for throwing or stabbing

spear VERB
to pierce with a spear or with something pointed

spearmint NOUN
mint used in cookery and for flavouring chewing gum

special ADJECTIVE
1 not ordinary or usual *a special occasion*
2 meant for a particular person or purpose *a special tool*

specialist NOUN
an expert in one subject or branch of a subject

speciality NOUN **specialities**
1 a special interest or ability
2 a special product

specialize VERB
to give particular attention or study to one subject or thing
specialization NOUN

specially ADVERB
1 in a special way
2 for a special purpose

species (spee-shiz) NOUN **species**
1 a group of animals or plants that are similar
2 a kind or sort

specific ADJECTIVE
definite or precise
specifically ADVERB

specification NOUN
a detailed description of something

specify VERB **specifies**, **specified**
to name or list precisely

specimen NOUN
1 a sample used for study
2 an example *a fine specimen*

speck NOUN
a small spot or particle

speckle NOUN
a small spot or mark
speckled ADJECTIVE

spectacle NOUN
1 an impressive sight or display
2 a ridiculous sight

spectacles PLURAL NOUN
a pair of glasses
spectacled ADJECTIVE

spectacular ADJECTIVE
impressive or striking

spectator NOUN
a person who watches a game, event, etc.

spectre NOUN
a ghost
spectral ADJECTIVE

spectrum NOUN **spectra** or **spectrums**
1 the bands of colours seen in a rainbow
2 a wide range of things, ideas, etc.

speculate VERB
1 to form opinions without any definite evidence
2 to invest in money markets in the hope of making a profit but with the risk of loss
speculation NOUN **speculator** NOUN

speculative ADJECTIVE
involving speculation

sped *past tense* of **speed**

speech NOUN
1 the action or power of speaking
2 a talk to an audience
3 a group of lines spoken by a character in a play

speechless ADJECTIVE
too surprised or emotional to say anything

speed NOUN
1 a measure of the time in which something moves or happens
2 quickness or swiftness

speed VERB **sped** or, in senses 2 and 3, **speeded**
1 to go quickly
2 to make or become quicker
3 to drive faster than the legal limit
speeding NOUN

speedboat NOUN
a fast motor boat

speedometer NOUN
a device in a vehicle, showing its speed

speedway NOUN
a track for motorcycle racing

speedy ADJECTIVE **speedier**, **speediest**
quick or swift
speedily ADVERB

spell NOUN
1 a set of words supposed to have magical power
2 a period of time
3 a period of a certain work or activity etc.

spell VERB **spelled** or **spelt**
1 to put letters in the right order to make a word or words
2 (of letters) to form a word
3 to have as a result *Wet weather spells ruin for crops.*

spellbound ADJECTIVE
entranced as if by a magic spell

spelling NOUN
the way a word is spelled

spend VERB **spent**
1 to use money for payment
2 to use up energy etc.
3 to pass time

spendthrift NOUN
a person who spends money extravagantly

sperm NOUN
the male cell that fertilizes an ovum

spew VERB
1 to vomit
2 to send out in a stream

sphere NOUN
1 a perfectly round solid shape
2 a field of action or interest etc.
spherical ADJECTIVE

spheroid NOUN
a solid like a sphere but not perfectly round

sphinx NOUN
a stone statue with the body of a lion and a human head, especially a massive one from ancient Egypt

spice NOUN
1 a strong-tasting substance used to flavour food
2 something that adds interest or excitement

spice VERB
to flavour with spices

spick and span ADJECTIVE
neat and clean

spicy ADJECTIVE **spicier**, **spiciest**
having a strong flavour from spices

spider NOUN
a small insect-like animal with eight legs that spins webs to catch insects on which it feeds

spidery ADJECTIVE
(of handwriting) having long thin lines and sharp angles

spike NOUN
1 a pointed piece of metal
2 a sharp point
spiky ADJECTIVE

spike VERB
1 to fit with spikes
2 to pierce with a spike

spill VERB **spilt** or **spilled**
1 to let something fall out of a container
2 to become spilt
spillage NOUN

spill NOUN
1 the act of spilling
2 something spilt
3 a fall from a horse, bicycle, etc.

spin VERB **spinning**, **spun**
1 to turn round and round quickly
2 to make raw wool or cotton into threads by pulling and twisting its fibres
3 (of a spider or silkworm) to make a web or cocoon
spin out to make something last longer

spin NOUN
1 a spinning movement
2 a short outing in a car

spinach NOUN
a vegetable with dark green leaves

spinal ADJECTIVE
to do with the spine

spindle NOUN
1 a thin rod on which thread is wound
2 a pin or bar on which something turns

spindly ADJECTIVE
thin and long or tall

spin dryer NOUN
a machine in which wet clothes are spun round to dry them

spine NOUN
1 the line of bones down the middle of the back
2 a thorn or prickle
3 the edge of a book where the pages are joined

spine-chilling ADJECTIVE
frightening and exciting

spineless ADJECTIVE
1 without a backbone
2 lacking courage; weak

spinet NOUN
a small harpsichord

spinning wheel NOUN
a machine for spinning fibre into thread

spin-off NOUN
an extra benefit or result

spinster NOUN
a woman who has not married

spiny ADJECTIVE
covered with spines; prickly

spiral ADJECTIVE
going round a central point and becoming gradually closer to it or further from it
spirally ADVERB

spiral NOUN
a spiral line or course

spiral VERB **spiralling**, **spiralled**
1 to move in a spiral
2 to increase or decrease rapidly

spire NOUN
a tall pointed part on top of a church tower

spirit NOUN
1 the soul
2 a person's mood or mind and feelings
in good spirits
3 a ghost or a supernatural being
4 courage or liveliness
5 a kind of quality in something
6 a strong distilled alcoholic drink

spirit VERB
to carry off quickly and secretly

spirited ADJECTIVE
self-confident and lively

spirit level NOUN
a glass tube of liquid with an air bubble in it,
used to find out whether something is
completely level

spiritual ADJECTIVE
1 to do with the human soul; not physical
2 to do with religion
spirituality NOUN **spiritually** ADVERB

spiritual NOUN
a religious folk song, originally sung by black
Christians in America

spiritualism NOUN
the belief that the spirits of dead people
communicate with the living
spiritualist NOUN

spit[1] VERB **spat**
1 to send out drops of liquid etc. from the
mouth
2 to rain lightly

spit NOUN
saliva or spittle

spit[2] NOUN
1 a long thin metal spike put through meat
for roasting
2 a narrow strip of land extending into the sea

spite NOUN
a desire to hurt or annoy someone
in spite of not being prevented by *went out
in spite of the rain*

spite VERB
to hurt or annoy someone from spite

spiteful ADJECTIVE
wishing to hurt or annoy someone
spitefully ADVERB

spitting image NOUN
an exact likeness

spittle NOUN
saliva, especially when it is spat out

splash VERB
1 to make liquid fly about in drops
2 (of liquid) to fly about in drops
3 to make wet by splashing

splash NOUN
1 the action or sound or mark of splashing
2 a bright patch of colour or light

splatter VERB
to splash noisily

splay VERB
to spread or slope apart

spleen NOUN
an organ of the body, close to the stomach,
that helps to clean the blood

splendid ADJECTIVE
1 magnificent; full of splendour
2 excellent
splendidly ADVERB

splendour NOUN
a brilliant display or appearance

splice VERB
to join pieces of rope etc. by twisting the
strands together

splint NOUN
a straight piece of wood etc. tied to a broken
arm or leg to hold it firm

splinter NOUN
a thin sharp piece of wood, glass, stone, etc.
broken off a larger piece

splinter VERB
to break into splinters

split VERB **splitting**, **split**
1 to break apart along the length of
something
2 to divide into parts
3 to divide among several people
split up to end a relationship

split NOUN
a break or tear caused by splitting
the splits an acrobatic position in which the
legs are stretched widely in opposite directions

split second NOUN
a very brief moment of time

splodge NOUN
a dirty mark or stain

splutter VERB
1 to make a quick series of spitting sounds
2 to speak quickly but not clearly
splutter NOUN

spoil VERB **spoilt** or **spoiled**
1 to damage or make useless
2 to damage the character of someone by
pampering them

spoils PLURAL NOUN
things stolen or gained in war

spoilsport NOUN
a person who spoils other people's
enjoyment

spoke[1] NOUN
each of the bars or rods between the centre of
a wheel and the rim

spoke[2] *past tense* of **speak**

a b c d e f g h i j k l m n o p q r s t u v w x y z

spokesperson NOUN
a person who speaks on behalf of others
spokesman NOUN **spokeswoman** NOUN

sponge NOUN
1 a sea creature with a soft porous body
2 the skeleton of this creature, or a piece of a similar substance, used for washing
3 a soft lightweight cake or pudding
spongy ADJECTIVE

sponge VERB
1 to wipe or wash with a sponge
2 (informal) to get money or food without giving anything in return
sponger NOUN

sponsor NOUN
1 a person or organization that provides money for an activity
2 someone who gives money to a charity in return for something achieved by another person
sponsorship NOUN

sponsor VERB
to be a sponsor for a person or thing

spontaneous ADJECTIVE
happening or done naturally
spontaneity NOUN **spontaneously** ADVERB

spoof NOUN
1 a hoax
2 a parody

spook NOUN
(informal) a ghost

spooky ADJECTIVE **spookier**, **spookiest**
eerie or frightening

spool NOUN
a rod or cylinder on which something is wound

spoon NOUN
a small tool with a rounded bowl on a handle, used for lifting things to the mouth or for stirring

spoon VERB
to take or lift with a spoon

spoonful NOUN **spoonfuls**
the amount a spoon will hold

sporadic ADJECTIVE
happening or found at irregular intervals; scattered
sporadically ADVERB

spore NOUN
a tiny reproductive cell of a plant such as a fungus or fern

sporran NOUN
a pouch worn in front of a kilt

sport NOUN
1 an athletic activity; a game or pastime
2 games of this kind *keen on sport*
3 (informal) an obliging good-natured person

sport VERB
1 to amuse yourself
2 to wear

sporting ADJECTIVE
1 to do with or interested in sport
2 fair and generous

sporting chance NOUN
a reasonable chance of success

sports car NOUN
an open low-built fast car

sports jacket NOUN
a man's casual jacket

sportsman NOUN **sportsmen**
a man who takes part in sport

sportsmanship NOUN
fair and generous behaviour in sport

sportswoman NOUN **sportswomen**
a woman who takes part in sport

spot NOUN
1 a small round mark
2 a pimple
3 a small amount
4 a place
5 a drop
on the spot without delay or change of place

spot VERB **spotting**, **spotted**
1 to mark with spots
2 to notice or recognize
spotter NOUN

spot check NOUN
a random check on one of a group of people or things

spotless ADJECTIVE
perfectly clean

spotlight NOUN
a strong light that can shine on one small area

spotty ADJECTIVE **spottier**, **spottiest**
marked with spots

spouse NOUN
a person's husband or wife

spout NOUN
1 a pipe or similar opening from which liquid can pour
2 a jet of liquid

spout VERB
1 to come or send out as a jet of liquid
2 (informal) to speak for a long time

sprain VERB
to injure a joint by twisting it
sprain NOUN

sprat NOUN
a small edible fish

sprawl VERB
1 to sit or lie with the arms and legs spread out loosely
2 to spread out loosely or untidily
sprawl NOUN

spray *VERB*
to scatter tiny drops of liquid over

spray *NOUN*
1 tiny drops of liquid sent through the air
2 a device for spraying liquid
3 a liquid for spraying
4 a single shoot with its leaves and flowers

spread *VERB* **spread**
1 to open or stretch out to its full size
2 to make something cover a surface
3 to become longer or wider
4 to make or become more widely known

spread *NOUN*
1 the action or result of spreading
2 a thing's breadth or extent
3 a paste for spreading on bread
4 (*informal*) a large or grand meal

spreadeagled *ADJECTIVE*
with arms and legs stretched out

spreadsheet *NOUN*
a computer program for organizing figures
etc. in a table

spree *NOUN*
a period of carefree enjoyment

sprig *NOUN*
a small branch or shoot

sprightly *ADJECTIVE* **sprightlier,
sprightliest**
lively and full of energy

spring *VERB* **sprang, sprung**
1 to jump; to move quickly or suddenly
sprang to his feet
2 to originate or arise
3 to present or produce suddenly *sprang a
surprise on us*

spring *NOUN*
1 a coil of metal that returns to its original
size after being bent, squeezed, or stretched
2 a springing movement
3 a place where water comes up naturally
from the ground
4 the season when most plants begin to
grow

springboard *NOUN*
a springy board from which people jump in
diving and gymnastics

spring-clean *VERB*
to clean a house thoroughly in springtime

springy *ADJECTIVE* **springier, springiest**
able to spring back easily after being bent,
squeezed, or stretched

sprinkle *VERB*
to make tiny drops or pieces fall on
something
sprinkler *NOUN*

sprinkling *NOUN*
a small amount

sprint *VERB*
to run very fast for a short distance
sprint *NOUN* **sprinter** *NOUN*

sprite *NOUN*
an elf, fairy, or goblin

sprocket *NOUN*
each of the row of teeth round a wheel, fitting
into links on a chain

sprout *VERB*
to start to grow; to put out shoots

sprout *NOUN*
1 a shoot of a plant
2 a Brussels sprout

spruce [1] *NOUN*
a kind of fir tree

spruce [2] *ADJECTIVE*
neat and trim; smart

spruce *VERB*
to smarten *Spruce yourself up.*

spry *ADJECTIVE* **spryer, spryest**
active and lively

spud *NOUN*
(*informal*) a potato

spur *NOUN*
1 a sharp device worn on the heel of a rider's
boot to urge on a horse
2 a stimulus or incentive
3 a ridge that sticks out from a mountain
on the spur of the moment on an impulse

spur *VERB* **spurring, spurred**
to urge on

spurious *ADJECTIVE*
not genuine

spurn *VERB*
to reject scornfully

spurt *VERB*
1 to gush out
2 to increase your speed suddenly

spurt *NOUN*
1 a sudden gush
2 a sudden increase in speed or effort

sputter *VERB*
to splutter

spy *NOUN* **spies**
someone who works secretly to gather
information about another country,
organization, etc.

spy *VERB* **spies, spied**
1 to be a spy
2 to keep watch secretly
3 to see or notice

squabble *VERB*
to quarrel or bicker
squabble *NOUN*

squad *NOUN*
a small group of people working or being trained together

squadron *NOUN*
a part of an army, navy, or air force

squalid *ADJECTIVE*
dirty and unpleasant
squalidly *ADVERB*

squall *NOUN*
a sudden storm or gust of wind
squally *ADVERB*

squalor *NOUN*
dirty and unpleasant conditions

squander *VERB*
to spend money or time wastefully

square *NOUN*
1 a flat shape with four equal sides and four right angles
2 an area surrounded by buildings
3 the result of multiplying a number by itself
9 is the square of 3 (9 = 3 x 3)

square *ADJECTIVE*
1 having the shape of a square
2 forming a right angle *square corners*
3 equal or even *still square at full time*
4 used to give the length of each side of a square shape or object *The carpet is four metres square.*
5 used to give a measurement of an area
an area of 25 square metres

square *VERB*
1 to make a thing square
2 to multiply a number by itself *5 squared is 25*
3 to make or be consistent
4 to settle or pay a debt

square deal *NOUN*
a deal that is honest and fair

squarely *ADVERB*
directly or exactly *The ball hit him squarely in the mouth.*

square meal *NOUN*
a good satisfying meal

square root *NOUN*
the number that gives a particular number if it is multiplied by itself *3 is the square root of 9 (3 x 3 = 9)*

squash[1] *VERB*
1 to press something so that it becomes flat or out of shape
2 to force into a small space
3 to suppress or put an end to

squash *NOUN*
1 a crowded condition
2 a fruit-flavoured soft drink
3 an indoor game played with rackets and a soft ball

squash[2] *NOUN*
a kind of gourd used as a vegetable

squat *VERB* **squatting, squatted**
1 to sit on your heels
2 to live in an unoccupied building without permission
squat *NOUN*

squat *ADJECTIVE*
short and fat

squatter *NOUN*
someone who is squatting in a building

squawk *VERB*
to make a loud harsh cry
squawk *NOUN*

squeak *VERB*
to make a short high-pitched cry or sound
squeak *NOUN* **squeaky** *ADJECTIVE*

squeal *VERB*
to make a long shrill cry or sound
squeal *NOUN*

squeamish *ADJECTIVE*
easily disgusted or shocked

squeeze *VERB*
1 to press something from opposite sides
2 to force into or through a place *squeezed through a gap*

squeeze *NOUN*
1 the action of squeezing
2 an amount of liquid squeezed out
a squeeze of lemon
3 a time when money is difficult to get or borrow

squelch *VERB*
to make a sound like treading in thick mud
squelch *NOUN*

squid *NOUN*
a sea animal with tentacles

squiggle *NOUN*
a short curly line

squint *VERB*
1 to be cross-eyed
2 to look with half-shut eyes at something
squint *NOUN*

squire *NOUN*
1 a country landowner
2 a young nobleman who served a knight

squirm *VERB*
to wriggle about from embarrassment or awkwardness

squirrel *NOUN*
a small animal with a bushy tail and red or grey fur, living in trees

squirt *VERB*
to send or come out in a jet of liquid
squirt *NOUN*

St. or **St** *ABBREVIATION*
1 Saint
2 Street

stab *VERB* **stabbing**, **stabbed**
to pierce or wound with something sharp

stab *NOUN*
1 the action of stabbing
2 a sudden sharp pain
3 (*informal*) an attempt

stability *NOUN*
a stable or steady state

stabilize *VERB*
to make or become stable
stabilization *NOUN*

stabilizer *NOUN*
a device for keeping a vehicle or ship steady

stable *ADJECTIVE*
1 steady and firm
2 sensible and dependable

stable *NOUN*
a building where horses are kept

staccato *ADVERB, ADJECTIVE*
(*Music*) played with each note short and separate

stack *NOUN*
1 a neat pile
2 (*informal*) a large amount *a stack of work*

stack *VERB*
to pile in a stack

stadium *NOUN* **stadiums** or **stadia**
a sports ground surrounded by seats for spectators

staff *NOUN*
1 the people who work in an office, shop, etc.
2 the teachers in a school or college

staff *VERB*
to provide with a staff

stag *NOUN*
a male deer

stage *NOUN*
1 a platform for performances in a theatre or hall
2 a point or part of a process, journey, etc.

stage *VERB*
1 to present a performance on a stage
2 to organize *staged a protest*

stagecoach *NOUN*
a horse-drawn passenger coach

stagger *VERB*
1 to walk unsteadily
2 to shock deeply
3 to arrange working hours etc. to begin and end at different times
stagger *NOUN* **staggering** *ADJECTIVE*

stagnant *ADJECTIVE*
(of water) stale from not flowing

stagnate *VERB*
1 to be stagnant
2 to be dull through lack of activity or variety
stagnation *NOUN*

staid *ADJECTIVE*
steady and serious in manner; sedate

stain *NOUN*
1 a dirty mark
2 a blemish on someone's character or past record
3 a liquid used for staining

stain *VERB*
1 to make a stain on
2 to colour with a liquid that sinks into the surface

stained glass *NOUN*
pieces of coloured glass held together in a lead framework to make a picture or pattern

stainless *ADJECTIVE*
without a stain

stainless steel *NOUN*
steel that does not rust easily

stair *NOUN*
each of a set of fixed steps that lead from one floor to another

staircase *NOUN*
a set of stairs

stairway *NOUN*
a staircase

stake *NOUN*
1 a thick pointed stick driven into the ground
2 a post at which people were executed by burning
3 an amount of money bet on something
at stake being risked

stake *VERB*
1 to fix or mark out with stakes
2 to bet or risk money etc.

stalactite *NOUN*
a stony spike hanging like an icicle from the roof of a cave

stalagmite *NOUN*
a stony spike standing like a pillar on the floor of a cave

stale *ADJECTIVE*
1 not fresh
2 dull and lacking new ideas

stalemate NOUN
1 a drawn position in chess when a player cannot make a move without putting the king in check
2 a situation in which neither side in an argument can win

stalk[1] NOUN
a stem of a plant etc.

stalk[2] VERB
1 to track or hunt stealthily
2 to walk in a stiff or dignified way

stall NOUN
1 a table or counter from which things are sold
2 a place for one animal in a stable or shed

stall VERB
1 to lose power suddenly and stop
2 to delay or avoid giving an answer

stallion NOUN
a male horse

stalls PLURAL NOUN
the seats in the lowest level of a theatre

stalwart ADJECTIVE
strong and faithful

stamen NOUN
the part of a flower bearing pollen

stamina NOUN
strength and ability to endure hard effort

stammer VERB
to keep repeating the same syllables when speaking
stammer NOUN

stamp NOUN
1 a small piece of gummed paper stuck to a letter or parcel to show the postage has been paid
2 a small device for pressing words or marks on something
3 a distinctive characteristic *bears the stamp of truth*

stamp VERB
1 to bang the foot heavily on the ground
2 to walk with loud heavy steps
3 to stick a postage stamp on
4 to press a mark or design etc. on
stamp out to put an end to

stampede NOUN
a wild rush by animals or people

stampede VERB
to rush wildly in a crowd

stance NOUN
1 the way a person or animal stands
2 an attitude or point of view

stand VERB **stood**
1 to be on your feet without moving
2 to rise to your feet
3 to set or be upright

4 to stay the same
5 to be a candidate for election
6 to tolerate or endure
7 to provide and pay for
stand for to represent

stand NOUN
1 something made for putting things on
2 a stall for selling or displaying things
3 a grandstand
4 a stationary position *took his stand near the door*
5 resistance to attack *to make a stand*

standard NOUN
1 a level of achievement or quality *a high standard*
2 a thing used to measure or judge something else
3 a special flag

standard ADJECTIVE
1 of the usual or average quality or kind
2 regarded as the best and widely used *the standard book on the subject*

standardize VERB
to make things have a standard size, quality, etc.
standardization NOUN

standard lamp NOUN
a tall upright lamp that stands on the floor

standard of living NOUN
the level of comfort and wealth that a country or person has

standby NOUN
something or someone kept to be used if needed

stand-in NOUN
a deputy or substitute

standing NOUN
1 a person's status or reputation
2 the period for which something has existed

stand-offish ADJECTIVE
cold and formal; not friendly

standpoint NOUN
a point of view

standstill NOUN
a complete stop

stanza NOUN
a verse of poetry

staple[1] NOUN
1 a small piece of wire pushed through papers and clenched to fasten them
2 a U-shaped nail

staple VERB
to fasten with a staple or staples

staple[2] ADJECTIVE
(of food or diet) main or usual

stapler NOUN
a device for stapling papers together

star NOUN
1 a large mass of burning gas seen as a bright light in the night sky
2 a shape with points or rays sticking out from it
3 a famous performer or celebrity

star VERB **starring**, **starred**
1 to be one of the main performers in a film or show
2 to have as a main performer
3 to mark with a star symbol

starboard NOUN
the right-hand side of a ship or aircraft facing forward

starch NOUN
1 a white carbohydrate in bread, potatoes, etc.
2 a substance used to stiffen clothes
starchy ADJECTIVE

starch VERB
to stiffen with starch

stardom NOUN
the state of being a star performer

stare VERB
to look at something intensely
stare NOUN

starfish NOUN
a sea animal shaped like a star with five points

stark ADJECTIVE
1 complete or unmistakable
2 desolate and bare *a stark landscape*

stark ADVERB
completely *stark naked*

starlight NOUN
light from the stars

starling NOUN
a noisy black bird with speckled feathers

starry ADJECTIVE
full of stars

starry-eyed ADJECTIVE
made happy by foolish dreams or unrealistic hopes

start VERB
1 to begin or cause to begin
2 to make a machine begin running
3 to jump suddenly from pain or surprise

start NOUN
1 a beginning
2 the place where a race starts
3 an advantage that someone starts with *ten minutes' start*
4 a sudden movement

starter NOUN
the first course of a meal

startle VERB
to surprise or alarm

starve VERB
1 to suffer or die from lack of food
2 to deprive someone of something they need
starvation NOUN

starving ADJECTIVE
(*informal*) very hungry

stash VERB
(*informal*) to store safely in a secret place

state NOUN
1 the quality or condition of a person or thing
2 an organized community under one government or forming part of a republic
3 a country's government
4 a grand style *arrived in state*
5 (*informal*) an excited or upset condition *got into a state*

state VERB
to express in spoken or written words

stately ADJECTIVE **statelier**, **stateliest**
dignified or grand

statement NOUN
1 words stating something
2 a formal account of facts

statesman NOUN **statesmen**
someone who is skilled in governing a country
statesmanship NOUN

static ADJECTIVE
not moving or changing

static NOUN
crackling or hissing on a telephone line, radio, etc.

static electricity NOUN
electricity that is present in something, not flowing as current

station NOUN
1 a stopping place for trains, buses, etc. with platforms and buildings for passengers and goods
2 a building equipped for certain activities *police station*
3 a broadcasting company with its own frequency
4 a place where a person or thing stands

station VERB
to put someone in a certain place

stationary ADJECTIVE
not moving
Do not confuse this word with *stationery*.

stationer NOUN
a shopkeeper who sells stationery

stationery NOUN
paper, envelopes, and other articles used in writing or typing
Do not confuse this word with *stationary*.

statistic NOUN
a piece of information expressed as a number
statistical ADJECTIVE

statistics NOUN
the study of information based on numbers

statue NOUN
a stone or metal object in the form of a person or animal

statuette NOUN
a small statue

stature NOUN
1 the natural height of the body
2 greatness gained by ability or achievement

status (stay-tus) NOUN
position or rank in relation to others

statute NOUN
a law passed by a parliament
statutory ADJECTIVE

staunch ADJECTIVE
firm and loyal

stave NOUN
a set of five lines on which music is written

stave VERB **staved** or **stove**
to dent or break a hole in
stave off to keep something away

stay VERB
1 to continue to be in the same place or state
2 to spend time in a place as a visitor

stay NOUN
a time spent in a place

stead NOUN
in a person's stead instead of this person

steadfast ADJECTIVE
firm and not changing

steady ADJECTIVE **steadier**, **steadiest**
1 not shaking or moving
2 continuing the same *a steady pace*
steadily ADVERB

steady VERB **steadies**, **steadied**
to make or become steady

steak NOUN
a thick slice of meat or fish

steal VERB **stole**, **stolen**
1 to take and keep something dishonestly
2 to move quietly

stealth NOUN
quiet or furtive action or movement

stealthy (stelth-ee) ADJECTIVE **stealthier**, **stealthiest**
quiet or furtive
stealthily ADVERB

steam NOUN
1 gas or vapour produced by boiling water
2 power produced by steam

steam VERB
1 to produce steam
2 to move by the power of steam
3 to cook or treat with steam

steam engine NOUN
an engine driven by steam

steamer NOUN
a ship driven by steam

steamroller NOUN
a heavy vehicle with a large roller used to flatten road surfaces

steamship NOUN
a ship driven by steam

steamy ADJECTIVE **steamier**, **steamiest**
1 covered in or full of steam
2 passionate

steed NOUN
(*literary*) a horse

steel NOUN
a strong metal made from iron and carbon

steel VERB
steel yourself to find courage

steep¹ ADJECTIVE
1 sloping sharply
2 (of a price) unreasonably high
steeply ADVERB

steep² VERB
to soak thoroughly

steepen VERB
to make or become steeper

steeple NOUN
a church tower with a spire at the top

steeplechase NOUN
a race across country or over hedges or fences

steeplejack NOUN
a person who climbs tall chimneys or steeples to make repairs

steer¹ VERB
to make a vehicle go in a certain direction

steer² NOUN
a young castrated bull kept for its beef

steering wheel NOUN
a wheel for steering a car, boat, etc.

stellar ADJECTIVE
to do with a star or stars

stem¹ NOUN
1 the main central part of a tree or plant
2 a thin part on which a leaf, flower, or fruit is supported
3 a thin upright part of something
4 (*Grammar*) the main part of a word, to which endings are attached

stem VERB **stemming**, **stemmed**
to stop the flow of
stem from to have as a source

stench NOUN
a strong unpleasant smell

stencil NOUN
a piece of card, metal, or plastic with pieces cut out of it, used to produce a picture, design, etc.

stencil VERB **stencilling**, **stencilled**
to produce or decorate with a stencil

step NOUN
1 a movement made by lifting the foot and setting it down
2 the sound of a person walking or running
3 a level surface for placing the foot in climbing
4 each of a series of things in a process

step VERB **stepping**, **stepped**
to tread or walk
step in to intervene **step up** to increase

stepbrother NOUN
the son of your stepmother or stepfather

stepchild NOUN **stepchildren**
a child of your husband or wife from an earlier marriage
stepdaughter NOUN **stepson** NOUN

stepfather NOUN
a man who is married to your mother but is not your natural father

stepladder NOUN
a folding ladder with flat treads

stepmother NOUN
a woman who is married to your father but is not your natural mother

steppe NOUN
a grassy plain with few trees

stepping stone NOUN
1 a stone for crossing a shallow stream
2 a stage in achieving something

steps PLURAL NOUN
a stepladder

stepsister NOUN
the daughter of your stepmother or stepfather

stereo ADJECTIVE
stereophonic

stereo NOUN **stereos**
1 stereophonic sound or recording
2 a stereophonic CD player, record player, etc.

stereophonic ADJECTIVE
using sound that comes from two different directions to give a natural effect

stereotype NOUN
a fixed widely held idea of a type of person or thing

sterile ADJECTIVE
1 not fertile; barren
2 free from germs
sterility NOUN

sterilize VERB
1 to make free from germs
2 to make a person or animal unable to reproduce
sterilization NOUN

sterling NOUN
British money in international trading

stern [1] ADJECTIVE
strict and severe
sternly ADVERB

stern [2] NOUN
the back part of a ship

steroid NOUN
a substance of a kind that includes certain hormones

stethoscope NOUN
a device used for listening to sounds in a person's body

stew VERB
to cook slowly in liquid

stew NOUN
a dish of stewed meat or other food

steward NOUN
1 an official who looks after the passengers on a ship or aircraft
2 an official who looks after arrangements at a large public event

stewardess NOUN
a female official on an aircraft

stick [1] NOUN
1 a long thin piece of wood
2 an implement used to hit the ball in hockey, polo, etc.
3 a long thin piece of something

stick [2] VERB **stuck**
1 to push a thing into something
2 to fix or be fixed by glue etc.
3 to become fixed and unable to move
4 (*informal*) to endure or tolerate
stick to to refuse to change

sticker NOUN
an adhesive label or sign

sticking plaster NOUN
a strip of adhesive material for covering cuts

stick insect NOUN
an insect with a long thin body and legs, resembling a twig

stickleback NOUN
a small fish with sharp spines on its back

stickler NOUN
a person who insists on something *a stickler for punctuality*

sticky ADJECTIVE **stickier**, **stickiest**
1 able or likely to stick to things
2 (of weather) hot and humid
3 (informal) difficult or awkward *a sticky situation*

stiff ADJECTIVE
1 not bending or moving easily
2 thick or dense
3 difficult *a stiff climb*
4 formal in manner
5 severe or strong *a stiff fine*

stiffen VERB
to make or become stiff

stifle VERB
1 to suffocate
2 to suppress *stifled a yawn*

stigma NOUN
1 a mark of disgrace
2 the part of a pistil that receives the pollen

stigmatize VERB
to regard something as bad

stile NOUN
an arrangement of steps or bars for climbing over a fence

stiletto NOUN **stilettos**
a shoe with a high pointed heel

still ADJECTIVE
1 not moving
2 silent
3 (of water) not fizzy

still ADVERB
1 without moving *standing still*
2 up to this or that time *were still young*
3 in a greater amount or degree *can do still better*
4 even so

still VERB
to make or become still

still NOUN
a photograph from a cinema film

stillborn ADJECTIVE
(of a baby) born dead

still life NOUN **still lifes**
a painting of lifeless things such as ornaments and fruit

stilted ADJECTIVE
stiffly formal

stilts PLURAL NOUN
posts or poles for supporting a person or building above the ground

stimulant NOUN
something that stimulates

stimulate VERB
1 to make someone excited or enthusiastic
2 to make more lively or active
stimulation NOUN

stimulus NOUN **stimuli**
something that stimulates or produces a reaction

sting NOUN
1 a sharp-pointed part of an animal or plant that can inject poison
2 a painful wound caused by this

sting VERB **stung**
1 to wound or hurt with a sting
2 to feel a sharp pain
3 to make someone feel upset or hurt *I was stung by this criticism.*

stingy (stin-jee) ADJECTIVE **stingier**, **stingiest**
mean; not generous

stink NOUN
an unpleasant smell

stink VERB **stank** or **stunk**
to have an unpleasant smell

stint NOUN
an amount or period of work

stint VERB
to restrict to a small amount

stipulate VERB
to insist on as part of an agreement
stipulation NOUN

stir VERB **stirring**, **stirred**
1 to mix a liquid or soft mixture by moving it round
2 to start to move
3 to excite or stimulate
stirring ADJECTIVE

stir NOUN
1 the action of stirring
2 a fuss or disturbance

stirring ADJECTIVE
exciting; rousing

stirrup NOUN
a metal part hanging from each side of a horse's saddle, as a support for the rider's foot

stitch NOUN
1 a loop of thread made in sewing or knitting
2 a sudden sharp pain in the side of the body

stitch VERB
to sew or fasten with stitches

stoat NOUN
a kind of weasel, also called an ermine

stock NOUN
1 items kept ready to be sold or used
2 a line of ancestors
3 a number of shares in a company's capital
4 liquid for soup, made by stewing meat, fish, or vegetables
5 the main stem of a tree or plant
6 the base, holder, or handle of an implement, weapon, etc.
7 a garden flower with a sweet smell

stock VERB
1 to keep goods in stock
2 to provide a place with a stock of

stockade NOUN
a fence made of stakes

stockbroker NOUN
a broker who deals in stocks and shares

stock car NOUN
an ordinary car strengthened for use in races where bumping is allowed

stock exchange NOUN
a country's central place for buying and selling stocks and shares

stocking NOUN
a piece of clothing covering the foot and part or all of the leg

stock market NOUN
1 a stock exchange
2 the buying and selling of stocks and shares

stockpile NOUN
a large stock of things kept in reserve

stocks PLURAL NOUN
a wooden framework with holes for a person's legs, in which offenders were formerly made to sit as a punishment

stock-still ADJECTIVE
completely still

stocky ADJECTIVE **stockier**, **stockiest**
short and solidly built

stodgy ADJECTIVE **stodgier**, **stodgiest**
(of food) heavy and filling

stoical (stoh-ik-al) ADJECTIVE
accepting pain or difficulty without complaining
stoically ADVERB **stoicism** NOUN

stoke VERB
to put fuel in a furnace or on a fire

stole [1] NOUN
a wide piece of material worn round the shoulders

stole [2] past tense of **steal**

stomach NOUN
1 the part of the body where food starts to be digested
2 the abdomen

stomach VERB
to endure or tolerate

stone NOUN
1 a piece of rock
2 stones or rock as material, e.g. for building
3 a jewel
4 the hard case round the kernel of fruit
5 a unit of weight equal to 14 pounds (6.35 kg)

stone VERB
1 to throw stones at
2 to remove the stones from fruit

Stone Age NOUN
the earliest period of human history, when tools and weapons were made of stone

stone cold ADJECTIVE
extremely cold

stoned ADJECTIVE
(informal) under the influence of drugs or alcohol

stone deaf ADJECTIVE
completely deaf

stony ADJECTIVE **stonier**, **stoniest**
1 full of stones
2 hard like stone
3 unfriendly *a stony silence*

stooge NOUN
(informal) an assistant who does the routine work

stool NOUN
a movable seat without arms or a back

stoop [1] VERB
1 to bend the body forwards and down
2 to lower your standards *would not stoop to lying*
stoop NOUN

stop VERB
1 to bring or come to an end
2 to be no longer moving or working
3 to prevent or obstruct
4 to stay for a time
5 to fill a hole

stop NOUN
1 the act of stopping
2 a place where a bus or train etc. stops
3 a full stop
4 a lever or knob that allows organ pipes to sound

stopcock NOUN
a valve controlling the flow of liquid in a pipe

stopgap NOUN
a temporary substitute

stoppage NOUN
1 an interruption in the work of a factory etc.
2 a blockage

stopper NOUN
a plug for closing a bottle etc.

stopwatch NOUN
a watch for timing, which can be started and stopped

storage NOUN
the storing of things

store NOUN
1 a supply of things kept for future use
2 a place where things are kept until needed
3 a large shop
in store soon to happen
store VERB
to keep things until needed

storey NOUN **storeys**
one whole floor of a building
Do not confuse this word with *story*.

stork NOUN
a large bird with long legs and a long beak

storm NOUN
1 a strong wind usually with rain, snow, etc.
2 a violent attack or outburst
stormy ADJECTIVE
storm VERB
1 to rush violently or angrily
2 to attack and capture a place

story NOUN **stories**
an account of a real or imaginary event
Do not confuse this word with *storey*.

stout ADJECTIVE
1 rather fat
2 thick and strong
stoutly ADVERB
stout NOUN
a kind of dark beer

stove¹ NOUN
1 a device containing an oven or ovens
2 a device for heating a room

stove² *past tense* of **stave**

stow VERB
to pack or store something away

stowaway NOUN
someone who hides on a ship or aircraft to
avoid paying the fare

straddle VERB
1 to sit or stand astride something
2 to be built across something

straggle VERB
1 to grow or spread in an untidy way
2 to lag behind
straggler NOUN

straight ADJECTIVE
1 going continuously in one direction
2 level, horizontal, or upright
3 tidy; in proper order
4 honest and frank *a straight answer*
straight ADVERB
1 in a straight line or manner
2 directly; without delay *Go straight home.*
Do not confuse this word with *strait*.

straight away ADVERB
immediately

straighten VERB
to make or become straight

straightforward ADJECTIVE
1 easy, not complicated
2 honest and frank

strain¹ VERB
1 injure or weaken something by stretching
or working it too hard
2 to stretch tightly
3 to make a great effort
4 to put through a sieve or filter
strain NOUN
1 the act or force of straining
2 an injury caused by straining
3 something that uses up strength,
resources, etc.
4 exhaustion

strain² NOUN
1 a breed or variety of animals, plants, etc.
2 an inherited characteristic

strainer NOUN
a device for straining liquids

strait NOUN
a narrow stretch of water connecting
two seas
Do not confuse this word with *straight*.

straitjacket NOUN
a jacket with the sleeves tied round the sides
for restraining a violent person

strait-laced ADJECTIVE
very prim and proper

straits PLURAL NOUN
1 a strait
2 a difficult condition *found ourselves in dire
straits*

strand¹ NOUN
each of the threads or wires etc. twisted
together to form a rope or cable

strand² NOUN
a shore

stranded ADJECTIVE
1 left on sand or rocks in shallow water
2 left in a difficult or helpless position

strange ADJECTIVE
1 unusual or surprising
2 not known or seen before
strangely ADVERB

stranger NOUN
a person you do not know, or a person in a
place they do not know

strangle VERB
to kill by squeezing the throat to prevent
breathing

stranglehold NOUN
complete control over a person or process

strap NOUN
a flat strip of leather etc. for fastening or holding things

strap VERB **strapping**, **strapped**
to fasten with a strap

strapping ADJECTIVE
tall and healthy-looking

strata *plural* of **stratum**

stratagem NOUN
a cunning plan or trick

strategic ADJECTIVE
1 to do with strategy
2 giving an advantage
strategically ADVERB

strategy NOUN **strategies**
1 a plan or policy designed to achieve something
2 the planning of a war or campaign

stratosphere NOUN
a layer of the atmosphere between about 10 and 60 kilometres above the earth's surface

stratum NOUN **strata**
a layer or level

straw NOUN
1 dry cut stalks of corn
2 a narrow tube for drinking through

strawberry NOUN **strawberries**
a small red juicy fruit, with its seeds on the outside

stray VERB
to leave a group or proper place and wander

stray ADJECTIVE
1 lost *a stray cat*
2 separated *a stray sock*

stray NOUN
a stray animal

streak NOUN
1 a long thin line or mark
2 a trace
3 a spell of success, luck, etc.
streaky ADJECTIVE

streak VERB
1 to mark with streaks
2 to move very quickly

stream NOUN
1 a small river
2 a flow of water, light, etc.
3 a constant passing of people or vehicles etc.

stream VERB
1 to move in or like a stream
2 to produce a stream of liquid
3 to organize pupils according to ability

streamer NOUN
a long narrow ribbon or strip of paper etc.

streamline VERB
1 to give something a smooth shape to help it to move easily through air or water
2 to organize a process to be more efficient
streamlined ADJECTIVE

street NOUN
a road with houses beside it in a city or village

strength NOUN
1 the state of being strong
2 how strong a person or thing is
3 an ability or good quality

strengthen VERB
to make or become stronger

strenuous ADJECTIVE
needing or using great effort
strenuously ADVERB

stress NOUN
1 a force that presses, pulls, or twists
2 the extra force with which part of a word is pronounced
3 distress caused by the problems of life
stressful ADJECTIVE

stress VERB
1 to pronounce part of a word with extra emphasis
2 to emphasize a point or idea
3 to cause stress to

stretch VERB
1 to pull something or be pulled so that it becomes longer or larger
2 to extend or be continuous
3 to push out your arms and legs as far as you can
4 to make high demand on resources, ability, etc.

stretch NOUN
1 the action of stretching
2 a continuous period of time or area of land or water

stretcher NOUN
a framework for carrying a sick or injured person

strew VERB **strewn** or **strewed**
to scatter things over a surface

stricken ADJECTIVE
badly affected by injury, illness, grief, etc.

strict ADJECTIVE
1 demanding obedience and good behaviour
2 complete or exact
strictly ADVERB

stride VERB **strode**, **stridden**
to walk with long steps

stride NOUN
1 a long step when walking or running
2 progress

strident ADJECTIVE
loud and harsh

strife *NOUN*
conflict; fighting or quarrelling

strike *VERB* **struck**
1 to hit with force
2 to attack or afflict suddenly
3 to make an impression on the mind
They strike me as being useful.
4 to light a match
5 to refuse to work as a protest
6 to produce by pressing or stamping
7 (of a clock) to sound
8 to find gold or oil etc. by digging or drilling
strike off or **out** to cross out

strike *NOUN*
1 a hit
2 an attack *an air strike*
3 refusal to work as a protest
4 a sudden discovery of gold or oil etc.

striker *NOUN*
1 a worker who is on strike
2 a football player whose role is to score goals

striking *ADJECTIVE*
1 impressive or attractive
2 noticeable
strikingly *ADVERB*

string *NOUN*
1 thin cord made of twisted threads, used to fasten or tie things
2 a piece of wire or cord etc. stretched and vibrated to produce sounds in a musical instrument
3 a line or series of things

string *VERB* **strung**
1 to fit or fasten with string
2 to thread on a string

stringed *ADJECTIVE*
(of a musical instrument) having strings

stringent (**strin**-jent) *ADJECTIVE*
(of rules) strictly enforced

strings *PLURAL NOUN*
stringed instruments

stringy *ADJECTIVE* **stringier**, **stringiest**
1 like string
2 containing tough fibres

strip *VERB* **stripping**, **stripped**
1 to take a covering or layer off something
2 to undress
3 to deprive a person of something

strip *NOUN*
1 a long narrow piece or area
2 the distinctive outfit worn by a sports team

strip cartoon *NOUN*
a series of drawings telling a story

stripe *NOUN*
1 a long narrow band of colour
2 a band of cloth on the sleeve of a uniform showing rank
striped *ADJECTIVE* **stripy** *ADJECTIVE*

strive *VERB* **strove**, **striven**
to try hard

strobe *NOUN*
a light that flashes on and off continuously

stroke[1] *NOUN*
1 a hit
2 a movement of the arms and legs in swimming
3 an action or effort *a stroke of genius*
4 the sound made by a clock striking
5 a sudden illness that often causes paralysis

stroke[2] *VERB*
to move the hand gently along a surface
stroke *NOUN*

stroll *VERB*
to walk in a leisurely way
stroll *NOUN* **stroller** *NOUN*

strong *ADJECTIVE*
1 having great power or effect
2 not easy to break, damage, or defeat
3 great in intensity *strong feelings*
4 having a lot of flavour or smell
5 of a certain number *an army 5,000 strong*

stronghold *NOUN*
a strong fortified place

strove *past tense* of **strive**

structure *NOUN*
1 something that has been built
2 the way something is built or organized
structural *ADJECTIVE*

structure *VERB*
to organize or arrange into a system or pattern

struggle *VERB*
1 to move about violently in trying to get free
2 to make strong efforts to do something
3 to try to overcome an opponent or difficulty

struggle *NOUN*
1 the action of struggling
2 a hard fight or great effort

strum *VERB* **strumming**, **strummed**
to sound a guitar by running your fingers across the strings

strut *VERB* **strutting**, **strutted**
to walk proudly or stiffly

strut *NOUN*
1 a bar strengthening a framework
2 a strutting walk

stub *NOUN*
1 a short stump left after use
2 the part of a cheque, ticket, etc. for keeping

stub *VERB* **stubbing**, **stubbed**
to bump a toe painfully

stubble NOUN
1 short stalks of corn left after harvesting
2 short hairs growing after shaving

stubborn ADJECTIVE
1 refusing to give way; obstinate
2 difficult to remove or deal with

stubby ADJECTIVE **stubbier, stubbiest**
short and thick

stuck *past tense and past participle* of **stick**

stuck ADJECTIVE
unable to move or make progress

stuck-up ADJECTIVE
(*informal*) conceited or snobbish

stud[1] NOUN
a small curved lump or knob

stud VERB **studding, studded**
to set or decorate with studs etc.

stud[2] NOUN
a stallion

student NOUN
a person who studies a subject, especially at a college or university

studio NOUN **studios**
1 the room where a painter or photographer etc. works
2 a place where cinema films are made
3 a room from which radio or television programmes are broadcast

studious ADJECTIVE
studying hard

study VERB **studies, studied**
1 to spend time learning about something
2 to look at carefully

study NOUN **studies**
1 the process of studying
2 a subject studied
3 a room used for studying
4 a piece of music for playing as an exercise
5 a drawing done for practice

stuff NOUN
1 a substance or material
2 possessions

stuff VERB
1 to fill tightly
2 to fill with stuffing
3 to push a thing into something
4 (*informal*) to eat greedily

stuffing NOUN
1 material used to fill the inside of something
2 a savoury mixture put into meat or poultry etc. before cooking

stuffy ADJECTIVE **stuffier, stuffiest**
1 lacking fresh air
2 with blocked breathing passages
3 formal and uninteresting
stuffily ADVERB

stumble VERB
1 to trip and lose your balance
2 to speak hesitantly or uncertainly
stumble across or **on** to find accidentally
stumble NOUN

stump NOUN
1 the bottom of a tree trunk left in the ground
2 something left when the main part is cut off or worn down
3 each of the three upright sticks of a wicket in cricket

stump VERB
1 to put a batsman out by knocking the bails off the stumps
2 to be too difficult or puzzling for

stumpy ADJECTIVE **stumpier, stumpiest**
short and thick

stun VERB **stunning, stunned**
1 to knock unconscious
2 to daze or shock

stunt[1] VERB
to prevent from growing or developing

stunt[2] NOUN
1 a daring action
2 something done to attract attention

stupefy VERB **stupefies, stupefied**
to make a person dazed
stupefaction NOUN

stupendous ADJECTIVE
amazing or tremendous
stupendously ADVERB

stupid ADJECTIVE
1 not clever or thoughtful
2 without reason or common sense
stupidity NOUN

stupor (stew-per) NOUN
a dazed condition

sturdy ADJECTIVE **sturdier, sturdiest**
strong and solid
sturdily ADVERB

sturgeon NOUN
a large edible fish

stutter VERB
to stammer
stutter NOUN

sty[1] NOUN **sties**
a pigsty

sty[2] or **stye** NOUN **sties** or **styes**
a sore swelling on an eyelid

style NOUN
1 the way something is done, said, or written
2 fashion or elegance
stylistic ADJECTIVE

style VERB
to design or arrange something
stylist NOUN

s

stylish *ADJECTIVE*
elegant or fashionable

suave (swahv) *ADJECTIVE*
smoothly polite

sub *NOUN* (*informal*)
1 a submarine
2 a subscription
3 a substitute

subconscious *ADJECTIVE*
to do with mental processes of which we are not fully aware
subconscious *NOUN*

subcontinent *NOUN*
a mass of land smaller than a continent

subdivide *VERB*
to divide into smaller parts
subdivision *NOUN*

subdue *VERB*
1 to overcome or bring under control
2 to make quieter or gentler
subdued *ADJECTIVE*

subject (sub-jekt) *NOUN*
1 the person or thing being talked or written about or dealt with
2 something that is studied
3 (*Grammar*) the word or words naming who or what does the action of an active verb, e.g. *The dog* in *The dog bit him*
4 someone who is ruled by a monarch or government

subject (sub-jekt) *ADJECTIVE*
ruled by a monarch or government; not independent
subject to 1 having to obey **2** liable to **3** depending on

subject (sub-**jekt**) *VERB*
1 to make a person or thing undergo something
2 to bring a country under your control
subjection *NOUN*

subjective *ADJECTIVE*
1 existing in a person's mind
2 depending on a person's own taste or opinions etc.

subjunctive *NOUN*
the form of a verb used to indicate what might happen, e.g. *were* in *if I were you*

sublime *ADJECTIVE*
noble or impressive

submarine *NOUN*
a ship that can travel under water

submarine *ADJECTIVE*
under the sea

submerge *VERB*
to go or put under water

submission *NOUN*
1 the act of submitting to someone
2 something offered for consideration

submissive *ADJECTIVE*
willing to obey

submit *VERB* **submitting**, **submitted**
1 to let someone have authority over you
2 to put forward for consideration

subordinate *ADJECTIVE*
1 less important
2 lower in rank

subordinate *NOUN*
a person working under someone's authority or control

subordinate *VERB*
to treat as being less important
subordination *NOUN*

subordinate clause *NOUN*
(*Grammar*) a clause which adds details to the main clause of the sentence, but cannot be used as a sentence by itself

subscribe *VERB*
1 to pay regularly for a service, membership, etc.
2 to contribute money
3 to say that you agree *We cannot subscribe to this theory.*
subscriber *NOUN*

subscription *NOUN*
money paid to subscribe to something

subsequent *ADJECTIVE*
coming after in time or order
subsequently *ADVERB*

subside *VERB*
1 to become less strong or intense
2 to sink

subsidence *NOUN*
the gradual sinking of an area of land

subsidiary *ADJECTIVE*
less important; secondary

subsidize *VERB*
to pay a subsidy to

subsidy *NOUN* **subsidies**
money paid to help or support a person or group

subsist *VERB*
to keep yourself alive
subsistence *NOUN*

substance *NOUN*
1 matter of a particular kind
2 the essential part of something

substantial *ADJECTIVE*
1 of great size, value, or importance
2 solidly built

substantially *ADVERB*
mostly; essentially

substantiate *VERB*
to produce evidence to prove something
substantiation *NOUN*

substitute *NOUN*
a person or thing that replaces another
substitute *VERB*
to put or use one person or thing instead of another
substitution *NOUN*

subterfuge *NOUN*
a trick or deception

subterranean *ADJECTIVE*
underground

subtitle *NOUN*
words shown on the screen during a foreign-language film, translating the words spoken

subtle (sut-el) *ADJECTIVE*
1 slight and difficult to detect or describe
2 faint or delicate
subtlety *NOUN* **subtly** *ADVERB*

subtotal *NOUN*
the total of part of a group of figures

subtract *VERB*
to take away a part or number from a greater one
subtraction *NOUN*

suburb *NOUN*
a district outside the central part of a city
suburban *ADJECTIVE*

subversive *ADJECTIVE*
tending to weaken or overthrow authority

subvert *VERB*
to weaken or overthrow
subversion *NOUN*

subway *NOUN*
1 an underground passage for pedestrians
2 an underground railway

succeed *VERB*
1 to achieve what you wanted or intended
2 to come after another person or thing
3 to become the next king or queen

success *NOUN*
1 the achievement of something wanted
2 a person or thing that does well

successful *ADJECTIVE*
having success; being a success
successfully *ADVERB*

succession *NOUN*
1 a series of people or things
2 the process of following in order
3 the right of becoming the next king or queen
in succession one after another

successive *ADJECTIVE*
following one after another *on successive days*
successively *ADVERB*

successor *NOUN*
a person or thing that comes after another

succinct (suk-**sinkt**) *ADJECTIVE*
expressed briefly

succour (**suk**-er) *NOUN*
help given in time of need

succulent *ADJECTIVE*
1 juicy and tasty
2 (of plants) having thick juicy leaves or stems

succumb (suk-**um**) *VERB*
to give way to something overpowering

such *ADJECTIVE*
1 of the same kind; similar
2 of the kind described *There's no such thing.*
3 so great or intense
such as for example

suchlike *ADJECTIVE*
of that kind

suck *VERB*
1 to take in liquid or air through almost-closed lips
2 to hold in the mouth and draw flavour from
3 to pull or draw in
suck up to absorb
suck *NOUN*

sucker *NOUN*
1 an organ or device that can stick to a surface by suction
2 a shoot coming up from a root
3 (*informal*) someone easily deceived

suckle *VERB*
to feed on milk from the mother's breast or teat

suction *NOUN*
1 the process of sucking
2 production of a vacuum so that things are sucked into the empty space

sudden *ADJECTIVE*
happening or done quickly or without warning
suddenly *ADVERB* **suddenness** *NOUN*

suds *PLURAL NOUN*
froth on soapy water

sue *VERB*
to start a lawsuit to claim money from

suede (swayd) *NOUN*
leather with one side rubbed to make it velvety

suet *NOUN*
hard fat from cattle and sheep, used in cooking

a
b
c
d
e
f
g
h
i
j
k
l
m
n
o
p
q
r
s
t
u
v
w
x
y
z

suffer _VERB_
1 to feel pain or sadness
2 to experience something bad
3 to become worse or be badly affected

suffering _NOUN_
pain or hardship

suffice _VERB_
to be enough

sufficient _ADJECTIVE_
enough
sufficiency _NOUN_ **sufficiently** _ADVERB_

suffix _NOUN_
(_Grammar_) a word or syllable joined to the
end of a word to change or add to its
meaning, as in suffi*ciently* and suffo*cation*

suffocate _VERB_
1 to prevent someone from breathing
2 to suffer or die because breathing is
prevented
suffocation _NOUN_

suffrage _NOUN_
the right to vote in political elections

suffuse _VERB_
to spread through or over something

sugar _NOUN_
a sweet food obtained from the juices of
various plants
sugary _ADJECTIVE_

suggest _VERB_
1 to put forward an idea or plan for someone
to consider
2 to cause an idea or possibility to come into
the mind
suggestive _ADJECTIVE_

suggestion _NOUN_
1 the act of suggesting
2 something suggested

suggestive _ADJECTIVE_
suggesting something, especially something
indecent

suicide _NOUN_
1 the act of killing yourself deliberately
2 a person who does this
suicidal _ADJECTIVE_

suit _NOUN_
1 a matching set of clothes worn together
2 each of the four sets of cards (clubs, hearts,
diamonds, spades) in a pack of playing cards
3 a lawsuit

Do not confuse this word with *suite*.

suit _VERB_
1 to be suitable or convenient for a person or
thing
2 to make a person look attractive

suitable _ADJECTIVE_
satisfactory or right for a particular person,
purpose, or occasion
suitability _NOUN_ **suitably** _ADVERB_

suitcase _NOUN_
a travelling case for carrying clothes

suite (_say as_ sweet) _NOUN_
1 a set of furniture
2 a set of rooms
3 a set of short pieces of music
Do not confuse this word with *suit*.

suitor _NOUN_
a man who wants to marry a particular
woman

sulk _VERB_
to be silent and in a bad mood because you
are cross about something

sulky _ADJECTIVE_ **sulkier**, **sulkiest**
silent and in a bad mood
sulkily _ADVERB_

sullen _ADJECTIVE_
sulking and gloomy

sulphur _NOUN_
a yellow chemical used in industry and
medicine
sulphurous _ADJECTIVE_

sulphuric acid _NOUN_
a strong colourless acid containing sulphur

sultan _NOUN_
the ruler of certain Muslim countries

sultana _NOUN_
a raisin without seeds

sultry _ADJECTIVE_ **sultrier**, **sultriest**
1 hot and humid
2 passionate

sum _NOUN_
1 an amount of money
2 a total
3 a problem in arithmetic
sum _VERB_ **summing**, **summed**
sum up to give a summary

summarize _VERB_
to make or give a summary of

summary _NOUN_ **summaries**
a statement of the main points of something
summary _ADJECTIVE_
1 brief
2 done or given hastily
summarily _ADVERB_

summer _NOUN_
the warm season between spring and autumn
summery _ADJECTIVE_

summit _NOUN_
1 the top of a mountain or hill
2 a meeting between world leaders

summon VERB
1 to order someone to come or appear
2 to call people together
summon up to find strength or courage or energy

summons NOUN
a command to appear in a lawcourt

sump NOUN
a metal case holding oil at the bottom of an engine

sumptuous ADJECTIVE
splendid and expensive-looking

sun NOUN
1 the star round which the earth travels
2 light and warmth from the sun

sunbathe VERB
to expose your body to the sun

sunbeam NOUN
a ray of sun

sunburn NOUN
redness of the skin caused by the sun
sunburnt ADJECTIVE

sundae (sun-day) NOUN
a mixture of ice cream and fruit, nuts, cream, etc.

Sunday NOUN
the first day of the week, for Christians a day of rest and worship

sundial NOUN
a device that shows the time by a shadow on a dial

sundown NOUN
sunset

sundries PLURAL NOUN
various small things

sundry ADJECTIVE
various or several

sunflower NOUN
a tall flower with golden petals

sunglasses PLURAL NOUN
dark glasses to protect the eyes from strong sunlight

sunken ADJECTIVE
sunk deeply into a surface

sunlight NOUN
light from the sun
sunlit ADJECTIVE

sunny ADJECTIVE **sunnier**, **sunniest**
1 full of sunshine
2 cheerful

sunrise NOUN
the rising of the sun in the morning

sunset NOUN
the setting of the sun in the evening

sunshine NOUN
sunlight with no cloud between the sun and the earth

sunstroke NOUN
illness caused by too much exposure to the sun

suntan NOUN
a brown colour of the skin caused by the sun
suntanned ADJECTIVE

sup VERB **supping**, **supped**
to drink liquid in sips or spoonfuls

super ADJECTIVE
(*informal*) excellent or superb

superb ADJECTIVE
magnificent or excellent

supercilious ADJECTIVE
haughty and scornful

superficial ADJECTIVE
1 on the surface
2 not deep or thorough
superficially ADVERB

superfluous ADJECTIVE
more than is needed

superhuman ADJECTIVE
1 beyond human ability
2 divine

superimpose VERB
to place one thing on top of another

superintend VERB
to supervise

superintendent NOUN
1 a supervisor
2 a police officer above the rank of inspector

superior ADJECTIVE
1 higher in position or rank
2 better than another person or thing
3 showing conceit
superiority NOUN

superior NOUN
a person or thing that is superior to another

superlative ADJECTIVE
of the highest degree or quality

superlative NOUN
the form of an adjective or adverb that expresses 'most' , e.g. *biggest*, *most quickly*

supermarket NOUN
a large self-service shop that sells food etc.

supernatural ADJECTIVE
not having a natural explanation

superpower NOUN
one of the most powerful nations of the world

supersede VERB
to take the place of something

supersonic ADJECTIVE
faster than the speed of sound

a b c d e f g h i j k l m n o p q r **s** t u v w x y z

superstition NOUN
a belief or action that is not based on reason or evidence
superstitious ADJECTIVE

superstore NOUN
a large supermarket

supervise VERB
to be in charge of a person or activity
supervision NOUN

supervisor NOUN
a person who supervises others

supper NOUN
a meal eaten in the evening

supplant VERB
to take the place of a person or thing

supple ADJECTIVE
bending easily; flexible
supplely ADVERB

supplement NOUN
1 something added
2 an extra section of a book or newspaper
supplementary ADJECTIVE

supplement VERB
to add to something

supply VERB **supplies**, **supplied**
to provide what is needed
supplier NOUN

supply NOUN **supplies**
1 an amount available for use
2 the action of supplying

support VERB
1 to keep something from falling or sinking
2 to give help or encouragement to
3 to provide with the necessities of life
supporter NOUN **supportive** ADJECTIVE

support NOUN
1 the action of supporting
2 a person or thing that supports

suppose VERB
1 to think that something is likely to happen or be true
2 to consider as a suggestion *Suppose you tell them.*
be supposed to to be expected to
supposition NOUN

supposedly ADVERB
so people suppose or think

suppress VERB
1 to put an end to something by force
2 to keep something from being known
suppression NOUN

supremacy NOUN
highest authority or power

supreme ADJECTIVE
1 most important or highest in rank
2 greatest *supreme courage*

surcharge NOUN
an extra charge

sure ADJECTIVE
1 completely confident of being right
2 certain to happen or do something
3 reliable; undoubtedly true

surely ADVERB
1 certainly or securely
2 it must be true *Surely you were there.*

surf NOUN
the white foam of waves breaking on a rock or shore

surf VERB
1 to go surfing
2 to browse through the Internet

surface NOUN
1 the outside of something
2 any of the sides of an object
3 an outard appearance

surface VERB
1 to put a surface on a road, path, etc.
2 to come up to the surface from under water

surfboard NOUN
a board used for riding on the waves

surfeit (ser-fit) NOUN
too much

surfing NOUN
the sport of riding on a surfboard
surfer NOUN

surge VERB
1 to move powerfully forward
2 to increase dramatically
surge NOUN

surgeon NOUN
a doctor who treats disease or injury usually by cutting open and repairing the affected parts of the body

surgery NOUN **surgeries**
1 the work of a surgeon
2 the place where a doctor or dentist treats patients

surgical ADJECTIVE
to do with surgery

surly ADJECTIVE **surlier**, **surliest**
bad-tempered and unfriendly
surliness NOUN

surmise VERB
to guess or suspect

surmount VERB
to overcome an obstacle or difficulty

surname NOUN
the name held by members of a family

surpass VERB
to do or be better than others

surplus NOUN
an amount left over after spending or using all that was needed
surplus ADJECTIVE

surprise NOUN
1 something unexpected
2 the feeling caused something unexpected
surprise VERB
1 to be a surprise to
2 to come upon or attack unexpectedly

surprising ADJECTIVE
causing surprise; unexpected
surprisingly ADVERB

surreal ADJECTIVE
using images from dreams and the subconscious

surrealism NOUN
a surreal style of painting etc.
surrealist NOUN **surrealistic** ADJECTIVE

surrender VERB
1 to stop fighting and give yourself up to an enemy
2 to hand something or someone over to another person
surrender NOUN

surreptitious ADJECTIVE
stealthy

surrogate (su-rog-at) NOUN
a deputy or substitute
surrogate ADJECTIVE

surround VERB
to come or be all round a person or thing

surroundings PLURAL NOUN
the conditions or area around a person or thing

surveillance (ser-vay-lans) NOUN
a close watch kept on a person or thing

survey (ser-vay) NOUN
1 a general look at something
2 an inspection of an area, building, etc.
survey (ser-vay) VERB
to make a survey of; to inspect

surveyor NOUN
someone qualified to make a survey of land, buildings, etc.

survival NOUN
1 the process or likelihood of surviving
2 something that has survived

survive VERB
1 to stay alive; to continue to exist
2 to remain alive after an accident or disaster
3 to live longer than
survivor NOUN

susceptible (sus-ept-ib-ul) ADJECTIVE
likely to be affected by something
susceptibility NOUN

suspect (sus-pekt) VERB
1 to have reason to think a person guilty of something
2 to believe that something is possible
suspect (sus-pekt) NOUN
a person who is suspected of a crime etc.
suspect (sus-pekt) ADJECTIVE
thought to be dangerous or unreliable
a suspect package

suspend VERB
1 to hang something up
2 to stop something for a time
3 to remove a person from a position for a time
4 to keep something from falling or sinking in air or liquid

suspender NOUN
a fastener to hold up a sock or stocking by its top

suspense NOUN
an anxious or uncertain feeling while waiting for something to happen

suspension NOUN
1 the act of suspending
2 the springs etc. in a vehicle that lessen the effect of rough road surfaces
3 a liquid containing pieces of solid material which do not dissolve

suspension bridge NOUN
a bridge supported by cables

suspicion NOUN
1 a feeling of doubt; a lack of trust
2 a slight belief

suspicious ADJECTIVE
feeling or causing suspicion
suspiciously ADVERB

sustain VERB
1 to keep someone alive
2 to keep something happening
3 to undergo or suffer
4 to support or uphold
sustainable ADJECTIVE

sustenance NOUN
food and drink; nourishment

svelte ADJECTIVE
slim and graceful

swab (swob) NOUN
a mop or pad for cleaning or wiping
swab VERB **swabbing**, **swabbed**
to clean or wipe with a swab

swagger VERB
to walk or behave in a conceited way
swagger NOUN

swallow [1] VERB
1 to make something go down your throat
2 to believe something improbable
swallow up to absorb completely
swallow NOUN

swallow[2] *NOUN*
a small bird with a forked tail and pointed wings

swamp *NOUN*
a marsh
swampy *ADJECTIVE*

swamp *VERB*
1 to flood
2 to overwhelm

swan *NOUN*
a large usually white waterbird with a long neck

swansong *NOUN*
a person's last performance or work

swap *VERB* **swapping**, **swapped**
to exchange one thing for another
swap *NOUN*

swarm *NOUN*
a large number of insects or birds etc. flying or moving together

swarm *VERB*
1 to gather or move in a swarm
2 be crowded with people

swarthy *ADJECTIVE* **swarthier**, **swarthiest**
having a dark complexion

swashbuckling *ADJECTIVE*
daring and fond of adventure

swastika *NOUN*
an ancient symbol in the form of a cross with its ends bent at right angles

swat *VERB* **swatting**, **swatted**
to hit or crush a fly etc.

swathe[1] *NOUN*
1 a broad strip or area
2 a line of cut corn or grass

swathe[2] *VERB*
to wrap in layers of bandages etc.

sway *VERB*
1 to move gently from side to side
2 to influence
sway *NOUN*

swear *VERB* **swore**, **sworn**
1 to make a solemn promise
2 to make a person take an oath *swore them to secrecy*
3 to use words that are rude or shocking

swear word *NOUN*
a word considered rude or shocking

sweat *NOUN*
moisture given off by the body through the pores of the skin
sweaty *ADJECTIVE*

sweat *VERB*
to give off sweat

sweater *NOUN*
a jersey or pullover

sweatshirt *NOUN*
a thick casual jersey

swede *NOUN*
a large kind of turnip with purple skin and yellow flesh

sweep *VERB* **swept**
1 to clean or clear with a broom or brush etc.
2 to move or remove quickly
3 to go smoothly and quickly *swept out of the room*
sweeper *NOUN*

sweep *NOUN*
1 the process of sweeping *Give this room a good sweep.*
2 a sweeping movement
3 a chimney sweep
4 a sweepstake

sweeping *ADJECTIVE*
general or wide-ranging *sweeping changes*

sweepstake *NOUN*
a form of gambling on sporting events in which the money staked is divided among the winners

sweet *ADJECTIVE*
1 tasting as if it contains sugar; not bitter
2 very pleasant *a sweet smell*
3 charming or delightful
sweetly *ADVERB*

sweet *NOUN*
1 a piece of sweet food made with sugar, chocolate, etc.
2 a pudding

sweetcorn *NOUN*
the juicy yellow seeds of maize

sweeten *VERB*
to make or become sweet

sweetener *NOUN*
an artificial substance used instead of sugar

sweetheart *NOUN*
a person's lover

sweet pea *NOUN*
a climbing plant with fragrant flowers

swell *VERB* **swollen** or **swelled**
1 to make or become larger
2 to increase in amount or force

swell *NOUN*
1 the process of swelling
2 the rise and fall of the sea's surface

swelling *NOUN*
a swollen place

swelter VERB
to feel uncomfortably hot
sweltering ADJECTIVE

swerve VERB
to turn suddenly to one side
swerve NOUN

swift ADJECTIVE
quick or rapid
swiftly ADVERB

swift NOUN
a small bird like a swallow

swig VERB **swigging, swigged**
(*informal*) to drink in large mouthfuls
swig NOUN

swill VERB
to pour water over or through something

swill NOUN
a sloppy mixture of waste food given to pigs

swim VERB **swimming, swam, swum**
1 to move the body through water
2 to cross by swimming
3 to float
4 to be covered with or full of liquid
eyes swimming in tears
5 to feel dizzy
swimmer NOUN

swim NOUN
the action of swimming *went for a swim*

swimming bath NOUN
a public swimming pool

swimsuit NOUN
a one-piece swimming costume

swindle VERB
to cheat a person in business etc.
swindle NOUN **swindler** NOUN

swine NOUN **swine**
1 a pig
2 (*informal*) an unpleasant person

swing VERB **swung**
1 to move back and forth or in a circle
2 to change opinion or mood

swing NOUN
1 a swinging movement
2 a swinging seat
3 the amount by which votes or opinions etc.
change
4 a kind of jazz music

swingeing (swin-jing) ADJECTIVE
severe or powerful

swipe VERB
1 to hit with a swinging blow
2 (*informal*) to steal
3 pass a credit card through an electronic
reading device
swipe NOUN

swirl VERB
to move round rapidly in circles
swirl NOUN

swish VERB
to move with a hissing sound
swish NOUN

swish ADJECTIVE
(*informal*) smart and fashionable

switch NOUN
1 a device pressed or turned to start or stop
something working
2 a change of opinion or methods
3 a mechanism for moving the points on a
railway track
4 a flexible rod or whip

switch VERB
1 to turn on or off with a switch
2 to change something suddenly
3 to replace one thing with another

switchback NOUN
a railway at a fair, with steep slopes

switchboard NOUN
a panel with switches etc. for making
telephone connections

swivel VERB **swivelling, swivelled**
to turn on a pivot or central point

swollen *past participle* of **swell**

swoon VERB
to faint
swoon NOUN

swoop VERB
1 to come down with a rushing movement
2 to make a sudden attack
swoop NOUN

swop VERB **swopping, swopped**
another spelling of **swap**

sword (sord) NOUN
a weapon with a long pointed blade fixed in a
handle or hilt

swordfish NOUN **swordfish**
a large sea fish with a long sword-like
upper jaw

sworn ADJECTIVE
1 given under oath *sworn testimony*
2 determined to remain so *sworn enemies*

swot VERB **swotting, swotted**
(*informal*) to study hard

swot NOUN
a person who studies hard

sycamore NOUN
a tall tree with winged seeds

sycophant NOUN
a person who tries to win favour by flattering
someone
sycophantic ADJECTIVE

syllable NOUN
a word or part of a word that has one vowel sound when you say it
syllabic ADJECTIVE

syllabus NOUN
a summary of the things to be studied in a course

symbol NOUN
1 a thing used as a sign
2 a mark or sign with a special meaning (e.g. +, -, and x , in mathematics)
Do not confuse this word with *cymbal*.

symbolic ADJECTIVE
acting as a symbol of something
symbolically ADVERB

symbolism NOUN
the use of symbols to represent ideas

symbolize VERB
to make or be a symbol of something

symmetrical ADJECTIVE
able to be divided into two halves which are exactly the same but the opposite way round
symmetrically ADVERB

symmetry NOUN
the quality of being symmetrical or well-proportioned

sympathetic ADJECTIVE
showing or feeling sympathy for someone
sympathetically ADVERB

sympathize VERB
to show or feel sympathy

sympathy NOUN **sympathies**
1 the sharing or understanding of other people's feelings
2 a feeling of pity or tenderness towards someone who is hurt or in trouble

symphony NOUN **symphonies**
a long piece of music for an orchestra, in several movements
symphonic ADJECTIVE

symptom NOUN
a sign that a disease or condition exists
symptomatic ADJECTIVE

synagogue (sin-a-gog) NOUN
a place where Jews worship

synchronize VERB
1 to make things happen at the same time
2 to put watches or clocks to the same time
synchronization NOUN

syncopate VERB
to change the strength of beats in a piece of music
syncopation NOUN

syndicate NOUN
a group of people or firms working or acting together

syndrome NOUN
1 a set of symptoms
2 a set of characteristic opinions, behaviour, etc.

synod (sin-od) NOUN
a church council

synonym (sin-o-nim) NOUN
a word that means the same or almost the same as another word
synonymous (sin-**on**-im-us) ADJECTIVE

synopsis (sin-**op**-sis) NOUN **synopses**
a summary

syntax (sin-taks) NOUN
the way words are arranged to make phrases or sentences
syntactic ADJECTIVE

synthesis (sin-thi-sis) NOUN **syntheses**
the combining of different things to make a whole

synthesize (sin-thi-syz) VERB
to make something by combining parts

synthesizer NOUN
an electronic musical instrument that can make a wide range of sounds

synthetic ADJECTIVE
artificially made; not natural
synthetically ADVERB

syringe NOUN
a device for sucking in a liquid and squirting it out

syrup NOUN
a thick sweet liquid
syrupy ADJECTIVE

system NOUN
1 a set of parts, things, or ideas organized to work together
2 a way of doing something

systematic ADJECTIVE
methodical; carefully planned
systematically ADVERB

Tt

tab NOUN
a small flap or strip that sticks out

tabby NOUN **tabbies**
a grey or brown cat with dark stripes

tabernacle NOUN
(in the Bible) the portable shrine used by the Israelites during their wanderings in the desert

table NOUN
1 a piece of furniture with a flat top on legs
2 a set of facts or figures displayed in columns

table VERB
to put forward for discussion

tableau (tab-loh) NOUN **tableaux**
a dramatic or attractive scene

tablecloth NOUN
a cloth for covering a table

tablespoon NOUN
a large spoon for serving food

tablet NOUN
1 a pill
2 a solid piece of soap
3 an inscribed piece of stone or wood etc.

table tennis NOUN
a game played on a table divided by a net, with bats and a small light ball

tabloid NOUN
a newspaper with small pages and many photographs

taboo ADJECTIVE
not to be done or used or talked about

taboo NOUN **taboos**
a subject or action that is disapproved of

tabular ADJECTIVE
arranged in a table or in columns

tabulate VERB
to arrange information in a table
tabulation NOUN

tacit (tas-it) ADJECTIVE
implied or understood without being spoken

taciturn (tas-i-tern) ADJECTIVE
saying very little

tack NOUN
1 a short nail with a flat top
2 a tacking stitch
3 a course of action or policy *to change tack*

tack VERB
1 nail something down with tacks
2 fasten material together with long stitches
3 sail a zigzag course to take advantage of what wind there is

tackle VERB
1 to try to deal with
2 to try to get the ball from an opponent in a game
3 to talk to someone about an awkward matter

tackle NOUN
1 equipment, especially for fishing
2 a set of ropes and pulleys
3 the act of tackling in a game

tacky [1] ADJECTIVE **tackier, tackiest**
sticky; not quite dry

tacky [2] ADJECTIVE **tackier, tackiest**
(*informal*) showing poor taste or style

tact NOUN
skill in not offending people

tactful ADJECTIVE
showing tact
tactfully ADVERB

tactical ADJECTIVE
to do with tactics
tactically ADVERB

tactics NOUN
1 the skilful arrangement of troops etc.
2 methods used to achieve something

tactile ADJECTIVE
to do with the sense of touch

tactless ADJECTIVE
showing a lack of tact

tadpole NOUN
the larva of a young frog or toad

taffeta NOUN
a stiff silky material

tag NOUN
1 a label fixed to something
2 a game in which one person chases the others

tag VERB **tagging, tagged**
1 to label with a tag
2 to add as an extra
tag along to go with other people

tail NOUN
1 the part at the end or rear of something
2 the side of a coin opposite the head

tail VERB
1 to remove stalks from fruit
2 to follow someone closely
tail off to become fewer, smaller, etc.

tailback NOUN
a line of traffic stretching back from an obstruction

tailless ADJECTIVE
not having a tail

tailor NOUN
a person who makes men's clothes

tailor VERB
1 to make or fit clothes
2 to adapt for a special purpose

taint VERB
to spoil with a small amount of a bad quality

taint NOUN
something that spoils

take VERB **took**, **taken**
1 to get something into your hands or possession or control etc.
2 to carry or convey
3 to make use of *to take a taxi*
4 to undertake or enjoy *to take a holiday*
5 to study or teach a subject
6 to make an effort *taking the trouble*
7 to experience a feeling *to take offence*
8 to tolerate
9 to need
10 to write down *to take notes*
11 to make a photograph
12 to subtract
13 to assume *I take it you agree.*
take after to resemble **take in** to deceive **take off** (of an aircraft) to become airborne **take on** to accept a task or challenge **take to** to develop a liking or ability for **take up 1** to occupy space or time etc. **2** to accept an offer

takeaway NOUN
1 a place that sells cooked meals for customers to take away
2 a meal from this

take-off NOUN
the process of an aircraft becoming airborne

takeover NOUN
the act of one business company taking control of another

takings PLURAL NOUN
money received by a business

talcum powder NOUN
a scented powder that is put on the skin

tale NOUN
a story

talent NOUN
a special ability
talented ADJECTIVE

talisman NOUN **talismans**
an object supposed to bring good luck

talk VERB
1 to speak or have a conversation
2 to be able to speak

talk NOUN
1 a conversation or discussion
2 an informal lecture
3 gossip or rumour

talkative ADJECTIVE
talking a lot

tall ADJECTIVE
1 higher than the average *a tall tree*
2 measured from the bottom to the top *10 metres tall*

tall story NOUN **tall stories**
(*informal*) a story that is hard to believe

tally NOUN **tallies**
the total amount of a debt or score

tally VERB **tallies**, **tallied**
to correspond or agree with something else

Talmud NOUN
writings containing Jewish religious law

talon NOUN
a strong claw

tambourine NOUN
a circular musical instrument with metal discs round it, tapped or shaken to make it jingle

tame ADJECTIVE
1 (of animals) gentle and not afraid of people
2 not exciting; dull

tame VERB
to make an animal become tame

tamper VERB
to meddle or interfere with something

tampon NOUN
a plug of soft material that a woman puts into her vagina to absorb the blood during menstruation

tan NOUN
1 a light brown colour
2 brown colour in skin exposed to the sun

tan VERB **tanning**, **tanned**
1 to make or become brown by exposing skin to the sun
2 to make an animal's skin into leather by treating it with chemicals

tandem NOUN
a bicycle for two riders, one behind the other

tandoori NOUN
a style of Indian cooking using a clay oven

tang NOUN
a strong flavour or smell

tangent NOUN
a straight line touching the outside of a curve or circle

tangerine NOUN
a kind of small orange

tangible ADJECTIVE
1 able to be touched
2 real or definite
tangibly ADVERB

tangle VERB
to make or become twisted and confused
tangle NOUN

tango NOUN **tangos**
a ballroom dance with gliding steps

tank NOUN
1 a large container for a liquid or gas
2 a heavy armoured military vehicle

tankard NOUN
a large drinking mug of silver or pewter

tanker NOUN
1 a large ship for carrying oil
2 a large lorry for carrying a liquid

tanner NOUN
a person who tans leather

tannin NOUN
a substance obtained from the bark or fruit of various trees (also found in tea), used in tanning and dyeing

tantalize VERB
to torment by offering something that cannot be reached

tantamount ADJECTIVE
equivalent *a request tantamount to a command*

tantrum NOUN
an outburst of bad temper

tap[1] NOUN
a device for letting out liquid or gas in a controlled flow

tap VERB **tapping**, **tapped**
1 to take liquid out of
2 to obtain supplies or information etc. from
3 to fix a device to a telephone line to overhear conversations

tap[2] NOUN
1 a quick light hit
2 tap-dancing

tap VERB **tapping**, **tapped**
to hit a person or thing quickly and lightly

tap dance NOUN
a dance performed wearing shoes that make elaborate tapping sounds on the floor
tap dancer NOUN

tape NOUN
1 a narrow strip of cloth, paper, plastic, etc.
2 a narrow magnetic strip for making recordings
3 a tape recording
4 a tape measure

tape VERB
1 fix, cover, or surround something with tape
2 record something on magnetic tape

taper VERB
to make or become thinner at one end

taper NOUN
a long thin candle

tape recorder NOUN
a machine for recording sound on magnetic tape

tapestry NOUN **tapestries**
a cloth with pictures or patterns woven or embroidered on it

tapeworm NOUN
a long flat worm that lives as a parasite in the intestines

tapioca NOUN
a starchy food in hard white grains obtained from cassava

tapir NOUN
a pig-like animal with a long flexible snout

tar NOUN
a thick black liquid made from coal or wood etc. and used in making roads

tar VERB **tarring**, **tarred**
to coat with tar

tarantula NOUN
a large poisonous spider

tardy ADJECTIVE **tardier**, **tardiest**
slow or late
tardily ADVERB

target NOUN
1 an object aimed at in shooting
2 a person or thing being criticized, ridiculed, etc.
3 a sum of money or other objective aimed at

target VERB
to aim at or have as a target

tariff NOUN
a list of prices or charges

tarmac NOUN
an area surfaced with tarmacadam, especially on an airfield

tarmacadam NOUN
a mixture of tar and broken stone, used for making a hard surface on roads, etc.

tarnish VERB
1 to make or become less shiny
2 to spoil or blemish

tarot (rhymes with *barrow*) PLURAL NOUN
a system of fortune-telling using special cards

tarpaulin NOUN
a large sheet of waterproof canvas

tarragon NOUN
a plant with leaves used to flavour salads etc.

tarry VERB **tarries**, **tarried**
to stay for a while; to linger

tart[1] NOUN
1 a pie containing fruit or a sweet filling
2 a piece of pastry with jam etc. on top

tart[2] ADJECTIVE
1 sour
2 sharp in manner

tartan NOUN
a pattern with coloured stripes crossing each other, especially one used by a Scottish clan

tartar NOUN
a hard chalky deposit that forms on teeth

task NOUN
a piece of work to be done

tassel *NOUN*
a hanging bundle of threads used as a
decoration

taste *VERB*
1 to take a small amount of food or drink to
try its flavour
2 to be able to perceive flavours
3 to have a certain flavour

taste *NOUN*
1 the feeling caused in the tongue by
something placed on it
2 the ability to taste things
3 the ability to judge beautiful or suitable
things well
4 a liking
5 a small amount of food or drink

tasteful *ADJECTIVE*
showing good taste
tastefully *ADVERB*

tasteless *ADJECTIVE*
1 having no flavour
2 showing poor taste

tasty *ADJECTIVE* **tastier, tastiest**
having a pleasant taste

tattered *ADJECTIVE*
badly torn or ragged

tatters *PLURAL NOUN*
badly torn pieces

tattoo *VERB* **tattoos, tattooing, tattooed**
to mark a design on the skin using a needle
and dyes

tattoo *NOUN* **tattoos**
1 a tattooed picture or pattern
2 an entertainment of military music,
marching, etc.

tatty *ADJECTIVE* **tattier, tattiest**
1 shabby and untidy
2 cheap and gaudy

taunt *VERB*
to jeer at or insult
taunt *NOUN*

taut *ADJECTIVE*
stretched tightly
tautly *ADVERB*

tautology *NOUN* **tautologies**
a form of saying the same thing twice in
different words, e.g. *a free gift*

tavern *NOUN*
(*old use*) an inn or public house

tawdry *ADJECTIVE* **tawdrier, tawdriest**
cheap and gaudy

tawny *ADJECTIVE*
a brownish-yellow colour

tax *NOUN*
1 money collected from the public by the
government, used for public purposes
2 a strain or burden

tax *VERB*
1 to put a tax on
2 to charge someone a tax
3 to put a strain or burden on

taxation *NOUN*
a system of collecting taxes

taxi *NOUN* **taxis**
a car that can be hired for short journeys for
payment

taxi *VERB* **taxies, taxiing, taxied**
(of an aircraft) to move along the ground
before or after flying

taxidermist *NOUN*
a person who stuffs the skins of dead animals
to make them lifelike
taxidermy *NOUN*

taxpayer *NOUN*
a person who pays tax

TB *ABBREVIATION*
tuberculosis

tea *NOUN*
1 the dried leaves of an evergreen shrub
2 a drink made from these
3 a meal in the afternoon or early evening

teacake *NOUN*
a kind of flat bun

teach *VERB* **taught**
to give a person knowledge or skill

teacher *NOUN*
a person who teaches at a school

teak *NOUN*
a hard strong wood

teal *NOUN*
a kind of duck

team *NOUN*
1 a set of players in certain games and sports
2 a group of people working together

team *VERB*
to put or join together in a team

teapot *NOUN*
a pot with a lid and a handle, for making and
pouring tea

tear[1] (teer) *NOUN*
a drop of the water that comes from the eyes
when crying

tear[2] (tair) *VERB* **tore, torn**
1 to pull apart or into pieces
2 to become torn
3 to run hurriedly

tear *NOUN*
a split made by tearing

tearful *ADJECTIVE*
crying easily
tearfully *ADVERB*

tear gas *NOUN*
a gas that makes the eyes water painfully

tease *VERB*
to amuse yourself by making fun of someone

tease *NOUN*
a person who often teases others

teasel *NOUN*
a plant with bristly heads

teaser *NOUN*
a problem or puzzle

teaspoon *NOUN*
a small spoon for stirring tea etc.

teat *NOUN*
1 a nipple through which a baby sucks milk
2 the cap of a baby's feeding bottle

technical *ADJECTIVE*
1 to do with technology
2 to do with a particular subject *technical terms*

technicality *NOUN* **technicalities**
a technical word, phrase, or detail

technically *ADVERB*
according to the strict facts, rules, etc.

technician *NOUN*
a person who looks after scientific equipment in a laboratory

technique *NOUN*
a method of doing something skilfully

technology *NOUN*
the study of machinery, engineering, and how things work
technological *ADJECTIVE*

teddy bear *NOUN*
a soft furry toy bear

tedious *ADJECTIVE*
annoyingly slow or long

tedium *NOUN*
a dull or boring time or experience

tee *NOUN*
1 the flat area from which golfers strike the ball at the start of play for each hole
2 a small peg for resting a golf ball to be struck

teem *VERB*
1 to be full of something
2 to rain very hard

teen *ADJECTIVE, NOUN*
(*informal*) a teenager

teenage *ADJECTIVE*
to do with teenagers
teenaged *ADJECTIVE*

teenager *NOUN*
a person in their teens

teens *PLURAL NOUN*
the time of life between 13 and 19 years of age

tee-shirt *NOUN*
another spelling of **T-shirt**

teeter *VERB*
to stand or move unsteadily

teeth *plural* of **tooth**

teethe *VERB*
(of a baby) to have its first teeth beginning to grow

teetotal *ADJECTIVE*
not drinking alcohol
teetotaller *NOUN*

telecommunications *PLURAL NOUN*
communications over a long distance, e.g. by telephone, telegraph, radio, or television

telegram *NOUN*
a message sent by telegraph

telegraph *NOUN*
a way of sending messages by using electric current along wires or by radio

telepathy (til-**ep**-ath-ee) *NOUN*
communication of thoughts from one person's mind to another without speaking, writing, or gestures
telepathic *ADJECTIVE*

telephone *NOUN*
a device or system using electric wires or radio etc. to enable one person to speak to another who is some distance away

telephone *VERB*
to speak to a person on the telephone

telephonist *NOUN*
a person who operates a telephone switchboard

telescope *NOUN*
an instrument using lenses to magnify distant objects
telescopic *ADJECTIVE*

telescope *VERB*
1 make or become shorter by sliding overlapping sections into each other
2 compress or condense something so that it takes less space or time

teletext *NOUN*
a system for displaying news and information on a television screen

televise *VERB*
to broadcast by television

television *NOUN*
1 a system using radio waves to reproduce a view of scenes, events, or plays etc. on a screen
2 an apparatus for receiving these pictures

tell *VERB* **told**
1 to use words to make a thing known to someone
2 to speak *telling the truth*
3 to order
4 to reveal a secret
5 to decide or distinguish
6 to have an effect *The strain was beginning to tell.*

tell off (*informal*) to scold or reprimand

telling ADJECTIVE
having a strong effect or meaning *a telling answer*

tell-tale NOUN
a person who tells tales

tell-tale ADJECTIVE
revealing or indicating something *a tell-tale spot of jam on his chin*

temerity NOUN
rashness or boldness

temper NOUN
1 a person's mood
2 an angry mood
lose your temper to become angry

temper VERB
1 to harden or strengthen metal etc. by heating and cooling it
2 to moderate or soften the effects of something *temper justice with mercy*

temperament NOUN
a person's nature and typical behaviour *a nervous temperament*

temperamental ADJECTIVE
1 likely to become excitable or moody
2 to do with temperament
temperamentally ADVERB

temperate ADJECTIVE
(of a climate) neither extremely hot nor extremely cold

temperature NOUN
1 how hot or cold a person or thing is
2 an abnormally high body temperature

tempest NOUN
a violent storm

tempestuous ADJECTIVE
1 stormy
2 violent or passionate

template NOUN
a thin sheet used as a guide for cutting or shaping

temple¹ NOUN
a building in which a god is worshipped

temple² NOUN
the part of the head between the forehead and the ear

tempo NOUN **tempos** or **tempi**
the speed or rhythm of music

temporary ADJECTIVE
lasting for a limited time only
temporarily ADVERB

tempt VERB
to try to to persuade or attract someone

temptation NOUN
1 the act of tempting
2 something that tempts

ten NOUN, ADJECTIVE
the number 10

tenable ADJECTIVE
able to be held or defended

tenacious ADJECTIVE
1 holding or clinging firmly to something
2 firm and determined

tenacity NOUN
firmness and determination

tenant NOUN
a person who rents a house, building, or land etc. from a landlord
tenancy NOUN

tend VERB
1 to be inclined or likely to do something
2 to look after

tendency NOUN **tendencies**
the way a person or thing is likely to behave

tender¹ ADJECTIVE
1 easy to chew
2 easily hurt or damaged
3 (of a part of the body) painful when touched
4 gentle and loving
tenderly ADVERB

tender² VERB
to offer formally *He tendered his resignation.*

tender NOUN
a formal offer to supply goods or carry out work at a stated price

tendon NOUN
a strong strip of tissue joining muscle to bone

tendril NOUN
1 a thread-like part by which a climbing plant clings to a support
2 a thin curl of hair etc.

tenement NOUN
a large house divided into flats

tenet NOUN
a firm belief

tenner NOUN
(*informal*) a ten-pound note

tennis NOUN
a game played with rackets and a ball on a court with a net across the middle

tenor NOUN
1 a male singer with a high voice
2 the general meaning or drift

tense [1] *NOUN*
the form of a verb that shows when
something happens: *past*, *present*, and *future*

tense [2] *ADJECTIVE*
1 tightly stretched
2 nervous or worried

tense *VERB*
to make or become tense

tension *NOUN*
1 how tightly stretched a rope or wire is
2 a feeling of anxiety or nervousness

tent *NOUN*
a movable shelter made of canvas or other
material

tentacle *NOUN*
a long flexible part of certain animals (e.g.
snails, octopuses), used for feeling or
grasping or for moving

tentative *ADJECTIVE*
cautious; trying something out *a tentative
suggestion*

tenterhooks *PLURAL NOUN*
on tenterhooks tense and anxious

tenth *ADJECTIVE, NOUN*
next after the ninth

tenuous *ADJECTIVE*
very slight or thin

tenure (**ten**-yoor) *NOUN*
the holding of a position of employment, or
of land, accommodation, etc.

tepee *NOUN*
a traditional Native American tent made with
animal skins

tepid *ADJECTIVE*
slightly warm

term *NOUN*
1 the period when a school or college is open
2 a definite period
3 a word or expression

term *VERB*
to call something by a certain term

terminal *NOUN*
1 the place where something ends
2 a building where air passengers arrive or
depart
3 a connection in an electric circuit or
battery etc.
4 a monitor and keyboard linked to a
computer network

terminal *ADJECTIVE*
(of a fatal disease) in the last stage
terminally *ADVERB*

terminate *VERB*
to stop finally
termination *NOUN*

terminology *NOUN* **terminologies**
the technical terms of a subject

terminus *NOUN* **termini**
1 the end of something
2 the last station on a railway or bus route

termite *NOUN*
a small insect that eats wood

terms *PLURAL NOUN*
1 a relationship between people *We are all on
friendly terms.*
2 conditions offered or accepted

tern *NOUN*
a seabird with long wings

terrace *NOUN*
1 a level area on a slope or hillside
2 a paved area beside a house
3 a row of joined houses
terraced *ADJECTIVE*

terracotta *NOUN*
1 a kind of pottery
2 a brownish-red colour

terrain *NOUN*
an area of land of a particular type *hilly terrain*

terrapin *NOUN*
a small turtle

terrestrial *ADJECTIVE*
to do with the earth or land

terrible *ADJECTIVE*
very bad; awful
terribly *ADVERB*

terrier *NOUN*
a kind of small lively dog

terrific *ADJECTIVE* (*informal*)
1 very great
2 excellent
terrifically *ADVERB*

terrify *VERB* **terrifies**, **terrified**
to make someone very afraid

territorial *ADJECTIVE*
to do with a country's territory

territory *NOUN* **territories**
an area of land belonging to a country or
person

terror *NOUN*
1 very great fear
2 a terrifying person or thing

terrorist *NOUN*
a person who uses violence for political
purposes
terrorism *NOUN*

terrorize *VERB*
to frighten someone by threatening them
terrorization *NOUN*

terse *ADJECTIVE*
using few words; concise or curt

test NOUN
1 a brief examination
2 a way of discovering the abilities or presence of a person or thing

test VERB
to carry out a test on

testament NOUN
1 a written statement
2 either of the two main parts of the Bible, the Old Testament and the New Testament

testicle NOUN
either of the two glands in the scrotum where semen is produced

testify VERB **testifies**, **testified**
1 to give evidence under oath
2 be evidence or proof of something

testimonial NOUN
a letter describing someone's abilities, character, etc.

testimony NOUN **testimonies**
evidence, especially given under oath

test match NOUN
a cricket match between different countries

testosterone (test-**ost**-er-ohn) NOUN
a male sex hormone

test tube NOUN
a tube of thin glass with one end closed, used for experiments in chemistry etc.

testy ADJECTIVE **testier**, **testiest**
easily annoyed; irritable

tetanus NOUN
a disease that makes the muscles stiff, caused by bacteria

tetchy ADJECTIVE **tetchier**, **tetchiest**
easily annoyed; irritable

tether VERB
to tie an animal with a rope

tether NOUN
a rope for tethering an animal
at the end of your tether unable to bear any more

text NOUN
1 the words of something written or printed
2 a novel, play, etc., studied for a course
3 a text message

text VERB
to send a text message by mobile phone

textbook NOUN
a book for teaching and learning about a subject

textiles PLURAL NOUN
kinds of cloth; fabrics

text message NOUN
a written message sent on a mobile phone

texture NOUN
the way that the surface of something feels

than CONJUNCTION, PREPOSITION
compared with another person or thing
Clare is taller than I am. Clare is taller than me.

thank VERB
to tell someone that you are grateful to them

thankful ADJECTIVE
grateful
thankfully ADVERB

thankless ADJECTIVE
not likely to win thanks from people

thanks PLURAL NOUN
1 statements of gratitude
2 (*informal*) thank you

thanksgiving NOUN
an expression of gratitude, especially to God

that DETERMINER, PRONOUN
the one there *That book is mine. Whose is that?*

that ADVERB
to such an extent *not that good*

that RELATIVE PRONOUN
which, who, or whom *the record that I wanted*

that CONJUNCTION
used to introduce a wish, reason, result, etc.
so hard that no one could solve it I hope that you are well.

thatch NOUN
straw or reeds used to make a roof

thatch VERB
to make a roof with thatch

thaw VERB
to stop being frozen

thaw NOUN
a period of warm weather that thaws ice and snow

the DETERMINER
a particular one; that or those

theatre NOUN
1 a building in which plays etc. are performed to an audience
2 the acting and production of plays
3 a hospital room for performing surgical operations

theatrical ADJECTIVE
1 to do with plays or acting
2 exaggerated and showy
theatrically ADVERB

thee PRONOUN
(*old use*) you (referring to one person and used as the object of a verb or after a preposition)

theft NOUN
stealing

a
b
c
d
e
f
g
h
i
j
k
l
m
n
o
p
q
r
s
t
u
v
w
x
y
z

their DETERMINER
belonging to them *Their coats are here.*
Do not confuse this word with *there*.

theirs POSSESSIVE PRONOUN
belonging to them *The coats are theirs.*
It is incorrect to write *their's*.

them PRONOUN
the form of **they** used as the object of a verb
or after a preposition *We saw them.*

theme NOUN
1 the subject of a piece of writing,
conversation, etc.
2 a melody

theme park NOUN
an amusement park with rides and
attractions based on a particular subject

theme tune NOUN
a special tune used to announce a particular
programme, performer, etc.

themselves PRONOUN
they or them and nobody else *They cut
themselves. They themselves have said it.*
by themselves alone; on their own

then ADVERB
1 at that time
2 after that; next
3 in that case

thence ADVERB
from that place

theologian NOUN
an expert in theology

theology NOUN
the study of religion
theological ADJECTIVE

theorem NOUN
a mathematical statement reached by
reasoning

theoretical ADJECTIVE
based on theory and not on practice or
experience
theoretically ADVERB

theorize VERB
to form a theory or theories

theory NOUN **theories**
1 an idea or set of ideas put forward to explain
something
2 the principles of a subject

therapeutic ADJECTIVE
treating or curing a disease etc.

therapy NOUN **therapies**
treatment of a physical or mental illness
without using surgery or artificial medicines
therapist NOUN

there ADVERB
1 in or to that place etc.
2 used to call attention to something
Do not confuse this word with *their*.

thereabouts ADVERB
near there

thereafter ADVERB
from then or there onwards

thereby ADVERB
by that means; because of that

therefore ADVERB
for that reason

therm NOUN
a unit for measuring heat, especially from gas

thermal ADJECTIVE
to do with heat; worked by heat

thermodynamics NOUN
the science of the relation between heat and
other forms of energy

thermometer NOUN
a device for measuring temperature

Thermos NOUN
(*trademark*) a kind of vacuum flask

thermostat NOUN
a device that controls the temperature of a
room or piece of equipment

thesaurus (thi-sor-us) NOUN **thesauruses**
or **thesauri**
a kind of dictionary listing words in sets
according to their meaning

these plural of **this**

thesis NOUN **theses**
1 a theory put forward
2 a long essay written for a university degree

they PRONOUN
1 the people or things being talked about
2 people in general
3 he or she; a person *If anyone is late they will
not be admitted.*

they're
they are
Do not confuse this word with *their* or *there*.

thick ADJECTIVE
1 measuring a lot between its opposite surfaces
2 measuring from one side to the other
ten centimetres thick
3 (of a line) broad, not fine
4 crowded with things; dense
5 not flowing easily
6 (*informal*) stupid
thickness NOUN

thicken VERB
to make or become thicker

thicket NOUN
a close group of shrubs and small trees

thickset ADJECTIVE
1 having a stocky or burly body
2 closely placed or growing

thief NOUN **thieves**
a person who steals

thieving NOUN
stealing

thigh NOUN
the part of the leg between the hip and
the knee

thimble NOUN
a small cap worn over the finger to push the
needle in sewing

thin ADJECTIVE **thinner, thinnest**
1 not thick; not fat
2 feeble *a thin excuse*
3 (of a liquid) watery

thin VERB **thinning, thinned**
to make or become less thick
thin out to make or become less dense or
crowded

thine POSSESSIVE PRONOUN
(*old use*) yours (referring to one person)

thing NOUN
an object; something which can be seen,
touched, thought about, etc.

things PLURAL NOUN
1 personal belongings
2 circumstances

think VERB **thought**
1 to use the mind to form connected ideas
2 to have as an idea or opinion
3 to intend or plan *thinking of buying a guitar*
think NOUN

third ADJECTIVE
next after the second
thirdly ADVERB

third NOUN
1 a person or thing that is third
2 one of three equal parts of something

Third World NOUN
the poorest countries of Asia, Africa, and
South America

thirst NOUN
1 a feeling of dryness in the mouth and
throat, causing a desire to drink
2 a strong desire

thirst VERB
to have a strong desire for something

thirsty ADJECTIVE **thirstier, thirstiest**
1 needing to drink
2 eager for something

thirteen NOUN, ADJECTIVE
the number 13
thirteenth ADJECTIVE, NOUN

thirty NOUN, ADJECTIVE **thirties**
the number 30
thirtieth ADJECTIVE, NOUN

this DETERMINER, PRONOUN
the one here *This house is ours. Whose is this?*

this ADVERB
to such an extent *not this big*

thistle NOUN
a prickly wild plant with purple, white, or
yellow flowers

thither ADVERB
(*old use*) to that place

thong NOUN
1 a narrow strip of leather etc. used for tying
and fastening
2 a style of knickers with just a narrow strip at
the back

thorax NOUN
the part of the body between the head or
neck and the abdomen
thoracic ADJECTIVE

thorn NOUN
1 a small pointed growth on the stem of a plant
2 a thorny tree or shrub

thorny ADJECTIVE **thornier, thorniest**
1 having many thorns; prickly
2 difficult *a thorny problem*

thorough ADJECTIVE
1 careful and detailed
2 complete in every way
thoroughly ADVERB **thoroughness** NOUN

thoroughbred ADJECTIVE
bred of pure or pedigree stock
thoroughbred NOUN

thoroughfare NOUN
a public road open at both ends

those DETERMINER, ADVERB, PRONOUN *plural* of
that

thou PRONOUN
(*old use*) you (referring to one person)

though CONJUNCTION
in spite of the fact that; even if *We can phone
them, though they may have left.*

though ADVERB
however *She's right, though.*

thought [1] NOUN
1 something you think; an idea or opinion
2 the process of thinking

thought [2] *past tense* of **think**

thoughtful ADJECTIVE
1 thinking a lot
2 showing consideration for other people
thoughtfully ADVERB

thoughtless *ADJECTIVE*
1 careless; not thinking of what may happen
2 inconsiderate

thousand *NOUN, ADJECTIVE*
the number 1,000
thousandth *ADJECTIVE, NOUN*

thrash *VERB*
1 to beat with a stick or whip
2 (*informal*) to defeat thoroughly
3 to move violently

thread *NOUN*
1 a length of cotton, wool, etc.
2 the spiral ridge round a screw
3 a theme or idea running through a story, argument, etc.

thread *VERB*
1 to put a thread through the eye of a needle
2 to pass a strip of film etc. through or round something
3 to put beads on a thread
4 to make your way through a crowd etc.

threadbare *ADJECTIVE*
(of cloth) having a worn surface

threat *NOUN*
1 a warning of harm or punishment
2 a sign of something undesirable
3 a person or thing causing danger

threaten *VERB*
1 to make threats against
2 to be a threat or danger to

three *NOUN, ADJECTIVE*
the number 3

thresh *VERB*
to beat corn to separate the grain from the husks

threshold *NOUN*
1 a slab of stone or board etc. under a doorway
2 a beginning of something great *on the threshold of a discovery*

threw *past tense of* **throw**

thrice *ADVERB*
(*old use*) three times

thrift *NOUN*
careful management of money or resources

thrifty *ADJECTIVE* **thriftier, thriftiest**
careful about spending money
thriftily *ADVERB*

thrill *NOUN*
a feeling of excitement

thrill *VERB*
to have or give a feeling of excitement

thriller *NOUN*
an exciting story about crime or spying

thrilling *ADJECTIVE*
very exciting

thrive *VERB* **throve, thrived** or **thriven**
to prosper or be successful

throat *NOUN*
1 the passage in the neck that takes food and drink down into the body
2 the front of the neck

throb *VERB* **throbbing, throbbed**
to beat or vibrate with a strong rhythm
throb *NOUN*

throes *PLURAL NOUN*
severe pain

thrombosis *NOUN*
the formation of a clot of blood in the body

throne *NOUN*
1 a ceremonial chair for a king, queen, or bishop
2 the position of king or queen *heir to the throne*

throng *NOUN*
a crowd of people

throng *VERB*
to crowd

throttle *NOUN*
a device that controls the flow of fuel to an engine

throttle *VERB*
to strangle

through *PREPOSITION*
1 from one end or side to the other end or side of *Light came through the window.*
2 by means of; because of *We lost it through carelessness.*

through *ADVERB*
1 from one end or side to the other *We squeezed through.*
2 with a telephone connection made *I'll put you through.*
3 finished *I'm through with the work.*

through *ADJECTIVE*
1 leading through *a through road*
2 not involving a change *a through train*

throughout *PREPOSITION, ADVERB*
all the way through

throve *past tense of* **thrive**

throw *VERB* **threw, thrown**
1 to send through the air
2 to put in a place carelessly or hastily
3 to move part of your body quickly *threw his head back*
4 to put someone in a certain condition etc. *threw us into confusion*
5 to confuse or upset
6 to move a switch or lever
7 to hold a party
throw *NOUN*

thrush *NOUN*
a songbird with a speckled breast

a
b
c
d
e
f
g
h
i
j
k
l
m
n
o
p
q
r
s
t
u
v
w
x
y
z

thrust VERB thrust
to push hard
thrust NOUN

thud VERB **thudding**, **thudded**
to make the dull sound of a heavy fall
thud NOUN

thug NOUN
a rough and violent person

thumb NOUN
the short thick finger set apart from the other four

thumb VERB
to turn the pages of a book etc. quickly with your thumb

thump VERB
1 to hit or knock heavily
2 to throb or beat strongly
thump NOUN

thunder NOUN
1 the rumbling noise heard with lightning
2 a loud noise

thunder VERB
1 to sound with thunder
2 to speak with a loud deep voice

thunderbolt NOUN
a flash of lightning with a simultaneous crash of thunder

thunderous ADJECTIVE
extremely loud *thunderous applause*

thunderstorm NOUN
a storm with thunder and lightning

Thursday NOUN
the day of the week following Wednesday

thus ADVERB
1 in this way
2 therefore

thwart VERB
to prevent from achieving something

thy ADJECTIVE
(*old use*) your (referring to one person)

thyme (*say as* time) NOUN
a herb with fragrant leaves

thyroid gland NOUN
a large gland at the front of the neck

tiara NOUN
a woman's jewelled ornament worn like a crown

tic NOUN
an unintentional twitch of a face muscle

tick¹ NOUN
1 a mark (✓) put by something to show that it is correct or has been checked
2 a regular clicking sound made by a clock or watch
3 (*informal*) a moment

tick VERB
1 to mark with a tick
2 to make the sound of a tick
tick off (*informal*) to scold or reprimand

tick² NOUN
a tiny bloodsucking insect

ticket NOUN
1 a printed piece of paper or card allowing a person to travel, enter a theatre, etc.
2 a notice of a traffic offence attached to a vehicle

tickle VERB
1 to touch a person's skin lightly to produce a slight tingling feeling
2 to amuse or please

ticklish ADJECTIVE
1 likely to react to tickling
2 awkward or difficult

tidal ADJECTIVE
to do with tides

tidal wave NOUN
a huge sea wave

tiddler NOUN
(*informal*) a small fish

tiddlywink NOUN
a small counter flicked into a cup by pressing with another counter

tide NOUN
1 the regular rise and fall in the level of the sea
2 (*old use*) a time or season *Christmastide*

tide VERB
tide someone over to provide them with their needs for a time

tidings PLURAL NOUN
(*formal*) news

tidy ADJECTIVE **tidier**, **tidiest**
1 neat and orderly
2 (*informal*) fairly large
tidily ADVERB **tidiness** NOUN

tidy VERB **tidies**, **tidied**
to make a place tidy

tie VERB **tying**
1 to fasten with string, ribbon, etc.
2 to arrange into a knot or bow
3 to have the same score as another competitor

tie NOUN
1 a strip of material worn under the collar of a shirt and knotted in front
2 a result when two or more competitors have equal scores
3 one of the matches in a competition
4 a close connection or bond

tier (teer) NOUN
each of a series of rows or levels
tiered ADJECTIVE

tiff *NOUN*
a slight quarrel

tiger *NOUN*
a large wild animal of the cat family, with yellow and black stripes

tight *ADJECTIVE*
1 fitting very closely
2 firmly fastened
3 fully stretched; tense
4 in short supply
5 mean; stingy
6 severe or strict *tight security*
7 (*informal*) drunk
tightly *ADVERB*

tighten *VERB*
to make or become tighter

tightrope *NOUN*
a rope or wire stretched tightly high above the ground, on which acrobats perform

tights *PLURAL NOUN*
an item of clothing that fits tightly over the feet, legs, and lower part of the body

tigress *NOUN*
a female tiger

tile *NOUN*
a thin square piece of baked clay or other material, used in rows for covering roofs, walls, or floors
tiled *ADJECTIVE*

till [1] *PREPOSITION, CONJUNCTION*
until

till [2] *NOUN*
a drawer or box for money in a shop; a cash register

till [3] *VERB*
to plough land for cultivation

tiller *NOUN*
a handle used to turn a boat's rudder

tilt *VERB*
to move into a sloping position

tilt *NOUN*
a sloping position
at full tilt at full speed or force

timber *NOUN*
1 wood for building
2 a wooden beam

time *NOUN*
1 all the years of the past, present, and future
2 a particular point or portion of time
3 an occasion *saw it for the first time*
4 a period available for something *not enough time*
5 (*Music*) rhythm depending on the number and stress of beats in the bar
in time 1 not late **2** eventually **on time** punctual

time *VERB*
1 to measure how long something takes
2 to arrange a time for

timeless *ADJECTIVE*
not affected by the passing of time

timely *ADJECTIVE*
happening at a suitable or useful time

timer *NOUN*
a device for timing things

times *PLURAL NOUN*
(*Maths*) multiplied by *Five times three is 15* ($5 \times 3 = 15$)

timetable *NOUN*
a list showing the times when things will happen, e.g. when buses or trains will arrive and depart, or when classes will take place

timid *ADJECTIVE*
easily frightened
timidity *NOUN*

timing *NOUN*
1 the choice of time to do something
2 the time when something happens

timorous *ADJECTIVE*
timid

timpani *PLURAL NOUN*
kettledrums

tin *NOUN*
1 a silvery-white metal
2 a metal container for food

tin *VERB* **tinning, tinned**
to seal food in a tin

tinder *NOUN*
a dry substance that burns easily

tinge *VERB* **tingeing**
1 to colour something slightly
2 to add a slight amount of another feeling *relief was tinged with sadness*
tinge *NOUN*

tingle *VERB*
to have a slight pricking feeling
tingle *NOUN*

tinker *NOUN*
(*old use*) a person travelling about to mend pots and pans etc.

tinker *VERB*
to work at something casually, trying to improve or mend it

tinkle *VERB*
to make a gentle ringing sound
tinkle *NOUN*

tinny *ADJECTIVE* **tinnier, tinniest**
1 like tin
2 (of a sound) unpleasantly thin and high-pitched

tinsel NOUN
strips of glittering material used for decoration

tint NOUN
a shade of colour, especially a pale one

tint VERB
to colour something slightly

tiny ADJECTIVE **tinier**, **tiniest**
very small

tip [1] NOUN
the part at the extreme top or end of something

tip VERB **tipping**, **tipped**
to put a tip on something

tip [2] NOUN
1 a small gift of money given to a waiter etc.
2 a small piece of advice

tip VERB **tipping**, **tipped**
1 to give a tip to
2 to name as a likely winner
tip off to give a hint or warning to

tip [3] VERB **tipping**, **tipped**
1 to tilt or topple
2 to dispose of rubbish

tip NOUN
1 the action of tipping something
2 a place where rubbish is tipped

tipple VERB
to drink small amounts of alcohol
tipple NOUN

tipsy ADJECTIVE **tipsier**, **tipsiest**
slightly drunk

tiptoe VERB **tiptoes**, **tiptoeing**, **tiptoed**
to walk quietly on your toes

tiptop ADJECTIVE
(informal) very best in tiptop condition

tirade (ty-**rayd**) NOUN
a long angry speech

tire VERB
to make or become tired
tiring ADJECTIVE

tired ADJECTIVE
feeling that you need to sleep or rest
tired of bored or impatient with

tireless ADJECTIVE
having a lot of energy

tiresome ADJECTIVE
annoying

tissue NOUN
1 tissue paper
2 a paper handkerchief
3 the substance forming part of the body of an animal or plant

tissue paper NOUN
thin soft paper used for wrapping and packing

tit [1] NOUN
a kind of small bird

tit [2] NOUN
tit for tat something equal given in return

titanic (ty-**tan**-ik) ADJECTIVE
huge; gigantic

titbit NOUN
a small amount of something

tithe NOUN
a tax of one-tenth of a year's income formerly paid to support the church

titillate VERB
to stimulate or excite pleasantly
titillation NOUN

title NOUN
1 the name of a book, film, song, etc.
2 a word used to show a person's rank or position
3 a sports championship
4 a legal right

titled ADJECTIVE
having a title as a member of the nobility

titter VERB
to giggle
titter NOUN

TNT ABBREVIATION
trinitrotoluene, a powerful explosive

to PREPOSITION
1 used to show direction or arrival went to Australia
2 used to show a limit worked to midnight
3 used to show giving or receiving lent it to them
4 used to show a ratio three to one
5 used to show a connection the key to the door
6 used in comparisons was nothing to what might happen
7 used before a verb, forming an infinitive hope to see you

to ADVERB
nearly closed Push the door to.
to and fro backwards and forwards

toad NOUN
a animal like a frog that lives mainly on land

toadstool NOUN
a fungus, usually poisonous, with a round top

toast VERB
1 to heat bread etc. to make it brown and crisp
2 to drink in honour of someone

toast NOUN
1 toasted bread
2 a call to drink in honour of someone

toaster NOUN
an electrical device for toasting bread

tobacco NOUN
the dried leaves of certain plants used for smoking

tobacconist NOUN
a shopkeeper who sells cigarettes, cigars, etc.

toboggan NOUN
a small sledge used for sliding downhill
tobogganing NOUN

today NOUN, ADVERB
this present day

toddler NOUN
a young child who has just started to walk

to-do NOUN **to-dos**
a fuss or commotion

toe NOUN
1 each of the separate parts at the end of the foot
2 the front part of a shoe or sock
on your toes alert

toffee NOUN
a sticky sweet made from heated butter and sugar

toga (toh-ga) NOUN
a long loose piece of clothing worn by men in ancient Rome

together ADVERB
with another person or thing

toggle NOUN
a short piece of wood etc. used like a button

toil VERB
to work or move with great effort

toil NOUN
hard work

toilet NOUN
1 a bowl connected by pipes to a drain, used for disposing of urine and faeces
2 a room containing a toilet

toiletries PLURAL NOUN
soap, cosmetics, etc.

token NOUN
1 a piece of metal etc. that can be used instead of money
2 a sign or signal of something

tolerable ADJECTIVE
able to be tolerated
tolerably ADVERB

tolerant ADJECTIVE
willing to accept other people's behaviour and opinions
tolerance NOUN

tolerate VERB
1 to allow something you do not approve of
2 to put up with something unpleasant
toleration NOUN

toll [1] NOUN
1 a charge made for using a road, bridge, etc.
2 loss or damage caused

toll [2] VERB
to ring a bell slowly

tom NOUN
a male cat

tomahawk NOUN
a small axe used by Native Americans

tomato NOUN **tomatoes**
a soft round red or yellow fruit eaten as a vegetable

tomb NOUN
a place where someone is buried

tombola NOUN
a kind of lottery

tomboy NOUN
a girl who enjoys rough noisy games etc.

tombstone NOUN
a memorial stone set up over a grave

tome NOUN
a large heavy book

tomorrow NOUN, ADVERB
the day after today

tom-tom NOUN
a drum beaten with the hands

ton NOUN
1 a unit of weight equal to 2,240 pounds or 1,016 kilograms
2 a large amount

tone NOUN
1 a sound in music or of the voice
2 each of the five larger intervals between notes in a musical scale
3 a shade of a colour
4 the quality or character of something
tonal ADJECTIVE

tone VERB
be harmonious in colour
tone down to make quieter or less intense

tone-deaf ADJECTIVE
unable to distinguish different musical notes

tongs PLURAL NOUN
a tool with two arms joined at one end, used to pick up or hold things

tongue NOUN
1 the long soft muscular part that moves about inside the mouth
2 a language
3 the leather flap on a shoe or boot under the laces

tonic NOUN
1 a medicine etc. that restores strength
2 anything that makes a person more energetic or cheerful
3 (Music) the keynote of a scale
tonic ADJECTIVE

a
b
c
d
e
f
g
h
i
j
k
l
m
n
o
p
q
r
s
t
u
v
w
x
y
z

tonic water *NOUN*
a fizzy mineral water with a slightly bitter taste

tonight *NOUN, ADVERB*
this evening or night

tonne *NOUN*
a metric ton (1,000 kilograms)

tonsil *NOUN*
either of two small masses of soft tissue at the sides of the throat

tonsillitis *NOUN*
inflammation of the tonsils

too *ADVERB*
1 also *Take the others too.*
2 more than is wanted or allowed etc.
too much sugar

tool *NOUN*
a device or instrument for doing a particular job

toolbar *NOUN*
(*ICT*) a row of icons on a computer screen, selected with the mouse or cursor

toot *NOUN*
a short sound produced by a horn

tooth *NOUN* **teeth**
1 each of the hard white bony parts rooted in the gums, used for biting and chewing
2 each of the sharp parts on a saw, cog, etc.

toothache *NOUN*
a pain in a tooth

toothbrush *NOUN*
a brush for cleaning the teeth

toothpaste *NOUN*
a paste for cleaning the teeth

toothy *ADJECTIVE* **toothier, toothiest**
having large teeth

top¹ *NOUN*
1 the highest part of something
2 the upper surface
3 the covering or stopper of a bottle, jar, etc.
4 an item of clothing for the upper part of the body
on top of in addition to

top *ADJECTIVE*
highest or best

top *VERB* **topping, topped**
1 to put a top on
2 to be at the top of
top up to fill something partly empty

top² *NOUN*
a toy that can be made to spin on its point

topaz *NOUN*
a kind of gem, often yellow

top hat *NOUN*
a man's tall stiff black or grey hat

top-heavy *ADJECTIVE*
too heavy at the top and likely to overbalance

topic *NOUN*
a subject to write, learn, or talk about

topical *ADJECTIVE*
connected with things that are happening now *a topical film*

topless *ADJECTIVE*
naked on the top half of the body

topmost *ADJECTIVE*
highest

topping *NOUN*
food that is put on the top of a cake, pudding, pizza, etc.

topple *VERB*
1 to totter and fall
2 to overthrow someone in authority

topsy-turvy *ADVERB, ADJECTIVE*
upside down; muddled

Torah (**tor**-uh) *NOUN*
in Judaism, the law of God as given to Moses

torch *NOUN*
1 a small electric lamp held in the hand
2 a stick with burning material on the end

torment *VERB*
1 to make someone suffer greatly
2 to keep annoying someone
tormentor *NOUN*

torment *NOUN*
great suffering

torn *past participle* of **tear**²

tornado (tor-**nay**-doh) *NOUN* **tornadoes**
a violent whirlwind

torpedo *NOUN* **torpedoes**
a long tube-shaped missile fired under water

torpedo *VERB* **torpedoes, torpedoing, torpedoed**
to attack or destroy a ship with a torpedo

torrent *NOUN*
1 a rushing stream or flow
2 a heavy downpour of rain

torrential *ADJECTIVE*
(of rain) pouring down violently

torrid *ADJECTIVE*
1 hot and dry
2 passionate

torso *NOUN* **torsos**
the trunk of the human body

tortoise *NOUN*
a slow-moving animal with a shell over its body

tortoiseshell NOUN
a mottled brown and yellow shell or colour

tortuous ADJECTIVE
1 full of twists and turns
2 complicated *tortuous logic*

torture VERB
to make a person feel great pain or worry
torture NOUN

Tory NOUN **Tories**
a Conservative
Tory ADJECTIVE

toss VERB
1 to throw into the air
2 to spin a coin to decide something
according to which side of it is upwards after
it falls
3 to move restlessly or from side to side
toss NOUN

toss-up NOUN
1 the tossing of a coin
2 an even chance

tot[1] NOUN
1 a small child
2 (*informal*) a small amount of spirits
a tot of rum

tot[2] VERB **totting, totted**
tot up (*informal*) to add up

total ADJECTIVE
1 including everything
2 complete
totally ADVERB

total NOUN
the amount reached by adding everything

total VERB **totalling, totalled**
1 to add up the total
2 to have as a total

totalitarian ADJECTIVE
having a form of government that does not
allow opposition

totality NOUN **totalities**
the whole of something

totem pole NOUN
a pole carved or painted by Native Americans
with the symbols (*totems*) of their tribes or
families

totter VERB
to walk unsteadily

toucan (*too-kan*) NOUN
a tropical American bird with a huge beak

touch VERB
1 to put the hand or fingers lightly on
something
2 to be or come together with no space
between
3 to move or meddle with something
4 to affect someone's feelings

5 to reach a certain level
touch and go uncertain or risky **touch on**
to discuss briefly **touch up** to improve
something slightly

touch NOUN
1 the action of touching
2 the ability to feel by touching
3 a small thing done *finishing touches*
4 a special skill or style of workmanship
hasn't lost her touch
5 communication with someone *have lost
touch with him*
6 the part of a sports field outside the playing
area

touching ADJECTIVE
causing pity or sympathy

touchline NOUN
one of the lines that mark the side of a sports
pitch

touchy ADJECTIVE **touchier, touchiest**
sensitive; easily offended

tough ADJECTIVE
1 strong; difficult to break or damage
2 difficult to chew
3 able to tolerate hardship
4 firm or severe
5 difficult to do

toughen VERB
to make or become tough

tour NOUN
a journey visiting several places

tour VERB
to make a tour

tourism NOUN
the industry of providing services for tourists

tourist NOUN
a person who visits places for pleasure

tournament NOUN
a series of games or contests

tourniquet (*toor-nik-ay*) NOUN
a strip of material pulled tightly round an arm
or leg to stop bleeding from an artery

tousled ADJECTIVE
untidy or ruffled

tout VERB
to try to sell something or get business

tout NOUN
a person who sells tickets for an event at
more than the official price

tow[1] (*rhymes with go*) VERB
to pull something along behind you

tow NOUN
an act of towing

tow[2] (*rhymes with go*) NOUN
short light-coloured fibres of flax or hemp

a
b
c
d
e
f
g
h
i
j
k
l
m
n
o
p
q
r
s
t
u
v
w
x
y
z

toward PREPOSITION
towards

towards PREPOSITION
1 in the direction of
2 in relation to; regarding *behaved kindly towards us*
3 as a contribution to *some money towards a new bicycle*

towel NOUN
a piece of cloth for drying the skin after washing

towelling NOUN
thick material used for towels

tower NOUN
a tall narrow building

tower VERB
to be very high

town NOUN
a place with many houses, shops, offices, and other buildings

town hall NOUN
a building with offices for the local council

towpath NOUN
a path beside a canal or river, originally used by horses towing barges

toxic ADJECTIVE
poisonous; caused by poison
toxicity NOUN

toxin NOUN
a natural poisonous substance in the body

toy NOUN
a thing to play with

toy ADJECTIVE
1 made as a toy
2 (of a dog) of a very small breed

toy VERB
toy with to handle or consider idly

trace NOUN
1 a mark left by a person or thing
2 a small amount

trace VERB
1 to copy a picture or map etc. by drawing over it on transparent paper
2 to find a person or thing by following evidence

traceable ADJECTIVE
able to be traced

track NOUN
1 a mark or marks left by a moving person or thing
2 a rough path made by regular use
3 a road or area of ground specially prepared for racing
4 a set of rails for trains or trams etc.
5 each of the songs or pieces of music on a CD, tape, etc.

6 a continuous band round the wheels of a tank or tractor etc.
keep or **lose track of** to stay or fail to stay informed about something

track VERB
1 to follow the tracks left by a person or animal
2 to follow or observe something as it moves

tracksuit NOUN
a warm loose suit worn by athletes for training or jogging

tract NOUN
1 an area of land
2 a pamphlet containing a short religious essay

traction NOUN
1 the action of pulling
2 the ability of a vehicle to grip the ground
3 a medical treatment in which an injured arm, leg, etc. is pulled gently for a long time

tractor NOUN
a motor vehicle for pulling farm machinery and loads

trade NOUN
1 the buying and selling of goods
2 an occupation or craft

trade VERB
to buy and sell things

trademark NOUN
a firm's registered symbol or name used to distinguish its goods etc. from others

tradesman NOUN **tradesmen**
a person who sells or delivers goods

trade union NOUN
a group of workers organized to help and protect workers in their own trade or industry

trader NOUN
a person who buys and sells

tradition NOUN
1 the passing down of beliefs or customs etc. from one generation to another
2 something passed on in this way

traditional ADJECTIVE
1 belonging to a tradition
2 established over a long period
traditionally ADVERB

traffic NOUN
1 vehicles, ships, or aircraft moving along a route
2 illegal trading

traffic VERB **trafficking**, **trafficked**
to trade in something illegally

traffic lights PLURAL NOUN
coloured lights used as a signal to traffic at road junctions etc.

tragedy NOUN **tragedies**
1 a play with unhappy events or a sad ending
2 a sad or distressing event

tragic ADJECTIVE
1 sad or distressing
2 to do with tragedies *a tragic actor*
tragically ADVERB

trail NOUN
1 a track, scent, or other sign left where something has passed
2 a path or track through the countryside

trail VERB
1 to follow the trail of
2 to drag or be dragged along behind
3 to follow someone more slowly or wearily
4 to hang down or float loosely
5 (of a voice) to become fainter

trailer NOUN
1 a truck or other container pulled along by a vehicle
2 a short extract advertising a film or television programme

train NOUN
1 a railway engine pulling a line of linked carriages or trucks
2 a number of people or animals moving in a line
3 a series of things
4 part of a long dress or robe that trails behind

train VERB
1 to give a person instruction or practice
2 to practise for a sporting event
3 to make something grow in a particular direction
4 to aim a gun or camera etc.

trainee NOUN
a person who is being trained

trainer NOUN
1 a person who trains people or animals
2 a soft rubber-soled shoe

traipse VERB
to walk wearily; to trudge

trait (*say as* tray *or* trayt) NOUN
one of a person's characteristics

traitor NOUN
someone who betrays their country or friends

trajectory NOUN **trajectories**
the path taken by a moving object such as a bullet or rocket

tram NOUN
a public passenger vehicle running on rails in the road

tramp NOUN
1 a homeless person who walks from place to place
2 a long walk
3 the sound of heavy footsteps

tramp VERB
1 to walk with heavy footsteps
2 to walk for a long distance

trample VERB
to tread heavily on something

trampoline NOUN
a large piece of canvas joined to a frame by springs, used in gymnastics for bouncing on

trance NOUN
a dreamy or unconscious state like sleep

tranquil ADJECTIVE
calm and quiet

tranquillity NOUN
a state of calm

tranquillizer NOUN
a medicine used to make a person feel calm

transact VERB
to conduct business

transaction NOUN
an item of business

transatlantic ADJECTIVE
across or on the other side of the Atlantic Ocean

transcend VERB
to go beyond or do better than

transcribe VERB
to copy or write out
transcription NOUN

transcript NOUN
a written copy

transfer VERB **transferring, transferred**
1 to move a person or thing to another place
2 to hand over
transferable ADJECTIVE **transference** NOUN

transfer NOUN
1 the transferring of a person or thing
2 a picture or design transferred to another surface

transfix VERB
to make unable to move because of fear or surprise etc.

transform VERB
to change completely the form or appearance of
transformation NOUN

transformer NOUN
a device used to change the voltage of an electric current

transfusion NOUN
the process of transferring blood taken from one person into another person

transgress VERB
to break a rule or law etc.
transgression NOUN

transient *ADJECTIVE*
not lasting or staying for long

transistor *NOUN*
a tiny semiconductor that controls a flow of electricity

transit *NOUN*
the process of travelling from one place to another

transition *NOUN*
the process of changing from one condition or form etc. to another
transitional *ADJECTIVE*

transitive *ADJECTIVE*
(of a verb) having a direct object, e.g. *hear* in *we can hear you*

transitory *ADJECTIVE*
existing for a time but not lasting

translate *VERB*
to put something into another language
translator *NOUN*

translation *NOUN*
1 the process of translating
2 something translated

transliterate *VERB*
to write a word in the letters of a different alphabet or language
transliteration *NOUN*

translucent *ADJECTIVE*
allowing light to shine through but not transparent

transmission *NOUN*
1 the process of transmitting
2 a broadcast
3 the gears by which power is transmitted from the engine to the wheels of a vehicle

transmit *VERB* **transmitting, transmitted**
1 to send or pass on from one person or place to another
2 to send out a signal or broadcast etc.
transmitter *NOUN*

transparency *NOUN* **transparencies**
1 the state of being transparent
2 a transparent photograph viewed on a screen

transparent *ADJECTIVE*
able to be seen through

transpire *VERB*
1 (of information) to become known
2 to happen

transplant *VERB*
1 to move a plant to another place to grow
2 to transfer a body part to another person or animal
transplantation *NOUN*

transplant *NOUN*
1 the process of transplanting
2 something transplanted

transport *VERB*
to take from one place to another
transportation *NOUN*

transport *NOUN*
the process or means of transporting people, animals, or things

transpose *VERB*
1 to change the position or order of
2 to put a piece of music into a different key
transposition *NOUN*

transverse *ADJECTIVE*
lying across

trap *NOUN*
1 a device for catching and holding animals
2 a plan or trick for detecting or cheating someone
3 a two-wheeled carriage pulled by a horse

trap *VERB* **trapping, trapped**
1 to catch or hold in a trap
2 to prevent someone from escaping an unpleasant situation

trapdoor *NOUN*
a door in a floor, ceiling, or roof

trapeze *NOUN*
a bar hanging from two ropes as a swing for acrobats

trapezium *NOUN*
a figure of four sides of which two are parallel

trapezoid *NOUN*
a figure of four sides, none of them parallel

trapper *NOUN*
someone who traps wild animals for their fur

trappings *PLURAL NOUN*
clothes or possessions showing rank or position

trash *NOUN*
rubbish or nonsense
trashy *ADJECTIVE*

trauma *NOUN*
a shock that produces a lasting effect on the mind

traumatic *ADJECTIVE*
very unpleasant or upsetting

travel *VERB* **travelling, travelled**
1 to move from place to place
2 to go on a journey
travel *NOUN*

traveller *NOUN*
1 a person who travels
2 a person who does not settle in one place

traverse *VERB*
to go across something
traversal *NOUN*

travesty *NOUN* **travesties**
a bad or ridiculous form of something
a travesty of the truth

trawl *VERB*
to fish by dragging a large net along the
bottom of the sea

trawler *NOUN*
a boat used in trawling

tray *NOUN*
a flat piece of wood, metal, etc. usually with
raised edges, for carrying cups, plates,
food, etc.

treacherous *ADJECTIVE*
1 betraying someone
2 dangerous

treachery *NOUN*
betrayal

treacle *NOUN*
a thick sticky liquid produced when sugar
is purified
treacly *ADJECTIVE*

tread *VERB* **trod**, **trodden**
to walk or put your foot on something

tread *NOUN*
1 a step in walking
2 the top surface of a stair
3 the part of a tyre that touches the ground

treadle *NOUN*
a lever pressed with the foot to work a
machine

treadmill *NOUN*
1 a mill wheel turned by the weight of
people or animals treading on steps fixed
round its edge
2 monotonous work

treason *NOUN*
the act of betraying your country
treasonable *ADJECTIVE*

treasure *NOUN*
1 a store of precious metals or jewels
2 a precious thing or person

treasure *VERB*
to value greatly

treasurer *NOUN*
a person in charge of the money of a club,
society, etc.

treasury *NOUN* **treasuries**
a place where money and valuables are kept
the Treasury the government department
in charge of a country's income

treat *VERB*
1 to behave in a certain way towards
2 to deal with a subject
3 to give medical care to
4 to put through a chemical or other process
5 to pay for something pleasant for someone
to have

treat *NOUN*
1 something special that gives pleasure
2 the process of treating someone

treatise *NOUN*
a book or long essay on a subject

treatment *NOUN*
1 the process or manner of dealing with a
person, animal, or thing
2 medical care

treaty *NOUN* **treaties**
a formal agreement between two or more
countries

treble *ADJECTIVE*
three times as much or as many

treble *NOUN*
1 a treble amount
2 a person with a high-pitched or soprano
voice

treble *VERB*
to make or become three times as much or
as many

tree *NOUN*
a tall plant with a thick trunk and many
branches

trefoil *NOUN*
a plant with three small leaves (e.g. clover)

trek *NOUN*
a long walk or journey

trek *VERB* **trekking**, **trekked**
to go on a long walk or journey

trellis *NOUN*
a wooden framework of crossing bars
supporting climbing plants

tremble *VERB*
to shake gently, especially with fear
tremble *NOUN*

tremendous *ADJECTIVE*
1 very large; huge
2 excellent

tremor *NOUN*
1 a shaking or trembling movement
2 a slight earthquake

tremulous *ADJECTIVE*
trembling from nervousness or weakness

trench *NOUN*
a long narrow hole cut in the ground

trenchant *ADJECTIVE*
strong and effective

trend *NOUN*
the general direction in which something is going

trendy *ADJECTIVE* **trendier**, **trendiest**
(*informal*) fashionable

trepidation *NOUN*
fear and anxiety

trespass *VERB*
to go on someone's land or property unlawfully
trespasser *NOUN*

trespass *NOUN*
(*old use*) wrongdoing; sin

tress *NOUN*
a lock of hair

trestle *NOUN*
each of a set of supports on which a board is rested to form a table
trestle table *NOUN*

triad *NOUN*
a group or set of three things

trial *NOUN*
1 a legal process of deciding whether a person is guilty of a crime
2 a test
3 an annoying person or thing

triangle *NOUN*
1 a flat shape with three sides and three angles
2 a percussion instrument made from a metal rod bent into a triangle

triangular *ADJECTIVE*
having the shape of a triangle

triathlon *NOUN*
an athletic contest consisting of three events

tribal *ADJECTIVE*
to do with or belonging to a tribe

tribe *NOUN*
1 a group of families living in one area as a community
2 a set of people

tribesman or **tribeswoman** *NOUN*
tribesmen or **tribeswomen**
a member of a tribe

tribulation *NOUN*
great trouble or hardship

tribunal (try-**bew**-nal) *NOUN*
a committee appointed to hear evidence and give judgements when there is a dispute

tributary *NOUN* **tributaries**
a river or stream that flows into a larger one

tribute *NOUN*
1 something said, done, or given to show respect or admiration
2 payment formerly made by a country or ruler to a more powerful one

trice *NOUN*
in a trice instantly

triceps (**try**-seps) *NOUN*
the large muscle at the back of the upper arm

trick *NOUN*
1 a crafty or deceitful action
2 a skilful action done for entertainment
3 the cards picked up by the winner in a round of a card game

trick *VERB*
to deceive or cheat by a trick

trickery *NOUN*
the use of tricks; deception

trickle *VERB*
to flow or move slowly
trickle *NOUN*

trickster *NOUN*
a person who tricks or cheats people

tricky *ADJECTIVE* **trickier**, **trickiest**
difficult; needing skill or tact

tricolour (**trik**-ol-er) *NOUN*
a flag with three coloured stripes

tricycle *NOUN*
a vehicle like a bicycle but with three wheels

trident *NOUN*
a three-pronged spear

trifle *NOUN*
1 a pudding of sponge cake with custard, fruit, cream, etc.
2 a small amount
3 something of little importance or value

trifle *VERB*
trifle with to treat with little seriousness

trifling *ADJECTIVE*
small in value or importance

trigger *NOUN*
a lever that is pulled to fire a gun

trigger *VERB*
trigger off to start something happening

trigonometry *NOUN*
the calculation of distances and angles by using triangles

trill *VERB*
to make a quivering musical sound
trill *NOUN*

trillion *NOUN*
1 a million million
2 formerly, a million million million

trilogy *NOUN* **trilogies**
a group of three stories, poems, or plays etc. on the same theme

trim *ADJECTIVE*
neat and orderly

trim *VERB* **trimming**, **trimmed**
1 to cut the edges or unwanted parts off
2 to decorate a piece of clothing

trim NOUN
1 the act of cutting or trimming
2 lace, ribbons, etc. used as decoration

trinket NOUN
a small ornament or piece of jewellery

trio NOUN **trios**
1 a group of three people or things
2 a group of three musicians
3 a piece of music for three musicians

trip VERB **tripping, tripped**
1 to catch the foot on something and fall
2 to move with quick light steps
3 to operate a switch
trip up to stumble

trip NOUN
1 a journey or outing
2 the action of tripping; a stumble
3 (*informal*) hallucinations caused by taking
a drug

tripe NOUN
1 part of the stomach of a cow etc., used
as food
2 (*informal*) nonsense

triple ADJECTIVE
1 consisting of three parts
2 three times as much or as many
triply ADVERB

triple VERB
to make or become three times as much or
as many

triplet NOUN
each of three children or animals born to the
same mother at one time

triplicate NOUN
in triplicate as three identical copies

tripod (**try**-pod) NOUN
a stand with three legs, e.g. to support a
camera

tripper NOUN
a person who is making a pleasure trip

trite (rhymes with *kite*) ADJECTIVE
not interesting, as a result of constant
repetition; hackneyed *a few trite remarks*

triumph NOUN
1 a great success or victory
2 a celebration of a victory

triumph VERB
1 to be successful or victorious
2 to rejoice in success or victory

triumphal ADJECTIVE
celebrating a success or victory

triumphant ADJECTIVE
1 victorious
2 rejoicing over a success or victory

trivia PLURAL NOUN
unimportant details or pieces of information

trivial ADJECTIVE
having little value or importance
trivially ADVERB

troll NOUN
(in myths and legends) a giant or a friendly
but mischievous dwarf

trolley NOUN **trolleys**
1 a small table on wheels or castors
2 a small cart or truck
3 a basket on wheels, used in supermarkets

trolleybus NOUN
a bus powered by electricity from overhead
wires

trombone NOUN
a large brass musical instrument with a
sliding tube

troop NOUN
1 an organized group of soldiers
2 a number of people moving along together
Do not confuse this word with *troupe*.

troop VERB
to move along as a group

trooper NOUN
a soldier in the cavalry or in an armoured unit

troops PLURAL NOUN
armed forces

trophy NOUN **trophies**
1 a cup etc. given as a prize
2 something taken in war or hunting

tropic NOUN
a line of latitude about 23° north of the
equator (**tropic of Cancer**) or 23° south of the
equator (**tropic of Capricorn**)
the tropics the hot regions between these
two latitudes

tropical ADJECTIVE
to do with the tropics *tropical fish*

trot VERB **trotting, trotted**
1 (of a horse) to run at a medium pace lifting
the feet high
2 to run slowly with short steps

trot NOUN
a trotting run

trotter NOUN
a pig's foot used for food

troubadour (**troo**-bad-oor) NOUN
a travelling singer in medieval France

trouble NOUN
1 difficulty or distress
2 a cause of these
take trouble to take great care

trouble VERB
1 to cause trouble to
2 to make the effort to do something
Nobody troubled to ask.

troublesome *ADJECTIVE*
causing trouble or annoyance

trough (trof) *NOUN*
1 a long narrow open container of water or food for animals
2 the low part between two waves or ridges
3 a long region of low air pressure

trounce *VERB*
to defeat heavily

troupe (*say as* troop) *NOUN*
a company of actors, dancers, etc.
Do not confuse this word with *troop*.

trousers *PLURAL NOUN*
a piece of clothing worn over the lower half of the body, with a separate part for each leg

trousseau (troo-soh) *NOUN* **trousseaus** or **trousseaux**
a bride's collection of clothing etc. for married life

trout *NOUN*
a freshwater fish used for food

trowel *NOUN*
1 a small garden tool with a curved blade for lifting or scooping
2 a small tool with a flat blade for spreading mortar

truant *NOUN*
a pupil who stays away from school without permission
play truant to be a truant
truancy *NOUN*

truce *NOUN*
an agreement to stop fighting for an agreed time

truck *NOUN*
1 a lorry
2 an open railway goods wagon

truculent *ADJECTIVE*
defiant and aggressive
truculence *NOUN*

trudge *VERB*
to walk slowly and heavily

true *ADJECTIVE* **truer**, **truest**
1 representing what has really happened or exists
2 genuine or proper
3 accurate
4 loyal or faithful

truffle *NOUN*
1 an underground fungus with a rich flavour
2 a soft chocolate sweet

truism *NOUN*
a statement so obviously true that it is not worth making it

truly *ADVERB*
1 truthfully
2 sincerely or genuinely
3 accurately
4 loyally or faithfully

trump *NOUN*
a playing card of a suit that ranks above the others for one game

trump *VERB*
to beat a card by playing a trump

trumpet *NOUN*
a brass instrument with a narrow tube that widens near the end

trumpet *VERB*
1 to blow a trumpet
2 (of an elephant) to make a loud sound with its trunk
trumpeter *NOUN*

truncated *ADJECTIVE*
made shorter

truncheon *NOUN*
a short thick stick carried as a weapon by police officers

trundle *VERB*
to roll along heavily

trunk *NOUN*
1 the main stem of a tree
2 an elephant's long flexible nose
3 a large box for transporting or storing clothes etc.
4 the human body except for the head, arms, and legs
5 (*American*) the boot of a car

trunks *PLURAL NOUN*
shorts worn by men and boys for swimming

truss *NOUN*
1 a bundle of hay etc.
2 a padded belt worn to support a hernia

truss *VERB*
to tie up securely

trust *VERB*
1 to believe that a person or thing is good, truthful, or reliable
2 to let a person have or use something believing they will treat it well
3 to hope
trust to to rely on *is trusting to luck*

trust *NOUN*
1 the belief that a person or thing can be trusted
2 responsibility
3 a legal arrangement in which money is entrusted to a person with instructions on how to use it

trustee *NOUN*
a person who looks after money entrusted to them

trustful *ADJECTIVE*
willing to trust
trustfully *ADVERB*

trustworthy *ADJECTIVE*
able to be trusted; reliable

trusty *ADJECTIVE* **trustier**, **trustiest**
trustworthy or reliable

truth *NOUN*
1 something that is true
2 the quality of being true

truthful *ADJECTIVE*
1 telling the truth
2 true *a truthful account*
truthfully *ADVERB*

try *VERB* **tries**, **tried**
1 to make an effort to do something
2 to test something by using or doing it
3 to decide in a lawcourt whether a person is
guilty of a crime
4 to be a strain on

try *NOUN* **tries**
1 an attempt
2 (in rugby football) a score achieved by the
putting the ball down behind the opposing
goal line

trying *ADJECTIVE*
tiresome or annoying

tsar (zar) *NOUN*
the title of the former ruler of Russia

tsetse fly (tet-see) *NOUN* **tsetse flies**
a tropical African fly that can cause sleeping
sickness

T-shirt *NOUN*
a short-sleeved shirt shaped like a T

tsunami *NOUN* **tsunamis**
a huge sea wave caused by an underwater
earthquake

tub *NOUN*
a round open container

tuba (tew-ba) *NOUN*
a large brass instrument with a deep tone

tubby *ADJECTIVE* **tubbier**, **tubbiest**
short and fat

tube *NOUN*
1 a long hollow piece of metal, plastic,
rubber, glass, etc., for liquids or gases to pass
along
2 a flexible container with a screw cap

tuber *NOUN*
a short thick rounded root or underground
stem of a plant (e.g. a potato)

tuberculosis *NOUN*
a disease of people and animals, affecting
the lungs

tubing *NOUN*
tubes; a length of tube

tubular *ADJECTIVE*
shaped like a tube

tuck *VERB*
1 to push a loose edge into something
2 to put something away in a small space

tuck *NOUN*
1 a flat fold stitched in a piece of clothing
2 (*informal*) sweets and cakes etc.

Tuesday *NOUN*
the day of the week following Monday

tuft *NOUN*
a bunch of close threads, grass, hair, etc.

tug *VERB* **tugging**, **tugged**
1 to pull something hard or suddenly
2 to tow a ship

tug *NOUN*
1 a hard or sudden pull
2 a small powerful boat used for towing
larger ones

tug of war *NOUN* **tugs of war**
a contest between two teams pulling a rope
from opposite ends

tuition *NOUN*
teaching, especially of a small group

tulip *NOUN*
a large cup-shaped flower on a tall stem
growing from a bulb

tumble *VERB*
1 to fall or roll over suddenly or clumsily
2 to move or push quickly and carelessly
tumble *NOUN*

tumbledown *ADJECTIVE*
falling into ruins

tumbler *NOUN*
a drinking glass with no stem or handle

tummy *NOUN* **tummies**
(*informal*) the stomach

tumour (tew-mer) *NOUN*
an abnormal lump on or in the body

tumult (tew-mult) *NOUN*
an uproar; a state of noisy confusion

tumultuous *ADJECTIVE*
noisy and excited

tun *NOUN*
a large cask or barrel

tuna (tew-na) *NOUN* **tuna**
a large edible sea fish with pink flesh

tundra *NOUN*
a vast Arctic region with no trees

tune *NOUN*
1 a pleasant series of musical notes
2 the music of a song
in tune at the correct musical pitch

tune VERB
1 put a musical instrument in tune
2 adjust a radio or television set to receive a certain channel
3 adjust an engine so that it runs smoothly
tuner NOUN

tuneful ADJECTIVE
having a pleasant tune

tungsten NOUN
a grey metal used to make steel

tunic NOUN
1 a jacket worn as part of a uniform
2 a piece of clothing reaching from the shoulders to the hips or knees

tunnel NOUN
an underground passage
tunnel VERB **tunnelling**, **tunnelled**
to make a tunnel

turban NOUN
a covering for the head made by wrapping a strip of cloth round a cap

turbine NOUN
a machine or motor driven by a flow of water, steam, or gas

turbot NOUN **turbot**
a large flat edible sea fish

turbulence NOUN
violent and uneven movement of air or water

turbulent ADJECTIVE
1 moving violently and unevenly
2 involving much change and disagreement

tureen NOUN
a deep dish with a lid, for serving soup

turf NOUN
short grass and the earth round its roots
turf VERB
to cover the ground with turf

turgid ADJECTIVE
1 swollen and thick
2 pompous and tedious

turkey NOUN **turkeys**
a large bird kept for its meat

turmoil NOUN
wild confusion or agitation

turn VERB
1 to move round or to a new direction
2 to change in appearance etc. *turned pale*
3 to make something change
4 to move a switch or tap etc. to control something
5 to pass a certain time *It has turned midnight.*
6 to shape something on a lathe
turn down 1 to reduce the flow or sound of something 2 to reject **turn out** to happen in a certain way **turn up** 1 to appear or arrive 2 to increase the flow or sound of something

turn NOUN
1 a turning movement
2 a place where there is a change of direction
3 an opportunity or duty etc. that comes to each person in succession
4 a short performance in an entertainment
5 (*informal*) an attack of illness
in turn in succession; one after another

turncoat NOUN
someone who changes their principles or beliefs

turning NOUN
a place where one road meets another

turnip NOUN
a plant with a large white root used as a vegetable

turnout NOUN
the number of people who attend a meeting, vote at an election, etc.

turnover NOUN
1 the amount of sales achieved by a business
2 the rate at which workers leave and are replaced

turnpike NOUN
(*old use*) a road at which a toll is charged

turnstile NOUN
a revolving gate that lets one person through at a time

turntable NOUN
a circular revolving platform or support

turpentine NOUN
a kind of oil used for thinning paint, cleaning paintbrushes, etc.

turps NOUN
(*informal*) turpentine

turquoise NOUN
1 a sky-blue or greenish-blue colour
2 a blue jewel

turret NOUN
1 a small tower on a castle or other building
2 a revolving structure containing a gun

turtle NOUN
a sea animal that looks like a tortoise

tusk NOUN
a long pointed tooth sticking out from the mouth of an elephant, walrus, etc.

tussle NOUN
a struggle or conflict
tussle VERB
to struggle or fight

tutor NOUN
1 a private teacher, especially of one pupil
2 a teacher of students in a college or university

tutorial NOUN
a meeting for students to discuss a subject with their tutor

tutu (too-too) NOUN **tutus**
a ballet dancer's short stiff frilled skirt

TV ABBREVIATION
television

twaddle NOUN
(*informal*) nonsense

twain NOUN, ADJECTIVE
(*old use*) two

twang NOUN
1 a sharp sound like that of a wire when plucked
2 a nasal tone in a person's voice

twang VERB
to make a sharp sound like that of a wire when plucked

tweak VERB
to pinch and twist or pull something sharply
tweak NOUN

tweed NOUN
thick woollen material of mixed colours

tweeds PLURAL NOUN
clothes made of tweed

tweet VERB
to make the chirping sound of a small bird
tweet NOUN

tweezers PLURAL NOUN
small pincers for picking up or pulling out small things

twelve NOUN, ADJECTIVE
the number 12
twelfth ADJECTIVE, NOUN

twenty NOUN, ADJECTIVE **twenties**
the number 20
twentieth ADJECTIVE, NOUN

twice ADVERB
1 two times; on two occasions
2 double the amount

twiddle VERB
to turn something round or over and over in an idle way

twig[1] NOUN
a small shoot on a branch or stem of a tree or shrub

twig[2] VERB **twigging**, **twigged**
(*informal*) to realize what something means

twilight NOUN
dim light from the sky after sunset or before sunrise

twill NOUN
material woven with a diagonal pattern

twin NOUN
either of two children or animals born to the same mother at one time

twine NOUN
strong thin string

twine VERB
to twist or wind together or round something

twinge NOUN
a sudden sharp pain

twinkle VERB
to shine with tiny flashes of light
twinkle NOUN

twinned ADJECTIVE
forming a pair; matching

twirl VERB
to twist quickly
twirl NOUN

twist VERB
1 to turn the ends of something in opposite directions
2 to turn round or from side to side
3 to bend out of the proper shape
4 to pass threads or strands round something or each other
5 to distort the meaning of

twist NOUN
1 a twisting movement or action
2 an unexpected development in a story

twit NOUN
(*informal*) a silly or foolish person

twitch VERB
to move or pull with a slight jerk
twitch NOUN

twitter VERB
to make quick chirping sounds
twitter NOUN

two NOUN, ADJECTIVE
the number 2

two-faced ADJECTIVE
insincere or deceitful

tycoon NOUN
a rich and influential business person

tying *present participle* of **tie**

type NOUN
1 a kind or sort
2 letters or figures etc. designed for use in printing

type VERB
to write something by using a typewriter or computer

typecast VERB **typecast**
to keep giving an actor the same kind of role to play

typewriter NOUN
a machine with keys that are pressed to print letters or figures etc. on paper
typewritten ADJECTIVE

typhoid fever NOUN
a serious infectious disease with fever, caused by bacteria

typhoon NOUN
a violent hurricane in the western Pacific or East Asian seas

typhus NOUN
an infectious disease causing fever, weakness, and a rash

typical ADJECTIVE
1 having the usual characteristics or qualities
2 usual in a particular person or thing *It was typical of him to forget.*
typically ADVERB

typify VERB **typifies, typified**
to be a typical example of something

typist NOUN
a person who works with a typewriter

tyrannical or **tyrannous** ADJECTIVE
harsh and cruel

tyrannize VERB
to rule harshly

tyrannosaurus NOUN
a huge flesh-eating dinosaur that walked upright on large hind legs

tyranny NOUN **tyrannies**
rule by a tyrant

tyrant NOUN
a person who rules cruelly and unjustly

tyre NOUN
a rubber covering round a wheel of a road vehicle

Uu

ubiquitous (yoo-**bik**-wit-us) ADJECTIVE
existing or found everywhere

udder NOUN
the bag-like part of a cow, ewe, female goat, etc. from which milk is taken

UFO ABBREVIATION
unidentified flying object

ugly ADJECTIVE **uglier, ugliest**
1 unpleasant to look at or hear
2 hostile and threatening *ugly scenes*
ugliness NOUN

UK ABBREVIATION
United Kingdom

ukulele (yoo-kul-**ay**-lee) NOUN
a small guitar with four strings

ulcer NOUN
a sore on the inside or outside of the body

ulterior ADJECTIVE
beyond what is obvious or stated *an ulterior motive*

ultimate ADJECTIVE
furthest in a series of things; final
ultimately ADVERB

ultimatum NOUN
a final demand or statement with a threat of action if it is not followed

ultramarine NOUN
a deep bright blue

ultrasonic ADJECTIVE
(of sound) beyond the range of human hearing

ultrasound NOUN
sound with an ultrasonic frequency

ultraviolet ADJECTIVE
(of light rays) beyond the violet end of the spectrum and not visible to the human eye

umber NOUN
a kind of brown pigment

umbilical cord NOUN
the long tube through which an unborn baby receives nourishment in the womb

umbrage NOUN
take umbrage to be offended

umbrella NOUN
a circular piece of material stretched over a folding frame with a central stick as a handle, used for protection from rain

umpire NOUN
a referee in cricket, tennis, and some other games

umpire VERB
to act as an umpire

umpteen ADJECTIVE
(*informal*) many; a lot of

UN ABBREVIATION
United Nations

unable ADJECTIVE
not able to do something

unaccountable ADJECTIVE
1 unable to be explained
2 not accountable for what you do
unaccountably ADVERB

unadulterated ADJECTIVE
pure; not mixed with other things

unaided ADJECTIVE
without help

unanimity NOUN
a state of complete agreement

unanimous *ADJECTIVE*
with everyone agreeing *a unanimous decision*
unanimously *ADVERB*

unassuming *ADJECTIVE*
modest; not arrogant or pretentious

unavoidable *ADJECTIVE*
not able to be avoided

unaware *ADJECTIVE*
not aware

unawares *ADVERB*
unexpectedly; without warning

unbalanced *ADJECTIVE*
1 not balanced
2 slightly mad or mentally ill

unbearable *ADJECTIVE*
not able to be endured
unbearably *ADVERB*

unbeatable *ADJECTIVE*
unable to be defeated or surpassed

unbeaten *ADJECTIVE*
not defeated or surpassed

unbecoming *ADJECTIVE*
1 not making a person look attractive
2 not suitable or fitting

unbeknown *ADJECTIVE*
unbeknown to without someone knowing

unbelievable *ADJECTIVE*
not able to be believed; incredible
unbelievably *ADVERB*

unborn *ADJECTIVE*
not yet born

unbridled *ADJECTIVE*
not controlled or restrained *unbridled rage*

unbroken *ADJECTIVE*
not broken or interrupted

uncalled for *ADJECTIVE*
not justified or necessary

uncanny *ADJECTIVE* **uncannier**, **uncanniest**
strange or mysterious

unceremonious *ADJECTIVE*
offhand or abrupt

uncertain *ADJECTIVE*
1 not known certainly
2 not sure
3 not reliable
uncertainty *NOUN*

uncle *NOUN*
1 the brother of your father or mother
2 your aunt's husband

uncomfortable *ADJECTIVE*
not comfortable
uncomfortably *ADVERB*

uncommon *ADJECTIVE*
not common; unusual

uncompromising *ADJECTIVE*
not allowing a compromise; inflexible

unconcerned *ADJECTIVE*
not caring about something

unconditional *ADJECTIVE*
without any conditions; absolute
unconditionally *ADVERB*

unconscious *ADJECTIVE*
1 not conscious
2 not aware of things

uncontrollable *ADJECTIVE*
unable to be controlled or stopped
uncontrollably *ADVERB*

uncooperative *ADJECTIVE*
not cooperative

uncouth *ADJECTIVE*
rude and rough in manner

uncover *VERB*
1 to remove the covering from
2 to reveal

undecided *ADJECTIVE*
1 not yet settled or certain
2 not having decided

undeniable *ADJECTIVE*
impossible to deny; clearly true
undeniably *ADVERB*

under *PREPOSITION*
1 below or beneath
2 less than
3 governed or controlled by
4 in the process of *under repair*
5 according to the rules of *permitted under the agreement*
under way in motion or in progress

under *ADVERB*
in or to a lower place or level or condition
The diver went under.

underarm *ADJECTIVE, ADVERB*
moving the hand and arm forward and upwards

undercarriage *NOUN*
an aircraft's landing wheels and their supports

underclothes *PLURAL NOUN*
clothes worn next to the skin, under other clothing
underclothing *NOUN*

undercover *ADJECTIVE*
done or doing things secretly

undercurrent *NOUN*
1 a current below the surface
2 an underlying feeling or influence

undercut *VERB* **undercutting**, **undercut**
to sell at a lower price than a competitor

underdeveloped *ADJECTIVE*
1 not fully developed or grown
2 (of a country) poor and lacking modern industrial development

underdog *NOUN*
a person or team regarded as likely to lose

underdone *ADJECTIVE*
not fully cooked

underestimate *VERB*
to make too low an estimate of

underfoot *ADVERB*
on the ground; under your feet

undergarment *NOUN*
an item of underwear

undergo *VERB* **undergoes, undergoing, underwent, undergone**
to experience or endure

undergraduate *NOUN*
a university student studying for a first degree

underground *ADJECTIVE, ADVERB*
1 under the ground
2 done or working in secret

underground *NOUN*
a railway that runs through tunnels under the ground

undergrowth *NOUN*
bushes and other plants growing closely

underhand *ADJECTIVE*
sly or secretive

underline *VERB*
1 to draw a line under
2 to emphasize

underling *NOUN*
a subordinate

underlying *ADJECTIVE*
forming the basis of something *the underlying causes*

undermine *VERB*
to weaken something gradually

underneath *PREPOSITION, ADVERB*
below or beneath

underpants *PLURAL NOUN*
an item of men's underwear covering the lower part of the body

underpass *NOUN*
a road that passes under another

underpin *VERB* **underpinning, underpinned**
to strengthen or support

underprivileged *ADJECTIVE*
lacking the normal standard of living or rights in a community

underrate *VERB*
to have too low an opinion of

undersized *ADJECTIVE*
of less than the normal size

understand *VERB* **understood**
1 to know what something means
2 to know how someone feels or why they behave in a certain way
3 to have been told
4 to take for granted

understandable *ADJECTIVE*
1 able to be understood
2 reasonable or natural
understandably *ADVERB*

understanding *NOUN*
1 the power to understand or think
2 sympathy or tolerance
3 agreement

understanding *ADJECTIVE*
sympathetic and helpful

understatement *NOUN*
an incomplete or restrained statement of facts or truth

understudy *NOUN* **understudies**
an actor who learns a part to be able to play it if the usual performer is ill or absent

undertake *VERB* **undertook, undertaken**
1 to agree or promise to do something
2 to take on a task or responsibility

undertaker *NOUN*
a person who arranges funerals and burials or cremations

undertaking *NOUN*
1 a job or task being undertaken
2 a promise or guarantee

undertone *NOUN*
1 a low or quiet tone
2 an underlying quality or feeling

underwater *ADJECTIVE, ADVERB*
beneath the surface of water

underwear *NOUN*
clothes worn next to the skin, under other clothing

underweight *ADJECTIVE*
not heavy enough

underwent *past tense* of **undergo**

underworld *NOUN*
1 the world of crime
2 (in myths and legends) the place where the spirits of the dead exist

undesirable *ADJECTIVE*
not wanted; objectionable

undo *VERB* **undoes, undoing, undid, undone**
1 to unfasten or unwrap
2 to cancel the effect of

undoing *NOUN*
be someone's undoing to be the cause of their ruin or failure

undoubted ADJECTIVE
not doubted; accepted
undoubtedly ADVERB

undress VERB
to take your clothes off

undue ADJECTIVE
excessive; too great

undulate VERB
1 to move like waves
2 to have a wavy appearance
undulation NOUN

unduly ADVERB
excessively; more than is reasonable

undying ADJECTIVE
lasting forever

unearth VERB
1 to dig up
2 to find by searching

unearthly ADJECTIVE
strange and frightening

uneasy ADJECTIVE
1 worried or anxious
2 uncomfortable
uneasily ADVERB

uneatable ADJECTIVE
not fit to be eaten

uneconomic ADJECTIVE
not profitable

unemployed ADJECTIVE
not having a job
unemployment NOUN

unending ADJECTIVE
not coming to an end

unequal ADJECTIVE
1 not equal in amount, size, or value
2 not giving the same opportunities
unequalled ADJECTIVE

unequivocal ADJECTIVE
completely clear; not ambiguous

unerring ADJECTIVE
making no mistake

uneven ADJECTIVE
1 not level or regular
2 not equally balanced
unevenly ADVERB

unexceptionable ADJECTIVE
not in any way objectionable

unexceptional ADJECTIVE
not exceptional; quite ordinary

unexpected ADJECTIVE
not expected
unexpectedly ADVERB

unfair ADJECTIVE
not fair; unjust
unfairly ADVERB **unfairness** NOUN

unfaithful ADJECTIVE
not faithful or loyal

unfamiliar ADJECTIVE
not familiar
unfamiliarity NOUN

unfasten VERB
to open the fastenings of

unfavourable ADJECTIVE
not favourable
unfavourably ADVERB

unfeeling ADJECTIVE
not caring about other people's feelings

unfit ADJECTIVE
1 not suitable
2 not in perfect health from lack of exercise

unfold VERB
1 to open or spread out
2 to make or become known slowly *as the story unfolds*

unforeseen ADJECTIVE
not foreseen; unexpected

unforgettable ADJECTIVE
too good to forget

unforgivable ADJECTIVE
not able to be forgiven

unfortunate ADJECTIVE
1 unlucky
2 unsuitable or regrettable
unfortunately ADVERB

unfounded ADJECTIVE
not based on facts

unfriendly ADJECTIVE
not friendly

unfurl VERB
to unroll or spread out

ungainly ADJECTIVE
awkward or clumsy

ungracious ADJECTIVE
not kindly or courteous

ungrateful ADJECTIVE
not showing thanks

unguarded ADJECTIVE
1 not guarded
2 without thought; indiscreet

unhappy ADJECTIVE
1 not happy; sad
2 unfortunate or unsuitable *an unhappy coincidence*
unhappily ADVERB

unhealthy ADJECTIVE
1 not healthy
2 likely to damage health *an unhealthy diet*

unheard of ADJECTIVE
never known or done before

unhinged ADJECTIVE
mentally ill or unbalanced

unicorn NOUN
(in legends) an animal like a horse with a straight horn growing from its forehead

uniform NOUN
special clothes worn by members of an organization, school, etc.

uniform ADJECTIVE
always the same; not varying *of uniform size*
uniformity NOUN

unify VERB **unifies**, **unified**
to make into one thing
unification NOUN

unilateral ADJECTIVE
done by one person or group or country etc.

unimportant ADJECTIVE
not important; trivial

uninhabited ADJECTIVE
with nobody living there

uninhibited ADJECTIVE
having no inhibitions

uninterested ADJECTIVE
not interested; showing or feeling no concern

union NOUN
1 the joining of things together
2 a trade union

Union Jack NOUN
the flag of the United Kingdom

unique ADJECTIVE
being the only one of its kind
uniquely ADVERB

unisex ADJECTIVE
suitable for both sexes

unison NOUN
1 agreement
2 harmony of speaking or singing

unit NOUN
1 an amount used as a standard in measuring or counting
2 a single item of equipment used with others *a sink unit*
3 (*Maths*) any whole number less than 10

unite VERB
1 to join together
2 to make or become one thing

unity NOUN **unities**
1 complete agreement
2 something whole that is made up of parts
3 (*Maths*) the number one

universal ADJECTIVE
to do with everyone or everything
universally ADVERB

universe NOUN
everything that exists, including the earth and all the stars and planets

university NOUN **universities**
a place where people study at an advanced level after leaving school

unjust ADJECTIVE
not fair or just

unkempt ADJECTIVE
looking untidy or neglected

unkind ADJECTIVE
not kind
unkindly ADVERB

unknown ADJECTIVE
not known or named

unlawful ADJECTIVE
not legal

unleaded ADJECTIVE
(of petrol) without added lead

unleash VERB
1 to release a dog from a leash
2 to show an emotion

unleavened (un-**lev**-end) ADJECTIVE
(of bread) made without yeast or other substances that would make it rise

unless CONJUNCTION
except if; if ... not *We cannot go unless we are invited.*

unlike PREPOSITION
not like; not typical of *It was unlike him to say that.*

unlike ADJECTIVE
not alike; different

unlikely ADJECTIVE **unlikelier**, **unlikeliest**
not likely to happen or be true

unlimited ADJECTIVE
very great or very many

unload VERB
to remove the cargo from a ship, vehicle, etc.

unlock VERB
to open by undoing a lock

unlucky ADJECTIVE
having or bringing bad luck
unluckily ADVERB

unmarried ADJECTIVE
not married

unmask VERB
1 to remove a person's mask
2 to reveal what a person or thing really is

unmentionable ADJECTIVE
too bad or embarrassing to be spoken of

unmistakable ADJECTIVE
not able to be mistaken for another person or thing
unmistakably ADVERB

unmitigated ADJECTIVE
total and absolute *an unmitigated disaster*

unnatural ADJECTIVE
not natural or normal
unnaturally ADVERB

unnecessary ADJECTIVE
not necessary; more than is necessary

unnerve VERB
to make someone lose courage or determination

unoccupied ADJECTIVE
not occupied

unofficial ADJECTIVE
not official
unofficially ADVERB

unorthodox ADJECTIVE
not generally accepted

unpack VERB
to take things out of a suitcase, bag, box, etc.

unpaid ADJECTIVE
1 not yet paid
2 not receiving payment

unparalleled ADJECTIVE
having no parallel or equal

unpick VERB
to undo the stitching of

unpleasant ADJECTIVE
not pleasant; nasty

unpopular ADJECTIVE
not much liked

unprecedented ADJECTIVE
never having happened before

unprepossessing ADJECTIVE
not attractive

unprincipled ADJECTIVE
lacking good moral principles

unprofitable ADJECTIVE
not producing a profit or advantage
unprofitably ADVERB

unqualified ADJECTIVE
1 not officially qualified
2 not limited *unqualified approval*

unravel VERB **unravelling**, **unravelled**
1 to disentangle
2 to undo something knitted
3 to solve a mystery

unreal ADJECTIVE
not real; imaginary

unreasonable ADJECTIVE
1 not reasonable
2 excessive or unjust
unreasonably ADVERB

unreliable ADJECTIVE
not reliable or trustworthy

unremitting ADJECTIVE
never stopping or relaxing; persistent

unrequited ADJECTIVE
(of love) not returned or rewarded

unrest NOUN
trouble or rioting by people who are dissatisfied

unripe ADJECTIVE
not yet ripe

unrivalled ADJECTIVE
having no equal

unroll VERB
to open something that has been rolled up

unruly ADJECTIVE
difficult to control; disorderly
unruliness NOUN

unsaturated ADJECTIVE
(of fats) forming cholesterol in the blood

unsavoury ADJECTIVE
unpleasant or disgusting

unscathed ADJECTIVE
not harmed

unscrew VERB
to undo something that has been screwed up

unscrupulous ADJECTIVE
having no scruples about doing wrong

unseemly ADJECTIVE
not proper or suitable; indecent

unseen ADJECTIVE
not seen; invisible

unselfish ADJECTIVE
not selfish; generous

unsettle VERB
to make someone feel uneasy or anxious
unsettling ADJECTIVE

unsettled ADJECTIVE
1 not settled or calm
2 (of weather) likely to change

unshakeable ADJECTIVE
strong and firm *an unshakeable belief*

unsightly ADJECTIVE
ugly

unskilled ADJECTIVE
not having or not needing special skill

unsolicited ADJECTIVE
not asked for *unsolicited advice*

unsound ADJECTIVE
1 not reliable
2 not firm or strong
3 not healthy *of unsound mind*

unspeakable ADJECTIVE
too bad to be described

unsteady ADJECTIVE
not steady or secure

unstinting ADJECTIVE
giving generously

unstuck ADJECTIVE
come unstuck (*informal*) to fail or go wrong

unsuccessful ADJECTIVE
not successful
unsuccessfully ADVERB

unsuitable ADJECTIVE
not suitable

unsure ADJECTIVE
not confident or certain

unsuspecting ADJECTIVE
unaware of a danger etc.

untenable ADJECTIVE
not able to be justified or defended

unthinkable ADJECTIVE
too bad or too unlikely to be worth
considering

unthinking ADJECTIVE
thoughtless

untidy ADJECTIVE **untidier, untidiest**
not tidy; in a mess
untidily ADVERB

untie VERB **unties, untied**
to undo something that has been tied

until PREPOSITION, CONJUNCTION
up to a particular time or event

untimely ADJECTIVE
happening too soon or at an unsuitable time

unto PREPOSITION
(*old use*) to

untold ADJECTIVE
1 not yet told
2 too great to be counted *untold wealth*

untoward ADJECTIVE
inconvenient or unfortunate

untrue ADJECTIVE
not true

untruth NOUN
an untrue statement; a lie

untruthful ADJECTIVE
not telling the truth
untruthfully ADVERB

unused ADJECTIVE
1 (un-**yoozd**) not yet used *an unused stamp*
2 (un-**yoost**) not accustomed *unused to*
flying

unusual ADJECTIVE
not usual; strange
unusually ADVERB

unveil VERB
1 to remove a veil or covering from
something
2 to reveal

unwanted ADJECTIVE
not wanted

unwarranted ADJECTIVE
not justified; uncalled for

unwary ADJECTIVE
careless about danger

unwell ADJECTIVE
not in good health

unwieldy ADJECTIVE
awkward to move or handle because of its
size or shape
Do not spell this word *unwieldly*.

unwilling ADJECTIVE
not willing
unwillingly ADVERB

unwind VERB **unwound**
1 to pull out from a reel etc.
2 (*informal*) to relax after work or stress

unwise ADJECTIVE
not wise; foolish
unwisely ADVERB

unwitting ADJECTIVE
unintended
unwittingly ADVERB

unworn ADJECTIVE
not yet worn

unworthy ADJECTIVE
not worthy or deserving

unwrap VERB **unwrapping, unwrapped**
to open something that is wrapped

up ADVERB
1 to or in a higher place or position or level
Prices went up.
2 so as to be upright *stand up*
3 out of bed *not up yet*
4 completely *eat it up*
5 finished *Time is up.*
6 (*informal*) happening *Something is up.*
up to 1 until **2** occupied with something
3 capable of **4** needed from *up to us to help*

up PREPOSITION
upwards along *A lizard ran up the wall.*

up-and-coming ADJECTIVE
(*informal*) likely to become successful

upbringing NOUN
the way someone is educated as a child

update VERB
to bring up to date
update NOUN

upgrade VERB
1 to improve a machine by installing new
parts
2 to promote to a higher rank
upgrade NOUN

upheaval NOUN
a sudden violent change or disturbance

uphill ADVERB
up a slope

uphill ADJECTIVE
1 going up a slope
2 difficult *an uphill struggle*

uphold VERB **upheld**
to support or maintain a decision or belief etc.

upholster VERB
to put a soft padded covering on furniture

upholstery NOUN
soft covering and padding on furniture

upkeep NOUN
1 the process of keeping something in good condition
2 the cost of this

uplands PLURAL NOUN
the higher parts of a country or region
upland ADJECTIVE

uplifting ADJECTIVE
making you feel more cheerful

upload VERB
(*ICT*) to move data from a personal computer to a computer network

upon PREPOSITION
(*formal*) on

upper ADJECTIVE
higher in place or rank etc.

upper-class ADJECTIVE
belonging to the highest class in society

uppermost ADJECTIVE
highest

upright ADJECTIVE
1 vertical or erect
2 honest or honourable

upright NOUN
an upright post or rod forming a support

uprising NOUN
a rebellion or revolt

uproar NOUN
an outburst of noise or excitement or anger

uproarious ADJECTIVE
very noisy

uproot VERB
1 to remove a plant and its roots from the ground
2 to make someone leave their home

upset VERB **upsetting**, **upset**
1 to overturn or knock over
2 to make a person unhappy or distressed
3 to disturb or disrupt plans etc.

upset ADJECTIVE
1 unhappy or distressed
2 slightly ill *an upset stomach*

upset NOUN
1 a slight illness
2 an unexpected result or setback

upshot NOUN
the eventual outcome

upside down ADVERB, ADJECTIVE
1 with the upper part underneath
2 in a mess; very untidy

upstairs ADVERB, ADJECTIVE
to or on a higher floor

upstart NOUN
a person who has risen suddenly to a high position and behaves arrogantly

upstream ADJECTIVE, ADVERB
in the direction from which a stream flows

uptake NOUN
quick on the uptake quick to understand

uptight ADJECTIVE
(*informal*) tense and nervous

up to date ADJECTIVE
1 modern or fashionable
2 having or providing the most recent information

Use hyphens before a noun: *an up-to-date edition* but *an edition that is up to date.*

upward ADJECTIVE, ADVERB
towards what is higher
upwards ADVERB

uranium NOUN
a radioactive grey metal used as a source of nuclear energy

urban ADJECTIVE
to do with a town or city

urbane ADJECTIVE
having smoothly polite manners
urbanity NOUN

urbanize VERB
to change a place into a town-like area
urbanization NOUN

urchin NOUN
a poor child wearing dirty or ragged clothes

urge VERB
1 to try to persuade a person to do something
2 to drive people or animals onward
3 to recommend or advise

urge NOUN
a strong desire or wish

urgent ADJECTIVE
needing to be done or dealt with immediately
urgency NOUN **urgently** ADVERB

urinal NOUN
a bowl or trough fixed to the wall in a public toilet, into which men may urinate

urinate VERB
to pass urine out of your body
urination NOUN

urine NOUN
waste liquid that collects in the bladder and is passed out of the body
urinary ADJECTIVE

urn NOUN
1 a large metal container for heating water
2 a vase holding the ashes of a cremated person

US or **USA** ABBREVIATION
United States (of America)

us PRONOUN
the form of **we** used when it is the object of a verb or after a preposition

usable ADJECTIVE
able to be used

usage NOUN
1 the way something is used
2 the way words are used in a language

use (yooz) VERB
to perform an action or job with something
used to 1 was or were in the habit of doing *We used to go by train.* **2** accustomed to *I'm used to their rudeness.*

use (yooss) NOUN
1 the action of using something
2 a purpose *another use for the box*
3 the quality of being useful *It is no use at all.*

used (yoozd) ADJECTIVE
not new; second-hand

useful ADJECTIVE
able to be used effectively
usefully ADVERB

useless ADJECTIVE
having no use or effect

user NOUN
a person who uses something

user-friendly ADJECTIVE
designed to be easy to use

usher NOUN
a person who shows people to their seats in a theatre etc.

usher VERB
to lead or escort someone

usual ADJECTIVE
happening or done always or most of the time
usually ADVERB

usurp VERB
to take power or a right etc. illegally
usurpation NOUN **usurper** NOUN

utensil (yoo-ten-sil) NOUN
a tool or device used in a house *cooking utensils*

uterus NOUN
the womb

utility NOUN **utilities**
1 usefulness
2 an organization that supplies water, gas, electricity, etc. to the public

utilize VERB
to find a use for

utmost ADJECTIVE
extreme or greatest *with the utmost care*
do your utmost to do all you can

Utopia NOUN
an imaginary place where everything is perfect
Utopian ADJECTIVE

utter[1] VERB
to say or speak

utter[2] ADJECTIVE
complete or absolute
utterly ADVERB

utterance NOUN
something said

uttermost ADJECTIVE, NOUN
extreme; utmost

U-turn NOUN
1 a U-shaped turn made by a vehicle
2 a complete change of policy

Vv

vacancy NOUN **vacancies**
1 a job that has not been filled
2 an available room in a hotel etc.

vacant ADJECTIVE
1 empty; not filled or occupied
2 (of a look) showing no interest or expression

vacate VERB
to give up a place or position

vacation NOUN
1 a holiday time
2 the act of vacating a place etc.

vaccinate VERB
to inoculate with a vaccine
vaccination NOUN

448

vaccine (vak-seen) *NOUN*
a substance used to provide immunity against a disease

vacillate *VERB*
to keep changing your mind

vacuous *ADJECTIVE*
empty-headed; unintelligent

vacuum *NOUN*
a space with no air in it

vacuum cleaner *NOUN*
a machine for sucking up dust and dirt etc.

vacuum flask *NOUN*
a container with double walls that have a vacuum between them, for keeping liquids hot or cold

vagabond *NOUN*
a person with no settled home or regular work

vagaries *PLURAL NOUN*
strange features or whims *the vagaries of fashion*

vagina *NOUN*
the passage leading from a woman's vulva to the womb

vagrant (vay-grant) *NOUN*
a person with no settled home or regular work
vagrancy *NOUN*

vague *ADJECTIVE*
1 not definite or clear
2 not thinking clearly or precisely
vaguely *ADVERB*

vain *ADJECTIVE*
1 useless *vain attempts*
2 conceited, especially about your appearance
in vain with no result; uselessly
vainly *ADVERB*
Do not confuse this word with *vane* or *vein*.

valance *NOUN*
a short curtain round the frame of a bed or above a window

vale *NOUN*
a valley

valentine *NOUN*
1 a card sent on St Valentine's day (14 February) to a loved person
2 a person who receives a valentine

valet (val-ay *or* val-it) *NOUN*
a man's personal servant

valiant *ADJECTIVE*
brave or courageous
valiantly *ADVERB*

valid *ADJECTIVE*
1 legally able to be used *a valid passport*
2 (of reasoning) sound and logical
validity *NOUN*

valley *NOUN* **valleys**
a long low area between hills, often with a river flowing through it

valour *NOUN*
bravery

valuable *ADJECTIVE*
worth a lot of money; of great value
valuably *ADVERB*

valuables *PLURAL NOUN*
valuable items

value *NOUN*
1 the price or worth of something
2 how useful or important something is *the value of regular exercise*
3 (*Maths*) the number or quantity represented by a figure etc.

value *VERB*
1 to think something to be valuable or important
2 to estimate the value of
valuation *NOUN*

valueless *ADJECTIVE*
having no value

valve *NOUN*
1 a device for controlling the flow of gas or liquid
2 a flap in the heart or in a vein, controlling the flow of blood
3 a device controlling the flow of electricity in old televisions, radios, etc.
4 either of the two parts of the shell of oysters etc.

vampire *NOUN*
a dead person who is supposed to rise at night and suck blood from living people

van[1] *NOUN*
1 a covered vehicle for carrying goods
2 a railway carriage for luggage or goods

van[2] *NOUN*
the vanguard

vandal *NOUN*
a person who deliberately damages public property
vandalism *NOUN*

vandalize *VERB*
to damage things as a vandal

vane *NOUN*
1 a weathervane
2 the blade of a propeller, sail of a windmill, etc.
Do not confuse this word with *vain* or *vein*.

vanguard *NOUN*
1 the leading part of an army
2 the first people to adopt a practice or idea

vanilla *NOUN*
a flavouring obtained from the pods of a tropical plant

vanish *VERB*
to disappear completely

vanity *NOUN*
conceit; a state of being vain

vanquish *VERB*
to defeat completely

vantage point *NOUN*
a place offering a good view of something

vapid *ADJECTIVE*
dull and uninteresting

vaporize *VERB*
to change or be changed into vapour

vapour *NOUN*
a visible gas to which some substances can be converted by heat

variable *ADJECTIVE*
likely to vary; changeable

variable *NOUN*
something that varies or can vary

variance *NOUN*
a state of differing or disagreeing

variant *NOUN*
a different form of something
variant *ADJECTIVE*

variation *NOUN*
1 the amount by which something varies
2 a different form of something

varicose *ADJECTIVE*
(of veins) permanently swollen

varied *ADJECTIVE*
of different sorts

variegated (vair-ig-ay-tid) *ADJECTIVE*
having patches of different colours

variety *NOUN* **varieties**
1 a set of different things of the same type
2 the quality of not always being the same; variation
3 a particular kind
4 an entertainment with various short acts

various *ADJECTIVE*
1 of several kinds
2 several
variously *ADVERB*

varnish *NOUN*
a liquid that dries to form a hard shiny coating

varnish *VERB*
to cover with varnish

vary *VERB* **varies, varied**
1 to make or become different
2 to be different

vascular *ADJECTIVE*
consisting of tubes or similar vessels for circulating blood, sap, or water in animals or plants *the vascular system*

vase *NOUN*
a tall open container for holding flowers

vast *ADJECTIVE*
very great in area
vastly *ADVERB*

VAT *ABBREVIATION*
value added tax; a tax on goods and services

vat *NOUN*
a large container for liquid

vaudeville (vawd-vil) *NOUN*
a kind of variety entertainment

vault *VERB*
to jump over something while supporting yourself on your hands or with a pole

vault *NOUN*
1 a vaulting jump
2 an arched roof
3 an underground room or burial chamber

vaulted *ADJECTIVE*
having an arched roof

VDU *ABBREVIATION*
visual display unit

veal *NOUN*
calf's flesh used as food

vector *NOUN*
(*Maths*) a quantity that has size and direction, such as velocity (which is speed in a certain direction)
vectorial *ADJECTIVE*

Veda *NOUN*
the most sacred literature of Hindus

veer *VERB*
to change direction

vegan *NOUN*
a person who does not eat or use any animal products

vegetable *NOUN*
a plant that can be used as food

vegetarian *NOUN*
a person who does not eat meat or fish
vegetarianism *NOUN*

vegetate *VERB*
to live a dull or inactive life

vegetation *NOUN*
plants that are growing

vehement *ADJECTIVE*
showing strong feeling
vehemence *NOUN* **vehemently** *ADVERB*

vehicle *NOUN*
a machine with wheels used for transport on land

veil *NOUN*
a piece of thin material worn to cover the face or head

veil *VERB*
1 to cover something with a veil
2 to hide something partly

vein *NOUN*
1 any of the tubes that carry blood to the heart
2 a line or streak on a leaf, insect's wing, etc.
3 a long deposit of mineral or ore in rock
4 a mood or manner *in a serious vein*
Do not confuse this word with *vain* or *vane*.

vellum *NOUN*
smooth parchment or writing paper

velocity *NOUN*
speed in a given direction

velvet *NOUN*
a woven material with soft furry fibres on one side
velvety *ADJECTIVE*

vendetta *NOUN*
a long-lasting bitter quarrel or feud

vending machine *NOUN*
a slot machine for buying drinks, chocolate, etc.

vendor *NOUN*
a seller, especially of a house

veneer *NOUN*
1 a thin layer of fine wood covering the surface of a cheaper wood
2 an outward show *a veneer of politeness*

venerable *ADJECTIVE*
worthy of respect or honour, especially because of great age

venerate *VERB*
to honour with great respect
veneration *NOUN*

venereal disease (vin-**eer**-ee-al) *NOUN*
a disease passed on by sexual intercourse

venetian blind *NOUN*
a window blind of adjustable horizontal strips

vengeance *NOUN*
action taken in revenge

vengeful *ADJECTIVE*
seeking revenge

venison *NOUN*
deer's flesh as food

Venn diagram *NOUN*
(*Maths*) a diagram of circles showing the relationships between sets

venom *NOUN*
1 poison produced by snakes, scorpions, etc.
2 hatred or spite
venomous *ADJECTIVE*

vent *NOUN*
an opening to let out smoke or gas etc.
give vent to to express feelings openly

vent *VERB*
to express feelings openly

ventilate *VERB*
to let air move freely in and out of a room etc.
ventilation *NOUN*

ventilator *NOUN*
a device or opening for ventilating a room

ventriloquist *NOUN*
an entertainer who makes their voice sound as if it comes from another source
ventriloquism *NOUN*

venture *NOUN*
a risky undertaking

venture *VERB*
to dare or be bold enough to do or say something

venue *NOUN*
the place where a meeting, sports match, etc. is held

veracity *NOUN*
truthfulness

veranda *NOUN*
a terrace with a roof, along the side of a house

verb *NOUN*
a word that shows what a person or thing is doing, e.g. *bring, came, sing, were*

verbal *ADJECTIVE*
1 to do with or in words
2 spoken, not written *a verbal statement*
3 to do with verbs
verbally *ADVERB*

verbatim *ADVERB, ADJECTIVE*
in exactly the same words

verbose *ADJECTIVE*
using more words than are needed

verdant *ADJECTIVE*
(of grass or fields) green

verdict *NOUN*
a judgement or decision made after consideration, especially that made by a jury

verge *NOUN*
1 a strip of grass along the edge of a road or path
2 the extreme edge or brink of something

verge *VERB*
verge on to be close to

verger *NOUN*
a church caretaker and attendant

verify *VERB* **verifies, verified**
to check or show that something is true or correct
verifiable *ADJECTIVE* **verification** *NOUN*

veritable ADJECTIVE
real; rightly named *a veritable villain*
veritably ADVERB

vermicelli (verm-i-**chel**-ee) NOUN
pasta made in long thin threads

vermilion NOUN, ADJECTIVE
a bright red colour

vermin PLURAL NOUN
animals or insects that cause damage or carry
disease, such as rats and fleas
verminous ADJECTIVE

vernacular NOUN
the ordinary language of a country or district

verruca NOUN
a wart on the sole of the foot

versatile ADJECTIVE
able to do or be used for different things
versatility NOUN

verse NOUN
1 writing arranged in short lines with a
particular rhythm
2 a group of lines forming a unit in a poem
or song
3 a numbered section of a chapter in the Bible

versed ADJECTIVE
versed in knowledgeable about

version NOUN
1 a particular person's account of something
2 a special or different form of something

versus PREPOSITION
against; competing with

vertebra NOUN **vertebrae**
each of the bones forming the backbone

vertebrate NOUN
an animal that has a backbone

vertex NOUN **vertices**
the highest point of a cone or triangle, or of a
hill etc.

vertical ADJECTIVE
at right angles to the horizontal; upright
vertically ADVERB

vertigo NOUN
a feeling of dizziness and loss of balance

verve (verv) NOUN
enthusiasm and liveliness

very ADVERB
1 to a great amount; extremely
2 (used for emphasis) *the very next day*

very ADJECTIVE
1 exact or actual *her very words*
2 extreme *the very end*

vessel NOUN
1 a ship or boat
2 a container for liquid
3 a tube carrying fluid in the body of an animal
or plant

vest NOUN
a sleeveless item of underwear worn on the
upper part of the body

vestibule NOUN
an entrance hall or lobby

vestige NOUN
a trace of something that once existed

vestment NOUN
a ceremonial garment worn by the clergy or
choir at a service

vestry NOUN **vestries**
a room in a church where the vestments
are kept

vet NOUN
a veterinary surgeon

vet VERB **vetting**, **vetted**
to make a careful check of a person or thing

vetch NOUN
a plant of the pea family

veteran NOUN
a person who has long experience, especially
an ex-member of the armed forces

veterinary surgeon NOUN
a person trained to give medical treatment to
animals

veto (**vee**-toh) NOUN **vetoes**
1 a refusal to let something happen
2 the right to prohibit something

veto VERB **vetoes**, **vetoing**, **vetoed**
to refuse or prohibit something

vex VERB
to annoy or cause worry to
vexation NOUN

vexed question NOUN
a problem that is difficult or much
discussed

via PREPOSITION
1 through; by way of *London to Exeter via
Bristol*
2 by means of

viable ADJECTIVE
able to work or exist successfully
viability NOUN

viaduct NOUN
a long arched bridge carrying a road or
railway over a valley

vibrant ADJECTIVE
full of energy; lively

vibrate VERB
1 to shake rapidly to and fro
2 to make a throbbing sound
vibration NOUN

vicar NOUN
a member of the Church of England clergy in
charge of a parish

vicarage

vicarage *NOUN*
the house of a vicar

vice[1] *NOUN*
1 evil or wickedness
2 a bad habit or fault

vice[2] *NOUN*
a device for gripping something and holding it firmly while you work on it

vice versa *ADVERB*
the other way round

vicinity *NOUN* **vicinities**
the area near or round a place

vicious *ADJECTIVE*
1 cruel and aggressive
2 severe or violent
viciously *ADVERB*

vicious circle *NOUN*
a situation in which a problem produces an effect which in turn makes the problem worse

victim *NOUN*
someone who is killed or harmed

victimize *VERB*
to single out for cruel or unfair treatment
victimization *NOUN*

victor *NOUN*
the winner

Victorian *ADJECTIVE*
belong to the time of Queen Victoria (1837–1901)
Victorian *NOUN*

victory *NOUN* **victories**
success won against an opponent in a battle, contest, or game
victorious *ADJECTIVE*

video *NOUN* **videos**
1 a video recorder or cassette
2 a recording on videotape

video *VERB* **videos, videoing, videoed**
to record on videotape

video recorder or **video cassette recorder** *NOUN*
a device for recording and playing video cassettes

videotape *NOUN*
magnetic tape suitable for recording television programmes

vie *VERB* **vies, vied**
to compete

view *NOUN*
1 what can be seen from one place
2 range of vision
3 an opinion
in view of because of

view *VERB*
1 to look at
2 to consider or regard

vineyard

viewer *NOUN*
someone who watches a television programme

viewpoint *NOUN*
1 an opinion or point of view
2 a place giving a good view

vigil *NOUN*
a period of staying awake to keep watch or to pray

vigilant *ADJECTIVE*
watchful; alert
vigilance *NOUN*

vigilante (vij-il-an-tee) *NOUN*
a member of an unofficial group organized to try to prevent crime in a community

vigorous *ADJECTIVE*
full of strength and energy
vigorously *ADVERB*

vigour *NOUN*
strength and energy

Viking *NOUN*
a Scandinavian trader and pirate in the 8th–10th centuries

vile *ADJECTIVE*
1 extremely disgusting
2 very bad or wicked
vilely *ADVERB*

vilify *VERB* **vilifies, vilified**
to say unpleasant things about
vilification *NOUN*

villa *NOUN*
a house, especially a holiday home abroad

village *NOUN*
a group of houses in a small country district
villager *NOUN*

villain *NOUN*
a wicked person or a criminal
villainous *ADJECTIVE* **villainy** *NOUN*

vindicate *VERB*
1 to clear of blame or suspicion
2 to prove to be true or worthwhile
vindication *NOUN*

vindictive *ADJECTIVE*
wanting revenge; spiteful
vindictively *ADVERB*

vine *NOUN*
a climbing or trailing plant producing grapes

vinegar *NOUN*
a sour liquid used to flavour food or in pickling

vineyard (vin-yard) *NOUN*
a plantation of vines for making wine

vintage *NOUN*
1 the harvest of a season's grapes
2 the wine made from this
3 the year or period from which something comes

vinyl *NOUN*
a kind of plastic

viola[1] (vee-**oh**-la) *NOUN*
a musical instrument like a large violin

viola[2] (**vy**-ol-a) *NOUN*
a plant of the kind including violets and pansies

violate *VERB*
1 to break a law, agreement, etc.
2 to treat a person or place with disrespect or violence
violation *NOUN*

violence *NOUN*
1 physical force that causes harm or injury
2 strength or intensity

violent *ADJECTIVE*
1 using or involving violence
2 strong or intense *a violent dislike*
violently *ADVERB*

violet *NOUN*
1 a small plant with purple flowers
2 purple

violin *NOUN*
a musical instrument with four strings, played with a bow
violinist *NOUN*

VIP *ABBREVIATION*
very important person

viper *NOUN*
a small poisonous snake

virgin *NOUN*
a person who has never had sexual intercourse
virginity *NOUN*

virgin *ADJECTIVE*
not yet touched or used *virgin snow*

virile *ADJECTIVE*
having masculine strength or vigour
virility *NOUN*

virtual *ADJECTIVE*
being something in effect though not strictly in fact

virtually *ADVERB*
nearly or almost

virtual reality *NOUN*
an image or environment produced by a computer that is so realistic that it seems to be part of the real world

virtue *NOUN*
1 moral goodness, or a particular form of this
2 a good quality or advantage
by virtue of because of

virtuoso *NOUN* **virtuosos**
a person with outstanding skill in singing or playing music
virtuosity *NOUN*

virtuous *ADJECTIVE*
morally good
virtuously *ADVERB*

virulent *ADJECTIVE*
1 strongly poisonous or harmful
2 bitterly hostile
virulence *NOUN*

virus *NOUN*
1 a tiny living thing smaller than a bacterium, which can cause disease
2 a hidden set of instructions in a computer program that is designed to destroy data

visa *NOUN*
an official mark put on a passport to show that the holder has permission to enter a foreign country

viscount (**vy**-kownt) *NOUN*
a nobleman ranking below an earl

viscous *ADJECTIVE*
(of a liquid) thick and gluey
viscosity *NOUN*

visibility *NOUN*
the distance you can see clearly

visible *ADJECTIVE*
able to be seen or noticed
visibly *ADVERB*

vision *NOUN*
1 the ability to see
2 something seen in the imagination or in a dream
3 foresight and wisdom
4 a beautiful person or thing

visionary *ADJECTIVE*
imaginative or fanciful

visionary *NOUN* **visionaries**
a person with imaginative ideas and plans

visit *VERB*
1 to go to see a person or place
2 to stay somewhere for a while

visit *NOUN*
1 the act of going to see a person or place
2 a short stay

visitation *NOUN*
an official visit

visitor *NOUN*
someone who visits

visor (**vy**-zer) *NOUN*
1 a part of a helmet that can be pulled down to cover the face
2 a shield to protect the eyes from bright light

vista NOUN
a long view

visual ADJECTIVE
to do with or used in seeing; to do with sight
visually ADVERB

visual display unit NOUN
a device like a television screen that displays
computer data

visualize VERB
to form a mental picture of
visualization NOUN

vital ADJECTIVE
1 necessary for life
2 essential; very important
vitally ADVERB

vitality NOUN
liveliness or energy

vitamin NOUN
any of a number of chemical substances that
are essential to keep people and animals
healthy

vitriolic ADJECTIVE
fiercely critical

vivacious ADJECTIVE
happy and lively
vivacity NOUN

vivid ADJECTIVE
1 bright and strong or clear
2 clear and lively
vividly ADVERB

vivisection NOUN
the practice of performing experiments on
live animals

vixen NOUN
a female fox

vocabulary NOUN **vocabularies**
1 all the words used in a particular subject or
language
2 the words a person uses
3 a list of words with their meanings

vocal ADJECTIVE
to do with or using the voice
vocally ADVERB

vocalist NOUN
a singer

vocation NOUN
1 a person's job or occupation
2 a strong desire to do a particular kind of work

vocational ADJECTIVE
teaching the skills needed for particular work
vocational training

vociferous ADJECTIVE
expressing views noisily and forcefully

vodka NOUN
a strong alcoholic drink made from potatoes
or grain

vogue NOUN
the current fashion

voice NOUN
1 sounds uttered by the mouth, especially in
speaking, singing, etc.
2 the ability to speak or sing
3 the right to express an opinion

voice VERB
to express something in words

void ADJECTIVE
1 empty
2 having no legal validity

void NOUN
an empty space or hole

volatile ADJECTIVE
1 (of a liquid) evaporating quickly
2 changing quickly in mood or behaviour
volatility NOUN

volcano NOUN **volcanoes**
a mountain with an opening from which lava,
ashes, and hot gases are thrown out when it
erupts
volcanic ADJECTIVE

vole NOUN
a small animal like a rat

volition NOUN
of your own volition choosing for yourself

volley NOUN **volleys**
1 a number of bullets or shells etc. fired at the
same time
2 a return of the ball in tennis etc. before it
touches the ground

volley VERB
to send or hit something in a volley or volleys

volleyball NOUN
a game in which two teams hit a large ball
over a net with their hands

volt NOUN
(*Science*) a unit for measuring electric force

voltage NOUN
electric force measured in volts

voluble ADJECTIVE
talking a lot
volubly ADVERB

volume NOUN
1 the amount of space filled by something
2 an amount or quantity *the volume of work*
3 the strength of sound
4 a book, especially one of a set

voluminous ADJECTIVE
large or bulky

voluntary *ADJECTIVE*
1 done or acting willingly
2 (of work) done without pay
voluntarily *ADVERB*

volunteer *VERB*
1 to offer to do something without being asked
2 to provide willingly or freely

volunteer *NOUN*
a person who volunteers

voluptuous *ADJECTIVE*
1 giving a luxurious feeling
2 (of a woman) having an attractively curved figure

vomit *VERB*
to bring up food from the stomach through the mouth
vomit *NOUN*

voodoo *NOUN*
a form of witchcraft and magic especially in the West Indies

voracious (vor-**ay**-shus) *ADJECTIVE*
1 having a large appetite
2 very eager *a voracious reader*
voracity *NOUN*

vortex *NOUN* **vortices**
a whirlpool or whirlwind

vote *VERB*
to show which person or thing you prefer by putting up your hand, marking a paper, etc.
voter *NOUN*

vote *NOUN*
1 the action of voting
2 the right to vote

vouch *VERB*
vouch for to support or guarantee

voucher *NOUN*
a piece of paper that can be exchanged for goods or money

vow *NOUN*
a solemn promise, especially to God

vow *VERB*
to make a vow

vowel *NOUN*
any of the letters *a, e, i, o, u,* and sometimes *y*

voyage *NOUN*
a long journey on water or in space

voyage *VERB*
to make a voyage
voyager *NOUN*

vulgar *ADJECTIVE*
1 rude or indecent
2 lacking good manners
vulgarity *NOUN*

vulgar fraction *NOUN*
a fraction shown by numbers above and below a line (e.g. ½)

vulnerable *ADJECTIVE*
able to be hurt or harmed or attacked
vulnerability *NOUN*

vulture *NOUN*
a large bird that feeds on dead animals

vulva *NOUN*
the outer parts of the female genitals

vying *present participle* of **vie**

Ww

wad *NOUN*
a pad or bundle of soft material, banknotes, papers, etc.

wadding *NOUN*
soft material used for padding

waddle *VERB*
to walk with short swaying steps like a duck
waddle *NOUN*

wade *VERB*
1 to walk through water or mud etc.
2 to read through something long or difficult

wafer *NOUN*
a kind of thin biscuit

waffle [1] *NOUN*
a small cake made of batter and eaten hot

waffle [2] *VERB*
(*informal*) to speak or write in a meaningless way
waffle *NOUN*

waft *VERB*
to carry or float gently through the air or over water

wag [1] *VERB* **wagging, wagged**
to move quickly from side to side
wag *NOUN*

wag [2] *NOUN*
a person who makes jokes

wage *NOUN* or **wages** *PLURAL NOUN*
a regular payment in return for work

wage *VERB*
to carry on a war or campaign

wager *NOUN*
a bet

wager *VERB*
to bet

waggle *VERB*
to move quickly to and fro
waggle *NOUN*

wagon *NOUN*
1 a cart with four wheels, for carrying loads
2 an open railway truck

waif *NOUN*
a homeless or neglected child

wail *VERB*
to make a long sad cry
wail *NOUN*

wainscot or **wainscoting** *NOUN*
wooden panelling on the wall of a room

waist *NOUN*
the narrow part in the middle of your body
Do not confuse this word with *waste*.

waistcoat *NOUN*
a short close-fitting jacket without sleeves, worn under a jacket

wait *VERB*
1 to stay or delay action until something happens
2 to be left to be dealt with later
3 to be a waiter or attendant

wait *NOUN*
an act or time of waiting *a long wait*

waiter *NOUN*
a man who serves food and drink in a restaurant

waitress *NOUN*
a woman who serves food and drink in a restaurant

waive *VERB*
to be willing to go without a benefit or privilege

wake [1] *VERB* **woke**, **woken**
1 to become conscious after sleeping
2 to revive from sleeping
wake *NOUN*
a gathering by the coffin of a dead person

wake [2] *NOUN*
1 the track left by a moving ship
2 currents of air left by a moving aircraft
in the wake of coming after

wakeful *ADJECTIVE*
unable to sleep

waken *VERB*
to wake

walk *VERB*
to move along on the feet at an ordinary speed
walker *NOUN*

walk *NOUN*
1 a journey on foot
2 the manner of walking
3 a path for walking

walkabout *NOUN*
an informal stroll among a crowd by an important visitor

walkie-talkie *NOUN*
a small portable radio transmitter and receiver

walkover *NOUN*
an easy victory

wall *NOUN*
1 an upright structure, forming a side of a building or room or enclosing an area
2 the outside part of something
the stomach wall
wall *VERB*
to enclose or block with a wall

wallaby *NOUN* **wallabies**
a kind of small kangaroo

wallet *NOUN*
a small flat folding case for holding banknotes, credit cards, etc.

wallflower *NOUN*
a garden plant with fragrant flowers, blooming in spring

wallop *VERB*
(*informal*) to hit or beat
wallop *NOUN*

wallow *VERB*
to roll about in water, mud, etc.

wallpaper *NOUN*
paper covering the inside walls of rooms

walnut *NOUN*
1 an edible nut with a wrinkled surface
2 the wood from the tree that bears this nut

walrus *NOUN*
a large sea animal with two long tusks

waltz *NOUN*
a dance with three beats to a bar
waltz *VERB*
to dance a waltz

wan (wonn) *ADJECTIVE*
pale from being ill or tired

wand *NOUN*
a thin rod used by a magician or conjuror

wander *VERB*
1 to go about without reaching a particular place
2 to leave the right route
3 to be distracted or digress
wanderer *NOUN*

wander *NOUN*
a wandering journey

wane *VERB*
1 (of the moon) to appear gradually smaller after being full
2 to become less or weaker

wane _NOUN_
on the wane becoming less or weaker

wangle _VERB_
(_informal_) to arrange something by trickery or clever planning

want _VERB_
1 to wish to have something
2 to be without something

want _NOUN_
1 a wish to have something
2 a lack or need

wanted _ADJECTIVE_
(of a suspected criminal) sought by the police

wanting _ADJECTIVE_
lacking in what is needed or usual

wanton _ADJECTIVE_
pointless; without a motive _wanton damage_

war _NOUN_
1 fighting between nations or groups
2 a struggle or effort against crime, disease, etc.

warble _VERB_
to sing with a trilling sound
warble _NOUN_

warbler _NOUN_
a kind of small songbird

ward _NOUN_
1 a room with beds in a hospital
2 a child looked after by a guardian
3 an area electing a councillor

ward _VERB_
ward off to keep something away

warden _NOUN_
an official in charge of a hostel, college, etc.

warder _NOUN_
a guard in a prison

wardrobe _NOUN_
1 a cupboard for hanging clothes
2 a stock of clothes or costumes

ware _NOUN_
manufactured goods of a certain kind
hardware
wares goods offered for sale

warehouse _NOUN_
a large building for storing goods

warfare _NOUN_
the act of fighting a war

warhead _NOUN_
the part of a missile etc. containing the explosive

warlike _ADJECTIVE_
1 fond of making war
2 threatening war

warm _ADJECTIVE_
1 fairly hot
2 keeping the body warm
3 friendly or enthusiastic
4 close to the right answer

warm _VERB_
to make or become warm

warm-blooded _ADJECTIVE_
(of animals) having blood that is constantly warm

warmth _NOUN_
1 gentle heat
2 friendliness

warn _VERB_
1 to advise someone about a possible danger or difficulty
2 to give cautionary advice _warned us not to be late_
warn off to advise someone to keep away or to avoid something

warning _NOUN_
advice about a possible danger or difficulty

warp _VERB_
1 to bend or twist out of shape
2 to distort a person's ideas, judgement, etc.

warp _NOUN_
1 a warped condition
2 the lengthwise threads in weaving

warpath _NOUN_
on the warpath angry and ready for a fight or argument

warrant _NOUN_
a document authorizing a person to act in some way _a search warrant_

warrant _VERB_
1 to justify
2 to guarantee

warranty _NOUN_ **warranties**
a guarantee

warren _NOUN_
1 a network of rabbits' burrows
2 a building or place with many winding passages

warring _ADJECTIVE_
involved in war

warrior _NOUN_
a person who fights in battle

warship _NOUN_
a ship used in war

wart _NOUN_
a small hard lump on the skin

wartime _NOUN_
a time of war

wary _ADJECTIVE_ **warier, wariest**
cautious and aware of possible danger or difficulty
warily _ADVERB_

w

wash VERB
1 to clean with water or other liquid
2 to flow against or over something
3 to carry along by a moving liquid
was washed overboard
4 (*informal*) to be believed *an excuse that won't wash*
wash up to wash the dishes after a meal

wash NOUN
1 the action of washing
2 clothes etc. being washed
3 the disturbed water behind a moving ship
4 a thin coating of colour

washbasin NOUN
a small sink for washing the hands and face

washer NOUN
a small ring of rubber or metal etc. placed between two surfaces to fit them tightly together

washing NOUN
clothes etc. being washed

washing machine NOUN
a machine for washing clothes etc.

washing-up NOUN
dishes and cutlery to be washed after a meal

washout NOUN
(*informal*) a complete failure

wasn't
was not

wasp NOUN
a stinging insect with black and yellow stripes

wastage NOUN
loss of something by waste

waste VERB
1 to use something extravagantly or without effect
2 to fail to use an opportunity etc.
3 to become gradually weaker or thinner

waste ADJECTIVE
1 left over or thrown away
2 not used or usable *waste land*

waste NOUN
1 the wasting of a thing
2 things that are not wanted or not used
3 an area of waste land
Do not confuse this word with *waist*.

wasteful ADJECTIVE
using something extravagantly or to no effect
wastefully NOUN

wasteland NOUN
a barren or empty area of land

wastrel NOUN
a person who does nothing useful

watch VERB
1 to look at closely
2 to be on guard or ready for something
3 to pay careful attention to something
Watch where you put your feet.
4 to take care of

watch NOUN
1 a small clock worn on the wrist
2 the action of watching
3 a turn of being on duty on a ship

watchdog NOUN
1 a dog kept to guard property
2 an official person or committee that monitors the activities of business companies

watchful ADJECTIVE
watching closely; alert
watchfully ADVERB

watchman NOUN **watchmen**
a person employed to patrol an empty building

watchword NOUN
a motto or slogan

water NOUN
1 a colourless tasteless liquid that is a compound of hydrogen and oxygen
2 a lake or sea
pass water to urinate

water VERB
1 to sprinkle or supply with water
2 (of the eyes or mouth) to produce tears or saliva
water down to dilute

water closet NOUN
a toilet with a pan flushed by water

watercolour NOUN
1 paint made with water and not oil
2 a painting done with this paint

watercress NOUN
a kind of cress that grows in water

waterfall NOUN
a place where a river or stream flows over the edge of a cliff or large rock

water lily NOUN **water lilies**
a water plant with broad leaves and large flowers

waterlogged ADJECTIVE
completely soaked or swamped in water

watermark NOUN
a design that can be seen in some kinds of paper when they are held up to the light

watermelon NOUN
a large melon with a smooth green skin, red flesh, and watery juice

watermill NOUN
a mill worked by a waterwheel

water polo NOUN
a game played by teams of swimmers with a ball like a football

waterproof *ADJECTIVE*
keeping out water

watershed *NOUN*
1 a ridge from which streams flow down on each side
2 a major change in events

water-skiing *NOUN*
the sport of riding on water on a pair of skis, towed by a boat

watertight *ADJECTIVE*
1 made or fastened so that water cannot get in or out
2 (of an excuse etc.) completely convincing

waterway *NOUN*
a river or canal for ships

waterwheel *NOUN*
a large wheel turned by a flow of water

waterworks *PLURAL NOUN*
a place with pumping machinery etc. for supplying water

watery *ADJECTIVE*
1 like water
2 full of water
3 containing too much water

watt *NOUN*
(*Science*) a unit of electric power

wattle *NOUN*
1 sticks and twigs woven together to make fences
2 an Australian tree with golden flowers
3 a red fold of skin hanging from the throat of a turkey

wave *NOUN*
1 the action of waving
2 a ridge moving along the surface of the sea etc.
3 a curling piece of hair
4 (*Science*) the wave-like movement of heat, light, sound, etc.
5 a sudden build-up of emotion

wave *VERB*
1 to move the hand to and fro as a greeting etc.
2 to move loosely to and fro
3 to curl

wavelength *NOUN*
the distance between corresponding points on a sound wave or electromagnetic wave

waver *VERB*
1 to be unsteady
2 to hesitate

wavy *ADJECTIVE* **wavier**, **waviest**
having waves or curves

wax [1] *NOUN*
1 a soft substance that melts easily, used to make candles, crayons, and polish
2 beeswax
3 a sticky substance in the ear
waxy *ADJECTIVE*

wax *VERB*
to coat or polish with wax

wax [2] *VERB*
(of the moon) to appear gradually larger

waxen *ADJECTIVE*
1 made of wax
2 like wax

waxwork *NOUN*
a model of a person etc. made in wax

way *NOUN*
1 how something is done
2 a manner *spoke in a friendly way*
3 a path or road
4 a route or direction
5 a distance to be travelled
6 an aspect *a good idea in some ways*
7 a condition or state *in a bad way*
give way 1 to collapse **2** to yield **in the way** forming an obstacle

waylay *VERB* **waylaid**
to wait for someone and stop them

wayside *NOUN*
fall by the wayside to fail to keep going

wayward *ADJECTIVE*
wilfully doing what you want

WC *ABBREVIATION*
water closet

we *PRONOUN*
a word used to refer to the person speaking or writing together with others

weak *ADJECTIVE*
1 having little power or effect
2 easy to damage or defeat
3 not great in strength or intensity

weaken *VERB*
to make or become weaker

weakling *NOUN*
a weak person or animal

weakness *NOUN*
1 a lack of strength
2 a liking for something

weal *NOUN*
a ridge raised on the flesh by a cane or whip etc.

wealth *NOUN*
1 a lot of money or property
2 a large quantity

wealthy *ADJECTIVE* **wealthier**, **wealthiest**
having wealth; rich

wean *VERB*
to make a baby take food other than its mother's milk

weapon *NOUN*
a device used to harm or kill people in a battle or fight
weaponry *NOUN*

wear *VERB* **wore**, **worn**
1 to have clothes, jewellery, etc. on your body
2 to have a certain expression
3 to damage or become damaged by use
4 to last while in use
wear off to become less intense **wear out**
1 to use or be used until it is useless 2 to exhaust

wear *NOUN*
1 clothes of a certain kind *evening wear*
2 gradual damage caused by use

wearisome *ADJECTIVE*
causing tiredness or boredom

weary *ADJECTIVE* **wearier**, **weariest**
1 tired from exertion
2 tiring *weary work*
wearily *ADVERB*

weary *VERB* **wearies**, **wearied**
1 to make weary
2 to grow tired of something

weasel *NOUN*
a small fierce animal with a slender body and reddish-brown fur

weather *NOUN*
the rain, snow, wind, sunshine, etc. at a particular time or place
under the weather feeling unwell

weather *VERB*
1 to expose to the effects of the weather
2 to survive a danger *to weather a storm*

weather-beaten *ADJECTIVE*
damaged or affected by the weather

weathercock or **weathervane** *NOUN*
a pointer that turns in the wind and shows its direction

weave *VERB* **wove**, **woven**
1 to make material or baskets etc. by crossing threads or strips under and over each other
2 to put a story together
3 (*past tense and past participle* **weaved**) to twist and turn *weaving through the traffic*
weaver *NOUN*

web *NOUN*
1 a cobweb
2 something complicated *a web of lies*
the Web the World Wide Web

webbed or **web-footed** *ADJECTIVE*
having toes joined by pieces of skin

weblog *NOUN*
a personal diary or journal put on the Internet

web page *NOUN*
a document forming part of a website

website *NOUN*
a place on the Internet giving information about a subject, company, etc.

wed *VERB*
to marry

wedding *NOUN*
the ceremony at which a man and a woman get married

wedge *NOUN*
1 a piece of wood or metal etc. that is thick at one end and thin at the other, used to force surfaces apart or keep something in place
2 a wedge-shaped thing

wedge *VERB*
1 to keep something in place with a wedge
2 to pack tightly together

wedlock *NOUN*
the state of being married

Wednesday *NOUN*
the day of the week following Tuesday

wee *ADJECTIVE*
(*Scottish*) small; little

weed *NOUN*
a wild plant that grows where it is not wanted
weed *VERB*
to remove weeds from the ground

weedy *ADJECTIVE* **weedier**, **weediest**
1 full of weeds
2 thin and weak

week *NOUN*
a period of seven days, especially from Sunday to the following Saturday

weekday *NOUN*
a day other than Saturday or Sunday

weekend *NOUN*
Saturday and Sunday

weekly *ADJECTIVE, ADVERB*
happening or done once a week

weeny *ADJECTIVE* **weenier**, **weeniest**
(*informal*) tiny

weep *VERB* **wept**
1 to shed tears; to cry
2 to ooze moisture

weeping *ADJECTIVE*
(of a tree) having drooping branches

weevil *NOUN*
a kind of small beetle

weft *NOUN*
the threads on a loom that are woven across the warp

weigh *VERB*
1 to measure how heavy something is
2 to have a certain weight *weighs six kilograms*
3 be important or have influence
weigh up to estimate or assess

a b c d e f g h i j k l m n o p q r s t u v **w** x y z

weight NOUN
1 the amount that something weighs
2 a piece of metal of a specific weight, used in weighing things
3 a heavy object
4 importance or influence

weight VERB
to attach a weight to

weighty ADJECTIVE **weightier**, **weightiest**
1 heavy
2 important or serious

weir (weer) NOUN
a dam across a river or canal

weird ADJECTIVE
very strange; uncanny

welcome NOUN
a greeting or reception, especially a friendly one

welcome ADJECTIVE
1 pleased to receive or see
2 freely allowed *You are welcome to come.*

welcome VERB
1 to show pleasure when a person or thing arrives
2 to accept gladly

weld VERB
1 to join pieces of metal or plastic by heating and pressing them
2 to join into a whole

welfare NOUN
people's health and happiness

welfare state NOUN
a system in which the government funds health care, social services, etc.

well [1] NOUN
1 a deep hole dug to bring up water or oil from underground
2 a deep space, e.g. containing a staircase

well VERB
to rise or flow up

well [2] ADVERB **better**, **best**
1 in a good or suitable way
2 thoroughly *Polish it well.*
3 probably or reasonably *may well be the last chance*

well ADJECTIVE
1 in good health
2 satisfactory

well-being NOUN
good health and comfort

wellingtons PLURAL NOUN
rubber or plastic waterproof boots

well-known ADJECTIVE
1 known to many people
2 known thoroughly

well-meaning ADJECTIVE
having good intentions

well-nigh ADVERB
almost

well off ADJECTIVE
fairly rich and comfortable

well-read ADJECTIVE
having read many books

well-to-do ADJECTIVE
fairly rich

welsh VERB
to cheat someone by avoiding paying a debt

welt NOUN
1 a strip or border
2 a weal

welter NOUN
a confused mixture

wench NOUN
(*old use*) a girl or young woman

wend VERB
wend your way to go slowly but steadily

weren't
were not

werewolf NOUN **werewolves**
(in stories) a person who can change into a wolf

west NOUN
1 the direction where the sun sets
2 the western part of a country, city, etc.

west ADJECTIVE, ADVERB
towards or in the west; coming from the west

westerly ADJECTIVE
1 coming from the west
2 facing the west

western ADJECTIVE
of or in the west

western NOUN
a film or story about cowboys in western North America

westward ADJECTIVE, ADVERB
towards the west
westwards ADVERB

wet ADJECTIVE **wetter**, **wettest**
1 soaked or covered in liquid
2 (of paint etc.) not yet dry
3 (of weather) raining a lot
wetness NOUN

wet VERB **wetting**, **wet** or **wetted**
to make wet

wet suit NOUN
a close-fitting rubber suit worn by divers etc. to keep the body warm and dry

whack *VERB*
(*informal*) to hit hard
whack *NOUN*

whale *NOUN*
a large sea mammal

whaler *NOUN*
a person or ship that hunts whales

whaling *NOUN*
the hunting of whales

wharf (worf) *NOUN* **wharves** or **wharfs**
a quay for loading and unloading ships

what *ADJECTIVE*
1 used to ask the amount or kind of
something *What book is that?*
2 used to express degree *What a time we had!*

what *PRONOUN*
1 what thing or things *What did they say?*
2 the thing that *This is what you must do.*

whatever *PRONOUN*
1 anything or everything *whatever you like*
2 no matter what *whatever happens*

whatever *ADJECTIVE*
of any kind or amount *Take whatever books
you need.*

whatsoever *ADJECTIVE*
at all

wheat *NOUN*
a cereal plant from which flour is made
wheaten *ADJECTIVE*

wheedle *VERB*
to persuade by coaxing or flattering

wheel *NOUN*
1 a disc-shaped device that turns on a shaft,
fitted to something to make it move
2 a steering wheel
3 a revolving disc used in shaping pottery

wheel *VERB*
1 to push a bicycle or trolley etc. along
2 to move in a curve or circle

wheelbarrow *NOUN*
a small hand-pushed cart with a wheel at the
front

wheelchair *NOUN*
a chair on wheels for a disabled person

wheeze *VERB*
to make a hoarse sound in breathing
wheeze *NOUN* **wheezy** *ADJECTIVE*

whelk *NOUN*
a shellfish that looks like a snail

when *ADVERB*
at what time *When can you come?*

when *CONJUNCTION*
1 at the time that *The bird flew away when I
moved.*
2 although; considering that *Why stay when
there's nothing to do?*

whence *ADVERB, CONJUNCTION*
from where; from which

whenever *CONJUNCTION*
at whatever time; every time

where *ADVERB, CONJUNCTION*
in or to what place or that place

whereabouts *ADVERB*
in or near what place

whereabouts *PLURAL NOUN*
the place where something is

whereas *CONJUNCTION*
but in contrast *Some people like sport, whereas
others do not.*

whereby *ADVERB*
by which

whereupon *CONJUNCTION*
after which; and then

wherever *ADVERB*
in or to whatever place

whet *VERB* **whetting, whetted**
to sharpen a knife etc.
whet your appetite to make you hungry

whether *CONJUNCTION*
as one possibility; if *I don't know whether to
believe them or not.*

whey (*say as* way) *NOUN*
the watery liquid left when milk forms curds

which *ADJECTIVE*
what particular *Which way did he go?*

which *PRONOUN*
1 what person or thing *Which is your desk?*
2 the person or thing referred to *the film,
which is a western*

whichever *PRONOUN, ADJECTIVE*
no matter which; any which

whiff *NOUN*
a puff or slight smell of smoke, gas, etc.

while *CONJUNCTION*
1 during the time that; as long as
while you work
2 although; but *She is dark, while her sister
is fair.*

while *NOUN*
a period of time *a long while*

while *VERB*
while away to pass time idly

whilst *CONJUNCTION*
while

whim *NOUN*
a sudden wish

whimper *VERB*
to cry or whine softly
whimper *NOUN*

whimsical *ADJECTIVE*
quaint and playful

whine *VERB*
1 to make a long high miserable cry
2 to complain in a petty way
whine *NOUN*

whinge *VERB* **whinging** or **whingeing**
(*informal*) to grumble persistently
whinge *NOUN*

whinny *VERB* **whinnies**, **whinnied**
to neigh gently
whinny *NOUN*

whip *NOUN*
1 a strip of leather fixed to a handle and used
for hitting people or animals
2 an official of a political party in Parliament
3 a pudding of whipped cream and flavouring

whip *VERB* **whipping**, **whipped**
1 to hit with a whip
2 to beat cream until it is thick
3 to move or take suddenly *whipped out
a knife*
4 (*informal*) to steal
whip up to stir up people's feelings etc.

whippet *NOUN*
a racing dog like a small greyhound

whirl *VERB*
to turn or spin quickly
whirl *NOUN*

whirlpool *NOUN*
a whirling current of water

whirlwind *NOUN*
a strong wind that whirls round a central
point

whirr *VERB*
to make a continuous buzzing sound
whirr *NOUN*

whisk *VERB*
1 to move or take away quickly and lightly
2 to beat eggs etc.

whisk *NOUN*
1 a kitchen tool used for whisking
2 a whisking movement

whisker *NOUN*
1 a long bristle growing near the mouth of
a cat etc.
2 each of the hairs growing on a man's face
whiskery *ADJECTIVE*

whisky *NOUN* **whiskies**
a strong alcoholic drink made from grain

whisper *VERB*
1 to speak very softly
2 to talk secretly
whisper *NOUN*

whist *NOUN*
a card game for four people

whistle *VERB*
to make a shrill sound by blowing through the
lips or an instrument

whistle *NOUN*
1 a whistling sound
2 a device that makes a whistling sound

white *ADJECTIVE*
1 of the lightest colour, like snow or salt
2 having light-coloured skin
3 very pale from the effects of illness or
fear etc.
4 (of coffee or tea) with milk

white *NOUN*
1 the lightest colour
2 the transparent part round the yolk
of an egg

white elephant *NOUN*
a useless possession that causes the owner a
lot of trouble

white-hot *ADJECTIVE*
extremely hot; so hot that heated metal looks
white

white lie *NOUN*
a harmless or trivial lie

whiten *VERB*
to make or become whiter

whitewash *NOUN*
a white liquid containing lime or powdered
chalk, used for painting walls etc.

whitewash *VERB*
1 to cover with whitewash
2 to conceal a mistake

whither *ADVERB, CONJUNCTION*
(*old use*) to what place

whiting *NOUN*
a small sea fish with white flesh

Whitsun *NOUN*
Whit Sunday and the days close to it

Whit Sunday
the seventh Sunday after Easter

whittle *VERB*
1 to shape wood by trimming
2 to reduce something gradually

whizz or **whiz** *VERB*
1 to sound like something rushing through
the air
2 to move very quickly

who *PRONOUN*
which person or people; the particular person
or people *the person who gave the money*

whoever *PRONOUN*
1 any or every person who
2 no matter who

whole *ADJECTIVE*
1 complete
2 not injured or broken

a
b
c
d
e
f
g
h
i
j
k
l
m
n
o
p
q
r
s
t
u
v
w
x
y
z

whole NOUN
1 the full amount
2 a complete thing
on the whole considering everything

wholefood NOUN
naturally produced food

wholehearted ADJECTIVE
without doubts or reservations

wholemeal ADJECTIVE
made from the whole grain of wheat

whole number NOUN
a number without fractions

wholesale NOUN
the selling of goods in large quantities to
shops for selling to the public
wholesaler NOUN

wholesale ADJECTIVE, ADVERB
1 on a large scale *wholesale destruction*
2 in the wholesale trade

wholesome ADJECTIVE
good for health; healthy

wholly ADVERB
completely or entirely

whom PRONOUN
the form of **who** used when it is the object of
a verb or comes after a preposition

whoop NOUN
a loud cry of excitement

whoop VERB
to make a whoop

whooping cough (hoop-ing) NOUN
an infectious disease that causes coughing
spasms and gasping for breath

whopper NOUN
(*informal*) something very large

whopping ADJECTIVE
(*informal*) very large or remarkable

who's
who is; who has *Who's there? I don't know
who's done it.*
   Do not confuse this word with *whose*.

whose PRONOUN
belonging to whom or which *Whose house is
that? He's a man whose opinion I respect.*
   Do not confuse this word with *who's*.

why ADVERB
for what reason or purpose *Why did you do it?
This is why I came.*

wick NOUN
the thread in the middle of a candle or in a
lamp etc. that carries the fuel to the flame

wicked ADJECTIVE
1 morally bad or cruel
2 mischievous *a wicked smile*
3 (*informal*) excellent
wickedness NOUN

wicker NOUN
thin canes or twigs woven together to make
baskets or furniture etc.
wickerwork NOUN

wicket NOUN
1 a set of three stumps and two bails used
in cricket
2 the strip of ground between the wickets

wide ADJECTIVE
1 measuring a lot from side to side
2 measuring from side to side *one metre wide*
3 covering a great range
4 missing the target *wide of the mark*

wide ADVERB
1 to the full extent *wide open*
2 missing the target *a shot that went wide*
3 over a large area *far and wide*

widely ADVERB
among many people

widen VERB
to make or become wider

widespread ADJECTIVE
existing in many places or over a wide area

widow NOUN
a woman whose husband has died
widowed ADJECTIVE

widower NOUN
a man whose wife has died

width NOUN
how wide something is

wield VERB
1 to hold and use a weapon or tool
2 to have and use power or influence

wife NOUN **wives**
the woman to whom a man is married

Wi-Fi NOUN
(*ICT*) a system of transferring data from one
computer to another using radio waves
instead of wires

wig NOUN
a covering of artificial hair

wiggle VERB
to move from side to side
wiggle NOUN **wiggly** ADJECTIVE

wigwam NOUN
a traditional Native American tent made with
animal skins

wild ADJECTIVE
1 living or growing in its natural state
2 not cultivated *a wild landscape*
3 not controlled; violent or excited
4 strange or unreasonable *wild ideas*
wildly ADVERB

a
b
c
d
e
f
g
h
i
j
k
l
m
n
o
p
q
r
s
t
u
v
w
x
y
z

wilderness *NOUN*
a wild uncultivated area

wildfire *NOUN*
spread like wildfire (of rumours etc.) to spread quickly

wild goose chase *NOUN*
a futile search

wildlife *NOUN*
wild animals in their natural setting

wile *NOUN*
a piece of trickery

wilful *ADJECTIVE*
1 obstinately determined
2 deliberate *wilful damage*
wilfully *ADVERB*

will [1] *AUXILIARY VERB*
used to express the future tense, questions, or promises *They will arrive soon. Will you shut the door? I will get my revenge.*

will [2] *NOUN*
1 the mental power to decide what you do
2 a chosen decision *against my will*
3 determination *set to work with a will*
4 a written statement of what is to happen to a person's property after their death

will *VERB*
to use your will power *was willing you to win*

willing *ADJECTIVE*
ready and happy to do what is wanted
willingly *ADVERB*

will-o'-the-wisp *NOUN*
a flickering spot of light seen on marshy ground

willow *NOUN*
a tree with long flexible branches

will power *NOUN*
strength of mind to control what you do

willy-nilly *ADVERB*
whether you want to or not

wilt *VERB*
1 to lose freshness
2 to lose strength or energy

wily *ADJECTIVE* **wilier**, **wiliest**
cunning or crafty

wimp *NOUN*
(*informal*) a weak or timid person

win *VERB* **winning**, **won**
1 to defeat opponents in a battle, game, or contest
2 to get or achieve by a victory or by using effort or skill
win over to gain someone's favour or support

win *NOUN*
a victory

wince *VERB*
to make a slight movement from pain or embarrassment etc.

winch *NOUN*
a device using a rope or cable for lifting or pulling things

winch *VERB*
to lift or pull with a winch

wind [1] (rhymes with *tinned*) *NOUN*
1 a current of air
2 gas in the stomach or intestines
3 breath used for running or speaking
4 the wind instruments of an orchestra

wind *VERB*
to make a person out of breath

wind [2] (rhymes with *find*) *VERB* **wound**
1 to go or turn in twists, curves, or circles
2 to tighten the spring of a clock or watch
3 to wrap round
wind up (*informal*) to end up in a place or condition

windfall *NOUN*
1 a piece of unexpected good luck, especially money
2 a fruit blown off a tree by the wind

wind instrument *NOUN*
a musical instrument played by blowing into it

windmill *NOUN*
a mill worked by the wind turning its sails

window *NOUN*
1 an opening with glass in a wall or roof etc. to let in light and air
2 (*ICT*) a framed area on a computer screen

windpipe *NOUN*
the tube by which air passes from the throat to the lungs

windscreen *NOUN*
the window at the front of a motor vehicle

windsurfing *NOUN*
the sport of riding on water on a board with a sail
windsurfer *NOUN*

windward *ADJECTIVE, ADVERB*
facing the wind

windy *ADJECTIVE* **windier**, **windiest**
with a lot of wind

wine *NOUN*
1 an alcoholic drink made from grapes or other plants
2 a dark red colour

wing NOUN
1 each of the limbs of a bird, bat, or insect used for flying
2 each of the long flat parts on either side of an aircraft that support it in the air
3 a part extending from the main part of a building
4 the part of a vehicle body above a wheel
5 a player positioned at the edge of the pitch in football or hockey etc.
6 a section of a political party
7 each side of a theatre stage out of sight of the audience

wing VERB
1 to travel by means of wings
2 to wound a bird in the wing

winged ADJECTIVE
having wings

wink VERB
1 to close and open the eye quickly
2 (of a light) to flicker or twinkle

wink NOUN
the action of winking

winkle NOUN
a kind of edible shellfish

winkle VERB
winkle out to get hold of information etc. with difficulty

winner NOUN
1 a person or animal etc. that wins
2 something successful

winnings PLURAL NOUN
money won in gambling

winter NOUN
the coldest season of the year, between autumn and spring

wintry ADJECTIVE
cold and wet

wipe VERB
to dry or clean by rubbing
wipe out to cancel or destroy
wipe NOUN

wiper NOUN
a device fitted to a vehicle's windscreen to wipe it

wire NOUN
1 a strand of metal
2 a length of this carrying an electric current

wire VERB
1 to fit with wires to carry electric current
2 to fasten or strengthen with wire

wireless NOUN
(old use) a radio

wireless ADJECTIVE
not using electrical wires

wiring NOUN
the system of electrical wires

wiry ADJECTIVE **wirier, wiriest**
1 like wire
2 lean and strong

wisdom NOUN
1 the quality of being wise
2 wise sayings or writings

wisdom tooth NOUN
a molar tooth at the back of the jaw of an adult

wise ADJECTIVE
1 judging well; showing good sense
2 knowledgeable
wisely ADVERB

wish VERB
1 to feel or say what you would like to do or happen
2 to hope for someone *I wish you luck.*

wish NOUN
1 something wished; a desire
2 the action of wishing

wishbone NOUN
a forked bone between the neck and breast of a chicken

wishful ADJECTIVE
wanting something

wishful thinking NOUN
the act of believing something to be true just because you want it to be

wisp NOUN
1 a few strands of hair or bits of straw etc.
2 a small streak of smoke or cloud etc.
wispy ADJECTIVE

wistful ADJECTIVE
sadly longing for something
wistfully ADVERB

wit NOUN
1 intelligence or cleverness
2 a clever kind of humour
3 a witty person

witch NOUN
(in stories) a woman with magic powers

witchcraft NOUN
the use of magic for bad purposes

witch doctor NOUN
a person who is believed to use magic to heal people

with PREPOSITION
1 in the company of *Come with me.*
2 having *a man with a beard*
3 using *hitting it with a hammer*
4 because of *shaking with laughter*
5 towards *angry with him*
6 against *was arguing with me*
7 separated from *had to part with it*

withdraw _VERB_ **withdrew, withdrawn**
1 to take back or away
2 to go away

withdrawal _NOUN_
1 the act of withdrawing
2 a sum of money taken out of an account
3 the process of no longer taking addictive drugs, often with unpleasant reactions

withdrawn _ADJECTIVE_
shy or reserved

wither _VERB_
to shrivel or wilt

withering _ADJECTIVE_
(of a remark or look) scornful or sarcastic

withhold _VERB_ **withheld**
to refuse to give or allow something

within _PREPOSITION, ADVERB_
inside; not beyond

without _PREPOSITION_
1 not having _without food_
2 free from _without fear_

withstand _VERB_ **withstood**
to endure or resist

witness _NOUN_
1 a person who sees or hears something happen
2 a person who gives evidence in a lawcourt

witness _VERB_
1 to be a witness of
2 to sign a document to confirm that it is genuine

witticism _NOUN_
a witty remark

witty _ADJECTIVE_ **wittier, wittiest**
clever and amusing
wittily _ADVERB_

wizard _NOUN_
1 (in stories) a magician
2 a person with amazing abilities
wizardry _NOUN_

wizened _ADJECTIVE_
full of wrinkles

woad _NOUN_
a kind of blue dye formerly made from a plant

wobble _VERB_
to move unsteadily from side to side
wobble _NOUN_ **wobbly** _ADJECTIVE_

woe _NOUN_
1 sorrow or misfortune
2 a cause of this

woebegone _ADJECTIVE_
looking unhappy

woeful _ADJECTIVE_
1 sorrowful
2 deplorable
woefully _ADVERB_

wok _NOUN_
a Chinese cooking pan shaped like a large bowl

wolf _NOUN_ **wolves**
a wild animal of the dog family that hunts in packs

wolf _VERB_
to eat greedily

woman _NOUN_ **women**
a grown-up female human being

womanly _ADJECTIVE_
having qualities typical of women

womb _NOUN_
the organ in a female's body in which young develop before they are born

wombat _NOUN_
an Australian animal like a small bear

wonder _NOUN_
1 a feeling of surprise and admiration
2 something that causes this

wonder _VERB_
1 to feel that you want to know
2 to feel wonder

wonderful _ADJECTIVE_
marvellous or excellent
wonderfully _ADVERB_

wonderment _NOUN_
a feeling of wonder

wondrous _ADJECTIVE_
(old use) wonderful

wont (wohnt) _ADJECTIVE_
(old use) accustomed _was wont to dress in rags_

won't
will not

woo _VERB_ **woos, wooing, wooed** (old use)
1 to court a woman
2 to seek favour or support

wood _NOUN_
1 the substance of which trees are made
2 a large group of trees

wooded _ADJECTIVE_
covered with growing trees

wooden _ADJECTIVE_
1 made of wood
2 showing no expression or life

woodland _NOUN_
wooded country

woodlouse _NOUN_
a small crawling creature able to roll into a ball

woodpecker _NOUN_
a bird that taps tree trunks with its beak to find insects

woodwind NOUN
wind instruments that are usually made of wood, e.g. the clarinet and oboe

woodwork NOUN
1 the making of wooden objects
2 things made out of wood

woodworm NOUN
the larva of a beetle that bores into wood and damages it

woody ADJECTIVE **woodier**, **woodiest**
1 like or made of wood
2 having many trees

woof NOUN
the gruff bark of a dog

wool NOUN
1 the thick soft hair of sheep and goats etc.
2 thread or cloth made from this

woollen ADJECTIVE
made of wool

woolly ADJECTIVE
1 covered with wool or hair
2 like wool; woollen
3 vague or confused
woolliness NOUN

word NOUN
1 a set of sounds or letters with a meaning
2 a brief conversation
3 a promise
4 a command or spoken signal
5 a message *to send word*

word VERB
to express in words

wording NOUN
the way something is worded

word processor NOUN
a type of computer or program used for editing and printing documents

wordy ADJECTIVE **wordier**, **wordiest**
using many words; not concise

wore *past tense* of **wear** VERB

work NOUN
1 something you have to do that needs effort or energy
2 a job; employment
3 (*Science*) the result of applying a force to move an object
4 a piece of writing, painting, music, etc.
the works of Shakespeare

work VERB
1 to do work
2 to have a job
3 to act or operate correctly
4 to operate a machine etc.
5 to shape or press etc.
6 to move gradually into a particular position
The screw had worked loose.

work out 1 to find an answer by thinking or calculating 2 to have a particular result

workable ADJECTIVE
that can be used or done; practical

worker NOUN
a person who works in a particular industry

workforce NOUN
the number of people who work in a particular place

working class NOUN
people who are employed in manual or industrial work

workmanship NOUN
skill in working; the result of this

work of art NOUN
a fine picture, building, etc.

workout NOUN
a session of physical exercise

works PLURAL NOUN
1 the moving parts of a machine
2 a factory or industrial site

workshop NOUN
a place where things are made or mended

world NOUN
1 the earth with all its countries and peoples
2 all the people on the earth
3 a planet
4 everything to do with a certain activity *the world of sport*
5 a large amount *will do them a world of good*

worldly ADJECTIVE
1 to do with material things on earth
2 interested only in money, pleasure, etc.

worldwide ADJECTIVE, ADVERB
over the whole world

World Wide Web NOUN
a vast information system that connects sites and documents on the Internet

worm NOUN
1 a creeping animal with a long soft rounded or flat body and no backbone or limbs
2 an unimportant or unpleasant person

worm VERB
to move along by wriggling or crawling
worm out to get information from someone by constant questioning

worn *past participle* of **wear** VERB

worn out ADJECTIVE
1 tired and exhausted
2 damaged by use

worried ADJECTIVE
feeling or showing worry

worry VERB **worries**, **worried**
1 to be troublesome to someone
2 to feel anxious
worrier NOUN

worry NOUN **worries**
1 the condition of worrying; anxiety
2 something that makes a person worry

worse ADJECTIVE, ADVERB
more bad or more badly
worse off less fortunate or well off

worsen VERB
to make or become worse

worship VERB **worshipping**, **worshipped**
1 to give praise or respect to God or a god
2 to love or admire greatly
worshipper NOUN

worship NOUN
1 the act of worshipping
2 a title of respect for a mayor or certain magistrates

worst ADJECTIVE, ADVERB
most bad or most badly

worsted NOUN
a kind of woollen material

worth ADJECTIVE
1 having a certain value *is worth £100*
2 good or important enough for something *a book worth reading*

worth NOUN
1 value or usefulness
2 the amount that a certain sum will buy *five pounds' worth*

worthless ADJECTIVE
having no value; useless

worthwhile ADJECTIVE
deserving the time or effort needed

worthy ADJECTIVE **worthier**, **worthiest**
having great merit; deserving respect or support
worthy of deserving *a charity worthy of our support*
worthiness NOUN

would AUXILIARY VERB
1 used as the past tense of **will**[1] *We said we would do it.*
2 used in questions and requests *Would you like to come? Would you come in, please?*
3 used to express a condition *They would tell us if they knew.*

would-be ADJECTIVE
wanting or pretending to be *a would-be artist*

wouldn't
would not

wound[1] (woond) NOUN
1 an injury caused by a cut, stab, or hit
2 a hurt to a person's feelings

wound VERB
1 to cause a wound to a person or animal
2 to offend someone

wound[2] (wownd) *past tense* of **wind**[2]

wraith NOUN
a ghost

wrangle VERB
to have a noisy argument or quarrel
wrangle NOUN

wrap VERB **wrapping**, **wrapped**
to put paper or cloth etc. round something as a covering
wrap up to put on warm clothes

wrap NOUN
a shawl, cloak, etc. worn for warmth

wrapper NOUN
a piece of paper etc. wrapped round something

wrapping NOUN
material used to wrap something

wrath (rhymes with *cloth*) NOUN
fierce anger

wrathful ADJECTIVE
fiercely angry
wrathfully ADVERB

wreak (*say as* reek) VERB
to inflict or cause *wreaked havoc*

wreath (reeth) NOUN
a circle of flowers or leaves etc.

wreathe (reeth) VERB
1 to surround or decorate with a wreath
2 to cover *faces wreathed in smiles*

wreck VERB
to damage or ruin something completely

wreck NOUN
1 a wrecked ship or building or car etc.
2 a person who is left very weak *a nervous wreck*
3 the wrecking of something

wreckage NOUN
the remnants of something wrecked

wren NOUN
a very small brown bird

wrench VERB
to twist or pull violently

wrench NOUN
1 a wrenching movement
2 pain caused by parting
3 an adjustable tool like a spanner

wrest VERB
to take something away using force

wrestle VERB
1 to fight an opponent, trying to throw them to the ground
2 to struggle with a problem or difficulty
wrestle NOUN **wrestler** NOUN

wretch *NOUN*
1 a miserable or pitiful person
2 a person who is disliked

wretched *ADJECTIVE*
1 miserable or unhappy
2 of bad quality

wriggle *VERB*
to move with short twisting movements
wriggle out of to avoid work or blame etc.
wriggle *NOUN*

wring *VERB* **wrung**
1 to twist and squeeze water out of
2 to clasp the hands firmly
3 to get something by a great effort
wringing wet wet enough for water to be squeezed out

wringer *NOUN*
a device with a pair of rollers for squeezing water out of washed clothes etc.

wrinkle *NOUN*
1 a small furrow or ridge in the skin
2 a small crease in something

wrinkle *VERB*
to make wrinkles in; to form wrinkles

wrist *NOUN*
the joint that connects the hand and arm

wristwatch *NOUN*
a watch for wearing on the wrist

writ (rit) *NOUN*
a formal written command issued by a lawcourt etc.

write *VERB* **wrote**, **written**
1 to form letters or words etc.
2 to be the author or composer of
3 to send a letter
4 to enter data into a computer
write off to regard as lost or useless
writer *NOUN*

writhe *VERB*
1 to twist the body in pain
2 to wriggle

writing *NOUN*
something written; a way of writing

wrong *ADJECTIVE*
1 incorrect; not true
2 not fair or morally right
3 not working properly
wrongly *ADVERB*

wrong *ADVERB*
wrongly *You guessed wrong.*

wrong *NOUN*
something morally wrong; an injustice

wrong *VERB*
to do wrong to someone

wrongdoer *NOUN*
a person who does wrong
wrongdoing *NOUN*

wrongful *ADJECTIVE*
unfair or unjust; illegal
wrongfully *ADVERB*

wrought *ADJECTIVE*
(of metal) worked by being beaten out or shaped by hammering or rolling etc.

wry *ADJECTIVE* **wryer**, **wryest**
1 slightly mocking or sarcastic
2 twisted or bent out of shape
wryly *ADVERB* **wryness** *NOUN*

WWW *ABBREVIATION*
World Wide Web

Xx

xenophobia *NOUN*
a strong dislike of foreigners

Xmas *NOUN*
(*informal*) Christmas

X-ray *NOUN*
a photograph or examination of the inside of the body, made by a kind of radiation that can penetrate solid objects

X-ray *VERB*
to make an X-ray of

xylophone (zy-lo-fohn) *NOUN*
a musical instrument with a row of wooden bars struck with small hammers

Yy

yacht (yot) *NOUN*
1 a sailing boat used for racing or cruising
2 a private ship
yachting *NOUN*

yachtsman or **yachtswoman** *NOUN*
yachtsmen or **yachtswomen**
someone who sails yachts

yak *NOUN*
an Asian ox with long hair

yam *NOUN*
the starchy potato-like tuber of a tropical plant

Yank or **Yankee** NOUN
(*informal*) an American

yank VERB
(*informal*) to pull strongly and suddenly
yank NOUN

yap VERB **yapping**, **yapped**
to bark shrilly
yap NOUN

yard NOUN
1 a measure of length, 36 inches or 91 centimetres
2 a long pole stretched out from a mast to support a sail
3 an enclosed area used for a special purpose *a timber yard*

yardstick NOUN
a standard by for measuring or judging

yarn NOUN
1 thread spun by twisting fibres together
2 a long tale or story

yashmak NOUN
a veil worn by Muslim women in some countries

yawn VERB
1 to open the mouth wide and breathe in deeply when feeling sleepy or bored
2 to form a wide opening *a yawning gap*
yawn NOUN

ye PRONOUN
(*old use*) you (referring to two or more people)

yea (yay) ADVERB
(*old use*) yes

year NOUN
1 the time the earth takes to go round the sun, about 365.25 days
2 a period of 12 months, especially the time from 1 January to 31 December
yearly ADJECTIVE, ADVERB

yearling NOUN
a one-year-old animal

yearn VERB
to long for something

yeast NOUN
a substance used to ferment beer and wine and to make bread etc. rise

yell VERB
to give a shout
yell NOUN

yellow ADJECTIVE
1 of the colour of buttercups and ripe lemons
2 (*informal*) cowardly

yellow NOUN
the colour of buttercups and ripe lemons

yelp VERB
to give a shrill bark or cry
yelp NOUN

yen [1] NOUN **yen**
a unit of money in Japan

yen [2] NOUN
a longing

yeoman (yoh-man) NOUN **yeomen**
formerly, a man who owned a small farm
yeomanry NOUN

yes ADVERB
used to agree to or accept something

yesterday NOUN, ADVERB
1 the day before today
2 the past

yet ADVERB
1 up to this time; by this time
2 eventually
3 in addition; even *found yet more of them*

yet CONJUNCTION
nevertheless *It is strange, yet it is true.*

yeti NOUN
a large animal thought to live in the Himalayas

yew NOUN
an evergreen tree with green leaves and red berries

yield VERB
1 to give in or surrender
2 to agree to do what is asked
3 to produce as a crop or profit

yield NOUN
the amount yielded or produced

yob NOUN
(*informal*) an aggressive lout

yodel VERB **yodelling**, **yodelled**
to sing with the voice continually varying in pitch

yoga NOUN
a Hindu system of meditation and self-control, with physical exercises

yogurt or **yoghurt** NOUN
milk thickened by the action of bacteria, giving it a sharp taste

yoke NOUN
a curved piece of wood across the necks of animals pulling a load
Do not confuse this word with *yolk*.

yoke VERB
to harness or join with a yoke

yokel (yoh-kel) *NOUN*
a simple country person

yolk (rhymes with *poke*) *NOUN*
the round yellow part inside an egg
Do not confuse this word with *yoke*.

Yom Kippur (yom kip-**oor**) *NOUN*
the Day of Atonement, a Jewish religious festival

yonder *ADJECTIVE, ADVERB*
(*old use*) over there

yore *NOUN*
of yore of long ago *days of yore*

you *PRONOUN*
1 the person or people being spoken to *Who are you?*
2 anyone or everyone; one *You can never tell.*

young *ADJECTIVE*
having lived or existed for only a short time

young *PLURAL NOUN*
children or young animals or birds

youngster *NOUN*
a young person; a child

your *ADJECTIVE*
belonging to you
Do not confuse this word with *you're*.

you're
you are
Do not confuse this word with *your*.

yours *POSSESSIVE PRONOUN*
something belonging to you
It is incorrect to write *your's*.

yourself *PRONOUN* **yourselves**
you and nobody else *You've cut yourself. You yourselves said it.*
by yourself or **yourselves** alone; on your own

youth *NOUN*
1 the time of being young
2 a young man
3 young people

youthful *ADJECTIVE*
young or looking young

youth hostel *NOUN*
a hostel for young people hiking or on holiday

yo-yo *NOUN* **yo-yos**
a round wooden or plastic toy that moves up and down on a string

Yule or **Yuletide** *NOUN*
(*old use*) the Christmas festival

zany *ADJECTIVE* **zanier**, **zaniest**
funny in a crazy way

zap *VERB* **zapping**, **zapped** (*informal*)
1 to attack or destroy forcefully
2 to change television channels rapidly with a remote control
zapper *NOUN*

zeal *NOUN*
enthusiasm or keenness

zealot (**zel**-ot) *NOUN*
a zealous person

zealous (**zel**-us) *ADJECTIVE*
keen; enthusiastic

zebra *NOUN*
a striped African animal of the horse family

zebra crossing *NOUN*
a street crossing for pedestrians, marked with black and white stripes

zenith *NOUN*
1 the part of the sky directly above someone looking at it
2 the highest point

zephyr (**zef**-er) *NOUN*
a soft gentle wind

zero *NOUN* **zeros**
1 nought; the figure 0
2 the point marked 0 on a scale

zest *NOUN*
1 great enjoyment or interest
2 orange or lemon peel

zestful *ADJECTIVE*
full of enjoyment
zestfully *ADVERB*

zigzag *NOUN*
a line or route turning sharply from side to side

zigzag *ADJECTIVE*
turning sharply from side to side

zigzag *VERB* **zigzagging**, **zigzagged**
to move in a zigzag

zinc *NOUN*
a white metal

zip *NOUN*
1 a fastener consisting of two strips with rows of small teeth made to interlock with a sliding tab
2 a sharp sound like a bullet going through the air

zip *VERB* **zipping, zipped**
1 to fasten with a zip
2 to move quickly with a sharp sound

zither *NOUN*
a musical instrument with strings stretched over a shallow body

zodiac (zoh-dee-ak) *NOUN*
a strip of sky in which the sun, moon, and main planets are found, divided into twelve equal parts (called *signs of the zodiac*), each named after a constellation

zombie *NOUN*
1 (*informal*) a person who acts without thinking, from tiredness
2 (in voodoo) a corpse revived by witchcraft

zone *NOUN*
an area set aside for a particular purpose

zoo *NOUN* **zoos**
a place where wild animals are kept so that people can look at them or study them

zoology *NOUN*
the scientific study of animals
zoological *ADJECTIVE* **zoologist** *NOUN*

zoom *VERB*
1 to move rapidly with a low buzzing sound
2 (in photography) use a zoom lens
zoom *NOUN*

zoom lens *NOUN*
a camera lens that can be adjusted continuously to focus on things that are close up or far away

a
b
c
d
e
f
g
h
i
j
k
l
m
n
o
p
q
r
s
t
u
v
w
x
y
z